The History of
BRITISH RAILWAY CARRIAGES
1900—1953

DAVID JENKINSON

PENDRAGON

© David Jenkinson and The Pendragon Partnership, 1996

Published by the Pendragon Partnership, PO Box No.3, Easingwold, York, YO6 3LF. All rights reserved

Jacket and other supplementary design by Barry C. Lane, Sutton-in-Craven

Printed by the Amadeus Press Ltd., Huddersfield, West Yorkshire

British Cataloguing-in-Publication Data: a catalogue refer-ence for this book is held by the British Library

ISBN No. 1 899816 03 8

The LYR adopted the gangwayed centre-aisle open saloon type of carriage in 1901 and continued to build ever improved designs of this type through to the grouping. Early types had the arc roof and inset doorways but the semi ellipti-cal roof pattern was introduced in 1906. This example was built in 1913 as part of several sets of matching vehicles for the better intercity services. Oddly enough, all such saloons were panelled in contrast to the smooth sided profile of the company's other stock.

Publisher's Notes:

1. This survey was first issued by Patrick Stephens Ltd in the 1980s as a two volume review. The pre-sent publisher would like to thank PSL (now part of the Haynes Group) for its courtesy in relinquishing its rights in the work to enable this new single vol-ume edition to be published

2. This book is, in content terms, a reprint of the original version, save for the necessary changes to page numbering and cross-references to suit a sin-gle volume format, and the publisher apologizes in advance for any omissions which may have occurred during this process. The two parts into which this new version has been divided reflect the original two volumes, but for convenience, figure and table reference numbers start again at No.1 in Part II.

3. Unacknowledged pictures in the book are from the author's and/or publisher's collections, many of them coming originally from various official BR sources via the regional PRO's offices. Since these sources no longer exist in their historic form, there is little point in quoting them(!); but it is likely that many images are still available via the National Railway Museum, to which all enquiries should be addressed. It is regretted that copies of pho-tographs and drawings in this book cannot be made available to readers by either publisher or author.

Contents

Author's Introduction to the Second Edition

It is said that Brahms, when explaining why he waited until he was in his early 40s before writing his first symphony, remarked that it was because he was aware of the spirit of Beethoven looming over his shoulder. Now apart from a great love of his music, I have little in common with Brahms save for a beard; but I know how he felt — let me explain.

Anyone attempting to write a general account of British railway carriages cannot help but feel the presence of that superb artist/author, the late Cuthbert Hamilton Ellis, the first to try and till the soil of carriage history to any depth and still, in my view, the best role model to follow. His definitive review·of the nineteenth century, in its revised form taking the story to 1914, appeared back in 1965 and is still the standard work. It was therefore with some anxiety and apprehension that I first received an invitation to compile this follow-on some ten years ago, especially when given vast amounts of words and hundreds of pictures to play with. It seemed an awful lot of space to fill, yet I very soon had to come to terms with what to leave out, so a few words of explanation as to emphasis seem prudent.

In my view, the railway carriage is, above all, something in which people travel. It is also, of course, a piece of applied technology and I am well aware that some carriages carry no people at all, being filled with luggage, parcels, mail or what have you; but when a 'bottom line' is drawn, the railway carriage functions as a socio-economic artefact in a way which the locomotive can never imitate and the freight vehicle only rarely. Of all the plant and machinery which make up the complexities of the railway, the passenger carriage is always that which is most familiar to most people — excepting dedicated railway enthusiasts who will regularly know more about most aspects of the railway than the typical traveller; but I hope that they too will find my remarks of interest.

There are thus no great fleet lists in these pages, nor have I attempted to mention every single carriage ever built, given the considerable writing devoted to this sort of thing — see Bibliography. But there is much reference to people, be it their travelling needs, changing attitudes, criticisms and the like or, in a more practical sense, the skills of those many, largely anonymous folk, who built some of the vehicles to be featured. There is also a fair bit of technology, for one cannot write of vehicles without explaining some of the 'how and why it works' aspects. Here, in trying not to assume too much pre-knowledge, I have attempted to explain the essential technology in terms which do not demand an engineering or applied physics degree. I therefore hope that those readers who do have this knowledge will make the necessary allowances.

Overall, I have tried to give an overview, concentrating on major trends, developments and principles which seem valid rather than address the minutiae. I have also tried to inject a historical perspective — hence my setting the scene by devoting the first chapter to the 'Victorian Inheritance'. History rarely obliges us by sorting itself out in terms of precise and tidy calendar dates and the railway carriage is no exception. But the story would be incomprehensible without first reviewing those years when the carriage 'grew up'. Much that was Victorian lasted into our time and it would be wrong to leave it out; railway technology is rarely of the 'throw away after use' kind!

When I first started to prepare this account over ten years ago, nobody could have foreseen the changes which would overtake the British railway system in the next decade, not least the reversion to private ownership. The opportunity to re-issue the survey therefore brought with it a temptation to make revisions in the light of recent changes; but on reflection, this seemed to be historically inappropriate, so this new edition is exactly as first written at a time when it was fully expected that the review would continue into BR days via a last volume — until a thing called the recession got in the way! My story therefore ends for the moment — maybe appropriately enough — at the start of the second Elizabethan period, mainly because 1952-3 marked the end of company style railway carriages as we once knew them. Needless to say, all references to the corporate 'British Railways' have been left as written and should be read in their historic context.

During the last ten years, rapid changes have conspired to make it hard to know just where to finish the BR carriage story. But privatisation seems to offer a suitable marker; so if I manage to reach the new millenium, the second half of the 20th Century carriage story might then be clear enough to put on record, and I might just be tempted...

David Jenkinson
Raskelf, North Yorkshire
June 1996

PART I — THE END OF AN ERA: 1900-22

At the end of the Victorian period, the railway carriage had emerged from the 'dark ages' to become the precursor of many present day ideas which the traveller now takes for granted. Between the turn of the century and the 1923 grouping, huge advances in carriage design and technology were made and travellers were offered ever more sophisticated facilities as the many private companies vied with each other for custom. Corridor bogie carriages, dining and sleeping cars, not to mention ever more sumptuous upholstery combined with decent toilets and electric lighting, all reached a high state of maturity in the last flowering of the semi-monopolistic railway era before the universal motor age.

'. . . the railway carriage is above all something in which people travel.' And if you were a reasonably well-heeled family in 1911, even the rather unfashionable Lancashire and Yorkshire Railway could offer this stylish Family Saloon for your delectation. It was wholly typical of the best achievements of British carriage builders during the first quarter of the twentieth century.

1. The Victorian inheritance

Unlike many manifestations of human ingenuity, the railway carriage has a fairly precise beginning. While the railway idea, as such, may be lost in the mists of antiquity — it certainly goes back some 4-500 years — the history books tell us that the first *people* officially to travel on a railway train did so in South Wales between Swansea and Mumbles in 1807, drawn by a horse. Prior to that time, railways were purely for things and the human species came a very poor second place in the reckoning.

The development of the 'steam railway' proper, in effect from the opening of the Liverpool and Manchester Railway in 1830, was very much a Victorian phenomenon, and it is a matter of fact that the enthusiastic demand for railway transport by people came as something of a surprise to certain parts of contemporary society. That it still does so in some establishment circles is, perhaps, outside this immediate discussion! Be that as it may, however, the railway carriage 'came of age' during the Victorian expansion of the mechanized railway and it is impossible to comprehend its twentieth century development without devoting some small space to 'setting the background'.

The railway carriage drew its main inspiration from the early nineteenth-century road coach — indeed, the words 'coach' and 'carriage' have their origins in the road transport business. The two words are more or less interchangeable and both will be used, somewhat indiscriminately, in this compilation. Indeed, much of the vocabulary, specific to the subject, derives from other sources, so it will not do any harm to start with a few more definitions of terms which will appear quite regularly in these pages. Take, for instance, windows, which were always called 'lights' because they let in the light. There were 'fixed lights' (ie non-openable), usually surrounded by some sort of frame; there were 'drop lights' (windows which opened by being lowered, ie 'dropped', in their surrounds); and there were 'quarter lights', usually set on either side of a door and so called because, initially, they were shaped like a quarter circle, harking back to stagecoach days again. There were also 'top lights', 'deck lights' and several others — more of which in their proper time.

This terminology withstood the transfer to the railway environment, even after carriage shapes had changed quite markedly. So too did other words and phrases which were often either anatomically or architecturally derived. Thus the 'waist' of a carriage was its middle portion just below the window; while 'eaves', 'cornice', 'gutter', 'floor', 'ceiling', 'dado' and even 'clerestory' had obvious roots in buildings and retained their basic connotations virtually unaltered.

The carriage itself started its purely railway form as a somewhat basic box, in effect three stagecoach bodies joined together and mounted on one set of four wheels. Each section was called a compartment and the whole unit was essentially a pure conveyance with not much thought for added amenity; thus it remained, in essence, for some forty years or so. But there were boxes and boxes, some distinctly better than others — and this was almost entirely as a result of the differential price structure in terms of paying for one's journey. The various distinctions were designated by the word 'class' which has developed unfortunate sociological connotations in recent decades, yet whose origins are no more than the root of the perfectly logical 'classification'.

The railways 'classified' their passengers according to how much the customers were prepared to pay, and in this they did no more than follow accepted road custom. Thus, first class developed from the old 'inside' seats of the stage coach. There could be no rooftop 'outside' seats on a steam-drawn train — the speed was too great and the danger of hitting fixed structures too high — so a cheaper option was offered in the form of a covered compartment of a considerably more spartan nature. Typically it would have wooden seats, few, if any, windows (save for those in the door) and probably little or nothing in the way of artificial light. Since more people could be packed in, the status and price somewhat equated with the old rooftop conveyance of the stagecoach. It was known as second class.

The cheapest form of conveyance was a third class carriage. This was the absolute provisioning — an open-topped box on wheels, frequently devoid of seats and possibly with a few holes in the floor to let out the rain-water. It was frightful but, amazingly

Top left *Archetypal Victorian four-wheeler from the Midland & Great Northern Joint Railway — third class No 3. The five-compartment third class was probably the most common single type at this time, whether on four or six wheels. Note the retention of oil lamps.*

Middle left *'Chariot ended' six-wheel first class No 15, with two lavatories and featuring half-compartments ('coupés') at the vehicle end, was an unusual but nevertheless typical nineteenth-century Highland Railway coach.*

Left *This North Eastern Railway six-wheel third class No 1453 with two central lavatories was a quite 'up-market' third class type in late Victorian times. Its body styling is wholly characteristic of traditional British practice — see Chapter 7.*

to modern-day travellers, it was popular. But then, the alternative form of conveyance in pre-railway days for the least wealthy, other than walking, was to ride on the slow moving (maybe 1-2 mph average) 'commercial' horse-drawn merchandise wagons which plodded their way along our roads. The increased speed of the railway and its eventual cheapness compared with road would obviously commend itself even in those spartan circumstances, however basic the accommodation offered. In due course, Gladstone's famous 1844 Act compelled the often reluctant railways to roof over even the third class carriages, but it was well into the last quarter of the nineteenth century before these miserable vehicles improved much further on a nationwide basis.

If there was a significant date above others, it was probably the year 1875 when the Midland Railway decided to abolish second class by upgrading its third class carriages to 'better than second class' standards but without increase in charge. Simultaneously — or near enough as to make no practical difference — it admitted third class passengers to *all* its trains and this again was something almost revolutionary. Hitherto, third class passengers were more often than not accepted only grudgingly by the railways. Obliged as they were by Gladstone's 1844 Act to provide at least *one* third class service per day at one old penny (0.4p) per mile, stopping at all stations — the famous 'Parliamentary' trains — many railways fulfilled their obligation but literally, interpreting the word 'day' as embracing 24 hours, thus allowing them to run the 'Parliamentary' at the most inopportune times — often in the middle of the night. Not without reason did the immortal W.S. Gilbert write those words into the Mikado's 'punishment and crime' song: '. . . we only suffer to ride on the buffer of a Parliamentary train'! They were pretty awful.

It was against this sort of background that the Midland delivered its *coup de théâtre*. When the Midland, having abolished second class, additionally reduced first class fares to second class levels without loss of carriage quality, the shock waves reverberated round the railway world. Of course, the effect on other systems was not immediate. Some improvements would have happened anyway and it is always dangerous for a historian to try and date with precision the point at which quantum changes occur; but if one wants to assign a 'conception' date for the first essentially twentieth-century *attitude* to rail passenger travel, then the activities of the English Midland Railway during the late 1870s seem to mark as good a single point in time as any.

In effect, the MR introduced a two-class only approach — the basic twentieth-century subdivision — with a built-in assumption that the lower of these two classes still merited essentially comfortable accommodation. However, the high quality of the 'soft third class' of the British railways — most of them eventually copied the Midland — was still a source of wonderment in many overseas countries well into the present century. That it took until as late as 1956 for the last vestiges of three-class accommodation to vanish in Britain (mostly retained on a few boat trains) is part of the main story to be considered later. But for older readers who remember it and have perhaps wondered at this curiosity, it does explain why during much of the first half of the present century, most British trains were, somewhat puzzlingly, labelled 1st and 3rd Class only.

So much, for the moment, for the social aspect of the railway carriage; in this survey, classes of accommodation will be quoted as they were known at the time the vehicle was built. 'Third' class did not become 'second' in Britain until well into the period which follows this volume, so references to 'second' class in this first part do, indeed, relate to a threefold subdivision.

Just as it took nearly half a century for the railways to develop a fairly civilized attitude to people, so too did it take longer than is generally realized for the vehicle itself to improve. The basic four-wheeler had a long and not entirely praiseworthy run in the nineteenth century, and many were built in the early part of the twentieth too, but eventually the demand for greater speed and safety gradually caused changes to occur. The combination of factors was a little subtle, involving both social and technological aspects, but the end product was to set the pattern for twentieth-century development just as in the socio-economic field thus far discussed.

The railway carriage is, fundamentally, a very stable vehicle and can be made very large and very heavy, subject mainly to the maximum dimensions imposed by fixed structures (bridges, tunnels, etc) and the maximum weight per axle permitted by the railway itself. The extent to which the carriage could be 'expanded' was probably not fully appreciated in early steam days, and in any case the early locomotives were often too feeble to pull much above a string of typical four-wheelers; but the potential for development was there.

The first increase in size was generally to a six-wheel type, often with enhanced width and height as well. This would clearly allow more 'people per carriage', but it is doubtful if the actual cost or weight per seat was less than with the four-wheeler. In fact, the contrary was probably the case. However, the six-wheeler was more comfortable at the higher speeds which competition (and the passenger) was forcing; its greater weight gave it greater safety in the case of accidents and there was, in general, rather

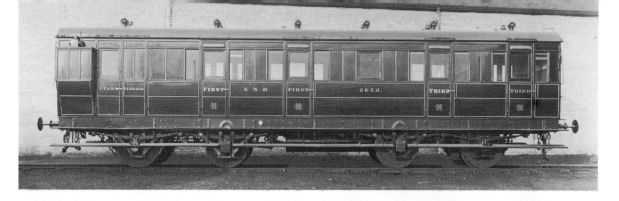

Top *Great Northern Railway No 2653, built in the late 1890s, was one of the several approaches to the use of eight wheels which did not involve the use of bogies. Only the first class had access to the lavatories. Some of these carriages lasted until the 1930s.*

Above *London & North Western Railway 42-foot eight-wheeler No 469 was one of many hundreds which employed Francis Webb's patent 'radial' axle at both ends of the vehicle as an alternative to pivoting bogies — see Figure 2a, page 16. It has lavatories and luggage space as well as three classes of accommodation.*

more space below the floor to fit the various ancillary equipment which was increasingly being provided, particularly in the realm of braking.

It is not too widely known that the legalized automatic braking of all passenger trains was quite a late arrival on the scene. Not until well after the Newark Brake Trials of 1875 did the railways seriously address themselves to the problem. It took some time to get things organized, nationally, after this date and even then there was not total agreement about the best system (see Chapter 2); but as far as the carriage was concerned, it meant that extra equipment had to be carried, increasing the weight.

The demands for increased amenities (see below), the growing need in absolute terms for more passenger capacity and the desire for still greater speeds together combined to force the carriage above the six-wheel configuration during later Victorian days. The Americans had had an answer since the 1830s, but Britain was slow to take it up. Essentially it involved mounting a much longer carriage on two separate sets of wheels (known as 'bogies' in Britain but, confusingly, 'trucks' in America), one at each end and free to pivot relative to the carriage body itself. Once again, applied technology provided part

of the reasoning. The typically British six-wheeler, like its four-wheeled counterpart, had a virtually rigid wheelbase (see Chapter 2). This meant that there were restrictions regarding the radius of curvature it could traverse. The precise mathematics need not concern us for the moment but suffice to say that in the context of British civil engineering it posed no serious problems. British lines were well engineered (some would even say 'over engineered'), had gentle curvature and were generally easily graded.

In America, by contrast, as part of the 'opening up' process of that vast continent, the early railways tended to be pushed through as expeditiously as possible and this included a 'low cost' element. More pronounced curvature and more severe gradients were accepted (to save money) and this had important consequences in both locomotive and carriage develevopments in North America, one early end product of which was the carriage bogie. This device was introduced in order to permit larger vehicles to traverse more severe curves than they could do were the wheelbase rigid. Each pivoting bogie acted as an independent four-wheel 'carriage' so, self evidently, the bogie coach could get round a sharper corner than a rigid six-wheeler.

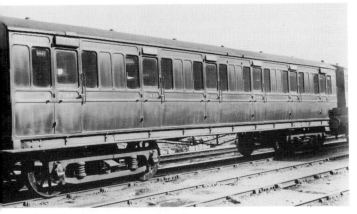

William Stroudley's London Brighton & South Coast Railway first class carriage No 77 built in 1889. The bogies were quite primitive (note the spoked wheels), but for their time the vehicles were very spacious, each compartment being almost eight feet square.

This was not such an acute problem on the well engineered lines in Britain, the six-wheeler was a cheaper option than the bogie carriage and the British railways muddled along quite happily as before. Thus, it was not until 1874 that the first bogie carriages appeared in Britain and, yet again, it was the English Midland Railway which introduced them into this country. That the bogies were also of patently American inspiration was no coincidence either, and bogie vehicles eventually became the norm in the twentieth century.

What took some time for the British railways to appreciate — and in this respect it is worth recalling that even the enterprising Midland built mostly six-wheelers down to 1900 — was that the bogie carriage had other advantages besides that of getting round curves more easily. For one thing, its 'ride' quality (ie freedom from unwanted jerks and jolts) was better, since it could be made larger and heavier; also, because of the vast area of empty 'sub-floor' space between the bogies, it could also have attached to it, a fair quantity of ancillary equipment. This latter advantage was to become dominant, which conveniently links to the third principal twentieth-century feature established in late Victorian days — improved passenger amenity.

The human species is a curious animal. Give it something better and it immediately bends its mind to thinking of yet further improvements, and railway carriages are no exception to the general rule. Thus, no sooner had the railways demonstrated that a better standard of seat comfort was possible than the passengers began to ask or even demand that other things, too, be considered. These grouped themselves into three principal categories, all connected with fundamental bodily functions — some almost unmentionable in polite Victorian circles — but none the less vital!

There was the lavatory for starters. The ever expanding railway network, together with the consequential longer transit times between more distant centres, meant that calls of nature could not be ignored. The train (unlike its stagecoach predecessor) was not able to call at any convenient roadside hostelry, so travellers had to rely on the often inadequate provisioning at station stops and risk the train leaving too soon! This was not really very dignified, so some of the more enterprising railways in the long-distance business started to incorporate lavatories on their trains.

In 1873, the North British Railway (NBR), closely followed by the London and North Western Railway (LNWR) in the same year, introduced sleeping cars to cater for a second vital bodily function and in 1879 the Great Northern Railway (GNR) put into service the first British dining car service between London and Leeds, which took care of the third basic bodily need. Hamilton Ellis has dealt with much of this in his own books so there is no need to concern ourselves further here, but sufficient has probably been said by now to appreciate that much which we now take for granted in the late-twentieth-century travelling environment was established by the privately-owned railways of later Victorian Britain from the 1870s onwards. Of course, it was stimulated by competition for patronage between the various private systems and often had to await the ability of the mechanical engineers to provide more swift-moving and powerful locomotives to haul the extra weight, but very little that we now regard as 'normal' in terms of twentieth-century rail travel had not been foreseen by our Victorian predecessors.

Naturally, although the fundamental ideas were first sown in the 1870s, it took some time for them to be universally adopted. Take inter-vehicle connections, for example. Clearly, if all passengers were to be able to gain access to a lavatory or partake of the facilities of the dining car, some means of getting from one carriage to another was essential. This meant a 'gangway' between the ends of adjacent vehicles and some form of passageway (or 'corridor') along the length of the vehicle itself to gain access to the gangway. Interestingly, the first recorded British example of this facility was on the pair of Royal Saloons provided for Queen Victoria in 1869 by the LNWR. It is said that she would not use it, save when the train was stationary!

We shall have cause to re-consider Royal travel later, more than once, but it is interesting to note that when the LNWR pioneered inter-vehicle connections in 1869, it transpired, and not for the last time, that where the Monarch led, the subjects followed. Thus, by the end of the nineteenth century it was becoming the norm that on long distance trains it should be possible to move along the length of any one vehicle without hindrance and, preferably, be able to move *between* vehicles, by means of a gangway, to gain access to other facilities.

It took time, and full 'corridor' trains were not really introduced to any real extent until the 1890s — and then not for all services. Indeed, the pioneering Midland did not venture its first corridor train until 1898 and in this rather significant respect it was behind some of its larger, longer distance rivals, notably the Great Western Railway (GWR) and the LNWR.

Now, although so far mention has not been made of other late Victorian improvements such as better lighting and heating — these will be considered in later chapters because they continued to form the basis of the first twentieth-century developments — what should now seem abundantly clear is that the railway carriage 'came of age' during late Victorian times and, in its bogie form, became the basis of most of the important twentieth-century innovations. The bogie carriage allowed for the insertion, between the bogies and below the floor, of most of the extra

equipment needed for the 'servicing' of the more elaborate vehicles, such as gas cylinders (for cooking and lighting), batteries (for storage of electricity) and brake apparatus. By the end of the last century, most of the bigger railways had 'adopted' the bogie carriage, or were in the process of so doing, simply because it made sense so to do. The four-wheel and six-wheel vehicles were not dead, but they were surely dying. That they took so long about it may be attributed perhaps more to the innate conservatism of the British than to any particular merits the carriages may have possessed. They were still, of course, cheaper to build, but that was not everything when the new century dawned.

Thus, on the first day of the twentieth century the 'nature of the beast' was probably apparent to all who took interest in these things and, by way of preliminaries, there only remains one final area to consider before launching into our main subject area. I refer to the 'train' itself.

The 'train' is a fundamental word in the study of railways. That a vast number of people use it when they really mean 'locomotive' or 'carriage' is beside the point — the 'train' is the end product when it comes to carrying the people about in rail-borne vehicles. In railway terms, the word means an assembly of vehicles, connected together and doing,

American influence on British practice during the nineteenth-century was particularly represented by the importation of typically American-styled carriages. Pullman was the best known practitioner (see Chapter 12), but this view shows South Eastern Railway first class 'Car No 35', built by the rival American Gilbert Car Company for the SER boat trains in 1892. The livery and decoration, also typically American, were applied in the USA before shipment and were described at the time as being dark lake, almost chocolate, with sage green bogies. The cars were later acquired by Pullman.

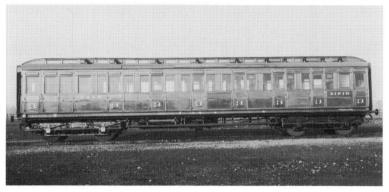

Classic late Victorian practice with profound twentieth-century influence — East Coast Joint Stock third class No 13, with side corridor and lavatories, built in 1898 and shown here as LNER No 41810. Its 'twin', ECJS No 12, is preserved at the National Railway Museum, York.

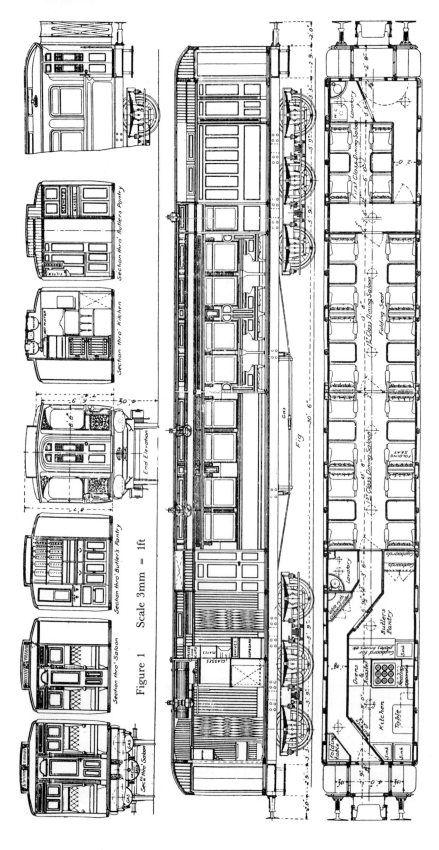

Figure 1 Fin de siècle — *the late Victorian twelve-wheeler in the form of the classic Wolverton (LNWR) 65 ft 6 in long dining and sleeping carriages, introduced in the mid-1890s. This drawing shows details and layout of the first type built, the first class dining cars of 1895. A slightly later example is shown in the picture on page 108.*

Above right *Victorian inheritance I — the long-lived characteristics of many typically humble Victorian-styled carriages are exemplified by this view of no fewer than a dozen of them at Kittybrewster as late as the mid-1920s on the former Great North of Scotland Railway, then part of the LNER. Some of the carriages still carry GNSR livery.*

Right *Victorian inheritance II — the Great Western Railway found considerable use for its turn-of-the-century clerestory coaches for many decades after they had seen the first flush of their youth. Here, at Southcote Junction, Reading, is a typical cross-country working to Newbury in 1931. Note the much shorter windows of the centre vehicle, of older vintage than the two end examples.*

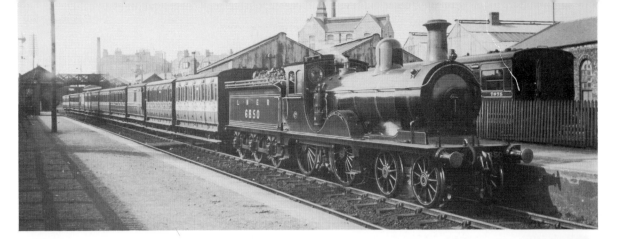

collectively, a useful job of work. In the beginning of passenger railways it merely reflected, in passenger terms, a number of vehicles (of whatever class) whose sole object was to convey people from 'A' to 'B'. In the fundamental sense it still does, but by later Victorian times, three quite distinctively different categories had begun to emerge in Britain and are relevant to the twentieth-century story.

Firstly, the long-distance train is totally different from its short-distance 'home to work' counterpart. This was not at first apparent (surprisingly), but by the start of the present century the railways appreciated the fundamental difference which existed between a vehicle in which one was anticipating to spend several hours (or even the bulk of one day) and that with which one's acquaintanceship was but transitory, for maybe an hour or even less. In between the two was a sort of intermediate third category — not quite long-distance and not quite transitory, but nevertheless distinguishable. These three broad categories are fundamental to the understanding of British railway carriage design, for they resulted in the provision of distinctly different vehicle types.

Put at its simplest, the long-distance train is 'strong' in amenity and the short-distance train is 'high' in seating capacity, with the intermediate train lying somewhere between the two. In British terms, the ultra-long-period operations (several days and nights) of the Americas, Australia or Asia were not relevant, but the railways were more than aware of the differing needs of potential patrons at an early stage; their response varied accordingly.

All these various differentiations had been identified — and the solutions to some extent arrived at — by the start of the twentieth century, so the 1900s started, in effect, with the various problems identified. The carriage had 'grown up' and the new century dawned with all to play for. It will be the object of the remainder of this survey to review the extent to which it was successful.

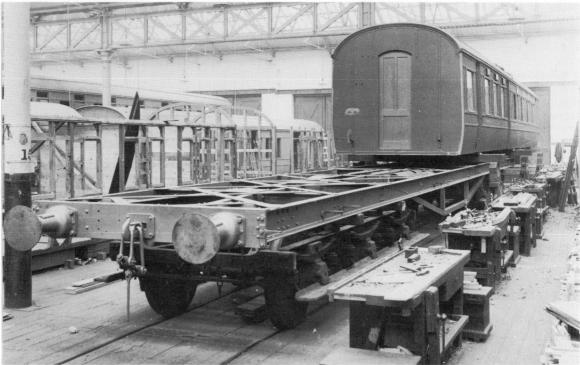

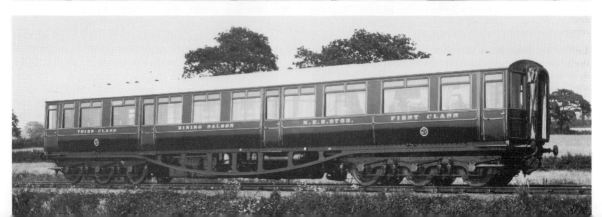

2. The carriage as a vehicle

The traditional British railway carriage consisted of two basic components, the chassis and the body. It was normal to build the two components separately and then, at some quite late stage in the process, offer up the body for fixing to the chassis, at which point the final stages of adding interior fitments, ancillary components, etc could begin, finishing with the all-essential painting and decoration. This approach, while not uniquely British, was in marked contrast to the form of construction generally adopted in America, where a form of 'integral' construction was adopted from an early stage. Although used widely in North America and possessing several advantages, this form of construction only achieved significance in Britain during the period covered by the first part of this survey in the shape of Pullman Cars (Chapter 12), and is therefore left out of consideration until that part of the book.

Bearing in mind the dangers of such a generalization, the railway carriage tended to be either British (perhaps, more accurately, European) or American in terms of its basic structural form for something like the first half of the twentieth century and, certainly as far as British practice is concerned, the separate body/chassis form was all but universal until the 1960s. Although a great number of detailed variations did exist, not to mention an ever-increasing move towards extensive pre-fabrication of components and semi-mass production of whole vehicles in the case of the larger companies, the fundamental structure of the vehicle itself remained little changed. It happily withstood the changeover from 'all-wood' bodies through 'part-wood/part-metal' to 'all-metal' without significant alteration to the basic principles. Consequently, given a

Above left *Six-wheel underframes, both all-steel (left) and composite wood and steel (right), under construction at the York works of the former North Eastern Railway.*

Middle left *The classic British form of carriage construction — body unit mounted on a separate chassis. The example illustrated is a twelve-wheel M & GSW first class dining carriage at Derby works in 1920, and the underframe itself is of the angle-trussed kind — see page 18. To the left can be seen the framing of a typical compartment coach*

Left *A somewhat dramatic solution to the underframe of heavy twelve-wheelers was adopted at York by the NER, and was likened by many to the girder construction of the various Tyne bridges! The style is well shown on NER first and third class dining car No 3753. Note the almost complete filling of the space between the bogies with ancillary apparatus. This type of underframe may still be examined in the preserved East Coast Royal Saloons at the NRM — see Chapter 13.*

fundamental understanding of how the early twentieth-century coach was put together, it is readily possible to appreciate the subsequent evolutionary stages. These latter were really quite slow and the late Victorian/early Edwardian carriage builders would have had little real difficulty in comprehending the vehicles of the mid-1950s. They might have been surprised at their greater size, the considerable changes in their interior decor and the move towards considerably simpler colour schemes, but that would be about all.

It has been seen in outline how the twentieth-century railway carriage was born during the last decade of the previous century in terms of concept and utilization. It is now necessary to turn to a consideration of how it actually worked. As in the case of concept, so too in the case of constructional methods, the ideas stemmed from late Victorian times. This detailed account, therefore, must also commence with a look at the turn of the century situation in terms of carriage building. For ease of comprehension, the various principal elements are separated into chapter and sub-headings; the various specific words and terms will be introduced as they become relevant and since the railway carriage is, in all its manifestations, always a vehicle, it seems logical to look first at its fundamental component, the vehicle chassis.

The underframe

The largest single part of the vehicle chassis is known as the underframe. It is the essential foundation of the whole vehicle, regardless of the precise body type, and to it are fixed, in one form or other, all the other components (wheels, axles, brakes, etc) which go to make up the whole. Frequently, the word underframe is used to denote the whole assembly, but in this book the word 'chassis' will be used to differentiate the whole from its constituent parts.

The underframe itself is basically a rectangular structure, the size of which reflects the length and width of the body which will, in due course, be fixed to it. Most railways arrived at various standardized sizes to suit several different body configurations, but few if any of the individual companies settled down to one basic underframe for all requirements. Neither did the different railways agree between themselves as to the optimum length which should be used for a particular carriage type. There was thus considerable variation in length and width at all times, even though all of them had to fulfil the same basic purpose.

The underframe had to have, above all, great

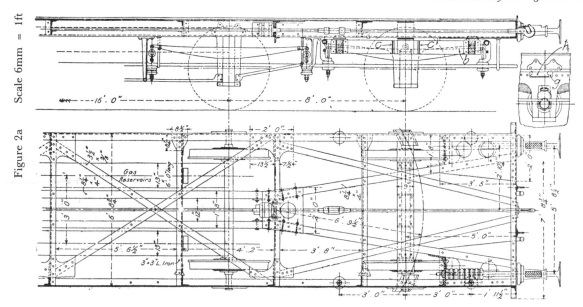

Scale 6mm = 1ft

Figure 2a

Figure 2a *Probably the most sophisticated of the non-bogie eight-wheel carriage underframes was Webb's LNWR radial pattern. Although by then obsolete, it was still quite widespread on the parent system at the start of the twentieth century.*

strength. To achieve this it was built in the form of a horizontal girder with very strong outer side-members (known as 'solebars') and equally strong outer end cross-members ('headstocks'). There would, typically, be additional longitudinal and cross-members, often associated with diagonal 'braces' to give extra strength in the more vulnerable areas where greater stress might be expected to occur. The essential requirement was to produce a framework which remained rigid and free from distortion. In this latter context, the most likely eventualities to be guarded against were too much drooping at the ends and rising in the middle (known as 'hogging' or 'hog-backed'), the opposite effect (known as 'sagging or 'sway-backed'), or a tendency to get out of square horizontally as a result of the forces exerted by the buffing and drawgear (see page 25). In point of fact, it was common for underframes to be constructed with a deliberate amount of 'hogging' which would be forced horizontal by the weight of the bodywork on top; otherwise 'sagging' would result!

In terms of material, underframes progressed from all-timber, via a combination of timber and iron (later steel) to all-steel. All three approaches could be seen at the start of the century but the all-steel underframe fairly rapidly assumed dominance. The all-wood underframe can be regarded as basically obsolete in carriage terms by the twentieth century, but many

carriages which spent most of their lives operating between 1900 and the mid-1930s (often later) did make use of a composite form. In most cases these would employ oak, reinforced with iron or steel plates and brackets.

The precise nature of a particular underframe was governed by two principal considerations, namely the nature of the buffing and drawgear (see below) and the length, wheelbase and number of wheels to be employed. In this latter context, there was a fundamental distinction between a four-wheel or six-wheel chassis and one which was to be carried on a pair of bogies.

The four-wheel and six-wheel arrangements carried the wheels and their supporting equipment mounted directly on the underframe. This type of arrangement had been virtually, but not quite, superseded by the present century for most of the better passenger-*carrying* vehicles, but remained in use for some lesser services and for passenger-*type* vehicles (luggage vans, etc) well into the modern age. The presence of either the centre set of wheels (six-wheelers) or the relatively short length of the vehicle (four-wheelers) meant that there was less intrinsic risk of sagging at the centre.

The bogie underframe, however, was different. The underframe was supported at each end on the bogies and, in the case of longer carriages, there was a considerable unsupported length between the bogies which would have a natural tendency to sag. To prevent this, the underframe was strengthened along the solebars (and sometimes also along the centre longitudinals) by an ancillary framework, usually

Figure 2b *These two part elevations and plans show characteristic 'round bar and queen-post' bogie underframes of the Midland (54-footers, circa 1910) and the LNWR (57-footers, circa 1913) respectively. Their considerable similarities are far more important than the superficial differences.*

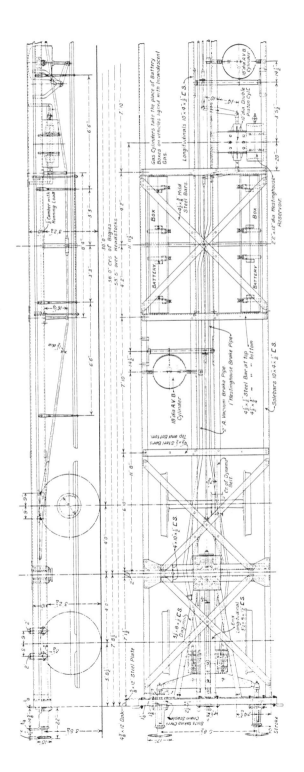

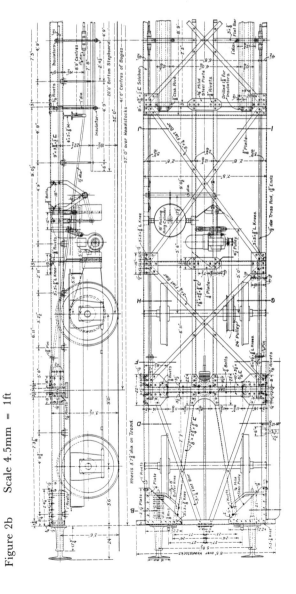

Figure 2b   Scale 4.5mm = 1ft

known as 'trussing'. This consisted of vertical members (usually referred to as 'queen-posts') and horizontal or slightly diagonal members known as 'truss-rods'. The appended diagrams and pictures show some typical arrangements.

The tendency for the underframe to drop in the centre puts the queen-posts into compression and the truss-rods into tension and, provided the stresses and dimensions are calculated properly, this combination of forces maintained the top of the underframe in a flat horizontal configuration. In Britain, this was normally achieved by one of two basic methods. The older solution — and entirely typical of the start of the century — was to make the queen-posts quite substantial (sometimes even decorative) and to make the truss-rods of round bar section, typically 1-1½ inches in diameter. Somewhere along its length, the truss-rod would be 'broken' and a 'turnbuckle' inserted. This and the end of the truss rod itself were threaded in the manner of a conventional nut and bolt so that when the turnbuckle was rotated it either increased or decreased the tension in the truss rods, the latter being fixed at their outer ends (ie those nearest to the bogies) to the underframe itself. Thus the integrity of shape of the underframe could be maintained.

This method (generally known as a 'roundbar and queen-post' or 'turnbuckle' underframe) was augmented and finally superseded by the second common method — the so-called 'angle-trussed, all-steel' underframe. In this arrangement, the stresses were met in more or less the same way but without the need for adjustment by turnbuckle. This was achieved by making the whole of the trussing out of angled steel sections, usually 'L'-shaped and permanently bolted together in such a way as to ensure almost total rigidity of the whole assembly with almost no distortion — other than any which had been 'planned in' — taking place when the body-work was put on top. This form of construction appeared quite early in the century — well before the railway grouping — and had become the British norm by the Second World War.

By this time, experiments in integral construction had begun to appear and welding was replacing the bolted-together form of fixing in some cases. These developments will be mentioned in their due historical sequence.

Springing and suspension

The carriage wheel was fixed to the underframe in one of two ways. It was either attached direct (in the case of four-wheelers and six-wheelers) or fixed to the bogie frame which in turn was separately attached to the underframe. Either way, the first and most critical factor was to fix the wheel in a firm housing

which would nevertheless allow it to accept some form of springing to cushion the shocks. Known as primary suspension, this was the only form of wheel suspension which could be contrived on a non-bogie vehicle.

The method adopted could trace its beginning to the very origins of the steam railway and, in the use of leaf springs, to the preceding road-coach era. As a principle it more than stood the test of time, increased weights and stresses being regularly matched by improved materials and methods of manufacture. Basically, two wheels were mounted on an axle which was allowed to project well beyond the outer faces of the wheel itself. These outer extensions (known as 'journals') were machined to the appropriate diameter and were carried inside an axlebox — a closed container in which were the axle bearings. Within the axlebox, the journals were kept cool in rotation against their bearings by means of lubricating oil. In earlier days, lubrication had been achieved by 'packing' or 'stuffing' the axlebox with semi-solidified grease, relying on frictional heat to melt the grease and afford lubrication. This method was still quite widespread at the turn of the century on freight vehicles, but the oil axlebox was much better and almost universally employed for passenger stock during the period of this survey. It was essential for really high-speed operation.

The axlebox itself was carried in a rigid metal frame — or axleguard — fixed to the underframe (or to the bogie side), within which it was free to slide up and down between parallel vertical 'guides'. Shocks were usually taken up by means of a leaf spring fixed to the top of the axlebox and anchored to the underframe or bogie frame at the outer ends by means of movable links or 'scroll irons'. It will be appreciated that as a spring flexes its length varies slightly, so the outer ends must be given some free-dom of movement. The term 'spring hanger' is often used as an alternative to scroll iron.

The axlebox itself should be not only free to move up and down in the axleguard but also have some lateral movement — quite commonly the groove in the axlebox is about 1 inch wide while the guide itself would be some ¾ inch thick. On six-wheelers, the centre axle had to be given rather more lateral movement, or side play, typically ⅝ - ¾ inch either side of the centre line in order to assist in traversing curves; as a result of this, the centre scroll irons were often of different design to allow for this extra lateral movement which, of course, also applied to the ends of the springs themselves.

With a bogie vehicle, each bogie acted as an inde-pendent four-wheel truck and in most British examples the primary suspension was exactly as described above using leaf springs. However, many bogies in North America used a form of compensating beam between the two axleguards on the same side of the frame as a substitute for two independent leaf springs — see Figure 6. Each end of this compensating (or equalizing) beam was anchored to one axlebox. Therefore, when, for example, the left-hand axlebox rose in its guide, the right-hand box would fall and the vertical shocks were most commonly damped by coil springs between the equalizing beam and the fixed frame. This type of bogie was used in

Britain, but to nothing like the extent of the leaf spring version. It was particularly popular with the Pullman Company (Chapter 12) and, indeed, was the first type of bogie used by the Midland Railway in 1874. All references in this book to 'American' pattern bogies should be taken to infer this form of springing.

Regardless of its primary suspension, the bogie itself was a sort of miniature underframe and was built along much the same principles, although some

Figure 3 *Oil axleboxes were developed late in Victorian times and in widespread use at the start of the present century. The examples shown are the LNWR standard and the Attock (Lancashire and Yorkshire Railway) types; other railways mostly used similar forms.*

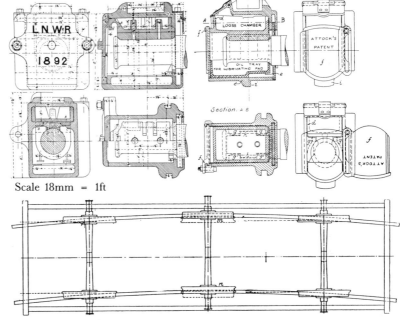

Scale 18mm = 1ft

Figure 4 *Exaggerated diagram showing the behaviour of a typical six-wheel chassis on a curve. This drawing shows, at 'm' and 'n', the lateral displacement of the centre axle.*

Scale 4mm = 1ft

Right *Detail view showing the leaf springs, spring hangers, axlebox and axleguard of a typical NER six-wheel carriage.*

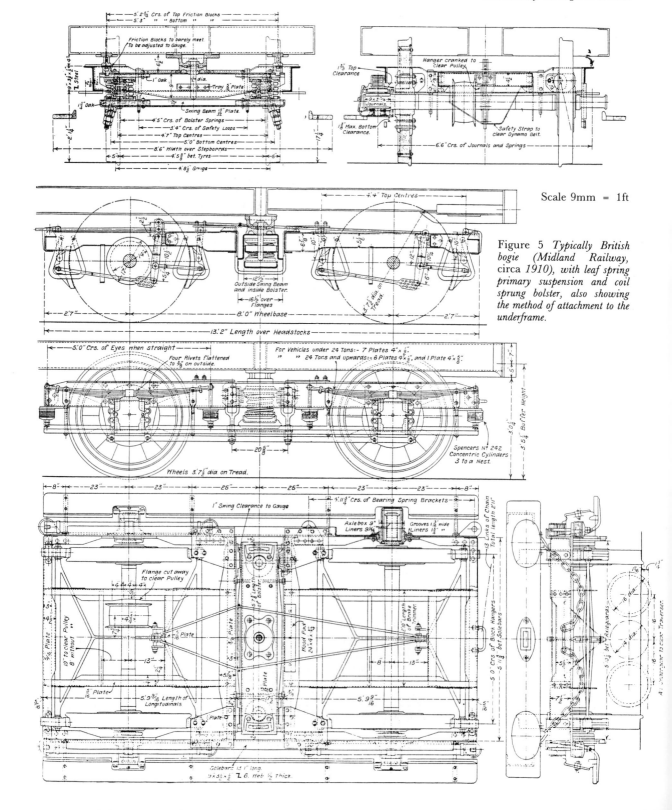

Scale 9mm = 1ft

Figure 5 *Typically British bogie (Midland Railway, circa 1910), with leaf spring primary suspension and coil sprung bolster, also showing the method of attachment to the underframe.*

bogies — again often the American type — were built with a mainframe cast in a single piece. It was, however, in its mode of attachment to the main underframe that the bogie displayed its advantages, in suspension terms, over a rigid wheelbase vehicle.

The essential component was known as a 'bolster'. This was a form of metal swinging plank set between and parallel to the two axles. It 'hung' from the bogie mainframe, usually on four rods (two at each end) known as 'swing links'. The centre of the top of the bolster carried the pivoting mechanism, the other part of which was fixed to the main underframe. Thus the weight of the carriage was carried through the pivot to the bolster and, via the swing links, to the bogie frame itself. In effect, the carriage, although appearing to bear down on top of the bogie, actually hung from it.

The swing links themselves were set in a trapezoidal shape which assisted the carriage on corners, when there is a natural tendency for the body and underframe to move to the outside of the curve by centrifugal force. This movement caused the outer swing links to adopt a more vertical position and the inner ones a slightly more inclined orientation. As a result, the bolster itself (to which was fixed the carriage body and underframe) tilted slightly inwards and the whole carriage 'leaned' into the curve — precisely what the passenger wanted for greater comfort and somewhat analogous to the leaning action of a cyclist or the banking of an aeroplane when cornering.

Although free to move within the bogie frame, the bolster itself was not permitted unlimited freedom. There were usually restraining blocks fitted to the carriage at each side to limit the maximum amount of 'tilt' — mainly to prevent the carriage underframe coming into contact with the wheel rim — and the bolster itself carried its own independent springing at each of the outer ends of the swing plank. This 'secondary' suspension, as it is known, was either in the form of transverse double leaf elliptical or powerful coil springs. Thus on a bogie carriage there were, interposed between the passenger and the wheel, at least three devices all of which helped to smooth the ride — the primary suspension, the tilting action of the bolster and the secondary suspension.

Thus, the bogie carriage was intrinsically more comfortable, particularly on curves, than a four or six-wheeler, quite apart from its other advantages. It also meant that curves could be taken more quickly without causing passenger discomfort. It can be demonstrated that the discomfort threshold is reached far sooner than the safety equivalent as far as vehicle speed is concerned so the bogie coach really did allow much higher speeds to be achieved. In practice, of course, the natural tendency of the bogie carriage to

LNWR carriage bogies undergoing overhaul at Wolverton Works during early LMS days, August 1930. Little had changed for thirty or more years — neither would it do so for a similar or longer period. The nature of the swing bolster plank itself is very apparent from the example in the foreground.

adopt a leaning position on curves was often supplemented by raising the outer rail of the track itself — superelevating as it is known.

Finally, although written in the past tense, it should perhaps be made clear that the substance of the above paragraphs still applies to the bulk of bogie vehicles on the modern railway — refined, of course, by many later improvements.

Before leaving the bogie itself, a few words about the effect of axle loading will not come amiss. The main purpose of adding wheels to a carriage was to ensure that no one axle bearing was subject to overload as weight increased. A typical turn-of-the-century British figure for coaching stock in this respect was about 6 tons per axle or a little more. This gave, typically, 12, 18 and 24 tons as fairly characteristic weights for carriages of four, six or eight wheels respectively. The railways, however, were having to build coaches heavier than 24 tons, so the next logical step was to introduce *six*-wheel bogies, capable of carrying up to 36-40 ton carriages. As the twentieth century progressed, permitted axle loadings gradually increased until some 10 or more

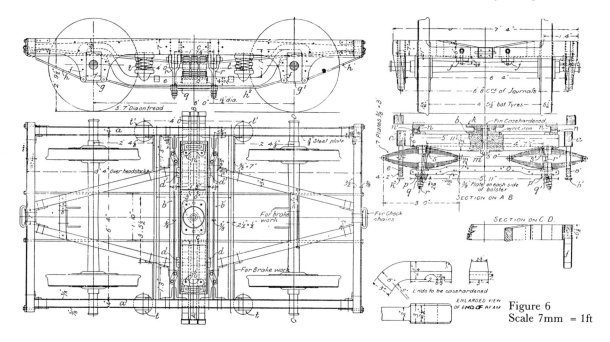

Figure 6
Scale 7mm = 1ft

Figure 6 *'American' pattern bogie with compensating beam primary suspension and transverse leaf bolster springing. The cross-section at AB shows the characteristic trapezoidal nature of the swing links on the bogie bolster, regardless of the form of primary suspension adopted.*

Figure 7 *These two diagrams show typical British six-wheel bogie designs. They represent (above) the Caledonian 'Grampian' stock of 1905 and (below) the final LNWR design of 1907, used for almost twenty years and even being fitted to some early LMS standard stock.*

tons per axle could be accepted. Thus, by the late 1930s it was possible to put 40-ton coaches on eight wheels — a weight which would have been pushing at the limits for a *twelve*-wheeler at the start of the century. Not surprisingly, the late twentieth century figure is higher still.

The six-wheel bogie itself was much the same as the four-wheel version and came in conventional or 'American' pattern as far as primary suspension was concerned. In the case of the American type, each side of the bogie carried two equalizing beams (one between each adjacent pair of wheels), both of which were anchored to the centre axlebox but free to move semi-independently. The bolster of a six-wheel bogie followed similar principles as for a four-wheeler but generally took an 'H' shape in plan — two transverse planks between and parallel to the axles joined by a central longitudinal member which carried the bogie pivot. This would have eight rather than four swing links and two sets of bolster springs on each side.

Carriage wheels and axles

These, the most fundamental components of the carriage chassis, are of far more than passing interest. They bear the brunt of the 'wear and tear' and, since even at 60 mph a typical 3 ft 6 in wheel makes 480 revolutions per minute, it is subjected to considerable stress. It must therefore be both strong and well balanced, not to say adequately supported by its bearings and springs.

Today, carriage wheels are made from cast steel discs on to which are 'shrunk' the separate steel 'tyres' which carry the wheel tread and flange, and this has been true for much of the present century. However, the era dawned with a very different sort of wheel in general use for carriages, the so-called 'Mansell' wheel, named after its inventor and characterized by its wooden centre section (see Figure 8).

Visitors to the National Railway Museum at York find it a constant source of surprise that quite heavy carriages were mounted on what they describe as 'wooden wheels' and there seems to be some lack of understanding of the considerable advantages possessed by the Mansell wheel. Although steel wheels were introduced very soon, the Mansell wheel was still being fitted to some new carriages until at least the late 1930s and remained in service for many years beyond that. Indeed, at least two of the NRM's Mansell-wheeled carriages withstood the full rigours

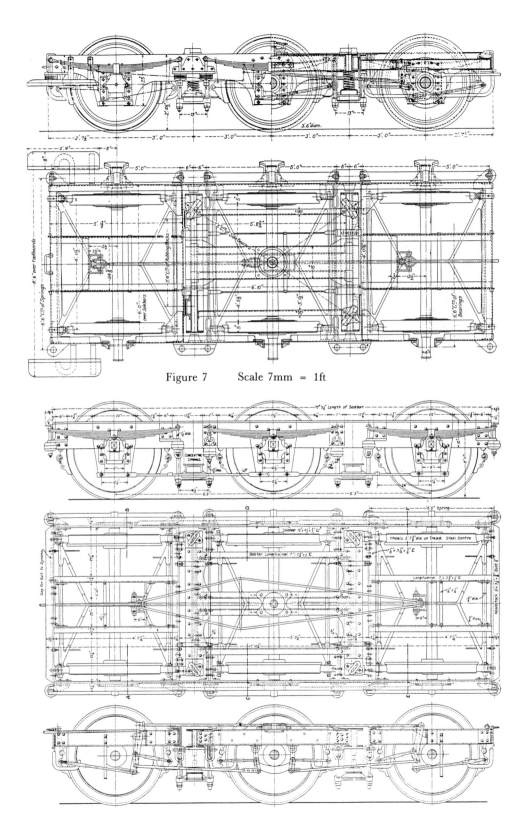

Figure 7   Scale 7mm = 1ft

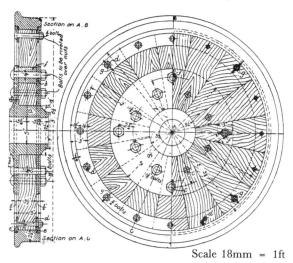

Scale 18mm = 1ft

Fitting carriage wheels to axleboxes at Wolverton, circa 1930; once again a practice hardly changed for nigh on a century, save for the method of wheel construction.

Figure 8 *Typical Mansell wheel construction as adopted by the Great Eastern Railway.*

of the current BR examination and were cleared for 70 mph running as recently as 1979.

The Mansell wheel was not solid wood. It consisted of a forged iron centre boss round which was fitted the wooden disc proper which itself was made from many separate timber segments (normally 16) which in turn were surrounded by retaining iron rings at the outer circumference. These rings also held the outer circumferential *steel* tyre. Individual railways adopted their own slight detailed design variations, but did not part from the general principle.

Turning now to the advantages of this somewhat complex wheel form, they were considerable when viewed against contemporary criteria:

1 The tyre fastening was very safe even if the tyre should break into a number of separate pieces — a real enough if not very common risk — because each separated piece would remain attached to the wheel unless the retaining ring also broke. This was a very unlikely eventuality.

2 The whole circumference of the tyre was supported by the wooden disc. This somewhat 'insulated' the tyre and caused less noise transmission to the carriage interior and less of the characteristic 'ringing' sound.

3 The tyres could be allowed to wear down in thickness to a considerable extent without danger.

4 The wheels were relatively easy to make and needed little skilled labour.

5 The slight elasticity of the wooden centre, compared with a rigid steel disc, probably made the wheels somewhat less vulnerable to the

stresses and shocks caused by passing over the very numerous rail joints (characteristic of the early part of the century) at the higher speeds then becoming common.

In due course, the obvious advantages (to modern-day eyes) of the one-piece cast steel disc wheel gradually became paramount in new vehicle construction, but this had to await the ability to make the right sort of steel; and it is not too fanciful to state that without the Mansell wheel, the early twentieth-century railways would have found it much harder to meet the ever growing public demand for more amenities (ie heavier coaches) and higher speeds (ie more stress on the moving parts).

Regardless of wheel type, the twentieth-century carriage always employed steel axles and even at the turn of the century a desired tensile strength of some 40 tons per square inch was required for any one axle. At this time, several interesting tests were demanded of the steel, including the ability to be bent double when cold without fracturing and an ability to withstand, also without fracturing, a ton weight dropped on it from a height of 20 ft, five times in succession, the axle being turned between each blow and supported only on two bearings some 3 ft 6 in apart.

It was thus an extremely rare thing for axle failure to occur, and such was the quality of workmanship that axles bearing a date stamp as early as 1908 have fully withstood the full rigours of present-day BR scientific ultrasonic stress testing when such institutions as the National Railway Museum have sought to operate vintage vehicles on the main lines.

Buffing and drawgear

The buffing and drawgear represent, after the wheels themselves, the most important part of the carriage chassis.

The traditional British coach carried buffers mounted on the headstock, one at each at the four corners of the underframe. Their purpose was multi-fold. Firstly they existed to absorb the momentum of moving vehicles by forming an elastic medium between carriages and wagons as they came into contact. For this reason they needed to be strongly sprung, and thus acted as a form of shock-absorber.

A second function was to stabilize the coach in motion in several important ways. The conventional British form of coupling carriages together was by means of an adjustable screw coupling (see below) and this was tightened up so as just to bring the buffer heads of adjacent vehicles into contact, or even slight compression. The friction generated by this contact, albeit usually made less by 'greasing' the buffer heads, tended to keep carriages steady when running at speed, particularly on curves and when negotiating pointwork and junctions. Additionally, the compression between the buffer heads also damped down most of the tendency for any vehicle to oscillate too much, particularly to 'roll' about its longitudinal axis. Thus, by preventing excessive to-and-fro movement and reducing the lateral tendency to oscillate, the buffers of a railway carriage materially assisted the train itself to behave as a unit rather than as a series of independently-minded wayward vehicles! During the early part of this century, this effect could most readily be appreciated by comparing the generally quite stately motion of a passenger train with the 'jack-rabbit' antics of the trucks in a typical loose-coupled goods train. In the latter case, the buffers merely prevented end shocks and were not always particularly successful even in this role.

A further characteristic of the tightly-coupled passenger train was that, if properly assembled, the buffer heads would not even separate when the train started, thus giving even more benefit to the passenger. The smooth starting and stopping of most British passenger trains was an oft-remarked aspect of railway operation in this country, much appreciated by overseas visitors. However, so much was this

form of train assembly taken for granted by the British travelling public that should a set of carriages be less than perfectly coupled together the resulting 'snatches' and 'jerks' between carriage ends — not abnormal in other lands — would probably precipitate some sort of adverse comment. Even the *Times* correspondence columns were not free from barbed shafts should the railways thus fall from grace.

With the advent of bogie stock on a more general basis, particularly the longer (60-70 ft) vehicles, the buffer heads became quite large and, viewed end-on, frequently assumed oval form with the major axis horizontal. This was to cope with the mathematical problems caused by long, straight vehicles rounding curves. A study of Figure 9 will reveal that the lateral displacement relative to the track centre-line could be considerable at the vehicle ends, and this was exaggerated if a reverse curve was encountered. If the carriages were being drawn along there would normally be no problem, but when being propelled, in sidings for example, the buffers were in compression and could quite easily slide laterally relative to each other sufficient for one to 'lock' behind the other. This would almost certainly cause derailment when the carriages met the next length of straight track. Larger buffer heads generally resolved this problem, as indeed did an alternative form of carriage coupling — the 'buckeye' type, which will be dealt with later.

The buffer springs themselves were contained behind the headstock or in the buffer housing itself. In earlier days (particularly, but not exclusively, on four-wheel and six-wheel stock), it was quite common to have buffers bearing against a transverse leaf spring, but this gradually gave way to independent springing, generally a longitudinal India rubber or coil spring behind the solebar, and some vehicles had self-contained semi-pneumatic springing within their casings.

Coupling between carriages was made for the most part by a pair of forged links with an adjustable screw

Figure 9 *Diagram showing the geometry of a typical bogie carriage on a curve. The lateral offset of the headstock is shown, dotted, at 'a' and 'b', the bogie pivots are at 'c' and the position of the bogie, relative to the curve centre, is indicated by lines 'd' and 'e'.*

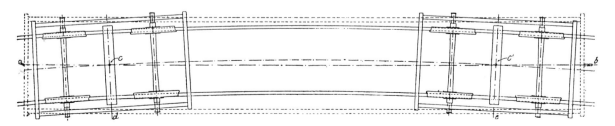

Scale 42mm = 1ft

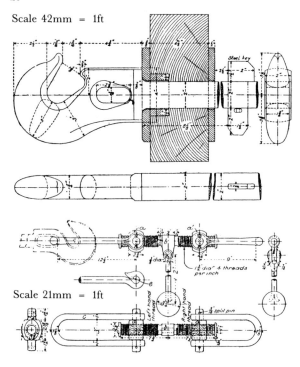

Scale 21mm = 1ft

Figure 10 *Typically British pattern draw-hook and adjustable screw coupling.*

thread linking the two to tighten them up — the so-called screw coupling (Figure 10). The carriages would be coupled with the links slack (for ease of handling) and then the screw thread would be tightened up, after which all necessary brake, heating, electrical and gangway connections could be made. This was, needless to say, a somewhat tedious and time consuming process, and moreover one which needed to be done with considerable care in order to impart the stability already discussed. There was, therefore, every reason to cut down the number of times when carriage formations were changed, and for this reason many railways utilized fixed 'sets' of coaches which were rarely split up. This was particularly valuable in the case of intensive suburban workings, but even on the main-line services it was quite common for at least part of the train to be in 'fixed formation', to which could be added extra stock to meet specific needs.

The screw coupling itself was carried through the headstock and either anchored securely to a suitable part of the underframe or connected with its opposite number at the other end of the carriage, the latter being referred to as 'continuous' drawgear. In either case, the coupling hooks were spring loaded to provide a little 'give' when starting from rest. Several alternative methods were available, well described in numerous technical journals of the day.

With discontinuous drawgear, the front coupling

of the leading carriage had to withstand the whole weight of the train behind it, the progressive strain on each coupling becoming less as the rear of the train was approached. With continuous drawgear, the actual pull was distributed down the train through the various drawbars and each coupling had, in effect, to contend with only the weight of its own coach. Before underframes were made exclusively of steel, the rather more sophisticated continuous pattern drawgrear was preferred, but with the much stronger steel underframe capable of withstanding immense strains this was less critical.

Finally, the screw coupling was sometimes permitted a degree of side to side movement within the headstock. This was to help adjust to line curvature, particularly in the case of long carriages. Typically, for example, the London and North Western Railway permitted some 5 inches of lateral movement of the coupling hook on its long twelve-wheelers.

There was an alternative to the screw coupling/side buffer method and, like the carriage bogie, it was American in its origins. In North America, the Pullman Car Company was probably the principal trend-setter in carriage design and in its carriages it had introduced, from the 1880s, a centre automatic coupling and a new type of gangway — the so-called 'Pullman vestibule' (see page 47). Henry Howard Sessions the superintendent of the Pullman Company in the 1880s, was the leading figure in this improve-

ment, but it was not until the early twentieth century that something similar became widespread in Britain.

This was the so-called Gould or 'buckeye' coupling. It took the form of a movable knuckle-shaped hook in the centre of the headstock, and the mere act of propelling two similarly equipped vehicles together, one of which should have the hook 'open', causes the hooks to spring back behind each other when the joint is made. It can best be envisaged by locking the curled fingers of both hands together. There was, inevitably, a degree of longitudinal tolerance, but most of this was taken up, once the buckeye coupling was 'made', by the compression together of the two Pullman-type gangways. It was in all important respects a better arrangement.

The principal British protagonist of this type of coupling was the celebrated Nigel Gresley (later Sir Nigel) who, when carriage superintendent of the English Great Northern Railway, standardized the Gould coupling on main-line stock. It had, in fact, been used earlier but not universally. It became the standard form on the LNER after grouping and was used exclusively by the English Pullman Company and widely adopted by the English Southern Railway in later years. However, many British companies, notably the Great Western and the principal constituents of what was to become Britain's largest railway, the LMS, remained faithful to the screw coupling and old-style gangway connection.

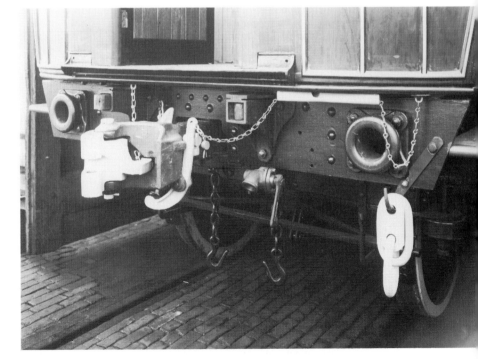

Far left *Midland Railway corridor carriage No 2845 shows a typical British arrangement of carriage end detail features. Note particularly the screw couplings, large oval-shaped buffer heads, vacuum brake (upper) and steam heat connection hoses and gangway detail — see also Chapters 3 and 4. The coach itself, a brake composite, contained first, third and guard/brake compartments .*

Left *A complete view of the whole buckeye system on GNR twelve-wheel clerestory dining car No 2993, including Pullman-type gangways (see also Chapter 3, page 47). The side buffers themselves, of quasi-oval shape, are extended and the buckeye is dropped for attachment to a conventionally equipped carriage.*

Right *Typical buckeye coupling on a Gresley carriage. The movable hook and the lever to activate it are painted white. Pulling on the lever of the mechanism will open the hook to allow the coupling to be made with a similarly equipped vehicle. Note also the fairly wide slot in the headstock to allow some lateral movement of the drawgear. Buffers and gangway are still to be fitted.*

There were thus two widely disparate standards in use in Britain and they needed to be reconciled in some way for through working if nothing else. This merits clarification, for the two forms of coupling and their associated gangways (where present) were fundamentally incompatible. The gangway aspect is considered in Chapter 3, as part of the discussion of bodywork, but we can conveniently deal with the coupling problem here.

It is a characteristic of the buckeye coupling that it does not actually need corner buffers to stabilize the vehicle. Thus, in an 'all-buckeye' environment, side buffers are not fitted. This has been true for generations past in North America and has become so in Britain in all cases where vehicles can be guaranteed some form of exclusivity in use. However, when it is necessary to couple a buckeyed vehicle to a conventional one, a regular routine throughout much of this century, it is the buckeyed vehicle which needs to be modified. This is done by means of 'unlocking' the centre knuckle coupler and allowing it to hinge down out of the way. This done, there stands revealed a conventional hook to which the adjustable screw link can be attached from the adjacent vehicle.

Additionally, the buckeyed vehicle has to be fitted with side buffers, normally idle and kept retracted close to the headstock and well out of contact range with an adjacent vehicle. To render them operational, the buffer heads are pulled out by some 6-9 inches and a metal collar placed over the exposed shank to prevent it from re-retracting too far. The buffer then functions normally and can be brought into compression with the conventional vehicle.

Somewhat surprisingly, since the buckeye also has considerable advantages in terms of absorbing end impact (eg collision damage), the British did not adopt the system as standard for new construction until well after the railways were nationalized in 1948. Even as these words are written some forty years later still, many vehicles carry the older type of arrangement and it is not possible to predict when, or even if, it will totally vanish. It should, however, be stated that in 1988 no non-buckeyed long-distance passenger-carrying coaches are to be found in regular main-line service in Britain.

Brakes

While no carriages can operate without wheels and drawgear, it is a sad fact that for much of the early phase of nineteenth century history, they managed quite well without any really effective form of braking. However, by the start of the present century, automatic braking became required by law on all passenger trains, and moreover at least one vehicle per train had to be fitted with an auxiliary handbrake.

It was in this vehicle that the 'guard' rode. This legal requirement arose from a serious accident at Armagh in 1889, even though the technical problem itself had been addressed some considerable time earlier at the Newark brake trials of 1875.

Although strictly outside the general period of this book, these continuous brake trials merit a brief mention here. They were held on the Midland Railway route between Nottingham and Newark in June 1875 and involved locomotives and trains from six companies. Eight different systems were evaluated, some of more than somewhat dubious merit, and although no very conclusive recommendations came out of the trials, they did serve to demonstrate quite clearly to all save the most partisan the superiority of the Westinghouse air brake over all the others. There were, however, other considerations at work, some of which had little or nothing to do with the relative efficiency of the brakes. Vested interest was also present in such measure that no harmonization was achieved and an opportunity was lost to standardize on an efficient air brake more than a century before it finally came exclusively into its own on BR in the 1980s.

The Newark trials are well recorded elsewhere, but, in spite of the many systems tried, only two forms of braking sufficiently stood the test of time in the twentieth century context to merit our concern here, the vacuum and the air brake; even this was one too many. Inevitably, of course, both existed side by side (as with couplings and gangways) and since they were essentially incompatible, the harmonization of braking systems in Britain was bedevilled for generations. Furthermore, just as with couplings, most British companies adopted the somewhat less effective of the two alternatives, the so-called automatic vacuum brake. Not that there was anything wrong with it *per se* — it was a very good and reliable system, and totally fail safe. It was simply that the air brake was, all round, rather better. The latter type has now become a British standard but it was as recently as 1987 that regular use of the vacuum brake finally terminated. Before describing the systems, it may be helpful to list the conditions, laid down by the Board of Trade, which automatic braking had to fulfil at the end of the Victorian period:

1   In case of accident, the brakes are to be instantaneously self-acting.
2   The brakes are to be capable of being put 'on' and taken 'off' on the engine and every vehicle of the train.
3   The brakes are to be efficient, instantaneous in action and capable of application without difficulty by driver or guard.

Figure 11 *The vacuum brake apparatus.*
The detail drawings show the 'universal'
connecting hose attachment between
vehicles (a), the ball valve mechanism (b)
and the vacuum cylinder itself (c). The
main diagram (d) shows the configuration
of the whole system.

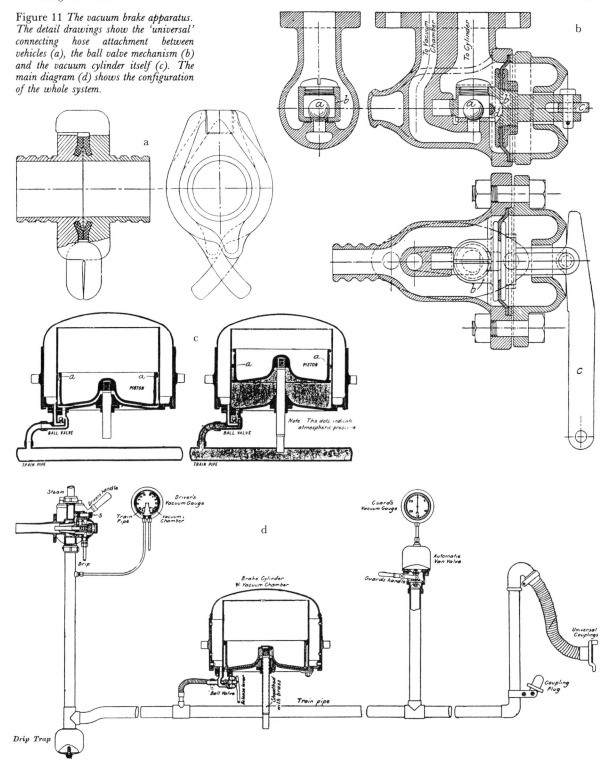

4   The brakes are to be regularly used in daily working.

5   Materials are to be durable and easily maintained in working order.

In both systems, the operation of the brake is brought about by creating a pressure difference on either side of a moving piston enclosed in the brake cylinder. The normal position (ie brakes not applied or 'off') occurs when the pressure (or lack of it) is equal on either side of the piston. Creation of the pressure difference, by accident or design, causes the piston to move, and by means of mechanical linkages (attached to the piston rod(s)) applies the brakes to the wheels. In the vacuum system the pressure difference is, theoretically, that between a perfect vacuum and normal atmospheric pressure (say 1 atmosphere at the very best). In the compressed air system, the pressure difference is between that of the compressed air itself (usually some 80-100 psi) and the atmosphere. This is some 4-6 times more than the pressure of the atmosphere acting against even a perfect vacuum; the air brake therefore possesses intrinsically more power. Indeed, it is a not very dissimilar principle which differentiates the huge and cumbersome low-pressure stationary steam engine from a smaller, but equally powered, high-pressure steam locomotive. The price paid is increased mechanical complexity and the same is true of brakes. It will therefore be helpful to outline some of the processes involved, if only to help explain the reasons for the choice between the two systems.

Dealing first with the vacuum brake, this apparatus works on the basis that a vacuum is created throughout the length of the train braking system from engine to last carriage. This is achieved by means of a continuous tube (or 'train pipe') from one end of the train to the other; vehicles are connected by flexible hoses each of which is equipped with a special connector to avoid ingress of atmospheric air. Below each carriage there is fixed the brake cylinder itself (normally one on a four-wheeler or six-wheeler and two on a bogie coach) which is connected with and 'open' to the train pipe and is thus also maintained in a state of vacuum.

When air enters the train pipe, thus destroying the vacuum, it can only reach one side of the brake piston because inside the brake cylinder is a simple non-return device — typically a ball valve — which only permits the incoming air access to one side of the piston, normally the underside. Thus the pressure difference is created within the brake cylinder which will apply the brakes. This can be achieved either deliberately, by driver or guard by means of a brake control which allows air into the brake pipe, or by accident, should the integrity of the train pipe be destroyed if, for example, two connecting hoses should separate.

This is the essential 'automatic' or 'fail safe' situation. It will be appreciated that a sudden accidental influx of air to the train pipe will apply the brakes more rapidly than the controlled influx by the driver or guard; but this is all to the good, since the train will stop more quickly. It is also possible for the driver to make a firm but controlled 'emergency' application by letting in air more rapidly than he would normally do for a routine stop. Likewise, when a passenger pulls the emergency alarm cord (chain) in a carriage, this has the effect of *partially* destroying the vacuum, thus alerting the driver who will then stop the train at the first safe place, ie within the protection of signals.

To free brakes applied by this system, it is necessary to re-establish the equilibrium in the brake cylinder(s), thus allowing the piston to resume its normal position. This can be done either by re-creating the vacuum in the train pipe or by admitting air to the normally 'vacuum only' side of the brake piston. This latter procedure is normally only carried out after vehicles have finished operating and are safely 'parked' in a siding with a handbrake applied. It is usually achieved by unseating the ball valve from its socket, thus allowing atmospheric air to reach both sides of the piston, and can be speedily effected by pulling a cord release provided for this purpose situated below the carriage floor.

To work the automatic vacuum brake, the only piece of ancillary apparatus other than the brake equipment itself, is a means to create the vacuum. This is normally achieved on the locomotive by means of an 'ejector', a mechanism which, as its name implies, ejects air from the train pipe. Sometimes the ejector was supplemented by a vacuum pump, which could maintain but not create the vacuum.

Turning now to the air brake, its intrinsically quicker-acting nature is obvious from the greater pressure difference already explained, but unlike the vacuum brake, which uses as its operating 'fluid' the universally available atmospheric air, the air-braked train must not only create but also carry with it a supply of compressed air, always available for instant use and readily replenishable. Thus, the first requirement is an air pump or compressor to create and maintain the supply of this working 'fluid'. This is an essentially more bulky and complex mechanism than the vacuum ejector, and when in operation it produces its own distinctly characteristic sounds. These were well in evidence on any steam locomotive to which one was fitted, and, indeed, on modern-day Southern Region electrics and the London Underground trains, to mention but two, the

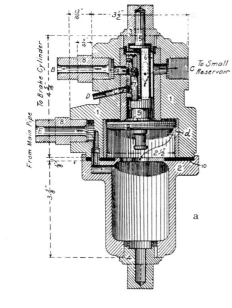

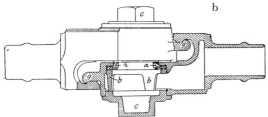

Figure 12 *The air brake apparatus. The detail drawings show the triple valve (a), the hose connection between vehicles (b) and the arrangement of the whole set-up (c).*

characteristic 'chunk-a-chunk-a-chunk' of the air compressors emanating from somewhere in the bowels of the vehicle is sufficient indication that one is riding an air-braked train!

Having created a supply of compressed air, it must then be stored and made available for use. This is usually achieved by means of a main reservoir on the engine and a series of individual auxiliary reservoirs on each coach, all interconnected. It is the small auxiliaries which actually apply power to the train brakes and they are replenished after a brake application by the compressor via the main reservoir. Already, this is a more complex set of equipment than for vacuum operation and the actuating mechanism itself is also more sophisticated, but again it makes use of the fact that, as with the vacuum brake, should air be allowed into the system (by accident or design), or more correctly should compressed air be allowed *out* of the sytem, the equilibrium is broken within the brake cylinder, the piston within is thereby caused to move and the brakes are applied. In essence, the cycle is as follows:

1   At the start of a journey, the compressed air from the engine's main reservoir is turned into the train pipe and, through branch pipes, 'charges' all the auxiliary reservoirs; but there is at this stage *no compressed air in the brake cylinder itself*, which is separated from both the main pipe and the auxiliary reservoirs by a triple valve (see step 3 below).

2   If the integrity of high pressure within the train pipe is now broken, by brake application or by severance of the flexible hose, the compressed air is released from the system and the state of equilibrium is broken. At this point the triple valve comes into play.

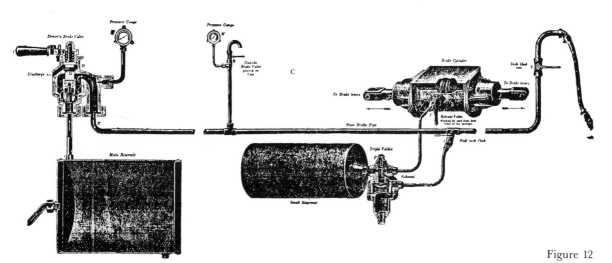

Figure 12

3 Attached to the brake cylinder is a fairly complex triple valve, connected, as its name suggests, to three outlets, the brake cylinder itself, the train pipe and the auxiliary reservoir, only two of which outlets are in mutual contact at any one time. When air is released from the train pipe, the compressed air in the auxiliary reservoir is now at a higher pressure than that in the train pipe, but is prevented from leaving the system by the triple valve. Instead, the air in the reservoir can now react against the lower pressure within the brake cylinder and thus apply the brakes.

Once again, the precise working of the various mechanisms need not concern us, but in essence whereas the vacuum brake works by increasing pressure on the *active* side of the brake cylinder piston, the air brake works by reducing pressure on the *passive* side. To do this requires a much more complicated mechanism to create and maintain the essential compressed air; so it may reasonably be asked why did *any* railway adopt the air brake, a clearly more expensive solution?

The reasons are bound up with train working, for the air brake is essentially quicker acting and this could be an important operational factor. Each auxiliary reservoir functions as an independent power source when the train pipe pressure is reduced, thus producing a well nigh instantaneous reaction down the train. With the vacuum system, the operating medium, air, comes from within the single train pipe and thus takes a measurable, if brief, time to be brought to bear on all vehicles. It is an altogether gentler sort of brake for the passenger and was, for this reason, often preferred. Indeed, when BR finally went over to air braking on most of its hitherto 'vacuum' main lines, many were the jerks and judders to be felt as drivers took time to appreciate the generally fiercer characteristics of the new air brakes compared with the older system.

It was, of course, these very characteristics which caused the air brake to be adopted in Britain by those railways which favoured it. The quick application and quick release offered a much more sensible choice where systems had a high proportion of intensive 'stop and start' suburban operations. Thus, it became an obvious choice for several of the steam railways radiating from London and elsewhere. It was also a natural choice wherever service frequency indicated that the even higher capital cost of electrification was justified, hence the London

Underground and Southern Railway examples already mentioned.

The air brake is also advantageous, for reasons already stated, where normal train lengths are considerable and/or where higher speeds are contemplated. Thus, in North America, with its immensely long trains, it has always been favoured (for both passenger and freight), and in Britain its ability to bring a train to a halt from higher speed but at no sacrifice in braking *distance* has been crucial to the speed-up of both passenger and freight operations since the late 1950s and early 1960s.

Before leaving the subject of brakes, one or two more points need making. To expedite through working between vacuum-braked and air-braked railways, it was often necessary for carriages to carry both types of equipment. In this case, the vehicle was said to be 'dual braked' and revealed its status by even more flexible hoses dangling from the carriage ends than either system would require on its own. To avoid wrong hose connections — and this point at least *was* standardized in Britain — the air hoses were normally of smaller diameter than the vacuum hoses, and carried a differently shaped connector.

Finally, for the bulk of the vehicles covered in this survey, the brakes themselves were in the form of friction blocks rubbing against the wheel tread and activated by a series of rods and levers connected to the brake cylinder(s). One set of 'brake rodding' normally sufficed on each carriage, in the case of dual fitted carriages being independently connected to both the vacuum and the air cylinders but, of course, only operated by whichever system was in use at the time.

In the case of so-called 'brake vans', a brake wheel in the guard's compartment could apply the brakes independently, by acting mechanically on the same set of rodding. If this form of handbrake was applied, it could not of course be released by simply pulling an external string, for it had to be physically released from within the vehicle. It was the railway equivalent, if you like, of a parking brake, and was mostly used to hold carriages stationary on gradients or in sidings when not connected to a locomotive. Needless to say, incidences of trains moving off without the handbrake being released were not uncommon and could result, *in extremis*, in the wheels being dragged along the rails for a distance. The resulting 'flat' on the wheel circumference, even if only small, could be disturbing to the passengers and could take several hundreds of miles to be worn away.

3. The carriage body

We must now turn our attention to that part of the carriage which, for most people, gives it character — the main body shell. In Britain, unlike many countries, carriages were usually designed by the railways that operated them rather than being purchased 'off the peg' from a range of manufacturer's standard types. Most were also built by the companies themselves, but even where railways felt the need to go to outside contractors, the carriages were still mostly built to the company's rather than the contractor's design. Of course this was true also for locomotives and as in the latter sphere so too in the carriage field, the British scene was characterized by its infinite variety both in style and decorative treatment. Some railways followed broadly similar lines while others were markedly different, and there were always subtle distinctions to be seen. There was no way, for example, that a London and North Western carriage could be mistaken for a Great Western example, or a Midland one confused with a Great Northern product; and Pullman was different from them all. One suspects that the companies preferred it that way!

Yet within all this manifold variety there was an underlying consistency of approach which this chapter attempts to distil, with the sole exception of the Pullman type, a vehicle of markedly American inspiration in both style and construction which will therefore be considered separately in Chapter 12.

The 'British' carriage made use of a separate body shell, mounted on an appropriate underframe. At the start of the twentieth century, wooden construction was the normal practice and remained the dominant material for most of the period covered by this first volume. Even though certain railways, for example the LNWR, GWR, Midland, Lancashire and Yorkshire and London and South Western, occasionally assayed the use of metal sheeting for parts of the outer 'skin' and added metal reinforcements to the framework, a wooden structure was the basis. After the grouping in 1923, the LMS did not really abandon what was, basically, a wooden-bodied coach until after 1930, while the LNER clung on to solid teak for the vast majority of its coaches until as late as 1941. Even then, both of these great companies still remained faithful to mostly timber frameworks, albeit with metal skins. Nor did techniques vary too much. The late Victorian period had seen the establishment of most of the principles which remained sound for many decades into the new century; they stood the test of time.

The body proper: floors, sides and ends

British carriages at the start of the present century were mostly built on the compartment principle embodying many outside doors. The need to thus interrupt the framing to make way for doorways rather inhibited the more integral type of construction favoured by Pullman (whose carriages generally had end doors only) and was one of the major reasons for the continued use of separate bodies, certainly during the 'wooden' era.

The starting point was the floor itself, a typical form of contemporary turn-of-the-century construction being shown, largely self-explanatory, in Figure 13. The main point to make is that the floor itself was designed to suit the configuration of corridors, partitions, lavatories, etc which were eventually to be erected upon it, and careful marking out and preliminary joinery had to be carried out to make sure that all subsequent components were a precise fit. Most of the actual joinery embodied quite simple forms of construction in order to expedite manufacture by machinery. Normal rules of carpentry applied in terms of the thickness of tenons, depth of mortices and grain direction relative to the joints in question. The aim was to ensure that pieces connected together were weakened as little as possible. The timber most commonly used for floor framing was oak or teak, the floor itself being made of deal, as were the internal partitions. Additionally, metal angle corner brackets (or 'knees') were often used to reinforce right-angle (and other) joints, and many sections were bolted together — indeed, the term 'coach bolt' provides its own explanation.

Above the floor, the side and end framing had to be designed so as to maintain its proper formation as well as support the covering panels. Again, oak or teak was the preferred choice for framing, with some preference for teak which keeps its form better during climatic changes, endemic, of course, as far as British railway carriages were concerned. Typical turn-of-the-century arrangements, giving all the associated nomenclature, are shown in Figure 14.

In general, it was customary to build the side and end frames as a series of sub-assemblies before offering up each completed frame to the floor. The analogy with a modelmaker's 'kit of parts' comes to mind and is a not wholly inappropriate way of visualizing the process. The order of assembly was usually to erect the ends first, followed by the corner panels and all the side sections containing fixed lights. The 'cantrail' was then added along the top of the side sections, thus securing the vertical pillars and forming

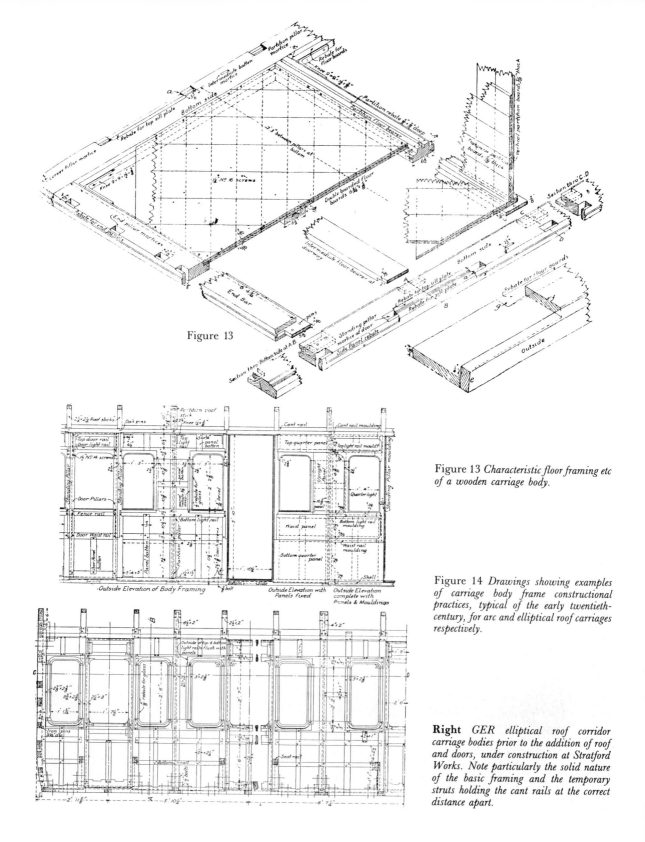

Figure 13

Figure 13 *Characteristic floor framing etc of a wooden carriage body.*

Figure 14 *Drawings showing examples of carriage body frame constructional practices, typical of the early twentieth-century, for arc and elliptical roof carriages respectively.*

Right *GER elliptical roof corridor carriage bodies prior to the addition of roof and doors, under construction at Stratford Works. Note particularly the solid nature of the basic framing and the temporary struts holding the cant rails at the correct distance apart.*

the base of the roof. At this point, and before adding the roof and doors, it was customary practice to 'straighten' the coach body if necessary. If it was found that any part of the framing was bulging outwards or inwards it was either cramped or forced out, and temporary battens or stretchers were fixed across between the side pillars to hold the assembly straight. The datum line for straightness was struck at waist level, for if the body was not straight at this point it would be difficult for the pre-assembled doors to be properly fitted.

At this intermediate stage the body was also kept square by placing temporary struts either between the cantrails or diagonally from the foot of a pillar at one side to the opposite side cantrail. Clearly, once all the internal partitions, seat rails, roof sections and panels had been added, the integrity of the shape would be permanently assured, so it was important to start from a properly 'trued-up' framework. Once a truly square and straight assembly had been achieved, the framing was then cleaned at the joints and tested (with a straight-edge) to ensure that the foundation for the outer panels was level. If not, the panels would twist and possibly split. Moreover, the resultant uneven surface would display itself badly under paint or varnish, and this was most certainly *not* to be desired. This, after all, was the part of the carriage which the customer registered first — its outer 'skin'!

Before the days of the metal-skinned coach, outside panels were usually made of either Moulmein teak or Honduras mahogany. The latter was favoured if a painted finish was desired because it took the paint well, while although the natural oils in teak made it less suitable (when very new) for a paint finish it was an admirable candidate for a varnished finish, its normal treatment. Finally, while it was rare for a new teak-panelled carriage to be *painted*, there were examples of mahogany-panelled carriages being *varnished*, for instance on the London Brighton and South Coast Railway at the turn of the century.

Regardless of timber choice, the selection of the right piece for a particular location was a matter of some skill. Firstly, the correct part of the trunk of the tree had to be used for such panels as needed to be curved (eg the bottom panels below fixed lights and at the bottom of doors). A near-contemporary description states that such panels 'should not be cut from the middle of the tree but from the sides and should have the heart side outwards as the natural law which governs the shrinkage of timber will then tend to keep the panel in the direction in which it is bent'.

Having established the correct shape for the panels

it was then not uncommon, if a varnished finish was to be given, to consider the grain pattern. Builders of wooden-bodied coaches had something of a passion for symmetry, and if grain pattern could enhance such effects it was often felt desirable, especially for the better coaches, to choose and place adjacent panels in harmonizing or matching pairs or triples, depending on the grain pattern.

Before being actually applied to the carriage framing, mahogany and teak panels required rather different treatment. Mahogany is very durable when dry but does not, unless protected by paint or varnish, stand up too well to weather. Moreover, it can become brittle when older, even though retaining its durability. For this reason, mahogany panels had to be additionally treated before fixing to avoid splitting. This was normally achieved by backing them with a canvas layer, thoroughly soaked with hot glue. When this was pressed into the back of the panel it became almost bedded into the wood surface which had been left rough finished just for this very purpose. The outer face of the panel was, of course, scraped or sandpapered.

If the panel was to be one of the curved variety, it was often fixed in position while quite warm, before the glue had set; it bent more readily in this condition and would dry out in the 'curved' configuration. Flat panels were allowed to dry out before fixing, and in either case the body framing was normally treated with white lead paint before the panels were fixed

into position. The fixing was done by means of carriage pins set round the edges of the panels (copper was preferred to iron for the best work since it avoided rust). Curved panels were usually fixed from the bottom edge, working upwards.

When positioned, the panels were further stiffened at the back by blocks of wood glued at intervals into the corners formed by the panel and the pillars, rails or battens forming the framework; this was to prevent splitting. Any remaining panel areas unsupported by such blocks were then covered by flat wooden pieces, about 2 inches square, glued in position with their grain running diagonally to that of the panel. When dry, the whole (of the inside surface) was given several coats of protective white lead paint.

All told, it was such an immensely careful procedure as to make one wonder at times why mahogany was used at all compared with teak. The latter wood is much less liable to split and does not necessarily need to be glued; in fact, it was usually so oily when new that contemporary glues would not adhere properly for any length of time anyway. Thus teak panels were often only pinned in position, supported solely by the main framework — a much less time consuming procedure. Again, the inside faces were coated with white lead.

I have been quite unable to determine the reasons why the different railways chose these two disparate

Lower body panel replacement on Queen Alexandra's (ex-LNWR) Royal Saloon at the National Railway Museum during 1981. These curved profile lower panels were always the most difficult to make and, in consequence, often the most likely to need constant attention due to splitting for instance.

Figure 15 *Typical cross-section of the upper part of a wooden-bodied carriage side showing the framing, panel and window bolection treatment.*

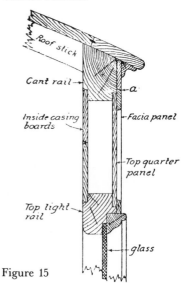

Figure 15

The panel beading, window frame and other characteristic details of a typical Edwardian wooden-bodied carriage are well exemplified in this view of London & South Western Railway tri-composite (1st/2nd and 3rd class) brake No 3598 in process of restoration at the National Railway Museum during 1986.

timbers. Economics or merely the desire to have a painted finish may have had something to do with it. Labour, of course, was relatively cheap at the time and even tradition cannot be discounted. Furthermore, mahogany is known to be a lovely wood to work compared with teak, so it may, all in all, have been something of a swings and roundabouts situation.

Once panelled, the outside body (except the doors) could be finished off. This normally took the form of applying outside mouldings (usually of the same ⅜ inch thickness as the panels proper) to cover each of the panel joins, which gave further scope for embellishment. While it may have been necessary to put some sort of moulding on the carriage to protect the panel joins, there were no rules as to the precise shape or profile they should follow. Thus these moulding strips (or 'beading' strips as they were sometimes called) could be round or square cornered, or both in combination; in profile they could be half round, flat or 'D' shaped; and in width could vary from about 1 inch to more than 2 inches. They were pinned into position using pins sufficiently long to penetrate both panel and framework. Each railway adopted somewhat different approaches to set its own hallmark on its carriages (see Chapter 7) and the pictures with this chapter show other possible variations within what was, in all essentials, the same basic process.

The same was true of the fixed quarter lights and other fixed windows. The glass itself was bedded in the aperture on either felt, putty or India rubber and held in position by 'picture frame' type mouldings — sometimes called bolections (Figure 15) — fixed from the outside. In this case, the mouldings were fixed with brass screws so that they could be removed easily when new glass was required. If the screw head was to be left visible (rather than countersunk, filled over and painted), a more decorative screw might be adopted and it was a fair certainty that the craftsmen of the day would then take particular care that all the slots in the screw heads were identically aligned, possibly changing orientation as they went round a corner!

The carriage roof

Yet another distinctive and often distinguishing feature of the railway carriage was its roof. Its purpose was, of course, to protect the interior and its construction was fairly standardized, but its shape was almost as varied as the railways were numerous. So, before going any further this aspect had better be clarified — it will recur regularly in these pages.

Essentially, when discussing roof shape one is referring to its cross-profile, ie viewed from the end. There were two fundamental sorts, the plain roof profile and the clerestory section. Both could exhibit several variations in curvature, but the essential difference was that the clerestory roof had a raised centre section and its employment forced a change in constructional technique.

Taking the plain roof first, this could vary from being almost flat (the British carriage never, as far as is known, employed a flat roof) to a deep, almost (but not quite) semi-circular profile. Generally, the plain roof could be grouped into three broad families, whose characteristics are summarized below:

1 *The 'arc' or 'compass' roof* (Figure 16) This roof shape usually displayed a perfect arc of a circle, of differing radii depending on the individual company. In some cases, the curvature sharpened a little as it approached the carriage side, but the genuine arc roof was always characterized by meeting the side proper at a quite definite angle. The arc roof was essentially a nineteenth-century style, but some coaches were built to this profile in the twentieth.

2 *The 'low elliptical' or 'cove' roof* (Figure 17) This roof shape had an 'arc' type centre section (again of varying radius depending on the company), but the junction between the main roof curve and the top of the cantrail was in the form of a radius of

Scale 7mm = 1ft

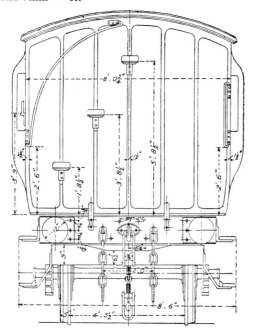

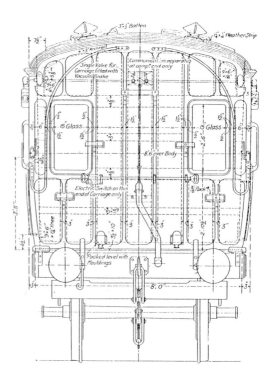

Figure 16 *Typical arc roof profile displayed on a Caledonian Railway brake-ended carriage.*

Figure 17 *A turn of the century 'cove' or low-elliptical roof profile as adopted by the Great Central Railway.*

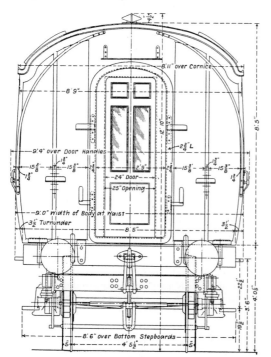

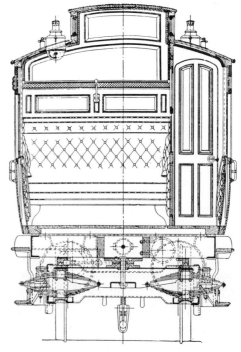

Figure 18 *The most typically twentieth-century roof shape was the fully elliptical form, as characterized here by an LNWR example.*

Figure 19 *Cross-sectional drawing of a typical British 'add-on' clerestory roof, in this case a late-nineteenth-century NER example. Further drawings of this particular type are shown in Figure 32 (page 66).*

a circle (often quite small) which was actually directed almost vertically where the roof met the side. This style also dated back to the nineteenth century but remained in use for new construction for some little time after 1900.

3 *The 'high-elliptical' or 'full elliptical' roof* (Figure 18) This section was, in all its subtle variations, by far the most typical British twentieth-century roof shape and after the railway grouping of 1923 no other type was built. Indeed, many companies had adopted it much earlier in the century.

The word 'elliptical' is something of a misnomer. For a start, it was, in fact, only at best a semi-elliptical shape, but even allowing for this well accepted form of linguistic impurity it is doubtful if the so-called 'elliptical' roof ever bore much more than a passing resemblance to the pure mathematical form from which it took its name. It was, of course, a sort of 'half oval', but the actual shape was usually derived by setting out a series of genuine circular arcs linked together.

If to these three categories one adds various other qualifying adjectives, one can readily imagine the descriptive situation quickly getting out of hand, but oddly enough this does not seem to have caused too much actual confusion — so this book will continue the tradition.

The 'add-on' clerestory style is well exemplified by NER composite (first/third) No 3414. This was a particularly opulent vehicle for its time, having lavatories for both classes but no draughty outside doors for either category. The carriage displays typical David Bain panelling — see page 110 — and its stylistic similarity, roof excepted, to the picture on page 40 is readily apparent.

Turning now to the clerestory roof (Figure 19), its ecclesiastical nomenclature is obvious. The raised centre section, ie the clerestory proper, had vertical sides, sometimes fitted with windows known as 'deck lights'. Two main forms of clerestory were to be seen in Britain, once again with considerable subtle variations within each. The older type simply added the clerestory to the top of an arc roof section, the clerestory roof itself also displaying an arc profile. The North Eastern Railway was rather fond of this shape, as was the nineteenth-century Midland (in small doses).

Later clerestories were often of much more subtle contour, generally employing a more rounded (or 'shouldered') lower roof profile together with a clerestory top which could either be a perfect arc or, as in the case of the later Midland examples, of more subtle compound curvature. The London and North Western and Great Northern Railways produced some particularly nice examples, while the Great Western entered the twentieth century with its own distinctive form which did not quite fit either category.

On most British carriages until quite modern times, the roof cross-profile continued to the carriage end unmodified and was reflected in the detail treatment given to this part of the vehicle. However, some railways adopted a down-curved roof at the ends of the coach (viewed from the side). This is usually referred to as a 'domed' roof, once again employing a not wholly accurate descriptive word. Some particularly beautiful effects were often created, both with plain and clerestory profiles, possibly the most celebrated examples of which on a plain roof were the many teak-bodied coaches built for the GNR and

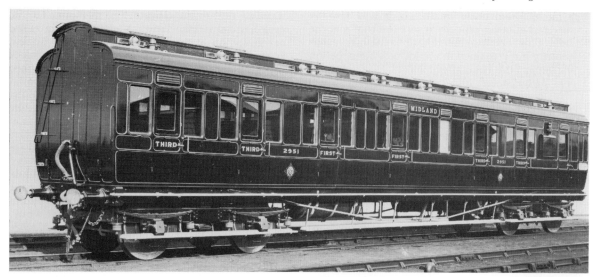

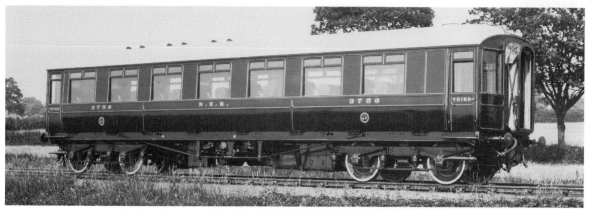

LNER by Nigel Gresley in the pre-grouping and post-grouping period, which became a real hallmark of the LNER main lines in the 1920s and 1930s. The North Eastern also produced a rather similar roof, as did the GWR in the 1940s.

On the clerestory side, the 'doming' could be either on both the lower roof *and* the clerestory, or on the clerestory roof only. In the former category, outstanding examples were the LNWR dining and sleeping cars whose construction just extended into the twentieth century, while in the second category the later LNWR clerestories and those of the East Coast Joint Stock were as good as any to serve as quick examples at this point in the narrative.

So to the building of the roof itself. For a plain roof without a domed end, the essential requirement was to establish the correct profile at the carriage end and then repeat it at intervals throughout the length of the vehicle, thus establishing the basic skeletal shape on to which the roof covering was to be fixed. Starting with the carriage end framing, the top member known as the 'arch rail' was the key. It was a substantial component, often sawn out of a single piece of wood. Sometimes, for economy, particularly with more curvaceous roof sections, several pieces of wood were employed, carefully jointed together. Like all other members of the carriage framework it could be — and usually was — rebated at the lower edge to accept the various pieces of panel timber and, as with the sides, joints were covered with beading strips.

Between the two end arch rails were situated a series of 'roof sticks' across the carriage, fixed to the tops of the cantrails. These copied exactly the curve of the arch rail and were rarely more than 2 or 3 feet apart. For example, above a typical compartment of say 6 feet between partitions, each partition would be surmounted by a roof stick and there would be at least one and commonly two sticks between the partitions. Roof sticks were sometimes made of ash, sawn to the curve of the roof, but this was rather wasteful of timber so a common solution was to bend roof sticks on a machine.

The machine itself was a device rather resembling a longitudinal slice from the outside of a cylinder whose radius was somewhat less than that of the roof. The roof sticks were placed on top of this curved surface and then bent down to meet the curve, being held in position by rollers which were screwed down from above. To provide the right conditions for bending, the roof sticks, before being put on the machine, were place in a closed steam chamber for about 2 hours at some 50 psi. They were then clamped to the machine and left for at least 6 hours to cool down. Even so, there was still a natural tendency for them to straighten partially as the drying out continued. In part this was allowed for by making the radius of the bending machine smaller than that of the coach roof, but just to make sure a straight lath was placed across the ends of the roof sticks and pinned to them to prevent further straightening. They were then allowed to dry completely and only at this point were they cut to finished section with all necessary grooving or shaping.

When fixing the roof sticks to the cantrails, it was common to make a slight modification to the usual rectilinear framing joints. The natural tendency of the roof stick would still be to push the cantrails away from each other, so the joint was often made in the form of a dovetail whose shape, acting as a wedge, would serve to prevent the sides from spreading.

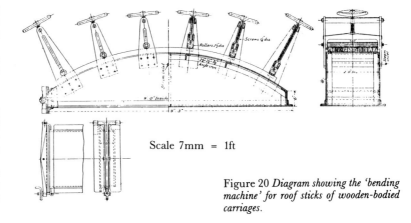

Scale 7mm = 1ft

Figure 20 *Diagram showing the 'bending machine' for roof sticks of wooden-bodied carriages.*

Ready for canvassing — the NRM's LSWR tri-composite No 3598 (see the picture on page 37). Again note the variable width roof boards.

Interior view of an elliptical roof carriage before the addition of interior fittings. Note the metal reinforced roof sticks and the variable width roof boards, narrower at the more curved portion, wider in the centre. The carriage is an MR-design gangwayed open third class of the type shown in the picture on page 191.

Roof sticks were, quite clearly, not the easiest of components to make, particularly as the demand arose for deeper and more curvaceous roofs. They were at their simplest in the pure arc roof form and it is not without significance that even before the end of the nineteenth century, several railways had begun to use rolled metal bars of angle, 'T' or channel section to support the roof, and this ability to use an alternative material may have helped the move to the semi-elliptical roof. Certainly this was one of the first areas where an alternative to wood was used as part of the basic constructional framework of the vehicle. Even where a fully metal roof stick was not employed, it became increasingly common to reinforce the conventional wooden version with a flat metal plate along the whole length.

For a domed roof, it was the roof sticks only which established the cross-profile, since the arch rail followed the contour of the lowered outer end. In these cases, the normal procedure was to fill in the space between the last proper roof stick and the arch rail with a series of shorter curved pieces (at right angles to the roof stick and arch rail) whose curvature matched the desired shape at the point on the roof.

The roof was normally covered with tongue and groove boarding, fixed longitudinally between the roof sticks, utilizing the latter as formers. The width of the boarding varied according to the curvature of the roof; for instance, a coved roof would have quite narrow boards round the sharper curve of the roof

edge and considerably wider ones at the more gently curved centre section. When the roof was boarded over, the gaps between the boards were stopped up and then the whole roof was covered in canvas, well impregnated with a fairly gruesome and messy mixture of linseed oil, white lead and putty. This substance oozed into all the crevices and through the canvas itself to form a waterproof seal. Further layers were added on top of the fixed canvas and a study of preserved coaches reveals that this was one area where perfection of appearance was often sacrificed to expediency. Perhaps it was the unpleasant nature of the work or maybe simply 'out of sight, out of mind'.

As a general rule the roof edge along the cantrail was finished off in one of two ways. The edge of an arc roof overhung the cantrail and the canvas went round to the underside. This sort of overhanging eaves effect was normally considered sufficient to protect the side panelling, and no separate gutter was provided by most companies. However, the LNWR (and a few others) did fix a moulding along the outer edge which in part prevented water from dripping on to passengers' heads in wet weather.

On a cove or elliptical roof coach, the lower edge of the canvas where it met the cantrail was trapped in position by a longitudinal gutter moulding, often of quite generous proportions and sometimes given quite a decorative cross-sectional shape. Such gutters

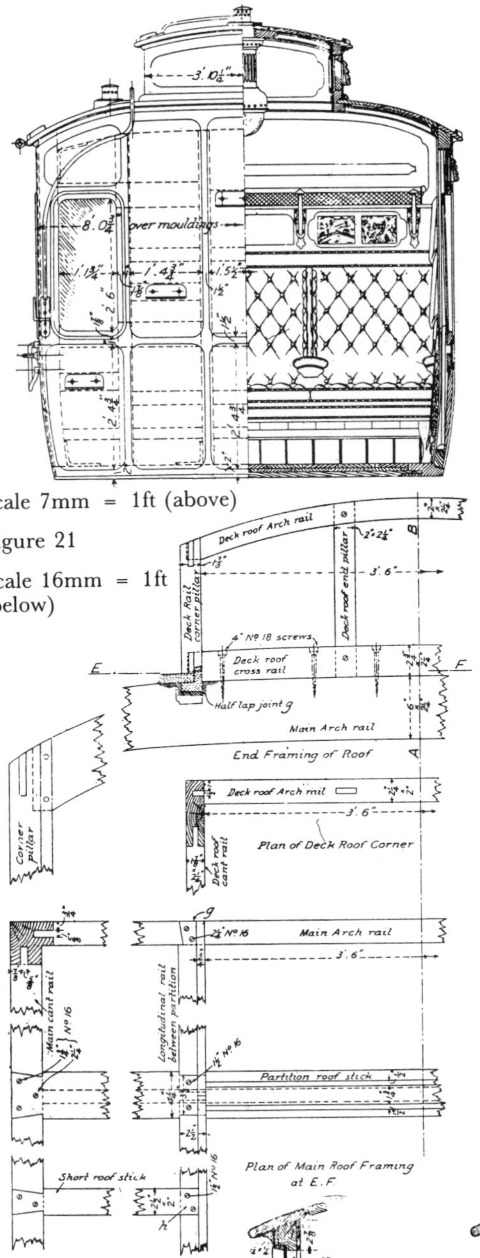

Scale 7mm = 1ft (above)

Figure 21

Scale 16mm = 1ft (below)

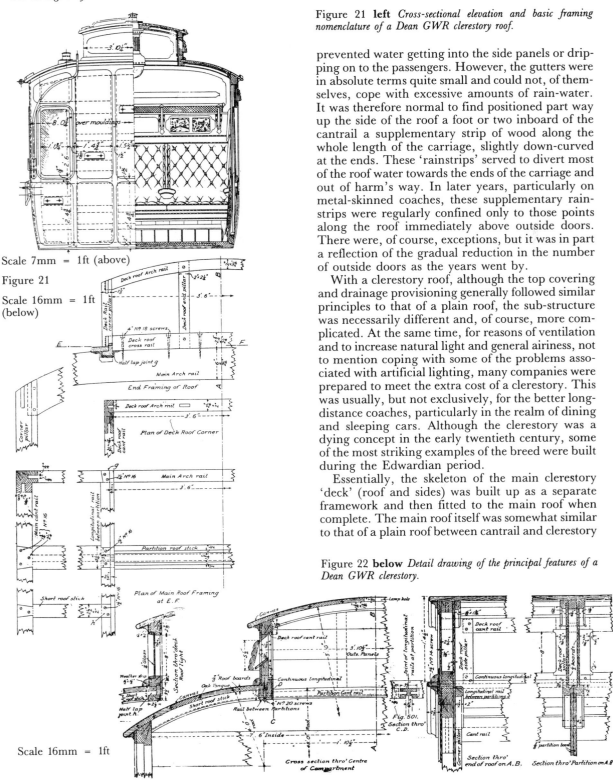

Figure 21 **left** *Cross-sectional elevation and basic framing nomenclature of a Dean GWR clerestory roof.*

prevented water getting into the side panels or dripping on to the passengers. However, the gutters were in absolute terms quite small and could not, of themselves, cope with excessive amounts of rain-water. It was therefore normal to find positioned part way up the side of the roof a foot or two inboard of the cantrail a supplementary strip of wood along the whole length of the carriage, slightly down-curved at the ends. These 'rainstrips' served to divert most of the roof water towards the ends of the carriage and out of harm's way. In later years, particularly on metal-skinned coaches, these supplementary rainstrips were regularly confined only to those points along the roof immediately above outside doors. There were, of course, exceptions, but it was in part a reflection of the gradual reduction in the number of outside doors as the years went by.

With a clerestory roof, although the top covering and drainage provisioning generally followed similar principles to that of a plain roof, the sub-structure was necessarily different and, of course, more complicated. At the same time, for reasons of ventilation and to increase natural light and general airiness, not to mention coping with some of the problems associated with artificial lighting, many companies were prepared to meet the extra cost of a clerestory. This was usually, but not exclusively, for the better long-distance coaches, particularly in the realm of dining and sleeping cars. Although the clerestory was a dying concept in the early twentieth century, some of the most striking examples of the breed were built during the Edwardian period.

Essentially, the skeleton of the main clerestory 'deck' (roof and sides) was built up as a separate framework and then fitted to the main roof when complete. The main roof itself was somewhat similar to that of a plain roof between cantrail and clerestory

Figure 22 **below** *Detail drawing of the principal features of a Dean GWR clerestory.*

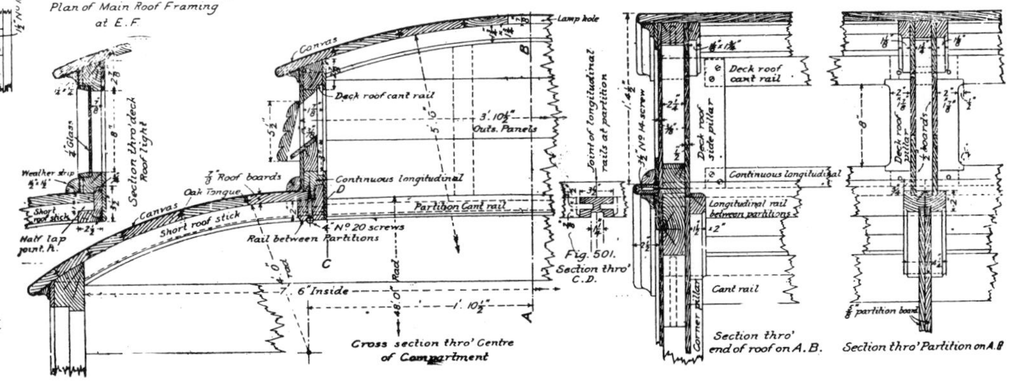

Scale 16mm = 1ft

deck, but obviously there could be no series of continuous roof sticks in the conventional sense spanning the carriage at the lower level of the main roof between cantrails — it would have negated the whole purpose of adopting the clerestory in the first place. Clearly there would be some degree of transverse support for the clerestory deck wherever there were partitions, but this was not sufficient; in any case, many clerestory coaches had large open saloons, so further strengthening was always essential. This took the form of a substantial and continuous longitudinal rail where the main roof met the clerestory deck, usually supplemented by a second longitudinal immediately below it and fixed between the partitions. Straight-grained pitch-pine was preferred for this continuous longitudinal since it not only had the desired grain structure but the length of available logs also regularly made it possible for there to be no need to splice two pieces together to span the whole of the carriage from one end to the other.

Additionally, where clerestory carriages had very long open saloon interiors, it was common to incorporate what were known as 'carlines' made of iron and fixed at roughly 6 feet intervals to hold the sides together. These carlines were bent to conform with the shape of the main and deck roofs from side to side of the carriage, the outer ends being bolted to the cantrail. This added to the rigidity of the structure, but even so there was always the risk of a sagging roof on a clerestory coach with the passage of time, as study of the preserved Midland dining car (built in 1914) at the National Railway Museum will reveal.

Doors and other external fittings

Even a cursory glance at a typical railway carriage by a non expert will reveal the numerous 'bits and pieces' which are regularly carried on the outside of the vehicle. Many of these are quite simple fittings whose purpose was self evident. Amongst these can be included footstep boards, end steps (to enable railwaymen to gain access to the roof top), handrails and door handles, door stops, brackets for destination boards, external lighting control gear (including electrical connections to the next carriage if required and relevant) and so forth. Their purpose was self evident and need not take any further explanatory space. Neither, for that matter, need the rather more subtle variations which were used from time to time, to provide a better 'look out' for the guard or, in their outward appearance, to hint at other semi-specialized functions for the vehicle in question. These will be dealt with as they become relevant in context.

However, two external features of the carriage do need a little more amplification: the outside doors (for

This view of a Dean GWR family saloon gives a very clear impression of the roof structure of a typical open clerestory interior. The noticeably more substantial profile piece spanning the vehicle from side to side some three windows from the extreme end was known as a 'carline'.

all vehicles) and the gangway connection (for those vehicles offering inter-vehicle communication).

Starting with the doors, these components were not normally fitted until almost the end of the body construction process. In part this was to enable the craftsmen to move more readily between the inside and outside of the vehicle as construction continued, but it was also because the door itself, along with its fittings, was quite a complex component involving, relative to its size, considerably more work than the plainer parts of the carriage. It was in fact easier to make the doors separately, virtually to completion apart from painting, and then fit them late in the building phase.

A fairly typical turn-of-the-century pattern of wooden door is shown in Figure 23, and the basic style hardly changed, save for the outer skin, for the first half of the century — or even longer. Quite apart from its obvious function, the door was also used (when closed) as a prime means of increasing ventilation. It always carried a 'drop light' and regularly a ventilator at the top as well. These features are both shown on the drawing. Additionally, the door had to be immensely strong to withstand hard usage. During most of the twentieth century, the carriage door was fitted with a 'slam lock' mechanism for safety, but this meant that the doors experienced little in the way of gentle handling when they were closed. Even in the 1980s, many suburban and cross-country trains have this type of door and there can be few rail travellers, particularly through London, who have not heard the fusillade of slamming doors which was and often still is the almost mandatory sound accompanying a train of workbound commuters on arrival at places like Waterloo, Charing Cross, Victoria and elsewhere!

Perhaps the most characteristic yet at times bewildering feature of the carriage door is the drop light — characteristic because it is always there but bewildering to many people because of its mode of operation. The drop light derives from the door of the old stagecoach, and although one of its functions is to allow fresh air inside the vehicle, an important secondary function is to allow the door to be opened from within. For safety reasons, many British carriage doors could only be opened by using the outside handle (and this is as true on the HSTs of the 1980s as it was on an Edwardian express, in both cases it being almost impossible to open a door accidentally from inside). It was and is, therefore, necessary to lower the drop light from within to allow the outer handle to be reached.

As a slight aside, this configuration, while not exclusively British, was typically so and can still cause confusion, especially to overseas visitors or those who use trains but rarely. Many are the puzzled looks on the faces of inexperienced passengers when faced at a station stop with an apparently handleless door! Moreover, the lack of an inside handle also carries with it a strong likelihood that an embarking passenger will either fail to close the door behind him or do so incompletely. For this reason, the slam lock is almost universal and has been so on most British carriages this century. It is nothing more than a spring loaded conventional latch arrangement which, if the door is slammed, automatically springs into its final resting place. It is connected directly with the outer handle, and a quick visual check by the station staff of the handle position can readily reveal an improperly closed door. Unless the handle is horizontal, the door latch is not properly engaged.

However, back to the drop light. Traditionally this was a wood-framed sliding window fitted at the bottom with a strong strap. In the fully closed position it was normally held in position by its lower edge resting on a ledge in the window frame often assisted by a spring mechanism. To lower the drop light it had first to be lifted off its ledge, pulled slightly towards the inside of the door and then lowered by the strap, the latter being sufficiently long that its free end was still accessible even with the drop light fully lowered. The strap had large holes at intervals which could be located over a brass pin on the garnish rail to hold the drop light in one of several intermediate positions. Should the drop light lose its strap (and they did make very good honing strops for cut-throat razors!), life became difficult although not necessarily impossible, especially if, as was often the case, an auxiliary 'finger pull' was affixed to the top of the drop light frame.

There were several slight variations within this general principle, and, as years went by, some railways introduced spring-loaded drop lights which would 'stay' in any given position and employed a finger pull at the top. Wooden frames sometimes gave way to metal and, later, a 'frameless' drop light of strong plate glass made its appearance. This latter is the common type to be found on the doors of modern BR stock. The drop light principle was not confined to the door, and many railways used them in other parts of the carriage for enhanced ventilation, sometimes with various additional operational subtleties.

The door top ventilator was often a characteristic stylistic feature. As with external beading, its basic

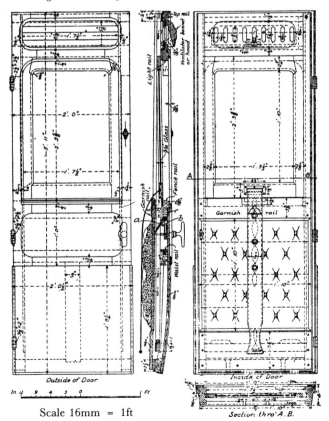

Figure 23 *Carriage door detail.*

Scale 16mm = 1ft

structure and function was virtually the same wherever it appeared — essentially, a moving 'hit and miss' wooden slide, protected on the outside by a bonnet or hood. The physical appearance of this bonnet could, however, be anything within reason provided it functioned properly and was of a size appropriate to the door. It thus gave scope for considerable stylistic variation. Not all railways used them, and with some railways they tended to be either removed or blanked off in later years or even not fitted at all.

Finally, before leaving the door, it should be mentioned that the lack of internal door handles was not universal. Several railways employed a spring loaded internal sliding door catch which, with some effort, could be used to open the door. It connected directly with the door latch and was virtually impossible to make work, except deliberately, so was not really a safety hazard. These door catches were, and still are, commonly fitted to suburban and commuter trains since they do materially speed up the door opening procedure, an important aspect of operation when a 'high frequency, short station stop' service is desired.

The last principal feature to be mentioned in this

GER third class carriage door showing the drop light strap and the internal spring-loaded door opening catch. The semi-circular door top was a feature of much GER suburban stock.

section is the end gangway. It has already been mentioned in Chapter 2 that two incompatible styles were adopted in Britain, the so-called and traditional 'British Standard' and the more effective 'Pullman' type. In either case, there had, of course, to be a door frame put into the end of the carriage and this would normally be closed from within the vehicle by means of either a conventional hinged or sliding door. These doors were lockable, a very essential feature when a vehicle formed the last coach of the train, even if an 'end board' was fitted (see below).

The external gangway structure was, however, markedly different and somewhat easier to visualize than actually to describe. In essence, however, the British Standard type was pulled out to meet its opposite number on an adjacent coach whereas the Pullman type projected slightly beyond the centre buckeye coupling and was compressed when two vehicles were connected together. This fundamental operational difference was reflected in the outside structural framework.

The British Standard gangway was supported by a massive metal 'housing' — almost a shallow box — mounted on the carriage end and around the door frame. It was about 3 feet wide, 7 feet high and had an almost semi-circular top. It projected anything from about 9 inches to almost 2 feet from the carriage end. Connected to this fixed housing was a movable outer frame, made of 'T' or 'L' section, whose elevation matched that of the housing. The connection was made by means of 'scissor' irons, sometimes called 'lazy tongs', whose nomenclature, for once, is descriptively apt. This allowed the outer frame to be moved outwards from the carriage end to meet the next vehicle, the two movable frames being held together by 'side' or 'gangway' clips, one being fitted permanently to the right hand edge of each frame when looking at the carriage end.

The movable frame carried a stiff horizontal metal plate at the bottom, at right angles to the frame itself and projecting back towards the fixed housing. This formed the floor of the gangway and slid over the top of the floor of the housing. Its length was such that even at maximum extension there was always an overlap between the moving and fixed parts, although accidents could (and did) happen, sometimes with interesting consequences to the three-dimensional geometry of the whole set-up! The floor was normally covered by a loose carpet or mat, to give some sort of additional protection to the customers passing through.

To those who have never encountered such a feature, it must sound a mite hazardous but was not, in fact, anything like as risky a business as it might seem. Once the train was assembled, the tight screw coupling and the side buffers imparted considerable

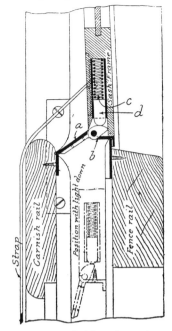

Figure 24 *A typical late-nineteenth-century carriage door dust and draught excluder to Telling's patent. When the drop light was closed, spring 'c' held the closing plate 'a' (pivoted on hinge 'b') in contact with the garnish rail by means of pin 'd'. This idea was used on carriage doors of* inter alia *the GWR, LNWR and LB & SCR.*

British Standard gangway components under construction at the Wolverton works of the LNWR, later LMS. Prominent in the foreground is the housing which will later be affixed to the carriage end.

stability, and although there was movement it was rarely excessive enough to cause alarm. In this respect it was considerably better than some of the abominable contraptions to be found on some continental coaches which not only moved about a great deal more but which also forced the passenger to walk, as it were, up, through and down the other side!

Weather protection for the gangway itself was formed by a flexible 'bellows' connection, made of leather and fitted between the fixed housing and movable frame, *inside* the lazy tongs. The whole was surmounted on top by a second cover sheet which gave double weather protection at the most vulnerable part. The only significant change to this style of gangway was introduced by the GWR (later copied by the LMS) in the early part of the post-grouping period. This replaced the scissors type extension by a spring suspension mounted at the top of the gangway frame. These were sometimes known as 'suspended' gangways but otherwise functioned much as before. When not actually in use, the British Standard gangway was pushed fully 'home' towards the housing and the movable frame was held in position against the fixed housing by retaining hooks on

each side. At the outer ends of a set of gangwayed carriages an 'end board' would be fitted, completely covering the full area of the outer frame.

By contrast with all this, the Pullman gangway was amazingly simple. It too had a metal housing on the carriage end and a movable frame connected to the housing by means of leather with additional top weather protection. At its base it was supported by a spring loaded platform and by additional springs at the top. These springs were set so as to allow the gangway to project in front of the coupler. When two such coaches were buckeyed together, the gangway springs went into slight compression and no gangway clips or other restraints were required.

The real fun began when examples of each of these two types of gangways were to be put together in a train. The previous chapter explained the dropping of the buckeye and the extending of the buffers, but the gangway connection could also cause problems. For one thing, the Pullman type gangway was generally wider than the BS type — and often taller too. Its outer frame was generally more substantial so there was a total mis-match as far as shape was concerned, and this meant that the BS gangway had to be adapted to suit the Pullman type. This was

A virtually complete corridor carriage body and underframe about to be lowered on to its bogies at the Stratford works of the old GER; the gangway apparatus is prominent. Although the underframe was built separately from the body proper, it was common practice at British carriage works for these two components to be kept fixed together after finishing and be lifted as a unit whenever it was necessary to attend to the bogies themselves. This particular process survives to the present day, even though integral carriage construction is now normal practice.

British Standard gangway connections between two corridor carriages of the LNWR. There is added interest in this picture in that the vehicle on the left is equipped for slip working and has a raised 'birdcage' guard's lookout for this purpose — see page 166

achieved firstly by welding an extra horse-shoe shape to the top of the BS gangway moving frame which effectively increased its height and top width closer to that of the Pullman version. Secondly, extension pieces were welded or bolted to each side of the BS gangway to increase the width at that point to that of the Pullman gangway. This was because these extensions each had to carry additional gangway clips in order to hold the BS gangway firmly against its non-compatible partner. Without the stabilising effect of the centre buckeye coupler, and given the total disparity of shape between the two gangways, there could easily be too much side play to allow 'unclipped' gangways to be used.

This somewhat extraordinary situation held sway in Britain well into the modern period and had some interesting consequences. For one thing, it was obviously uneconomical to adapt all the BS gangways in existence, so those railways which used them had to maintain a sort of pool of gangway-adapted vehicles for use with buckeyed stock. This must have

had some element of economic disadvantage in terms of lack of overall flexibility of use. Secondly, although strictly outside the timespan of this first volume, as the years went by and more and more buckeyed coaches came into use, it became more probable that some of the newer recruits in the carriage sidings would not be aware of the need to 'clip and adapt'! Thus, when uncoupling trains it was increasingly likely that the gangway clips would be forgotten, and should this happen, even though the carriages were *uncoupled*, the gangways were still connected. The next move of the shunting engine would almost inevitably pull the BS gangway clean off the end of its coach and dump it unceremoniously on to the ballast! It was, however, all very British.

Overall dimensions

Before leaving the question of carriage bodies, it should be pointed out that there were certain overall dimensional constraints to which every carriage had to conform. In Britain, by comparison with most overseas countries, these were relatively modest, although they grew a little more tolerant as the twentieth century progressed. Each railway therefore imposed its own 'loading gauge', as it was called.

Setting aside the few rather more generous and the few somewhat more restricted loading gauges imposed by a handful of companies, a typical British figure would be to permit an absolute maximum width of some 9 feet (or a little more) and a height of about 13 feet. However, these figures did not refer to a rectangular cross-section. The maximum height was only permissible close to the centre-line and the maximum width rarely applied much above 10 feet from the rail top or much below about 5-6 feet either for that matter. Over the years, attempts were made to harmonize between various parts of the system but there were always some exceptions.

In consequence, the end elevation of a typical British coach — again with some exceptions — showed certain characteristic features. It was normal for the carriage body to 'narrow' from the waist downwards — this feature, necessitating the curved panelling mentioned above, was either known as 'turn-under' or 'tumblehome'. Similarly, if a carriage was built to the full 9 feet waist width, it was common for the cantrail width to be a few inches less, typically about 8 ft 9 in. Thus the sides, above the waist, were often 'battered' (ie inclined inwards). A combination of inward batter plus marked tumblehome was often, in some descriptions, called 'clipper' shaped, presumably because it was vaguely reminiscent of the hull profile of a clipper ship.

At the turn of the century, vertically sided coaches were normal but, for structure gauge reasons, were generally confined to a maximum of 8 ft 6 in wide (8 feet being a particularly common figure). Virtually all had turned-under lower bodyside panels, but the true clipper shape was largely a twentieth-century feature. It was found that by increasing the waist width to a full 9 feet over the panels that an extra seat per side could often be incorporated and the slight reduction of width at the roof made little or no difference in this respect.

Because of the geometry of a vehicle on a curve, the dimensions quoted also allowed for a degree of lateral offset or 'throwover' at the vehicle ends (see Figure 9, page 25) and at the middle. This, in turn, imposed length limitations. Once again, a typical turn-of-the-century bogie vehicle would normally be within the 45-60 feet bracket, with a few pushing to 65 or 70 feet where either more specialized usage or limited spheres of operation thus allowed. This 65-70 feet length remained a *de rigueur* maximum until well into the 1970s, and it was only well into BR days that the somewhat longer MkIII coach could be accepted. Even so, there still has to be a modest inward taper at the carriage end to make allowances for the very long length (by British standards) of the MkIII carriage.

Above *This extraordinary cornucopia was the East Coast Joint Stock solution to the third class dining car challenge of its rivals at the turn of the century in 1900. It was built at Doncaster, and whatever one might think of the stylistic mishmash no one could seriously accuse the railways of not trying when the twentieth-century began. This design was surely one of the most comprehensive vehicles ever offered to third class passengers at this time — just look at those gas lamps!*

Left *The 'somewhat uneasy mixture of Victorian rectitude and art nouveau' is well exemplified by this interior view of the smoking compartment of an LNWR first class clerestory sleeping car of 1905. The cane chairs are very much à la mode as is some detail of the raised border patterns on the otherwise plain Lincrusta ceiling and wall panels, although the dark mahogany woodwork, the symmetry of the panel treatment and the fussy floor covering all betoken an earlier era. However, it seems to have worked — this was undoubtedly a pleasant room in which to linger over a malt whisky and a good cigar, watching the sun go down on a summer evening before turning in for the night! (BR LMR).*

4. Interior finishing and passenger amenities

If it is the exterior bodywork of the carriage which gives it character, distinction and, possibly, any aesthetic virtues it may have on first acquaintance, this appeal can only be 'skin deep' at the final analysis, for it is the interior arrangement which will create the most profound and long-lasting effect on its potential customer. Even speaking from a purely personal standpoint. I can remember the carriage *interiors* of my youth long after I have forgotten some of the more esoteric aspects of their exterior elevation. Moreover, beauty of exterior aspect can at times be utterly misleading. The sublime exterior elegance and symmetry of the Gresley LNER open thirds may be remembered, married to a quite diabolical degree of discomfort in their atrocious 'bucket' seats; the aesthetic pleasures of the ex-NER clerestories with their hard, horsehair benches; the often quite unharmonious 'look' of many GWR and LMS carriages which often belied a rather better interior and even, in much more modern days, the sleek, elegant style of the BR Blue Pullmans of the 1960s (both inside and out) but the more than adventurous nature of their suspension system!

Happy indeed was the traveller who could feast his aesthetic sensitivity as he boarded his carriage and have his delight further enhanced from within when the journey commenced. Fortunately, at least on their better trains, the British were rather good at satisfying both criteria, even for the third class passenger; it did not happen by accident.

The carriage interior must inevitably be a subtle combination of visual elements and practical provisioning, both being measured against a whole series of constraints covering such things as dimensional restrictions, weight limitation, seating capacity, envisaged usage, durability, economy of manufacture and so forth. It is always and quite inescapably a compromise between often contrary elements and can never be wholly perfect. Sometimes the constraints are few, sometimes many, and it is no small tribute to the designers — rarely even distinguished by name in contemporary accounts, unlike their privileged locomotive counterparts — that they so often managed to produce not only vehicles of great intrinsic beauty but also great practical virtue as well.

The story, as always, is one of continuous evolution both in style and technology, so yet again the starting point must be the situation broadly as it stood at the turn of the century. As with most aspects of the carriage, a basic understanding of the various practices which had developed by the end of Victoria's reign enables most of the rest of the story to be understood quite readily until well into the BR period.

Interior partitions and doors

The purpose for which the carriage was designed determined the exact layout of the interior partitions and doors, and these had to be pre-planned into the floor structure. Thereafter, partition framing was erected much as for the exterior, and both sides of the partition were then covered in by 'casing boards', often quite basic in their material, on top of which were then applied the visible decorative finishes. Interior doors were made in much the same fashion as for any domestic interior and arranged either to hinge or slide according to need. Naturally, the surface finishings of doors and interior walls were designed to harmonize.

In terms of wall finishes, most carriages reflected the fact that much of the furniture, paticularly the seating, was 'built in'. As a consequence, if one removed a complete seating unit there often stood revealed bare casing boards without the semblance of a finishing layer. However, where the walls revealed themselves above the seats, round the windows and in corridors and passageways, much flamboyance could be seen. It generally reflected the class of the carriage or compartment but was almost always done with care and, on the best carriages, with an astonishing attention to detail.

The favourite material was always wood, whether inlaid, panelled, veneered or, in later days, left relatively plain and simply polished to enhance its colour and/or grain pattern. It was not until well into the 1950s that extensive use was made of alternative materials to any great extent, and only in the 1970s and 1980s did one see any real diminution of the traditional wood finishes. Thus, during the period covering the first two of these three volumes, wood was king and the techniques of handling it hardly changed — only the design altered. Throughout this survey, examples of fine craftsmanship, even in the humblest of coaches, will regularly reappear, so there is no need to dwell too long at this point; but there are a few other preliminary remarks worth making.

The decorative wood treatment generally stopped at about cantrail or head height, above which it was customary practice to paint, in white or cream, the

'All-over-patterned' Lincrusta seems to have been just about the only wall and ceiling finish for everything but the wood framing in this Edwardian vintage LSWR corridor coach.

Austere finish in a GER third class suburban carriage. Even the partitions scarcely reached to mid-window height and the less said about those seats the better. Even so, however, the grain finish of the plain tongue and groove casing boards is likely to have been put there in paint — a small concession, but at least it was something.

upper wall sides (sometimes) and the ceilings (almost always). In this respect there was a conscious imitation of domestic interiors above and below the picture rail, so to speak. Not that there were hanging pictures or even a picture rail as such; but there *were* pictures and mirrors, often in abundance, whose fixed frames were often part of the panelling. These pictures could range from sepia-toned photographs of places served by the railway or specially made prints of original paintings, via colourful poster-type notices with an advertising flavour, to stark printed statements as to the policy of the railway itself. I feel that it is one of the more regrettable aspects of modern rolling-stock — which has many virtues not possessed by its ancestors — that pictorial decoration of the interior generally seems 'out' and that the railway's own 'in house' material is frequently applied by the cheap and nasty method of pasting an appropriate notice directly on to wall or window. It would cost so little and look so much better to do it properly.

Returning to wall finishes, a particularly popular alternative to wood — especially during the period covered by this first volume — was the use of textured Lincrusta, particularly on ceilings and top wall panels of compartments and on the dado (ie the area between waist and floor) of corridors and passageways. Like many things, it drew its basic inspiration from contemporary domestic interiors, and the new century dawned with a sort of mixed stylistic treatment best described as a somewhat uneasy mixture

of Victorian rectitude and art nouveau. Oddly enough, it generally worked rather well, even when to it was added the occasional Edwardian revival of Adam style decorative motifs in some of the best carriages. Stylistic purity of concept was never at the heart of railway carriage interior design but somehow it did not seem to matter too much. Symmetry of design pattern was, however, a well nigh universal feature if permitted by the carriage 'geometry'.

At the heart of it all was, in addition to wood, that wonderfully versatile material 'Lincrusta-Walton'. Unlike wood finishes, which are still very much a part of general interior design in the late twentieth century (even if not so prevalent in carriages), figured Lincrusta is a substance rarely met these days. In fact, and risking a somewhat irrelevant aside, it has proved to be quite a problem, when trying to restore vintage carriages at the National Railway Museum, to find anything which really encapsulates the character of Lincrusta, and the more modern and not quite so appropriate Anaglypta has had to be accepted. It therefore seems worthwhile to devote a few lines to the subject.*

Lincrusta-Walton was introduced in later Victorian days as a replacement for figured waxcloth.

*Since writing the above, genuine Lincrusta has come back on to the market!

It was just as readily fixed but rather more durable and its nature made it rather more versatile in terms of decorative possibilities. Essentially it was a heavy compressed composition paper, moulded (under pressure) to give the desired patterns. These could be either raised, the usual approach, or embossed. The non-textured part of the Lincrusta was known as the 'ground' and it was common to pick out the textured pattern in a different colour, or even gilt. Thus 'gilt on cream ground Lincrusta' inferred gilt patterns (raised or embossed) on a cream background.

It was supplied mounted on stout millboard and cut out to fit the various areas to which it was applied. It was treated very much like wood interior panelling — ie pinned in position on casing boards or under the roof framing — and the areas to which it was applied had to offer an even surface before the Lincrusta was added. There were other similar materials with their own brand names, but 'Lincrusta' became a sort of generic term to describe a process — much in the manner of 'Hoover' in our present day.

As a 'standard' treatment it had a pretty good run during the first twenty years or so of the century but tended to die out, following currently fashionable trends, during the 1920s. Of course, such was the longevity of carriages that quite a few Lincrusta-panelled coaches ran in service until after the Second World War — principally dining and sleeping cars and other more specialized vehicles.

Before completing this basic review of wall finishes it is also worth mentioning that in humbler coaches plain tongue and groove boarding was often used on top of the casing boards, sometimes grain painted to simulate something better. Plain boarding was equally often applied to the undersides of ceilings. There were no hard and fast rules, but there was plenty of scope for individual company variety.

Seat construction, trimming and other interior decoration

Save for those relatively rare cases where 'loose' furniture, of typical domestic kind, was incorporated in a carriage, the seats themselves were permanently fixed in place and were usually of a built-in nature. They were not, however, made *in situ*. Like many parts of the carriages, as much as possible of the seating was fabricated as a separate process and the finished unit added to the structure quite late in the assembly. In general, the backs and seat cushions were separate loose items and the seat base, although made outside the body, became a semi-permanent fixture once offered up to the carriage.

The seat base, frequently sprung, was anchored to the wall of the carriage by means of a rear seat

Although earlier than the two dining carriages pictured on page 56, this turn-of-the-century LNWR first class interior shows an altogether more enterprising use of trimming material. It could well have been the famous green Blenheim moquette, much quoted in contemporary accounts. Regardless of precise colour, however, the attention to detail was formidable

rail — a substantial timber section fixed to the wall. The front seat rail was a similar strong member, anchored to the sides of the compartment and sometimes supported, intermediately, by one or two legs to the floor. The seat back unit — sometimes called a back 'squab' — was a separate item which, unlike the seat base, usually carried the finishing material. It was designed so as to be able to be lifted clear of the wall in one piece without disturbing the trim.

On most first and many second class seats, the actual cushion on which the passengers sat was made up as a separate loose item, sometimes with its own interior springing and was removable for cleaning.

By contrast, third class seating units were often single-piece structures containing all the springs, and the seat base in these cases was merely a framework on which the whole seat unit rested. This sort of fixed seating was the normal practice in compartment and side corridor stock. Where a centre aisle was used, in the open interior configuration of a dining car for example, the seat units adjacent to the transverse partition walls were much as described, but the intermediate 'double-sided' units were slightly different. A fixed timber framework, with seat bases on both sides of a central vertical back-board, was installed on to which the seats and back squabs were fixed as for a conventional compartment. The inner end of

this unit (adjacent to the carriage side) was anchored to a seat rail, but the outer end, adjacent to the aisle, was a decorative member carrying legs, the whole being used as a principal design feature of the carriage interior.

A similar solution was also adopted in non-corridor compartment stock where a seat unit did not stretch from side to side of the compartment, for example in those cases where a break had to be made for an access door to a lavatory, for example.

The most obvious aspect of the seating was, of course, its upholstery, or 'trimming' to use the more common railway term. During most of the nineteenth century, railways had been somewhat unenterprising in this area and had employed relatively few different finishes. For example, 'blue cloth' was the most common first class trimming used by nearly all companies. It was quite plain with a sort of velour type finish and remained popular well into the present century. In fact, when the NRM was restoring its Midland six-wheeler of 1883, a suitable length of blue cloth was, happily, exhumed by Wolverton Works as late as 1974! The lower orders had to make do with plainer materials such as plush or rep, but sometimes velvet was used. Plain colours — usually brown or red — were most common.

This somewhat austere situation began to change in late Victorian days and the twentieth century dawned with a much more enterprising attitude to interior finishes, both in terms of quality and variety. Typical first class materials, in addition to the familiar blue cloth, could now embrace velvet, morocco and buffalo leather, moquette and sometimes even brocade. Floral and other patterns began to appear and the decorative braiding round seat

cushions and seat supports was often supplemented by decorative fringes, tassels or whatever.

An equal variety also began to appear in second and third class compartments, often of very high quality and regularly of some considerable variety. Regrettably, little dedicated research has been carried out on carriage interior materials and it is very difficult — save by means of the often fallible human memory — to establish precisely what materials were used. The situation has become progressively more bewildering during the subsequent decades and it is rarely possible to do more than generalize or try to make an intelligent guess as to colour from a black and white photograph.

However, regardless of precise pattern or type, carriage upholstery cloth had to fulfil certain fundamental criteria. It was originally some 60 inches wide — more recently 48 inches — and of durable weight per yard, about 24 oz being typical for the 60 inch width. Its strength was such that a strip of the weft, or cross threads (edge to edge), should not tear with a pull of less than 55 lbs, while a strip of the warp (longitudinal threads) had to withstand a 75 lb pull. This was to ensure, as far as possible, resistance to rough usage and also the inevitable strain when cloth was drawn down by button finishing or at cushion and seat edges. Woollen cloth was considered to be the most suitable and, in addition to strength, the cloth should have a clean, even surface well covered with nap, short and cleanly cut. Finally, the cloth should be evenly coloured throughout.

Leather, sometimes used for complete seats and regularly for armrests and other features, had to be of even thickness, free from cuts or cracks, and be able to withstanding bending or pleating without

Above left *This pair of views shows comparisons between the second and third class in an LSWR non-corridor lavatory-equipped carriage. One or two obvious differences are evident, but most are rather subtle; there was probably little to choose in terms of real comfort.*

Above *First and third class on the Cheshire Lines Committee. This agreeable design emerged from Doncaster in 1911, essentially to Gresley's GNR style of construction although vastly better than anything Doncaster ever built for the harassed King's Cross commuters. The lack of outer armrest in the third class is a bit unusual.*

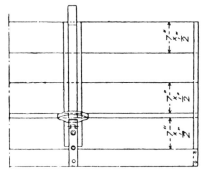

Figure 25 Scale 16mm = 1ft

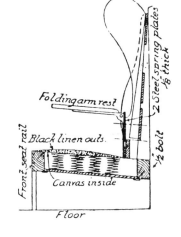

Figure 25 *General construction of a first class seat unit (with simple folding arms and a sprung permanent base) and, in enlarged detail, Attock's LYR pattern folding armrest. In this fitment, raising the arm caused part of the seat back to retract, leaving a space into which the arm could fit flush with the seat back, thus allowing more passengers to be seated at busy times. This, in one form or another became the normal British arrangement, especially in third class carriages during and after the 1930s.*

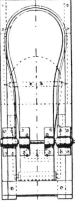

ARM REST CLOSED.

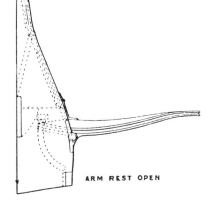

ARM REST OPEN

cracking. Laces and braid for finishing had to be perfect and straight to pattern, be of firm quality, even finish and good clean colour. Wool or silk were the customary materials.

The cushions and back squabs, in addition to the springing if present, were stuffed with best quality curled horsehair which, when uncurled for stuffing, retained its elasticity, sometimes too much so, as those of us who recall sitting on horsehair seats in short trousers remember only too clearly — the backs of the knees were distinctly vulnerable! A contemporary description states of horsehair that 'Inferior hair is knotty, dull, short and the ends are frequently split, indicating that the hair has not been obtained from

the horse, but probably from the hog or some other unsuitable animal'! On a fair number of carriages, horsehair stuffing without springs could often be considered adequate, particularly on seat backs. This practice was not customary in first class carriages, save in some cases for the loose cushions which sat on top of the sprung base, but third class seat backs were regularly stuffed only! It was comparatively rare in the twentieth century, however, to find a third class carriage without at least some form of springing in the seat itself.

This basic form of carriage seat construction stood the test of time well into the modern (post-nationalization) era and it was not really until the BR MkII

Left *Typical 'blue-cloth' seat trimming in a first class dining carriage of the Midland Railway, along with many other characteristic interior detail features, most of which were also offered to third class diners too — see the picture on page 50*

Below left *The 'Edwardian Adam' design influence may have been at work in this first class open carriage of the North Eastern Railway which conveys a somewhat less fussy impression than the previous MR example; both are good. Blue cloth is again the trim material, but the seats have loose cushions, the rather more customary practice in first class carriages. The dark mahogany is still there, however.*

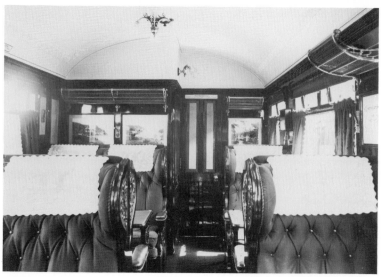

Above right *This 1914 lavatory compartment in an East Coast corridor carriage is rather more spacious than most and features a fixed ceramic wash basin rather than the more common folding type.*

Above far right *This well-appointed first class lavatory compartment of LYR non-corridor composite No 1085 as well as showing a cased in wash basin also features a drinking water filtration system.*

period (1960s onwards) that any significant structural changes were made — and then only slowly. Fashions changed, of course, as did the actual shapes and layouts of seats, but the interiors of BR MkI coaches almost always revealed their traditional origins — and there are still those of us who reckon that nothing subsequently has bettered the traditional first class compartments last employed for all practical purposes in the late MkI and early MkII BR stock.

In addition to the seats, armrests and other basic items of the carriage interior, there were numerous small fittings which could enhance the pleasure of the traveller. These could range from such vital components as window blinds for use in sunny weather to such pleasant touches as small courtesy shelves for the odd cup or glass, ashtrays for the smoker, folding tables — or even permanent ones — for more substantial use, luggage and parcel racks or shelves, coat-hooks (or even coat-hangers), luggage compartments and, very occasionally, even fold-away seats in the corridors. These latter were for use either at times of overcrowding or, more amenably, as a means of parking the derrière when the scenery on the corridor side was deemed more pleasant than that opposite! The railways seemed to think of most things which people might want and occasionally a few which were of less obvious practical value. There were, however, amongst all these items a few rather more general amenities which merit a little more detailed consideration.

Lavatories and toilets

Amongst all the vulgarities of humour contained in the British make-up — and one has only to read a few words of Shakespeare to realize how long-standing this has been — the subject of the toilet and its trappings has always been firmly at the top of the list for a spontaneous giggle; yet the start of the heyday of the railway carriage actually coincided with the curious period in history where one did not mention such things in polite society. Consequently, the providing of a lavatory in a train was fraught with social as well as practical problems in the early days.

It had largely been solved by the end of the Victorian period and Hamilton Ellis has virtually said all that needs to be stated of the pioneer developments*. By the twentieth century, the position of the lavatory had taken one of two basic arrangements. It was either located off the corridor at one or both ends of the carriage (sometimes intermediately as well) or, in the case of non-corridor stock, an individual compartment had its own provisioning, leading directly off the compartment. Centre-aisled carriages tended to follow the corridor style with lavatories at the coach ends.

Within the toilet compartment itself there would normally be found the usual pedestal fitting and some sort of washbasin facility, along with a towel and soap, provided that someone had not removed the

* Railway Carriages in the British Isles from 1830-1914

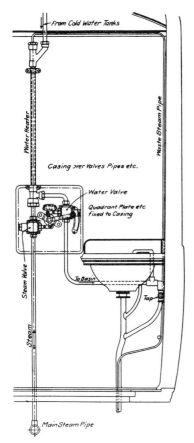

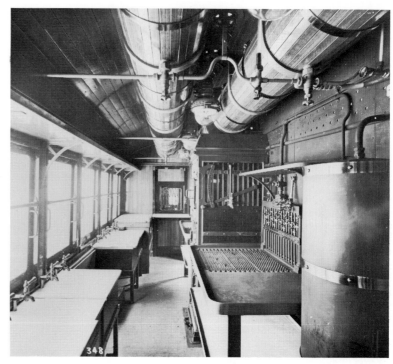

Figure 26 *Hot water heating system of the type fitted to East Coast carriages such as depicted in the picture on the previous page.*

Above *This interior view of an LNWR kitchen car for the American boat trains — see Chapter 13 — clearly shows the supplementary drinking water tanks suspended below the ceiling*

latter pair of items. Since the lavatory compartment took up floor space for essentially non-revenue-earning use, it was normally very cramped and folding washbasin units were commonplace. Especially typical, until very recent years, were those made by Beresford of Birmingham. They were usually of nickel-plated brass and they folded away against the wall when not in use, projecting only a few inches from the partition. The action of folding them away discharged the water from the back of the basin into a sort of reception chute and hence to the outside of the carriage below the floor. The basins had a deep lip round the rim to prevent spillage of water when the train was in motion.

Until quite recent days, generally post-nationalization, the fixed handbasin was a somewhat less common feature than a folding one. Where used, however, it was commonly placed in a corner angle of the toilet compartment and shaped to suit this location. It could be made either from metal or, more likely, a ceramic material. Regardless of washbasin type, however, only a cold water supply was provided at the start of the century in most cases. In later years,

some carriages were given a hot water supply as well, the heat being derived from the carriage steam heating system (see below).

The pedestal fitting — which doubled as a urinal — was generally earthenware, usually white glazed and, especially in earlier days, often of quite florid and spectacular vulgarity. Sometimes the whole was encased in a wooden housing.

The water supply for both fittings was gravity fed from tanks housed in the roof and was most certainly of non-drinking quality. The tanks were filled from the outside by hoses either directly into the top of the tank itself via an aperture in the roof (which had a detachable cover) or, later, by attaching the hose to a filler pipe which was fixed to the carriage end and went up the end and over the top of the roof to the water tank location(s). 'Carriage watering', as it was known, was and is an essential accompaniment to the operation of the railway, since water storage capacity is always limited.

Discharge (solid and liquid) from the toilet compartment, whether from washbasin or toilet, was always direct to the ballast of the track (below the carriage) which acted as a natural filter bed. The effluent was inevitably spread quite hygenically over many yards of track as the carriage moved along, but the nature of the effluent was, of course, such as to make immediately obvious the reasons for the familiar exhortation inside the vehicle not to use the facilities while the train was standing in the station! Amazingly, it was not until well into the MkIII era that BR began to use self-contained, below floor discharge tanks for lavatories, but in this respect it was and is no different from anywhere else in the world.

A somewhat less savoury sanitary fitting was the 'dry closet' which was more prevalent in countries with poor supplies of water. In these instances, discharge to the ground was achieved merely by opening a valve or hinged flap at the base of the pan (usually by foot treadle or hand lever) and allowing gravity to take over. In essence this was not too different in its mechanical operation from that of the water closet, but the lack of sluice water could cause it to be anything but pleasant. Happily, this sort of apparatus was considerably less common in Britain than elsewhere. It should be appreciated, of course, that the 'S'-bend trap at the base of the pedestal was not normally used in a train even if it was of the water closet variety.

The flushing mechanism itself was operated by foot treadle, lever or chain and, in some cases, by raising the seat of the pan to the upright position — a baffling situation to encounter for anyone with no experience of the process since there were no operating instructions! In general, however, during the twentieth century the British railway lavatory managed to get by better than most after its appallingly slow Victorian start, and it was only in the more modern era that major changes were made.

The actual position of the roof tanks was variable. They were often purpose-built in shape, to match the roof profile, and were incorporated in the roof structure. An alternative method, also used in a supplementary way if extra water capacity was needed, was to fit tanks inside the carriage, below the roof boards and covered with casing boards. In this position there was less likelihood of freezing in cold weather. Galvanized steel or iron, or sometimes copper, were the common materials, and in dining cars even more water provisioning was often provided by cylindrical tanks hanging from the kitchen and pantry ceilings. In these cases, some of the water supply was led through water filters to purify it and make it fit for drinking, and this practice could be found in some of the better quality ordinary stock as well, including sleeping cars.

Mention of the latter serves as a reminder that in this specific category of vehicle, the plumbing arrangements were normally much more sophisticated. These mobile 'hotels' were and are the most opulent general service vehicles built by the railways and are considered in more detail in Chapter 11.

Carriage heating

A particular problem which affected British carriages in the nineteenth century was the difficulty of heating an interior which, in almost all cases, was constructed on the compartment principle. An open saloon interior could be warmed by a stove, and this method was commonplace overseas. The problem in Britain was only solved in a satisfactory manner at the end of Victoria's reign and fully effective carriage heating is thus, in British terms, very much a twentieth-century development. However, since it took time to be fully developed, the older methods remained in use during the earlier part of the period under survey and warrant a brief word.

Firstly was the so-called 'foot warmer', an individual flat metal cannister of quite substantial size and vast inconvenience. Originally they were filled with hot water by means of a screw top aperture, much in the manner of a hot water bottle; by 1900, they had developed to a sealed form containing soda acetate crystals. These were pre-heated before being distributed to the passengers and continued to give out heat as the solution re-crystallized. By giving them a good shake from time to time they could, to some extent, be made to give warmth for several

Figure 27 *Typical arrangement of the steam heating system in a compartment carriage. The two main steam pipes 'a' and 'd' are connected by individual valves 'b' to the heaters 'c'. The whole system can be drained by valves 'e' and 'f', one for each of the main feed pipes.*

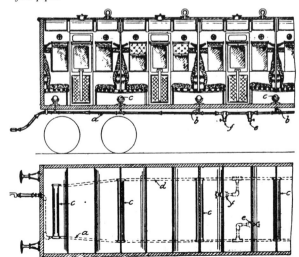

hours. They did not long survive the introduction of steam heating. The alternative older method, used in a few carriages, was some form of circulating hot water system fed by a small boiler. Pullmans were often equipped with this system — of essentially American origin — as were some of the better late Victorian sleeping cars. It, too, was superseded by the steam heating method. Rarely if ever did a British passenger-carrying vehicle make use of the iron stove, radiating its heat directly to the interior, which was so popular elsewhere, not least on the brake vans of British goods trains.

A variant of the circulating hot water system was tried out, experimentally, by the Midland Railway late in the nineteenth century using hot water from the locomotive, but the best solution was that of feeding a supply of steam to the train. Several systems were developed late in Victorian days and all were very similar in principle. Steam from the locomotive was passed through a pressure reducing valve to a continuous pipe below the carriages, the linkage between each carriage being by means of flexible hose couplings similar to the brake connections (see Chapter 2). From each pipe, a feeder led to a radiator inside the compartment. These were usually located either below the seats or, in some open stock, were located in the angle between the floor and the side of the carriage. In this variation, the radiators were generally covered by means of a pierced metal grille which served both as a decorative feature in its own right and as a protection both for the radiator itself and the feet of the passenger.

The radiator itself could sometimes be of the storage type and filled with a soda acetate solution working in much the same way as a foot warmer, ie absorbing heat from the steam supply and then giving it off as it cooled. Fresh steam was automatically admitted when the cooling reached a predetermined point. More often, however, the system was non-storage with live steam in the radiator itself. Supplementing these radiators many railways also used the steam pipe itself — along corridors for example — protecting it, and the passengers, by means of covers or grilles.

In many carriages, the supply of steam to the radiators could be adjusted by the passenger by means of a control knob or lever and this method of heating remained standard throughout the steam period. Indeed, the first generation diesel locomotives in Britain were often equipped with auxiliary boilers to provide a supply of steam for the heating system. In all cases, drain cocks were provided in every carriage to avoid condensing steam freezing solid in the pipes during cold weather, especially when standing in the sidings.

The principal exception to steam heating during the early days was to be found in electrically-propelled stock which, not surprisingly, was also electrically heated; this has now become the accepted modern method for almost all trains in Britain.

Ventilation

The object of carriage ventilation is to get a free circulation of air without either draught or dust. This was not really possible with the traditional drop light type of opening window, or indeed some of the later styles of opening window. Any form of opening window was bound at some stage to admit not only draughts and dust but also rain, and was often a frequent cause of argument between passengers who wanted it open and those who preferred it closed. The matter was never really settled and only became a dead issue with the introduction of permanently sealed windows, allied with air-conditioning, in more recent times, although there are still many who yearn for an openable window in those coaches which have none.

There were, however, other forms of carriage ventilation. The door top version with its sliding 'hit and miss' shutter has already been mentioned in connection with body construction. It had a series of holes or slots in a sliding panel which, when open, coincided with similar apertures in the door top panel. On the outside these ventilators were covered by decorative hoods, and could also be found over many of the fixed lights. There was, however, no special device for extracting stale air.

A variation of this type was the Anderson ventilator which did have extractor capability — see Figure 28. From the outside, the hood (or 'bonnet') looked much the same but, be it metal or wood, was open at both ends. Behind the hood there was a flattened suction tube of a kind of double conical shape rather like a semi-collapsed diabolo, while inside the carriage a deflector tube, which prevented the incoming fresh air mixing with the outgoing stale air, was sometimes fitted. When the carriage was moving, the outer suction tube created a partial vacuum at the rear end which sucked out the stale air as the fresh air entered the carriage. The arrows on the diagram show the various directions of movement.

Another quite popular form of carriage side ventilator was the glass vane type (see Figure 29), particularly favoured by the LMS in the 1920s but which actually came into use during pre-grouping days on several railways. These units were mounted above some of the windows in the eaves panel and had a series of vertical glass vanes, all held in place at the top and bottom by individual brass castings which could pivot in a common frame. All the vanes

This pair of glass vane ventilators surmounting the large picture window of a North Eastern first class open carriage were described, somewhat puzzlingly, as 'Patent louvre ball-bearing hit and miss ventilators'!

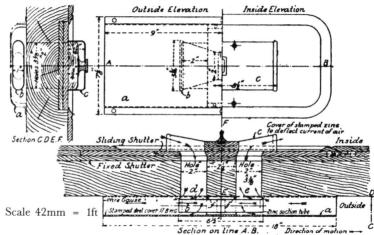

Figure 28 *Diagram of the Anderson extractor ventilator.*

Scale 42mm = 1ft

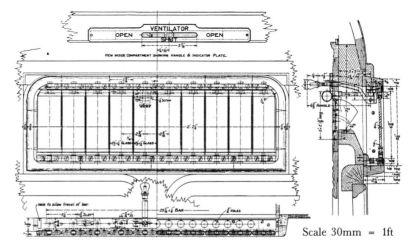

Figure 29 *Diagram of Great Eastern Railway pattern glass vane ventilator.*

Scale 30mm = 1ft

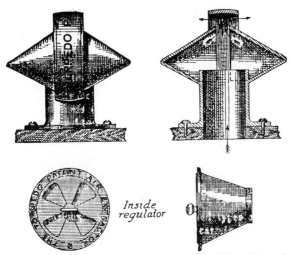

*Inside
regulator*

Figure 30 *The original Laycock's patent 'Torpedo' roof
ventilator.*

were arranged to move simultaneously by means of
a linkage attached to an interior handle, so that they
could be set either flush with the carriage side, in
which position the edges of the vanes almost touched
and admitted but little air, or they could be swivelled
to either face or trail the airstream at an angle, thus
producing either an incoming or outgoing air current. Inside the carriage, the ventilator aperture was
oten fitted with a small secondary window, hinged
at the lower edge, which could be kept closed by a
catch at the top edge. To make use of the glass vane
facility, this inner window had first to be opened.

Further forms of carriage side ventilation appeared
down the years and will be considered in their proper
chronology, but one final and almost universal form
which lasted throughout the century (save in air-
conditioned stock) must be mentioned here. It was
perhaps the most characteristic of them all and was
fitted to the top of the roof, often to the sides of
clerestories if present, and was generally known as
the 'Torpedo' ventilator.

There were, in fact, many subtle variations on the
theme both in shape and size, and the shape, disposition and number of roof ventilators could be just as
distinctive a visual characteristic of a particular
railway as its panelling style or carriage livery. All
the varieties worked in much the same way, but
strictly speaking the 'Torpedo' name is properly
applied only to that type invented and patented by
Laycock in the nineteenth century.

Essentially, the 'Torpedo' was an extractor unit
and worked by the creation of a partial vacuum
between the outer band and the inner cones when
the train was moving. To close it, an interior 'hit and
miss' revolving shutter was fitted, yet another gadget

which could give an imaginative carriage builder
some scope for decorative innovation. The shutters
were normally finished in brass or bronze but some
were wood and other materials could also be found.
The outer unit was normally cast iron.

Lighting

At the start of the present century, carriage lighting
for new construction had settled down to one of two
main alternatives, gas or electricity. There were still
surviving examples of the older oil lamps in use, but
many formerly oil-lit carriages had been converted
to the more modern form by the start of the period,
and this obsolete form need not concern us save to
note its occasional continuance. Of the two more
recent methods, gas was the older. During the last
quarter of the nineteenth century, several experiments in gas lighting were conducted, some involving
coal gas carried in a separate vehicle, but by 1900
the railways had pretty well standardized on
compressed oil gas if they had not moved over to
electricity. Compressed oil gas as a method of lighting
was first introduced to Britain in 1876 on the
Metropolitan Railway which adopted a system
developed by Julius Pintsch. This and the
contemporary Pope's system differed only in a few
details at the distillation stage and a general outline
of the basic principles should suffice for both.

Oil gas was made in a separate gas plant by means
of distillation, and the railways often built their own
gasworks for this purpose. Various heavier tars and
impurities were removed during the distillation
process and the 'cleaned' gas was then passed to a
gasholder prior to its transfer to the carriages. In
order not to take up too much space on the carriages
and to enable the supply to last for a considerable
time, the gas was compressed into cylindrical holders
at a pressure of some 10 atmospheres (about 140-150
psi).

Transfer to the gas reservoirs of the carriages
themselves was by one of two methods. When a major
carriage servicing depot was close to the gas plant,
a direct pipeline supply was laid to the depot
terminating in gas charging standards which could
be connected directly to the carriages. Equally
common, however, were the travelling gasholders
(gas wagons) which were positioned up and down the
railway system wherever carriages may have need to
be 'topped up'. Clearly, more remote locations were
served exclusively by such wagons, but at many busy
stations it was normal to have a few gas wagons at
strategic locations in order to avoid wasting time by
sending stock to the depot, even if the latter was only
a mile or two away. Needless to say, the tanks of these
wagons had to be strong enough to withstand the high
pressure; some railways favoured a single tank on the

Figure 31 *These drawings show (right) the Pope's and (far right) the Pintsch's form of 'butterfly burner' gas lamp. The arrows indicate the general direction of air circulation. The Pintsch lamp also shows the form of construction adopted when such lamps were fitted in the elevated centre roof section of a clerestory carriage.*

Below right *Pintsch gas lamps are prominent in this more than adequately equipped third class Midland and Glasgow & South Western Joint Stock dining carriage. Although dating from the mid-1890s, this was still very much 'state of the art' gas lighting technology at the start of the twentieth century (BR LMR).*

wagon, others opted for two or more smaller ones.

On the carriage itself, there were reservoirs suspended from the underframe, the size of which depended on the number of gas appliances to be served and the desired time between 'refills'. If more than one gas reservoir was carried, they were interconnected. It would be normal to carry sufficient supplies for at least one or two days of the darkest possible conditions, ie midwinter. For example, a fairly typical reservoir some 6 ft long by 1 ft 9 in diameter would contain about 12 cubic feet which, at the designed pressure, could supply three 8-candle-power burners for some 36-40 hours at full gas pressure (the gas pressure in the carriage reservoirs was somewhat less than that of the main storage tanks, typically about 60-70%, ie about 80-100 psi). The carriage reservoirs were charged from the tank wagons or depot pipelines through valves and hose-pipes and a pressure gauge was placed close to the inlet valve to show when the required pressure had been reached, at which point the valve was closed. Once again, the Pintsch and Pope systems varied only slightly, mainly in the design of the valves.

From the reservoirs, the gas was taken to the lamps in small-bore piping, usually externally mounted on the roof. A regulating valve kept the supply pressure constant and a pull-out handle at the carriage end enabled platform staff to turn on or off the main gas supply to the interior. This action controlled all the lamps simultaneously, since they usually had small permanently lit pilot flames fed by a secondary supply. Without pilot flames, lamps had to be individually turned on and lit from within the compartment; this cumbersome and time-wasting process

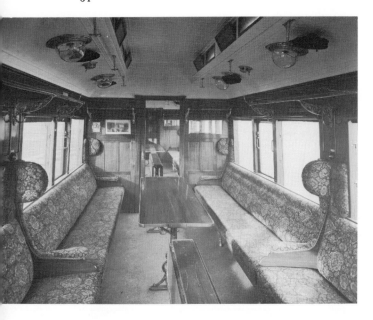

and this, in spite of the considerable fire risk which several railways, particularly the Midland, had good cause to appreciate. Grantham on the GNR (1906), together with Hawes Junction (1910) and Ais Gill (1913), both Midland, were three thoroughly embarrassing 'mishaps', to use the typically understated and favourite railway euphemism for what was often a cataclysmic accident, and did not enhance the reputation of gas. But the LYR in 1913, rather than go all-electric, persevered with a 'fireproof' gaslit train — see page 190 — and repeated the exercise in 1917.

In part, the reason was the lighter weight of the gas equipment compared with electric, not to mention the considerable capital investment made by many railways in their gas-producing plants. Moreover, in spite of several possible alternatives, compressed oil gas was still far and away the best solution to on-train cooking. Consequently, the death throes of oil gas were drawn out, extending well beyond the period of this first book. The LMS was still installing gas lights in its otherwise thoroughly modern flush-sided kitchen cars in the 1930s and as a cooking medium oil gas did not actually vanish until the much more recent introduction of bottled gas. Moreover, many gaslit coaches remained thus to the end — well into the 1930s and 1940s.

In this context, although a bit outside the immediate period of this survey, it might be worth pointing out the fundamental difference between compressed oil gas and bottled gas as applied to railways. Both types were petroleum based, but whereas compressed oil gas was carried on the vehicles in *gaseous* form under pressure, modern bottled gas, be it propane, butane or merely described as lpg (liquefied petroleum gas), is actually stored as a liquid until it passes from its pressurized container to the 'user' end.

In the latter part of the twentieth century, we are accustomed to constant media exhortations as to the virtues of electricity and take it for granted, but there was still a sort of 'magical mystery' surrounding the subject at the start of our survey and, yet again, the seminal period was late Victorian. Hamilton Ellis has, as usual, reviewed the ground most thoroughly in his work so there is no need for undue repetition here. Suffice it to say that by the start of our period, most experiments were over and a fairly standardized system patented by J. Stone in the 1890s became by far the most widely used.

Setting aside for the moment the sheer convenience factor of electric lighting, the main problem with using it on a moving vehicle is that of current storage, in the absence of a regular outside supply such as that provided to our homes and workplaces. Even if the railway is itself electrified, this does not really solve the problem of supply since a typical locomotive-

was virtually obsolete by the end of the nineteenth century.

The lamps themselves were relatively simple, comprising a pipe and burner below a chimney. The burners were initially of the 'butterfly' type, so-called because the shape of the flame was somewhat like a butterfly's wing. One of these burners gave about 7 candlepower, but many lamps were fitted with duplex burners — one pipe fed two 'butterfly' flames and this doubled the light intensity. There was usually a pivot mechanism allowing the whole of the pipe/burner apparatus to be hinged out of the way to allow for cleaning the lamp and also, in the days before pilot lights, for easier lighting as well. From about 1905 onwards, gas mantles often replaced the open flame burners to give a further improvement in light intensity.

Inside the carriage, it was not always possible for the flame size to be adjusted — save by railway staff — or for the light to be extinguished, so hinged cloth covers were often provided to shroud the gas globe and dim the compartment. Another interesting aspect of gas lighting was its ability to augment the warmth of the carriage, not to mention the scope it gave for exuberant decorative treatment of the light fittings themselves.

The basic simplicity of the gas lighting system, together with its ability to produce quite bright light, especially after the introduction of gas mantles, gave it a long life, even in the twentieth century. Some railways were particularly wedded to gas lighting, even after electric light systems had become more reliable, noteworthy being the GWR and Midland;

Left *This Midland picnic saloon of 1907 displays gas lamps with mantles, now fitted to the main roof and almost flush with the ceiling, thus leaving the clerestory itself free to provide perhaps better ventilation than when the lamps were mounted there*

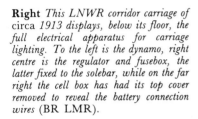

Right *This LNWR corridor carriage of circa 1913 displays, below its floor, the full electrical apparatus for carriage lighting. To the left is the dynamo, right centre is the regulator and fusebox, the latter fixed to the solebar, while on the far right the cell box has had its top cover removed to reveal the battery connection wires* (BR LMR).

hauled railway carriage could well find itself operating in all parts of the system, whether it be electrified or not. It is therefore not a totally practical proposition for a locomotive-hauled railway carriage to pick up current from outside. The system must be self-contained and therein lies the basic problem. The fact that it still bedevils the road vehicle industry's attempts to harness electric power for traction purposes is sufficient proof of this.

If there is no 'mains supply', electricity can only be stored in some form of accumulator or battery and these things take up much space and contribute considerable weight if they are to have any reasonable storage potential. Indeed, one of the more noteworthy nineteenth-century efforts — Stroudley's on the LB & SCR — realized this problem and made a valiant attempt to solve it by putting a generator in the guard's van. This was the key.

The best way to reduce the need for battery storage of electricity is to generate it as you go along. This can be done by means of a completely self-contained unit (eg the diesel-powered generators in modern diesel-electric locomotives) or by harnessing the motion of the train itself. In the former case, the electricity generation is independent of the movement of the train but incurs a severe weight penalty by the need to have a separate 'engine' to drive the generator. If on the other hand one drives a generator by harnessing the rotary motion of the wheels and axles, the generation stops when the vehicle is not moving. Nevertheless, it was the latter mode which Stone developed in the 1890s and which became standard until well into BR days.

In Stone's system, a generator (dynamo) was mounted beneath the carriage and the moving parts given rotary motion by connecting them via pulleys and a belt to the nearest axle. The dynamo had to be manufactured in such a way that it functioned properly regardless of the direction of travel which, of course, would determine whether the rotation was clockwise or anticlockwise.

The rate of electricity generation was, of course, determined by the speed of the rotation of the wheels, so there was an undesirable variation in the rate. Thus, before the current was fed to the lights a voltage regulator was inserted — in effect a variable resistance — so that the supply to the lights was kept constant. Now this arrangement was fine so long as the vehicles were moving fast enough for current to be generated, but there comes a point (when either the vehicle speed is too low or the carriage is stationary) at which the dynamo ceases to provide enough current to keep the lights going. To overcome this, a battery supply was still needed, albeit nothing like as large as it would have been if there was no generator capacity. Thus, the complete Stone's system embodied dynamo, regulator *and* batteries, the latter being housed in one or more 'cell boxes' fixed below the underframe. The lights took their current either from the dynamo via the cells (when moving normally) or the cells alone (when moving slowly or stationary). The generating capacity of the dynamo had of course to *exceed* the demands of the lights when running at normal speeds so that the excess generating capacity could be diverted into the important business of re-charging the batteries in the

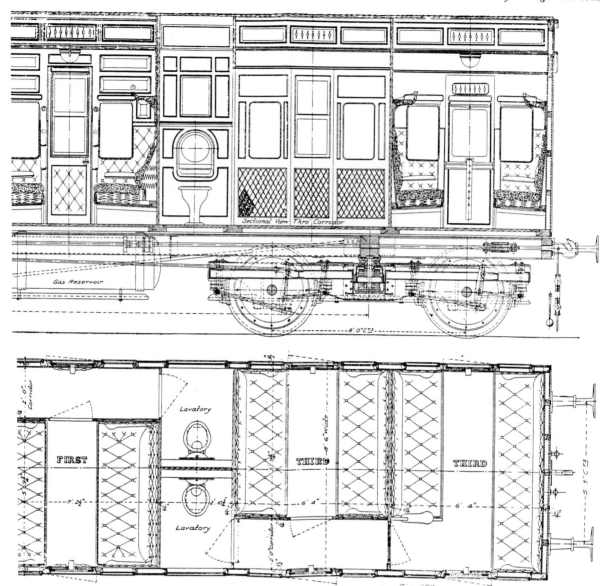

Scale 6.5mm = 1ft

Figure 32 *This and the next two drawings show something of the total design integration achieved by British carriage builders at their best. This one is a very late Victorian NER clerestory non-corridor with lavatories, a type which set standards for many decades both on the NER and elsewhere. An end elevation can also be found in Figure 19.*

cell boxes. The dynamo capacity varied, according to need, and sometimes (for instance in suburban trains), one dynamo could serve two coaches.

The batteries themselves were conventional lead-acid accumulators and were quite heavy, especially if the demands of the carriage itself were greater than normal due to extra lights, electric fans and so on. Nevertheless, the system stood the test of time, although it did add more weight to the carriage than the gas lighting apparatus already considered. It began to run into trouble when the demand for electricity exceeded its intrinsic capability, such as when all-electric cooking was adopted to some extent in the 1930s.

So successful was the basic Stone's principle,

Figure 33 *Right at the turn of the century, the GCR produced some small but stylish side-corridors of somewhat 'continental' aspect for the London Extension. These cross-sections show* *something of the detail which went into them. The seat design and toilet fittings encapsulate most of the issues discussed in this chapter. For plans, see Figure 44 (page 168).*

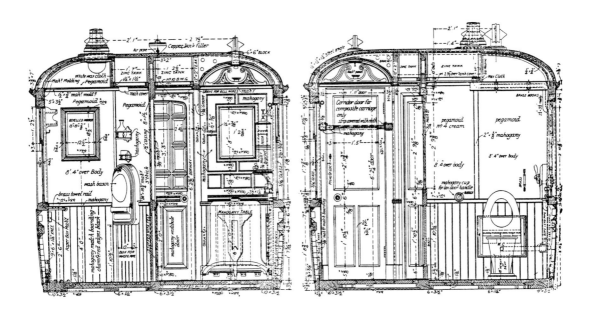

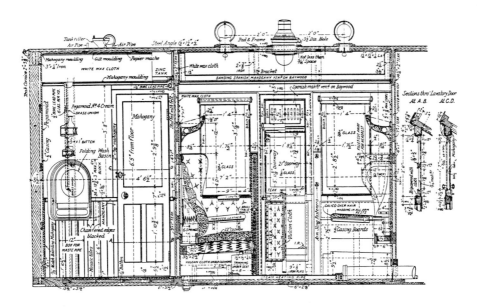

Scale 8mm = 1ft

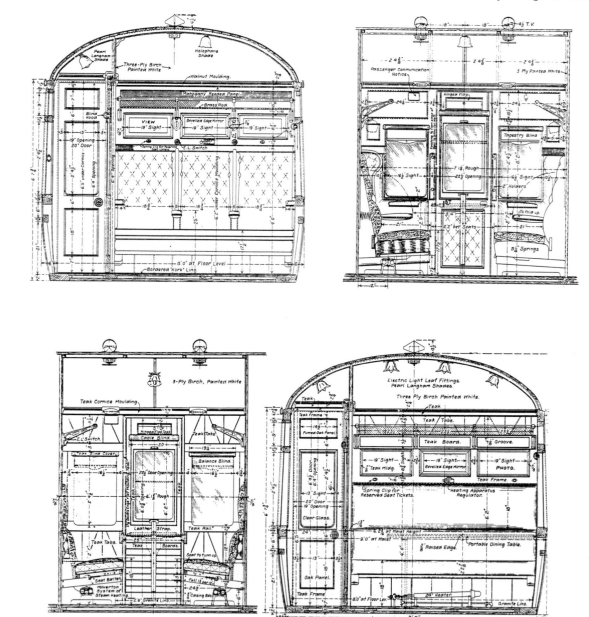

Scale 8mm = 1ft

Figure 34 *Compartment details of a West Coast Joint Stock corridor carriage of 1913. These and dozens more like them from many railways established standards which were not significantly bettered until the 1930s. Indeed, most better carriages of this period were not scrapped until well into BR days, surely adequate testimony to the essential quality of their original design.*

whether in its original form or as somewhat modified in later years by the LMS into what was known as the 'Wolverton' system, that there was no need to make any really fundamental changes for decades. In fact, the BR MkI period still utilized an essentially similar method during the 1950s and early 1960s to that which had existed since the turn of the century.

The carriage itself carried its electric supply cables either concealed beneath the inside panelling or sometimes in conduits on the roof top, and the 'supply side' voltage was normally quite low (24-28 volts) compared with domestic electric equipment. Light bulbs were normally about 25 watts with a pearl finish but they could be found in light fittings of infinite variety and style.

One particular advantage of electric lighting as compared with gas was the much simpler process of turning it on or off by means of a simple switch. It is therefore not at all surprising that the onset of electrically-lit coaches pretty well coincided with the increasing use of auxiliary optional (or 'courtesy') lights. These might be individual wall lights, separate table lamps, bedhead lights in sleeping cars and so forth, all under passenger control. It became possible to dim the lights at night or take the option between full or partial lighting, and there were few more pleasurable experiences than to ride in an electrically-lit Pullman or dining car with all the lights extinguished save for the cosy table lamp. The modern BR coaches do not offer this option — more's the pity!

The really significant changes in carriage electrics did not generally appear until the 1960s and 1970s with the onset of fluorescent lighting, air-conditioning and so on which also demanded changed methods of power generation. They will not, therefore, be

It should perhaps be repeated that the above account of electric lighting applies only to locomotive-hauled stock. Where carriages formed a permanent part of electrically-propelled multiple unit formations (EMUs), their lighting current could, of course, be supplied from the conductor rail (or wire). Although this supplied traction current at high voltage, by means of suitable voltage reduction apparatus it could also be used to light the train, hence the occasional momentary 'dimming or blacking out' sometimes experienced when EMUs negotiate a break between two electrical supply sections.

Before concluding this review of interior amenities, it is worth adding a short note simply to point out that certain types of vehicle, by virtue of their specialized nature, regularly carried more interior fittings — both in terms of quantity and variety — than did ordinary day coaches. Dining cars, for example, had to carry extra water supplies and extra gas cylinders for the kitchen, while the latter itself often added weight to the carriage by virtue of its heavy equipment. Sleeping cars had a plethora of partitions and cupboards, not to mention extra water, lavatory and lighting facilities, and so forth. In consequence, the need to contain elaborate interior equipment could spill over into the basic design of the vehicle itself, thus explaining the larger and heavier characteristics of many specialized carriages (12 rather than 8 wheels, for example).

There was, in fact, a tremendous degree of integration between all the three aspects of vehicle design (chassis, body and interior) which have been for convenience sake separated for analysis in this and the previous two chapters. The complete vehicle was a total synthesis of many differing requirements, and at times a compromise between disparate sets of conditions — and it does no harm to be reminded of this point from time to time if only more fully to appreciate the ingenuity with which the railways regularly solved the problems.

5. Livery, painting and decoration

Throughout most of their history the railways of Britain have been quite notably colourful, in the literal sense of the word, and happily, as these words are written in the later 1980s, there are many encouraging signs of a rebirth on the railways of something of the colourful variety which was once so characteristic of the company era. Nowhere was the use of colour more strikingly manifest than in the liveries adopted for the adornment of carriages, whether it be the humblest of suburban conveyances or the most grandly finished special saloons.

The tradition undoubtedly goes back to the horse-drawn road-coach era where rival coach operators often decorated their vehicles with a high degree of flamboyance. In part this was an expression of pride but it also had the practical virtue of identification, whether it be for the company in question or the service which was operated. Since they drew much of their early carriage inspiration from the road-coach business, the railways, not surprisingly, copied the ideas with a considerable degree of fidelity, even to the extent of giving names to some of their carriages. By the start of the twentieth century, although the practice of naming had become all but exclusive to Pullman cars, the distinctively different basic liveries remained as prevalent as ever.

By this time, livery was most definitely associated with specific companies rather than particular types of vehicles or services. With relatively few exceptions which can, realistically, be ignored, there was no longer a significant livery differentiation between, say, first and second class vehicles, but there was considerable variation between the colour schemes adopted by the individual private systems. In modern jargon it would be called 'house style'; in those days it was sufficient simply to refer to 'Midland red'. 'Great Western chocolate and cream', Great Northern teak', or whatever, to establish, beyond peradventure, the system on which one was travelling.

As an aside, it is interesting to note that the modern (ie 1985 onwards) re-introduction of colourful variety in carriage livery is almost a

Furness Railway six-wheel composite No 57 shows the customary method of applying a two-colour livery, in this case blue and white, to a wooden-panelled coach. Most companies put fine lining round almost every piece of panel moulding, and the main point of variation, colours apart, was whether or not the waist panel was painted the darker or lighter of the two shades. This picture represents the slightly more common approach, but some very famous railways, for example the GWR with its famous chocolate and cream, adopted the alternative course, ie with a dark waist panel. This FR carriage has a very long wheelbase for a rigid six-wheeler; secondly, and unusually for an English railway, it features what I have called the 'Scottish' style of twin-layer body panelling — see page 103

On LNWR tri-composite (three-class) corridor brake carriage No 900, the two-colour livery (carmine lake and white) also confined the darker shade to the bottom panels only but the Wolverton panelling (see page 103) gives it quite a different look. Because there was relatively little panel beading carrying a darker shade above the waist, LNWR carriages were often called 'white' trains, exaggerated if, as was often the case, the roof was also painted white

reversion to a very early form of vehicle identification by service or carriage type, rather than to identify the company itself. There is thus no longer a universal BR carriage livery *as such,* but we now have 'Network SouthEast', 'ScotRail', 'InterCity' and many other similar terms, all serving as justification for the various colour schemes currently adopted by the unified BR system. Whatever the reasoning, it is a very welcome change.

Until recently, this colourful variety of exterior treatment was a somewhat peculiarly British manifestation of train travel. It was not that other countries never employed colourful styles, but they rarely went to such extravagant extremes as did the British companies, and this characteristically 'British' approach to carriage decoration was very much in evidence during and very typical of the first few decades of the present century.

Essentially, of course, the primary object of painting a carriage is to preserve the material so painted from climatic and other deterioration as a result of prolonged exposure to open-air conditions. Therefore, the first property of a carriage livery was to be of sufficient substance to protect and seal the structure of the vehicle. In Britain, the two most favoured approaches were to use either a colour base or a varnished wood treatment and the decorative possibilities were very much secondary, yet they inevitably achieved more public attention simply because of their nature. By the start of the twentieth century, fairly standardized methods of treatment had been established by the railway industry,

Top *The LYR adopted a two-colour system which took its darker livery colour to window level. For photographic purposes, it also painted the odd carriage in various shades of 'works grey' to display more clearly the details and livery style, the 'Lanky' carriage colours, carmine lake and dark tan, being hard for contemporary photographic emulsions to separate. This produced a very clear impression of the character of the carriage, in this case tri-composite corridor brake No 1061. It would have received the proper livery before entering service.*

Above *A less common variant of the two-colour style was adopted by the LSWR, represented by arc roof bogie first class non-corridor No 175. Not only were the colours unusual (salmon pink and dark brown), but the practice of painting the upper panel beading the same colour as the panels themselves, rather than the darker body colour, was comparatively rare and followed by few other railways.*

regardless of specific livery style, and these painting and varnishing methods lasted throughout the first half of the century, largely unchanged, right into early BR days. They were slow to change even after the 1950s and, in certain particulars, have continued in use to the present days; needless to say, the origins were firmly Victorian.

The traditional method of coach painting as practised by the railways is as much art as science and its full appreciation by the onlooker can be much enhanced by a basic understanding of two fundamental and closely related aspects of the subject, namely the materials themselves and their method of application. This, therefore, will be the starting point.

Carriage painting materials

The basic ingredients

From the outset it should be understood that unlike modern paints, which make extensive use of synthetic chemical constituents, the materials used by coach painters during the first half of the century were based on naturally occurring substances falling into three broad categories. These gave way but slowly to the modern materials and, in some cases, what might be termed 'older fashioned' paint, provided it does not offend some modern 'health and safety' regulation, is still preferred by a real craftsman.

1 *Basic pigments* These constituents, which imparted colour and covering power to the finished product, were the fundamentals of paint. Indeed, they were often called 'bases', the term 'pigment' being reserved to designate those which actually imparted the finished colour. The commonly used bases were such as white and red lead, oxide of iron, zinc white, various blacks and the umbers. A more detailed analysis of the various bases and their colours is given below. They were often supplied in non-liquid form — solid, paste or powder being characteristic.

2 *Vehicles, mixes and solvents* These were the substances which, when mixed with the chosen basic pigment(s), turned them into a consistency which was recognizably 'paint', Various oils or spirits of turpentine were the norm.

3 *Driers* These, as the name implies, were substances added to the paint to hasten the drying or hardening process. Such materials as litharge, zinc sulphate or lead acetate were commonly used.

4 *Stoppers and fillers* Prior to application of any paint or varnish finishes, much less the final decorative embellishments, blemishes on the carriage surface had to be stopped or filled to give a smooth surface. The materials used were closely allied to the paints themselves and three sub-categories can be identified.

a) *Putty* This was a substance formed by mixing dried 'whiting' (fine powder produced from pure white chalk) into a stiff paste with raw linseed oil and then kneading well. A little white lead added prior to kneading improved matters and the putty could be tinted by adding colouring pigments if required. It was, of course, principally used for glazing purposes. Whiting on its own, incidentally, when rubbed on to a surface, could be used to prepare it for gilding or varnishing, having the interesting property of imparting a texture to the surface which allowed the varnish, gold size or whatever to 'lay' properly; it did not affect the finished texture and/or colour of the top coating.

b) *'Hard stopping'* This was the form of hard-drying putty, made from dry white lead mixed with gold size or varnish, and used to fill cracks, crevices and so forth. When dry, it could be smoothed down ('faced down') with pumice stone prior to painting. If a little turpentine and whiting were added, it was possible to face down the stopping with sandpaper rather than pumice stone and in this form it was called 'sandpaper stopping'. In general, hard stopping was preferred for rectifying blemishes in panels and the like because of its ability to be rubbed down to a very smooth finish. However, most carriage painters would choose to use a normal putty for major defects in joints, since this material was far less likely to become completely brittle and fall out of the crevice when subjected to the vibrations of the carriage in traffic.

c) *'Knotting'* The third filling material — something of a misnomer in this case — was used only on wooden components. The object of this substance was to 'kill' any knots in the wood (ie prevent any subsequent exudation of turpentine or resin) and also to prevent the knots absorbing paint or causing discoloration on the surface when painted. The first application was made from a mixture prepared by grinding red lead in water, mixing with glue size and applying when hot; it dried in about ten minutes. The second application was of red lead ground in oil and thinned with either boiled linseed oil or turpentine. There was also a patent form of knotting consisting of shellac dissolved in naphtha. In all its forms, knotting had no real filling power; it merely served as protection.

The art of the coach painter, in every sense, was a combination of his ability to mix these materials properly for the required purpose and his skill in applying effectively 'his' mixes to the surface in question. Used in various combinations, the above materials could provide not only the means whereby the final finish was obtained but they could also assist in the preparation process. The coach painter had to master it all.

The bases and pigments

The most commonly occurring constituent of traditional coach painting was white lead, a mixture of lead hydrate and lead carbonate. This was an extensively used substance, whether as base or pigment. When combined with oil it possessed great permanency and covering power as a base and it was unequalled amongst the various available whites as a pigment. In dry form, it could be used for stopping up cracks in the woodwork, and in any form it could be tinted with other pigments to provide many desired finishing colours. Used in small quantities, it tended to make paint somewhat easier to work with the brush and it is said that the Caledonian Railway locomotive painters at Perth were more than adept at using it in this mode. As a result they went to such extremes that, over the years, they managed to produce a somewhat lighter shade of Prussian blue than the official version — 'Perth blue' as it was sometimes called. It later became the recognized Caledonian locomotive colour, or so it is said... At the same time, however, who is to say that painters in the carriage works did not resort to the same trick with official carriage colours as well? For painting use, white lead was normally provided in 'tub' form (ie mixed with some 8-15% oil in the form of a paste).

Lead-based paint, as it was often called when white lead was a principal constituent, was poisonous and its manufacture is no longer permitted, but it had a long run as an essential basis for exterior painting. Its toxic properties were known, if not quite so feared as in our often over-sensitive modern era, and for interior use a common, non-poisonous alternative was based on zinc sulphide, frequently known as 'enamel' white. There was also a non-poisonous lead white (lead sulphate) but neither of these non-toxic white bases was quite as good as the traditional white lead, always the favoured choice of the best coach painters.

The second very common base was red lead, this time an oxide of the metal. Like white lead, it mixed well with oil, had good covering power and dried quickly. For these reasons it was a popular undercoat or primer and was particularly suited to metal components. However, unlike white lead, it could only be mixed safely (in regard to permanence of colour) with ochres, earths and blacks. Mixed with other pigments (including white lead), it went 'fugitive' — in other words, it lost colour permanence.

To obtain the vast range of different colour shades so characteristic of railway liveries, other pigments had to be added, and although this survey is not meant to be a paint manufacturing manual, a brief summary of the more common colour pigments will not be out of place. For one thing, even a slight knowledge of the considerable complexity of the pigments employed can only serve to enhance the appreciation of the skills applied by those really competent coach painters who knew how to use them properly. The various pigments group themselves into broad colour categories, in each of which such qualities as beauty and depth of colour, 'body' (ie covering power), ease of application, durability and permanence were all sought-after characteristics.

Blacks

Several kinds of black pigment were used by the railway painters. 'Lamp' and 'vegetable' black, usually containing 98% or more carbon, were obtained from the soot formed by burning various substances such as coal, tar, oil or tallow. The superior version (vegetable black) was that obtained from the burning of pure vegetable oil. Another common type was 'ivory' or 'bone' black obtained by burning (calcining) ivory or bone in closed vessels and then grinding it to a fine powder. Ivory was considered superior to other bone and produced an intense black pigment. A description often encountered was 'drop black', referring to the practice of selling the black pigment in pear-shaped drops of exceedingly fine quality, easily fractured prior to grinding and mixing with the appropriate 'vehicle'.

Browns and yellows

These pigments came in a variety of forms, mostly derived from natural earths and clays whose colours were mainly due to the presence of oxides of iron and manganese. Common names found in this category were the 'umbers', a large class of natural dark earths found in many places, particularly Turkey; the 'ochres', somewhat similar natural clays of rather lighter tone, often used as a basis for a yellow colour; and the 'siennas', close allies of both, a warmer shade lying somewhere between them in tone. 'Burnt' as opposed to 'raw' umbers and siennas were produced by burning to give a darker colour, while 'Vandyke brown' was a naturally occurring dark brown mineral pigment.

The brown family in its more or less natural state graded at one end into a sort of yellow and at the other end into red, while the darkest browns could be given all manner of subtle hues by amalgamation with blacks or greens. The permutations were infinite but a particularly good example of what could be achieved is the elusive and indescribable shade used for the lower panels in the distinctive two-tone carriage livery adopted by the London and South Western Railway. To call it 'dark brown' begs the question. In some conditions it could seem almost black, while in others, by all accounts, it took on a sort of greenish hue. It has proved a very difficult colour to reproduce with modern synthetics at the National Railway Museum.

The other principal source of yellow pigmentation was from chromate of lead (chrome yellow), much used in the preparation of green shades (see below).

Reds

Red, together with blue and yellow, is one of the three primary colours and, along with green in some form or another, was probably the most common railway livery colour. Even those railways which never adopted it as a basic livery tone always used some form of red for items such as locomotive buffer planks, signals and so on, and also quite regularly for lining out an otherwise 'red-free' colour scheme. Reds varied from the near-brown to a bright vermilion bordering on orange, and in the darker part of the spectrum some singularly beautiful and rich shades were to be seen.

At the 'red/brown' end were to be found a series of fine powders prepared from antimony sulphide which required little or no grinding and mixed readily with oil. They had great covering power as did the reds obtained from iron oxides. They were also very durable, hence the common use of red oxide as suitable finish for tens of thousands of humble goods wagons. Red/brown in its most celebrated form was often known as 'Indian red', a name which in theory should only be applied to those red pigments obtained by grinding Bengalese haematite ore to a fine powder. There were, however, many substitutes to be found, possibly the best of them being calcined sulphate of iron. The red/browns were rarely used as a basic livery colour for carriages, save perhaps for picking out window frames and other details, but were a common form of undercoat, particularly for the rich, dark shades of red wherein the warmth of the red/brown undercoat would transmit its richness through the final, almost semi-translucent quality of the top coat.

The brightest of the reds was vermilion, a naturally occurring sulphide of mercury known as cinnabar,

Liveries involving dark red and black, especially those using a single basic colour, were difficult to photograph before colour sensitive photographic emulsions came to the rescue. However, when the odd picture was taken using material which could differentiate the shades, the result could give a crystal clear indication of the disposition of both main colour and lining. This is clearly shown on Midland Railway corridor third class brake No 1617 in 1916. Even the two-colour roof (black and grey) is differentiated.

and the best came from China. When prepared with sulphide of potassium, it could rarely be bettered for sheer brilliance of colour. Once again, it was rarely a basic livery colour, but applied in the form of fine lining at the edge of gilt-embellished panel beading, it imparted an unparalleled opulence to the finished carriage. Not surprisingly, many railways used it for just this purpose.

The 'real' railway reds (ie those used as basic colours for the final liveries) were usually classified as 'lakes'. The word really describes a process rather than a substance and was used to denote the method whereby organic colouring substances were precipitated by potassium carbonate or a solution of alum from a variety of raw materials, the nature of which gave the lake its essential colour. Thus, such sources as the 'coccus cacti' insect would produce carmine, cochineal would produce crimson, the madder plant would produce the lake of the same name, and so on. Several other lakes could be manufactured from coal tar colours and, again, the varieties and their descriptions were endless.

In purely British railway carriage terms, the most commonly found lakes were the famous crimson, particularly associated with the Midland Railway and, later, the LMS, but also used in near identical shade by the North British, North Eastern and Glasgow and South Western Railways, to mention but three. A very dark lake — almost purple-brown — was carmine, particularly associated with the London and North Western and Lancashire and Yorkshire companies, but also used in a slightly lighter form by the Caledonian Railway. Lying somewhat between these two colours in the spectrum was a third basic dark shade of red, described, probably correctly, as madder lake on the North Staffordshire system but also used in near identical shade on the

South Eastern and Chatham Railway and even, for a short time between 1913 and 1922, on the Great Western in replacement of the famous 'chocolate and cream'. The latter, of course, came back at the 1923 grouping of the railways.

We are now, of course, in the highly subjective area of colour description, a topic pretty well guaranteed to cause argument and controversy. It is, in fact, well-nigh impossible to describe colours in words with any real precision, but the mere fact that even in the 1980s the topic of Edwardian liveries still causes such endless debate merely reinforces the fact that railway colour schemes were and are a prime aspect of the railway scene in Britain. The next group of colours was no different from the reds in this respect.

Greens

In theoretical colour terms, green, although the most widely occurring colour in nature, is not a primary shade and is in fact composed of a mixture of blue and yellow in various proportions. The natural green sources for paint pigments reflected this situation, being classified in two main groups. Those manufactured from sulphates were generally classed as 'Brunswick' greens and originated from barytes, gypsum or lead sulphates, acted upon by Prussian blue (see below) or chrome yellow. Those derived from chrome oxide, were unsurprisingly, classified as the 'chrome' greens. For the most part, and accepting the subjective and somewhat sweeping nature of the comment, Brunswick greens often seemed to possess a slightly colder quality than chrome greens, the latter tending rather more towards the yellow end of the spectrum.

Green was much more a locomotive than a carriage colour and many were and are the arguments surrounding the precise shades used. Indeed, I cannot resist commenting that the famous GWR locomotive green was of the chrome variety rather than oft-quoted Brunswick version! In the context of this book, however, its more subtle nuances need rarely concern us since few railways used green either as a basic carriage colour or even for decoration.

Prior to the grouping, the only major railways which adopted the shade were the Cambrian, Highland, Maryport & Carlisle, and (for some stock only) the London and South Western. After 1922, the Southern Railway, in succession to the LSWR, was the only major user of green for carriages, by which time the whole issue was further confused by the insertion of additional adjectives such as 'olive', 'malachite' and so forth.

Blues

Blue is one of the three primary colours but until fairly recent BR days (1965 onwards) it did not find too much favour as a carriage colour. In fact, it was even less popular than green. Before 1923 only the Furness Railway and the Somerset and Dorset Joint Railway used it to any great extent for carriages and, prior to 1965, its only other significant appearance was in the form of the somewhat specialized liveries adopted by the LMS and LNER for their streamlined trains of the 1930s, neither of which had any great claim to aesthetic distinction. Even as a locomotive colour, blue was not much more widespread and, risking a personal opinion, I find blue to be a somewhat less attractive shade than most for railway use, its only redeeming manifestations being perhaps the locomotive liveries of the Great Eastern and Caledonian Railways. It nearly always has a 'cold' quality to it.

At the same time, when added to other pigments blue can impart real quality to the end product. The famous LNWR 'white', for example, used on the upper panels of its carriages, could never have achieved its fame but for the addition of a mere pound weight of ultramarine to each hundredweight (112 lb) of white tub lead.

In natural form, blue pigments were most commonly (in railway usage) of either 'Prussian' or 'ultramarine' type. Prussian blue was the complex chemical result of adding proto-sulphate of iron to a solution of potassium ferro-cyanide to which, when precipitated, was further added a small amount of a solution of bichromate of potash and sulphuric acid, the whole process resulting in the familiar deep blue shade. Ultramarine, on the other hand, was prepared from alum, sulphur, soda and silica, acids being used to completely deodorize the end product. A third natural blue, known as 'Brunswick' blue and, of course, used in preparation of the green bearing the same prefix, was made from barytes, green copperas, china clay and yellow prussiate.

These, then, were some of the natural sources of the various colours used by the railways. Many of them were mixed by the paint manufacturers before being supplied to the users, but within the railway paintshop itself the painters too had to be well versed in the art of paint mixing, partly for matching purposes when rectifying worn or damaged paintwork, or possibly even to get a more precise match between two separate batches of a nominally identical colour. It should be appreciated that it was much more difficult to fix a precise shade using natural sources, however carefully prepared, than it is to do so with modern synthetic chemicals.

Vehicles, mixes and solvents

Most of the real skill of the painter was bound up closely with his knowledge and appreciation of the various oils, solvents and driers, the vehicles used for rendering the various paints workable. Most of them were either fixed or volatile oils of either the linseed or turpentine families. They came in varying properties and qualities and were chosen according to precise needs. However, they all had to work freely, display drying power and be transparent, preferably as near colourless as possible.

Linseed oils

Linseed oil is obtained from flax seed and was traditionally imported from the Baltic and Black Sea areas and also from India, the latter source generally being regarded as somewhat inferior. It could be processed in various different ways to produce three main sub-forms:

1 *Raw linseed oil (cold drawn oil)* This variety, the best quality, was obtained by crushing, grinding and pressing the oil from the seed *without heat*. It was pale, transparent, viscous and almost odourless. It did not keep as well as oil produced by heating, nor did it yield much more than 20% oil, but it was the preferred choice for the best work, although somewhat slow drying by nature.

2 *Ordinary linseed oil* This was a similar product but the seed was steam heated to about 200° F. The yield was better at some 25-30%, but the oil was less viscous and had a much darker colour — a sort of amber shade.

3 *Boiled linseed oil* This was obtained by mixing linseed oil with lead oxide (litharge) or other additives and heating to about 400° F, a process which drove off those substances which impeded oxidation, thus improving the drying powers. Even without additives, boiled linseed oil would dry more rapidly and was sometimes called 'drying oil', but the additives made the drying process even quicker and some of them altered the oil's consistency in important ways. Lead acetate, for example, would produce a lighter shade than litharge, while for use with zinc-based paints the oil had to be free from lead oxide altogether and was boiled instead with about 5% manganese peroxide.

In any form, linseed oil, although it would not keep for ever, had to be at least six months old before it was fit for use with paint, during which time it was stored in tanks to allow it to purify and mature, so to speak. Any residual water or impurities would settle as a precipitate, a sort of gooey mass called 'foots'. Sometimes white lead (about 1 lb per gallon) was also added and allowed to settle out. This improved the colour and also the drying properties of the oil and the white lead 'foots' could later be used for rough work. Oil could even be bleached by putting it in shallow, lead-lined troughs and covering

it with glass, the lead aiding the bleaching process.

Linseed oil, on final exposure to the air, oxidizes and becomes thicker. In its purest form it is quite slow to dry, but even the best quality, when used in paint, should have dried out within two or three days. Anything longer was an indication of poor quality, as was too dark a colour.

Of the three varieties, raw and ordinary linseed oils, preferably the former, were, of course, the obvious choice for the main colour pigments, while the boiled variety was confined to paint destined for carriage roofs or any other areas which received 'rougher' preparation. In addition to helping make paint pigments, linseed oil was also used in manufacture of putty and other fillers (see page 72).

Oil of turpentine

Turpentine, or 'turps', is a volatile oil obtained by tapping pine and larch trees — much in the manner of tapping rubber trees — and then distilling the raw turpentine. The residue after distillation is common resin and traditionally the best quality came from America.

Turpentine is used as a solvent in painting and in the manufacture of varnish; it also has a slight bleaching quality which, to some extent, tends to correct the colouring effect of the linseed oil with which it is mixed. It is used to 'flatten' white and make quicker drying paints, but it is merely a solvent to enable paint to work more freely and is no use on its own. Since in due course it will evaporate, it actually weakens the paint pigment, hence its best-known everyday function — cleaning brushes. However, it also has an interesting property of preventing the blistering of paint so, used in the correct quantity, it was an obvious valuable ingredient of those paints and varnishes which were exposed to the sun — hence its value in carriage painting.

Paint driers

These have already been mentioned, and they worked on the principle that the maximum drying power in oils is achieved by adding atmospheric oxygen to them. This was best done by using metallic substances which acted as 'carriers' of atmospheric oxygen and if, in addition, these substances themselves contained oxygen, so much the better. The best were therefore the metallic oxides such as the above-mentioned litharge (lead oxide), the most common single variety. Other driers in the traditional paint business included lead acetate, zinc sulphate, manganese sulphate and manganese oxide. As already mentioned, *lead* oxides were not used for zinc-based paint. Some driers, like manganese oxide, although quick in effect, were dark tones and could only be

This is pure 'signwriting'. On the original print, the brush marks can be seen as can the variations in the hand-applied gold leaf. The picture was taken to illustrate the GNR's new-style elongated insignia introduced in 1906 — see the picture on page 82. Later, of course, transfers would be made, but it was normal and cheaper to use the signwriter when new styles were first evaluated.

used for dark-coloured paints. Paint dryers were often supplied ready for use, ground and mixed in oil.

Regardless of type, driers had to be handled carefully. Only the absolute minimum quantity was needed since, paradoxically, if used in too great amounts, in spite of their name they actually slowed down the drying process! With finishing coats, little or any was used, especially if the tint might be affected, and in all cases driers were mixed into the colour at the very last moment prior to use. There were several different kinds of driers, most of which could not be used together and amongst the best known varieties were 'japan' and 'gold size'. The former was much used for tinting greens and browns but was particularly associated with black whenever a good high finish was required. Gold size, as its name implies, was used for picking out gilded areas, where its particular ability to become tacky quite speedily was of value in laying on the subsequent gold leaf (see below). Used on its own as a drier, gold size blended well with varnish, did not affect the brilliancy of the finished coat and did not become brittle with weathering. There were various types of gold size according to specific needs.

Gold leaf and transfers, and their application

Gold leaf, and its close ally the 'varnish fix' transfer, were used quite regularly in the process of gilding and decorating carriages. Gold leaf itself is beaten out of a thin sheet of pure gold until it is only a few thousandths of an inch thick and is normally supplied in books containing individual leaves some 3-4 inches square, each placed between a tissue layer coated with chalk to prevent the gold itself sticking to the paper.

The precise shade could vary from very pale to almost an orange-red. Some suppliers offered 'ribbon' gold, a long roll of gold leaf some ⅜ - ½ inch wide, ideally suited to carriage lining. Application to the carriage was by means of gold size. The area to be gilded was treated with gold size and, while the size was still tacky, the gold leaf was rubbed into place through the carrying tissue, the size acting as an adhesive. It demanded skilful judgement on the part of the painter to know precisely the right moment at which to apply the gilding. Gold leaf was easier to apply if it was slightly warmed so as to be perfectly dry and when the process was completed, a gentle wipe down was all that was normally required prior to covering with varnish.

It is surprising how often gold leaf was used for picking out lining, even on quite humble carriages, at the start of the century. Although many railways used yellow painted lines for their vehicles, many others preferred gilt lining throughout. Other systems reserved gilding for their particularly important special vehicles while some railways used gold for their corridor coaches but not for their shorter-distance stock which was down-market! Although gilding was durable it was undoubtedly expensive

This close-up view of a well-weathered NER carriage clearly shows the use of transfer insignia, the texture of the letters RAI being particularly clear. The lining, however, can scarcely be distinguished; it was there! This view also gives good detail of typical carriage bodyside features — see Chapter 3. Note particularly the 'frameless' drop light in the door.

and painters, rather than waste any, would save the 'scrapings' from the gold sheets for touching up purposes elsewhere.

That said, however, gilding as a *routine* decorative procedure began to decline quite early in the century — largely because of the expense — but it continued to be quite common on the better stock throughout the period of this first volume. In fact, it was not really until the later 1930s that it became a particularly rare process in the carriage works. It has not been possible to discover the precise cost of gilding a typical carriage of the Edwardian period, but it might be of interest to reveal that in the 1980s the cost of re-gilding a historic twelve-wheel bogie vehicle of that same Edwardian period using the traditional techniques and materials can be some £1,000-£1,500 *more* than for plain painted lining!

Gold leaf was also used to a very considerable extent in the manufacture of the characteristic transfer emblems, heraldic devices and carriage insignia, once so common. This form of establishing company identity and the like was a far less time-consuming process than hand lettering, but needed economies of scale to make the often high cost of the transfers themselves justifiable. For this reason, in our modern age the old insignia which increasingly appear on vintage vehicles have to be put there by hand, thus keeping alive yet another of the sub-skills of the traditional carriage painter, that of signwriting. As the years went by, the use of gold leaf in the transfers inevitably gave way, through rising costs of material, to the use of gold powder (a rather inferior substitute) and eventually yellow pigments, but it was not until very recently that BR abandoned the traditional type of transfer insignia. There are still quite a few practitioners around in the preservation movement and the 'old-fashioned' transfers are still made from time to time.

Transfer manufacture, an art in itself, is usually carried out by specialist firms. The transfer itself consists of multiple layers of coloured pigments, one each for *every single* colour called for by the finished device. These are laid down in careful register in reverse order and mirror-image configuration so that the first layer to go on the carrying paper is that which will eventually form the outer side of whatever emblem is represented. The transfer is actually 'printed' on to a quite thin tissue backing layer to which is bonded a thicker protective layer for ease of preliminary handling. As with gold leaf, the face of the transfer which will be applied to the carriage side is normally protected with a loose sheet of tissue to avoid the delicate detail being damaged. Transfers made in this way are normally called 'varnish fixing' and they are applied to the carriage in much the same way as gold leaf.

Transfers were not always easy to distinguish from the hand-written equivalent on a well-finished vehicle, but if something went wrong in the paintshop it could sometimes be revealed by accident. On this LYR steam railmotor, the misalignment between the 'Luggage' and 'Compartment' wording suggests that someone got the transfers in the wrong position and did not discover it until too late! The picture also shows excellent detail of a typical fully panelled carriage body; note particularly the substantial hinges and door stops.

The first process is to partially separate the heavier protective paper layer from the transfer-carrying tissue layer by gently teasing one corner free, the full separation of carrying tissue from protective layer coming later. The transfer is then attached to the carriage by applying varnish or gold size to the transfer itself and waiting for it to become tacky, a process, as with gold leaf application, requiring some considerable judgement on the part of the painter. When reckoned to be ready, the transfer is then pressed into position on the correct part of the carriage side and pressed down firmly, taking particular care to expel any air bubbles which might be trapped between transfer and panel. Sometimes a particularly recalcitrant air bubble could be persuaded to vanish by pricking a hole through the backing paper. The heavy supporting paper layer is then carefully peeled from the tissue-carrying layer, leaving the latter, with its transfer, on the coach side. When properly dry, the tissue layer can then be swabbed down with a damp cloth impregnated with turpentine so as to soak it thoroughly, thus rendering it capable of easy removal. A gentle wipe down with the same or a similar damp cloth would normally remove any vestiges of gum or varnish.

It sounds tedious and certainly took time, but to watch a real expert carry out the process was to marvel at the sheer skill and dexterity with which it could be carried out. Normally, some sort of 'production line' procedure would be adopted so as not to waste too much time waiting for things to be right. It would thus be normal, for example, to apply the whole of the required transfers to one coach, or even several coaches, in sequence, starting at one end of the vehicles and progressing down the line.

Varnishes

Varnishes imparted the final finish, whether on unpainted or painted material, and served to protect surfaces from atmospheric weathering. They also required to be such that the surface can be cleaned or washed without damage. Such was their importance in the paint-makers' repertoire that their precise preparation was not always specified. In fact, a contemporary description states: 'The manufacture of varnishes is more or less a complicated and to some extent a secret process, which cannot be dealt with...'!

The principle constituent of varnish in its natural form was 'gum', the fossil exudation of certain trees. When a surface was varnished, the solvents eventually evaporated from the mixture leaving the gum as a thin transparent film of resin-like quality. Varnishes were named according to their gum (eg amber, copal, etc), their usage (finishing, fine-coating, etc), the solvent which held the gum in solution (oil, spirit, etc) or even by their brand names.

The best suited for outside work and for areas needing frequent cleaning and polishing were the oil varnishes made from the hardest gums; they took time to dry but were the most durable in service. They were best for being kept as long as possible before use and were never less than three months old. In carriage terms, two main qualities prevailed, known as 'first coat' (or 'rubbing') varnishes and 'second coat' (or 'finishing') varnishes. The former had a greater proportion of gum to aid drying and hardening, while the latter were paler and more brilliant in gloss, giving a durable top surface.

Spirit varnishes (or lacquers) were made by dissolving softer gums in spirit and they dried through evaporation rather than by oxidation. They were more brilliant than oil and turpentine varnishes and had a harder surface. However, being more brittle and liable to crack or break off the surface, they were only really suited to inside work.

The move towards synthetic materials

Progressively through the century, and particularly since the Second World War, the natural materials from which traditional coach paints were made have given way to purely chemically prepared synthetic substances, and modern paint technology is vastly different from that of a century ago. In particular, the ability of the modern paint technologist to fix a shade and then specify its precise formulation so as to be capable of repetition time after time has much reduced the individual painter's need to be able to 'mix and match' his own materials. Of course, the art of the colour mixer in the first stage is much as it always was, but the vastly increased range of both paint shades and varnishes (for all manner of purposes) has undoubtedly reduced the need for the individual craftsman to have the deep knowledge of materials and their properties which his early twentieth-century predecessor had to have. There is nowadays probably a whole generation of painters which knows not the virtues of lead-based paint, having been thoroughly brainwashed by our frequently over-neurotic society into an attitude conditioned solely by its admittedly toxic qualities! Furthermore, changes in livery styles themselves have also reduced the need for mastery of the skills of lettering and lining to not much more than a pale shadow of that which was needed in former times.

These two factors accepted, however, the painting of a railway carriage, even in the modern era, is not the same sort of business as that of spraying or dipping a car body. Although the paints themselves may have changed and the styles of decoration have become simpler, the actual process of putting the paint on to the vehicle was and still is a skilled and specialized matter, for the railway carriage has to withstand a pretty tough life. For one thing, it is not cosseted and coddled like the domestic motor car, nor does it live most of its life sheltered in a nice garage. It is expected to be able to run almost as many millions of miles as the car will run thousands and is considered something of a failure if its useful lifespan is not twice or three times that of a road vehicle.

To enable it to do this, it needs regularly to be fully repainted, a typical interval being about five to seven years; between these full repaints, an intermediate touch up and re-varnish would be normal. This aspect of the subject must now be considered, concentrating as before on the traditional early twentieth century way of doing things. Sadly, it has to be said that the demands for cost-effectiveness by the modern railway do not permit of quite the same degree of thoroughness, nor do modern synthetics wholly compensate for its absence.

Carriage painting methods

The painting of a railway carriage may be divided into three categories, of which the third, interior painting, was so indistinguishable from conventional interior decorating as to concern us not at all, save to record that it took place during the interior finishing stages already described. The other two categories were concerned with the exterior finishing of the carriage and came in two quite specific stages, perhaps best summarized by the words 'preparation' and 'finishing'.

Preparation

The preparatory, preliminary or plain painting (all three descriptions were used) was relatively straightforward, consisting mainly of the application of various primers — usually lead-based — to act as protection for framework, insides of panels, ironwork and so on. Much of this work was carried out as construction took place and the general aim was to ensure that *no* materials or surfaces, however difficult of access, remained unprotected. This made sound economic sense in that any protective coating, be it on metal or wood, kept out the air and prevented, or at least delayed, the onset of decay, rot and rust.

A typical process would be to thoroughly clean all grease, oil, rust, scale, glue and so forth from the bodywork and then treat any appropriate areas with knotting, followed by overall coats of a lead based primer. For any ferrous surfaces, red lead mixed with linseed oil gave a good protection and for wood a grey base was fairly common. Quite often, these priming paints were mixed in the paintshop from left overs and 'foots' from other purposes, provided they were of the right constituency. Their colour was less critical than their purpose (protection) and generalization would be pointless save to say that a typical body primer would be about 3½ lbs of tub lead with one pint of linseed oil and relatively little drier. Mixed into a stiff paste, it would be thinned with turpentine to help it penetrate the joints. The only exception to this basic priming process was of course on the *visible* surfaces of any carriage which was to receive a natural varnished wood finish. The special circumstances of this type of finish will be considered after the analysis of the methods used to apply a fully painted livery.

Finishing

In a curious way, the actual process of 'finishing',

The paintshop at York carriage works during NER days. On the left, a humble six-wheel brake van is receiving the full treatment — note the chalk marks indicating where further attention is needed. On the right, another similar vehicle is almost finished. The gloss is such that one can almost use the carriage side as a mirror.

in coach painting terms, was, in fact, a series of preparation processes carried out with the next stage in mind and generally obscured by it. The only finish one saw was the very last coat of paint (as well as varnish, of course) and anything up to 90% or more of the effort which went before was buried below; but this was the nature of coach painting — and woe betide the painter who did not tackle the job thoroughly and properly, for the eventual finish would all too easily reveal any poorly executed preliminaries.

It is probable that no two railways followed precisely the same processes of painting their carriages in every detail, but they all adopted very similar principles and it is these which guaranteed the end product.

After the first primer coat, one or two more coats of similar colour would be applied, properly brushed out and 'laid off' (that is *across* the grain of the timber areas, if present), free from heavy brush marks. At this point, all holes, blemishes and the like would be filled with hard stopping applied with a sort of palette-knife. Sometimes, several more coats of 'brush filler' would be applied. This was basically the same as normal filler save for being thinned to allow it to be brushed rather than spread with a knife. When the supervisor judged that the stopping and filling process had gone far enough, the filler would be allowed to harden, at which point the surfaces were faced down with pumice stone and water and dried off with chamois leather. The modern substitute is, of course, 'wet and dry' abrasive paper, but the process is much the same.

Next came the 'guide' or 'disguise' coat — again usually of lead colour — and this gave the final opportunity to examine the surface for any uneven parts which may have been overlooked. Further stopping (if need be) and rubbing down (always) was followed by a final lead colour coat and a last rub down.

In this view at Eastleigh, LSWR-pattern 1st/3rd non-corridor carriage No 7627 is being finished off with lining pencils by two craftsmen prior to the final varnishing. It now carries the all-green livery which, although adopted by the Southern Railway in 1923, was introduced by the LSWR in 1915 when many former non-corridor coaches were converted or rebuilt to electric multiple unit form. No 7627 was one such — note the modified headstock for close coupling.

By now, counting in the preparation phase, a typical carriage would have from five to seven layers of paint on its surface, and it was only at this point that any real thought was given to the final body colour. The appropriate undercoat would go on first, followed by two or more coats of the final colour (it was usually more than two!). Between each coat it was customary to 'flat down' the surface to remove minor imperfections. This was a similar if rather less aggressive process to facing down and produced a nice matt surface for the next layer. It was common practice for the very last layer of finish coat to be mixed with varnish and if so, to be referred to as a 'glaze coat'.

There would now be at least ten layers of paint on the carriage and only then did the final decoration begin. The final body coat would again be flatted down and the lettering, lining and other decoration applied, including gilding and transfers if called for,

as already described. Lining was invariably hand applied, whether in paint or gilt, and for this purpose special brushes known as 'lining pencils' were used; the length of the bristles could be anything up to 3 inches long and their number depended upon the thickness of the desired line. Many carriages carried what were known as 'picking-out' lines at the edge of the main lining, the width of which was only 1/8 inch or less, and for these lines the pencils had very few bristles indeed. The paint for lining was usually

The full treatment has been given to the pioneer GNR carriage to receive the new type of insignia in 1906, first and third class dining saloon No 3039. The GNR (and later the LNER) standardized this attractive style of lettering, but in this particular instance it was probably a bit 'over-the-top'. The carriage itself is very stylish but a little more decorative restraint might have been beneficial.

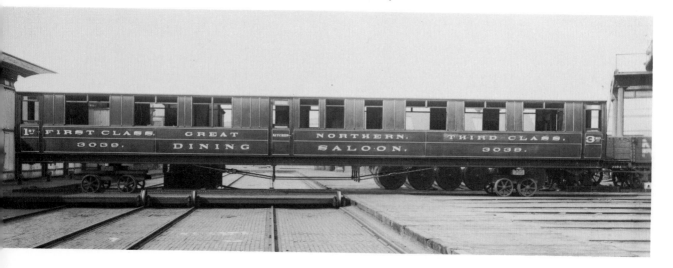

mixed by the individual painter on a palette and the pencil drawn across the palette to charge it with paint. If lining was to be of the gold leaf variety, the gold size was applied using the lining pencil technique. Once again, to watch the real expert at work on this kind of process is an education in itself.

When all lining and decoration was dry, all was dusted off and preparation for final varnishing begun. This would normally involve a re-washing of the carriage which was also commonly rubbed with fine pumice dust or a whiting rag as well in order to provide an absolutely clean, dry surface for the varnish, but taking great care not to damage the decorative embellishments.

The first varnish coat was applied thinly to prevent ridges, stains or 'tear drops' and was allowed to dry thoroughly before the next coat was applied. Only after the second varnish coat was it safe to rub down again — any earlier rubbing down might damage the lining and other decoration. Once protected with two layers of varnish, however, the carriage received its most thorough rub down since the pre-guide-coat stage, using ground pumice dust and water applied by cloth or pad, the aim being to produce an impeccably smooth and clean surface for the final varnish coat(s). A total of three or four further coats of finishing varnish was then normal for all railways, after which the carriage was allowed to harden off before going into traffic.

Roof tops, after canvassing if applicable (see Chapter 3), were generally finished with white or grey lead paint, the final coat being mixed with varnish. External underframe surfaces after priming, were usually painted with two or three coats of black. Sometimes parts of the underframe (eg solebar faces and headstocks) would be given a colour to harmonize with the main body shade.

A fully-varnished exterior, such as found on the characteristic East Coast teak carriages, was dealt with in a somewhat similar way to that of painted carriages save that varnish was used at all stages rather than the primers, guide coats and top coats. Stopping and filling was, naturally, tinted to match the colour of the wood. Typically, after the first varnish coat and any stopping and filling, anything up to six coats of hard drying varnish would be applied and individually rubbed down *before* the lining and lettering was added. The paint for any ironwork and so on was tinted to match the basic wood shade and sometimes referred to as 'teak' or 'mahogany' colour. After the decorative phase, much the same procedure was followed as for a painted carriage.

Either way, the end result was usually a mirror-like finish of great beauty and high durability, perhaps the most revealing point being that it was given to all carriages from the most humble to the most mighty. The secret was not to hurry the work and to allow ample time for drying out — normally at least a day between each process. It was especially necessary for the last coat of varnish to harden thoroughly before the carriage was sent into traffic. Even in the 1930s, a typical new carriage would be allotted some three weeks to go through the paint-shop, and this was little changed when the first metal-panelled vehicles began to replace their wooden-bodied forebears.

Repainted carriages were normally treated in much the same way as new work. Quite regularly, the new coat would be applied over the remains of the old one which formed a sound base from which to start and avoided much stopping and filling. It did, of course, need to be well rubbed down first to get back to the desired smooth surface, and it was not unusual for the top layers of the old paint to be burned before starting the whole process again. Sometimes it was necessary to go to bare timber or metal, especially if structural repairs were called for. The state and, indeed, the status of the vehicle would also come into play in this respect. A fairly new, or, if not fairly new, then a more important vehicle, would obviously rate more attention than one which was near the end of its life or only destined for limited or relatively 'down market' usage. Considerable discretion was allowed to the paintshop foreman in this respect, but such was the pride in their job that few of them would permit even the humblest of carriages to leave 'their' shop in a form which reflected adversely upon either them or their painters.

That then was coach painting. It was a technique which had developed over a long period of time and had withstood the test of many changes both in paint technology and livery styles. The full procedure remained normal in railway workshops until well into the BR period and although today it is not practised to the full degree, a railway paintshop still reveals evidence of the long-standing traditions which it has inherited. Furthermore, that the techniques can still be practised to the full when and if called for is only too apparent by even the most cursory glance at some of the restored carriages in such places as the National Railway Museum. Even though the painter of today has to use modern synthetic materials, the old techniques of application have well and truly stood the test of time and probably always will.

6. Patterns of passenger traffic 1901-21

It should be something of a *non sequitur* that since most carriages are meant to carry people, their design should reflect the patterns of traffic which the passenger generates. Yet rarely in any books on historic railway carriages does one see more than passing mention of the subject and I find this surprising. After all, there is little point in building exotic and expensive dining and sleeping cars if one's business is mainly in the field of conveying thousands of home-to-work travellers over distances of less than ten miles. Likewise, if one's business lies mainly in the long-distance field, there may be less financial necessity, or even generated demand, for the high-capacity 'maximum seating at all costs' type of vehicle. Now there can be no doubt that the different private railways realized this and adopted very different approaches to their carriage provisioning. This inevitably affected the *sort* and quantities of carriages they built, so it will be the purpose of this chapter to analyse the traffic itself in order to set the background against which this carriage building took place.

We shall, of course, have to resort to statistics to reveal the story, and the British scene is particularly well served by the surviving records kept (as a requirement by Parliament) in the form of Board of Trade and other statutory returns. At the turn of the century, every railway was required by law to submit at *yearly* intervals a mass of data to the Board of Trade. At first glance, these masses of data can seem indigestible, but, given the effort, they are wonderfully revealing. For this analysis, I have taken all

Above left *Vintage North Western — a typical array of gangwayed carriage styles is presented by the first four vehicles of the 'Sunny South Special', a through working to the south coast from Manchester, at Rugby circa 1912. Arc, elliptical and clerestory roof profiles, along with 50-foot, 57-foot and 65 ft 6 in lengths and either eight or twelve wheels are all seen, a sort of mixture characteristic of many British main-line railways in the first half of the century*

Left *This view of a southbound Midland train in 1910 near Cotehill on the Settle and Carlisle line is of interest both for the variety and number of vehicles present in what was, after all, a mere stopping train through a sparsely populated area. There are two quite new horseboxes, a less than five-years-old 1st/3rd corridor clerestory, two 20-30-year-old arc roof bogie non-corridors, two ten-year-old clerestories (six-wheel luggage/brake van and bogie non-corridor with lavatories) and three more nineteenth-century arc roof carriages with, respectively, six, eight and four wheels. It is quite possible that the load would not have taxed the capacity of the first three passenger-carrying vehicles!*

those railways which had a route mileage greater than 100 in 1901 and 1911, and these are summarized at Table 1, taking ten-year intervals. This chosen interval and the 100 route mile rule are slightly arbitrary and may conceal some subtle changes, but the main pattern is clear.

The country was dominated by nine companies whose individual route mileage was some 800 or more, and their 'pecking order' never changed in twenty years. Following these was a second tier of more or less 400-800-mile companies whose order of mileage tended to fluctuate a little, while bringing up the rear was a third group of eight, under-400-mile railways which again showed a remarkable consistency in their relative rankings.

It might be supposed at first glance that this classification of the railways might be reflected in the carriage situation, but Table 2 reveals a slightly different story. In terms of vehicle fleets, one of the second group of companies, the LYR, comes well up on the list, while the two biggest Scottish companies drop from fifth and seventh to eleventh and twelfth overall. The bottom group, however, is identifiably much the same set of companies whether by route mileage or carriage fleet.

Other railways showing well in this second analysis relative to route mileage include the SE & CR and the LB & SCR, and this is further reinforced by Table 3 wherein the volume of passenger traffic is analysed. Only four of the top seven route mileage companies now qualify for a high ranking, but the three middle-sized concerns already mentioned are all performing well relative to the bigger companies. The Caledonian and the NBR are still well down the list and the famous Midland does not get above ninth place until 1921 when it suddenly comes third behind the GWR and LNWR. This is almost certainly explained by its absorption in 1912 of the London Tilbury and Southend Railway (LT & SR), a system which was not in the '100-plus' route mile category but which contributed a considerable volume of short-range commuter type traffic.

In this context, it should be pointed out that the LT & SR was one of a few companies excluded from this survey which, proportional to length, added quite substantially to the stock of carriages and particularly to the total number of passengers carried. The excluded companies were mostly of an urban nature and, apart from the LT & SR, perhaps the most important were the various 'underground' systems in and around London, both the surface and 'tube' construction. The nearest to a main line system of any of these railways was probably the Metropolitan,

Table 1 Railways by route mileage 1901-1911-1921

Notes:
1. This table includes only those railways (including joint lines) whose route mileage was 100 or more in both 1901 and 1911 and is confined to the mainland of Great Britain.
2. Railways are listed in 1901 order of route mileage.

Company	1901 order	1901	1911	Change (%) (1901-1911)	1911 order	1921	Change (%) (1911-1921)	1921 order
				Route miles and changes				
GWR	1	2627	3006	+ 379 (14.4)	1	3005	− 1 (.03)	1
LNWR	2	1937	1966	+ 29 (1.5)	2	2045	+ 79 (4)	2
NER	3	1654	1728	+ 74 (4.5)	3	1757	+ 29 (1.7)	3
MR	4	1437	1532	+ 95 (6.6)	4	1731	+ 199 (13)	4
NBR	5	1242	1339	+ 97 (7.8)	5	1376	+ 37 (2.8)	5
GER	6	1110	1133	+ 23 (2.1)	6	1187	+ 54 (4.8)	6
CR	7	939	1072	+ 133 (14.1)	7	1114	+ 42 (3.9)	7
LSWR	8	898	964	+ 66 (7.3)	8	965	+ 1 (0.1)	8
GNR	9	825	856	+ 31 (3.8)	9	905	+ 49 (5.7)	9
SE & CR	10	609	629	+ 20 (3.3)	11	638	+ 9 (1.4)	11
LYR	11	556	591	+ 25 (6.3)	12	601	+ 10 (1.7)	12
GCR	12	494	757	+ 263 (53.2)	10	804	+ 47 (6.2)	10
HR	13	485	485	—	13	506	+ 21 (4.3)	13
LB & SCR	14	448	454	+ 6 (1.3)	15	457	+ 3 (0.7)	15
GSWR	15	399	466	+ 67 (16.18)	14	493	+ 27 (5.8)	14
GNSR	16	331	333	+ 2 (0.6)	16	335	+ 2 (0.6)	16
Cambrian	17	252	283	+ 31 (12.3)	17	296	+ 13 (4.6)	17
NSR	18	193	216	+ 23 (11.9)	18	212	− 4 (2)	18
M & GN*	19	182	194	+ 12 (6.6)	19	194	—	19
CLC*	20	140	142	+ 2 (1.4)	20	143	+ 1 (0.7)	21
FR	21	134	134	—	21	158	+ 24 (17.9)	20
TVR	22	124	124	—	22	125	− 1 (0.7)	22
S & DJR*	23	101	106	+ 5 (5)	23	106	—	23

Totals:

Lines listed	1901		1911			1921	
England & Wales	13721		14815	+ 1094 (8%)		15329	+ 514 (3.5%)
Scotland	3396		3695	+ 299 (8.8%)		3824	+ 129 (3.5%)
Great Britain	17117		18510	+ 1393 (8.1%)		19153	+ 643 (3.5%)

All lines							
England & Wales	15187		16200	+ 1013 (6.7%)		16401	+ 201 (1.2%)
Scotland	3485		3815	+ 330 (9.5%)		3880	+ 65 (1.7%)
Great Britain	18672		20015	+ 1343 (7.2%)		20281	+ 266 (1.3%)

* denotes a jointly-owned line.

but the circumstances of operation of most of these urban lines, and their regular early involvement with electrification, makes their nature somewhat untypical of the nation as a whole and they will be dealt with later. Interestingly, however, in view of the above comment, the middle-ranking main-line systems mentioned in the previous paragraphs (LB & SCR, LYR and SE & CR), along with the LSWR (almost middle rank!) represented the main areas in which suburban electrification was seriously entertained in the pre-BR period. Tables 2 and 3 certainly help to explain why.

Before leaving this particular point, it is interesting to compare the total figures in Table 3 for the 23 listed railways with the totals for the country as a whole. Whereas in most of the summaries in this chapter,

Table 2 Passenger rated rolling-stock 1901-1911-1921

Note: Companies are listed in 1901 order of ranking in *each* category.

Passenger carriages

1901 order	Company	1901	1911[1]	1911 order	1921[2]	1921 order
1	LNWR	6092	5880	1	6239	1
2	GWR	4495	5321	2	5646	2
3	LYR	3950	4181	3	3749	5
4	GER	3685	3829	4	3970	4
5	MR	3511	3637	6	4331	3
6	SE & CR	3286	2961	7	2766	7
7	NER	2997	3675	5	3106	6
8	GNR	2559	2508	9	2639	9
9	LSWR	2515	2841	8	2649	8
10	LB & SCR	2398	2313	10	1871	12
11	NBR	1995	2301	11	2424	10
12	CR	1796	1925	12	2290	11
13	GCR	998	1489	13	1694	13
14	GSWR	935	990	14	1187	14
15	GNSR	423	427	15	454	16
16	CLC	345	345	16	462	15
17	HR	295	324	17	303	19
18	NSR	281	287	18	341	17
19	FR	277	249	20	269	20
20	Cambrian	201	225	21	221	21
21	TVR	198	285	19	316	18
22	S & DJR	127	127	23	131	23
23	M & GN	33	173	22	173	22

Other coaching stock

1901 order	Company	1901	1911	1911 order	1921	1921 order
1	LNWR	3455	3503	1	3320	1
2	GWR	2103	2524	2	3100	2
3	MR	1863	1849	3	1790	3
4	LSWR	1470	1383	5	1416	5
5	GER	1378	1468	4	1683	4
6	SE & CR	1059	1090	7	1047	7
7	NBR	1008	1170	6	1277	6
8	NER	982	985	8	1012	9
9	GNR	804	733	10	868	10
10	LB & SCR	777	806	9	734	11
11	LYR	563	557	11	579	13
12	CR	474	515	12	732	12
13	GSWR	340	320	14	421	15
14	GNSR	306	309	15	319	16
15	GCR	172	342	13	1031	8
16	NSR	141	149	17	193	17
17	HR	127	160	16	496	14
18	CLC	122	102	19	91	21
19	FR	99	99	20	93	20
20	Cambrian	83	116	18	116	18
21	TVR	68	78	21	96	19
22	S & DJR	52	65	22	70	22
23	M & GN	24	53	23	49	23

Total coaching stock

1901 order	Company	1901	1911[1]	1911 order	1921[2]	1921 order
1	LNWR	9547	9383	1	9559	1
2	GWR	6599	7845	2	8746	2
3	MR	5374	5486	3	6121	3
4	GER	5063	5297	4	5653	4
5	LYR	4513	4738	5	4328	5
6	SE & CR	4345	4051	8	3813	8
7	LSWR	3985	4224	7	4065	7
8	NER	3979	4660	6	4118	6
9	GNR	3363	3241	11	3507	10
10	LB & SCR	3175	3119	12	2605	13
11	NBR	3003	3471	9	3701	9
12	CR	2270	2440	13	3022	11
13	GSWR	1275	1360	14	1608	14
14	GCR	1170	1831	13	2725	12
15	GNSR	729	736	15	773	16
16	CLC	467	447	17	553	17
17	HR	422	484	16	799	15
18	NSR	422	436	18	534	18
19	FR	376	348	20	362	20
20	Cambrian	284	341	21	337	21
21	TVR	266	363	19	412	19
22	S & DJR	179	192	23	201	23
23	M & GN	57	226	22	222	22

Totals

Passenger carriages

Lines listed	1901	1911	1921
England & Wales	37948	40325	40573
Scotland	5444	5967	6658
Great Britain	43392	46292	47181

All lines	1901	1911	1921
England & Wales	41431	43916	42232
Scotland	5503	6028	6714
Great Britain	46934	49944	48946

Other coaching stock

Lines listed	1901	1911	1921
England & Wales	15216	15902	17288
Scotland	2255	2524	3245
Great Britain	17471	18426	20533

All lines	1901	1911	1921
England & Wales	15648	16371	17661
Scotland	2256	2525	3246
Great Britain	17904	18896	20907

Total coaching stock

Lines listed	1901	1911	1921
England & Wales	53164	56227	57861
Scotland	7699	8491	9903
Great Britain	60683	64718	67764

All lines	1901	1911	1921
England & Wales	57079	60287	59893
Scotland	7759	8553	9960
Great Britain	64838	68840	69853

1 Including steam railmotor carriages.
2 Including steam railmotors, but *excluding* electrical multiple unit stock.

Table 3 Passenger bookings by class 1901-1911-1921

Note: Companies are listed in 1901 order of ranking of *total* number of passengers.

1901 order	Company	1901 (1000's) 1st	2nd	3rd	Total	1911 (1000's) 1st	2nd	3rd	Total	1911 order	1921 (1000's) 1st	2nd	3rd	Total	1921 order
1	GER	2040	4868	113810	120718	1548	2229	94554	98331	2	1444	1471	75719	78634	4
2	LNWR	1912	5369	74231	81512	1245	3391	69917	74553	3	1158	—	82301	83459	2
3	GWR	1406	6103	72664	80173	1749	439	100335	102523	1	1081	1572	89863	90944	1
4	SE & CR	2343	5263	65505	73111	1676	3942	54291	59909	6	1174	—	46965	49711	9
5	LSWR	2292	4754	54887	61933	2011	2544	63516	68071	4	1458	—	63536	64994	6
6	NER	1566	—	58833	60339	1202	—	59771	60973	5	796	—	60488	61284	7
7	LYR	908	4213	54386	59507	1129	3287	54540	58956	7	1897	100	69886	71783	5
8	LB & SCR	1920	4402	50349	56671	1628	2373	52997	56998	8	1328	—	55092	56520	8
9	MR	1370	—	50737	52107	900	—	49640	50540	9	907	—	80952	81859	3
10	CR	3137	—	41685	44822	2502	—	30732	33234	12	2487	—	33370	35857	10
11	NBR	1845	1261	38362	40207	1354	510	34323	35677	10	1791	209	32827	34618	11
12	GNR	924	—	35376	37561	753	—	34408	35671	11	563	—	27057	27829	12
13	GCR	372	—	18803	19175	453	—	24563	25016	13	294	—	20805	21099	13
14	GSWR	738	—	17680	18418	509	—	16232	16741	14	357	—	14649	15006	14
15	CLC	615	—	10014	10629	451	—	9934	10385	15	426	173	9732	10158	15
16	TVR	67	320	7497	7884	61	202	8105	8368	16	57	—	7792	8022	17
17	NSR	118	562	6442	7122	72	445	6485	7002	17	84	—	10058	10142	16
18	GNSR	102	15	3346	3448	99	—	3253	3352	18	101	—	3572	3673	18
19	FR	55	88	2615	2685	45	22	2906	2973	19	18	—	3415	3433	19
20	Cambrian	45	—	2295	2428	41	69	2634	2744	20	17	—	2134	2151	20
21	HR	92	—	2236	2328	75	—	2053	2128	21	38	—	1482	1520	21
22	M & GN	26	—	1584	1610	25	—	1871	1896	22	10	—	1218	1228	22
23	S & DJR	26	—	1150	1176	20	—	1327	1347	23	5	—	870	875	23

Totals:

		1901 1st	2nd	3rd	Total	1911 1st	2nd	3rd	Total		1921 1st	2nd	3rd	Total	
Lines listed	England + Wales	18005	37218	681178	736401	15009	19453	691794	726256		12717	3525	707883	724125	
	Scotland	5914	—	103309	109223	4539	—	86593	91132		4774	—	85900	90674	
	Great Britain	23919	37218	784487	845624	19548	19453	778387	817388		17491	3525	793783	814799	
All lines	England + Wales	27263	65227	1021179	1113669	24199	22573	1141432	1188204		19871	4546	1102679	1127096	
	Scotland	5937	—	118427	124364	4635	—	102663	107298		4777	—	97551	102328	
	Great Britain	33200	65227	1139606	1238033	28834	22573	1244095	1295502		24648	4546	1200230	1229424	

This particularly neat assembly on the SE & CR, circa 1908, pulled by one of his celebrated Class 'E' locomotives, is one of Harry Wainwright's stylish boat trains, composed entirely of matching non-corridor stock amply provided with lavatories, luggage space and comfortable seats — see also page 162.

Standing in marked contrast to its SE & CR equivalent of some ten years earlier is this equally neat 11-coach set of LYR gangwayed carriages of open interior rather than side-corridor configuration. Like the SE & CR, the LYR provided plenty of vehicles for its patrons and was justly proud of its best stock. This is a posed view, taken in 1921, of a new batch of so-called 'fireproof' coaches (see page 190), most of which were destined, initially, for boat train service.

the '100-plus' route mile railways accounted for some 90% or more of British activity, in terms of numbers of passengers the proportion was only some two-thirds. This rather suggests that further analysis is needed before firm conclusions can be drawn, and to this end Table 4 has been compiled.

In the first two categories, the dominance of what might be called the urban-based systems is clear. In the first summary, only the GER and LNWR of the 'big seven' by mileage manage to get into the top one-third while when it comes to passengers per route mile the GER alone retains its top ranking status. One of the most startling leaders now turns out to be the Cheshire Lines Committee along with the Taff Vale Railway, and these two are even higher when it comes to vehicle loading levels. This latter comparison is at first a little surprising since one might expect the railways with high 'per route mile'

figures to maintain a high level of loading, but this did not always happen.

Take the LYR, for example, (in both 1901 and 1911) or the SE & CR in 1921. These lines always made generous carriage provisioning in terms of vehicles per passenger and this seems reflected in their loading levels. Interestingly, conventional wisdom gives neither of them very much space in the story of carriage evolution but the figures suggest that one might have had a more comfortable (or at least *less crowded*) ride than on some more popularly favoured systems. At the very least, it suggests that railways such as these were more influential in establishing short to medium distance *standards* than is often supposed.

A caveat should perhaps be entered at this point about the sudden climb in ranking of some railways between 1911 and 1921. The noteworthy ones are

Table 4 Passenger and Vehicle comparisons 1901-1911-1921

Note: Companies are listed in 1901 order of ranking in *each* category.

Carriages per route mile

1901 order	Company	1901	1911	1911 order	1921	1921 order
1	LYR	7.10	7.07	1	6.24	1
2	SE & CR	5.40	4.70	3	4.33	2
3	LB & SCR	5.35	5.10	2	4.09	3
4	GER	3.32	3.38	4	3.34	4
5	LNWR	3.15	2.99	5	3.05	6
6	GNR	3.10	2.93	7	2.92	7
7	LSWR	2.8	2.95	6	2.75	8
8	CLC	2.46	2.43	8	3.23	5
9	MR	2.44	2.37	9	2.50	10
10	GSWR	2.34	2.12	12	2.41	11
11	FR	2.07	1.86	14	1.70	17
12	GER	2.02	1.97	13	2.11	12
13	CR	1.91	1.80	15	2.06	13
14	NER	1.81	2.13	11	1.77	15
15	GWR	1.71	1.77	16	1.88	14
16	NBR	1.61	1.72	17	1.76	16
17	TVR	1.60	2.30	10	2.53	9
18	NSR	1.46	1.33	18	1.61	18
19	GNSR	1.28	1.28	19	1.36	19
20	S & DJR	1.26	1.20	20	1.24	20
21	Cambrian	0.80	0.80	22	0.75	22
22	HR	0.61	0.67	23	0.60	23
23	M & GN*	0.18	0.89	21	0.89	21

Passengers per route mile

Company	1901	1911	1911 order	1921	1921 order
LB & SCR	126497	125546	1	123676	1
SE & CR	120050	95245	3	77917	3
GER	108756	86788	4	66245	6
LYR	107026	99756	2	119439	2
CLC	75422	73134	5	71035	4
LSWR	68967	70613	6	67351	5
TVR	63580	67484	7	64176	7
CR	47734	31002	16	32188	12
GSWR	46161	35925	10	30438	14
GNR	45528	41672	8	30750	13
LNWR	42556	37921	9	40811	10
GER	38815	33046	13	26242	16
NSR	36901	32417	15	47840	8
NER	36517	35285	11	34880	11
MR	36260	32990	14	47290	9
NBR	32372	26637	17	25158	17
GWR	30518	34106	12	30264	15
FR	20037	22187	18	21728	18
S & DJR	11643	12708	19	8255	20
GNSR	10417	10066	20	10964	19
Cambrian	9635	9696	22	7266	21
M & GN	8846	9773	21	6330	22
HR	4800	4388	23	3004	23

Passengers per carriage

Company	1901	1911	1911 order	1921	1921 order
TVR	39818	29361	2	25386	3
GER	32759	25681	3	19807	6
CLC	30809	30101	1	21987	5
NSR	25345	24397	5	29472	2
CR	24956	17264	9	15658	11
LSWR	24625	23960	6	24535	4
LB & SCR	23633	24642	4	30208	1
SE & CR	22249	20233	7	11972	17
NBR	20154	15505	13	14281	12
NER	20153	16591	12	19731	7
GSWR	19698	16910	10	12642	15
GER	19213	16801	11	12455	16
GWR	17836	19268	8	16108	10
LYR	15065	14101	15	19147	8
MR	14841	13896	16	18901	9
GNR	14678	14223	14	10545	18
LNWR	13380	12679	17	13377	13
Cambrian	12080	12196	18	9733	19
FR	9693	11940	19	12762	14
S & DJR	9260	10606	21	6679	22
GNSR	8151	7850	22	8090	20
HR	7892	6586	23	5017	23
M & GN*	61923	10960	20	7098	21

*1901 figures are distorted for this system as a result of widespread use of 'foreign' stock.

Averages

Carriages per route mile	1901	1911	1921
Lines listed			
England + Wales	2.77	2.72	2.65
Scotland	1.60	1.61	1.74
Great Britain	2.54	2.50	2.46
All lines			
England + Wales	2.73	2.71	2.57
Scotland	1.58	1.58	1.73
Great Britain	2.51	2.50	2.41

Passengers per route mile	1901	1911	1921
Lines listed			
England + Wales	53670	49022	47239
Scotland	32762	24664	23712
Great Britain	49403	44159	42542
All lines			
England + Wales	73330	73346	68721
Scotland	35686	28125	26373
Great Britain	66304	64727	60619

Passengers per carriage	1901	1911	1921
Lines listed			
England + Wales	19405	18010	17847
Scotland	20063	15273	13619
Great Britain	19488	17657	17270
All lines			
England + Wales	26880	27056	26688
Scotland	22599	17800	15241
Great Britain	26378	25939	25118

Right *This gruesome, albeit tidy-looking collection of soul-destroying six-wheelers on the London, Tilbury & Southend Railway was typical of inner suburban working and by no means the worst which could be seen in the London area in and after 1900. However, this one, seen near Leigh on Sea, was a Southend bound express! The MR, when it took over the Tilbury system in 1912, decided that enough was enough as far as the native stock was concerned and rapidly consigned the worst of them to unmourned oblivion, replacing them by the type shown in the next picture.*

Right *This posed shot, taken in the Derbyshire area, is in fact one of the new sets of replacement bogie carriages for the Tilbury line which entered service around the time of the 1923 railway grouping. The train, in new LMS colours, still has a massive carrying capacity and there is only one lavatory-equipped carriage in the whole set, but it is a considerable improvement on its forebears.*

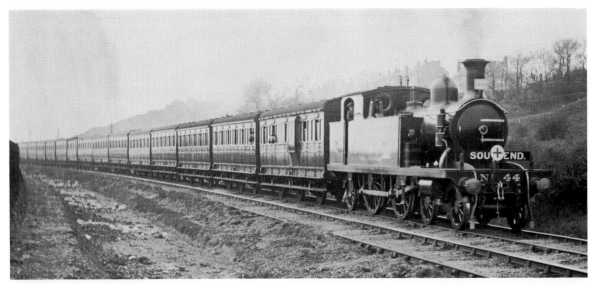

Table 4A Electrically-propelled stock 1921

LSWR	317
LYR	241
LNWR	185
LB & SCR	134
NER	125
MR	117
GWR	60
GCR	16
Subtotal	1195
Non-listed lines	2123
Grand total	3318

Note: The figures relate only to those eight of the 23 companies listed in Table 1 which owned electric stock in 1921. They are listed in descending order of magnitude. All were in England, but the MR, GWR and GCR figures need qualifying. The MR total was mostly made up of tramcars (Burton and Ashby line) plus its share (with the District Railway) of the London area Whitechapel and Bow stock, arising from the takeover by the MR of the LT & SR in 1912. The Lancaster, Morecambe and Heysham route — see page 255 — was the only uniquely Midland example of anything even remotely approaching conventional main-line electrification. The GWR total was entirely made up of its share (with the Metropolitan Railway) of the stock on the Hammersmith and City line, while the GCR fleet consisted entirely of 'tramcars' used between Grimsby and Immingham.

the LB & SCR, LSWR and LYR, but this reflects the fact that passenger levels were recorded in absolute terms regardless of carriage fleet whereas the carriage *totals* refer to 'hauled stock' only. By 1921, several railways, including all of these three, were carrying many of their urban passengers in electric trains, whose stock is not reckoned. Proof of this is the still low position of the SE & CR whose area was not electrified until after the formation of the Southern Railway in 1923. Other interesting 'climbers' in 1921 were the MR (probably reflecting the LT & SR again) and the NER which, by then, had a substantial (unrecorded) Tyneside electrification supplementing its locomotive-hauled fleet. For this reason, Table 4A has been added, giving the electrical multiple unit (EMU) stock as at 1921.

Particularly interesting in this matter of 'passengers per carriage' is the position of two of the English 'giants', the LNWR and MR, in 1901-1911, roughly equal at some 13-15,000 or so passengers (annually) per carriage owned. If one assumes some 300 working days per year, then the 'per day' loading is less than 50 passengers per carriage compared with some twice that total at the top of the list. However, what the raw statistics do *not* tell is how many seats per carriage were available or, even more important, how many times per day a carriage might be expected to be used. It is a fair inference that since the MR and LNWR had a considerably greater number of long-haul journeys than most, their carriages were, on average, less spartan in 'space per passenger' terms or even seats per vehicle and were used less intensively as well. If so, the apparently lowly position is less surprising.

Even so, however, a low load factor does not, in purely fiscal terms, betoken an efficient railway,

Left *The best GER expresses could rival those of most railways. This is a Liverpool Street to Clacton train on Brentwood Bank in 1910 formed of distinctly superior (and new) corridor stock for what was really quite a short-distance operation.*

Below left *There is a splendid 'time warp' quality to this GWR train between Reading and Basingstoke in July 1932; the carriages, a neat and tidy collection of William Dean's non-corridor clerestories, could well have been seen on the same task some 25-30 years earlier, as, indeed, could the engine. The carrying capacity of such a train was formidable and demonstrates the long-lasting nature of the travel styles originated in the Edwardian era.*

Above right *Many smaller railways, although building coaches for their own local services, often relied on the larger companies for most carriage provisioning for through services. One such was the Furness Railway, exemplified at Barrow circa 1920. The train about to leave behind an imposing 4-6-4T consists of a four-coach LNWR corridor set branded 'Liverpool and Barrow', while at the rear, almost lost in the shadow of the station roof, are the two FR 'local' non-corridors which probably went no further than Carnforth. Another 'home' product stands in the bay to the right.*

Right *A variation on the 'borrowing' theme was often seen with the several 'Joint Stock' operations, particularly between Scotland and England. The Caledonian Railway held a one-third share in the West Coast Joint Stock, all the excuse it needed to use them whenever possible. A typical example is seen here, circa 1920. If there are any CR carriages at all in this northbound nine-coach corridor express, they can only be the final pair. The rest are a typical mixture of either West Coast Joint vehicles to LNWR design or even the LNWR's own products (R.J. Essery collection).*

Right *Although the Highland Railway was the archetypal 'borrower' of other people's coaches, especially when it trundled north from Perth to Inverness with through carriages from (almost) all parts of the Kingdom, when it had to be self-sufficient in the more far-flung reaches of the system it was probably the last bastion of the pure Victorian railway. This mixed train from Kyle of Lochalsh to Dingwall in the early 1900s probably changed little for many a year afterwards — not a lavatory in sight and the best vehicle, the second one, an archaic six-wheel luggage 1st/3rd!*

Table 5 Passenger revenue 1901-1911

1901 order	Company	1901 (£1000s) Passenger	Other coaching	Total	1911 (£1000s) Passenger	Other coaching	Total	1911 order
1	LNWR	4815	1248	6063	5248	1583	6831	1
2	GWR	4329	1006	5335	5361	1440	6801	2
3	MR	2873	754	3627	3255	903	4158	3
4	SE & CR	2757	393	3150	3031	575	3606	4
5	GER	2726	345	3071	2725	431	3156	7
6	LSWR	2614	445	3059	2905	597	3502	5
7	NER	2532	482	3014	2761	625	3386	6
8	LB & SCR	2095	221	2316	2236	288	2524	9
9	LYR	2057	257	2314	2269	322	2591	8
10	GNR	1783	384	2167	1922	498	2420	10
11	CR	1512	327	1839	1530	429	1959	11
12	NBR	1450	288	1738	1498	358	1856	12
13	GCR	692	236	928	1024	394	1418	13
14	GSWR	629	129	758	674	156	830	14
15	CLC	348	60	408	373	62	435	15
16	HR	217	113	330	235	116	351	16
17	NSR	215	53	268	223	61	284	17
18	GNSR	187	59	246	192	71	263	18
19	TVR	190	22	212	193	29	222	19
20	Cambrian	137	41	178	144	46	190	20
21	FR	112	25	137	114	26	140	21
22	M & GN	79	19	98	106	30	136	22
23	S & DJR	65	18	83	78	23	101	23

Totals

Lines listed	1901 Passenger	Other	Total	1911 Passenger	Other	Total
England + Wales	30419	6009	36428	33968	7433	41901
Scotland	3995	916	4911	4129	1130	5259
Great Britain	34414	6925	41339	38097	9063	47160

All lines

	Passenger	Other	Total	Passenger	Other	Total
England + Wales	33453	6156	39609	38194	8114	46308
Scotland	4084	930	5014	4215	1147	5362
Great Britain	37537	7086	44623	42409	9261	51670

however nice it might be for the passenger to find a higher proportion of vacant seats; so it suggests that yet other factors must have been present. In essence, and this is a point often overlooked, the railway was in business to make money. The slightly more modern 'social service' obligation was not really in the minds of the private companies, however laudable it may be in absolute terms. I happen to believe in the 'social factor' being applied to railways in the latter part of this century, especially if they are publicly owned, but at the time of this particular analysis it was not a prime consideration. That some of the early twentieth-century private railways managed to provide a better 'social' service in a thoroughly hard-nosed commercial environment than

their own nationalized successor can do in our present day society is another matter; this is a carriage history, not a socio-political analysis! However, such ramifications cannot help but impinge throughout the century whether it be the 'fair deal' campaigns of the 1930s or the post-Beeching 'social service' obligation of the last 15-20 years. Both of them in their different ways have affected carriage design.

At the root of it all was and is *money,* so the next series of summaries (Tables 5-9) are addressed to this aspect as it affected the Edwardian period. The official statistical basis of comparison was changed between 1911 and 1921 and, in any case, was probably distorted during and after the Great War when railways were being operated in the national interest as a single system. However, the figures quoted do give a pretty well undiluted picture of the position as it was when all the private companies really were independent.

Table 5 is an unqualified raw statement of revenue in absolute terms. Five of the seven high mileage companies are up at the top again and, significantly, the same middle rank systems by mileage (LB & SCR, LSWR, LYR, SE & CR) are doing just as well as they were in the previous analysis if revenue is related solely to route mileage, while the 'big two' in Scotland (NBR and CR) are down the list again. In fact, the average performances in Scotland were nearly always less than those in England and Wales,

Table 6 Passenger train miles 1901-1911

Note: Companies are listed in 1901 order of ranking.

1901 order	Company	Train miles (1000's) 1901	1911	1911 order
1	LNWR	26657	30705	2
2	GWR	23790	32761	1
3	MR	19899	22442	3
4	NER	15382	17419	4
5	LSWR	13029	15650	5
6	GER	12950	14030	6
7	LYR	12302	12705	9
8	GNR	12041	13054	7
9	SE & CR	11011	12867	8
10	CR	9535	10093	11
11	NBR	9246	9496	12
12	LB & SCR	8684	11088	10
13	GCR	5863	8790	13
14	GSWR	4077	4568	14
15	CLC	2516	2613	15
16	HR	1696	1750	16
17	GNSR	1421	1518	17
18	NSR	1241	1445	18
19	Cambrian	1033	1158	19
20	M & GN	907	1065	21
21	FR	702	738	23
22	TVR	675	1080	20
23	S & DJR	670	757	22

Totals		1901	1911	
Lines listed				
England + Wales		169352	200367	
Scotland		25975	27425	
Great Britain		195327	227792	
All lines				
England + Wales		185853	229958	
Scotland		27380	28972	
Great Britain		213233	258930	

regardless of how the comparison were drawn, which was probably a reflection of the different basic economic geography of the two statistical areas. This was, undoubtedly, one of the reasons why at the 1923 grouping it was felt inadvisable to have a separate fifth group for Scotland, however desirable this might have been on purely emotive grounds.

Table 6 is an equally raw statement of passenger train miles, and yet again the same companies dominate, save that the two large Scottish companies now come above the LB & SCR, a fact which, given the respective geographies, should occasion no surprise whatsoever. In this context, it should be mentioned that passenger train mileage figures did not differentiate between all-passenger operations, mixed formations involving some use of passenger-rated stock also conveying mail for instance, and completely non-passenger operations such as 'full' mail, milk or fish trains, for example. Perusal of both Table 5 and Table 2 will reveal what a considerable proportion of the total passenger-rated activity was involved with the handling of non-human cargoes, some 16-18% in revenue terms (on average), and no less than 25-30% in purely vehicular terms. Indeed, some railway companies would have suffered grievously had they not carried a solid non-passenger element. The GCR, for example, derived nearly 30% of its passenger-rated revenue from its non-passenger operations (probably reflecting the importance of the Grimsby fish traffic), the HR proportion was similar and the LNWR passenger-rated vehicle *fleet* was 37% non-passenger-carrying types in 1911 — probably a reflection of its importance in the mail and prize livestock business. The non-passenger element of the passenger-rated vehicle story was, in fact, of such importance that it spawned a whole range of specialized vehicles, some of which are considered later. The quoted figures, yet again, explain why.

If, however, one analyses the raw statistics on a comparative basis, a very different picture emerges. Tables 7-9 attempt to summarize the story and readers are left to form their own particular deductions. No doubt supporters of particular railways will find evidence to support whatever prejudices and preferences they may have, but overall a sort of pattern does emerge. Unsurprisingly, the revenue per route mile shows a strong dominance by the tightly knit urban/industrial companies, or those with a fair proportion of such routes. The revenue per train mile is not dissimilar, and once again the larger companies are not too high on the lists. The GWR and LNWR only reach the top five in Table 7, for example.

However, when the figures are split into passenger and non-passenger categories (Tables 8 and 9), a

Table 7 Total passenger-rated revenue rankings 1901-1911

Note: This table includes both passenger and non-passenger carrying coaching stock operated in passenger trains. Companies are listed in 1901 order of ranking per category.

1901 order	Per route mile (£)				Per vehicle owned (£)				Per train mile (£)			1911 order
	Company	1901	1911	1911 order	Company	1901	1911	1911 order	Company	1901	1911	
1	SE & CR	5172	5733	1	CLC	874	973	1	TVR	.314	.205	7
2	LB & SCR	5169	5559	2	CR	810	803	6	SE & CR	.286	.280	1
3	LYR	4162	4384	3	GWR	808	867	3	LB & SCR	.267	.228	2
4	LSWR	3407	3633	4	TVR	797	612	15	GER	.237	.225	3
5	LNWR	3130	3475	5	GCR	793	774	7	LSWR	.235	.224	4
6	CLC	2915	3063	6	HR	781	725	12	LNWR	.227	.222	5
7	GER	2767	2786	8	LSWR	767	829	4	GWR	.224	.208	6
8	GNR	2626	2827	7	NER	757	727	11	NSR	.216	.197	10
9	MR	2524	2714	9	LB & SCR	729	809	5	NER	.196	.194	12
10	GWR	2031	2262	10	SE & CR	725	890	2	FR	.195	.190	14
11	CR	1958	1827	13	MR	675	758	8	HR	.195	.201	9
12	GSWR	1899	1781	15	GNR	644	747	9	CR	.193	.194	13
13	GCR	1879	1873	12	LNWR	635	728	10	LYR	.188	.204	8
14	NER	1822	1959	11	NSR	635	651	14	NBR	.188	.195	11
15	TVR	1709	1790	14	Cambrian	627	557	18	GSWR	.186	.182	17
16	NBR	1398	1386	16	GER	607	596	17	MR	.182	.185	16
17	NSR	1389	1315	17	GSWR	595	670	13	GNR	.180	.185	15
18	FR	1023	1045	18	NBR	579	535	20	GNSR	.173	.173	18
19	S & DJR	822	953	19	LYR	512	547	19	Cambrian	.172	.164	20
20	GNSR	743	790	20	S & DJR	464	526	21	CLC	.162	.166	19
21	Cambrian	707	671	23	FR	364	402	22	GCR	.158	.161	21
22	HR	680	724	21	GNSR	337	357	23	S & DJR	.124	.133	22
23	M & GN	538	701	22	M & GN	1719*	602	16	M & GN	.108	.128	23

Averages Lines listed	Per route mile		Per vehicle		Per train mile	
	1901	1911	1901	1911	1901	1911
England + Wales	2655	2828	685	745	.215	.209
Scotland	1446	1423	638	619	.189	.192
Great Britain	2415	2548	681	729	.212	.207
All lines						
England + Wales	2608	2859	694	768	.213	.201
Scotland	1439	1406	646	627	.183	.185
Great Britain	2389	2582	688	751	.209	.200

* This figure is only explained by the fact that this company made much use of 'foreign' stock at this time. It is therefore listed *last* in this column.

somewhat different picture emerges. The Highland Railway, for example, suddenly climbs the table to the top of the league in revenue per passenger and also ranks high in revenue per non-passenger vehicle. In this latter category, the GCR suddenly seems a much more viable concern than its detractors might admit and the often high-ranking GER falls to bottom place in revenue per passenger. Some of the bigger English companies (for example the GWR, LNWR and MR) reveal their real strength in the revenue per passenger column, and the LNWR and MR also score well in the non-passenger revenue per route mile category. There are, of course, more than a few 'jokers', and although the much favoured GWR tends to bounce about yo-yo fashion, its position in any of the tables never falls below halfway — an underlying indication of its overall strength in all departments.

Overall, however, the various summaries tend to emphasize that there was more than a little of the 'horses for courses' element about the patterns of traffic generated. The dominance in England and Wales of the GWR, LNWR and MR in the 'size and distance' related statistics is clear, and the fact that these railways had a strong influence in the design and construction of main-line express stock is no longer surprising. The position of such lines as the LYR and SE & CR in the short/medium distance field has been commented upon, and the fact that the LB & SCR never assayed corridor stock is more than adequately explained. In Scotland, the NBR and CR never performed quite as well as English systems of similar size, for a variety of reasons, but their dominance north of the border is clearly apparent save in a few isolated instances. Which leads, fairly naturally, to a final question — was there any such thing as a 'typical' pre-1923 railway, as far as passenger carriage activities were concerned, taking all matters into account?

Perceptive readers will, perhaps, have noted that so far in this analysis no specific mention has been made of the two principal constituents of the English

Table 8 Passenger revenue rankings 1901-1911

Note: Companies are listed in 1901 order of ranking per category.

1901 order	Per route mile (£)				Per passenger booked (£)				Per carriage owned			
	Company	1901	1911	1911 order	Company	1901	1911	1911 order	Company	1901	1911	1911 order
1	LB & SCR	4676	4925	1	HR	.093	.110	1	LSWR	1039	1023	3
2	SE & CR	4527	4818	2	LNWR	.059	.070	2	CLC	1009	1081	1
3	LYR	3700	3839	3	Cambrian	.056	.052	8	GWR	963	1008	4
4	LSWR	2911	3013	4	MR	.055	.064	3	TVR	960	677	16
5	LNWR	2486	2669	5	S & DJR	.055	.058	4	LB & SCR	874	967	5
6	CLC	2486	2627	6	GWR	.054	.052	9	NER	844	751	11
7	GER	2456	2405	7	GNSR	.054	.057	5	CR	842	795	8
8	GNR	2161	2245	8	M & GN	.049	.056	6	SE & CR	839	1024	2
9	MR	1999	2125	9	GNR	.047	.054	7	MR	818	895	6
10	GWR	1648	1783	10	NER	.042	.045	12	LNWR	790	893	7
11	CR	1610	1427	14	LSWR	.042	.043	13	NSR	765	777	9
12	GSWR	1576	1446	13	FR	.042	.038	19	GER	739	712	13
13	TVR	1532	1556	12	SE & CR	.038	.051	10	HR	736	725	12
14	NER	1531	1598	11	LB & SCR	.037	.039	17	NBR	727	651	17
15	GCR	1401	1353	15	NBR	.036	.042	14	GNR	697	766	10
16	NBR	1167	1119	16	GCR	.036	.041	15	GCR	693	688	14
17	NSR	1114	1032	17	LYR	.035	.038	18	Cambrian	682	640	18
18	FR	836	851	18	CR	.034	.046	11	GSWR	673	681	15
19	S & DJR	644	736	19	GSWR	.034	.040	16	LYR	521	543	21
20	GNSR	565	577	20	CLC	.033	.036	20	S & DJR	512	614	19
21	Cambrian	544	509	22	NSR	.030	.032	21	GNSR	442	450	23
22	HR	447	485	23	TVR	.024	.023	23	FR	404	458	22
23	M & GN	434	546	21	GER	.023	.028	22	M & GN	2394*	613	20

Averages Lines listed	Per route mile		Per passenger		Per carriage	
	1901	1911	1901	1911	1901	1911
England + Wales	2217	2293	.041	.047	802	842
Scotland	1176	1117	.037	.045	734	692
Great Britain	2011	2058	.041	.047	793	823
All lines						
England + Wales	2203	2358	.030	.032	807	870
Scotland	1172	1105	.033	.039	742	699
Great Britain	2010	2119	.030	.033	800	849

* This figure is so exceptional that it can only reflect the fact that at this period most trains on the M & GN were composed of other companies' stock. For this reason it is listed *last* in this column.

A typical scene in the year of the grouping on the East Coast Main Line. The main train is a mixture of GNR styled elliptical roof and clerestory carriages but the leading vehicle is the NER clerestory Dynamometer car, the engine, a former NER 4-6-2, being under test.

North British Railway passenger trains changed little until several years after the grouping. This southbound express at Inverkeithing in the 1920s is typical, for, although now in LNER colours, the whole train consists of NBR stock. The main portion consists of standard robust NBR corridors with, just under the bridge, one of the newer NBR steel-panelled dining cars (see page 125). However, the principal operating interest lies in the leading carriage. It is older, of lesser quality, all third class and still gas lit, but at least it has a lavatory. The fact that it is separated from the main train by a six-wheel van suggests that it was added at the last moment as a 'strengthener' to meet some unexpectedly heavy traffic. This sort of operational opportunism was a widespread British practice.

part of the East Coast Main Line, the GNR and the NER. Both these systems were big ones; the NER was in the top three by mileage and rarely out of the top seven on any of the absolute criteria analysed, while the GNR was also always there or thereabouts. Taken overall, the GNR probably came nearer to average more often than any other railway and is as nearly typical as one is likely to get. The LSWR came quite close in this respect as also, to some extent, did the MR. In all cases, these railways operated long-distance trains as well as being heavily involved with suburban operations in the major conurbations and operating a fair proportion of non-passenger stock. This was true also of the GWR and LNWR but these two systems were in fact well ahead in terms of absolute size and would obviously dominate to some extent, however one defines the situation.

The point is that carriage design of necessity was a combination of what might be called ephemeral matters (body style, livery and decoration) combined with practical considerations (seats per passenger, type of vehicle needed and so forth). While all railways had a fairly free hand in the first of these areas, some lines needed only to consider certain aspects of the more economically based criteria. Thus, those railways which had to address *all* (or most) aspects of the passenger train field were, fairly naturally, likely to dominate those whose horizons were more restricted. This, naturally, assumed rather more importance when the railways were amalgamated in 1923, and the recorded statistics give ample evidence as to *why* certain company's design styles and approaches predominated in the post-grouping period. It was not simply a matter of *force majeure* as is sometimes supposed, but also a question of relevant experience in the context of a larger amalgamated railway. These matters will be dealt with more comprehensively in the next chapter; in the meantime, it is probably sufficient to state that the patterns of passenger traffic as revealed by the recorded statistics were there for all to see even before the 1914-18 holocaust disrupted matters in many more areas than that of the mere railway carriage.

Nevertheless, these factors, while perhaps fairly apparent in retrospect, were by no means obvious to contemporary society in the 1901-14 period. The private railways were then at the zenith of their prosperity and reputation. They were still fiercely independent and vying with each other for public patronage and approbation, even though they had no serious competition from other *forms* of transport (eg road and air) in the long and medium distance field. The railway carriage door was the point of contact with much of the public, and in consequence

many railways felt obliged, for strictly business reasons, to produce something that little bit better than that of their rivals. It led to a superb flowering of elegant vehicles, superb craftsmanship, pride in the task and not a little merit. It is doubtful whether the men of Swindon, Eastleigh, Wolverton, Derby, Doncaster, York, Cowlairs et al saw it this way at the time — it was merely the norm in relation to their time. But it *was* also the end of an era (as I have entitled this *whole part*), and it will be the object of the rest of this part of the survey to record something of the superb contribution to transport history which these carriage builders made.

Table 9 Non-passenger-coaching revenue ranking 1901-1911

Note: Companies are listed in 1901 order of ranking per category.

1901 order	Company	Per route mile (£) 1901	Per route mile (£) 1911	1911 order	Company	Per vehicle owned (£) 1901	Per vehicle owned (£) 1911	1911 order
1	SE & CR	645	914	1	GCR	1372	1152	1
2	LNWR	644	805	2	HR	890	725	3
3	MR	525	589	5	M & GN	792	566	8
4	LSWR	496	619	4	CR	690	833	2
5	LB & SCR	493	634	3	Cambrian	444	397	16
6	GCR	478	520	8	CLC	492	608	5
7	GNR	465	582	6	NER	491	635	4
8	LYR	462	545	7	GWR	478	571	7
9	CLC	429	437	10	GNR	478	506	10
10	GWR	383	479	9	LYR	456	578	6
11	CR	348	400	11	MR	404	488	11
12	GSWR	323	335	14	GSWR	379	488	12
13	GER	311	380	12	NSR	376	409	15
14	NER	291	362	13	SE & CR	371	528	9
15	NSR	275	282	15	LNWR	361	452	13
16	HR	233	239	17	S & DJR	346	354	19
17	NBR	232	267	16	TVR	324	372	17
18	FR	187	194	21	LSWR	302	432	14
19	GNSR	178	213	20	NBR	286	306	20
20	S & DJR	178	217	19	LB & SCR	284	357	18
21	TVR	177	234	18	FR	253	263	22
22	Cambrian	163	163	22	GER	250	294	21
23	M & GN	104	155	23	GNSR	193	230	23

Averages Lines listed	Per route mile 1901	Per route mile 1911	Per vehicle 1901	Per vehicle 1911
England + Wales	438	535	395	499
Scotland	270	306	406	448
Great Britain	405	490	396	492
All lines				
England + Wales	405	501	393	496
Scotland	267	301	412	454
Great Britain	379	463	396	490

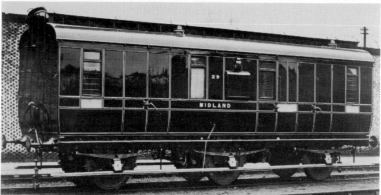

The traditional British style of panelling displayed on Caledonian Railway third class corridor saloon No 46. The absence of ventilator bonnets over the door drop lights was unusual, but not uncommon on Caledonian elliptical roof stock.

The MR was probably the best known of those British companies which adopted fully square-cornered standard panelling. This six-wheel passenger brake No 29 gives a good impression of the style

In 1912, the LNWR adopted a partially square-cornered variant of the traditional style. This view shows one of a series of four-wheelers built to this new style by the LNWR for its associated North London Railway. New four-wheel carriages were rather less usual after the turn of the century but by no means unknown (R.J. Essery collection).

7. The companies and their styles

The nature of the railway carriage during the 'company' period reflected a combination of what might be called stylistic preference and practical provisioning required by the traffic. In general, the visual styling (which included the livery) transcended the utilization factor so one could find a particular visual style of treatment applied 'across the board' to all types of carriage, whereas a specific type of carriage could be interpreted in a variety of different visual styles. The situation was not very dissimilar to that which influences the designer of the modern motor car or road coach. Thus, the end product tended to be a subtle combination of company stylistic preference married to an internal layout which most accurately catered for the prescribed needs of the passengers of that particular company. Small wonder that the permutations were endless and that the variety was enormous.

Attempting to bring order out of what might be regarded as incipient chaos, this analysis will first consider the various different *stylistic* approaches (regardless of company) and then consider both the *types* and styles of carriage preferred by specific companies. To further simplify the analysis, the company treatment will reflect the groupings into which they were placed in 1923. The specific circumstances applicable to self-propelled (including electric) stock, Pullman and other more special-purpose vehicles will be considered separately, while the particular unique matter of those London area suburban and city lines which were amalgamated to form London Transport in 1933 will, for chronological reasons, be considered fully in Chapter 22 although the origins are touched on in Chapter 15.

Vehicle styling

Basically, for the bulk of the period covered by this first volume vehicle styling was dominated by the nature of the wooden-bodied carriage. Even when the occasional use of sheet steel was adopted for the outer skin, the traditional approach died hard. Thus, many companies merely substituted steel for wood on the outside skin without real change in stylistic approach. Eventually, the different characteristics of sheet steel began to influence outward styling, but this was not a particularly significant factor during the first part of the century for most of the bigger companies.

Although the wooden-bodied carriage was put together in much the same way regardless of length, width or company, its outward styling gave considerable scope for decorative variation in such matters as panel shapes and sizes and the precise arrangement of the protective beading strips, ventilator bonnets, window frames and so forth. Virtually every individual railway adopted its own house style to a greater or lesser degree in these matters, whether it made its own carriages or had them built by contractors. Some lines maintained a recognizably similar treatment for a considerable period of time while others tended to alter the visual lines quite regularly. In the latter case, this could either take the form of a radical change or a progressive modification or refinement of existing norms. However, in spite of the many variations, most carriage styles fall into one or other of a rather smaller number of categories than one might expect. Some of these were more widespread than others, but it will help to enumerate their basic characteristics so as to avoid constant repetition later. The nomenclature adopted is that of the author and has no 'official' status in terms of historic usage.

The traditional British style

The most widespread form of body treatment took the form of a series of panels the edges of which were protected by beading strips with *rounded* corners. There would normally be a row of *eaves* panels above window level below the roof edge, a second row of panels the same depth as, and located between the windows, a third row of panels roughly matching the eaves panel along the *waist* of the carriage and a fourth row of lower body panels between the waist and the bottom edge of the body.

Within the broad definition, there was considerable scope for individual development in such matters as panel depth (top to bottom), the radius of the corner curvature of the beading, the precise location and style of the ventilator bonnets along the eaves panel and whether or not supplementary windows could (or should) be fitted above the main windows. The style went back well into the nineteenth century and did not vanish for new construction until the 1930s.

Of the more important railways, the GWR, NER, MR, LSWR and Caledonian were widespread users of the style. There were, of course, others.

The 'modified' British style

Given the traditional panel layout (eaves, window, waist and lower body), two principal variations were not uncommon, the differences usually being in the treatment of the beading. One of two common variations was adopted — all the panel corners were square or some corners only were squared off. In the latter case, it was more usual to find only the window level panels so treated, although some companies treated the eaves and waist panels in like manner.

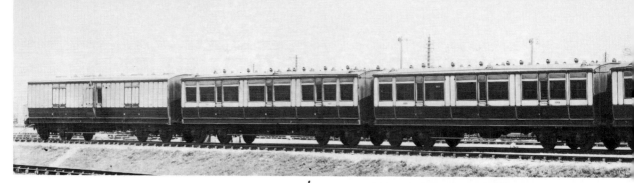

Some distinctly pleasant visual variations could be seen with this sort of approach as many of the pictures in this book will reveal. Railways adopting the fully squared corners with the traditional panel layout were rather few, but included some notable companies like the MR (during the 1896-1905 period) and the NER for a short while. The GER, too, came up with its own very distinctive form of treatment which was, if you like, an 'alternative modified' style!

The 'low-waisted' or 'Wolverton' style
On some railways, especially the LNWR, the traditional style of panelling was further modified to eliminate the eaves and waist panels (except on the doors) and to extend the bodyside panelling from the cornice to the waist rail between the doors. This gave a quite different visual appearance and, by virtue of reducing the quantity of beading strips, often tended to look rather more modern — or at least less fussy. The style is believed to have originated at Wolverton (LNWR) in mid-Victorian times and was copied later by several other companies, the SE & CR and its predecessor the South Eastern Railway being perhaps the most important of the others.

The twin-layer 'Howlden' or 'East Coast' style
At Doncaster on the GNR, Mr Howlden introduced a very distinctive form of bodyside treatment for the

famous varnished teak coaches built there. The panelling was square cornered but was in effect in two layers, that above the waist being set back slightly from the panelling below the waist. The beading profile also varied — flat with rounded edges above the waist, half round below. Being varnished teak, opportunity was also taken to feature the grain direction as part of the treatment, horizontal in the waist and lower body panels, vertical above the waist. The style was later adopted as standard for the East Coast Joint Stock, whether built at Doncaster, York (NER) or Cowlairs (NBR).

In due course Gresley adopted it, virtually unchanged, for his own build of GNR, ECJS and LNER carriages and it remained in use until 1941, having become by then probably the longest lasting of any individual form of wooden bodyside treatment in Britain. At that time, the LNER was the only British main-line company still building traditional all-wood carriage bodies.

The twin-layer 'Scottish' style
This strictly unofficial definition seems apposite because it was particularly characteristic of several Scottish companies, especially the NBR. The 'layering' followed much the same principles as the 'Howlden' style but visually it was more like the

Top *Wolverton style LNWR panelling is displayed on this train of four gangwayed arc roof carriages in the early 1900s*

Above left *This spartan four-wheeled second class carriage No 198 shows one of the several characteristic GER variations of traditional panelling to be seen during the early part of the twentieth century.*

Left *Typical Howlden GNR panelling on a composite brake of circa 1897, No 314. It was a slip carriage (see page 166) and ran until 1950.*

Right *The 'Scottish' style of twin-layer panelling on yet another economical gas-lit suburban four-wheeler, NBR third class No 1072.*

traditional British panelling with rounded corners to the beading. The GNSR and the Highland also produced a few vehicles of this kind but it was less often seen in England.

Flush-sided and semi-flush-sided styles

One or two railways eschewed the use of beading strips for the most part and, even with wooden bodies, managed to produce carriages whose side surfaces were rather more akin to those of modern metal-skinned vehicles. Of course, the general shape and nature of the coaches remained similar to that of many other railways. The most noteworthy exponent was the LYR, whose carriage styling was wholly unique for many years because of this fact. In later days, one or two railways took a slightly different approach by suppressing *some* beading in favour of a more flush-clad treatment, sometimes allied to the use of *some* metal sheeting. The GWR and Caledonian were both exponents of this approach, but tended to confuse matters by continuing with a painted livery suggestive of normal traditional panelling.

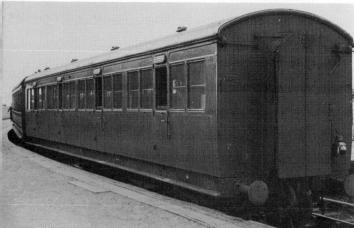

Above left *These elliptical roof non-corridors, photographed soon after 1923, show the nature of orthodox LYR carriage styling with its twin-level outer sheeting. The leading coach has received new LMS colours which do not seem to have taken too well. The inward taper towards the guard's lookout was a distinctive feature of many LYR carriages, an idea also used on the LSWR 'Ironclads' — see page 128.*

Left *This 'matchboard'-panelled, cove-roofed Highland Railway corridor third was photographed in BR days at Wormit, Fife (ex-NBR), proof that not all ex-HR carriages were short-lived after 1923 (Gavin Wilson).*

Below *A massive but visually well-balanced GCR 'matchboard'-sided corridor composite built in 1911 for the Manchester-London services.*

A third variant, though perhaps not really qualifying as flush-sided, was the use of a vertical tongue and groove boarding, sometimes from the waist downwards and sometime for the whole depth of the carriage side. The HR, SE & CR and GCR all, at times, built examples of 'matchboard-panelled' stock as it was known, while in pre-metal days it was always one of the characteristic features of Pullman car styling.

*   *   *

The above six categories probably embrace the vast majority of carriages built in Britain during the first quarter of the twentieth century and there were, additionally, styles which do not really lend themselves to analysis. These were regularly, but not exclusively, found on the newly developing electric stock (especially in London, Merseyside and Tyneside) but sometimes on particularly important special stock such as the West Coast sleeping and dining saloons. Taken with the considerable variations in roof profile and height, not to mention the infinite variety of window arrangements and carriage lengths to be seen and the multiplicity of liveries, the railway carriage scene was a decidedly colourful and cosmopolitan business before the grouping.

Against this background it may be supposed that generalization is a bit of a forlorn hope, but in fact there were many points of similarity within the apparent disparity. Most railways built broadly the same types of stock for the same sorts of services, and

Until 1910, the NLR — see also the picture on page 100 — had built its own unique four-wheelers for almost forty years to a style which does not really fit any of the categories defined in the text. This is first class No 99, built in 1906.

these will be examined in detail in the next few chapters. However, before tackling this job, it will be helpful to give a broad company-by-company review. Clearly it is not possible to mention them all or even give a proportionally correct amount of space to those which are mentioned. Rather it will be the object to examine the dominant trends which were apparent in the 1901-22 period, for these mostly set the pattern for the rationalization of post-1922 design. For this reason, the companies will be considered in the groupings into which they were put in 1923, and in descending order of magnitude of carriage fleets.

The LMS group

In 1922, the constituent companies of the LMS whose route mileage exceeded 100 were as follows, the number of passenger-carrying vehicles owned in 1921 being listed alongside:

England	Furness Railway		269
	LYR		3749
	LNWR		6239*
	MR		4331†
	NSR		341
		Subtotal	14929
Scotland	CR		2290
	GSWR		1189
	HR		303
		Subtotal	3780
		Grand total	18709

*Includes former North London Railway stock.
†Includes former LT & SR stock.

Left *Britain's most numerous ever single bogie carriage type? LYR 49-foot bogie non-corridor third, LMS No 14493, seen in scruffy LMS livery sometime after 1933, unchanged from its original state. Note the air intakes to the Anderson ventilators — see page 60 — at the ends of the door-top bonnets*

Right *Visual proof that the LYR could rival the rest for styling when it so chose — first class dining car No 213, built in 1907. The styling may have been influenced by the Wolverton LNWR twelve-wheelers, the two companies being close allies in many things.*

From this analysis (an abstract from Table 2 on page 87), the dominance of the three big English constituents is noticeable, representing some 75% or more of the total. All three took a quite different approach to carriage building, the LYR being probably the most consistent overall.

This railway had adopted its basic body style as early as 1876, the originator being one Mr Attock. It was in all respects a far smoother-sided treatment than that adopted by most contemporary railways, and perhaps the most noticeable individual feature was the fact that the side sheeting below the waist was set back by the thickness of the sheeting from the waist upwards. The window treatment was also particularly distinctive and neatly arranged, and the whole effect (for its time) was quite a bit more modern than most railways.

This modernity was emphasized by the fact that the LYR was one of the earlier systems to adopt the bogie in a big way; its most numerous manifestation, the 49-foot eight-compartment non-corridor third, introduced as early as 1893, was not only built for some ten years but eventually totalled 808 vehicles. This is thought to have been the most numerous single type of bogie carriage built for any railway in Britain at any time. Many other types, including some corridor stock, were built to this basic house style and even when George Hughes (the CME of the LYR prior to the grouping) moved from the characteristic arc roof to the fully-elliptical style, the body panelling hardly changed on most coaches, save for the rounding off of the lower window corners and some trivial modifications to vertical heights.

The generally smooth appearance of a typical LYR carriage was enhanced by its livery, which has been in some sources unkindly described as 'two shades of ordure'! It was in fact carmine lake on the lower panels and a brownish-orange above, eminently practical for the industrial environment in which

most of them worked. The lighter colour was derived from the shade of varnished teak used in earlier days. The lining treatment was restrained compared with most contemporary systems but aesthetically very much in tune with the structural nature of the carriages. When the LYR did build a few fully-panelled vehicles in quasi-traditional style, it demonstrated that it was just as capable of delivering an elaborate fully-lined livery as anyone else when the carriage 'architecture' warranted it. The Fleetwood boat stock, for example, must have looked distinctly stylish. The LYR insignia was always very characteristic and with its white outlines set off the whole ensemble very well.

The LYR has always suffered a bad press for it carriages relative to the MR and LNWR, but this is not really fair. Its operating circumstances were very different and it was obliged to concentrate heavily on short-distance, high-capacity coaches — hardly the most suitable candidates for large-scale experimentation. Its hard horsehair third class seats became almost legendary, almost as if it was the only railway to adopt such practice, and its liking for gas lighting has sometimes been regarded as a black mark. But the MR, GWR and LNWR, to mention but three, were not exactly known for the rapidity with which they abandoned gas! Had the LYR been the sort of railway which needed, proportionally, the same number of long-distance carriages as were built by those other railways with large carriage fleets, then the available evidence suggests that it would have more than held its own. Its best corridor, and particularly first class, carriages were both luxurious and sumptuous; there simply were not many of them. Furthermore in its unwillingness to disguise its carriages with pseudo-panelling (in paint), the LYR adopted a distinctly modern approach and it was not really followed by any other railway until well after the grouping.

Although the LYR had a lot of carriages and, as Chapter 6 has endeavoured to demonstrate, generally provided a more than adequate number of seats for its patrons, it must be conceded that in terms of variety, relative to the larger amalgamated LMS, its contribution was possibly doomed to take a relatively minor place. However, its carriage works at Newton Heath remained one of only three locations which went on building new stock in LMS days (the others being Derby and Wolverton), and the operating requirements of the Central Division of the LMS (the post-1923 nomenclature of the former LYR area) were equally central to the precise provisioning of new non-corridor stock in LMS days. Furthermore, in its adoption of gangwayed centre-aisle open stock, its final experimentation with angle-trussed underframes and its eventual settling on a 56-57 foot carriage with fully-elliptical roof, it was not too far out of line with the post-1923 LMS policies which will be discussed in later chapters.

It was, however, (and hardly surprisingly) the LNWR and MR approach to carriage building which was more in tune with the overall national picture during the first quarter of the century. Both companies operated just about every sort of passenger service from long-distance expresses to high-density suburban trains. Their carriages were, however, distinctly different.

The larger of the two, the LNWR, was possibly (along with the GWR) the most comprehensive railway system in Britain before 1923, impregnated with the sort of tradition which was well reflected in its carriages. From way back in Victorian times it had adopted a quite distinctive low-waisted form of carriage architecture which was hardly changed when the new century dawned. Allied to its equally long-lived and famous livery of carmine lake lower panels and white (actually white 'broken' with blue — see Chapter 5), it probably entered the twentieth century

seeming to the outside world to have all the permanence of the Rock of Gibraltar. For the first decade or so, thus it remained. The carriage roof profile changed from arc roof to a superb low-elliptical form in early Edwardian days and became fully elliptical in 1907/8. Carriage length crept up from a sort of standard 50-foot form in 1900-1 to a 57-foot norm by 1905-10, and width increased from 8 ft 6 in to 9 ft during the same time; but the livery and decorative treatment scarcely change.

There was, however, one area where the LNWR really 'went to town', and that was in its more specialized vehicles, be they sleeping cars or Royal Saloons. They were mostly twelve-wheelers, and arguably Wolverton works, the celebrated LNWR carriage building establishment, built more elaborate twelve-wheelers than anywhere else in Britain. They will, quite properly, be given more space later in this survey, but at this point it is sufficient to state that they displayed a wholly unique visual stylistic approach, quite unlike normal LNWR practice; they rode like a dream on some of the finest permanent way in the world and can lay sound claim to having been the visual and mechanical high point of British carriage construction in the pre-grouping period. That this is a strong assertion cannot be denied, but their only serious rivals in this respect were the East Coast twelve-wheelers (see page 119) and, possibly, some of Churchward's magnificent 70-footers for the GWR (see page 135). I propose to stick my neck out and give Wolverton the accolade if only because it built rather more of them than anyone else.

As for ordinary coaches, the LNWR suddenly changed course in 1912-13 when it adopted to all intents and purposes the traditional style of panelling for almost all its general service stock. This seems to have been at the behest of Mr H.D. Earl, the carriage superintendent in succession to the famous C.A. Park, who had, *inter alia*, devised the immortal

This page top to bottom *Traditional Wolverton-style panelling on elliptical roof stock is represented by this pair of first class LNWR luxury club saloons — see also Chapter 13 — built in 1908*

This unique form of LNWR panelling, though not confined to vehicles with six-wheel bogies, is often referred to as the 'twelve-wheel' style. It was introduced in 1892 and current for more than thirty years. This example, clerestory roof 2nd/3rd class dining car No 290, built in 1904, represents possibly the most stylish single variant of this distinctive treatment

The post-1912 standard LNWR body architecture is exemplified by 'Toplight'-styled WCJS corridor composite No 275, built in 1913 as part of two new sets for the morning London-Glasgow service.

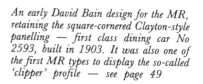

An early David Bain design for the MR, retaining the square-cornered Clayton-style panelling — first class dining car No 2593, built in 1903. It was also one of the first MR types to display the so-called 'clipper' profile — see page 49

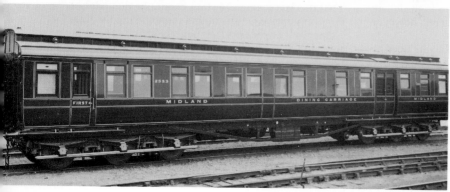

Right *First class corridor carriage No 2671 was built to Bain's design in 1911 and is probably everyone's image of a typical Midland vehicle; yet it was a rare type, one of only four such carriages owned by the MR, and there were only three more in the Midland's Joint stock. This picture shows the almost unchanged livery adopted in LMS days.*

twelve-wheelers. Earl did not dare — or so it would seem — to change the twelve-wheel style (save for giving them elliptical roofs from 1907 onwards), but his later LNWR ordinary stock was, it has to be said, visually somewhat undistinguished. Being the LNWR, its new-style carriages naturally retained certain traditional features unchanged, such as door ventilators and handles, not to mention the famous livery. Earl also indulged (for a year or two) in a sort of modified style with square, lower cornered window and eaves panelling; but the last decade of LNWR coach building was a sort of uneasy visual compromise (probably unconscious) between the Churchward (GWR) and Bain/Reid (MR) style with few of the redeeming virtues of either. For example, compartment sizes in corridor stock became distinctly parsimonious compared with earlier twentieth century LNWR standards.

However, in one respect the LNWR influence was never diluted. It was of all the LMS constituents by far the most experienced in long-distance operations. In consequence, it had developed by 1922 a far more sophisticated approach to corridor coach design than almost any other British company (see Chapter 10). Its only serious rival was possibly the GWR, and this is not relevant in the LMS context. Thus, the LNWR approach to internal vehicle *layout* was of prime value in the 1920s and 1930s, and its general espousal of 57-foot (ordinary) and 68-foot twelve-wheel dining and sleeping cars became the LMS standard, probably much to the chagrin of the Midland followers. In fact, such was the dominance of the LNWR in the long-distance field that its corridor thirds *alone* outnumbered the whole of the Midland Railway fleet of gangwayed long-distance coaches.

At this point, dedicated followers of the third principal English constituent of the LMS, the Midland Railway, are perhaps muttering furiously in their armchairs! Traditional wisdom has it that the MR was the most noteworthy of the pre-1923

railways in terms of passenger comfort not just in the LMS but in Britain as a whole. It is a nice thought and I am not unknown for my espousal of many aspects of the Midland cause; but it is not quite accurate.

The MR certainly deserves total credit for its emancipation of the third class passenger from the mid-1870s (see Chapter 1), but by the start of the present century it had been somewhat overtaken in certain respects. For instance, the GWR, LNWR and even the GER had all adopted corridor trains well before the Midland. Moreover, at that time Midland carriage *design* was in a state of transition. During 1896-7, its famous carriage designer Thomas Clayton had introduced the celebrated and unique clerestory profile, and by 1900-1 this had become the standard for all new MR coaches. It was associated with the square-cornered modification of the traditional panel style and the end product was a series of highly distinctive carriages, mostly non-corridor but with a few corridor and dining car examples. The Midland was, however, in spite of its forward-looking image, somewhat conservative in terms of carriage *type* and still built a fair number of four-wheel and six-wheel carriages, some of them incorporating the pre-1896 'traditional' style of Clayton round-cornered panelling with arc roof profile. In fact, just before the turn of the century it had produced some singularly uninspiring *four-wheelers* for the Metropolitan line services to the City of London which were every bit as awful as those of the GNR or North London lines!

These facts must be put into the equation when considering MR coaching stock and it was not until David Bain (ex-North Eastern) took over from Clayton in 1903 that the MR really began to move forward again. By now, the LNWR had been building corridor coaches for itself and the West Coast Joint Stock for some years, whereas the MR had only constructed a few corridors, mainly for the Scottish Joint Stock, and even these only appeared

as late as 1898. Bain lengthened the corridor stock from 48 feet to 50-54 feet and the twelve-wheelers from 60 feet to 65 feet but retained the square-cornered panelling for a short period. He then completely revised the Midland styling to his own version of the traditional round-cornered pattern (basically brought with him from the NER) and applied it to both long-distance and suburban coaches. The main-line and some of the non-corridor lavatory stock retained the 1896-7 Clayton clerestory profile (slightly modified), but the more suburban vehicles reverted to an arc roof profile.

Ten years or so after this, the Midland, by now the last major user of the clerestory, adopted the full elliptical roof for all stock, but this was almost half a generation later than the LNWR, GWR, LYR and several others. Moreover, it was never particularly widespread and elliptical-roof corridors did not appear until after the Great War. In consequence, Midland carriages were not quite as tidy in visual style as sometimes supposed and there were still a lot of four-wheelers and six-wheelers to be seen, some going well back into the nineteenth century. However, the final MR carriage designer, R.W. Reid, had by the end of the pre-group period moved MR carriage design into something recognizably similar to that pursued by the LNWR. The standard length became 57 feet for corridor stock while 65 feet was retained for twelve-wheelers. The roof profile was consistently elliptical by now, the underframe had developed into an angle-trussed form and the panelling was basically David Bain-style with slight modification.

It is part of accepted folk myth that these features were adopted unchanged by the LMS in 1923, largely because of the dominance of many MR officers in the post-1922 management of the new company; indeed, Reid became the new LMS carriage supremo and instituted new and more cost-effective constructional methods in the 1920s which will be discussed in Chap. 16. It is, therefore, not surprising that MR stylistic features were copied (they were, at the time, probably the best of all the LMS constituents), as was its magnificent all-lake livery — one of the most distinguished and practical carriage finishes of all time — but that is about as far as it went. The MR interior design concepts very soon vanished — they were basically not as well thought out or as versatile as those of the LNWR — and overall carriage dimensions and seating capacity became much nearer the LNWR/LYR standards than those of the Midland. To be fair, the Midland offered generous space in its passenger provisioning and made good-looking carriages, but after 1923 its influence was more aesthetic than practical as the very cost-conscious LMS quite speedily demonstrated

during the 1920s.

These, then, were the three primary contributions to the LMS scene; but what of the remaining 20-25%? Dominant here were the Caledonian and GSWR contingents; the former was the more significant, not simply because it had twice as many carriages, but also because the GSWR was not, if we are to be honest, a profoundly significant railway in terms of its carriage stock. At the turn of the century it was producing some very neat stock of the 'modified traditional' kind, designed by James Manson (or at least attributed to him). They were neat and well finished and by no means unattractive visually, but they showed no real innovatory features compared with those of the larger companies. The GSWR lived, in carriage terms, somewhat 'under the shadow' of its English ally the Midland. It was, however, much smaller and did not get itself involved in the design of the Scottish Joint Stock — that was very much a Derby prerogative and MR designs were actually built at Kilmarnock in the late nineteenth century for Joint Stock working. Furthermore, the GSWR and MR had wished to amalgamate in the 1870s and, even though foiled in this endeavour, they remained very close associates. The GSWR adopted the MR carriage livery (to all intents and purposes) and its carriages were very Midland-like in both appearance, amenity and dimension during the Manson period. Take away the square lower corner panelling of a Manson GSWR carriage and one almost has a pre-clerestory Clayton MR coach.

Funnily enough, it was the much-maligned Peter Drummond — who made something of a 'porridge' of GSWR locomotives — who gave the company such carriage distinction as it was able to offer to the new LMS. He produced a distinctly attractive, almost fully elliptical carriage style which retained the basic Manson panelling (now rounded at all corners) but increased the overall size to something approaching modern dimensions. His use of pressed steel bogies was almost 'avant garde' and the vehicles were most certainly in the front rank for the time. But, as with the LYR considered earlier, there were not too many of them and their influence could be but minor after 1922.

It is an odd thought that the Caledonian Railway, though a fierce rival of the GSWR, suffered much the same sort of fate after 1922 as far as carriage design was concerned, even though its engines fared rather better. The 'Caley' was a much larger railway (second only in Scotland after the NBR) but, in carriage terms, it suffered from several dis-advantages. Firstly, to all intents and purposes it left the design of the West Coast Joint Stock to its English partner, the LNWR. It even adopted virtually the same livery, believed to be in

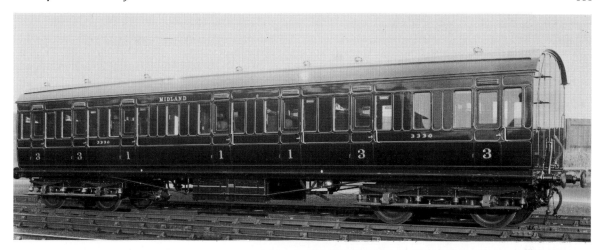

Top to bottom *The Midland's elliptical roof carriages, such as lavatory non-corridor composite No 3330, retained Bain-style panelling and became the visual models on which early LMS stock was based*

Characteristic Manson-styling on the GSWR is shown by arc roof non-corridor third class No 693. The apparent lack of lining suggests that it may have been a 1914-18 wartime repaint.

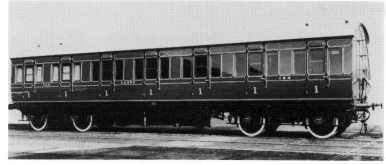

The visual style of Peter Drummond's new stock for the GSWR is well shown in this ex-works view of non-corridor first class No 194. The generally Midland nature of the livery is obvious, but the roof is white and there is a fine gilt line centrally on the beading, a feature not adopted by the MR (Staffordshire County Record Office).

Caledonian Railway corridor third No 982 typifies the turn-of-the-century style adopted by this famous company.

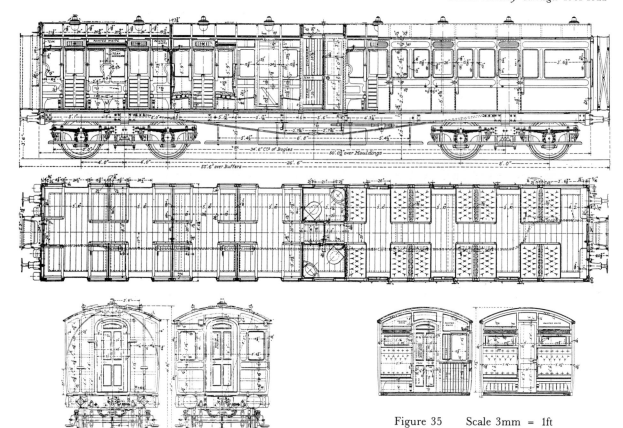

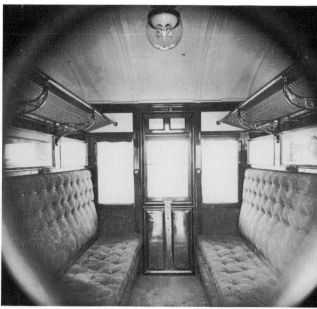

Figure 35   Scale 3mm = 1ft

consequence of the favourable reception given by the CR directors to some of the early WCJS stock when it first appeared north of the Border. In consequence, the Caledonian never really gained first hand experience of those two essentials of the true long-distance operation — sleeping and dining carriages. The former it left to the LNWR and the latter it sub-contracted to the Pullman Car Company (see Chapter 12). This meant inevitably that the Caledonian lacked what might be called the 'total experience' in 1923.

However, the Caledonian did produce some very fine carriages. Its turn-of-the-century style was 'arc roof traditional', but very soon it gained considerable favourable publicity with its magnificent 'Grampian' stock with an almost fully elliptical roof in 1903 (see also Chapter 10). Very soon afterwards, it went to the fully elliptical roof and began to suppress some of the raised panel beading. It also moved to a sort of standard 57-foot length as early as 1912 and, by the end of its independent existence, its basic profile was very close indeed to that of the MR, LNWR and LYR. In fact, it had also adopted the angle-trussed underframe and 'matchboard' end panelling, which features it shared particularly with the MR.

Thus it was that by 1923, four of the main constituents of the LMS (MR, LNWR, LYR and CR) had all, by various means, arrived at a broadly similar approach to carriage building. The 57 ft x 9 ft size, elliptical roof and angle-trussed underframe were now the common solution. The MR and LNWR were both building 'traditional' panelled

carriages, while the MR and CR had opted for the 'matchboard' ends and the MR and LYR had started to experiment with gangwayed open stock. Interestingly, the common factor was the MR. In this context, therefore, it is not very surprising that the LMS standard vehicle (see Chap. 17) took some of the forms it did — but what of the rest?

It has to be conceded that the smaller constituents of the LMS had little or no place in the post-1922 thinking — but how could they? In absolute terms they contributed few vehicles, and in design terms virtually nothing at all. Even if one adds the Maryport and Carlisle, North London and London, Tilbury and Southend Railways to the totals for the FR, NSR and HR (listed on page 105), they would barely exceed the smallest of the rest, the GSWR — and we have seen how little influence the latter really had. In essence, these smaller companies, however idiosyncratic and individualistic they may have seemed to their followers, had little real influence. The Highland, for example, was a fascinating company, but its carriages were anything but typical. If it had a particular style by LMS days, it was as much a second generation development (via Peter Drummond the Highland CME from 1896-1911) of ideas developed at Cowlairs and St Rollox (CR).

The HR was always 'strapped for cash', as they say, and it should occasion no surprise whatsoever that its carriages in the twentieth century revealed, in the interest of economy, the replacement of the panelled and beaded style of David Jones (nineteenth century) by the somewhat cheaper 'matchboard'

Figure 35 In 1902, the CR introduced some well-designed open third class gang-wayed carriages, described at the time as 'among the finest third class carriages in the country'. This drawing shows some of the details of what, along with the LYR's similar experiments (see page 189), turned out to be quite prophetic designs.

Left *These first and third class compartment interiors (composite No 362) reveal the high quality achieved in the elliptical roof stock built by the Caledonian Railway.*

Right *Typically spartan Highland Railway six-wheel, six compartment third class No 140, showing a combination of beading and 'matchboard' panelling (Gavin Wilson collection).*

Top to bottom *This fine view of Furness Railway six-wheel third class brake No 13 shows how close this company came to a 'carbon copy' of Wolverton's LNWR styling in most of its carriages*

The North Staffordshire Railway's version of Wolverton-style panelling was associated with an end arrangement which 'turned under' to the headstock in Midland fashion. This is shown on six-wheel brake third, LMS No 27775, taken in the mid-1930s. The centrally located guard's lookout, a common NSR feature, has had its original panelling replaced by metal sheeting (R.J. Essery collection).

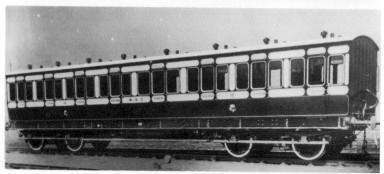

Maryport and Carlisle bogie tri-composite (1st/2nd/3rd class) No 15 was a neat enough carriage, but hardly of great design significance. The class breakdown is, however, interesting, one first, two second and five third, quite a good 'guesstimate', one feels, in relation to travelling needs — see page 165 (B.C. Lane collection).

Typical Tilbury line bogie stock headed by the highly decorated and now preserved 4-4-2T Thundersley at St Pancras in Coronation year 1911. Now, if only some of the effort obviously spent on the engine had been applied to the carriages . . .! (R.J. Essery collection).

styling adopted by Drummond. The extraordinary thing is that some of the HR stock *did* survive quite well and its admittedly small quota of corridor stock was not too bad. But the fact that the LMS, soon after the grouping, saw fit to allocate quite a volume of second-line former MR, LYR and LNWR stock to the Highland area seems to tell its own story of the general backwardness of the latter's overall fleet. Only the later Drummond stock enjoyed any real longevity.

The Furness and North Staffordshire Railways both rather favoured the 'Wolverton' (LNWR) style of carriage construction, but neither of them came up with anything better than that of the larger constituents. The Maryport and Carlisle had an attractive green and cream livery allied to 'traditional' or 'modified traditional' body style but not much else, while the LT & SR and NLR systems could hardly be expected to set the Thames on fire with their carriage designs. The MR had, long before 1922-3, decided to replace the indigenous LT & SR stock with something better, and maybe the less said about the NLR contribution the better! It is one of the more amazing facts of twentieth-century carriage history that the quite appalling four-wheelers of the NLR were, for a time (after the LNWR took over), replaced by *new* four-wheelers and these archaic concepts continued to trundle up the 'Northern Heights' of the London suburbs well into the 1930s. Mark you, the CR had also built some 'modern' four-wheelers right up to the time of the grouping, so perhaps one should not be too critical.

Obviously, in a general survey such as this the subtle nuances so beloved of the railway enthusiasts have little or no place, and it may be that some readers feel that this analysis is altogether too superficial. However, if one tries to extract, from a very complex story, some continuing threads which stood the test of time — the only *real* criterion for lasting influence — then the later development of the railway carriage in the twentieth century, as far as the LMS was concerned, was strongly biased in favour of the contributions made by the LNWR, MR and LYR. These were the three main contributors to the LMS fleet which, in turn, was the major single influence in the BR continuation. It may seem to be *force majeure* but, if so, the fact should not be too unsurprising. Remember that railways were in business to make money, and their carriages reflected this fact; if the present (1980s) shape of the open second class carriage on a MkIII HST set reveals its ancestry via the LMS/LYR, so be it. History is a continuum and railway carriages are no exception.

We now turn to the next in 1923 order of magnitude, the LNER.

The LNER group

Once again abstracting from Table 2, the 100-or-more-route-mile companies which came under the LNER ownership, along with their 1921 passenger carriage totals, are listed below:

England	GCR	1694
	GER	3970
	GNR	2639
	NER	3106*
	Subtotal	11409
Scotland	GNSR	454
	NBR	2424
	Subtotal	2878
	Grand total	14287

*This total includes vehicles from the Hull & Barnsley Railway, absorbed early in 1922.

Somewhat like the LMS group, three English companies dominated the scene, this time with some 68% of the total fleet, but there was only one smaller system compared with the considerable number of such railways in the LMS group. Five out of six companies owned quite large fleets and only the GER stood out numerically. However, its numerical ascendancy was not as significant as, say, that of the LNWR in the LMS system.

The GER total of carriages included a huge number of suburban vehicles reflecting its intensive London area services into Liverpool Street. In this context it enjoyed a near territorial monopoly, save for the LT & SR, somewhat comparable with the various constituents of the Southern Railway (see below). In this respect it was different from the two other London-based parts of the LNER which had to face rather more railway competition from such rival organizations as the Metropolitan, North London and Underground systems, not to mention a degree of territorial overlap with main-line companies like the Midland or LNWR.

In consequence, GER carriage design was dominated by the needs of suburban short-distance passengers. it adopted a traditionally British form of styling but with numerous distinctive variations all its own. The eaves and waist panels were notably deeper than those adopted by most railways and the division of the lower side sheeting into a series of vertical panels on many of its carriages was wholly unique. Its livery was varnished natural wood which, when kept clean, could be quite smart, but it was by

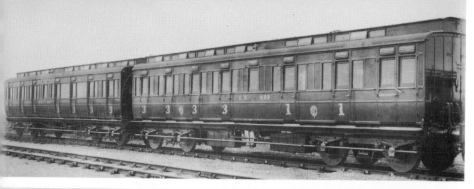

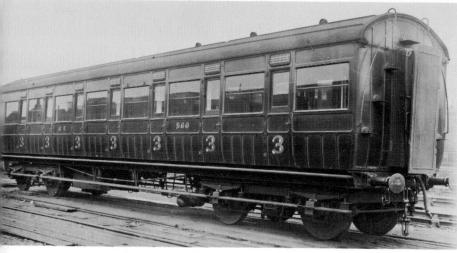

no means the most striking of such styles since it had nothing like the decorative embellishments carried by, say, the East Coast companies (see below). In 1919, the GER changed to a dark crimson lake colour for some of its carriages and at all times its use of large class-identifying figures on the doors was a dominant feature. In this particular, it was somewhat ahead of most companies during the early part of the period under review.

In spite of its large fleet, the GER suffered two principal drawbacks in terms of its future influence on things. Firstly, it was not a true long-distance railway in the sense of the GNR, MR or LNWR for instance, and its contribution in terms of gangwayed stock was, in consequence, relatively modest. Secondly, and in LNER terms of more than superficial importance, it was not involved with the design or operation of the East Coast Joint Stock. In both these respects, its position after 1922 was not dissimilar to that of the LYR. That it could build some very fine coaches is exemplified not just by its early use of corridor coaches and third class dining cars in late Victorian days, but also by its twentieth-century stock for the Continental boat trains and the services to the principal East Anglian cities like Ispwich and Norwich, not to mention Cambridge.

But these were all 2-3 hour sort of trips (even less in the case of Cambridge and the boat trains), and the GER rarely had to address the problem of designing what amounted to an all-day or all-night travelling environment.

Thus, like the LYR, its carriage designs tended to be ignored after the grouping although, just as with the LMS in the case of the LYR, the new LNER could not ignore the traffic *requirements* of the ex-GER lines and the post-1922 design of LNER suburban stock very much reflected this fact. Another interesting influence which was at first precipitated by GER requirements was the need to design a shorter version of the LNER standard corridor coaches for use on the Great Eastern system, parts of which could not accept the longer vehicles.

Turning now to some of the other English constituents of the LNER, two of them had main lines to London, but whereas that of the GCR was a sort of appendage grafted in 1899 on to a former provincial system (the Manchester Sheffield and Lincolnshire), the whole ethos of the GNR stemmed from its role as a main trunk route from the day it opened, halfway through the nineteenth century. 'Kings Cross for the North' had been almost written into its tablets of incorporation. However, notwithstanding this fundamental difference in history, both railways had to address similar, if not identical, operating problems. In terms of vehicle design response, they did so in markedly different ways.

The Great Central entered the new century flushed with pride at its recent change of title consequent upon its achievement of the London main line to Marylebone. However, as a newcomer it had to face formidable rivalry for long-distance traffic from the three existing and well-established systems whose trains were already in fierce competition for passengers from the same or similar catchment areas, ie the LNWR, MR and GNR. In trying to face these problems, the GCR came up with some very fine carriages indeed.

At the turn of the century, the new Great Central employed traditionally panelled coaches in a nice livery of chocolate brown and French grey, later brown and cream. It built some very well-equipped corridor coaches right at the close of the Victorian era which, although by no means to the maximum length adopted by some railways, offered distinctly spacious accommodation. At times, it also favoured the clerestory roof which was a rather elegant stylistic compromise between the Midland and Great Western approaches. Its clerestory non-corridors

were most definitely a cut above the average and could stand favourable comparison with anything in the land.

In 1907, the GCR went to the fully elliptical roof and a varnished natural wood livery appeared in 1910. This was accompanied by a change to a very distinctive body styling for some of its carriages combining vertical 'matchboard' treatment below the waistline and a general increase in the coach size, both in terms of length and cross-section. In the latter context, the GCR had built its London main line to a very generous structure gauge of almost continental proportions, and this permitted correspondingly generous internal provisioning for the passenger, including probably the widest internal side corridors ever offered to the British traveller.

However, the GCR loading gauge posed its own problems, just as did that of the GWR (page 134). Very large carriages could not pass freely over all 'foreign' systems, and since through coach working in Britain was a characteristic and important feature of railway working, the big GCR carriages, excellent though they were, could not offer the most effective solution after 1923. Moreover, in numerical terms they were considerably few in number compared with the GNR and/or NER fleets. Additionally, the GCR also retained a fair quantity of earlier and less worthy

This stylish GCR clerestory non-corridor third class brake with end lavatory was built in 1903. Compared with most of its third class short to medium-distance contemporaries, this must have been a more than amenable form of travel (B.C. Lane collection).

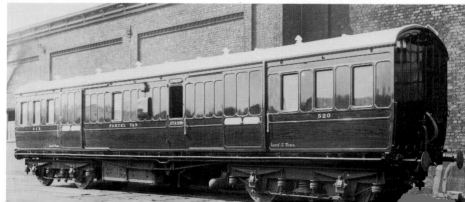

Considerable attention to detail is apparent in the finish of this attractive GCR bogie guard and parcels van, No 520, built in 1907. The carriage is unlined but the original picture clearly shows the beautifully applied grained finish of the post-1910 GCR livery. It is possible that this picture was taken to illustrate the new style.

Left *This appalling four-wheel monstrosity built by the GNR seated no fewer than 72 passengers in six compartments not much over 5 feet wide, and was one of forty such carriages when built in 1900. It was not untypical of the frugal nature of most GNR suburban stock.*

Right *In the long-distance field the GNR had to meet fierce competition, and only four years after building the four-wheelers in the previous picture it produced ten of these elegant gangwayed clerestory third class brakes with only 42 seats arranged in three open saloons and three-per-side seating, arranged 2 + 1 on either side of the central aisle.*

stock. But make no mistake about it, the Great Central carriage was by no means the inferior vehicle which its apparent eclipse after 1922 might suggest.

By contrast with the GCR, the GNR influence in carriage building throughout the first half of the twentieth century was profound — and this is somewhat surprising all things considered. In 1921 it came only third in the LNER constituent companies' carriage fleet 'pecking order', and only just above the stock of the NBR. However, numbers were not everything, as the LNWR had discovered *vis-à-vis* the Midland in the LMS group. The outcome, however, was not quite the same.

In many ways, the GNR was very like the LNWR, although considerably smaller in size. During much of the later nineteenth century they had both operated some quite dreadful carriages on their main lines considering the generally prestigious nature of both companies. However, they were both distinctly arrogant railways, full of self-satisfied complacency, and it was not until both were pushed into providing something better that improvement began to take place! In this, the competition offered by the Midland was probably pivotal to both the GNR and LNWR, while the new GCR did not exactly endear itself to any of its rivals with its rather good carriages. It is, one feels, more than significant that the GNR only began to sort matters out at the turn of the century (as indeed did the LNWR), by which time the MR had been offering superb comfort for nearly twenty years and, additionally, the new GCR was a possible threat to everyone.

The GNR responded with considerable éclat, which was to lay a firm foundation for East Coast and LNER carriage building for the best part of half a century, and its influence may, perhaps, best be summed up by the names of three people, Howlden, Gould and Gresley. Of these names, the first two are probably less well known than the last, yet they were

probably more influential, at least superficially. Firstly, it was Howlden who created the distinctive 'East Coast' carriage panelling style which was worn without significant change in either style or livery (varnished teak) from the 1880s until 1941. Gould we have also met in the context of the buckeye coupling and the Pullman gangway, both being eventually adopted by the GNR as standard for long-distance stock. Gresley's influence was, in turn, both more subtle and undoubtedly more long-lasting, even though the most ardent Gresley admirers must admit that he had a good foundation on which to work which only needed a bit of refinement.

In 'surface' terms, the only thing which made the body of a Gresley carriage look significantly different from its long-distance predecessors was its full height elliptical roof and its beautifully 'domed' roof ends. In this, it was quite an achievement to improve on its forbears, for the GNR corridor clerestory was itself a thing of great beauty dating back to the late 1890s. The less said about the pure 'Howlden' body the better, with its sort of flattened elliptical roof profile which was universally adopted for non-corridor stock and its quite regular association with the most diabolically cramped compartments! In this respect, Gresley's elliptical roof suburban non-corridors were not particularly marvellous either for the most part!

It was 'below decks', so to speak, that Gresley's carriage influence was most significant. He is, of course, most famous for his fine locomotives, but he actually came to the GNR as carriage and wagon chief and had trained on the LYR. Before he left this latter railway, it had begun to experiment with an outside frame 'wide bearing' bogie of monumentally ugly aesthetic aspect but considerable virtue in terms of its ride quality. While I have never seen documentary proof of the connection, it does not seem too wild a supposition to link this LYR wide bearing bogie with the altogether more elegant

outside frame *double* bolster bogie which Gresley fairly soon designed for the GNR after he had left the LYR. The two units looked remarkably different but the resemblance in principle is there for all to see.

Be that as it may, the Gresley bogie became the GNR norm, was adopted for the East Coast Joint Stock and later the LNER, was put under many hundreds of carriages of the LNER pre-group constituents and was still considered sufficiently sophisticated to be adopted by BR in the 1950s for some of its *new* multiple unit stock. This might not be quite so glamorous an achievement as a glossy streamlined 'A4' 'Pacific', but in sheer passenger comfort terms it was certainly of benefit to far more people — and I did say at the beginning that carriages were about people!

The Gresley bogie utilized probably the finest four-wheel suspension ever adopted in Britain until quite modern days. Speaking from personal experience, its only serious rivals during the company period were the heavy LNWR and LMS twelve-wheel bogies and the LMS 9-foot four-wheeler (itself derived from the MR and LNWR types), all of which needed the stabilizing effect of screw couplings and side buffers for the best effect (see page 25). I well remember travelling to Newhaven from Leeds in 1948 when the contrast between the almost floating quality of the LNER corridor stock on its Gresley bogies was in marked contrast to the frightful antics of the Southern Railway equivalent on the boat train! At the same time, I cannot resist commenting that there were occasions when one could have wished that the East Coast had put as much effort into the carriage *interior* as it did into the wheels and suspension; however, back to the GNR.

Gresley's other principal carriage contribution was also related to wheels and suspension, namely carriage articulation wherein two adjacent carriage ends are carried on a single shared bogie. This too was a GNR innovation and will be re-addressed in later chapters; suffice to say at this point that between 1900 and 1914 the total effect of the GNR carriage revolution — for thus it was — turned out to be the dominant factor in LNER thinking from 1923 onwards. Of course, the fact that Gresley became

The first example of Gresley articulation, using the earlier GNR bogie, was East Coast Joint Stock twin corridor composite No 202/6, converted in 1905 from two 1890-built six-wheelers. In about 1914 it was transferred to GNR stock.

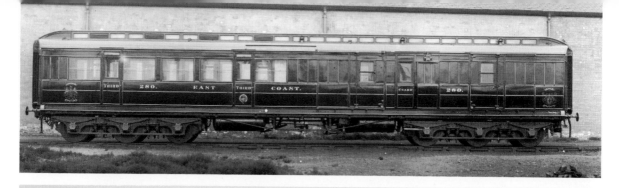

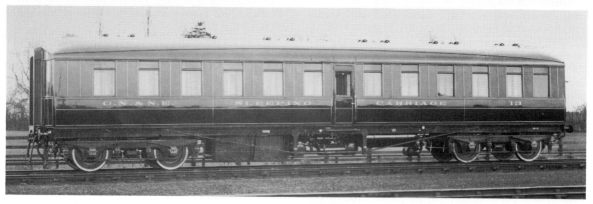

Top to bottom *GNR influence I — East Coast clerestory twelve-wheel corridor third class brake No 280 was one of five similar vehicles built at Cowlairs in 1901 to pure GNR style and outline.*

GNR influence II — ECJS kitchen car No 211 was built at York by the NER in 1914; again, the GNR stylistic influence is paramount. The NER-type chassis, full-length eaves panel and glass vane ventilators do, however, impart a slightly diluted GNR effect to the whole.

GNR influence III — Less well known than the ECJS was the GN/NER Joint Stock for the London-Newcastle route. GNR styling was again dominant as in this sleeping car, No 13 of 1909. The body is pure Gresley/GNR, but the NER bogies and chassis give it subtle points of difference. Identical carriages were also built on GNR chassis.

CME of the LNER may also have had something to do with it! But it was not without its technological justification.

A further contributory factor to the GNR stylistic dominance after 1922 was undoubtedly the East Coast Joint Stock. These vehicles, jointly owned by the GNR, NER and NBR, were used for the principal Anglo-Scottish services from King's Cross Although many were built at York (NER) and some at Cowlairs (NBR), the styling was normally standardized on GNR practice and coaches of basically GNR outline came out from all three locations. In fact, there is one still in existence at the NRM, a beautifully restored ECJS corridor third built by the NER at York as early as 1897 but to pure GNR style. It is true that some ECJS coaches (unlike their Midland or LNWR Scottish Joint Stock equivalent) were, during the twentieth century, built to non-GNR styling, but their influence was peripheral. This too is surprising, for the NER and NBR were by no means poor relations in the carriage field. Furthermore, whereas the LNWR and MR were absolutely dominant numerically in their respective Scottish Joint Stocks by comparison with their CR and GSWR partners, this did not really hold true for the East Coast triumvirate. Even now, therefore, it is still just a touch surprising that a railway like the GNR, which contributed less than 20% of the total LNER carriage fleet, should, in the event, have proved so dominant.

If any railway or its supporters had cause to be aggrieved by the GNR dominance in the LNER carriage field, it must surely have been the North Eastern. Second only to the GER amongst the LNER constituents in numerical terms, its carriages were, for the most part, vastly superior to most of those of the East Anglian company and, speaking from personal experience, infinitely preferable to most of those built by the GNR too. Of all the many individualistic aspects which ceased to exist at the 1923 grouping, the speedy decline of NER influence in purely carriage terms is in my opinion by a long way the most surprising of them all.

The NER was the largest of the LNER constituents, even Gresley allowed NER thinking to have more than a small place in locomotive affairs and its former officers achieved some management prominence in post-grouping days; yet its carriages seemed of little consequence after 1922 — extraordinary! This is even more inexplicable when one considers that at the turn of the century, the start of our story, NER carriage design was in the charge of that supreme carriage builder David Bain, later of Midland fame. In fact, there was more than a little collaboration between the NER and the Midland. In locomotive terms, the immortal Midland compounds were basically inspired by earlier NER experiments, and there was more than a little NER influence in latter-day Midland carriage design. Even their carriage liveries (crimson lake) were substantially similar — perhaps the 1923 grouping got it wrong!

I can offer no logical explanation for this seemingly anomalous state of affairs. It even transcended the eclipse of the LNWR styling by the MR version on the rival LMS for, as we have seen, the LNWR operating philosophy still tended to hold sway. All I can therefore do is to record the main elements of the situation as it seems from a distance of sixty or more years.

NER carriages were of the traditionally panelled kind in 1901. They were of either nineteenth century arc roof configuration or the more recent clerestory profile, a quite distinctive form which superimposed a clerestory deck on top of a basic arc roof shape without serious change of lower roof profile or bodyside styling. The latter was a particularly harmonious combination of eaves, window and waist panelling, largely attributable to David Bain. It withstood the transition to the MR in 1903, for many of Bain's carriages were not much more than NER-styled bodies married to Clayton's distinctive clerestory of 1896-7 vintage.

After Bain left, NER carriage design tended to become a bit confused — and maybe this was the problem. The roof profile became, fairly swiftly, the full semi-elliptical type, but the body styling, except for the livery, rang the changes in this manner of a debutante who could not quite make up her mind which dress she should wear for the Hunt Ball! There were experiments with straight-sided 'match-boarding' — somewhat aesthetically disastrous. There were also permutations within the 'traditional' field involving various combinations of square-cornered and round-cornered panelling; some carriages came out with top lights as an alternative to eaves panels and some did not, while corridor coaches could not quite make up their minds whether or not to suppress individual compartment doors — and so it went on. There was, in effect, no dominant and instantaneously recognisable NER approach in its latter years in the same sense as one can discern in, say, GNR, GWR, NBR or LSWR carriages, and this was a pity, for amongst all this confusion the NER built some quite splendid vehicles.

If there was a preferred single style towards the end of the pre-1922 era, it was perhaps best exemplified by the singularly well-proportioned gangwayed coaches which combined traditional panelling with something very closely approaching the Gresley pattern of elliptical roof with domed ends. The NER, possibly influenced by the GNR, adopted this profile with great enthusiasm and made some very beautiful carriages at its York works. Many of these were distinctly modern in their elimination of individual and draughty compartment doors and in their use of large picture windows. Unfortunately, the perverse British public was not always convinced (qv GWR developments — see page 136), so the poor old NER was forced to offer the older type as well; but in all essentials, the NER was probably rather more ahead of its time in terms of carriage amenity than most other companies. In terms of interior *layout* this was certainly so, and even after 1922 the Gresley-dominated LNER saw fit to continue building NER-styled corridor coaches for a year or two and to put a lot of ex-NER carriages on to Gresley pattern bogies. In this latter respect, of course, there was probably good technical reason,

as was also the case in the fitting of ex-NER corridor coaches with buckeye couplings and Pullman gangways after the grouping. Additionally, of course, this policy made economic sense. The NER had so many carriages that the LNER could not afford to ignore them, and their harmonization (in technical terms) with Gresley's GNR stock, combined with the relative newness of many of the carriage bodies, gave the LNER a substantial fleet, many of which lasted well into BR days.

North Eastern influence was also strong in the cross-country field (see Chapter 9), and its more specialized carriages, particularly its dining cars, could stand comparison with most. However, as with many other railways, it tended to lack the all round experience of such companies as the LNWR, GWR and MR — it was not a significant builder of sleeping cars, for example, save for its contribution to the GNR-dominated ECJS — so maybe its declining

influence, post-1922, is not totally inexplicable; but it still seems surprising in retrospect.

Not too far behind the NER and GNR came the NBR, the largest of the Scottish railways before 1923, a considerable builder of railway carriages and in numerical terms above the Caledonian, its principal Scottish rival. The NBR was of course the dominant Scottish constituent of the LNER, but like the Caledonian in the LMS group, its carriage construction was insufficiently comprehensive, viewed against the needs of the post-1922 situation, to have any real long-term significance. In many ways this was unfortunate, for the North British had developed a quite distinctive stylistic approach. In terms of *type*, it was not too different from many other British systems, but its visual style, if not quite unique, was very characteristic indeed.

The NBR was, in carriage terms, the archetypal

Below *'To door or not to door?'* — *that seems to have been the question on the NER when in came to corridor stock. These two first class brakes Nos 1950 and 1453 are typical, and both are, in all essentials, identical. Discounting the obvious door issue, other interesting detail differences are underframe design, the presence or absence of a guard's lookout, recessed doors and so on. Both versions also appeared with each other's style of panelling! At the same time, one cannot help but remark on the extremely stylish end product, no matter what the design minutiae may have been.*

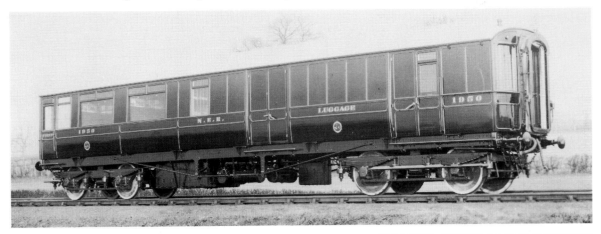

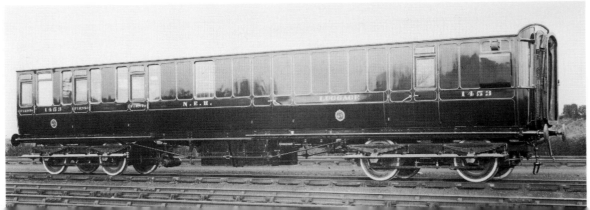

Left *The distinctive and very consistent NBR carriage styling is well seen in this period view of Tayport station* circa *1910. The scene is dominated by non-corridor four and six-wheelers, all embodying the familiar NBR cove roof profile and two-layer panelling*

Below *This crisp view of third class carriage No 1730 shows an interesting NBR alternative to the corridor approach. It is a lavatory carriage with an inter-mediate side corridor giving access to the one toilet at the left-hand end. Almost certainly, it is this type of vehicle which forms the leading carriage of the train pictured on page 98.*

Bottom *Typical of the best NBR corridor stock was full third No 1793, built in 1906 and branded for the 'Lothian Coast Express'. It was also photographed at the same time branded 'Fife Coast Express' and was actually built as part of a set of trains for the Aberdeen services!*

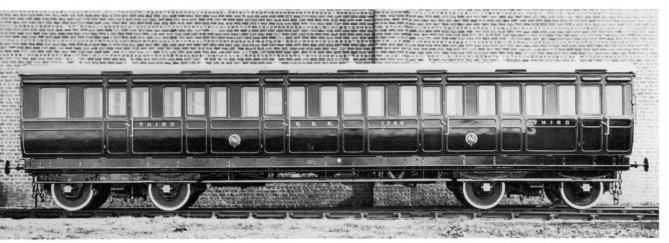

Scottish railway. Its twin-layer panelling style, while not quite unique to itself (the GNSR and HR had both tried it out to some extent), was most certainly the most dominant single visual influence in carriage terms north of the border before 1923 and was not really mirrored by any English railway. Its livery, however, like that of the rival Caledonian, was by no means innovative compared with its competitors. It was one of many systems which employed an all-red colour scheme (not very different from that of the MR and NER) and, to be frank, had no prime claims to virtue. In fact, the NBR was, in twentieth-century carriage terms, something of a low-key railway compared with the occasionally ostentatious characteristics of its Scottish rival, the Caledonian, or, particularly, its East Coast partners, specifically the GNR. For instance, just as in the case of the CR (West Coast Joint Stock) or the GSWR (Midland Joint Stock), it virtually abrogated East Coast Joint design to the GNR (usually) and NER (occasionally), and with far less cause, for it was larger than either of its Scottish contemporaries. All things being equal, one might have expected NBR influence to have been proportionally more dominant (*vis-à-vis* the CR or GSWR) than, in effect, it turned out to be after 1922, especially when one considers the fact that it was the NBR which first introduced sleeping carriages to Britain, way back in Victorian times.

Towards the end of its independent existence, the NBR was one of the earlier railways to experiment with metal-clad carriage exteriors. This it did with the same sort of dull and ponderous styling as was exemplified, for example, by the LSWR with its 'Ironclad' carriages (page 128). The LNER was not wildly impressed, unlike the Southern, and this pioneering use of 'new technology' was in the event not adopted by its post-1922 successor until some 25 or more years later, and then in very different style in the form of the much maligned but rather good-looking post-Second World War LNER carriages of the 1940s designed by Edward Thompson (see Chap. 29). Meantime, the NBR's best claim to fame

lay probably in its corridor express stock of *circa* 1906 — a series of distinctly attractive and well thought out carriages fully competitive and compatible with most of the opposition and, in most respects, well ahead of their time.

As for the other contributors to the LNER carriage story, there are but two serious contenders, the GNSR and the hitherto unmentioned Hull and Barnsley Railway. The latter of course was in the 'under 100 route miles' category; furthermore, it was absorbed by the NER *before* the 1923 grouping. For most of its independent life, it endured something of a hand to mouth existence and could never be regarded as one of the British 'blue chip' companies. Nevertheless, it did produce some quite well thought out carriages even though its long-term influence was negligible.

The GNSR was probably even more impecunious than the Highland. Its ambitions never ventured much further afield than its own somewhat restricted territorial area, and in consequence its carriages were never much more than were seemly in the immediately local context. It had a fairly unique livery of darkish red and cream (not dissimilar, in fact, to the first post-1947 BR standard style), but this sort of claim to distinction was far too ephemeral to be of any consequence after 1922. It was, in truth, one of those many railways which, in spite of their local following, contributed nothing of profound significance to subsequent developments. A harsh judgement? Maybe — but not without foundation.

The LMS and LNER constituents between them owned something like 70% of the total passenger-carrying vehicles in existence in Great Britain at the

Three austere, almost brutal-looking steel-panelled composite dining cars were built for the NBR by Cravens of Sheffield in 1919. They were reputedly, at 47 tons, the heaviest carriages inherited by the LNER, but their influence was not profound Although later given buckeye couplings and Pullman gangways, a common LNER modification, they lasted barely twenty years, not especially good for a carriage.

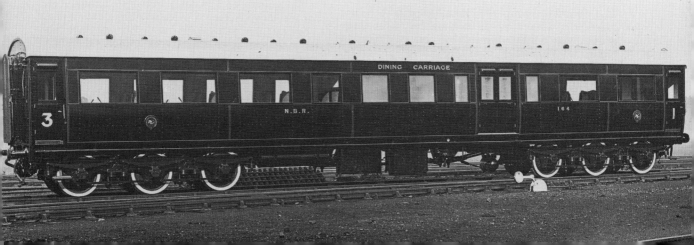

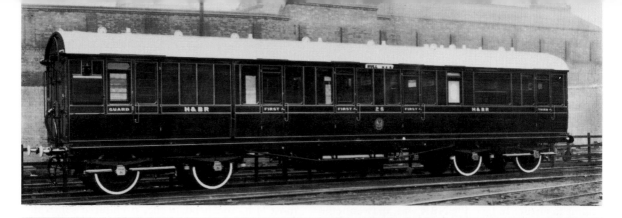

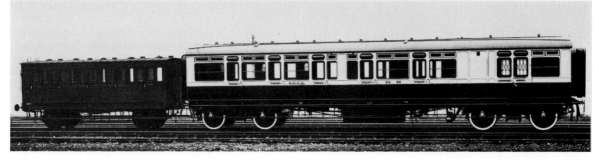

Top *The almost forgotten Hull and Barnsley Railway operated some quite well-equipped carriages in its later years. This is No 25, a non-corridor brake composite, with intermediate lavatories accessed by short internal passageways (Staffordshire County Record Office).*

Above *This picture seems, somehow, symbolic of the Great North of Scotland Railway. The chronically inadequate four-wheel third is probably the more typical, but the bogie corridor composite brake is very good in both visual and accommodation terms. Its livery (red and white) was unusual, attractive and distinctively applied — somewhat in the LSWR style (see opposite).*

time of the grouping, and by far the biggest single contribution to the rest was made by the Great Western Railway. At the same time, although this great company was second in number only to the LNWR in 1921, after the grouping it had to take fourth place below the Southern Railway in the carriage numbers game and it is with this latter company that we must first deal before going on to the unique situation which applied to the carriage policy of the GWR.

The Southern Group

The Southern group was the smallest of the 'Big Four' in 1923 and by far the smallest of the three groups which were formed by amalgamation of erstwhile somewhat similarly sized pre-group companies. Yet when its carriages were totalled, it came up into an easy third place, well above the GWR. The 1921 breakdown was as follows:

LB & SCR		1871
LSWR		2649
SE & CR		2766
	Total	7286

Two or three points should be made from the outset. First and most obvious is the fact that the Southern and its constituents were more passenger orientated than any other of the 'Big Four'. Allowing for the railway's absolute smallness, a carriage total greater by 1,000 or so than that of the GWR (which operated 1,000 more route miles than the SR) betokens a considerable difference in operating pattern. Not only that, but when it is further considered that there were more carriages on the newly-formed Southern Railway alone than in the whole of Scotland, which had nearly twice the railway route mileage (3,824 compared with 2,060), it will be seen how different indeed was this smallest of the amalgamated railways — and this was inevitably reflected in the carriage types it received from its constituents.

On the face of things, there was not too much disparity in totals between the SE & CR and the LSWR, and even the Brighton was not exactly an insignificant third, but there were important differences in emphasis. Two of the three systems were in essence suburban, and only one of them (the LSWR) was a 'main-line' railway in the accepted sense. This affected carriage designs and, in consequence, only the LSWR had what might be termed a comprehensive range of vehicle types comparable with those of the GWR or the other principal railways heading north and north-west from London. It might therefore be expected that, all things being equal, the LSWR would probably dominate, even though the SE & CR had marginally more carriages. To some extent this was true, but the actuality was rather more subtle and all three railways were very different.

The LSWR has embraced the traditionally panelled carriage with considerable enthusiasm and remarkable visual consistency. It entered the twentieth century with the fairly common arc roof profile which soon gave way to a sort of flattened elliptical shape very similar to that used by the GNR in the pre-clerestory, pre-Gresley days. Eaves and waist panels were quite deep and remained so while wooden bodies were made, and from the waist upwards the bodyside of an LSWR carriage was probably nearer to that of the GER than any other. There, however, most comparisons ended, for, like

quite a few British lines, the LSWR had a quite unique livery which virtually defies verbal description. 'Salmon pink and brown' is quite a common nomenclature, but both tones were more than normally subtle. The upper panels were a sort of orange —pink shade, but not really the colour of a salmon, either the fresh or the canned variety. The

Below *Arc roof bogie tri-composite (1st/2nd/3rd class) No 485, typifies the LSWR approach to carriage building as it entered the twentieth century. This type of carriage contained all the seeds of that which was to become characteristic of the South Western in later years.*

Bottom *This carriage style, in effect the older form with changed roof shape and deepened eaves panelling, is probably more characteristic of the LSWR than any other in the pre-1923 period. Lavatory tri-composite No 633 is also a reminder that the LSWR retained three classes for longer than many railways and regularly used non-corridor stock with lavatories rather than the gangwayed equivalent. This example had no fewer than six lavatories, one per compartment. Its brake-ended equivalent is preserved at the National Railway Museum.*

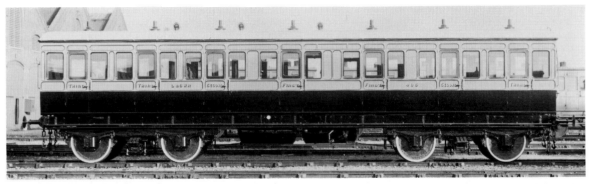

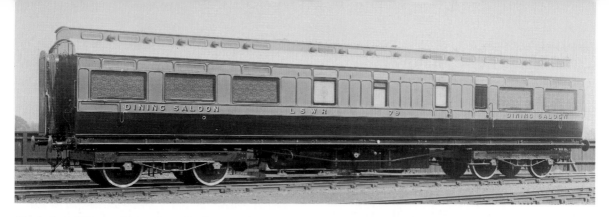

The basic LSWR panelling style lasted almost to the railway grouping, and on the way developed some distinctly good-looking variants, including two small batches of clerestory dining cars. No 79, one of the series given large picture windows, is shown here, carried on the new outside-framed bogies also adopted for the 'Ironclads'.

nearest fishy equivalent in colour terms is probably the smoked version! As for the brown —well, what is brown? It was very dark indeed and in some light conditions took on a dark reddish hue, reminiscent of, say, an even darker version of the LNWR carmine lake. In other light circumstances it could display sort of bronze-green overtones, and at its most extreme could seem almost black —'invisible' brown might be an appropriate phase. The combined effect of the two colours (if the NRM has got it even nearly correct on the restored LSWR tri-composite) was, however, an uncommonly handsome carriage finish, especially in association with a sage green engine.

This distinctive colour scheme was applied to a wide range of carriage types from suburban non-corridors to a small fleet of corridor carriages of particularly harmonious shape. The LSWR built its corridor coaches rather wider than its non-corridor stock and this allowed the slightly flattened elliptical roof to follow a somewhat more curvaceous profile

across the centre. The nearest contemporary equivalent was probably the cove roof corridor stock of the LNWR, and I consider both approaches to be amongst the aesthetic leaders at this time. The fact that both companies employed unique liveries may also have made a contribution.

Two main changes and a few minor ones took place during the pre-grouping period. Firstly was the electrification of some services from 1915 onwards, which will be considered in detail in Chapter 15. This went with a change from the two-colour livery to an all-over green shade on the electric lines. This, in the event, proved the dominant colour factor in the Southern Railway period. The second major change was the gradual introduction of steel sheeting for the outer body panels of LSWR coaches. At first this was associated with traditional woodern beading strips and, when painted, the carriages looked no different. However, when the raised beading was finally abandoned on later LSWR corridor stock, a somewhat different sort of carriage styling stood revealed.

Applied solely to corridor coaches which were quickly nicknamed 'Ironclads', this newer LSWR treatment produced a vehicle not all that different in shape from its forbears, but what might be termed their 'texture' was something new. To be honest,

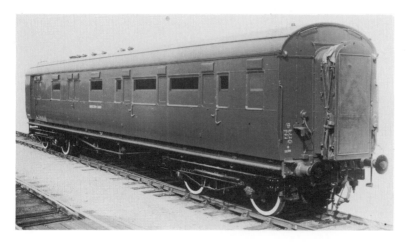

No ex-works pictures seem to have survived of the LSWR 'Ironclads' when new in 1921, but this view of Southern Railway No 7714 shows one of them, little changed externally when converted for inspection use many years later. It started life as a brake first with pantry and kitchen between the three compartments and the van. The inward taper towards the guard's lookout was a characteristic feature and similar to that of the LYR (see page 104). The general style of these carriages, including the lookout arrangement, became the basis of early Southern Railway developments after 1922.

they seemed to lack something of the visual finesse of earlier LSWR corridor coaches, but like most things South Western they were very solidly built and their influence was wholly dominant in the early stages of Southern Railway long-distance thinking. It could hardly have been otherwise, in retrospect. The LSWR was the only one of the SR constituents to have any real experience in the corridor field and even then not much. The Brighton had none at all, and the SE & CR only one complete train, so by adopting the LSWR corridor coach as the basis for this new design, the Southern CME (R.E.L. Maunsell) was taking the sensible option. He could hardly be accused of prejudice since he was an ex-SE & CR man.

Thus the LSWR carriage was highly influential in setting two aspects of post-1922 Southern thinking — livery and long-distance gangwayed stock. That, however, is about as far as it went. Unlike the LMS and LNER, the non-corridor story was quite a different matter and took a somewhat unusual and remarkable turn, the origins of which were firmly rooted in the carriages of the other pre-group constituents of the Southern system. There was no such thing as a 'standard' Southern non-corridor, nor even the semblance of one.

While most of the story must, perforce, wait until Part 2, one quite extraordinary fact must be stated at this point. The Southern Railway never built any locomotive-hauled non-corridor stock for the whole of its independent existence! It relied entirely on its pre-group inheritance. This was, of course, very much bound up with the continuous electrification of the SR which enabled pre-1923 stock to soldier on in the non-electrified areas. However, even in the electrified field, totally new stock of a purely suburban type was not found to be necessary in any great quantity until after the 1939-45 war.

However, we must leave it at that for the moment and revert to the discussion of the pre-1923 situation.

Second in size, but marginally first of the SR constituents, in carriage numbers was the SE & CR. This was a working partnership established in 1899 between the South Eastern Railway and the London Chatham and Dover Railway which remained nominally independent until the grouping. To all intents and purposes, however, the SE & CR functioned as a single railway during the twentieth century and it will be thus considered in this account.

The SE & CR inherited from its partners a motley fleet of pretty appalling carriages, it being a moot point in the 1890s which of the two was the more disgraceful (probably the LCDR). Fortunately, the SER had began to improve matters, and in Harry Wainwright, the SE & CR inherited from the SER the services of one of the most forward-looking engineers of the day. His locomotive artistry is well known (*vide* his preserved 4-4-0 No 737 at the NRM, one of the visual high points of the whole collection), but what is far less often recorded is his interest in carriage matters. He had in fact begun to take a grip on things when he became Carriage and Wagon Superintendent of the SER in 1896, and in carriage terms, there was no break in SER development when the SE & CR was formed.

Wainwright's preferred visual lines were the low-waisted type — very reminiscent of that pursued by the LNWR — and this became the SE & CR norm but with a roof profile somewhat more elevated, a sort of cross between the pure cove roof and the high elliptical form. A particularly distinctive visual point was the elevated guard's 'lookout' which projected above normal roof height on brake-ended carriages. It was, perhaps inevitably, referred to as a 'birdcage' and it remained thus named to the very end, well into BR days; these carriages lasted a very long time!

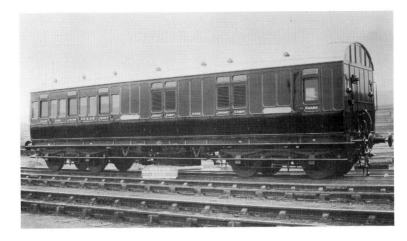

This neat 'birdcage' lookout non-corridor third class brake No 2299 is entirely typical of the vast improvement wrought by Harry Wainwright to the carriage affairs of the SE & CR. It is very 'Wolverton' in general appearance, but the roof profile and window bolection treatment are distinctive. The large luggage section undoubtedly reflects the needs of boat train travellers.

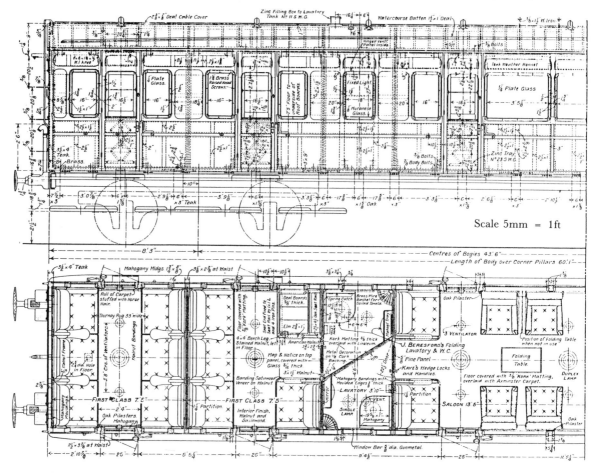

Scale 5mm = 1ft

Figure 36 *Elevation and plan of a typical, later vintage first and second class SE & CR bogie non-corridor, embodying the particularly distinctive SE & CR variation of traditional panelling. Even at first perusal, the self-evident high quality is apparent. Note, particularly, the spacious compartment dimensions.*

Below *Later SE & CR stock displayed a slightly flattened top to the raised guard's lookout such as shown by No S3321S, still looking remarkably good in early BR days. This type of lavatory non-corridor carriage was the favoured SB & CR type for most of its expresses; once again, note the long van portion. Just visible on the right is an example of the later SE & CR styling with modified traditional panelling.*

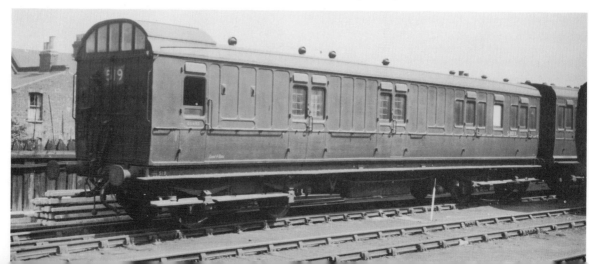

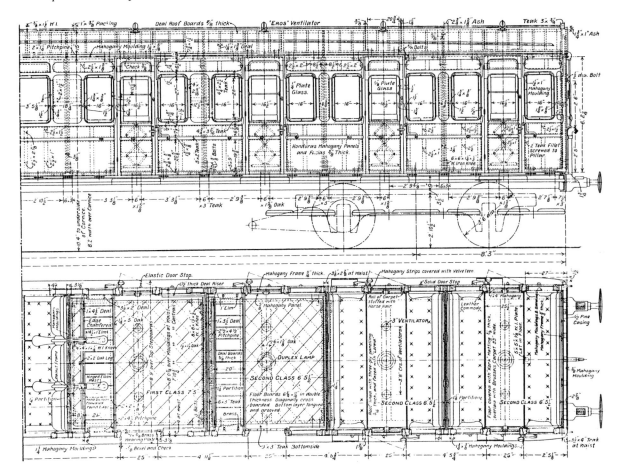

Decked out in rather austere dark lake livery of no particular distinction compared with that of, say, the MR or NER, SE & CR carriages were nevertheless distinctly well thought out in terms of passenger amenity. However, in one or two specifics the SE & CR carriages did not develop along quite such progressive lines as did those of the LSWR and this discrepancy was mainly in the long-distance field.

The SE & CR, like the LB & SCR, was a fairly tightly knit territorial company and had no really lengthy main line. London to the Channel ports of Kent was about its limit and its most prestigious services were its boat trains. Even these flagship turns (excusing the pun) were of relatively minor significance in numerical terms compared with the need of the SE & CR to provide thousands of suburban seats for the commuter services, particularly in replacement of some of the primeval relics built by its two constituents during Victorian days. In consequence, Wainwright placed very high priority in proving decent suburban stock, to the

almost total exclusion of more elaborate vehicles, and did so to good effect. Hundreds of bogie coaches were built, mostly formed into neat sets with 'birdcage' brakes, and although they were undoubtedly of high seating capacity, there were plenty of them and they were a distinct cut above their predecessors in all respects. They were also a fair bit better than the suburban stock of some other London-based lines too — the GNR and NLR spring readily to mind as being two of the worst offenders. Thus, by the time of the grouping the SE & CR had virtually replaced all the pre-Edwardian horrors and possessed a fine, modern fleet of substantial and well-built non-corridor coaches which formed the basis of the subsequent post-1922 electrification. Some later examples, although keeping the 'birdcages', abandoned the low-waisted style for a very neat, part-square-cornered traditional approach to the panelling.

Meanwhile, what of the more prestigious trains? In this context the SE & CR was disadvantaged in

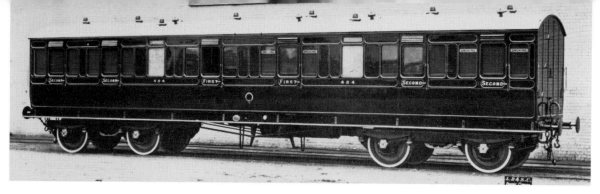

This turn-of-the-century bogie first/second class lavatory non-corridor in the old varnished mahogany livery is typical of the Stroudley carriage style as developed by Lawson Billinton in the 1890s for the Brighton line.

two respects — distance and catering. Dealing with the latter first, the SE & CR is only the second railway so far considered in this chapter where the role of the Pullman Car Company becomes relevant (the Caledonian was the other). The position of the Pullman Company was somewhat curious in the British context and is considered later, but as far as the SE & CR was concerned, its chief task was to provide the train catering and it was probably the principal provider of the up-market luxury as well. The preserved carriage *Topaz* in SE & CR colours at the NRM probably says all. Thus the SE & CR could not offer much experience in this field to the new Southern system. This in itself might not have mattered, but the distance factor made things more difficult, the SE & CR having no long-distance schedules of much more than 1½-2 hours maximum.

In spite of Wainwright's vast improvement in the suburban field, he seems to have seen no need to adopt corridors for the boat trains. Instead, he opted

for long-distance 'lavatory' stock and very good it was too, as might be expected of him. There was plenty of seating space and much provisioning of second class accommodation (important on boat trains), but not until the very end of the period under review, in 1920 after Wainwright had gone, did the company finally adopt corridor coaches for its better trains. To be fair, the SE & CR had built its first corridor coaches in 1907 — mainly to run through to other railways — but in terms of its own domestic needs it stayed faithful to the non-corridor lavatory alternative. The 1920 corridor carriages were few in number and steel panelled, but it was only at the very end of its independent existence that the company ordered some new corridor boat trains. They came out (mostly after the grouping) with very distinctive 'matchboard' lower panelling but they were too little and too late to have much lasting effect on SR design.

The third contributor to the Southern fleet was the LB & SCR, an even more territorially compact system than the SE & CR. It held (and still holds) a popular and romantic place in the minds of many railway enthusiasts, but it has to be said that the reality often belied the romance in purely carriage terms. The Southern inherited a distinctly mixed bag of assets from the Brighton line.

Its basic carriage style was unreservedly Victorian, owing most of its visual characteristics to William Stroudley, later modified by Robert Billinton in the

In 1903, this carriage was built for the LB & SCR with the new umber and cream livery. Although similar in style to that pictured above, the more cramped nature of this third class coach is readily apparent.

The so-called 'Balloon' stock of the LB & SCR undoubtedly displayed the most conspicuous variant of the full elliptical roof ever adopted in Britain. This is non-corridor tri-composite No 629, in which only the first class compartments could gain access to the lavatories. Regrettably, for they were by no means inferior vehicles, this style did not take really firm root on the Brighton system.

1890s. It was of traditionally panelled, arc roof configuration, and at the turn of the century by no means behind the times. Indeed, when fitted with a clerestory (as some vehicles were) it was a distinctly handsome profile, nowhere better exemplified than by the magnificent 1897 Royal Train. However, things tended to get stuck in a groove at this point, with only the occasional sporadic exceptions during the Edwardian period.

The 'Brighton' changed its livery from varnished mahogany to a pleasing umber and white (more or less matching that of the normal Pullman livery) in 1903, but little else seemed to change. In part, this must be put down to Billinton's quite remarkable efforts during the 1890s to replace earlier stock. He introduced bogie carriages in 1894 to a more or less standard 48 ft x 8 ft dimension and a wide variety of designs began to appear, mostly non-corridor, non-lavatory. These continued in construction well into the present century but with little real change or improvement in the types built. Some few types had lavatories, but none had corridors, and the Brighton never built a gangwayed train for itself although it did talk about it! Compartments were often cramped and the whole ethos seemed dominated by the suburban requirement of the South London area.

This in itself would not be particularly surprising but it was exacerbated by the generally short-distance trips which LB & SCR trains ran, combined with the fact, as on the SE & CR, the Pullman Company had carved quite a nice little niche for itself in terms of higher value trade. The 'Southern Belle' was a most famous LB & SCR train, but apart from its engine there was little that was 'Brighton' about it, save for its destination.

In 1905, the LB & SCR made one of its two or three pre-1923 attempts to break the mould when it leapt abruptly from the 'basic Victorian' to the 'Edwardian monumental' style by adopting an ultra-high elliptical roof for some of its carriages. This seemed something of a shock to the system and the vehicles were quickly nicknamed 'Balloons' because of their roof profile. Length and width also increased from the Billinton standard to some 54 ft x 8 ft 6 in, but not many were built even though the variety of types was quite comprehensive. They were used for the better, longer-distance trains and boat trains, and a nine-coach special set of broadly similar, first-class-only stock was used for the 'City Limited' in 1907; but there it seemed to stick, save for a few 'Balloon' railmotor coaches (see Chapter 15).

Part of the reason for the slow forward movement on the LB & SCR was the above-mentioned Billinton re-stocking and the creaming off of the best traffic by the Pullmans, but a second contributory factor was the introduction of electrification in 1909, for which services new stock was built. This is considered in Chapter 15, but it reduced, in absolute terms, the need for many new locomotive-hauled carriages to be put into service. It merely allowed the more notorious nineteenth-century examples to be removed from the scene as electrification advanced.

Thus, even more than the SE & CR, the Brighton company came to the Southern system with a very limited range of carriages, and most of these looked distinctly old-fashioned by comparison with those of the LSWR and SE & CR. However, as we have seen, many of them were in fact quite new and, like those of the other Southern constituents, survived well after the grouping and played their part as electrification expanded in the 1920s and 1930s.

In consequence of the widely disparate inheritances acquired by the system in 1923 — and their approximately equal balance in both age and numerical terms — the Southern Railway was not faced with any clear cut options as to future carriage policy. In the event, it followed the path of expediency and economy. Thus, in spite of the mild SE & CR experiment with corridor stock, LSWR practice dominated in the long-distance sphere; in the short distance field, however, all three companies had produced a fair quantity of quite new stock, none of which had any prime claim to consideration. That of the SE & CR was probably the best and that of the LB & SCR probably the most outdated. All had sufficient life left in them for the Southern not to have to spend too much time debating the point, especially when taken together with the complications of electrification — and there we must leave it for the moment.

The Great Western group

Finally we turn in this pre-1923 review of styles to that most idiosyncratic of all British railways, the Great Western, and to those companies which were absorbed into its activities in 1923. 'Absorbed' is not too strong a word to use, for the pre-1923 GWR was dominant in its group in a way unmatched by any other British company. It vied with the LNWR for dominance in the pre-1923 scene, but in route mile terms was undoubtedly 'King', so much so that when the new boundaries were drawn, the GWR group took the name of its largest constituent company. Psychologically, if nothing else, this gave it the edge over its newly formed competitors the LMS, LNER and SR, even though it had to fall to third place in the total hierarchy and last place in the numerical count of carriages owned. It was not often that the GWR came last in anything! However, it had 'history' on its side, a trump card which it played with a monotonous and at times irritating frequency, and not always justified by events, if truth be told.

The trouble with the GWR was that its many and real virtues were marred at times by an apparent inability on its part, or that of its supporters, to see any virtue in anything which did not emanate from the 'fount of all virtue', Swindon Works! Not for nothing was it nicknamed 'God's Wonderful Railway' — there were times when it thought it was. Only the GWR could celebrate its centenary (in 1935) rather less than 100 years after it opened for business — and the whole nonsense was repeated in 1985 with 'GW 150', no less than 37 years *after* the GWR had 'Gone With Regret', as someone put it!

Tongue in cheek though these remarks may be — and, when advanced by rival railways, tinged with not a little envy — they do encapsulate a kind of reality which must be accepted (and understood) if the GWR contribution is to be properly assessed. In this respect the carriage story is no different and, like so many things GW, its twentieth-century story cannot entirely be divorced from the aftermath of the nineteenth-century epic of Brunel and the Broad Gauge, well recorded elsewhere.

Brunel's broad gauge Great Western ran its last trains in 1892 but left three vital elements which were to pervade the twentieth-century story. Firstly it made the GWR *different* from the others, a point of emphasis which still seemed to have a positive virtue to the company even after it had to run its trains on the same 4 ft 8½ in track as everyone else. Secondly, it gave the railway a more generous structure gauge which allowed it to build bigger vehicles, in terms of height and width, than most of its rivals save possibly for the 'Johnny-come-lately' GCR (page 117). Lastly, and possibly of most significance in the twentieth-century context, the genuine sadness with which the 7-foot gauge was consigned to oblivion gave the GWR in the 1890s a once and for all chance of a new beginning which was, realistically, denied to its rivals. I am inclined to believe that the sheer dominance of GWR thinking in the early twentieth-century is not unconnected with a desire on the part of the company itself to prove something, having lost the 'Battle of the Gauges'! That it did most certainly 'prove something' is a matter of historical fact, and one could even draw interesting geo-political comparisons with the economic performance of West Germany and Japan in the aftermath of the 1939-45 disaster. In fact the comparison is not so wide of the mark, for we are back to the 'people' element again, and the GWR had some very strong people.

The first name to quote in the carriage context is William Dean. He had the unenviable task of seeing the GWR through the broad/standard gauge transition, and this meant not only new engines but new coaches as well. He came up with a distinctly clever 'pendulum' type of bogie suspension and some delectably styled clerestory carriages. They owed something to the broad gauge, not least their livery, but in most important aspects they were a new concept. Dean introduced corridors, built a splendid set of new vehicles for Queen Victoria (save for her own saloon whose carcass she insisted on having re-mounted on a new frame!) and, when the GWR moved into the 1900s, Dean had set the company on a new course which it never totally deserted until much later.

The Dean clerestories may have been nineteenth century in concept but they were very much an integral part of the early twentieth-century GWR. Of all the carriages mentioned so far, they probably encapsulate more than any others the essential 'Victorian Inheritance' which was addressed in Chapter 1. Their only serious rivals were probably the LNWR, MR and GNR clerestories, all of which had nineteenth-century origins but considerable twentieth-century ramifications. Roof shape excepted, the architecture of a Dean coach, in the form of the GWR version of traditional British panelling style, became 'standard GW' until the company abandoned raised panel beading strips on its carriages. Interestingly, too, even when the GWR went to an all-metal body covering with 'painted panelling', the actual proportions of the pseudo-panelling were pure Dean!

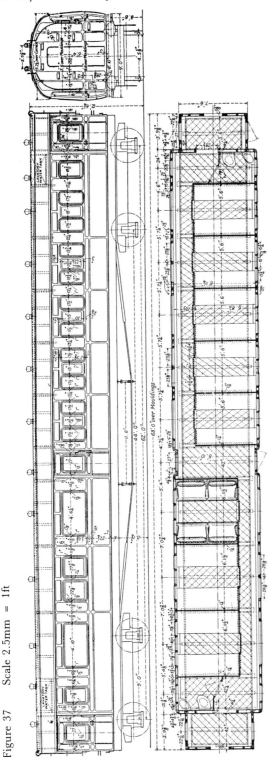

Figure 37   Scale 2.5mm = 1ft

Figure 37 *Great Western 68 ft by 9 ft 6 in 'Dreadnought' corridor composite gives a clear impression of all the significant features in Churchward's huge carriages of 1905. Individual compartment doors were omitted and the carriages given recessed entrances because of the great width. For all its great size, one must note the less than generous compartment dimension between partitions. Moreover, arising from the considerable width, the first class compartments were clearly intended to seat eight rather than the more customary four or six passengers favoured by other railways, and the thirds might even be expected to take five per side at busy times.*

Had it not been for the gigantic nature of his successor, William Dean may have given more credit in the whole business than has come his way, but the man who followed him was George Jackson Churchward. Now Churchward designed locomotives of more than seminal significance but he also put the GWR well to the fore in carriage design. At this range in time, it is a moot point just how much of a particular design concept is personally attributable to the man in charge, but it does seem that Churchward did take a more direct interest than many of his contemporaries. Be as it may, however, what is certain is that shortly after he arrived on the scene, GWR carriage design underwent a quantum change — at least superficially.

Retaining the Dean panelling, Churchward in 1904 superimposed a high elliptical roof and stretched the carriage length to no less than 70 feet and its width to 9 ft 6 in. Not surprisingly, in view of their incredibly massive size by any British standard, then or subsequently, they were known as 'Dreadnoughts', an allusion to a Royal Navy battleship design of the time. In fact, length apart, their absolute dimensions have never been exceeded in British carriage history. Even the modern-day BR MkIII carriage is contained within a sort of standard 9 ft wide by 12 ft 6 in high 'envelope', even though its length is greater.

The 'Dreadnoughts', splendid though they were — and we shall meet them again — went a bit too far for contemporary thought. Their 9 ft 6 in width meant that no company except the GWR would take them, and this, along with the 70 foot length, even caused problems on the GW itself. Churchward therefore tried again, this time with the so-called 'Concertina' approach, a curious and probably rather expensive alternative, whereby a 70 foot coach was combined with entrance doors set back from the main body line. This must have caused horrendous manufacturing complications and, of course, gave rise to the nickname. It was designed to keep the projecting exterior fittings (handles, etc) within the 9 foot width, a more acceptable system-wide standard, and it had some success although it was not universally accepted.

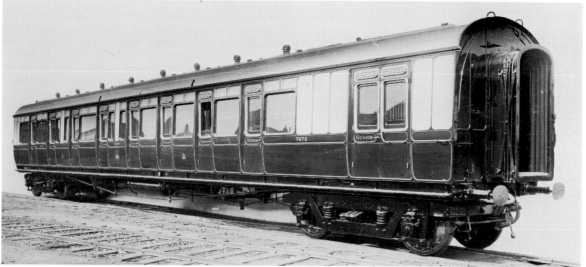

Top *Brake third No 950, photographed ex-works, gives a clear impression of the carriage styling adopted by the GWR under Dean. The more celebrated clerestories embodied the same lower roof shape with its compound curvature. Note particularly the considerable attention to livery and lining detail even on a humble four-wheeler.*

Above *This superb view of 'Concertina' brake composite No 7672 clearly shows the distinctive characteristics of Churchward's second essay into corridor coach construction.*

This sort of 'hit and miss' approach can seem, at times, to be at odds with the normally accepted view of Churchward's sureness of approach, but it was not until he finally gave up some of the delusions of grandeur that he finally arrived at a fairly universally acceptable norm in the shape of his 'Toplight' carriages, so called because of their upper windows in the zone of what would be the eaves panels of many coaches. The LNWR and NER, to mention but two, also tried this idea. The 'Toplight' stock became very characteristic of the pre-1923 GWR, whether in the gangwayed or non-corridor field, and established standards not incompatible with those elsewhere; but they were not perfect. For one thing, Churchward had to yield to pressure and reinstate doors to all the compartments of corridor coaches — a fact which will be further examined in Chapter 10. Secondly, the finished size of a standard 'Toplight' at 56-57 ft × 9 ft or so was not dissimilar to that arrived at by many other British companies which did not have the advantages of the generous GWR structure gauge. True, the 'Toplight' story had started with the 70-foot length, but common sense had to prevail. However, a 56-60 feet long by 9 feet wide carriage was pretty commonplace long before the grouping; at the end, therefore, the GWR was not greatly different.

The GWR further compromised its position by abandoning its distinctive chocolate and cream livery in 1908 during the 'Toplight' period in favour, at first, of an all-brown livery of catastrophic dullness which was only slightly redeemed when, in 1913, it moved to an all-over dark red livery whose shade was about that of the SE & CR or North Staffordshire, but lacked the essential richness of, say, that of the MR or NER. Fortunately, it was redeemed by a fair profusion of gilt lining and embellishment and the overall effect was pleasing. At the same time, one cannot help feeling that the abandonment of the historic chocolate and cream was a foolish thing to

do. The LNWR, for all its economy mindedness, would not, one feels, have so readily abandoned its own 'hallmark' livery and it is not without significance that at the time of the grouping the GWR grasped the nettle and reinstated its famous colour scheme.

Below *The first 'Toplights' retained the 70-foot length, thus allowing no fewer than ten compartments to be fitted into the full third.*

Bottom *The most familiar GWR 'Toplights' were the 57-foot corridors, here represented by one of the 1915 series of thirds, No 3923. By now, the GW had adopted angle-trussed underframes, an idea gradually taken up by most British companies. The carefully applied all-lake livery almost completely hides the fact that this is a flush-sided steel-panelled carriage (T.J. Edgington collection).*

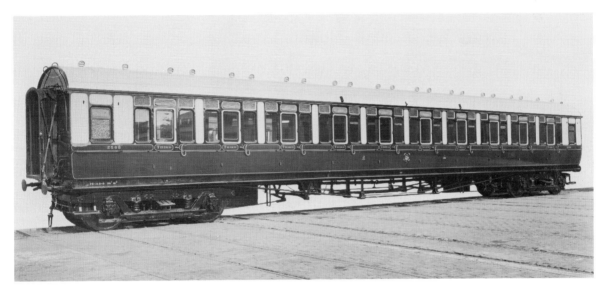

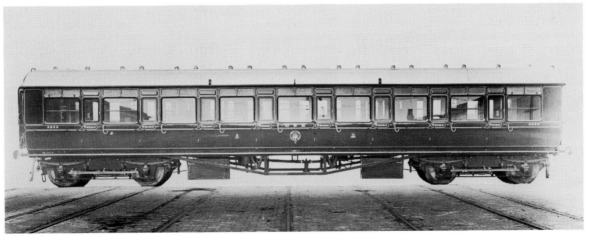

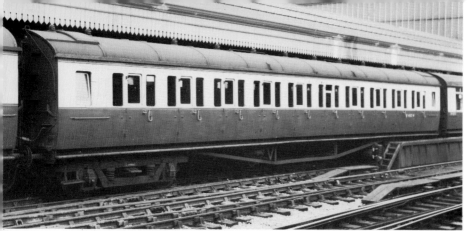

Compared with vehicles produced in the Edwardian era, GWR carriages at the end of the pre-group period became rather uninspired in visual terms. This is one of two somewhat experimental 1924 built 70 ft 8 ¼ in ten-compartment corridor thirds, No 4502 of the early bow-ended era, photographed at Birmingham Snow Hill in 1953. Vehicles of this general style superseded the 'Toplights'.
(T.J. Edgington collection).

This 1938 view on Aldermaston troughs shows three generations of GWR coaches. Leading is a clerestory non-corridor third, followed by a fully panelled 'Toplight' corridor brake composite with a post-grouping flush-sided non-corridor third brake bringing up the rear.

Below The Taff Vale Railway's most noteworthy contribution to carriage development was in the field of the steam railmotor, a concept fully explored in Chapter 15. This view shows one of the 1906 batch, engine unit No 14 with coachwork by Brush of Loughborough.

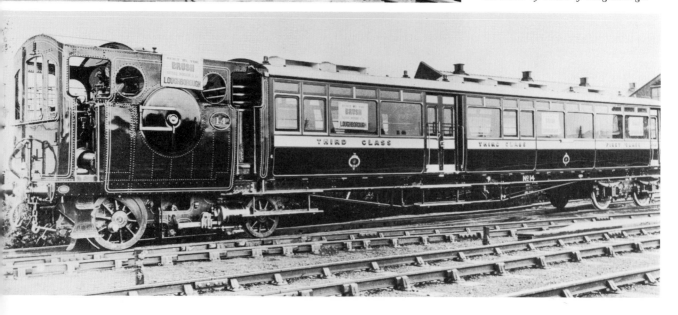

Meanwhile, carriage design itself tended to stagnate on the GWR after the 'Toplights'. There was an interesting and significant move towards steel panelling, replacing the erstwhile wood treatment, but stylistically a sort of dull complacency set in. 'Toplights' continued to be built with the new style steel-panelled treatment, but one gets the feeling, as with locomotive design, that some 20-25 years after the abolition of the broad gauge the GWR began to rest on its laurels and did not really take a subsequent firm grip on the situation until well after the grouping. What is certain is that other railways caught up and passed the GWR during the 1920s and 1930s in many respects, a point which will be taken up in more detail in the next volume.

Nevertheless, sheer size of operation decreed that the GWR influence would dominate after 1923, regardless of any inherent complacency, so it only remains to be seen what, if anything, its smaller constituent companies had to offer. The 1921 statistics for the '100-plus-route-mile' railways tend, in this context, to be all revealing in terms of passenger carrying vehicles:

GWR	5646
Cambrian	221
Taff Vale	316
Total	6183

Even if one adds even smaller concerns like the Barry Railway or the Rhymney Railway, their influence seems hardly likely to have been profound — and so it turned out to be.

We have already seen that even where one of the 'Big Four' such as the LMS or LNER absorbed several quite large fleets, the fate of the 'small fry' was pretty well guaranteed to a sort of oblivion. Only the Southern Railway showed signs of registering the nature of all its constituents, and it really had no 'small fry'. The GWR was diametrically opposite. All of its constituents could be catergorized as 'small fry', and they had no chance at all. Their eclipse was rapid and total, and in the long-term sense their influence on subsequent GWR thinking was utterly negligible They were, indeed, 'absorbed' in every sense of the word.

The Taff Vale was the largest numerically; but who, giving due respect to the sensitivities of the South Wales area, has ever seriously regarded the Taff Vale Railway as having had anything positive to contribute to the GWR, let alone the British carriage story? Even the trio of Highland TPOs is better known! This is very unfair, really, for the TVR had the longest independent history of the GWR constituents, its story going back to 1840. It did, however, in its later years, display a quite characteristic body style of by no means unpleasing aspect. Most of its carriages, though purchased from contractors, were, in fact designed by itself, and at Cathays, Cardiff, it possessed a works facility which even BR found to be of value. It adopted a similar livery to that of the GWR (chocolate and white) and in one respect was distinctive in that the upper panel beading was not always coloured black or to match the lower body panels (the normal British approach), but was simply picked out in the lining colour. It was an early user of a high elliptical roof and quite a pioneer in the steam railmotor business (see Chapter 15) but most of its carriages soon vanished. What is perhaps most surprising is that in converted form, its railmotors survived to BR days as sort of ersatz corridor thirds!

The Cambrian, alone of the small constituents of the GWR in 1923, could claim to be a genuine all-purpose railway. It showed distinct affinities with its Celtic contemporaries such as the Furness, Highland or even the GNSR — and its fate was not dissimilar. It was ignored! In stylistic terms it employed traditional panelling with an arc roof profile of somewhat Caledonian aspect. Apart from a fairly mandatory quota of conventional four-wheel and six-wheel carriages, it possessed a fair number of better vehicles such as saloons, lavatory stock and even the odd corridor coach. In fact, because of its geography, it probably possessed proportionally rather more of the better quality carriages than some of its contemporaries, but all to no avail. Its livery was quite distinctive (bronze green and 'white', later all-over green) but there is no evidence that its specific requirements loomed large after 1923. As a totally irrelevant aside, one of its more maverick acquisitions was the purchase, via the Highland Railway as agents, of the Duke of Sutherland's saloon, built in late Victorian days. The Duke had obtained in 1900 a new and opulent vehicle from Wolverton (now preserved by the NRM) and his slightly older saloon was therefore sold to the Cambrian for some reason. It became in due course GWR saloon No 9215, but in 1925 was relegated to 'fruit and parcels' status and was scrapped in 1931. This, of course, proves nothing, but is one of the many and various items of minutiae which the study of carriage history reveals.

As for the 'less than 100 route mile' constituents of the GWR, there were quite a number of them, but their influence was in all honesty peripheral to non-existent. The Barry Railway, quite a prosperous little concern, had some nice dark red carriages with electric lighting and automatic vacuum brakes but never bothered to provide carriage heating! Even so, one or two survived into BR days. A definitive history describes the Rhymney Railway as that which would

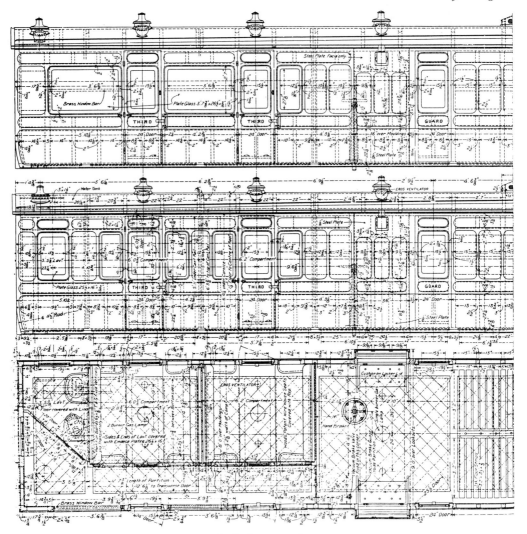

Scale 5mm = 1ft

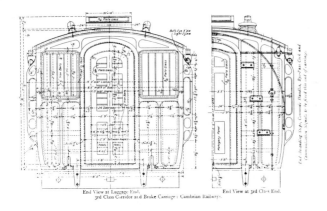

End View at Luggage End.
End View at 3rd Class End.
3rd Class Corridor and Brake Carriage : Cambrian Railways.

Figure 38 *The neat but hardly innovative carriage styling of the Cambrian Railway is well represented by these drawings of a corridor third brake of 1908 vintage. The central lookout is somewhat unusual and the large van suggests a form of dual purpose role. Designed as through carriages, they could clearly carry much more than the luggage of the dozen or so passengers who could be accommodated. The drain holes in the van floor suggest milk traffic (ie to cope with any accidental spillage).*

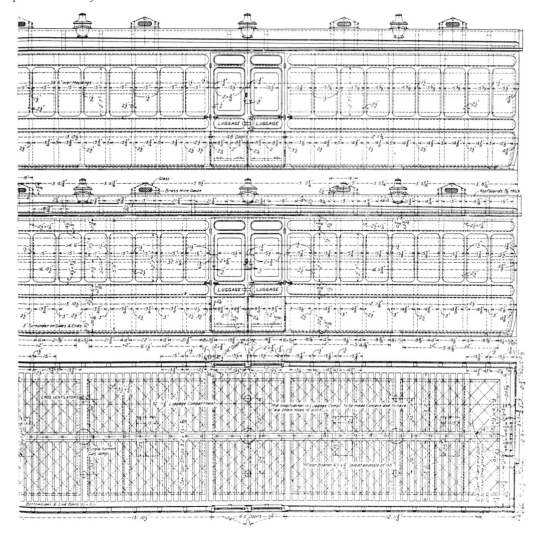

'never be described as having carriage stock that would have raised the enthusiasm of the weary traveller over its lines'! Even so, its own-design vehicles were of more than uncommonly neat outline with somewhat MR/GSWR visual overtones of the nineteenth-century kind, and a few survived to BR, generally those examples which were mounted on bogies. It was, *en passant,* the only GWR constituent to employ the Westinghouse brake and it adopted a rather attractive red and cream livery, later all red; but it signified nothing.

All told, therefore, it cannot be a source of any surprise that the 'greater' GWR, after 1923, chose to ignore any contribution made by its constituents, be it in locomotive or carriage affairs. It was in all senses rather inevitable and something of a foregone

conclusion. This had curious side effects after 1922. The GWR had gained so much of its own way at the grouping that it was probably less aware than the remainder of the 'Big Four' companies of the virtues of combining the experience of its various constituents. The LMS undoubtedly gained from an amalgamation of the carriage building experiences of its various larger companies as, in a different sense, did the LNER. We have also seen how the SR had to reconcile the disparate requirements of its trunk route constituent (LSWR) with those of its tightly-knit suburban partners; but the GWR sailed serenely on — or so it seemed. That it fell on its face in carriage terms during the 1920s must await Part II to analyse fully. The GWR was a magnificent railway, but in one sense the grouping did it no

Left *The later Rhymney Railway bogie vehicles lasted extremely well. This is third class No W1099W, built at Caerphilly in 1921 as RR No 58, still in service in 1954. It had an open interior with two saloons and far fewer than normal the number of outside doors for its time. The styling has a sort of GSWR look to it but the vertical sides were a distinctive, if not unique, RR feature (T.J. Edgington).*

Below right *Cheshire Lines carriages were either of GNR or GCR style. This stylish lavatory composite No 313, of typical GNR outline was built in 1911. Interior views of a similar vehicle can be seen on page 55.*

Bottom right *Like the GNR, the GCR also built spacious carriages for the CLC. This is composite No 9 of 1914 with only seven compartments in a 53-foot length. Note that CLC carriages wore the livery of the company which built them. This one is finished in post-1910 GCR style.*

favours. It was, in a phrase, too dominant by far for its own good — and therein lies the clue to the post-1922 story.

The Joint railways

It now only remains to consider the carriages of the various joint railways as they were contituted during the first quarter of the century. Effectively there were but three significant systems, the Cheshire Lines Committee, and the Midland and Great Northern and Somerset and Dorset Joint Railways.

Of the three, one of them tended towards its own design of carriages (S & DJR) while the others seemed quite content to accept the carriage designs of their owning partners. The CLC was a tri-partite concern whose owners were the GCR (formerly the MS & LR), the GNR and the MR. The M & GN was self-descriptive in ownership terms while the S & DJR was a Midland/LSWR operation. It is with the CLC, the most prosperous of the three, that we start the analysis.

The Cheshire Lines company was badly described, for much of the system was not based in Cheshire. The main artery was an alternative route between Liverpool and Manchester, and although owned by three railways the carriage stock was provided by but two of them, the GNR and GCR. The statistical summaries in the previous chapter reveal the considerable intensity of use to which the CLC was put and the carriages were dominantly of the suburban kind. In effect they mirrored contemporary

company style, be it GNR or GCR, and after grouping the system continued in joint ownership, two-thirds LNER and one-third LMS. In all conscience, and notwithstanding the fact that the CLC carried a high volume of presumably remunerative traffic, its influence on carriage design was almost non-existent.

The other two joint lines were not dissimilar, and only in one case (S & DJR) were some small original contributions made to carriage design. The M & GN was marginally the bigger of the two but in carriage terms it was utterly insignificant. During much of the twentieth century and well into the LNER/LMS ownership period, it tended to make use of 'hand me down' carriages from the parent systems. Its independent history as a fully fledged joint line went back no further than 1893 when it was first incorporated, so not surprisingly its carriages were not exactly epoch-making and nothing bigger than a six-wheeler was owned before 1923, or for a few years after for that matter. Much stock was of GNR pattern but there were some residual survivors from those companies which had preceded the M & GN and, according to H.C. Casserley[*] it had never had any new passenger coaches built for its own use at any time. Its livery was varnished teak (GN-type stock) or Midland red (MR-type and other stock).

By contrast with the CLC and M & GN, the Somerset and Dorset Joint Railway did have its own carriages, built new for the system and liveried in

[*]Britain's Joint Lines, Ian Allan, 1968.

a distinctive blue shade reserved to itself rather than simply aping the style(s) of the parent system(s). The vehicles were more closely allied to the nineteenth-century Midland styling of the pre-clerestory Clayton period than anything else but were not necessarily pure carbon copies, even in the arc roof period. However, later S & DJR carriages were fairly distinctive. They were mostly 46-foot bogie vehicles (plus a few six-wheelers) which combined Clayton's round-cornered traditional pre-1896 MR panelling style with a fairly high flattened elliptical roof profile of almost pure LSWR shape. They were all non-corridors, some with lavatories, and it was quite surprising how the mere change of roof profile could impart such a difference in overall appearance to what was, basically, a Midland type of carriage; but thus it was.

Conclusion

I am conscious that, lengthy though this review of the 1901-22 position has been, it has scarcely scratched the surface of a very complex situation, but I hope that a few basic trends have emerged, even though many small railways have been all but ignored and even the larger ones given only a brief consideration. However, unlike locomotives where one can occasionally discern truly epoch-making designs whose influence often transcended company boundaries (Churchward's on the GWR for example), there were few if any pre-1923 carriage trends which turned out to be way above the competition, even if superficial appearances seemed to suggest otherwise.

This is not to say that there were no patterns to

Top *M & GN six-compartment composite No 56 typifies the better 'native' stock of this long-gone system. The excessive end overhang of the body was a common M & GN practice with six-wheelers, presumably to keep the wheelbase within the acceptable geometry for the track curvature. Even so, the lateral displacement incurred at the carriage end — see also page 19 — was considerable, and the carriage was probably uncomfortable in consequence.*

Above *'Nineteenth-century Midland panelling with twentieth-century LSWR roofs' is an apt description of the styling of most Somerset and Dorset carriages of the present century, but the guard's lookout was most un-Midland. This is 46-foot brake third No 100; the early use of colour-sensitive photographic material enables the layout of the all-blue livery with its black and gold lined mouldings to stand out clearly.*

be observed. Churchward's work on the GWR clearly laid the foundation of all post-1922 developments on that system and, as we have seen, Gresley and the GNR proved dominant on the East Coast. The LMS developed a highly consistent house style in the 1920s based essentially on Midland exterior treatment allied to LNWR interior layout, while the Southern, in so far as it standardized at all, took its main lead from the LSWR. Within these broad stylistic outlines, however, there was much variety to be witnessed within the carriage walls, so to speak, and it took quite some time for even the post-1922 companies to settle down. In part, this was more than a little the consequence of the bewildering variety of carriage layouts favoured by even the smaller companies, which topic it will be the object of the next few chapters to analyse.

8. All stations

We have seen in the first chapter how the characteristic British non-corridor compartment coach evolved from the stagecoach in the 1830s, stagnated for the best part of half a century and was eventually supplemented by the more specialized late Victorian vehicles which formed the basis of twentieth-century development. However, it is important to remember that at the start of our period by far the largest number of passenger carriages were still of the traditional compartment type. Thus, although the age of the more specialized carriage for medium and long-distance trains had dawned, they had by no means fully taken over even on the most prestigious workings, and compartment coaches were most likely to be found in the vast majority of trains, no matter what the distance travelled.

Now, it is conventional wisdom that the non-corridor coach was the characteristic vehicle for the 'stopping at all stations' suburban and local trains. Well, it did for the most part become just that, during the twentieth century, but it should not be thought for a moment that this was its only role. Many late nineteenth century 'expresses', not to mention a few twentieth-century ones, were composed of non-corridor stock. However, having entered this important caveat, it will be convenient to divide the analysis in this and the next few chapters along the lines of customary twentieth-century usage, starting with the most basic and traditional form of non-corridor carriage — ie that without even the refinement of a lavatory.

Such carriages all derived from the fundamental 'three-box' four-wheeler whose origins go back to 1830, but by the end of Victoria's reign quite a few variations had occurred in length, interior accommodation, comfort, heating, lighting and so on, so a few more definitions will not be out of place. Normally a carriage was referred to by class of accommodation offered, first, second or third. Should a carriage have two classes of compartment then it was known as a 'composite'. In this group, the 1st/3rd mix was the most common, especially as many railways had abandoned second class, or did so during the first twenty years of the century. However, 1st/2nd or 2nd/3rd composites could also be seen, and if all three categories appeared then it was known as a tri-composite.

Those carriages which carried a handbrake and guard's compartment were known as 'brake' carriages; normally two were found in any train and one was always mandatory if passengers were to be carried (see also Chapter 2, page 28). The brake carriage could be exclusively occupied, guard's equipment excepted, by empty space for luggage, parcels and so on, in which case it was known as a 'full brake' or 'passenger full brake'. The word 'passenger' in this context was inserted to denote *not* that the vehicle carried people but that it could operate in a passenger train. Quite regularly — in fact more commonly — a brake carriage would incorporate passenger-carrying compartments as well as that for the guard and handbrake, in which case it was referred to as a 'brake third' or whatever, depending on the class(es) of compartments provided in addition to the guard/brake space. The latter accommodation could vary in size between the minimum space necessary — often no bigger than a normal compartment — to a quite capacious loading area for luggage and the like. This space was often known as the 'van' portion because of its general resemblance to the interior of a goods van. The size of the van portion often revealed the nature of the train, in that long-distance services would, in the natural order of things, need more luggage and parcels space than a short-haul suburban train.

Sometimes one could see carriages which looked superficially like brake coaches in that they possessed a windowless luggage space as well as passenger seats. However, if this was simply a luggage compartment, 'box' or 'locker' (all these terms were used) without any guard/handbrake facility, then it was a 'luggage third', 'locker composite' or some such.

Supervening these basic descriptions related to usage were the generic terms applicable to vehicle configuration in such matters as wheels or roof profile. Thus, as an extreme example one could theoretically have such a creature as a 'bogie clerestory luggage tri-composite brake'. It would still be as much a non-corridor compartment coach as the humble four-wheel ordinary third class coach with a nearly flat roof and bare-board seats.

Of all the possible permutations of length, accommodation and so forth, the most common by far was the humble third class, closely followed by the brake third. There were, in fact, a lot of brake carriages, most of them third class, largely because of the common practice observed by many railways of assembling their vehicles in semi-permanent 'sets' of carriages, three to six being most typical. Each 'set' customarily would have at least two brakes, and since there was an amazingly large number of these fixed formations, almost as many brake carriages were being built as non-braked versions. In point of fact, the great fondness of many railways for 'set' trains could become a dominant factor in the actual planning and building of carriages.

The chief virtue of the non-corridor third class compartment coach was its 'sardine can'-like capability for absorbing lots of people and loading them quickly. Not only did each compartment have a pair of facing seats along which sitting passengers could be packed, but there was also just enough space between the seats for a third row of 'standees' at busy times. Times were often busy, trains were often well used and crowding was not at all uncommon, so the additional fact that every compartment had its own door made this really quite unpleasant form of transportation additionally favoured by the railways, solely because there were so many doors available that they could be loaded, and unloaded expeditiously.

This was not the only reason the railways liked them; they were also cheap to build and, size for size, offered more passenger seats per ton weight of carriage than any other option. This point merits further amplification. If one takes a typical five-compartment six-wheel third class carriage of the type very common at the start of our period and typically weighing around 12 tons, it could absorb 50-60 seated passengers and at least another 20-30 standing customers for a dead weight of well under 5 cwt per passenger when fully loaded. A bogie corridor coach of broadly similar carrying capacity and fitted with lavatories as well could easily at least double this figure. This meant bigger and more powerful engines, thus more capital investment and higher motive power costs, not to mention the extra vehicle costs as well.

For many purposes, until forced into doing something better, there was every incentive for the railways to pack people in and keep carriage weights down. This they did to a remarkable degree. Because four-wheelers and six-wheelers were cheap to build and showed these better 'passenger to weight' ratios than did bogie carriages, their construction continued unabated for a while. If a railway could somehow

build carriages to take six per side in the third class (rather than five) without serious weight penalty then it did so. In fact, the GER even found it expedient to cut a lot of its carriages down the centre, splice in an extra foot width and put them back on the same chassis solely to get more seats without increasing train length and with very little increase in weight.

Other railways took the view that the closer you could make the distance between compartment partitions, the more of them you get per foot length of vehicle, and some very intimately sized horrors emerged in consequence. A fairly reasonable size for a third class compartment was some six feet between partitions. This allowed a 2 feet wide door between two seats, each of which occupied the space between door and partition. Five of them would just nicely complete a 30-foot vehicle, but some railways elected to put six *five-foot wide* compartments into the same space — or something equally spartan in space terms. Each compartment was still expected to carry the same number of people and on some of the more impoverished lines one could expect to have to travel quite some distance in them.

It is, of course, generally accepted that these miserably small compartments were not untypical of Victorian railways, but more than a few companies continued building them well into this century. Amongst the more notorious practitioners were the otherwise highly respected LB & SCR and GNR, neither of which donated too many favours in terms of space to the poor old third class non-corridor customer. We have seen how the GNR was dragged reluctantly into the twentieth century in terms of carriage design and eventually produced some gangwayed long-distance masterpieces — but tell that to the homeward bound traveller going to Hertford or Potters Bar! Mind you, if he was served by the North London Railway or Great Eastern he would not fare any better as many a vile four-wheeler continued to testify as it bumped and jolted its weary

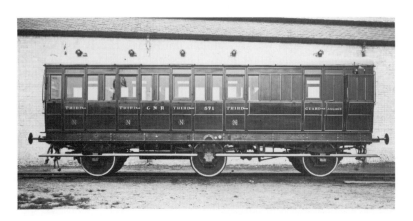

GNR brake third No 571, although built in the late 1890s, was typical of the basic and spartan suburban third class carriage at the start of the century. Over 300 were built, the ten-seat compartments were only about 5 feet between partitions, yet, astonishingly, this one remained in service until 1946!

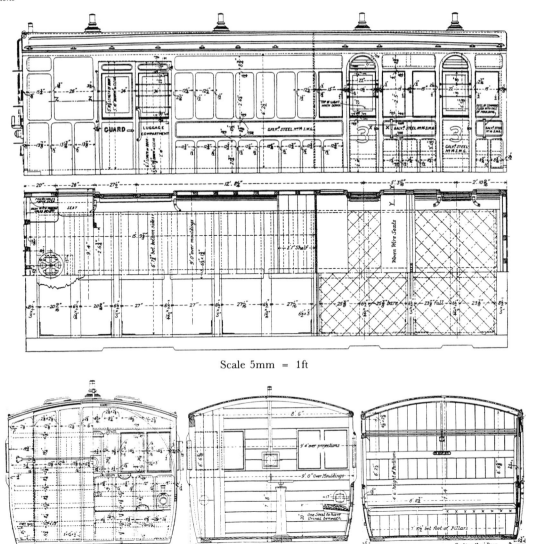

Scale 5mm = 1ft

Figure 39 *Early in the twentieth century, as well as widening older vehicles the GER also built some so-called 'wide' suburban carriages. This 1902 drawing reveals the rabbit-hutch-like quality of a brake third of this miserable four-wheel series. The use of galvanized steel panelling in some areas was adventurous but there is little else save cheapness to commend it.*

This NER elliptical roof carriage seen at Scarborough, is correctly described as a 'luggage composite' with three firsts and four thirds.

Top *Later in the twentieth century the GER joined together pairs of wide arc roof suburbans to make bogie carriages. This view shows an Enfield-bound suburban train composed entirely of such re-builds.*

Above *Like the GER (and many others), the LYR also carried vast numbers of passengers but generally gave them rather more breathing space; these views show typical examples. Third class brake No 1979 had bogies and approximately 6-foot compartments even in the early 1890s, and when the company was forced into something bigger, its elliptical roof ten-compartment thirds like No 3290 were at least 60 feet long. The latter vehicle is finished in works grey (see also the picture on page 71) and is gas-lit.*

way through the London suburbs.

Nor was it only a matter of space. Seats were not exactly renowned for comfort either, and this was not just in consequence of the interlocking nature of opposing feet and knees in the cramped compartments! The seats were frequently thinly cushioned with little more than a modest concession to a neck rest and were regularly full of dirt. A slightly more hygenic option — but hardly the acme of comfort — was the slatted wood seat. This railborne equivalent of a park bench is generally supposed to have been confined to that strange and relatively unknown phenomenon the 'workmen's' train — it had something to do with not transmitting dirt from greasy overalls, as it was once said. Well, it may have been, but if so there must have been a great number of greasy-overalled workmen in the most unlikely workplaces if the carriages were any indication!

Then there was the 'toffee paper, chewing gum and tobacco trap' — that thoroughly unpleasant and almost inaccessible gap between the rear of the seat itself and the base of the seat back. It would not have been so bad had there been any real aesthetic pleasure in observing the 'decor' of the compartment itself, but it seemed that visual self-denial was to be added to physical discomfort on many of our railways. Institutional cream or off-white paint was regularly married to matchboard casing boards to produce an interior of the most depressingly Dickensian nature, by no means redeemed by the occasional picture (if

you were lucky) or the generally poor quality of the lights.

Clearly, the early twentieth-century railways

Below *The NLR has received more than a few barbed comments in these pages, and these pictures may help to explain why. Composite No 18 dates from 1875 so its spartan nature, with only two lamps shared between three second class compartments, might be expected. However, it was still in use when the all-third No 245 was built in 1906 — five compartments, no change in style and still only three lamps! Note, too, the subtle class distinction on the outer doors — full heraldry on the firsts, elaborate monogram on the seconds, plain '3's' on the thirds. Astonishingly, they trundled on into the 1930s.*

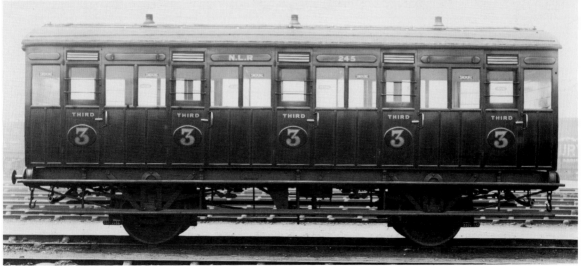

reckoned that the third class passenger's eyesight was twice as good as that of his second or first class contemporary, so they gave him only half as many lights. It was not (usually) back to the old one light per two compartments, uncomfortably puckered into a sort of hole in the compartment partition below the ceiling, but it was not much better. If you were lucky you would perhaps get one of the newfangled electric light bulbs whose wattage was obviously the lowest which was capable of manufacture. If the dynamo was not too good and the batteries a bit flat, you were in trouble. However, it is a moot point whether the romantic-sounding gas alternative was any better. Not for the humble third class suburban passenger the glories of the chandelier. If, as was often the case, the compartment partitions did not go fully to the roof, lighting provision could often get even worse!

That there were alternatives was demonstrated by a few more enterprising railways. The newly formed GCR had some very nice suburban carriages, the LNWR, not always famed for its lavish provisioning in the Victorian period, generally gave its early twentieth-century third class passengers a more or less standard 6-foot compartment, albeit in a somewhat old-fashioned looking vehicle, while up in the North of England, the NER's carriages were better than most, but then it did have David Bain

Figure 40 *The GCR demonstrated that not all London area services needed to be operated by cramped vehicles. This 1907 drawing shows a very well thought out third class brake — not quite as elegant as the GCR clerestories (see page 117) but more than adequate, nonetheless.*

in charge at the start of the century. Even the oft-maligned LYR had probably more suburban bogie coaches, *pro rata*, than most companies and, as we have seen, did provide more than generously in terms of seats per passenger.

If, however, one can single out one particular type of carriage in this category which stood out above the rest it was probably the Midland's bogie clerestories which were being built right across the turn of the century. They were non-corridor and non-lavatory but, this apart, their internal space was every bit as good as on the main line with 6 ft 6 in as the third class compartment size and usually at least 7 ft 6 in for the firsts. The trouble was that there were not enough of them and they had to run cheek by jowl with some of the Midland's earlier stock which, in the case of the late Victorian four-wheelers for the Metropolitan line services, were every bit as dreadful as those of the GNR, GER and NLR, having 5 ft 2 in thirds and *five*-a-side firsts in an 8 ft 6 in wide body!

These non-corridor bogie clerestories were only built for a year or two but had the curious effect of helping to brand the Midland, quite incorrectly, as a clerestory railway. Basically, however, their form of construction was too expensive and their finish rather too elaborate to be really justifiable in the short-haul context. Soon after his arrival on the scene in 1903, David Bain, for all his continuance of good quality carriages in the long-distance field, pretty soon put a stop to this extravagance in the suburban category and reverted to the cheaper-to-build arc roof style with considerably smaller compartments; but

Scale 3mm = 1ft

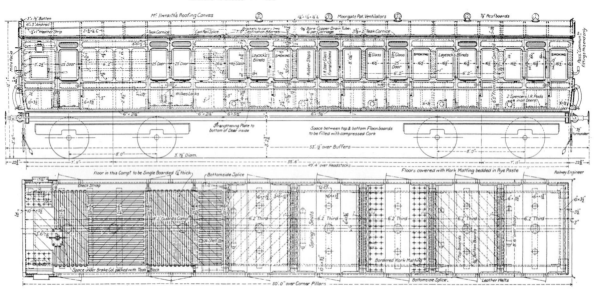

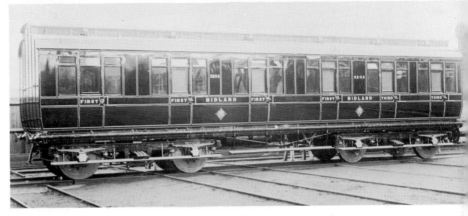

Above *Another more agreeable third class carriage in space terms was this nine-compartment NBR example of 1914, one of more than a hundred such. Interestingly, the nine-compartment third on a length of some 54-57 feet became a quite customary minimum standard for such vehicles on many railways, both before and after the railway grouping in 1923.*

Right *The best of the non-corridor breed? This is a standard 45-foot Midland clerestory suburban composite No 3205 of 1902. Its third class compartments were each 6 ft 6 in between partitions and its firsts 7 ft 9 in, both enhanced by the high clerestory roof*

they were nonetheless bogie coaches rather than six-wheelers, and were at least 8 ft 6 in wide. However, the clerestories had shown what could be done, and lucky indeed were the commuters in places like the West Riding of Yorkshire where the Midland and its LMS successor chose to operate a large proportion of them for many years.

Thus far, the discussion has concentrated heavily on the conditions of travel for the third class passenger, for he indeed was the main source of railway revenue in the short-distance field as Chapter 6 has already demonstrated. However, during most of the pre-grouping era, second class passengers were carried by many of the bigger railways and, of course, all of them provided first class carriages.

There is a certain degree of ambiguity about the position of the second class carriage during this period of railway history. It was certainly of declining importance but, nevertheless, certain lines clung to it with a degree of tenacity which its basic quality may scarce have deserved. When the Midland pioneered two class only travel in the 1870s by being the first system to abandon second class, it was also its declared intention to make its own third class as good as everyone else's second class. This, for the most part, it managed to achieve, and by the start

of our period there can be no doubt that except for those extreme cases of the third class 'dog boxes' already described, many railways had managed to produce quite a number of third class vehicles distinguishable from the second class only by virtue of the different designation on the doors.

At best, the second class passenger could expect little extra in the way of comfort over that provided in a decently upholstered third. There would be, perhaps, an official edict that one less passenger per side of the compartment should be conveyed (one wonders how often *that* was observed at busy times) and, in the better cases, this would be made more probable of achievement by inserting an arm rest somewhere along the length of the seat, thus reducing a five per side capacity to four, or some such. But that would be about all. If he was very lucky, the second class passenger might even get a slightly softer seat or better quality upholstery cloth, but there was not the real quantum difference between second and third class that there was between either of them and the first class carriages operated by most railways which were in most cases quite genuinely superior. In fact, when those railways which still had three classes of carriage finally abandoned second class, it was normal for them to simply downgrade the erst-

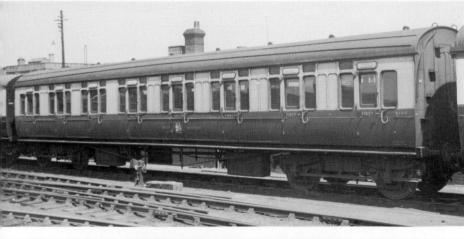

Left *In 1908, the GWR built twenty superb 60-foot 'Toplight' non-corridor firsts with no more than eight compartments, each seating eight. They were typical of the best British first class practice at the time, albeit larger than most. Such was their quality that more than forty years later they were still in first class service. This is No 8199 at Birmingham Snow Hill in 1950* (T.J. Edgington collection).

Centre left and below left *The LB & SCR 'Balloon' brake firsts of 1905 were certainly in the first rank, albeit only three in number. The exterior view shows No 27, the first of the series, containing only six seats in each of the four spacious 8 ft 6 in by 7 ft 3 in compartments; the interior view of a similar carriage shows what the passenger could expect to find when he boarded such a vehicle.*

Below right *High-capacity eight-compartment 70-foot 'Toplight' GWR brake third of 1913 marked up as 'Birmingham Division 5', its fixed set number. Note the painted panelling* (T.J. Edgington collection).

while seconds to thirds, and one doubts if many folk noticed much change. I am inclined to believe, therefore, that the perpetuation of the second class in the non-corridor field was, yet again, another example of the way in which the railway carriage related closely to the people who used it. There was a simultaneous element of both snobbery and economy about the second class carriage, and in some places it died hard.

As far as can be judged, two main groups of people used the second class. Firstly were the 'upwardly mobile' and growing middle classes. By travelling second class they asserted their better status over the hoi polloi — or maybe thought they did. Presumably one travelled with a better class of person in every sense of the word if one bought a second class season ticket! The retention of second class on the LNER in the London area until 1937 was, in fact, so as to provide a special class for season ticket holders. Secondly were those travellers who would, perhaps, travel first class on a long distance train but chose to travel second for reasons of economy. Presumably they *could* afford first class but chose to use their not inconsiderable spending power in other ways — or maybe the journey was too short for it to matter anyway. Furthermore, it was and still is characteristic of quite a few wealthy people *not* to be too liberal with their disbursements. That is how some of them became rich to start with and why so many of them managed to stay that way!

Be that as it may, the second class seems to have suffered erosion at both extremities of the social scale as the years went by and continued to decline. Interestingly, there has been a sort of contemporary replay of this phenomenon in more modern days (since the 1960s) with the gradual removal of the *first* class option altogether from many short-distance trains which are now very egalitarian one-class-only operations.

Sociologists may read what they may into the above analysis, but of one thing we can be certain, the first class carriage of the early part of the century was, almost always, exactly what it claimed to be. Very few railways failed to offer a distinctly superior conveyance for their up-market customers and there was, in truth, probably little to choose in quality between the best samples from any of them. Every passenger would normally have his own seating area defined by padded armrests and frequently by headrests as well. There would be a carpet on the floor, adequate lighting, beautiful detail treatment in the woodwork and often curtains and pictures too. There would rarely be more than three per side in an 8 feet wide carriage, or four at the most in a 9 feet vehicle, and if the compartments were much less than 7 feet between partitions, the company concerned was beginning to look distinctly parsimonious. In fact, corridors and lavatories excepted, there was little to choose between the first class compartments of ordinary non-corridor stock and that of the longer-distance equivalent.

There were, of course, a few exceptions in which the first class was not much better than the better second class offerings of those railways which retained three types, but in general, whether it be on four, six, eight or even twelve wheels, the first class non-corridor coach was no bad way to get to the office if you could afford the fare — and many could.

By the mid-Edwardian period, although vast numbers of suburban carriages were of the four-wheel or six-wheel type, there was gradually dawning a slow realization that bogie carriages were the way forward and most new building took this form. Noteworthy in this respect were, south of the Thames, the LSWR and SE & CR, both of which managed to introduce some really quite worthy carriages on their suburban services. North of the river, we have already noted the LNWR, MR and GCR, but what of the others? Well, the GWR went from almost the sublime to the ridiculous in the Birmingham area, changing rapidly from flat or clerestory roofed Dean-style four and six-wheelers (with a few bogies thrown in) to the non-corridor version of the 70 foot 'Toplights'. Their load-absorbing capacity was formidable. Even the brake thirds, for example, had no fewer than eight compartments, could seat 96 and possibly pack in 50 or more standing passengers as well.

Meanwhile, further north in Scotland, several railways leapt abruptly from spartan short carriages to quite gigantic bogie non-corridors, and the Caledonian, GSWR and NBR even put some of them on twelve wheels. Sadly, the HR and GNSR could not afford such grandiloquent gestures and neither could some of the smaller English or Welsh concerns, but, for the most part, one can at least say that the railways were trying harder than they had been. In part this was because they were facing real competition for the first time, and lest this statement should seem to be at odds with a railway network operated by apparently competing private

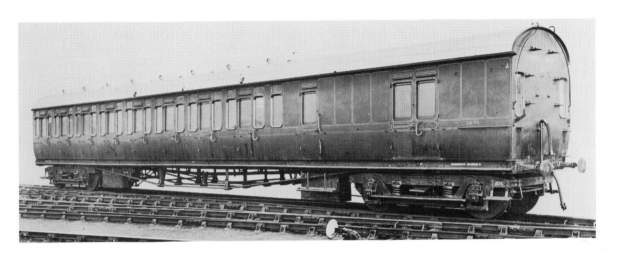

Another high-capacity suburban design — the Caledonian twelve-wheel non-corridors for its 'Glasgow and Edinburgh Direct' service in 1905 — seen here branded thus in the eaves panels as part of the livery treatment. The two eight-compartment third brakes and the nine-compartment full first seated 192 and 72 respectively.

companies, a few words of explanation are needful.

In the suburban field, the companies mostly enjoyed semi-territorial monopolies close in to the cities, quite unlike the longer-distance situation. Thus, while one could, for example, choose any one of four railways to take you from, say, London to Manchester (LNWR, GCR, MR, GNR), if you lived in the inner or outer suburbs, the chances were that you had only one of the competing companies within sensible walking distance of your home, whether you were a resident of the London region or any of the several industrial conurbations. In these circumstances, the only thing which could really change the situation as far as short-distance passenger comfort and convenience was concerned was a viable alternative *system* to the railway itself — and this is precisely what happened. It was called the street tramway.

The rapid growth and cheap operating costs of the electrified street tramways in the early part of the present century gave the complacent railways a considerable fright, and one can detect a very close correlation between the improved carriage stock already mentioned and the areas most affected by the new threat. Obviously, there were some kinds of service offered by the tramways (and later by the motor bus) which the railways could not match, but where the trams threatened to cream off more than

just the very short-distance passengers, then the railways responded either with better carriages or better services, sometimes both.

It was not, of course, quite as simple as that, for some railways had invested quite heavily in what were fast becoming outmoded vehicles only a few years before the perceived need to improve matters. In many cases, some considerable improvement could be effected by mounting two carriage bodies of what had thus far been two separate four or six-wheelers on to one new bogie underframe. As far as can be ascertained, this method was probably pioneered by the LNWR in 1895 when it did just this for the benefit of the reigning monarch, no less! This result may still be seen at the National Railway Museum and the idea quickly spread, though mainly confined thereafter to non-corridor stock.

However, there was one noteworthy and different approach to the problem of getting a better ride quality without the expense of scrapping fairly new four and six-wheelers. This was the particular *métier* of the GNR in the person of Nigel Gresley who, rather than put two bodies on to one bogie underframe, began to employ articulation to get the same effect. Anything between two and five vehicles could thus be joined together utilizing only one more bogie than the number of carriage body units in the formation. It did nothing to improve the often spartan quality of the interior compartment accommodation offered but undoubtedly made the otherwise spine-shattering progress better! Articulation also gave the means whereby a further lease of life could be given to redundant but still quite new steam railmotor bodies (see Chapter 15) and also allowed some of the better long-distance six-wheel and rigid eight-wheel carriage bodies to carry on in

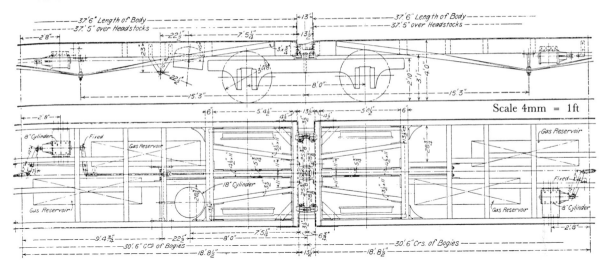

Figure 41 *Drawing of Gresley's articulated system as applied in 1908 to a pair of 37 ft 6 in carriages and utilizing the older GNR-type bogie.*

main-line service longer than might otherwise have been the case.

The problem with articulation was that if one bogie became defective, it put the whole set out of operation. If there was only a pair of vehicle bodies involved it might not be too bad, but if the ensemble was a four or five-unit formation, it could be serious and sometimes was. Nevertheless, the sheer weight-saving obviously persuaded Gresley to persevere for

Below *The picture on page 119 depicted the first quite typical form of articulation for older Howden stock. This view shows No 2116, a 'triplet composite brake' conversion in 1912 from three former six-wheelers, brake third, composite and full third, all dating from the 1890s.*

Bottom *Gresley's first purpose-built articulated carriages (as opposed to conversions) had elliptical roofs with old-style bogies. This is twin brake third No 3256 of 1912, still frightfully cramped with compartments no more than about 5 ft 3 in between partitions, each, however, now seating a dozen passengers because of the greater width. This pair were reformed in 1921 as one end of a 'Quad-Art' set, perhaps the best known form of Gresley's suburban articulated stock.*

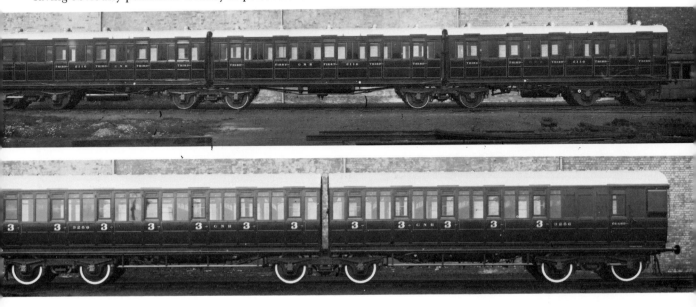

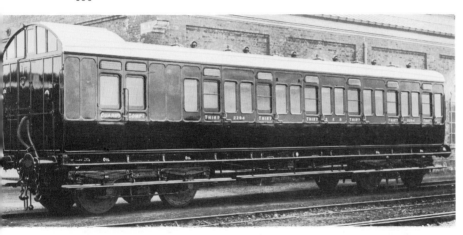

Left *This SER 'birdcage' suburban third brake was built just prior to the formation of the SE & CR and illustrates the short 'van', very typical of inner suburban stock.*

Below *LNWR suburban stock at the turn of the century is represented by this Broad Street and Willesden set which seems to have been first and second class only when built. Note the even shorter guard/brake compartment than the previous SER example*

many decades, and it was not until after he died that the LNER, as successor to the GNR, finally abandoned articulation. Of course, the high quality and general reliability of the Gresley bogie (page 119) must have had more than some influence on matters, but the GNR low-roof articulated sets were introduced well before the Gresley bogie was designed and, since they generally utilized the original type of bogie, the new Gresley version was usually confined to *new* articulated coaches, of which a fair number were also made.

Mention of the fixed nature of these GNR articulated sets, be they new or rebuilt, brings us finally in this section to the more general discussion of train formations and operations and the role of the 'set train', for it must never be supposed that the articulated combinations were the only examples of fixed formation working.

For reasons outlined in Chapter 2, the time taken for the coupling and uncoupling of individual

Below left *A close-coupled LSWR four-coach 'block' set No 1358, consisting of two third class brakes and two tri-composites. The latter were different, the leading example having two thirds, three seconds and three firsts, while the further carriage had four firsts, three seconds and one third.*

Bottom left *A third variety of four-coach set is represented by this late Midland example which actually entered service after the grouping. It has two third brakes, one full third and a composite (five firsts and three thirds). The MR, of course, had long abandoned three-class travel. Although the carriages are of the usual MR quality, the set is still gas lit.*

Below *The LYR had three-class travel in 1910, and its four-coach set was a little different from the LSWR version, viz two third brakes, one full third and one 1st/2nd class composite, the latter having four firsts in the centre with a pair of seconds at each end.*

passenger carriages tended to act against a speedy turn-round of coaches. Thus there was every reason *not* to reassemble trains on arrival at their destination; far better to have a fixed set of vehicles which would, all things being equal, meet with most demands likely to be made during a typical day. This philosophy was particularly applicable to the short-distance 'all stations' train where a rapid turn-round of a set of carriages was of considerable value in maintaining a high service frequency, especially at busy times. The GER undoubtedly holds the palm for virtuosity in this respect for its famous 'Jazz' steam suburban services out of Liverpool Street. Not only were the trains of fixed formation but the track layout at the terminus was also such as to allow the engine of the outgoing working to be attached to one end of the train at the same time as the newly arrived engine was uncoupled from the opposite end. This slick operation could, at its most efficient, send a train on its way out of the station well within five minutes of its arrival!

The GER was not, however, the only example of this sort of thing, even if it was perhaps the best known. Most railways, including even those with only a modest amount of suburban and stopping traffic, found the fixed formation train to be of considerable value, and in many cases ordered their new carriages with the express purpose of marshalling them into 'sets', as they were generally known. The make-up of these sets could simultaneously both reveal quite a bit about the nature of the envisaged traffic and also indicate something of the physical constraints of the owning company.

Firstly, the actual make-up of the train could vary considerably in terms of vehicle type, the proportions of first, second and third class seating being gauged to suit the pattern of traffic for the area in question. Secondly, the actual number of vehicles provided was

rarely more than necessary in terms of passenger volume regardless of class. For one thing this reduced, in absolute terms, the capital cost of vehicles and secondly, in motive power terms, the shorter the train, the less powerful and expensive was the locomotive needed to pull it. Naturally, there were 'peaks' and 'troughs' as a typical day went by — the rush-hour is no modern phenomenon — but then, as now, if one chose to travel at busy times, one could expect crowded trains. Even in Edwardian days the railways did not like to have too much stock lying idle and not earning revenue between periods of peak demand, although things were not quite so tight as in more modern times.

One feature was, however, quite usual. This was to have trains made up of two or three identical sets at peak periods, rather than one large single formation. This then allowed one or two of the sets to be detached at quiet periods, thus reducing vehicle mileage and extending the time interval between carriage overhaul, the latter being based on miles run. It also allowed essential maintenance to be carried out on the idle sets during the slack times as well as reducing the locomotive fuel bill. For this reason, three, four and five-coach formations were particularly popular since, when multiplied by repetition, they could easily generate most of the other requirements from six to fifteen vehicles — and there were some quite lengthy caravans formed in this way.

It mattered little whether the basic unit of a set was a four, six or eight-wheeler, as the principles remained much the same. Indeed, there could also be seen some mixed formations too, not all of the same age or body style; but there was usually method in the apparent diversity, regardless of outward appearance.

In one respect, overall train length, the physical nature of a set of carriages could also be affected. As traffic increased, the capital cost of extending platforms to accept longer trains had to be considered and sometimes was, but on many occasions the railways sought to maximize capacity without increase of train or platform length. This could be done in one of several ways. We have already seen how the GER managed it simply by widening the carriages to take one extra seat per side in every compartment. Other tricks were to reduce the guard's van to rudimentary size in order to allow more passenger compartments and even to shorten the distance between carriages by using some form of fixed coupling, often of a centrally located type without side buffers. Some railways, like the Midland, introduced what was known as 'short buffer' stock to reduce the distance between individual vehicles within the set, while it was not uncommon to find cases where the standard carriage length was reduced slightly but still contained the same number of compartments. By doing this, it was sometimes possible to gain one whole vehicle without serious enlargement of train length.

If the worst came to the worse, of course, most railways were in a position to add 'strengthening' vehicles at the end of a set or sets of carriages. These could be drawn from a pool of spare vehicles and could result in some quite curious visual effects from time to time. However, one of the more characteristic features of the stopping train at this time was its generally rather tidy appearance, consequent upon the use of these matching sets. The pictures within this chapter show some of the various solutions adopted and there were many more besides these. In fact, taken all in all, the operation of the humble stopping train was an altogether more sophisticated business than its apparently lowly status might lead one to suppose.

There was one final mode of operating suburban services not so far mentioned which came gradually into more prominence as the years went by. This was the electrification of the railways, but since this regularly went hand in glove with a total reassessment of the nature of the vehicle itself, it is dealt with later.

9. Semi-fast

One of the dangers in trying to establish some broad generalized patterns in a basically complex field is the definition of categories and the blurring of edges where one category merges into another. The so-called 'semi-fast' train was and still is a prime case in point. There was, however, a certain type of operation which developed in Britain during Victorian days which, while not being exactly an all-stations local was most certainly not a long-distance express either. In its most classical form, it would normally cover longer overall distances, typically in the 25-100-mile category and would omit stops at some or all of the smaller intermediate stations. It was fairly characteristic on the mid-distance cross-country routes and not at all uncommon in what might be called the 'outer suburban' commuting environment. In the latter case, a train would, typically, pick up its load at the outer stations of its route and then run non-stop through the inner suburbs. It is a practice still widespread in the modern era.

When this type of train first came to be recognized as a separate sort of creature is conjectural — probably quite early in Victorian times — but what is certain is that the carriages provided were, in the early days, no different from those used on any other services, and this remained the case for most of the last century. However, in the present century this intermediate range operation became increasingly the area wherein one could find that euphoniously sounding vehicle the 'lavatory non-corridor' carriage, and it is with these vehicles that this chapter is concerned. As usual, however, it is necessary to start with a few comments about the origins of the type.

The non-corridor lavatory-equipped carriage first appeared in the later nineteenth century when it was introduced as a first tentative step towards improving amenities on the long-distance trains. Indeed, the Midland Railway, which built some of the finest examples of the genre in the late 1890s, described many of them as 'Express Lavatory Stock' and put them on its main trunk services. Other railways did likewise and it was only with the establishment of the gangwayed corridor coach that the lavatory non-corridors began to be moved across to the intermediate distance services. This process of 'cascading', as it is now called, was only in its infancy during the first part of the twentieth century and, in fact, many railways deployed lavatory stock rather than corridor vehicles on their expresses well into the 1920s and 1930s. For the most part, these superficially less venturesome systems were those whose main lines did not offer really long-distance travel. Thus, for example, the SE & CR remained very much wedded

to the lavatory non-corridor style, even for its most prestigious boat trains, until almost the end of its independent existence — and they were often things of great luxury and splendour. However, even such giants as the Midland were by no means extravagant in corridor coach provisioning at this time and it was only a few systems, notably the GWR and LNWR, which had whole-heartedly embraced the corridor during the Edwardian period.

Thus it is probably most accurate to say that the more modern-day association of lavatory non-corridors with an intermediate sort of operational role was never more than a gradually evolving concept during the pre-grouping period. Many of the vehicles to concern us had actually been built, by and large, for express services and probably only a minority of lavatory non-corridors were actually designed and built purely for the intermediate tasks until after the railway grouping.

So much by way of background, but what of the vehicles themselves? Structurally, of course, they were little different from orthodox non-corridors save for the insertion of the lavatories in place of some of the passenger seating areas. They were built to the usual ad hoc mixture of lengths, roof profiles and wheel arrangements but there was never any one dominant approach as to what, precisely, constituted the ideal arrangement. In this respect, there was a fundamental difference between lavatory and non-lavatory stock. In the latter case, regardless of external stylistic difference there was a broad measure of consistency between railways as to the basic arrangement of the carriage. In truth, there could be little variation save the overall vehicle length and compartment size, but the lavatory non-corridor was a different creature altogether.

For one thing, there never seemed to be any measure of agreement either between railways or even within one railway as to whether all or merely some compartments should have access to lavatories and/or whether such provisioning should be exclusive to the upper passenger echelons or provided on a more egalitarian basis. Furthermore, even if one could detect a sort of underlying principle at work — by no means easy — there was still no dominant solution. Things had reached their most confusing right at the turn of the century and a few examples must serve to suffice for the whole; although late nineteenth century in origin, they more than typify the early twentieth century state of affairs.

Take the LNWR, for example, a railway which, like its GNR rival, seemed often to display a chronic indifference to the plight of its customers until late

Left *This Webb radial chassis West Coast Joint Stock tri-composite, No 25 dating from the late 1880s, is typical of the first use of lavatories, ie for express use in pre-corridor days. Only the first class has lavatories and there are two coupés (see page 165), one of which, at the far end, is the solitary second class provisioning. Converted to bogie form, this and many carriages like it enjoyed a considerable twentieth-century life in the intermediate role before eventual scrapping.*

Below left *Characteristic use of non-corridor lavatory stock in the early twentieth century — a Highland Railway express at Druimuachdar Summit, circa 1905. All but one of the carriages visible in the picture have some lavatory provisioning, many of them being quite generously served.*

Below and bottom *The LSWR clearly exemplified the indecision regarding the quantity of lavatory provisioning to be provided. Much early lavatory stock favoured the first class, as in arc roof tri-composite brake No 447, and this philosophy was repeated in the early cove roof stock. Later, carriages like full third No 390 gave four out of seven compartments the choice, one for ladies only. The final solution was lavatories for all — see the picture on page 127.*

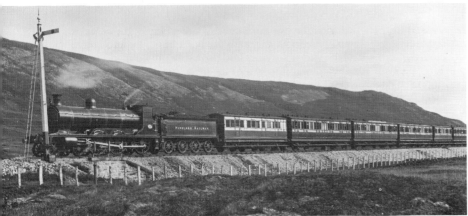

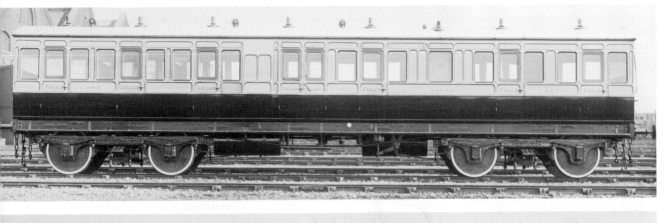

in Victorian days. It had obviously embraced the non-corridor lavatory carriage by the 1890s and had more or less settled on a standardized 42 foot or 45 foot length, but the variations of layout within that length defied all logical analysis; it was almost as if every single batch of carriages was built to fulfil slightly different criteria. Thus, totally new layouts were introduced for very minor changes in overall accommodation offered — all very confusing.

On the other hand, that much praised system, the Midland, seemed at times to get itself into a total confusion of principle. In 1896 and 1897 it had introduced some of the finest express trains seen in Britain between Bradford and Bristol and from London to Manchester. They were non-corridor but otherwise beyond comparison in their use of a dramatic new clerestory style and spacious compartment sizes. They were nominally two class only (first and third), but on more detailed analysis they actually turned out to be *six* class trains, viz first class dining and lavatory, first class lavatory only and first class non-lavatory, this whole threefold subdivision then being repeated in the third class end of the train! One needed to be something of a Sherlock Holmes to be able to find the right place in a train under these circumstances; yet this sort of nonsense went on right through the early decades of the present century. The obvious solution was the continuous corridor, already fully developed, but this did not always happen, so one must try to answer the question 'Why?'. It probably resulted from a complex interplay of public demand, economic factors and train weight considerations.

The provision of lavatories was an obvious first step in the improvement of travelling conditions for the long-distance traveller, but regardless of the precise layout adopted, the lavatories took up floor space at the expense of seats. They also involved extra fittings and internal doors, not to mention the essential plumbing, so foot for foot, a lavatory carriage was more expensive to build for less actual seats than its non-lavatory equivalent. This commercial disadvantage was set directly opposite the growing passenger demand for better facilities and it was probably a matter of fine judgement on the part of the railways when it came to assessing the balance between higher capital cost and the likely effect on passenger revenue if such cost was not incurred.

It was probably this specific aspect which caused many railways to come up with the already mentioned halfway solution, where some compartments did have lavatories and others did not. It showed willing if nothing else, one supposes, but at its more parsimonious could produce the sort of train where one carriage had a token lavatory or two, the rest being the mixture as before. The LYR was

rather fond of this solution and was by no means alone. We have already noted a Midland example and most railways could offer similar instances.

Another factor was overall train weight per passenger carried. Even if the economics of lavatory provisioning *vis-à-vis* passenger revenue could be accepted, the mere fact of reducing the number of seats within an otherwise unchanged carriage configuration to make room for the lavatories meant either that more carriages were needed for the same loading levels or that new and bigger carriages must be built. Either way, one had a heavier and probably larger train and this, in turn, posed questions of the locomotive fleet which, frankly, some railways were incapable of answering. It is not at all without significance that the move towards larger and more powerful locomotives took place at the start of the twentieth century when passengers were making more and more sophisticated demands on the companies in terms of carriage amenity.

In consequence, many lines, especially those with relatively shorter principal routes, tended to favour the lavatory non-corridor over the corridor alternative since it still offered an appreciable seat for seat weight advantage compared with the gangwayed carriage. However, in those instances where railways chose the lavatory alternative for express working, there was often a determined effort to provide every compartment with toilet facilities and this led to some very ingenious interior layouts showing probably more variety of approach than in any other generic type of carriage. Thus there gradually developed two quite separate strands of lavatory non-corridor design. Firstly, there were those where lavatory access was only provided for some of the compartments. These were often, but not always, of late nineteenth-century origin, but were used well into this century increasingly in the 'intermediate' role. Secondly were those carriages which offered lavatories for all. These were normally intended for express working and many remained thus employed well into the 1920s, albeit 'cascaded' later.

There were many ways by which lavatories could be incorporated in a carriage design and most possibilities seem to have been tried somewhere along the way. Most of them, however, fell into one of three principal categories:

1 *The 'between compartments' approach.* This traditional method, the simplest solution to the problem, undoubtedly derived from late Victorian practice wherein erstwhile non-lavatory coaches were converted to the lavatory style by the simple expedient of removing the seats from one compartment and converting it into a toilet or toilets. The LNWR and MR were masters of this particular technique and,

Left *This SER six-wheeler, No 21, is the classic example of the conversion of an original compartment into a pair of lavatories, probably in connection with its rostering as part of 'No 2 Boat Train'. The bar with handles across the carriage end was for turning on the gas lamps — see Chapter 4.*

Below left *LB & SCR brake tri-composite No 5189, built in 1905, bears all the stamp of the typical non-corridor lavatory fitted through carriage. It contained five first, five second and 26 third class seats, probably a fairly accurate breakdown of the likely customers. The one third class lavatory served all three compartments by means of intermediate connecting doors at the far side.*

Figure 42 This floor plan and some typical interior elevations show the very thoughtful provisioning in Wainwright's 1st/2nd class 'semi-corridor' lavatory composites for the SE & CR boat trains at the start of the century. It is no way inferior to contemporary corridor stock and, for once, gives specific details of upholstery: 'electric blue' velvet (2nd class) and figured claret velvet (1st class).

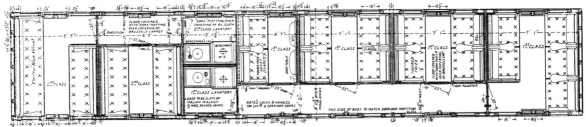

Scale 3.5mm = 1ft

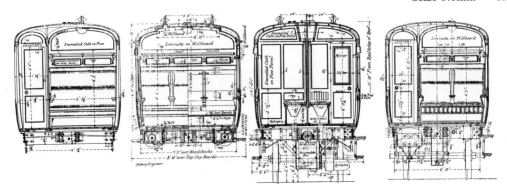

quite apart from its modest conversion cost, it also resulted in a quite spacious lavatory area. New carriages built to this principle generally saw a reduction in the size of the lavatory compartment (between partitions), often either to allow for some recovery of passenger seating space or to permit more lavatories to be incorporated.

2 The 'short passageway' approach. A disadvantage of the first solution was the fact that each lavatory could only really serve one compartment, therefore a common minimum provisioning had to offer at least two sets of toilet apparatus. This could be circumvented by two adjacent compartments sharing a single intervening lavatory, provided some sort of 'walk through' passageway could be offered. In effect it was a sort of mini-corridor, but saved a considerable number of lavatories.

3 The 'semi-corridor' approach. In this solution, much favoured by the NER and later the LNER, the short passageway was extended probably halfway along the carriage to allow all compartments to be served by fewer lavatories. Apart from the lack of connecting gangways, this type of carriage was close to being a true corridor vehicle but, properly planned, it could offer more seats than an orthodox corridor coach with

The lack of some outside doors at the left hand end of 'matchboard'-panelled NER lavatory third No 959 reveals it to be a typical 'semi-corridor' carriage wherein all compartments could gain access to a pair of centrally located lavatories. The passageway for the right-hand four compartments was on the far side of the vehicle, the general floor layout being much the same as shown in Figure 42.

fewer lavatories than the 'between compartment' type. For a given vehicle length, its seating capacity approximately equated to the 'full-lavatory-provisioned' version of alternative 1 above. This variation could in some cases lend itself to subsequent conversion to the full corridor form.

Apart from the semi-corridor type of solution either of the other two approaches could be used either in the partial or full provisioning of lavatories, and there were no really dominant styles. However, if full provisioning was wanted in the traditional mode, then anything up to six lavatories could be provided and considerable numbers of vehicles with just this sort of lavish facility were built for either all or one of the various classes of passenger. In this context, as might be supposed, the first class passenger was the best treated, but the days when this type of customer was the only one deemed to have such bodily needs had long gone. The second class (where it still remained) was usually well served and the third class by no means ill provided.

At their best, lavatory non-corridor coaches could provide a very civilized form of travel, provided there was no prima face need for mobility within the train (to a dining car, for example), and nowhere was this better exemplified than in the already-mentioned boat trains of the SE & CR. Study of the floor plans of a typical set of vehicles reveals considerable ingenuity, and it was normally achieved within a neat external style and considerable visual harmony. The SE & CR was by no means alone in this respect as some of the pictures in this book reveal, but it can stand as very typical of the best contemporary practice. In fact, this is one area in carriage design where

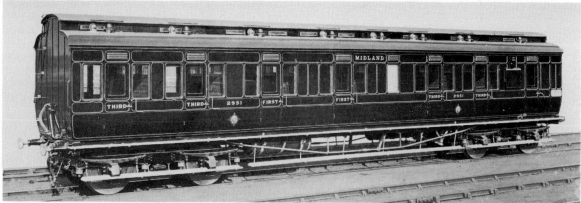

Top to bottom *GNR lavatory third brake No 3083, built in 1908 for the King's Cross to Cambridge and Grimsby services, shows an alternative style 'semi-corridor'. A pair of open saloons gained gained access to the lavatories by means of central aisles between the seats. It seated only 42.*

NER lavatory third class No 3712 shows the full side-corridor layout whereby all compartments were served by a single lavatory without the expense of end gangways. For some reason, these carriages are annotated on the record as being for 'emigrant traffic'!

This Midland composite solution dates from 1906. Clerestory brake composite No 2951 permits only one each of the two classes of compartment to gain access to the lavatories. This approach lingered until the end of the MR period and beyond, for example the picture on page 111.

This 'non-corridor five compartment, five lavatory "slip" composite brake' of the LNWR, No 6078, represents possibly one of the most extreme solutions to the through carriage business. It has two guard/brake compartments and a pair of 'birdcage' lookouts to assist the guard in the 'slipping' process. Only three were built to the new 1912 LNWR carriage panelling style, obviously intended for one specific service (two working, one spare — a common situation); it has not been possible to ascertain the service on which they ran.

the differences between the best and the worst companies were far less pronounced than in other fields. On the whole, they were all pretty reasonable.

An important use of the lavatory non-corridor coach was in providing through services, without change of vehicle, to a multiplicity of smaller destinations not served by a full train. In twentieth century terms, it no longer had the monopoly in this role, having first to share it with and then be supplanted by the corridor vehicle, but it led to a flowering of many ingenious composite carriage designs. The problem with a through coach was that it had to provide seats and lavatories for at least two and possibly three classes of passenger plus space for the luggage and, regularly, a guard's compartment as well. In this latter form it was known as a 'brake composite' or 'brake tri-composite', and the railways had real fun trying to get the balance right. This was equally true of the corridor equivalent, but the non-corridor was possibly the more catholic in terms of sheer variety.

For one thing, a through carriage probably mirrored in terms of its passenger load the economic breakdown of the two or three classes of traveller conveyed. However, the proportions of each were often difficult to achieve. Suppose that the numbers of first, second and third class travellers were likely to be in the ratio 2:1:8, for instance, a quite plausible division, then how do you get a single carriage to satisfy this demand? The fact is that most railways ten-

ded to take an inspired guess. Some companies contending three classes often provided equal numbers of compartments for all three, typically two of each. The LSWR was one such, and a real manifestation of this can still be seen at the NRM in the form of the preserved tri-composite brake No 3598 wherein are contained six compartments (two of each class), six lavatories, a luggage van and a guard's compartment. It is a real *tour de force* but by no means untypical. One does, however, suspect that until the second class compartments were downgraded to third class, the latter passengers probably had a bit of a raw deal in terms of the seats-per-passenger ratio.

Individual companies tended to favour different approaches in this matter of composite coach design. The Midland, for instance, having but two classes to cope with, tended to favour the first class customer both in terms of the proportion of compartments offered and in the provision of lavatories. In spite of its high reputation, it was distinctly parsimonious in the latter context, and the high seating quality of its third class could often be negated by some shortfall in lavatory provisioning in the long-distance trains — and it made very few carriages with lavatories for all compartments save in the corridor field.

Notwithstanding the above remarks, companies could go to some lengths to get the class balance more nearly correct and this led to that wonderful institution, the 'coupé' or 'half' compartment. This made tacit recognition of the fact that straight multiples of a whole compartment did not always get things right in terms of seat numbers, but that a half-compartment (ie one row of seats facing a plain partition wall) might just do the trick. It was, in fact, a bit wasteful of space, since two half-compartments (say first and third class) would each need a separate door and floor area and thus occupy more length than a single complete example of either type, but this did not seem to put the railways off. The idea originated in the nineteenth century and was probably inspired in the first place by the need to fill up the odd few residual feet of length in a carriage which could not, for some reason or other, be extended or reduced in length to accept a whole number of reasonably standard compartments. The oldest extant example is to be found at the NRM in the shape of Queen Adelaide's carriage (London and Birmingham Railway No 2) built as early as 1842, but the custom died hard.

At its most extreme — and some railways seemed to thrive on it — it could lead to a situation where in, say, a tri-composite there would be but two or three second class seats in a solitary second class half compartment, sometimes with an exclusive lavatory

Right *This early version of a so-called 'LBL' lavatory set dated from the three-class period on the LYR and was very sparing of lavatories, two first class compartments only being served. The seconds (in the middle carriage) and the thirds were denied, as were half the firsts!*

Below Figure 43 *In 1913, at about the same time as the LYR example, the SE & CR also introduced partial lavatory provisioning on some of its outer suburban and semi-fast services, but to slightly better effect. This floor plan shows a typical version made up from three 60-foot carriages of the style shown in Figure 36 (page 130).*

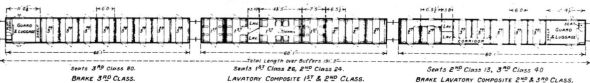

Seats 3RD Class 80.
BRAKE 3RD CLASS.
Seats with Lavatory Accomodation 14-1ST, 13-2ND, 20-3RD.

Seats 1ST Class 26, 2ND Class 24.
LAVATORY COMPOSITE 1ST & 2ND CLASS.
Summary of Seats 26-1ST, 37-2ND, 120-3RD, Total 183.

Seats 2ND Class 13, 3RD Class 40
BRAKE LAVATORY COMPOSITE 2ND & 3RD CLASS.

for those same few seats. Needless to say, under certain circumstances this could make the coupé very popular indeed; not for nothing were they often called 'honeymoon' compartments! The LNWR was particularly fond of them at the turn of the century.

Just as the lavatory non-corridor displayed many more subtle design variations than did the more suburban type of vehicle, so too did its operation defy simple analysis. Many of them were formed up into sets for the more important services, but a huge number were regarded as 'loose' vehicles to be added to or removed from trains at will. We have already seen their role as through carriages, conveyed perhaps at the end of a principal train and detached intermediately for working to a different destination. Sometimes this was achieved without stopping the main train by the ingenious process of 'slipping' the carriage from the rear. The GWR, LNWR and to a lesser extent the Midland were all rather fond of this technique. It later became commonplace with corridor carriages too, but certainly began with the lavatory non-corridor.

A 'slip carriage' had to be a self-contained 'train in one vehicle' and was, for the most part, a brake composite or brake tri-composite. It carried its own guard who, at the appropriate moment in the journey, could activate an ingenious mechanism whereby the slip carriage could be uncoupled from the main train while in motion without fracturing the train brake pipe (see page 30), thus allowing the slipped carriage (or carriages — there could be more than one) to freewheel into the station as the main

train receded into the distance. It saved much transit time for the main train but, of course, was impossible to repeat in the reverse mode when it came to attaching the carriage to an inbound service, but it was popular.

Another common use for the lavatory carriage — again with perhaps a slight emphasis on the composite type of vehicle — was in order to enhance the quality of a particular service without going to the expense of providing all lavatory stock. It was particularly common, for example, to find a lavatory composite sandwiched between two non-lavatory third class brakes for the sort of 25-50-mile trips quite common throughout Britain. In fact, the LYR actually built new sets of coaches to this philosophy for its not inconsiderable traffic across the Pennines between Leeds, Bradford and Liverpool (the 'LBL sets'). These could hardle be classed as short-haul suburban, but there they were, nonetheless, with but one or two first class lavatories puckered in amongst non-lavatory compartments!

Excursion trains were another likely spot for the odd lavatory coach. Here the objective was to maximize seating capacity but, perhaps, make a slight concession or two possibly for PR purposes. Thus a lavatory coach would find itself at the end of a string of suburbans on its way to Southend or the Clyde Coast for example. It was all rather random and there was little pattern to any of it. They could even be found quite regularly as 'strengtheners' on the end of corridor expresses.

This particular part of the narrative has dwelt at

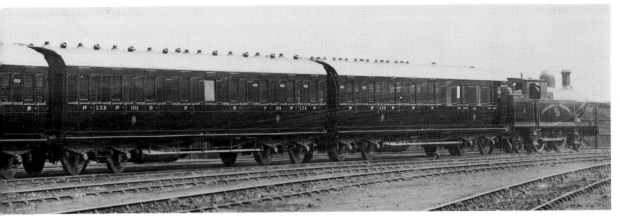

some length on the operational variety and particularly the variable internal arrangements within the non-corridor lavatory coach, for it is perhaps its most interesting single feature and much more could be said did space permit. However, it should be sufficiently clear by now that there was more than a degree of 'ad hoccery' about the whole business and it seems to me that this is symptomatic of some degree of uncertainty on the part of the railways themselves, individually and collectively, as to what should be the proper solution. However, such a statement presupposes that the nature of the problem was capable of precise identification, and there is little firm evidence that this was the case. A very wise, now, deceased, railway engineer once told me that he had found decision making to be easy; it was the identification of the *problem* that caused him all the headaches! This seems to be the key to understanding this very fascinating group of carriages.

There is no doubt that the railways moved quite sharply from a period of considerable complacency in the late nineteenth century to one of greater awareness in the early twentieth. Competition from the road was just beginning both in the field of public transport and in the slow but, as it was to prove, inexorable move towards private mobility in the shape of the motor car. One doubts if it was quantified with any great precision, but one can sense that the railways were beginning to feel that something ought to be done in terms of both meeting new competition and trying to satisfy greater customer expectation.

The difficulty was that any improvement to the carriage itself, or the services provided, would invoke greater capital expenditure, be it on vehicles, locomotives or infrastructure, and the railways were commercial companies trying to make profits. There was thus every incentive to keep expenditure within bounds, and against this background the lavatory non-corridor carriage must have seemed an attractive and less expensive option than the full corridor alternative. To this must also be added the fact that social habits and travel patterns were changing quite markedly in the Edwardian era. After sixty or more years of staid Victorian rectitude, the Edwardian period undoubtedly saw a considerable change in public attitudes from the Monarch downwards, and it would be ridiculous to think that this did not have its effect in the field of passenger travel. 'Emancipation' is not, perhaps, too strong a word.

In effect, therefore, the railways were faced with a period of great adjustment and change at all levels and had to try and respond, simultaneously, to all manner of different stimuli. That they managed to do so pretty effectively, all things considered, is one reason why the Edwardian era, short though it was, is often regarded as the high point of private railway development, particularly in the passenger vehicle field. In a sense it was inevitable since the pace of change was forcing the railways to pursue more experimentation than at any time in their previous history. This took on both a technological and sociological form in carriage terms and the lavatory non-corridor was a particularly good example of the interplay in the socio-economic field. The fact that it could appear in so many different forms was no more than a reasonable response to rapidly changing demands and expectations.

With the benefit of hindsight, one can realize that for all their valiant attempts the railways never got it quite right, and that the non-gangwayed lavatory vehicle, however well designed, could never really match the gangwayed alternative. This did not stop the railways trying until well beyond our immediate period, and many of the products of this particular school of carriage thinking continued in use until almost the end of the steam railway itself. But the real future lay with the gangwayed carriage and to this we must now turn attention.

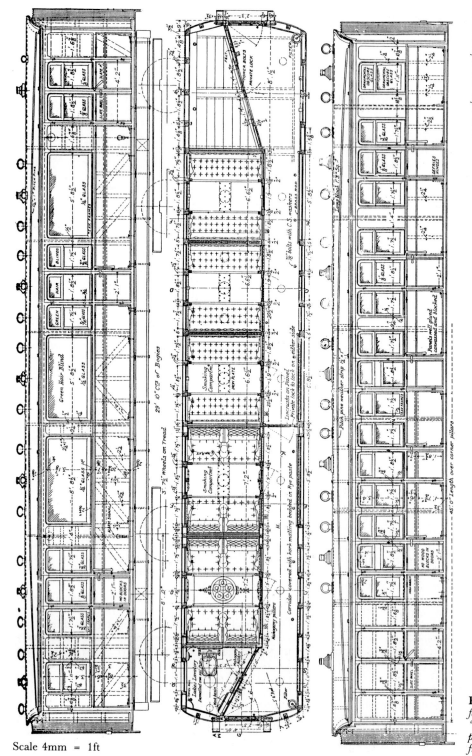

Figure 44 *These elevations and floor plans, albeit of a relatively small carriage (45 ft by 8 ft 6 in), show the essential layout of most British side-corridor stock of the twentieth century. It is, in fact, a GCR example from 1900, internal sections of which are featured in Figure 33 (page 67).*

Right *The essential difference between 'corridor' and 'open' stock is shown by this pair of GER interiors, dating from circa 1910.*

10. The general service long-distance carriage

There can be little doubt that the gangwayed bogie carriage has proved the most versatile single vehicle type which the railways, whether of Britain or elsewhere, have ever produced. Its adaptability seems virtually without limit and it is the essential common factor linking this and the next few chapters. It was the adoption of the gangway which made possible most of the amenities which we now take for granted on the train, and although in Britain such vehicles were by no means in the numerical ascendency over the already considered non-corridor types, their infinite variety was such that it is necessary to devote several chapters to them. Indeed, this particular section concerns itself only with what is usually called 'general service ordinary stock'.

The origin of the gangwayed carriage is firmly American, and we have already seen that the first British example was in 1869 with Queen Victoria's LNWR-built Royal Saloons in their original 'twin' form, now preserved united on a single 'modern' (1895) twelve-wheel chassis at the NRM. Somewhat more general use of the gangway did not occur in Britain until a generation or so later in the 1890s, but its well-nigh universality was very much a twentieth-century phenomenon, established as such beyond doubt in the period covered by this particular volume.

The technicalities of the gangway itself have been covered in Chapter 3, but a paragraph ot two must needs be added at this point by way of further definition. In the existing literature of railway carriages, words like 'corridor', 'gangway' and 'vestibule' are often hurled around with a careless disregard of their precise meaning. In fact, the same word can often be ascribed to entirely different features, or two different words used for the same feature!

As far as this book is concerned, the 'gangway' is the apparatus fixed to the carriage end by which the passenger moves from one vehicle to another — in other words, it is a technical term. The word 'corridor' refers to an internal passageway generally located *at one side* of a carriage from which access can be gained to compartments, kitchens, lavatories or whatever. The word 'vestibule', frequently used as a synonym for gangway (reflecting its American form of usage), is more correctly used (in the British context) in reference to an internal lobby, usually with outside doors, from which access can be gained to the internal corridor or the gangway between vehicles (or both simultaneously). So far so good, but there is the special case where the passageway for passengers runs along the longitudinal centre of the vehicle between seats on either side, such as are found in dining carriages and the like. This is the common

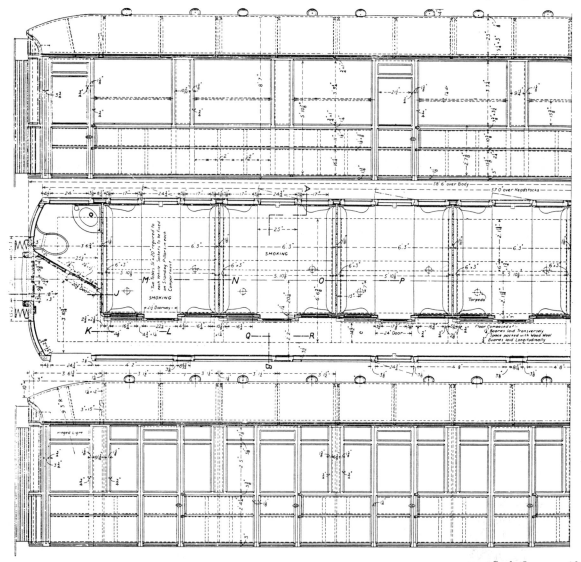

Figure 45 *Half elevations and plan of a typical Gresley styled 58 ft 6 in ECJS corridor third of 1907. The carriage was exactly symmetrical about its centre-line, and the basic design hardly changed for the next forty years.*

Scale 5mm = 1ft

Figure 46 *Third class carriages to an approximately 50-54-foot length usually had one less compartment than the 57-60-foot type. This plan shows a York-built ECJS example, contemporary with Fig 45 but only 53 ft 6 in long.*

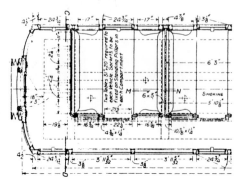

Scale 4mm = 1ft

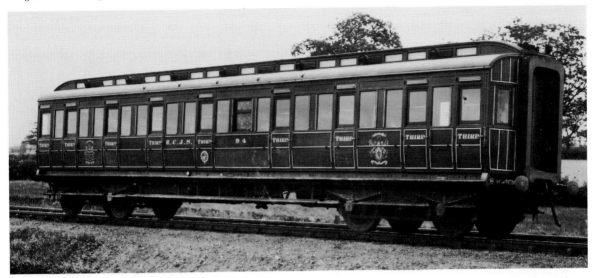

Above *The toilet layout shown in Figure 46 seems to have been something of an East Coast speciality. This is an earlier clerestory example, ECJS No 94, built in 1903 to the same 53 ft 6 in length, this time with only one intermediate lavatory and two end vestibules.*

modern approach but historically its nomenclature is confusing. Some railways, for instance the LYR, called it a 'centre corridor', but since it had no walls this seems a bit of a linguistic inaccuracy; others adopted the terms 'passageway' or 'gangway', while after 1922 the LMS use the word 'vestibule' to denote this *type* of carriage! Since its most obvious differentiated characteristic was the open nature of its interior (ie not cluttered with intermediate walls and partitions), it seems logical to use the word 'open' to define the type, whether or not it possessed vestibules or gangways! This, indeed, is current BR form, so let us use it throughout.

So much for the semantics; what of the vehicles themselves? Essentially they can be classified into two families, 'corridor' and 'open', and this will be the basis of our analysis of ordinary stock.

In the 1900-1925 period — and later, for that matter — by far the most typical gangwayed carriage was of side corridor configuration. Early pioneers were the GWR, LNWR and, surprisingly, the GER, but by the end of the nineteenth century most long-distance systems which had tried it out at all had copied the basic arrangement. For one thing, it was extremely logical. Take one ordinary non-corridor carriage composed of conventional compartments, add a lavatory at one or both ends, place a passageway along one side, encapsulate the whole within the confines of an acceptable overall carriage size, add gangways at both ends and there you have it — the basic gangwayed corridor coach. All else was mere adaptation, and still is to all intents and purposes. It is in the adaptation that the real interest lies, for the railways demonstrated a remarkable versatility in playing 'variations on a single theme'.

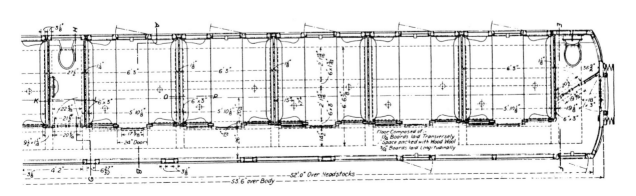

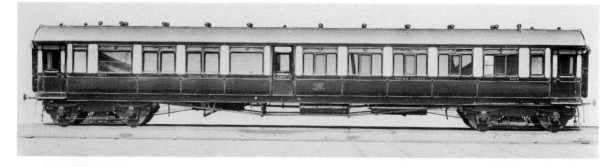

Firstly, it must be understood that in Britain the individual compartment was for the most part *de rigueur* in those days and woe betide the railway company which decided to break with tradition too dramatically. Thus, yet again, we come face to face with the interaction between people and vehicles as far as the railway carriage is concerned. Now, whether or not the reactions of individual companies were conscious or not is pretty well irrelevant at this distance in time, but they did reflect a genuine social reality in their almost universal adoption of the side corridor vehicle — and it was not solely a matter of practicality. The British liked their compartments.

They always had and, I guess, given a free choice, they probably still do today. Nor am I free of prejudice myself, for nothing delights me more than to find my train formed up from the increasingly rare side corridor vehicles still to be seen on BR. The British are not wildly sociable people, and the compartment offered a sort of privacy which was jealously guarded in railway carriage terms for more than half of the present century!

Why this should be so is beyond my competence to analyse, but it seems real enough — or else why would the railways have gone to the trouble of making vehicles by the thousand over the years which

Left *The classic GWR 'Toplight' corridors evolved from the 'Dreadnoughts' via the 'Concertinas', and these views show the start and finish of the process 'Dreadnought' full third No 3277 and 70-foot (actually 69 ft 11¼ in) 'Toplight' full first No 8337, brand new in lake livery in 1914. Note that as well as a full set of compartment doors on the far side, each of the eight compartments had a door on the corridor side as well, a somewhat outmoded practice at this time (Below T.J. Edgington collection).*

Below left *MR composite No 3421 — see the drawings on this page.*

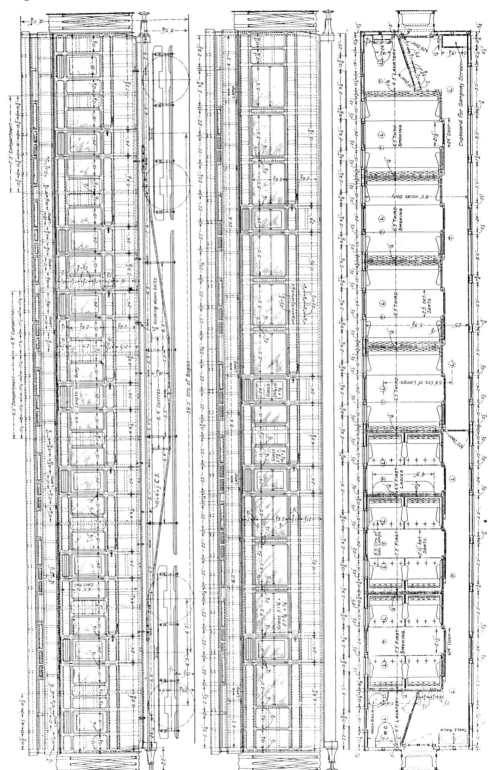

Figure 47 *Elevations and plan of a 54-foot Bain corridor composite built for the Midland Railway in 1909. Note the first class half-compartment*

Scale 3.5mm = 1ft

were intrinsically more expensive than their open equivalents? They needed more partitions, doors, fittings and so on, and regularly provided a smaller number of seats per vehicle; but that was what was wanted, so the railways tried their best to provide, and right royally they succeeded. This attitude extended, in fact, well beyond the period under immediate discussion, but it was firmly grounded in the Edwardian age.

Setting aside the superficialities of style, roof profile, livery and so on, the basic corridor carriage was designed so that within the defined company length and width the best use could be made of available space. Typically, two particularly characteristic forms emerged which were to stand the test of time, the full third and the composite. The style of the full third was normally some 7-8 compartments plus two lavatories within a 50-60 foot length and an 8 ft-8 ft 6 in width. A typical desired compartment dimension was about 6 feet long, and the lavatories were about 4 feet, so a seven-compartment third plus two lavatories nicely fitted into a 50ft length; this was a very common choice, give or take a foot or so, perhaps best exemplified by hundreds of LNWR vehicles. Add an extra compartment and the very common 56-57 foot dimension emerged in consequence and variations within this arrangement were based on similar principles.

Thus, for example, the Midland, which favoured a somewhat more spacious 6 ft 3 in to 6 ft 6 in third class compartment, tended to go for a six compartment 48-footer at the turn of the century, extended to about 54 feet for the seven compartment version of the 1903-10 period. At the other end of the scale, the GWR 'Dreadnoughts' could get nine third class compartments plus lavatories into their 70-foot length. These carriages also managed to incorporate a corridor which changed sides halfway down the vehicle and lobbies at each end.

The composite was rather more of a problem. For one thing, there was always present the need to assess the relative proportions allocated to the various classes in terms of compartment numbers. Even had

this basic decision been made with any degree of consistency, which was rarely the case, it could then be further confused by the need for *three* classes to be accommodated by those railways which still retained the second class option. Now, logic would suggest that the solution *should* have been to offer full first and second class carriages was well as full thirds, and this was a quite common solution in the four and six-wheel era. However, virtually all corridor carriages were of bogie type, and to allocate a complete vehicle of this larger type to either of the upper echelons would, in most cases, provide too many first and second class seats relative to the third class. The statistics analysed in Chapter 6 make this point only too clearly. Most railways did, in fact, build a few full firsts, but only used them on their heavier trains. For most purposes, three or four first class compartments within a composite would suffice to meet the need.

The main structural problem with a composite was to resolve the conflict between the increased length needed for the first class compartments and the understandable wish to use the same length of carriage in the interests of chassis standardization. The 'full' option was, of course, quite simple, in that six first class compartments, for example, would occupy much the same length as seven second or third class compartments, and this was the commonly adopted solution in these cases. The composite, however, was different, many indeed were the variations thereof and a few examples must needs serve to illustrate the whole.

For general use, a sort of half-and-half layout was adopted, typically 3 + 3 or 3 + 4 (either way round). Should this result in one fewer compartment overall than for a full third, the extra space gained, possibly 3 feet or so, could either be given to the lavatory compartments or provide, perhaps, extra internal luggage storing capacity. Thus, for instance, some of the six-compartment LNWR 50-foot composites had more or larger lavatories than the seven-compartment thirds. If, on the other hand, a company did not wish to reduce compartment numbers, it was

Left *This LSWR corridor composite No 999 has a fairly normal corridor side arrangement for the period, but displays a common stylistic variation, that of having drop lights opposite those compartments not served by outer doors — compare the picture on page 176.*

Below *The familiar corridor brake third could come in a variety of forms and compartment numbers. These three are typical, the references to 'handing' referring to the location of the brake end when viewed from the corridor side. They are: 50-foot three-compartment RH GER No*

31 (above); 57-foot four-compartment RH CR No 1365 (below); 57-foot five-compartment LH LNWR No 6742 (bottom). Note that all of them have individual doors to each compartment

sometimes possible to reduce (slightly) the dimensions of both compartments and lavatories to fit them all in. A parallel alternative to either of these solutions was to incorporate a coupé, rather than lose a whole compartment. The Midland was quite fond of this trick and its 54-foot composites often had two-and-a-half first plus four thirds.

The exact number of compartments could be misleading in terms of perceived class proportions in the vehicle. In a corridor carriage, a third class compartment would always be assumed to have six or even eight seats available (the latter being typical for stock 9 feet wide) whereas the first class would mostly have but four seats per compartment (up to 8 ft 6 in wide carriages) and either four or six for a 9 feet wide example. In fact, many a 9 feet wide carriage was given but four seats per first class compartment, and no better provisioning has ever been made for the first class traveller since then, save at times on 'supplementary fare' services. Thus, a three first plus four third composite (a very typical form) would have a seating capacity of some 12-18 plus 24-32.

These figures, of course, did not reflect the true balance of cutomers within the train itself, but then it would not be very likely that a composite would run on its own. It would typically be operated with several thirds, and many railways chose to operate mostly composites rather than full firsts on even their longer trains. Two composites, placed 'first class to first class', would give the same number of seats as a full first but offer greater flexibility of operation. The MR was paricularly wedded to this approach.

The brake-ended corridor coach came in all three principal varieties (first, third and composite), but dominant again were the thirds and composites. On most railways, a fairly standard brake third layout was adopted with a lavatory at the non-brake end, followed by as many or as few compartments as were thought desirable before the van portion was reached. In general, the size of the latter tended to reflect the probable amount of luggage anticipated for the whole train, so on longer-distance services there were as few as two or three compartments with a large van, while at the opposite extreme, five or six compartments

The five-compartment layout (two firsts and three thirds) was probably the most common form of corridor brake composite. Two of these three examples are of this kind, the third, the WCJS coach, having six compartments. In order, the types are: 65 ft 6 in twelve-wheel 'matchboard'-style LH ECJS No 142; 53 ft 6 in LH NER No 406; 57 ft RH WCJS No 398 (two firsts and four thirds). The layout of ECJS No 142 is given in Figure 48 and is reasonably typical for all, save for the precise location of toilets and first class compartments.

The much rarer corridor brake first is represented by these spacious examples, built within a year of each other in 1905-6. Both had but four seats per compartment. GNR No 217 is a five-compartment LH brake while MR No 2656 is a four-compartment RH example — this is the corridor side. Note the distinctive early MR practice of repeating quarter and drop lights opposite all compartments but without a full set of corridor doors; larger windows appeared later (see page 109)

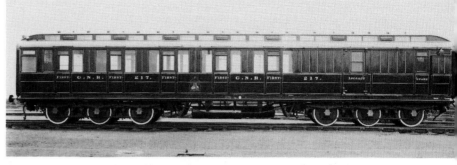

with a shorter van would be preferred. Most long-distance companies could offer examples of all types, three to five compartments being probably the most customary.

The brake first was something of a rare bird, and still is for that matter. Unlike the full first, the relative sparseness of the brake first had little or nothing to do with the problem of compartment numbers as such. In fact, one might argue that a three or four compartment brake first would be just about right for many services in terms of accommodation *vis-à-vis* the rest of the train, but this would put the first class customers at one end of the formation. Many railways, however, preferred to put their first class seats in the middle of the train, flanked by the seconds (if present) and thirds. This had the effect of giving the first class customers the shortest walk to the dining car, if provided, and, except at terminal stations, was likely to put the first class section nearest to the entrances and exits from the platforms — all most laudable, but not always as practical as it may seem.

The alternative solution of firsts at one end, thirds at the other and dining facilities between them is much more common these days in Britain (reading 'second' for 'third'), and is the standard method of forming up a gangwayed train. However, until BR days this was by no means always the case, so the brake first tended to have some rarity value. Insofar

as one dare generalize in these matters, it was probably the LNWR and particularly the MR which partially favoured the end location for the first class passenger, although neither did it exclusively. On their Anglo-Scottish trains, for example, it was quite common to see them formed up with the first class at the London end (avoiding a long walk from the platform barrier) then the diner(s) and then as many thirds as might be needed. In the case of the MR, since these trains often reversed their direction of travel at Leeds, the first class end was also at the platform end on arrival in Glasgow too — very clever! However, before taking this discussion of the complex business of marshalling a gangwayed train any further, we must first look into the role of that astonishingly versatile carriage, the corridor *composite* brake. Many railways had, or seemed to have, almost as many of these as they had brake thirds and the reason is not hard to find.

Like their non-corridor predecessors, corridor composite brakes were the logical choice for through workings. In fact they were even better, for the gangway allowed the passengers full use of the train's facilities right up to the point where the vehicle was detached to follow its own individual route to journey's end. Thus it was by no means uncommon to find trains carrying quite a number of such vehicles, each of which was bound for a different 'ultima

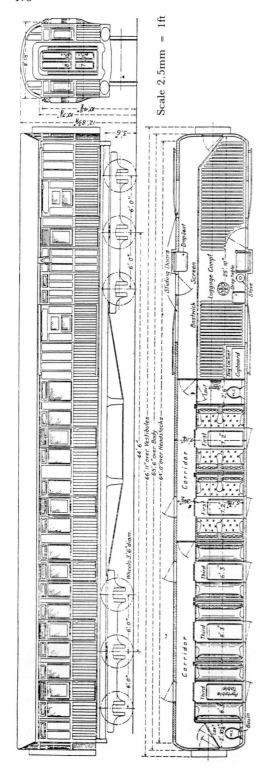

Scale 2.5mm = 1ft

Figure 48 *Elevation and plan of the ECJS corridor composite brake illustrated on page 176. In this case, the toilets were 'outside' the compartments and the first class at the 'van' end of the carriage.*

Thule'. Furthermore, on some services the first class accommodation within a typical single brake composite might even suffice for the whole train, in much the same manner as did the first class compartments within a non-brake composite under different circumstances.

In terms of interior layout, the brake composite followed that of the brake first or third, but normally the van was shorter and it was rare to have fewer than four compartments (1 + 3 or 2 + 2) and far more likely to be five or six (2 + 3 or 2 + 4). There would often be a second lavatory between the last compartment and the van and, hardly surprisingly, many railways made extensive use of coupés in their brake composites. At times it went to ridiculous extremes, but no one could argue that the railways were not trying their best. In fact, the sheer variety of corridor carriage layouts within the same set parameters is only explicable in terms of the railways making a conscious effort to match their carriage provisioning as precisely as possible to the nature of specific services. It reached its ultimate form in the 'dedicated' set formations for specific services (see Chapter 13) but, within the 'general service' category, most railways managed to provide themselves with a sufficient measure of choice in order to achieve, or try to achieve, a precisely correct mix for most purposes.

Take, for example, the matter of the 'handing' of brake carriages. Perusal of any corridor coach plan will reveal that the van can either be at the left-hand or right-hand end of the vehicle, relative to the corridor and passenger spaces. There is no hard and fast rule about it, but, to avoid ambiguity, references to 'left-handed' and 'right-handed' brakes in this survey will relate to the position of the van when viewed from the *corridor* side. There is no prima facie case for 'handing' a brake-ended carriage. The normal ramifications in service will pretty soon guarantee that the vehicle at some time in its life gets itself 'inside out', so to speak, as a result of negotiating loops, triangles, reversals of direction and all the other track complexities which the railways in their heyday could provide. So why was it done?

As far as I can determine, there were only two reasons for this phenomenon, both concerned with train marshalling. In a perfect world, a set of gangwayed carriages would normally have a brake vehicle at each end, van portions outwards. Now, some railways, particularly such influential concerns as the LNWR, liked to maintain the corridor down the

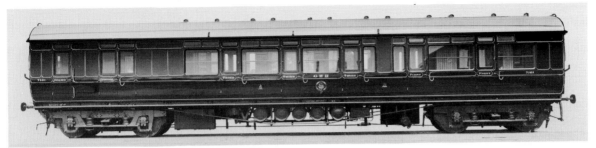

The corridor brake composite was ideally suited for slip working — see page 166 — and the GWR was probably the prime exponent. This is 'Toplight' 'slip brake composite' No 7101

same side of the train throughout. This was said to be because the LNWR wished to have the corridor on the 'west' side of its mainly north-south trains. Apparently it was to avoid passengers getting too hot on long sunny days! The LNWR certainly put most corridors on the west side on many occasions, but this inevitably meant opposite-handed brakes at the ends of the formation, however many intervening carriages might be present. This particular obsession even went as far as 'handed' composites from time to time in order to allow the first class portions of two adjoining coaches to be connected together with the corridor on the same side or to put them next to the diner(s). This was all most commendable, but rather presupposed that nothing would ever happen to alter the formation of the train — a vain hope in most cases.

Paradoxically, the second reason for 'handed' brakes arose from precisely opposite criteria, the wish to alternate the corridor from side to side between each vehicle. There was a sort of feeling, arising from the fact of the corridor coach having its passengers distributed towards one side of the vehicle, that it would, in some way, be loaded more heavily on the compartment side. The GWR 'Dreadnoughts' displayed a corridor which was switched across the vehicle at the mid point for this very reason. The effect was at best marginal, but took on somewhat absurd characteristics when some railways decided to balance the perceived asymmetric loading by alternating the corridor side between adjacent vehicles, as if it could in some magical way cancel out the lop-sidedness! I have never seen any good argument advanced for this quaint custom, but when allied with fixed sets of corridor coaches it inevitable meant that those sets containing an *odd* number of vehicles threw up opposite-handed brakes at their extremities.

The most noteworthy practitioner of this approach was probably the LSWR which set much store on five-coach sets (usually two brake thirds, two thirds

and one full first). In this it was often followed slavishly by the Southern in more recent times, but mercifully the more corridor-orientated railways fairly rapidly abandoned the nonsense and settled on a single configuration, dominantly right-handed. By BR days, all new side-corridor brake coaches of any type were exclusively right-handed. Mark you, there was still (save in BR days) much scope for variety in terms of compartment numbers and whether or not (in the case of a brake composite) the first class should be at the end of the vehicle or adjacent to the van. By means of such inconsequential ephemera,

First class two-seat coupé (for ladies only) in a Midland corridor composite brake of 1903

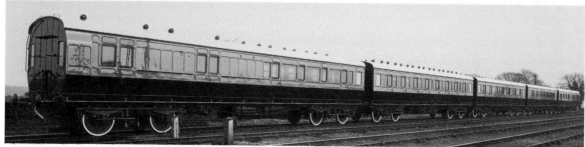

Top *This elegantly styled five-coach set of LNWR cove roof corridors clearly demonstrates the 'corridor down one side' principle. From the near end, the types are: brake first (two compartments), first (six compartments), two thirds (seven compartments), brake third (four compartments). All were 57-foot carriages and the small number of compartments was probably generous to a fault; but what a nice train for 1905! The formation also demonstrates the 'first class at one end' philosophy, and if a dining car was included it would have been inserted between the first and third class portions*

Above *Another elegant set, this time LSWR, illustrates the 'alternating side' corridor principle and a different class distribution. From the near end the types are: brake third, third, two composites (first class portions adjoining), brake third. In this case the firsts are in the middle of the train, and note also that the brake end has no gangway (it was later modified), symptomatic of the 'set' principle followed by the LSWR. Other LSWR sets had one full first and two thirds rather than as shown here. In my view, this and the preceding LNWR train represent some of the stylistic high points of the pre-group era.*

the delights of the carriage student were much enhanced!

It was, of course, the principal long-distance companies which led the way in terms of corridor coach design — and there seems to have been more than a bit of 'over the shoulder' looking at the offerings of the rival concerns. Thus, within broadly similar parameters, the companies came up with quite a few variations. The dominant concerns were, not unnaturally, the LNWR (including the West Coast Joint Stock partnership with the CR), GWR, Midland, GNR and NER (including their various joint activities) and, in Scotland, the CR and NBR, though the latter pair tended to be of lesser significance than their respective English partners.

This led to more than a few very splendid carriages being put into service on the longer-distance routes which, fashion apart, would not disgrace the modern railway. Take those arch rivals the MR and LNWR for example. They were in fierce competition for much of the traffic between London, the Midlands, the North and Scotland, and their carriages could not

have been more different during the Edwardian period. Both companies entered the century with a sort of 48-50 ft x 8 ft 6 in standard dimension, the LNWR with an arc roof profile, the Midland with its classic clerestory. In terms of compartment size and general elegance the MR probably held the edge, but in its espousal of the corridor principle the LNWR was second to none. In the early 1900s, both companies made changes. The MR extended its carriage length to 54 feet, retaining broadly the same stylistic features, but in 1905 the LNWR made a great leap forward with some of the finest corridor vehicles ever seen in Britain up to that time. They were 57 feet long by 9 feet inside with a handsome cove roof profile (see page 37) and extraordinarily spacious compartments. The full third had but seven of them and the full first only six, the latter, moreover, with but four seats per compartment. They also came in at over 30 tons per vehicle, an awful lot of weight for only 24 first class passengers; but they were sumptuous. In due course, they were built with full elliptical roofs but, interestingly, they

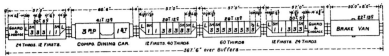

New Train, Day North Express, L. and N.W.R.   57ft. 0in. × 9ft. 0in. Stock.   Side doors.
36 First Class.   148 Third Class.   Total passengers 184.

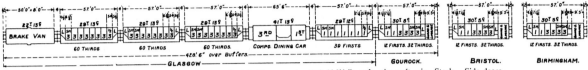

New Train for 10 a.m. ex-Euston, Scotch Express, L. and N.W.R. 57ft. 0in. × 9ft. 0in. Stock.   Side doors.
75 First Class.   276 Third Class.   Total passengers 351.

New Train, Scotch Express, Edinburgh Portion, L. and N.W.R. 57ft. 0in. × 9ft. 0in. Stock.   Side doors.
51 First Class.   220 Third Class.   Total passengers 271.

Figure 49 This contemporary drawing shows typical LNWR/ WCJS formations used in 1913. The trains were mostly new-styled carriages such as shown on page 108, save for the twelve-wheel diners and the full brakes.

were usually confined to the English routes where the LNWR met with competition from several rivals. The West Coast services, however, continued until about 1912-13 with the old arc roof style, save for one spectacular exception (see Chapter 13).

The MR and the GWR (also in rivalry with the LNWR) seemed unwilling to match this LNWR grandeur and continued to provide the mixture much as before, and even the LNWR seemed to think twice about these excessively generous compartment sizes before many years had lapsed. Interestingly, all three companies settled down to very similar provisioning,

based on a 57 feet by 9 feet dimension, during the Great War period. Exterior styling apart, there was little to choose between them by, say, 1918 in terms of their then current building programmes. As has already been mentioned, the GWR after the Dean period came to this situation by means of a short-lived experiment with 70 foot coaches ('Dreadnoughts' and 'Concertinas') before it finally settled down during the 'Toplight' era to something very close to the LNWR/MR approach.

Down the East Coast, as has been seen, the GNR

This 1908 53 ft 6 in NER corridor third No 1920, without compartment doors, was distinctly ahead of its time, and it was a generation later before its LNER successor standardized the same principle. Even the NER was forced into retaining an all-door configuration on many of its carriages (see the picture on page 123).

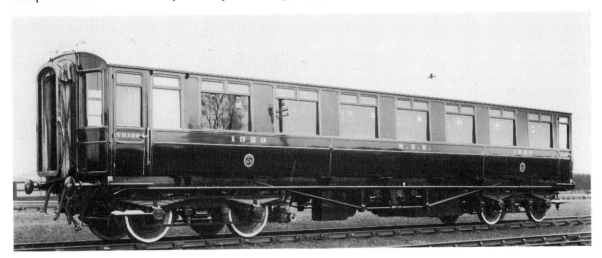

design influence gradually became dominant and this really started with some magnificent twelve-wheel corridors built at the turn of the century. There were not many of them, but in terms of the competition from the other Northern routes they were every bit as good and offered particularly welcome improvements in the third class — probably to meet the Midland's aggressive aompetition. These pioneer clerestories were, however, soon to be rendered obsolescent, if not obsolete, by Gresley's introduction of his new corridors with their very 'modern'-looking domed end roof shape, thereafter to become dominant both in ECJS and later LNER days. Their length tended to settle down at a foot or two longer than those of most companies at the time, eventually standardizing at around 58-61 feet, give or take a few inches.

In one respect, the companies so far considered had one particular design point in common, the retention of outside doors to all compartments. It is true that the GWR 'Dreadnoughts' abandoned this feature, but it turned out to be too advanced a concept for the time, so back came the doors with the 'Concertinas' and 'Toplights'. There was, however, one railway which made more than one valiant attempt to move forward. This was the NER which, for its own domestic use, produced a whole range of carriages especially attractive both outside and within. Those without compartment doors were a definite cut above most of the competition but clearly met with some resistance since the NER also felt obliged to produce some all but identical repeats with a full array of doors. In their liking for individual doors, one can only conclude that the British travelling public showed similar resistance to change as they did with the move to open carriages (see below).

The NER, for all its size, tended to live somewhat under the shadow of the GNR as far as long-distance carriages were concerned, especially in its jointly-owned operations. The ECJS examples are, of course, relatively well known, but the situation was further diluted from the NER standpoint by the GNR/NER joint stock which operated the London-Newcastle services. These too, although much less well known than the ECJS fleet, tended to follow the latter pattern, so the purely NER designs tended to be concentrated in the provinces where, perhaps inevitably, they received rather less attention than might have been the case had they been regularly seen in London. In this respect, the regional nature of the NER seemed to put it at a disadvantage, size of system notwithstanding. At the same time, it should be recorded that many GN-styled Joint Stock coaches were built by the NER to its own somewhat shorter length and on NER design chassis.

Right Figure 50 *Part elevations, plans and selected cross-sections of the celebrated Caledonian 'Grampian' corridor stock of 1905. Details of the bogie can be found in Figure 7 (page 23).*

A somewhat similar fate befell the two principal Scottish companies which operated corridors, the NBR and CR. Their services to England were largely in the hands of the ECJS and WCJS respectively, so their own individualistic contribution was generally confined to their purely domestic routes. In this context, they both proved capable of producing some quite splendid offerings of which perhaps the most celebrated were the Caledonian's 'Grampian' twelve-wheelers. These highly praiseworthy vehicles came out as early as 1905 and exhibited a near GWR size in terms of length and profile, being 65 feet by 9 feet with an almost fully elliptical roof. Internally they were conventional enough in layout, but their considerable length allowed a considerable enhancement in seating capacity. Unfortunately, as with many other rather good carriages, there were too few of them to count for much in subsequent years, and the CR soon went over to the 57 foot type, very similar to its English contemporaries.

The NBR's equivalents to the 'Grampians' were some rather stylish vehicles built for the Fife and Lothian Coast Expresses (and other purely Scottish services) in 1907. Like most railways at this time, the NBR had also decided to espouse the full height roof but came up with its own subtly distinctive form which, when allied to its equally characteristic panelling treatment, produced a rather different-looking vehicle — albeit with little in the way of interior innovation. Another disadvantage as far as the NBR was concerned in terms of long-term influence was the fact that not only did it participate in the ECJS, but also that its services via the Waverley route to England were in the hands of the so far unmentioned Midland-Scottish Joint Stock (MSJS), later renamed M & NB or M & GSW as appropriate. Just as with the other two Anglo-Scottish joint fleets, so too in the case of the MSJS, the English influence was dominant, this time pure Derby. This led, in time, to the somewhat amusing situation of Midland-designed vehicles being operated in LNER colours after the post-grouping division of the M & NB stock between its LMS and LNER partners.

Meanwhile, what of the smaller concerns, sparing the sensitivities of their followers? Here again there were quite perceptible differences both between Scotland and England and, south of the border, between the London-based and the provincial systems. Moreover, even the nature of the various London-based systems caused differences to appear.

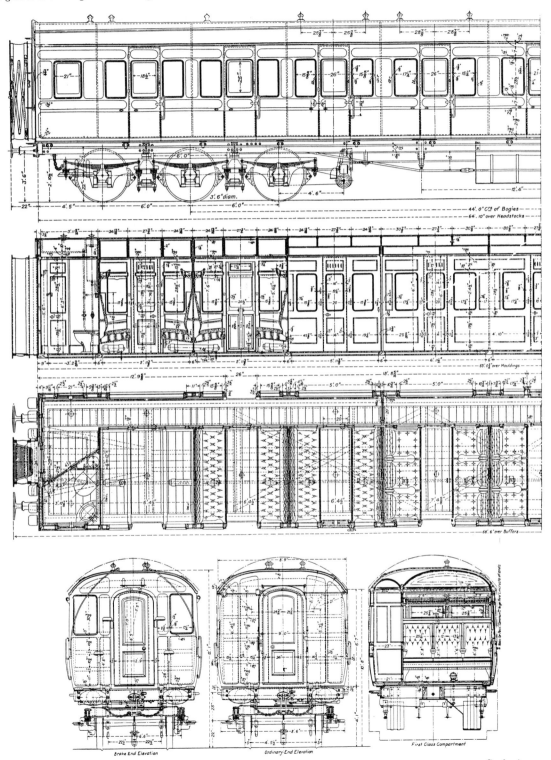

Brake End Elevation

Ordinary End Elevation

First Class Compartment

Scale 4mm = 1ft

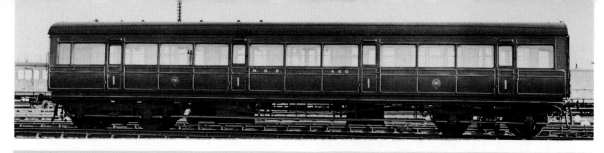

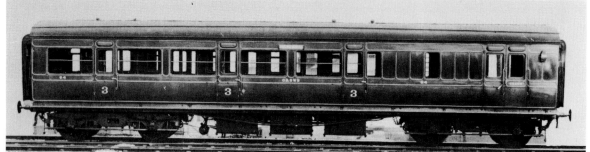

However, before considering these rather subtle influences, it will be convenient to conclude the Scottish survey.

Apart from the NBR and CR, the main Scottish user of corridor coaches was the GSWR and in Peter Drummond's time some very attractive vehicles emerged, somewhat in contradiction to his less than universally approved locomotive designs. However, like the other two big Scottish companies, any possible GSWR influence on a larger scale was heavily eroded by the dominance of the English element (Midland) in the M & GSW fleet of corridor coaches. These were always pure Derby and frequently identical to the domestic MR product. In fact, even before the grouping, the GSWR found itself operating Derby-designed vehicles under its own banner as a result of its share of 'cascaded' former M & GSW coaches. In this, of course, it was no different from the NBR or CR. Nevertheless, the Drummond coaches were good, and in their extensive use of pressed steel bogie frames distinctly ahead of much of the opposition.

Drummond, of course, had come to the GSWR from the Highland Railway, and one can detect some degree of design linkage between his latter-day HR coaches and those he built for his new company. However, the HR was a somewhat impecunious system and did not build many corridors on its own account. To be honest, it hardly needed to, being fed, so to speak, at Perth with the products of Derby, Wolverton, Doncaster et al as they converged from their various points of origin on to the Southern end of the famous Highland main line to Inverness and the far North. What a spectacle that must have been in its heyday! Thus, apart from a few carriages built for services between Inverness and Glasgow or Edinburgh, the HR did not bother too much with corridors and the GNSR was much the same, although it had produced some excellent examples of the type as far back as the 1890s.

Back in England, one can clearly differentiate between the provincial and the London-based systems. Thus, for example, although the GCR might not have been as important in absolute terms as, say, the LYR, the fact of its main line to Marylebone caused it to tackle the corridor coach problem with some vigour. In a sense it had no choice because it was entering an already competitive field against some real giants. In a fairly modest start at the turn of the century it displayed some imaginative internal touches, not least being the admirably wide corridors compared with the competition. This was a much appreciated improvement, albeit at the expense of compartment width. This, however, can be seen in retrospect to have been little more than a final flowering of the Manchester, Sheffield and Lincolnshire Railway approach (the pre-1899 name of the GCR). Once the GCR began to build to the limits of its structure gauge for the London Extension, its new 'matchboard'-sided corridor coaches commanded immediate attention. They were better than the more famous 'Barnums' (see below), not least in their styling — large, dignified and on the whole harmonious. They kept the wide corridors, and some of them even had a patent form of anti-telescoping device fitted to their headstocks which caused a great deal of contemporary technical interest. They certainly gave plenty of space inside for all their passengers.

The other two so far unconsidered London-based concerns with any pretensions to corridor coach status, the LSWR and the GER, could not have been more different. Alone of the constituents of what was to become the Southern Railway, the LSWR had trunk route status and, in consequence, started to tackle the corridor coach implications of its competition with the GWR for the West of England traffic. It did so in a distinctive way, not so much in terms of vehicle quantities, types or styling, but by a quite positive attempt to translate the undoubted advantages of set train formations (see Chapters 8 and 9) to the altogether more complicated business of long-distance operating. This has already been touched upon earlier in the chapter but this seems, perhaps, the best point at which to amplify the topic; the LSWR, while not alone in producing sets of corridor coaches, was undoubtedly the leader, as indeed was its Southern successor.

The practical advantages of set formation trains of time-saving on coupling, marshalling and so on, have already been discussed, particularly in the non-corridor field, but they are equally applicable to corridor vehicles if some sort of standardized pattern could be evolved. Interestingly, most of the 'corridor' lines tended, at best, to go for only a few regular sets of vehicles, each being 'dedicated' to one or two specific services, the LNWR, for example, being one such system. The balance of services on these lines would be operated more often than not by a suitable assemblage of vehicles formed up to meet specific operating requirements. The LSWR was different. It took the view, quite deliberately, that if one could arrive at a suitable fixed formation for most of the time, then at periods of pressure one could augment the principle either by having a few spare or 'loose' vehicles (dominantly thirds) or even use two identical

sets rather than one only. On the whole, it seems to have worked and the Southern continued the general idea right into the post-Second World War era. In fact, after the grouping the idea translated quite well across to such large systems as the LMS which became quite adept at using what it called 'Inter-Corridor sets' (an abbreviation for standardized Inter-District corridor formations of three or four coaches) for many services.

Back to the LSWR, however, and what can be said is that even the building of its corridor coaches was carried out with the deliberate intention of forming the vehicles into sets. The individual carriage running numbers, the 'handing' of the brakes (if relevant) and the fact that the sets were regarded for decades as having almost permanent status (they were branded by number on the the outer brake ends) were all reflected in the end product — and the vehicles themselves were not bad either. The earlier examples were typically LSW in styling (low elliptical roof, traditional panelling and so on) but were 9 feet wide and quite lengthy (57 feet) by company standards. However, before the grouping, the LSWR entered somewhat pioneering territory by being one of the first companies to experiment with the more widespread use of steel, particularly in the exterior panelling, in its so-called 'Ironclads'. They were hardly things of great aesthetic distinction — some would even call them dull and boring — but, like many things LSW, they were built like the proverbial battleship and stood the test of time. Southern Railway practice came much under their influence for many years and they too tended to the 57-foot length already considered above.

Top left *The NBR introduced this seven-compartment corridor first in 1907, but built a few more in 1921 so they must have been more than adequate. They certainly provided a very clear view on the corridor side as exemplified by No 460 of the 1921 series.*

Above left *Peter Drummond's GSWR corridor stock, though not particularly well known, was more than uncommonly handsome and spacious as well as being typically British, points well shown in this brake third No 64. The full thirds had only seven compartments in a 57-foot length. Most railways at this time would have used eight.*

Right *The spacious 2 ft 6 in wide corridors of the new GCR trains are shown clearly in this view of first class No 1299 of the 'armoured' series.*

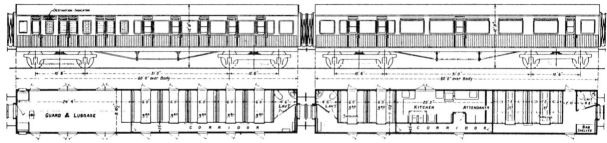

Corridor Third Brake Carriage. To carry 40 Passengers.   Corridor Composite Kitchen Car. To carry 12 First and 16 Third Class Passengers.

Diagram of London, Manchester and Bradford

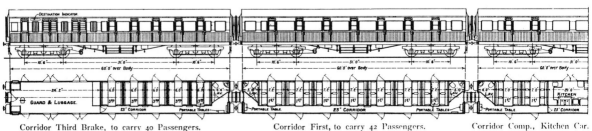

Corridor Third Brake, to carry 40 Passengers.   Corridor First, to carry 42 Passengers.   Corridor Comp., Kitchen Car.

Diagram of London and Manchester Armoured

Figure 51 *Floor plans and simplified side elevations of the trend-setting GCR 60-foot corridor trains of 1915, one of which was fitted with the so-called 'armoured' anti-telescoping device at the carriage ends, details of which are also shown (below).*

The GER, on the other hand, although having been an early pioneer of corridor stock, tended to remain somewhat on the periphery of things. Its vehicles, be they clerestory or elliptical, were always neat and unfussy, and some of the boat train formations were distinctly superior; but somehow they never seemed to catch on either in popular acclaim or in subsequent LNER days. Perhaps it was because few could believe that a railway capable of such diabolical atrocities as were provided for its suburban services could ever be capable of producing anything decent in the longer-distance field. It was manifestly unfair, as a study of some of the pictures in this book will reveal, but it seems to have been real enough. Nevertheless, after the grouping the impoverished LNER must more than once have had

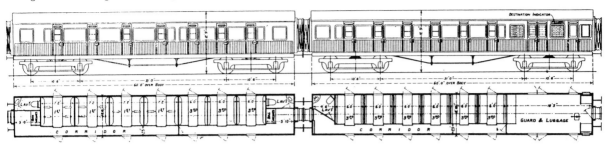

Corridor Composite Carriage. To carry 20 First and 24 Third Class Passengers. Express Train; Great Central Railway.

Corridor Third Brake Carriage. To carry 48 Passengers.

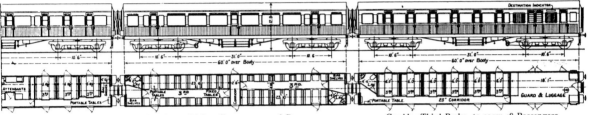

to carry 36 Passengers. Express Train, Great Central Railway.

Third Class Dining Car, to carry 48 Passengers.

Corridor Third Brake, to carry 48 Passengers.

cause to be grateful for the quality of the better GER corridors; they certainly lasted for a long time and were by no means the worst of their kind, although they tended to be shorter in length than most contemporary corridor coaches.

A rather different story is to be told of the SE & CR, a railway not renowned for its corridor stock. In fact, to all intents and purposes, it had none to speak of save for one or two rather curious exceptions, including an altogether rather splendid clutch of brake composites. Interestingly, these were not built for local consumption but more in accordance with a 'keep up with the Joneses' philosophy. We have seen how the SE & CR produced some distinctly superior non-corridors, but where through services were concerned it obviously felt it needed to be on a par with the companies with whom it exchanged traffic. It thereupon proved that it could come up with the goods if necessary. Its introduction of corridors for its own services was caught up inextricably with the grouping but, for the record at this point, it should be stated that the final SE & CR corridor designs were of distinctive 'matchboard' style which formed the pattern for the Eastern section of the SR after 1922, even if not in quite such a seminal way as did the 'Ironclads' of the LSWR.

As for the Brighton influence on corridor coach evolution, it may safely be ignored!

Corridor coaches on both the larger and smaller provincial companies, if built at all, tended in layout terms to copy the patterns of the larger concerns but

some interesting vehicles emerged. Even the Cambrian and Furness Railways had a few, but perhaps the most significant contribution, as far as future influence in Britain was concerned, was that of the LYR, an unlikely contender for honours one might feel. Over the years, the Lancashire and Yorkshire has been given less than due credit for its often innovative approach to the business of operating a railway. We have already noted its quite generous provision of bogie coaches in the non-corridor field and equally one could instance the work of George Hughes in the sphere of locomotive development. There will also be cause to come back to the LYR in the story of steam railmotors and electrification (in Chapter 15) but what is perhaps less well known is its influence in the field of gangwayed carriage design.

As fas as side corridors were concerned, the LYR examples were from the outset built to quite full dimensions — 56 feet by 9 feet. Originally with arc roofs, they went straight to the full elliptical style early in the century and thereafter mirrored contemporary fashion in terms of layout and operation. Thus far they would merit no more and no less attention than those of many another company, but in one important respect the LYR turned out to be a significant trendsetter on a nationwide basis, and this was its espousal of the open saloon interior as a common alternative to the conventional side corridor — which nicely sets the scene for a discussion of the second principal type of gangwayed ordinary mentioned early in this chapter.

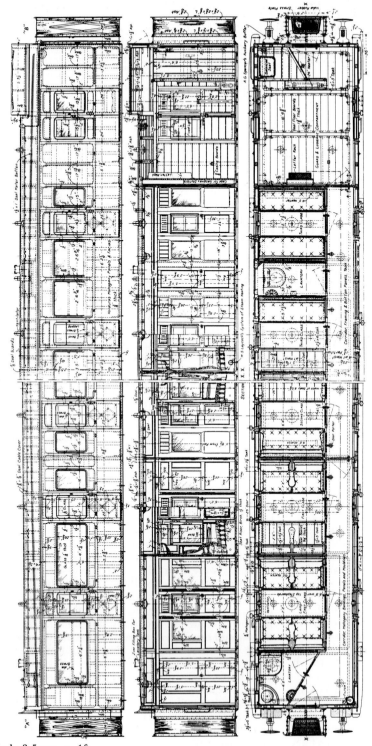

Scale 3.5mm = 1ft

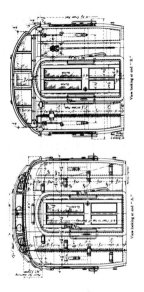

Figure 52 *A rare but by no means inferior essay into the side-corridor field — elevations and plan of the exceedingly well-appointed bogie tri-composite corridor carriages built by the SE & CR for through operation to the North and West via the LNWR, MR and GWR.*

Above right *Probably the first serious attempt at open stock was represented by six so-called 'Picnic' saloons by the LYR in 1900-01. They were true harbingers of the later and ubiquitous open third. No 2509 was the first and only one to be built without gangways (added later). The use of traditional panelling, a treatment always confined by the LYR to its carriages with open interiors rather than the orthodox LYR styling gave distinctive visual characteristics to the carriage.*

The open configuration began in the dining car field, having obvious practical advantages in the context of meal service, but for many years this was the only type of carriage which displayed this form of interior layout. Even those relatively few open carriages without a kitchen/pantry area were always regarded as dining carriages, and several railways built the odd example from an early date, back in the 1890s in some cases. However, as far as can be ascertained it was probably the LYR which first began to consider them as an alternative to side corridors for ordinary, as opposed to dining, use. The reasons cannot be determined exactly, but alone of the pre-grouping companies the LYR regarded them on virtually equal terms with the side corridor type, and thus began a trend which in BR days was virtually to eliminate the good old side corridor style for new construction. Of course, it was never quite as simplistic as this in real terms and for many decades open stock was regarded more as a supplement to rather than a replacement of the side corridor approach, particularly in the third (now second) class field.

Like them or loathe them — and both views have their adherents — the open carriage configuration

possesses certain advantages from the railway company's point of view. For one thing it is cheaper to make, having less internal partitions and, save for a few exceptions which can realistically be ignored, considerably fewer outside doors. Secondly, and this time from the passenger standpoint, if four per side seating is required in a gangwayed third class coach, then the 2 + 2 seating of an open carriage is marginally more comfortable than the four per side corridor style. If three per side in the third class compartment is favoured (common in later LMS, LNER and BR days), then an open 2 + 2 arrangement actually offers 33% more seats per vehicle without too much loss of comfort. These latter considerations have obviously proved decisive in modern BR planning, but it may well be that the LYR was the first company to see it that way.

In terms of styling, the LYR open stock generally differed from the side corridor equivalent in a number of ways, some significant, others not. For some reason, whether arc or elliptical roof, most of them abandoned the characteristic and somewhat spartan Attock styling (page 106) in favour of a more traditional style which embodied distinctly pleasing proportions and a somewhat more elaborate lining

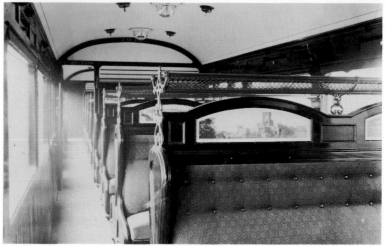

Above *Open composite No 865 typifies the later and more familiar elliptical roof 'fireproof' stock of the LYR. The large picture windows are prominent and, again, it was given traditional panelling.*

Left *Another LYR experiment in 1908-09 produced some fascinating carriages described as 'open side corridor', again with large windows. They displayed conventional LYR exterior styling, and the interior of the first example, No 1010, is illustrated. Although the general idea did not catch on, the LMS found use for them for many years.*

treatment. This may have been a shrewd publicity move, for when allied as it was in the elliptical roof variants with large 'picture' windows in each seating bay, it really did make the carriages look very modern by comparison with those of many other lines.

It was some of these open coaches which formed the basis of the celebrated LYR 'Fireproof' trains. In Chapter 4 the reluctance of some railways to abandon gas lighting was mentioned, and the LYR was one such. In 1913, it produced a series of metal-clad carriages with much supplementary fire-resistant material in an endeavour to stave off the need to move, exclusively, to electric lighting. They were distinctly attractive and gracious vehicles and, being placed on the prestigious residential expresses, sometimes known as 'Club' trains, operated by the LYR to Southport and Blackpool, they were given all the publicity which the company could muster. With an Aspinall 'Atlantic' or Hughes 4-6-0 in charge, they were no mean advertisement for a so-called 'provincial' railway. However, their influence in the 'fireproof' sense was far less significant than the implications of their layout. Indeed, it is not too

far fetched to presume that the LYR experience of ordinary open stock was by no means the least of the reasons why the LMS adopted the idea with great vigour after the grouping

Now, lest it should be thought that the LYR was the only major company to experiment with gangwayed open coaches for non-dining services, this impression must be corrected. Several of the pre-1923 companies tried the idea with a greater or lesser degree of success, including a few unlikely contenders such as the Caledonian. However, of those which did persevere, one can perhaps single out the Midland and the Great Central as being the most noteworthy.'

During 1909, the Midland Railway had put into service a handful of 'Vestibuled Excursion Coaches' as it called them. As mentioned on page 171, the use of the word 'vestibule' was somewhat misleading and the LMS took up the term after 1922 to denote the open configuration, but in essence they were gangwayed clerestories with open saloon interiors. Although relatively few were built, they must have struck something of a receptive chord because after the Great War, almost on the eve of the grouping, the MR repeated the exercise, this time using a 57 feet by 9 feet elliptical roof body as the basis. Their exterior treatment was entirely traditional and they employed a very characteristic twin window arrangement per seating bay (one fixed and one drop light) but their influence was profound. None had actually been built when the MR was succeeded by the LMS, but the new company promoted the designs with vigour, adopting them as the first of the new standard carriage types. There is a fair amount of evidence that they were intended primarily as excursion stock, but, no doubt bolstered by the LYR experience, the LMS quickly came to regard them

as one-for-one equivalents of side corridor coaches and used them accordingly, thus establishing the beginnings of the modern day 'open second' as it is now called.

It is, in fact, rather doubtful if these MR/early LMS open carriages were ever seen as particularly significant trendsetters at the time for, superficially, they did not look too different from most other coaches and there were not, until the 1920s, very many of them; but the same could not be said of the Great Central 'Barnums'. These huge vehicles, of quite distinctive, almost slab-sided construction with 'matchboard' panelling, emerged on the scene in

Right *The GWR did not really espouse open stock until after the grouping, but some of its turn-of-the-century so-called 'corridors' displayed semi-open interiors. This is an unidentified Dean clerestory third.*

Below *The true trend-setter? LMS 57 ft 56-seat open third No 4649 built to Midland design, was not put into service until after the grouping. Hundreds were built over the years, undoubtedly representing the most significant move away from side corridors thus far seen (BR LMR).*

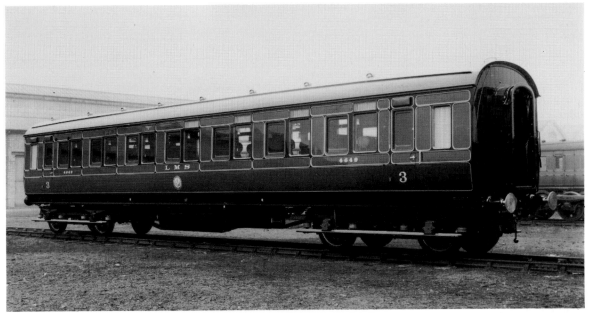

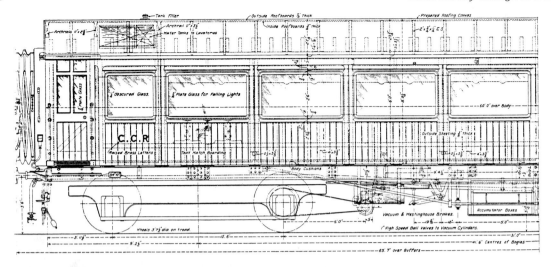

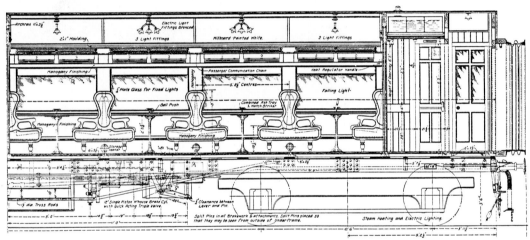

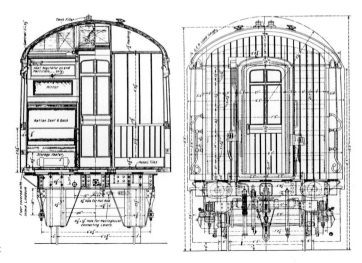

Scale 4.5mm = 1ft

Figure 53 *Selected drawings of the well-known GCR 'Barnums'. Never built in great quantity, many of their features, not least their large windows and overall size, anticipated several aspects of more modern practice.*

Right *The open version of a coupé is well shown in this NER elliptical roof first class example of* circa *1908. In open carriage parlance, this would be known as a 'half-bay'.*

1910. Built to the full dimensions of the GCR London Extension structure gauge, they offered open accommodation in a very spacious envelope. In all conscience they cannot be regarded as the most visually pleasing of coach design, or the most significant, but they were certainly noticed at the time and one or two still survive in preservation. Their nickname is believed to derive from the contemporary fame of the Barnum and Bailey circus elephants — an allusion to their great size. Such is the odd nature of popular perception that their historical relevance has regularly been over-emphasized. Interesting though they were, nothing quite like them was ever seen on British metals either before or since, but their fame seems assured.

Turning, finally, to the types and interior layouts of open general service coaches in the pre-grouping period, once again the early examples turned out to be prophetic. By far the most common was the full third, the ancestor of the modern open second. Typically it would have seven or eight bays of seats, two per side, in facing pairs and quite regularly with a table. Intermediately there would be one or possibly two transverse partitions defining smoking and non-smoking areas, and the lavatories would usually be at one or both ends of the carriage. Full firsts and composites would be much the same, the full first normally deploying one less seating bay for a given coach length just as in the side corridor equivalent,

and with the composite there was again the problem of organizing a mixture of first and third (second) class bays so as exactly to fit the carriage length. The open equivalent of a coupé was sometimes to be seen, ie two seats in a sort of half-bay, either side of the central aisle. First class bays almost always had an asymmetric aisle with single seats on one side, twins on the other — the 2 + 1 arrangement so familiar today. If, by any chance, one encountered a 2 + 1 *third* or even *second* class open coach one could be fairly sure it was either a non-kitchen dining vehicle or had started life as such.

Brake-ended open coaches were much fewer in number relative to their non-brake equivalents than in the side corridor field and were almost always third class. Open brake firsts were exceedingly rare as were open brake composites, and the latter were rarely if ever used in the same mode as the side corridor brake composite. This curious distinction remained right through the company period and into BR days. In later days one might have no choice but to occupy an open coach in the third (later second) class part of the main train, but if you were travelling in the through coach, detached *en route*, the compartments reigned supreme.

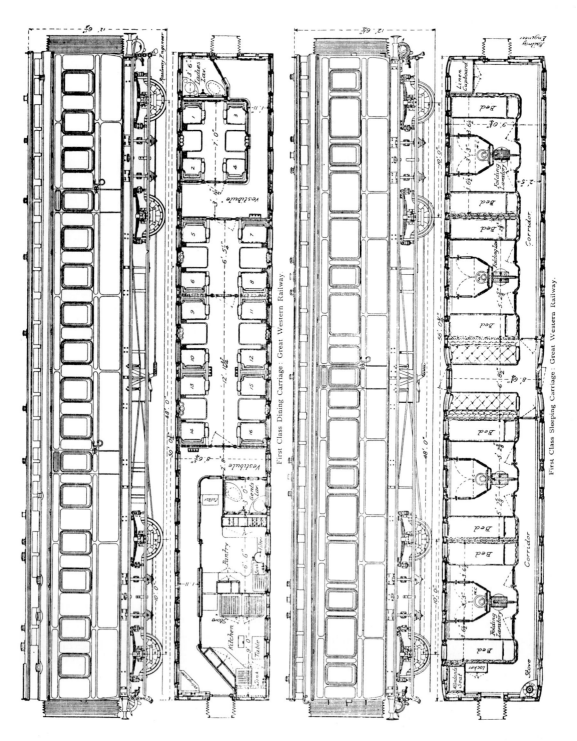

First Class Dining Carriage : Great Western Railway.

First Class Sleeping Carriage : Great Western Railway.

Scale 3mm = 1ft

11. Mobile hotels

With the possible exception of the ocean liner, there can have been few more gracious ways to travel than were provided by the Great Trains during the heyday of the mechanized railway. To be strictly truthful, one should perhaps say 'are' rather than 'can have been' since the modern railway is still quite capable of offering stylish travel when it so chooses. The trouble these days is that there are so many alternatives from which potential travellers may choose that, in proportionate terms, the railway's share of the market has declined and this has inevitably caused a reduction in the total number of prestigious trains. Moreover, life styles have changed and too many people nowadays seem to be in too much of a hurry to be able to enjoy the more leisured progress of a well-endowed train. 'Travelling hopefully', it would seem, has been thoroughly superseded by the wish to arrive, and this has just as inevitably caused changes to the nature of the railway carriage as it has in other walks of life. However, it was not always thus, and in terms of vehicles Britain made its own highly distinctive contribution.

Central to the whole business of civilized long-distance travel were two principal types of vehicle, supplemented occasionally by carriages of a third group. The two main categories were sleeping and dining cars, while the third and smaller group were the various forms of 'private' saloons, covered in Chapter 13, which could be hired by those who so wished. Together, these three types of operation inspired the building of vehicles which for the most part were both refined and beautiful and which have rarely, if ever, been surpassed in terms of sheer quality, be it inside or out.

The most sophisticated requirements of the long-distance traveller were first addressed beyond the shores of Britain, notably in America, and it has to be conceded that many of the early British dining and sleeping cars drew heavily on American experience, particularly influenced by the activities of the Pullman Car Company. In fact, so important was the influence of the latter that it has been felt desirable to include a separate chapter on this very theme. However, in the strictly British context things had settled down quite nicely to a recognizably 'modern' approach by the start of our period, most of the experimentation having been carried out, as in most other areas, during the last decade of Victoria's reign. This relatively late start can, for the most part, be attributed to the geographically small nature of Great Britain compared with many parts of the world. There were few journeys which lasted appreciably more than twelve hours, and none at all which spanned the twenty-four-hour spectrum, so the carriage needs in Britain were from the outset different in scope. Nowhere was this more true than in the field of sleeping cars, the first of the categories to be considered.

The British sleeping car began, so history tells us, with the North British Railway in 1873, closely followed by the LNWR and, two or three years later, the Midland, the latter in the form of its imported American Pullmans. For the rest of the nineteenth century, various different approaches were tackled, mostly concentrating on internal layout about which there seemed to be no single agreed solution. From the outset, however, it was a facility for first class passengers only and this did not change until as late as 1928. Part of the reason was cost, the other part being mostly related to the nature of the service and the social mores of the time.

It is an inescapable fact that a bed takes up more floor space than a chair, so, for a given size of carriage, fewer sleeping passengers can be accommodated at floor level than if they were sitting on conventional seats. There must, therefore, be a premium charge for the use of a sleeping carriage — but then one is saving the cost of a hotel room. There can be no doubt that the early railways concluded that only their first class clients would want to or be able to afford these extras and also that they would expect for their money a considerable degree of comfort, privacy and amenity. In consequence, the British sleeping car was always exceedingly well equipped, whatever its layout.

There was, in fact, a somewhat more economical alternative, the 'Pullman' section. This idea, imported from America, consisted of facing pairs of seats (on either side of a central aisle) which at night could be drawn towards each other to form a bed, and a second 'bunk' lowered from a folded position in the ceiling. This ensured that when converted for night use, a Pullman sleeper could carry as many recumbent passengers as it could seated customers by day — a very practical solution in the context of multi-day travel in North America. However, privacy at night was achieved by little more than curtains drawn down the aisle and shutters or screens between individual section. Moreover, there was no room to change into night attire and, frankly, the

Figure 54 *Elevations and floor plans of William Dean's splendid dining and sleeping cars for the GWR in 1896. Their internal arrangement set most of the basic standards for the next century, regardless of subsequent changes.*

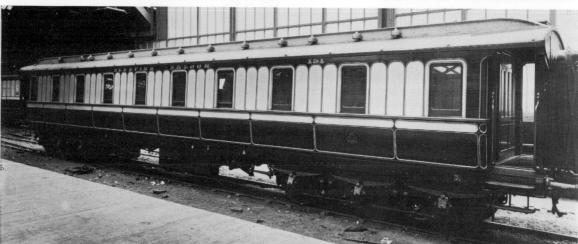

Left *Interior view of Pullman 'sections' made up for night use on the Midland Railway in the 1890s*

staid Victorians *did not like it!*

Although the MR persevered with this approach to some extent until the start of the present century, the typical British sleeping car was designed to provide a series of private bedrooms, each self-contained as far as possible. For one thing, there was scarcely any need for it to have a daytime function (journeys were too short) and the customers liked their privacy so from the start of the present century the sleeping car was almost always a purpose-built vehicle rather than one with a conversion option. It still is, for that matter, and during most of the last 100 years its interior layout has hardly changed, having settled down to one basic and overriding form in the 1890s with very few noteworthy exceptions.

The characteristic British sleeping car was and still is a side corridor compartment vehicle, each compartment functioning as an individual bedroom, with either single or double occupancy. There are the usual lavatories at the corridor ends and, regularly, an additional compartment for the travelling attendant. Frequently in Edwardian days there would be one non-sleeping compartment provided with a few comfortable seats for use as a smoking saloon, but this idea was quickly abandoned — it was a bit extravagant and the all-sleeping configuration (save for the attendant) became standardized.

Within each compartment, the railways spared no expense to make the facilities as self contained as possible — washbasins, coathangers, shelves, even hooks on which to hang the pocket watch being all provided. About the only thing which was not present on an individual compartment basis was a lavatory and given that the compartment was rarely more than about 6 ft 6 in by 4 ft 6 in (some doubles were about 6 ft 6 in square) this was hardly to be wondered at. Even so, there was usually what might best be called 'emergency provisioning' — at least for the men folk!'

All in all, the sleeping car was a masterpiece of compact planning and, in most cases, of considerable merit too. Of course, not all railways needed to (or did) provide such vehicles, so the design influence was dominated by the long-distance concerns, particularly the Great Northern (including its NER partner in the ECJS), the Great Western, the London

Centre and left *Classic twelve-wheel clerestory sleeping cars, LNWR No 151, built in 1904, and MR No 2767, seen in post-grouping LMS markings, built in 1911. Both could sleep eleven first class passengers, mostly in single berth compartments*

and North Western (including as it did all the designs for the WCJS) and the Midland (including all the MSJS designs). As we have seen, most of them had settled on a fairly universal layout by the start of the present century, but there were still some variations on the theme to be observed. Comparisons are always odious, but risking a personal view, it seems to me that the dominant influence, both in contemporary terms and in relation to their future influence, was provided in the fleets owned, maintained and operated by the East and West Coast rivals; they did, after all, operate the most numerous and the longest distance overnight operations.

Both organizations favoured the twelve-wheeler for a variety of reasons and, additionally, both of them also tended to be dominated by one only of the respective owning companies, the GNR (ECJS) and the LNWR (WCJS). The twelve-wheel preference is easy enough to explain, being mostly connected with matters of weight. If to a normal corridor coach one added the extra weight of washbasins, beds, sundry internal fittings and a whole host of additional ancillary features below the floor (eg heavier-duty batteries to cope with the greater demand), the weight limit for an eight-wheeler was soon exceeded, and if one was going to have to contemplate twelve wheels, one might just as well go for the largest and most versatile vehicle which *could* be carried on twelve wheels — typically about 65 feet long and 40 tons tare. In consequence, there were spawned some truly memorable carriages on both sides of the country, and it would be a brave man who attempted to adjudicate between them. If forced to a decision, I would favour those of the West Coast, not because I have specialized in their study but mainly because there were rather more of them, there was slightly more consistency in design and, on the whole, they did tend to be more influential in the design of subsequent LMS and BR vehicles than any of the others; but in truth there was little to choose.

Both favoured the clerestory at the start of our period, and beautifully elegant they were, an attribute which was not changed when, during the Edwardian period, the full elliptical roof was adopted. They literally (and most appropriately) rode like dreams, and in the case of the West Coast examples at least three of them were considered good enough to be transferred, without significant structural or mechanical modificaion, to the LNWR (later LMS and BR) Royal Train. This role they continued to fulfil until 1968, over sixty years after the first of them had been built. There can be little doubt that had the East Coast Royal Train (see Chapter 13) been used appreciably for overnight travel, some of the ECJS sleepers would have been similarly distinguished. Of all the lost causes in the field of

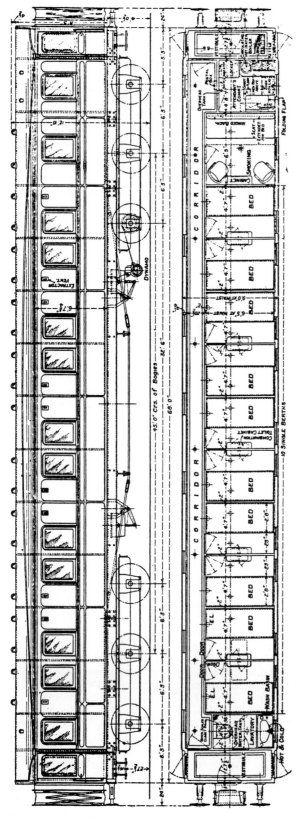

Figure 55 *The finest of the pre-group sleeping cars were probably the 68-foot twelve-wheelers introduced by the LNWR in 1914. This drawing shows the arrangement as built — little different from a modern-day plan. One survived in Royal Train use until 1968.*

railway carriage preservation — and there have been more than a few — the absence of a genuinely original Edwardian sleeping car is by far and away the most significant omission in my view — they were magnificent.

However, the East and West Coast routes did not have a total monopoly of the elegant overnight trade, a fairly respectable 'second eleven' being provided by the Great Western and the Midland. Each, in its own way, was distinctively different. The Great Western was in fact the first company to standardize the side corridor style, and during the Dean period its side corridor sleeping cars could stand comparison with any whether in terms of practicability or visual harmony. However, the GWR did not have the sheer distance of those routes which headed north from London, so its fleet was never anything like so big. Moreover, its few Edwardian sleepers did not stand the test of time as well as those of the East and West Coasts. There were four massive twelve-wheel 'Dreadnoughts' built in 1907 which lasted less than thirty years, and a pair of eight-wheel 'Toplights' of no great distinction which were later rebuilt into twelve-wheel composites of the most monumental dullness — and that was about all in the pre-group period.

The Midland was rather better, but if truth be told, not much. Its sleeping cars had initially mostly been in the Pullman mode with its centre aisle and 'pull-together' sections. Right at the start of the century, its latest offerings were still partly of this kind — a clutch of four Pullman-type twelve-wheelers containing a mixture of sections and individual compartments served by a side corridor. Visually they were most striking with a high clerestory roof, but were soon rebuilt to an all side corridor arrangement. Even so, they did not survive beyond the early 1930s, a similar fate to that which befell the more orthodox 'British' Midland sleeping cars of the Bain era. They too were often twelve-wheelers, typically elegant clerestories but finding little subsequent favour.

In one respect, however, the Midland was a bit more adventurous in its building of a composite sleeping car type, a handful of which were constructed during the Bain period. They were not true composites in the sleeping car sense because only the first class compartments had beds, third class being accommodated in conventional seated

compartments. However, they were quite spacious, had fewer than the normal number of outside doors and ample luggage space. In this respect they were distinctly better than some of the so-called composites of the West Coast, a series of distinctly peculiar vehicles, well recorded, which grafted a 9 feet wide first class portion containing sleeping compartments on to an 8 ft 6 in wide portion containing the orthodox third class seating accommodation. They were grotesque, and the true composite sleeping carriage had to await the post-grouping period for its appearance. Needless to say, the LMS, which inherited both the West Coast and Midland exemplars, had little time for either of them after the early 1930s.

Thus it was that the two principal Anglo-Scottish routes dominated the sleeping car scene in Britain, and continued to do so. What, however, of the rest?

Well, in point of fact there were not many of them and since it is not the purpose of this book to chronicle every single vehicle built by every individual company, two final examples of the genre must needs suffice. They could not have been more different or, in a sense, more surprising, coming as they did from the LSWR and HR respectively.

The LSWR examples were conventional enough but rather larger than most of the matching corridor fleet. In truth there can have been little use for them, and one suspects that it was more of a gesture to keep pace with the rival GWR than anything else. They were, however, rather handsome in a typically South Western way and their relatively few patrons to the deepest West Country must have been pleased enough at the time. They were, in fact, sold off later to the GWR itself.

It has already been remarked that the Highland

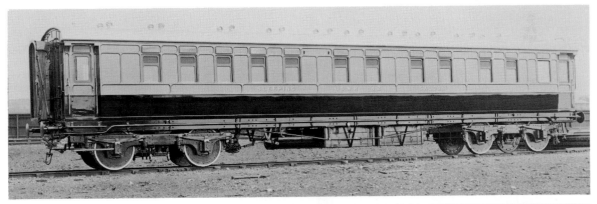

Most but not all sleeping cars were twelve-wheel types. Here are two eight-wheelers from companies not particularly famed for their sleeping car provisioning: the compartment side of LSWR No 42, one of four built in 1908, and the corridor side of Highland Railway No 8, one of this company's only excursions into the sleeping car field (Gavin Wilson Collection).

was served by through carriages from many parts of the kingdom, so its building of two sleeping carriages in 1907 was something of a surprise. They seem to have been dedicated to the overnight Inverness-Glasgow service (one each way each night) and were composites, first class sleeping, third class ordinary. Built in Drummond's rather distinctive 'matchboard' style, all but unique to the Highland, they did not last long in their original form and by LMS days they were operating as corridor third brakes with a very long van portion in place of the erstwhile first class sleeping accommodation.

If sleeping cars were most noteworthy for their limited nature (in terms of operating company), the same was not true of the second major category of mobile 'hotel' vehicle, the dining car. By the turn of the century, 'meals on wheels' had become an accepted part of longer-distance travelling, even for those railways which could not offer the sort of distances which would justify sleeping cars, and by the 1923 grouping there were relatively few of the major railways which could not offer at least one or two quite sumptuous catering vehicles. As with sleeping cars, there was a strong Pullman influence, deferred to the next chapter, and in the case of on-train catering, it was actually a Pullman service in 1879 between Leeds and London which began the whole business in Britain. From these tentative beginnings there had developed by the turn of the century a fairly characteristic dining car form which was to stand the test of time well into the modern era.

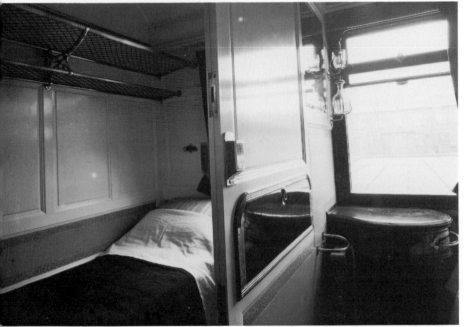

Above left and left *Contrasting compartment interiors of the LSWR carriage shown on page 199 and GN/NE joint car No 12 of 1909, the LSWR example having the wood panelling and brass bedstead. The GN/NE interior has interconnecting berths with the sliding door open between them; an exterior view of a similar type is shown on page 120.*

Right Figure 56 *This group of elevations and plans shows typical dining car arrangements, both centre and end-kitchen. It is noticeable that the greater size of the GWR 'Dreadnought' of 1904 permits more people to be seated, albeit at rather closer seating pitch than the 1912 GNR and NER examples. The NER car is illustrated on page 14.*

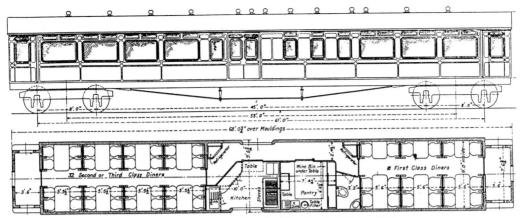

Composite Dining Cars, Great Western Railway.

'Dreadnought' Dining Car, Great Western Railway, 1904

Scale 2mm = 1ft

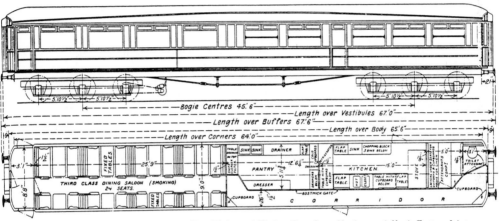

Third Class Dining and Kitchen Car; Great Northern and North Eastern Joint.

Third Class Dining and Kitchen Car, Great Northern and North Eastern Joint, 1912

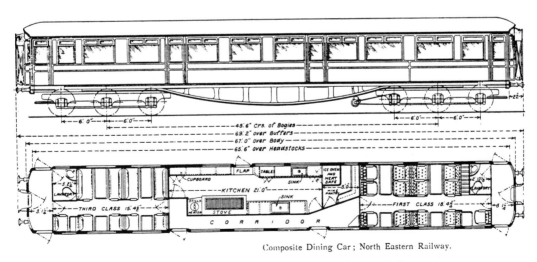

Composite Dining Car; North Eastern Railway.

Composite Dining Car, North Eastern Railway, 1912

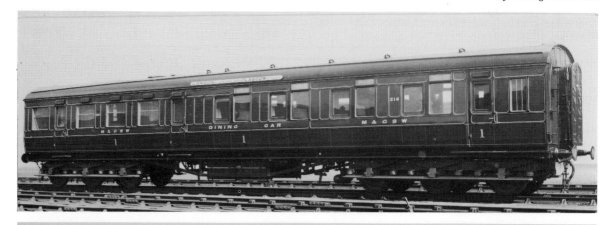

These dining cars, built for the M & GSW Joint services in 1920, formed a typical operating pair: kitchen first and open third. The vehicles are M & GSW Nos 216 and 394 respectively.

The typical British dining car consisted of a combination of food preparation and food serving areas, the kitchen and pantry commonly occupying anything from 25-50% of the length of the vehicle with the seating normally arranged in 2 + 1 form separated by an aisle. Four to six seating bays were the common standard, although there were exceptions at both ends of the scale and the seats could be arranged in one of two principal layouts. That with the kitchen/pantry portion at one end and the seats at the other was known as an 'end kitchen' vehicle, that with the service section in the middle, flanked by seating bays at both ends, was the 'centre kitchen' variant. The latter was almost invariably a composite with the kitchen and pantry separating firsts from thirds while the end kitchen type could be either one class only, divided by a partition into two classes, or even used for all classes, in which case it was known as a 'common' diner. From this it will be appreciated

that dining facilities in Britain were not confined to the first class passenger during this period, unlike the case with sleeping cars. Interestingly, this universal provisioning has been somewhat eroded by latter-day BR policy, and it is now quite regularly impossible to obtain a full meal service on a modern InterCity train without first taking a first class ticket — so much for late twentieth century egalitarianism!

Like sleeping cars, dining cars generally carried much more equipment than ordinary day carriages so, like their overnight contemporaries, they regularly displayed the twelve-wheel form. There was also much in common in terms of length and exterior styling but, of course, there the resemblance ended. However, before coming on to this aspect of the story, a few more general points need to be made.

Firstly, although all classes were catered for, the second class option was very much in decline even on those railways which still retained all three, so the dominant trend was first, third or 'common'. Secondly, it was found from experience that the typical kitchen of a dining car was well capable of serving more meals than there were seats in the diner itself. This gave rise to a second type of dining vehicle which had no kitchen but whose seating areas were arranged in the characteristic dining car form, ie open interior with central aisle. These were and are regularly referred to as 'open' diners as opposed to 'kitchen' diners. A fairly typical pairing might be a kitchen first with an open third, but there were many variations. In certain circumstances, it was possible to find a kitchen-only vehicle flanked by open coaches, but this practice did not become particularly widespread until after the grouping. An alternative solution, regularly practised on the LNWR for example, was to have two quite separate kitchen diners in different parts of the train and, if need arose, provide removable tables which could be fitted into some of the side corridor compartments for the overflow trade.

As for the vehicles themselves, it seems fair to state that with the exception of Royal and some special saloons the interior furnishing of a British dining car was the most splendidly opulent of any of the vehicles built by the railways. They moved slowly from ponderous late Victorian to a slightly less oppressive form during the period under review, but at all times

Style on the GCR. This splendid vehicle, open third class dining car No 1602, was built for the London Extension of the GCR right at the end of the last century. The interior was truly first class standard, while the exterior seems to have been inspired by Wolverton (LNWR).

GER kitchen interior of 1912. The ingenious storage arrangements for crockery etc are quite typical, and various utensils are seen hanging below the outer casing of an auxiliary water tank — see page 58.

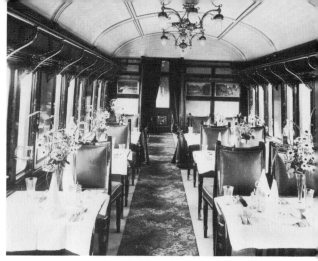

The GWR 'Concertina' period 70-foot first class dining cars of 1906 established a general end-kitchen layout on the GWR until the grouping. They were less spacious than the 'Dreadnoughts' but still rather larger than found anywhere else.

the use of decorative finishes was high on the priority list. Whether it be inlaid veneer, marquetry panels, flamboyant Lincrusta panelling or superb quality upholstery, the diners usually had some or all of them. Polished and carved wood detail was common, associated with delicate mouldings and decorative light fittings. Built-in bottle holders, courtesy lights and push-buttons to call the attendant were all commonly to be found and, particularly significant, there was much less difference between first and third class than in most carriages. Most third class diners were literally first class in their provisioning, and it was often difficult, if not impossible, to tell the difference. In fact, unless the first class diner was one of those relatively rare birds (inspired by Pullman) with single seats on both sides of the aisle, there often was no difference save, perhaps, for a slight reduction in the length of each seating bay in the third class section. They really were splendid and many railways vied with each other in terms of elegance and style.

As for kitchens and pantries, these were veritable masterpieces of ingenuity. They normally used compressed oil gas for fuel and literally every nook and cranny was pressed, cleverly, into service. This did, of course, lead to some particularly odd-shaped cupboards and storage areas, but space was at a premium and none was wasted. Thus, for example, in a kitchen not much more than 10 feet by 6 feet, one might regularly expect to find anything between six and twelve burner rings and at least two ovens, each capable of holding a 30 lb turkey.

It would be impossible to identify the best company in the dining car sense but, of course, matters of scale decreed that some railways needed to build more than others. In the purely numerical sense, the LNWR probably held first place and, at its peak building

period, it was sending new twelve-wheel diners into service at the rate of one per month. Splendid though they were, who is to say that they were better, in absolute terms, than the four cars which were all that were ever built by the LYR or the spectacular one or two individual vehicles of such railways as the GSWR.

The other big companies in the dining sense were the East Coast triumvirate (particularly the GNR and NER), the Midland and the Great Western, but the GER, the nineteenth-century pioneer of third class dining cars in 1891, had some quite incredibly good diners, particularly associated with its boat trains, while the LSWR slotted some distinctly stylish clerestories into the middle of several of its five-coach corridor sets. The 'upstart' GCR added its quota and, short of letting this chapter degenerate into a catalogue of vehicles built, it seems best, for once to let the pictures tell the story. Happily, dining cars were well-photographed vehicles (possibly because they had a sort of 'flagship' status) and it seems a pity not to give many of them an airing! If, however, I was forced to give an opinion, I would award the absolute decor prize to a quite splendid Adam-style one-off built by the GNR for its Harrogate service. From the outside it was rather ordinary, but inside it was a tour de force (see the picture on page 207) No doubt the Harrogate destination was not the least of the reasons for its styling!

At this point, and as a link to the Pullman chapter, it should perhaps be mentioned that several railways were quite content to leave the bulk, if not all, of their catering to the Pullman company, and amongst the more important lines in this respect were the LB & SCR, SE & CR and Caledonian, although there were others.

During the pre-group period, the full meal dining car was the archetypal catering vehicle, those passengers with less gastronomic propensities having to make do with either their own pre-packed picnics or the now long-gone railway picnic hamper, a thing of great splendour which, happily, I am just able to recall from the days of my childhood when my father would obtain one at London prior to a journey north. They were amazingly good value and it was always a moment of great excitement to see what might be contained therein. There were some surprises! These hampers were in a sense precursors of the modern buffet car, a vehicle which did not really achieve any great significance until the 1930s and which did not really come into its own until the modern day. However, this survey of the pre-group catering vehicle would be incomplete without mention of a few of the early attempts which were being made, even at the start of the period, to provide an alternative to the full meal. They were not very numerous, nor very well known, but were of interest, if only because they were ahead of their time.

Allowing a year or two of latitude in respect of its building date (1898), pride of place in the innovation stakes early in the century goes to the GCR which, coincidentally with the opening of its London Extension, not only built some exceedingly well-appointed conventional dining cars but added a buffet car design by way of bonus. This was regarded with considerable contemporary interest and was a very well thought out design, but it did not at the time start anything in the way of a trend, possibly because at that period even those third class passengers who partook of meals were solidly middle class and could readily afford the full meal option. In any case, the fad for 'fast food' is very much a modern innovation.

One of the nice things about the well-run dining car until, in fact, quite recently was the regular service of afternoon tea, and this seems to have inspired such railways as the LNWR to experiment with a minimum facility catering vehicle, usually called a 'tea car'. These were corridor thirds with two central compartments converted into a miniature kitchen/pantry/service area. They seemed to be used on cross-country journeys to provide a form of corridor refreshment service; one could not actually consume the food at its point of preparation since there were no dining seats as such. It was not a true buffet car but must have had some success, the

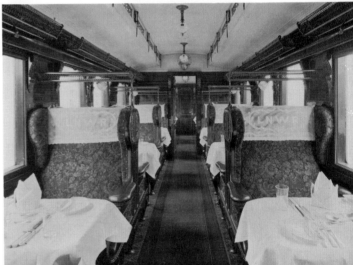

Right, top to bottom *Contrasting first class interiors of typical GNR and LNWR clerestory twelve-wheel dining cars* circa *1905, together with a comparative view of a GWR elliptical roof 'Toplight' period example, No 9561 built in 1922*

Top *Ten years or so after they were built, Gresley modified some of his GNR pre-decessor's twelve-wheelers to accept the new larger window style introduced* circa *1906. It gave an even more elegant look to what were already stylish vehicles. This is the centre kitchen composite No 2993, modified in 1913.*

Above and left *The GER built relatively few dining cars but this clerestory example for the Continental boat trains was very good. The company favoured leather upholstery in the first class, shown to good effect in the interior view of the same car, No 24. The later GER ellip-tical roof cars of 1912 were finished in almost identical manner.*

Right *This must surely have been Britain's most elegant dining car interior ever — GNR No 3250, the famous 'Harrogate' car built in 1912.*

Below right *The first LSWR dining car venture consisted of adding a clerestory to its basic corridor coach style. The centre kitchen composite was preferred and the result was pleasing (see the picture on page 128). This view shows the third class section of No 67, one of an earlier series with three windows per seating bay.*

LNWR eventually placing a dozen or so in service. They were not, however, repeated after the Great War.

The sleeping car and the dining car have stood the test of time, albeit with some minor changes, but the third category of travelling 'hotel' vehicle, the special saloon, was very much a child of its time. In the days when everyone from the highest to the most humble travelled by train, there was a small but identifiable demand by specific types of clientele for semi-private travel facilities, and the railways sought to meet this demand by offering as an alternative to the normal form of carriage the exclusive use of a special saloon in exchange for a specified number of fares. These vehicles are somewhat inextricably mixed up with the Royal saloons and are considered in Chapter 13.

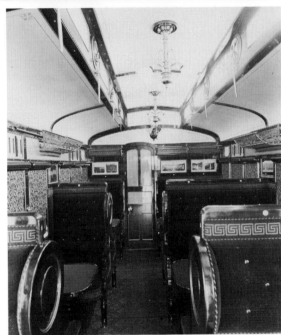

Below *The GCR's pioneering Buffet Carriage of 1898. From the left-hand end, it consisted of a buffet counter, a central kitchen with gas range, an attendant's compartment and three third class compartments plus lavatory. Strangely, this fundamentally sound idea did not catch on until more than a generation later in the 1930s.*

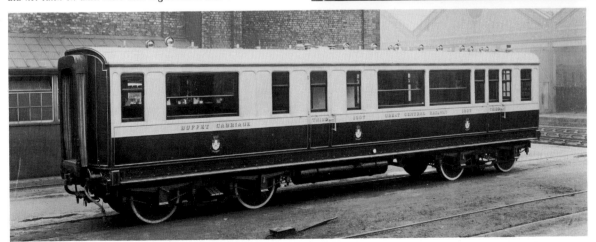

12. The Pullman contribution

There can be few more evocative yet misunderstood words in the field of travel than 'Pullman'. It can define a railway carriage, refer to a style of travel, be applied to other forms of transport than rail or even be used to designate an up-market waiting room, yet all in all it is no more than the surname of a famous American entrepreneur who had a vision back in the last century, one George Mortimer Pullman. No doubt Mr Hoover met with much the same problems in the field of domestic appliances as years went by.

Pullmans have been with us, in one form or another, for most of the twentieth century and long before, and it is vital that their place in railway history is properly understood. It is quite complex, but fortunately there is some considerable specialized literature on the subject (see the Bibliography) so we need only consider the essential outlines here, concentrating mainly on those relating to the vehicles themselves. Even in this context, however, there are two main strands of development to the story, the use to which the vehicles were going to be put and the nature of the vehicles built to fulfil this requirement. Logically, one should start with the nature of the services themselves; this time, however, we must spend a little more time than usual in the pre-twentieth century period.

Pullman carriages were developed by George Pullman himself in North America and were designed from the outset to offer extra comfort and amenity for those passengers who could and would pay for it; the 'would' is important in the British context! From the beginning, there was always an expectation of greater style and comfort in a Pullman vehicle, thereby explaining the subsequent adjectival use of the word. The first Pullman cars (always 'cars', by the way, *never* carriages) were imported into Britain by the Midland Railway in 1874 and put to work on its lines. They were owned by Pullman himself, in the shape of his American Pullman Car Company and 'plied for hire' on the lines of whichever railway system was prepared to accept them. Although the Midland ordered some almost identical carriages for itself, the name 'Pullman' could only be applied, strictly speaking, to those vehicles owned and operated by the Pullman Company. Thus, in effect, some Pullmans were not 'Pullmans' even though they looked as if they were! The subsequent confusion can readily be appreciated.

How, then, did the Pullman Company make its living, since it did not actually collect the fares for the journey itself, these being kept by the parent railway? The method was to charge a supplementary fee for the use of the Pullman Car and keep all the catering and other incidental revenue thus generated. Since people tend to part with their money rather more readily if treated in a civilized fashion, the emphasis in a Pullman was always firmly on the aspect of 'service'. The attendants were always attentive and always smart; they pandered to every wish of the passenger; they took pride in remembering the names, seating preferences and even the favourite drinks of their regular clientele — and so forth. There was, in truth, more than a bit of the snob element to it all, but interestingly it was eventually made available to third class passengers

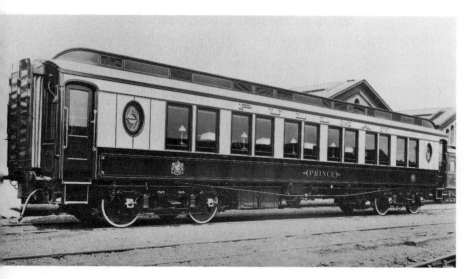

Left *Parlor Car 'Prince' was built in the USA in 1888 as part of the first British Pullman car set with 'closed' entrance vestibules. It is seen here as re-modelled in 1915, carrying the familiar umber and cream livery in its first variant, ie with a cream-coloured 'headboard' above the windows.*

Right *The stylish twelve-wheel 'Arundel', here seen at Brighton in the older Pullman colours, was a sumptuous parlor car imported from the USA in 1899. It did not remain long in this form, being rebuilt with a kitchen and renamed 'Majestic' in 1905. This and the previous view give a good comparison between the eight and twelve-wheel American style bogies regularly used for Pullmans at this time.*

too. Pullman cars, by tradition, concentrated on the dining and sleeping car side of things — this was, after all, a reflection of their American origin — and it stayed thus throughout, although in Britain it tended during the present century to be mostly a catering operation.

The independence of the Pullman Company from the various British railways remained intact throughout the company period and into early BR days, at which point it tended to become rather anachronistic and caused not a few problems until the company was taken over, absorbed, bought out, or call it what you will, by BR in 1954. Today the word is used solely to denote a style of travel and has no corporate meaning in Britain.

Because the Pullman Company relied heavily on the willingness of independent private railways to accept its cars, there was always a degree of *frisson* in its relationships with the companies. Some liked Pullman, others did not and the rest were indifferent, so the operations were never to be evenly spread throughout Britain. Wales, for example, was a Pullman 'desert' until a much later period and for rather different reasons. In fact, during the 1901-23 period, Pullman operations were mostly confined to the South of England, but more of these details anon.

The first Pullman cars to run in Britain were actually built in America but with dimensions to suit the smaller British structure gauge. They were shipped in component parts across the Atlantic where they were reassembled, initially at a special sub-section of the Midland Railway's main works at Derby. The cars were, therefore, thoroughly American in concept and design and they remained thus for some three-quarters of a century, long after all construction had moved to England.

The American influence was both conceptual and structural, the latter being somewhat a consequence of the former. Their layout almost always followed the open style with centre aisle and seats on each side. This was true whether the vehicle was a day carriage or a 'Parlor Car' as it was called — the spelling of 'parlor' was long kept in its original 'old English', later American form — or whether it was for sleeping purposes, in which form the Pullman 'section' was typical — see page 195. The Midland tried out both types, and just to proclaim its own independence called its own day carriages 'Midland Drawing Room Cars' rather than Pullman Parlors. They were, in fact, much the same sort of animal.

To be honest, The Midland did not find its espousal of Pullman-style travel to be a total success. The open plan and supplementary charges were both in the nature of mild disincentives in those days and seemed to supervene the improved facilities and vastly improved riding qualities of the vehicles themselves. The Midland was quite good at this sort of thing itself anyway, so maybe the comparisons were not quite as dramatic as they would have been on other lines. Be that as it may, during the rest of the nineteenth century, the various imported Pullmans tended to be shifted around from system to system, and although the MR remained half-heartedly faithful to at least a few Pullman sleeping cars, most of Pullman's fleet (if not sold to the Midland and others) tended to find a more welcome home in the south, particularly on the LB & SCR.

Below *The almost 'Gothick' interior of 'Arundel' typified most turn-of-the-century Pullman parlor cars. Two almost identical armchairs and a section of a similar interior survive at the National Railway Museum.*

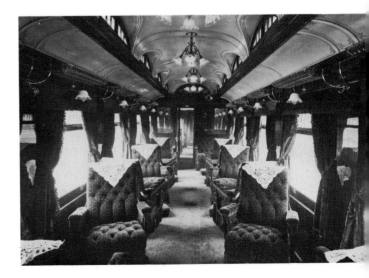

Thus matters remained, more or less, until George M. Pullman's death in 1897.

Meanwhile, the vehicles themselves were heavier and larger than anything else in Britain at the time of their introduction and for many years afterwards. They were also immensely stronger than British-built coaches. In part this was a consequence of both their layout and their ancestry. Their American origins decreed a much stronger basic construction because of the generally less well engineered lines on which they ran in the USA. Their open layout, devoid of too many intermediate partitions and with doors at the extremities only, meant in fact that their strength could be built into the sides, floor and roof uninfluenced by compartments and outside doors. In fact, the wooden-bodied Pullman carriage was built on the integral box-girder principle and had no separate underframe or chassis. The whole carcass was immensely rigid and most of the ancillary features were, literally, fixed to the outside. This structural form withstood the transition from open to closed vestibule entrance lobbies in 1888 and from the favoured clerestory from of the nineteenth century to the elliptical roof of the twentieth. Roof apart, the structure of the preserved 'Topaz' at the NRM (built in Britain in 1913) is all but identical to that of the first to be imported almost forty years earlier.

This integral box structure also withstood the transition from wood to steel at a later date, and it was not until well beyond the period of the first two volumes of this survey that Pullman actually made use of a standard British body form when the last vehicles were ordered in 1959 by the 'independent' Pullman concern, now wholly BR owned. Until then, Pullman was, to all intents and purposes, alone.

It was alone, too, in the realm of carriage styling. For some 75 years from the 1870s to the 1950s, Pullman cars were flat sided. One is tempted to call them 'slab sided', but this would be an insult to the decorative efforts of their makers. The styling was, in fact, a straight copy of contemporary American practice, miniaturized by about 10-15 per cent to suit the more restricted British loading gauge. In the wooden-bodied era, which lasted well into the present century, there was, typically, a lower body treatment of vertical 'matchboarding', above which was a definite waist rail followed by the window-level features. The windows and their intermediate panels were always decorated, at times flamboyantly, and until the 1950s the lavatories *always* displayed a lovely oval stained glass window. Above the windows was the headboard on which, most commonly, would be emblazoned the word 'PULLMAN' in an ostentatiously sized but stylishly executed elongated serif style of lettering. They often ran on American-pattern bogies, they almost always sported a highly finished and distinctive livery and they nearly always carried names, not numbers. It was not until Pullman cars entered the third class arena that 'Car No XXX' was seen on the sides of the vehicles; even then the first class cars continued to bear names.

The famous 'umber and cream' livery of the British Pullman car was not, as is often supposed, written into the tablets. In fact it did not become the normal scheme until the 1900s when the association with the LB & SCR was strong. As we have seen (page 133), the latter company introduced the livery early in Edwardian days and at this range in time it is a moot point whether Pullman copied Brighton or vice versa. The Pullman livery change is variously quoted as 1902 or 1906, the Brighton being 1903-4. What can be said is that prior to this time Pullman often used its own dark olive brownish-green colour scheme (as in North America) with a profusion of gilded scrolls and curlicues, the bane of the life of any modeller! In the 1901-23 period, those on the SE & CR and Metropolitan Railway carried a distinctive dark red scheme, in the former case matching that of the SE & CR and faithfully reproduced on the preserved 'Topaz' at York. It was not until the 1920s that all Pullmans became two-tone brown and cream.

So much for the (mostly) pre-twentieth century background to the twentieth century Pullman story. It is by no means simple and the continuation was less so. Allowing a bit of licence as to dates, the story of the present century began, for practical purposes, in the late 1890s, first with the death of Pullman himself and then with the introduction of a second complete train of Pullmans on the LB & SCR in 1898 supplementing the earlier 1888 set, the latter, incidentally, being Britain's first electrically-lit train.

Even so, by the turn of the century, Pullman's toe-hold on the British mainland was at best precarious, however defined. When the founder himself died, the pioneering Midland had already decided it could build its own diners and sleepers every bit as well as could Pullman, and either did so or bought the erstwhile Pullman vehicles rather than run them under Pullman's own banner after the original contract had expired. Since the Midland was the major long-distance user of Pullman cars, this was rather a blow, scarce mollified by a small purchase of four Pullman-bodied sleeping cars in 1900 which were actually put on Midland-pattern running gear and flew Midland insignia from the outset. By 1907, only the LB & SCR, LSWR and the Highland were operating Pullmans.

In fact, while drawing heavily on the Pullman influence in terms of vehicle types and, to some extent, styling, all the British long-distance companies tended to take the view that they preferred

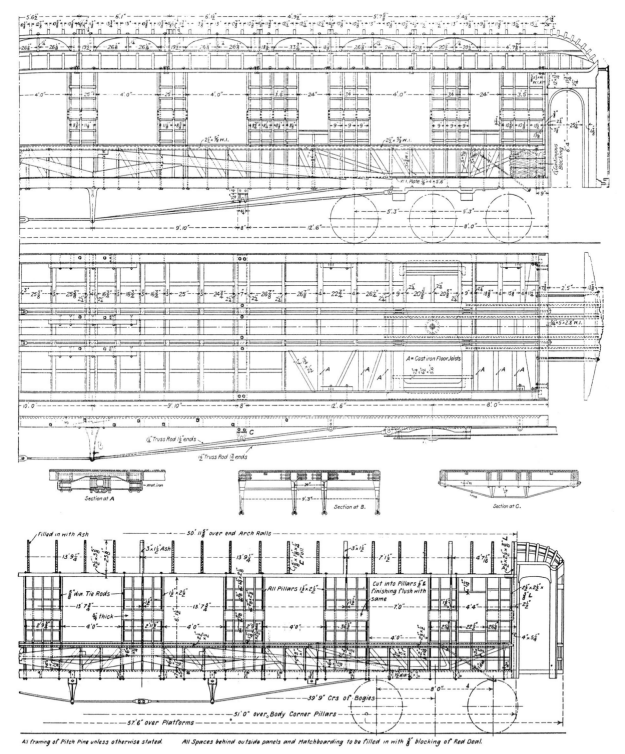

Figure 57 *The basic structure of wooden-bodied Pullman cars is shown in these drawings of a 1905-built clerestory American car and the similar but smaller British-built SE & CR example of 1913 with elliptical roof.*

Scale 4mm = 1ft

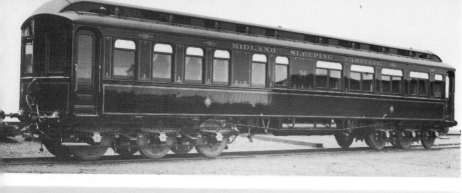

Left *The last Midland association with Pullman — sleeping car No 36, one of a batch of four introduced in 1900. Note that although still very American — the bodies were built there — the carriage is running on Midland pattern bogies*

Left *The famous pioneer 'Southern Belle' Pullman set of 1908, brake-ended 'Alberta' at the near end. This was a completely twelve-wheel formation embodying the new elliptical roof profile but still bearing all the traditional Pullman hallmarks. Note the lack of end gangway.*

Opposite page *Interior view of the bar counter in Pullman buffet car 'Mayflower', one of two built in 1910 by the Birmingham C & W Co and used on the Metropolitan Railway (Staffordshire County Record Office).*

to build and operate their own sleeping and dining vehicles, so Pullman was forced to look elsewhere. Its saviours turned out to be the mid-range companies, especially those in the London area. As has already been pointed out, few of the Southern companies themselves built either dining, sleeping or even gangwayed vehicles, and this gave Pullman the opening it needed. A fairly thorough and successful assault was made on these lines and the company which benefitted most was the Brighton concern, closely followed by the SE & CR. The LSWR began to build its own diners, but on the other two lines, increasingly after 1910, it was Pullman cars which provided most if not all of the catering right through into Southern Railway days, and it is no coincidence that its offices eventually settled down at London Victoria (jointly operated by the LB & SCR and SE & CR) and its repair works became located first at Longhedge (SE & CR) and later at Preston Park, Brighton (LB & SCR).

Thus began an association which lasted half a century or more and was bolstered by a fairly rapid seried of changes in the structure of the company following the death of the founder himself. The story is complex and well recorded elsewhere, but the salient facts are that in 1907 ownership of the company was transferred across the Atlantic to a new organization headed by Mr Davison Dalziel, who was also Chairman of the famous Wagons-Lits Company based in Belgium and founded by the celebrated George Nagelmackers. In fact, and brushing aside all the tortuous ramifications of company finances and organization, the so-called independent British Pullman Company was, as near as makes no odds, a wholly-owned subsidiary of Wagons-Lits until 1954, as anyone could guess who had travelled with either of them. Staff uniforms, crockery, cutlery, and even the basic *modus operandi*, although independently branded and marketed, were too close for it to be coincidence. It was, if you like, the railway equivalent of the familiar 'badge engineering' in the motor car business of the late twentieth century!

Pullman in Britain ceased to import American-built cars in 1906, thereafter relying on British works to satisfy the demand. Even this was not as simple as it may sound. Brand new vehicles were usually built by outside contractors such as, for example, Cravens of Sheffield and the Birmingham C & W Company, but they were still very American in concept and construction, and Pullman issued the specification; there was no 'off the peg' purchasing of standard designs. Pullman itself also built 'new' cars, but these were most difficult to define. Many of them were, in fact, comprehensive rebuilds of older cars while others were in the form of old underframes fitted with completely new bodies. For example, a particularly astute purchase by Pullman of some ex-Great War ambulance coaches provided some splendid underframes on to which were grafted new bodies to launch Pullman into the 1920s era. Obviously, by this time, the 'integral wood box girder' form of construction had been supplemented by this later subterfuge, but outwardly there was little apparent change in appearance.

Nor did it stop there. For all the outward opulence, Pullman was a very shrewd practitioner of 'make do and mend'. While it might be necessary, for technical reasons, to upgrade the running gear (possibly even the kitchen equipment), if the armchairs and other such fitments were still sound, reupholstery and reinstatement into a so-called 'new' car was quite customary. This went on right to the end and beyond, and is one of the reasons why the preserved 1913 'Topaz' was displayed for many years *sans* seats; when the 1960 Metro-Cammell cars were put into service by BR, their original loose armchairs were purloined from the vehicles they replaced! 'Topaz' lost most of its armchairs as a result and it was not until 1984-5 that the NRM was able to make restitution of this fine car by commissioning exact replicas of the original tables, table lamps and armchairs. However, back to the pre-group era.

The first manifestation of the new order was a splendid set of British-built cars for the LB & SCR 'Southern Belle', as it was called in 1908. It was the Brighton's third full Pullman set and became justly famous for both its quality and its clientele between London and Brighton. Its successor, the electrified 'Brighton Belle' of 1933 et seq, became equally celebrated, although this latter train must await Part II.

To be honest, London to Brighton was hardly the most suitable route to act as the standard-bearer for the Dalziel Pullman philosophy. For one thing, the distance was really too short to provide scope for all that Pullman could and would, given the chance, try to do. A fifty-mile run through the North and South Downs, lasting little more than an hour, was not really adequate time in which to deploy the particular style which was 'Pullman'. However, it does seem to have been the first twentieth century manifestation of that most distinctive feature of British Pullman operating — the provision of meals at all seats. This may, in the event, have turned out to be the most significant factor. In North America, 'Pullman' was synonymous with high-quality *overnight* travel; Dalziel made the British equivalent synonymous with day travel in association with 'refreshing the inner man'. The one feature which made British Pullman travel in the twentieth century so agreeable was the tacit assumption by Pullman that one would prefer to take a meal without having to go to a separate dining car. Even in North America this was a rare possibility. Thus, whether first or third class (practically speaking, second class may safely be ignored in this

context), this was what one expected of Pullman (and usually got) for one's supplementary payment.

Interestingly, the one main-line company which seemed to have grasped this point in relation to its own dining cars was the pioneering Midland. Almost alone in the pre-grouping period, the Midland encouraged 'all the way' travel in its dining cars and transmitted this idea to some extent to its LMS successor. One can perhaps conclude that the Midland's long association with Pullman in the last century may have had something to do with it.

The long-term effect, as far as Pullman was concerned, was that the provision of kitchens was a vital part of its operations. If a train was 'all Pullman', then every second or third vehicle (first *or* third class) would be a kitchen-equipped car, and if running singly there would almost always be some minimum catering facility as well as the passenger seats. Thus, for example, when Pullman managed to get a couple of cars on to the outer suburban services of the Metropolitan Railway, they were catering vehicles, albeit in modern parlance more correctly referred to as buffet cars. The same idea was translated with considerable success to the catering services of many trains on the post-1922 Southern Railway.

Meanwhile, the other two principal Pullman activities in the pre-grouping era of the this century could not have been more dissimilar or more widely geographically spread. Staying, for the moment, in the South of England, we must now address that most

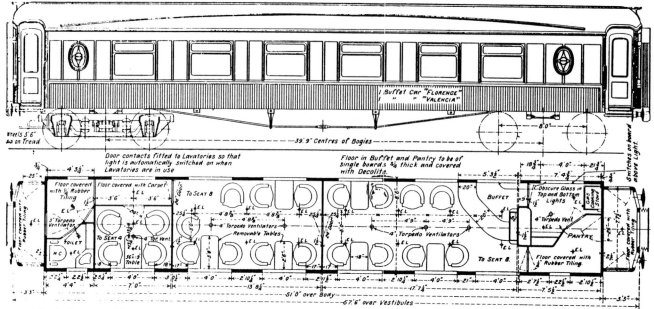

Scale 3mm = 1ft

Figure 58 *Elevations and plan of typical 57 ft 6 in buffet/parlor cars 'Florence' and 'Valencia', built in 1910 for the SE & CR. The preserved 'Topaz' of 1913, at the NRM, is an almost identical full parlor equivalent.*

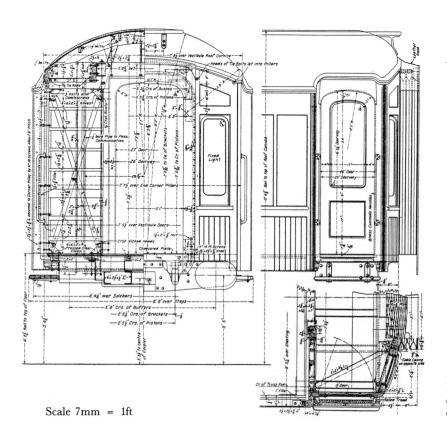

Scale 7mm = 1ft

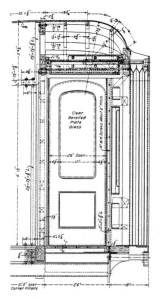

Figure 59 *Vestibule end and framing detail of the 1910 Pullmans for the SE & CR.*

Above *Parlor Car 'Emerald', built by the Birmingham C & W Co in 1910, was turned out in SE & CR dark red livery, carrying the somewhat rare circular Pullman badges used on a few vehicles at this time. It was replaced in 1960 by the modern 'Emerald', now preserved at the NRM.*

Below *The years between 1920 and 1924 saw a great upsurge in Pullman car building and refurbishments, most of the consequences being felt in the post-grouping era. It also saw the last flowering of the classic twelve-wheel wooden-bodied cars, two of which are featured here: 'Arcadia', built in 1920 by Clayton as a kitchen and*

parlor car and remodelled by Pullman in 1924, as shown, to a brake parlor first; 'Malaga', a kitchen/parlor car built by Pullman itself in 1921 and seen here on 'Golden Arrow' service in the post-1928 umber and cream colours with dark headboard. It survives in preservation, thanks to the Ian Allan organization.

interesting railway, the SE & CR. This company, even when operating as two separate systems (SER and LC & DR) during the nineteenth century, had always witnessed the SER part in some rivalry with the LB & SCR for cross-channel patronage, but in the 1890s the SER had gone to the rival American Gilbert Car Company to obtain some suitable vehicles by which to counter the Brighton Pullmans. These vehicles (see page 11) were very much like Pullmans, but it was not until 1910 that the SE & CR decided to throw in its lot with Pullman. There thus began a separate and profitable association (of which the preserved 'Topaz' is the prime exemplar) of Pullman with a second major part of the south-of-the-Thames railway scene. By 1922, all the best SE & CR boat trains were, like the best Brighton services, Pullman-operated and, with the limited continued espousal of Pullman by the LSWR for some services, the stage was set for the continued linkage between Pullman and the SR after the grouping.

While all this was happening in the south, the main trunk lines (LNWR, GWR, MR etc) were all busily developing their own 'in house' services without the help of Pullman, though doubtless influenced by some aspects of the Pullman style. It therefore must have seemed that the future of the Pullman Company lay within its southern redoubt; but this was to underestimate the tenacity of Dalziel's company. Pullman never stopped trying to persuade the various railways to accept its cars, and eventually an unlikely breakthrough was made in Scotland in the shape of the Caledonian Railway which entered into a twenty-year agreement with Pullman in 1914, embracing all its non-WCJS catering services. This led to the building of an opulent fleet of Pullman dining cars, all with suitably Scottish-sounding names of considerable resonance. Thus there entered the scene 'Flora McDonald', 'Lass o' Gowrie', 'Fair Maid of Perth' and many others, not the least of which was

the unique Pullman observation car 'Maid of Morven' which plied its trade on the Oban line, displaying a quasi art nouveau observation verandah to all and sundry and causing much comment both in the contemporary and subsequent railway press. It was the only British Pullman observation car until after the Second World War.

Now, apart from the 'Maid', the Scottish cars were quite different from what later became to be understood as normal Pullmans (ie parlour cars or parlour/kitchen cars). They were pure 'all-comers' dining cars in the best Wagons-Lits tradition (first and third class) and were simply slotted into normal Caledonian trains as required. Their umber and cream livery did not fight too strenuously with the Caledonian colour scheme, but in 1923, with ten years of the contract still to run, they began to look somewhat visually incongruous amongst the ever-increasing flood of LMS-liveried crimson lake coaches. In any case, the LMS did not favour Pullman, so when the contract came up for renewal, the LMS, like the nineteenth-century Midland a generation earlier, bought up the cars rather than renewing the contract, painted them red and proceeded to add them to its own not inconsiderable fleet of dining carriages. As such, some of them survived until well after nationalization.

Not for the first time, this part of the narrative has exceeded the strict bounds of the period covered by this first volume; thus was the nature of Pullman, however. It never quite followed the normal ground rules.

By the end of the pre-grouping period, Pullman had rather recovered from the low point of the early century. It was well established south of the Thames, had a firm foot-hold in Scotland, was one of the few civilizing influences on the Metropolitan Railway and was even beginning to make successful overtures into East Coast, later to become LNER, territory. This led to a considerable flowering of activity during the

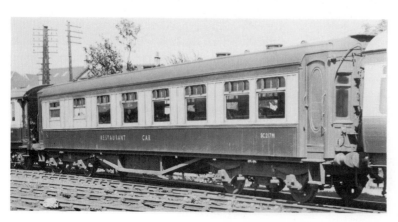

Left *This Pullman in BR red and cream livery, circa 1950, was one of the many pure dining cars built to a Caledonian Railway order. It entered service as 'Meg Dods' in 1923, was sold to the LMS in 1933, becoming LMS No 217 in the composite dining car series and was scrapped in the form seen here as Sc217M — quite a history!* (F.W. Shuttleworth).

Above right *Interior view of what is thought to be No Sc217M, circa 1950, scarcely changed from its original state and still in amazingly sound condition* (F.W. Shuttleworth).

1920s to 1950s period, but will have to await the next volume to resolve. The common factor in all these operations was catering, and by way of concluding this first encounter with the Pullman company, a few further words on the vehicles themselves will not be out of place.

One could always recognize a Pullman from the outside, partly from its livery but also from its shape, and this was just as true of the interior. We have seen how things began as a mixed day and night activity, but by the twentieth century Pullman was a dining operation. Its foundation was the full parlour car, with the kitchen/parlour as a close second, be it first or third class. Within the carriage, the layout was of the open configuration, dominantly individual armchairs in the first and 2 + 1 fixed seating in the thirds (introduced in 1915). A full parlour would almost always include two small compartments (or coupés) at the extremities between the main saloon and the end-located lavatory. These havens of privacy (almost always four-seaters) had a side corridor alongside and were much sought after. The name 'coupé' was very much a Pullman interpretation, for they were, in every respect, of full compartment size, unlike the honeymoon half compartments (page 165) normally called coupés. Kitchen/parlours had one such feature, the kitchen itself occupying the other end of the car, and this internal configuration remained very consistent throughout.

Other arrangements mostly followed either the individual dining car layout or the buffet car style, and for some 'all Pullman' sets a brake-ended version was also provided. These seem to have appeared originally as first class cars with 'Alberta' and 'Verona' on the 1908 'Southern Belle', but increasingly the brake-ended Pullmans were of the third class type. In fact, one of the first of the 'lower order' Pullmans was a brake third.

Within the carriage, first or third, the decor was unmistakable with its coved ceilings, considerable use of inlaid or carved woodwork (often both) and the ever-present table lamps, an indispensable accompaniment to Pullman travel and, in the pre-BR era, regularly stamped with the name of the car itself. A clock would normally be present (until more recent years), and floors would be carpeted. So good, in fact, were Pullmans that even the third class option was usually equatable with most *first* class diners in the non-Pullman field. That it could all be provided — and make money — at a cost of only a few shillings (10-30p) plus a meal price no more than that to be found on a normal railway-owned vehicle was one of the more astonishing facts of this highly idiosyncratic organization.

Pullmans were rarely built in vast batches, usually

coming into service only when specific needs arose. In consequence there were rarely more than a handful of identical specimens, and during the present century lengths varied between about 57 feet and some 68 feet, as did the choice between eight or twelve wheels; but they were all in the family. In consequence, when, as often happened, Pullman switched its cars from one service to another, it was not always possible that the more casual traveller would notice the change. Nor was it common for a complete set of new cars to be provided for a fresh service. It would, more typically, be a mix of new, refurbished and old. This too remained characteristic, but those readers who would know more will need to refer to the more detailed specialist works; it is a fascinating tale.

Pullman's influence was simultaneously both more and less significant than might be supposed. In the positive sense it showed what could be done, but some of Pullman's thunder was stolen, in the British context, when such systems as the GWR, Midland, East and West Coast Joint services and others demonstrated a quick ability to learn, copy and eventually replace Pullman with vehicles every bit as good. Thus Pullman never gained the same stranglehold on British train catering services as did its Wagons-Lits partner in many European countries. Even after the grouping, although Pullman maintained a high profile in certain areas, the traditional twentieth-century non-Pullman lines (essentially the LMS and GWR constituents of the post-1922 scene) were not involved until after nationalization, and for rather different reasons.

However, in spite of many disincentives, by the end of this first period of study, Pullman in Britain had well and truly arrived and still had its finest hours to come.

13. Special carriages for special purposes

We turn now and finally in this review of orthodox locomotive-hauled passenger carriages to those special vehicles which most railways could offer, even if only on a unitary basis, to those travellers who merited VIP or other special forms of treatment. By their very nature, they have always been at the forefront of such limited literature as the railway carriage has inspired, so I have tried hard to resist the temptation to wax too eulogistic and at too great a length about them. Much has been written already, and sheer repetition would border on plagiarism, but they cannot be ignored. For one thing, the various special and other carriages, however defined, were almost always at the apex of design, fashion and construction, and collectively they displayed in a far more tangible form than any other group of vehicles the sheer skills, ability and pride in the job which characterized the railway carriage builders. Limited they may have been in terms of those who were privileged enough to ride in them, but in all their glory they represented all that was best in British carriage building, and it would be unfair to those who built them not to comment on their place in the scheme of things. They were magnificent and, happily, one can still stand open-mouthed in admiration at the sheer quality of their workmanship, for many survive in preservation to the immense benefit of all.

At the top of the heap stood those vehicles built for or associated with the demands of the Monarchy, and there can be no doubt that during the Edwardian period of the pre-group age the ultimate high point of carriage design was reached in those vehicles provided for that most characterful of sovereigns, King Edward VII. The King liked trains and indeed had some splendid ones built for him — but they did not happen by accident, and yet again we must back off into the Victorian era to set the scene.

Queen Victoria embraced rail travel in the 1840s and was undoubtedly instrumental in helping to make railways respectable; she was, however, more than a bit conservative in her wishes and by the end of the nineteenth century had more than once frustrated those railways, notably the LNWR and GWR, which wanted to deploy their latest technology in the service of their Queen. She was more than happy to go on using her old vehicles, and the best that either the GWR or LNWR could do was to obtain her agreement to remount old carcasses on new running gear. The Queen was quite content with this compromise solution, the only genuine exemplar of which, the LNWR saloon, remains preserved for all time at the National Railway Museum. The

GWR equivalent is long gone, in spite of the valiant attempts by Tussaud's Waxworks to persuade us otherwise in their imaginative but artificial recreation of the 1897 GWR Jubilee train at Windsor station.

King Edward VII had none of his mother's inhibitions. His nineteenth-century carriages (provided for him as Prince of Wales) were generally rather more modern than the Queen's, and when he became King the approaches of the principal railway companies regarding new Royal Saloons were very well received. Indeed, it is said that he hated Queen Victoria's saloons and the NRM knows of only one recorded instance where her preserved saloon was used by the new King after her death.

First in the strictly twentieth-century field was the London and North Western Railway, the owner of Queen Victoria's principal saloon and the traditional provider of vehicles for the Windsor-Balmoral pilgrimage via Ballater (GNSR) station. However, before going on to the realization of this wish by both railway and sovereign, a brief last mention of the nineteenth century is necessary in the shape of two railways, the GWR and the LB & SCR. Both had built almost brand new Royal Trains of considerable distinction in 1897 and, the GWR Queen's Saloon excepted, these were all but twentieth century in concept and much to King Edward's liking. Not surprisingly they survived well, and, in fact, it would not be bending regal history too much to postulate that the elegant Brighton clerestory set was, to all intents and purposes, designed more to meet Edward's requirements than that of the elderly Queen. She was not best known for her pilgrimages to Brighton, or to the races for that matter!

However, the long-distance journeys north were not well provided for in terms of the new King, so the LNWR moved in swiftly, obtained approval in mid-1902 for a brand new Royal Train and managed to deliver the principal saloons by Christmas of the same year! These two fabulous twelve-wheelers were supplemented by no fewer than *six* matching a semi-royal carriages a year or so later, and the whole ensemble was a visual and technological *tour de force*, never surpassed and scarcely approached since. The LMS kept it intact until 1941, and some bits of it survived until the late 1960s in regular royal service. It was eventually augmented by the addition of matching sleeping and dining cars of the conventional Wolverton type together with a couple of brake vans for the train crew, the latter being superseded in 1923-4 by a pair of corridor first brakes. Amazingly, seven of these carriages survive, five in the NRM

Right *This view of the LB & SCR Royal Train of 1897 shows that the Brighton line was just as capable as anyone else of producing elegantly styled carriages if it so chose. However, only the Monarchy benefited!*

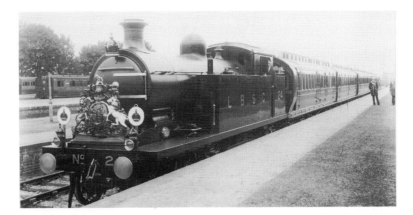

Right and below right *The 1897 GWR Royal Train embodied the so-called 'Royal' clerestory, a roof profile of great beauty with its distinctive overhanging domed-end shape. No new principal saloon was built, so the style was only used on new vehicles such as the Lords and Ladies in Waiting saloon No 9003, seen here in the new single-colour livery, sometime after 1909. The interior was every bit as elegant as the outside.*

collection (two Royal Saloons, both brake firsts and the royal dining car) and two (the staff diner and semi-royal) in private ownership.

The special vehicles themselves, although a mixture of eight and twelve-wheelers, were of the classic Wolverton 'twelve-wheel' exterior styling and entirely in tune with the style and fashion of the day. Their visual lines, both inside and out, broke away from the stuffy Victorian, and since they have been described many times in some detail I have let the pictures tell the story. What is, perhaps, most important about them is that they established the 'travelling palace' concept for the first time in a truly comprehensive way, by marrying the quite well established family saloon idea (see below) with all that was best in modern technology. Moreover, although their own clientele was very restricted, many of the ideas which they pioneered eventually became characteristic of much general service stock — much more quickly, in fact, than is often supposed. Indeed, the dining and sleeping cars allocated to the LNWR Royal Train from *circa* 1904 onwards were unmodified examples from the LNWR/WCJS fleet and little changed thereafter.

If, however, a single vehicle can be identified as being the most significant contribution to this essentially twentieth-century approach to the VVIP train, then there is only one serious contender — the magnificent carriage built across the turn of the century by the LNWR for the 4th Duke of

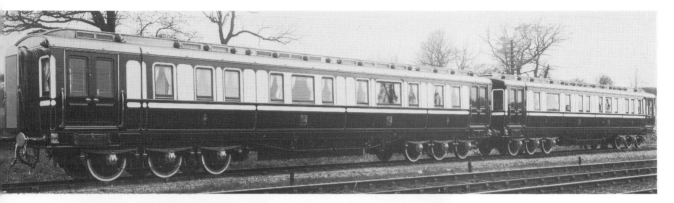

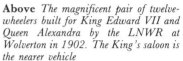

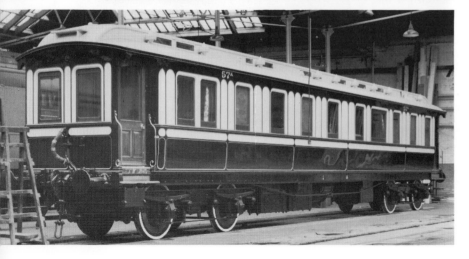

Above *The magnificent pair of twelve-wheelers built for King Edward VII and Queen Alexandra by the LNWR at Wolverton in 1902. The King's saloon is the nearer vehicle*

Left *Interior view of the 1902 LNWR Royal saloons taken from the Queen's parlour and looking through the vestibules to the King's lounge. As preserved at the NRM, these carriages display the later interior decor introduced by Queen Mary*

Below left *Saloon No 57A, the fine carriage built by the LNWR at Wolverton for the 4th Duke of Sutherland in 1899-1900, which established virtually all of the features subsequently to be found in most British Royal carriages. The picture was taken at Wolverton in 1958 when the saloon was first restored. It now resides at the NRM, York, having been further renovated during 1979-80 (F.W. Shuttleworth).*

Above right *East Coast Royal Saloon No 396, built at York by the NER in 1909 for Queen Alexandra. In LNER days it was converted to a dual purpose saloon for the King and Queen, and in 1962 it was again refurbished for Queen Elizabeth II and the Duke of Edinburgh. In this final form it, too, now resides in the NRM collection.*

Sutherland, again, happily, preserved in the NRM Collection. This was a family saloon writ very large indeed. It was, in truth, the final flowering of the Victorian era but spent the whole of its operational life (1900-48) in the twentieth century, and King Edward VII travelled in it from the very outset whenever he visited his aristocratic friend at Dunrobin Castle where it was housed. Small wonder that the LNWR Royal Train of 1902-4 drew heavily on the ideas first put into tangible form for this influential Scottish nobleman; the King was most impressed with its vastly better amenities than that of his mother's ancient conveyances and said so. Why, the Duke's saloon even had its own private kitchen! Furthermore, the Duke's unique facility to use his carriage on demand in the Highlands as a mobile home must further have appealed to the new King.

Thus it was that King Edward VII was the first beneficiary of the better technology and up market provisioning which the railways could now provide; but it did not stop there, this was merely the beginning.

It was not to be expected that the East Coast companies would stand idly in the wings allowing the LNWR to gain all the kudos from its new, very visible Royal Train, so in 1908-9 they replied in kind with another sumptuous pair of saloons for Edward VII and his Queen, accompanied by a handful of equally grand semi-royals. These carriages were, naturally, in the Gresley East Coast style, although one of the principal saloons was actually built at York (NER). These two saloons were regarded as East Coast Joint Stock, unlike those of Wolverton which were jealously protected by the LNWR and distinctly *not* joint stock! In exterior design terms, the East Coast pair (also preserved by the NRM) lacked a little of the delicacy and visual harmony of normal Gresley-styled vehicles, being somewhat overblown in their overall proportions and mounted on heavy NER-type chassis, but inside they were probably

unmatched for quality in the 'quasi-Adam' style. The wood veneers in the principal day compartment of the King's saloon, No 395, are probably without peer in any British-built carriage.

The East Coast set was in much demand for trips to Sandringham (King Edward VII's favourite abode), not to mention race meetings and the like, but it was never used quite so often in the overnight or long duration role. In consequence, it never acquired sleeping or dining cars on a permanent basis and was never quite as flexible in the operational sense as was the LNWR set. It was probably for this reason that it lasted even longer, making its final run in full formation as late as 1961 (for the Duke of Kent's wedding in York), the principal saloons themselves being used intermittently for yet another decade or more until the mid-1970s. Long before then, the original King's saloon had been converted for the fairly exclusive use of Queen Mary, and was later to be similarly employed by Queen Elizabeth the Queen Mother after the deaths of King George VI and Queen Mary in the early 1950s. However, the further adventures of these two splendid Edwardian Royal Trains will have to await the next volume.

By 1910, counting the late-nineteenth-century LB & SCR and GWR trains, the reigning monarch now had four complete sets of carriages to choose from, but still there was more. Early in the century the SE & CR had produced its own saloon for the King, and in 1910 the Midland Railway got into the act with a splendid Royal Saloon, No 1910. Surprisingly, given its reputation, the MR never built a full Royal Train, but could provide a more than passable substitute by combining this new carriage with its better family saloons, dining cars and corridor stock and occasionally did so. Likewise, too, sometimes the railways south of the Thames utilized their better saloon carriages in the service of the Monarch, rather than venture into exclusively royal provisioning. In this, they were often assisted by Pullman in the form

Above *Surprisingly, the MR Royal Train, apart from the principal saloon, No 1910, was formed from better quality general service stock. The main saloon, numbered for its year of manufacture, is seen formed up as the second vehicle. The rest of the train, save for the third carriage, a nineteenth-century Clayton clerestory dining car, is pure David Bain. No 1910 survives in preservation; sadly it no longer has its original interior fitments.*

Left *The King's ECJS Saloon No 395 of 1908 was later converted for HM Queen Mary's use and, later still, refurbished for HM Queen Elizabeth the Queen Mother. The furniture has changed but the fantastic sycamore wall panelling and 'Edwardian Adam' decor may still be admired at the NRM.*

Left *In 1914, the GNR built two almost identical first class saloons, Nos 3099/ 100. In practice, they turned out to be almost exclusively VIP saloons for use with the East Coast Train. This view shows the interior of No 3099.*

Right Figure 60 *Elevations, plans and sections of LNWR six-wheel Invalid/ Family saloon of 1902. Six wheelers were still quite common in the normal compartment coach field, but their continued use for a somewhat specialized vehicle was, by this time, somewhat rare.*

of its best parlour cars; the use of Pullman cars for royal journeys on the Southern lines continued well into the BR period.

As will be appreciated, Royal Saloons tended to be somewhat one-off vehicles and generalization is not readily possible. It therefore seems more sensible to cover some of their more noteworthy ramifications by using a rather higher proportion of illustrations to depict their considerable variety and the quality of their detail and finish. Much the same sort of approach also seems valid for the next group down the hierarchy, the many and various forms of private and family saloons. We have already encountered some of the grander examples of those built for use in support of the Royal Trains, and a point not often appreciated is the fact that most of these vehicles could be hired, if not required by the Royal Family, by any person willing to pay the cost — probably something in the order of 12-24 first class fares. After all, the Royal household paid and still does pay the railway for the provision of the Royal Train, so why should not this privilege be extended to anyone whose pocket was deep enough? The railways saw no reason why not.

The idea of a special saloon for private hire was a concept dating well back into Victorian days, and the majority of such vehicles were actually built during the nineteenth century. They did, however, reach their peak of luxury during Edwardian times before their inevitable and early decline in favour of the motor vehicle. After all, it was the more wealthy folk who would, all things being equal, be amongst the first to espouse the motor car. But the so-called family saloon, or whatever other name it was given, was often the carriage builders' *tour de force,* short, that is, of the even more elaborate Royal Saloons.

In this context, the word 'saloon' can be misleading. In railway terms it regularly described a complete vehicle (dining saloon, sleeping saloon and so on), but could also be used to indicate one specific area within the carriage, ie the 'day' saloon as opposed to the 'night' equivalent. In this work, the word will hopefully be confined to references to the whole vehicle.

The family saloon, with its close ally the so-called 'invalid saloon', can trace its origins back to the pioneer sleeping cars of the 1870s, and probably even earlier. Typically, the vehicle would have accommodation for the family itself, the servants (in a second or third class type of compartment of course) and all the luggage and paraphernalia of the late Victorian travelling entourage. There would be much luxury in the family compartment(s), characteristically armchairs and/or settees together with tables, carpets and

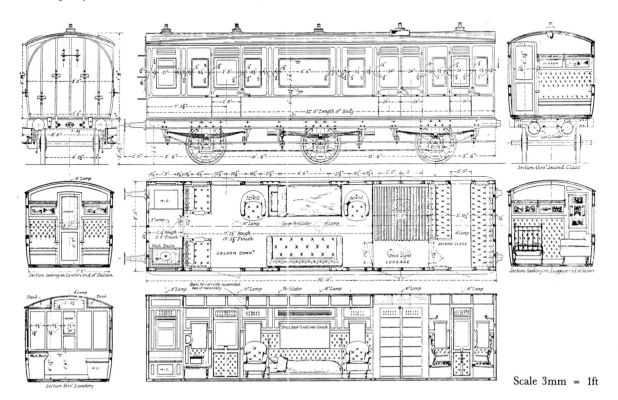

Scale 3mm = 1ft

Left Interior view of a Dean GWR family saloon with suspended couch for the use of invalids.

the many florid excesses of the time. The vehicle would have lavatories and usually be well lit and heated. Typically, the servants' compartment would be separated from the family apartment(s) by the luggage space, but at least the staff would usually have a lavatory. Most of these saloons contained the sort of furniture which could be turned into beds at night — hence the design linkage with sleeping cars — and the only significant difference between the pure 'family' and the specialized 'invalid' variant was the ability of the latter to admit a stretcher or wheelchair to the main compartment by means of wider doors. They would also, as a rule, have a proper bedstead for the invalid passenger. Some saloons, indeed, were convertibles.

The Victorian family saloon was normally a six-wheeler and, quite regularly, two or three would be seen on the longer-distance trains, but by the start of the present century a somewhat paradoxical situation was beginning to develop. On the one hand demand was reducing, probably because of the generally improved nature of general service sleeping and dining cars, while on the other those few vehicles which *were* built embodied even more luxury and were normally carried on bogies. However, Royal Trains excepted, it was a last desperate fling, and although such renowned companies as the Midland, LNWR, East Coast lines and GWR made valiant attempts to cater for this trade, it soon disappeared and the only really long-lasting special saloons were those considered for royal or VIP use. The remainder

were either scrapped, turned into railway officers' saloons or downgraded into third class vehicles with redesigned interiors

Lest it should be thought that the specialized saloon was the exclusive prerogative of the first class passenger, this might be an appropriate point at which to mention that other early twentieth-century oddity, the 'picnic saloon'. These were dominantly third class and were for hire by private parties for excursions, or even attached to service trains. Their layout was usually spartan but friendly, with seats round the periphery of the open interior and long tables down the centre. They were the precursors, one supposes, of the modern road coach which in turn has superseded the early-twentieth-century open-topped charabanc. Either way, just as with the more opulent saloons, the picnic versions did not long survive the onslaught of road motor transport, although at least they did last a bit longer, quite a number surviving even the Second World War. Some, indeed, were actually conversions of erstwhile first class family saloons.

There is a distinct 'grey area' dividing the generally available special saloons and those which were dedicated for the exclusive use of specific groups of people. Clearly, of course, these included those for the Royal Family, but there were other kinds too and these must now be considered, though they are, in truth, difficult to categorize. In the strictly pre-grouping context, there seem to me to be three areas of prime interest, two of which were available for public use, the third category most definitely not.

Dealing with the latter group first, this was the domain of the travelling boardroom, usually known as Officers' or Inspection Saloon. There were not many of them but when very senior railway management decided to inspect the line, they regularly travelled as well as Royalty, sometimes even as part of the Royal Train. The vehicles usually contained one or two lounges, one at each end, with panoramic views both from the sides and ends of the coach to aid the business of 'inspection'. Between these two areas there would usually be some sort of service facility, almost always including kitchen and toilet, sometimes even a sleeping berth or two or a bathroom. Within the confines of a normally-sized vehicle, little in the way of creature comfort was spared to create the most agreeable self-contained travelling environment for those privileged to use them — and they rarely had gangways to connect them to adjoining vehicles in the train. Most of the time this was not necessary because an 'Officers' Special' usually consisted of the saloon itself together with a well-turned-out locomotive and little else save for the chef and the rest of the train crew, in that order of priority for the most part, one suspects!

Most railways owned at least one of these rather self-indulgent vehicles and several still survive both in museum collections and private ownership. Naturally enough, the larger and more self-important railways produced the more grandiose and long-lasting specimens, but some of the really quite minor systems also went in for either delusions of grandeur beyond their status or the most extraordinary one-offs imaginable. Two must suffice as exemplars, one from each of the opposite extremities of the scale.

The so far scarce-mentioned Taff Vale Railway had a most comical set up — a rather grand, if somewhat ancient, clerestory officers' saloon permanently coupled to a separate 'dining room'. The latter was

Far left *'Spartan but friendly' — a typical picnic saloon interior, in this case a turn-of-the-century LYR six-wheeler*

Left *In 1912, the Cheshire Lines Committee obtained what it chose to call a first class family saloon, No 201, of typical GNR external style. In fact, it rather seems that this opulent vehicle was mainly used by railway officers. This interior gives an idea of the comfort in which they patrolled their domain. There was also, needless to say, a kitchen!*

Right *Lancashire and Yorkshire No 1 was, as its name implied, very much an 'Inspection Saloon' with its almost glasshouse-like array of windows. The folding steps allowed for between station stops and the central service area was small.*

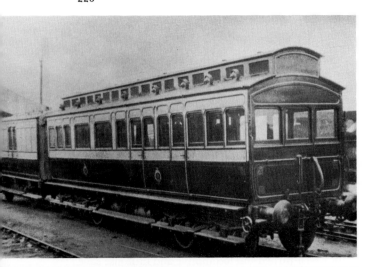

a converted six-wheel full brake with no windows, but which was wallpapered inside — one of only a very few British carriages ever to be so finished and almost certainly the only 'full' brake! Its curiosity value is such as to merit even the rather poor quality picture reproduced alongside. Equally bizarre in its own way was the principal saloon of the London, Tilbury and Southend Railway, a sort of mock 'Gothick' creation with elliptical roof, domed ends and a pair of extraordinary fireplaces, one in the centre of each end where the gangway would normally have been located. Again, visual confirmation is appropriate, since the Tilbury was hardly renowned for most of its carriages.

The more celebrated railways tended to build their officers' saloons in the general style of their main-line carriages, and the illustrations show something of the variety. Of those which survive for posterity, we might perhaps single out one or two. There is, for instance, a rather nice vehicle, No GE1 in private ownership, which, for all its latter-day alterations both by the LNER and BR, is still recognizably Great Eastern, even though its open verandah at one end gives it a vaguely American feel. Splendid too are a pair of ex-LNWR saloons — a massive twelve-wheeler now in private ownership and, most amazing of all, the former LNWR Chairman's saloon, built in 1920, which at the time of writing is still in service with the Royal Train, being used for its traditional purpose of carrying railway officers travelling with the Royal Train and cleared for 100 mph running, no less!

This astonishing vehicle has been used by all manner of people as well as railway officers — King Edward VIII, General Eisenhower and Winston Churchill to name but three. It is expected that by the time this book appears, it will have gone or be about to go into honourable retirement, having been earmarked by the NRM for permanent preservation in the National Collection.

In some respects, even more exclusive than the Officers' Saloons were those extremely rare creatures, the 'Club' saloons, if only because there were so few of them. Their origin is a bit obscure but casts a fascinating glimpse into the travelling mores of the day. In essence, they were used on public trains by fare-paying passengers on a regular daily basis, but there all resemblance to normal commuting ends. They were firmly, if not exclusively, a Northern phenomenon, closely connected with the prosperity of the Yorkshire and Lancashire textile industries. Within these areas, many of the more wealthy businessmen chose to live away from their 'dark satanic mills' in more salubrious places such as Blackpool, Southport, Morecambe, Llandudno, Windermere and so on. If sufficient patrons were agreed as

Left *The curious Taff Vale Railway inspection ensemble referred to in the text. The 'dining car' is at the far end*

Below left *Exterior and interior views of the amazing LT & SR Directors' saloon, complete with its internal fireplaces. The outside shows it in the 1920s as LMS No 2799, and the interior view shows the far end of the vehicle (Top R.J. Essery collection).*

This page *This trio of Club saloons from the NER, MR and LYR respectively were used on the Hull to Bridlington, Morecambe to Leeds and Manchester to Blackpool services. Apart from the MR example, an ex-family saloon, the other two were purpose-built*

Left *Club chairs in a club carriage — a view of the inner sanctum of another NER vehicle.*

Below right *LB & SCR continental boat express at Newhaven Harbour, 1908. Note the Pullman car midway down the formation.*

Bottom right *This view of WCJS No 386, the 'Aberdeen' brake composite from the '2 pm' train, shows the basic carriage styling used on the famous Wolverton trains of 1907-08. The large-size windows were usually found only on the corridor side of the side-corridor vehicles.*

to their times of travel, it was not particularly difficult to persuade the railways to provide a special saloon for this distinguished and usually first class clientele. It was known as a 'Travelling Club' and was attached to a regular morning and evening working to and from centres like Leeds, Bradford, Manchester, Liverpool and the like. Club saloons were either purpose-built or converted from other conventional stock, and were dominantly of open configuration, a sort of cross-breed between the more common family and officers' saloons. The LYR, LNWR, MR and NER were quite good at this sort of thing and there were others.

The third category of carriages in the pre-grouping period were those provided for particular services only. In a sense, this is an appropriate group with which to conclude this chapter for these carriages bring us back to a somewhat more democratic patronage than the exclusive vehicles so far considered. The only thing which governed their use was whether or not one's travelling needs coincided with the services to which the carriages were allocated. If so, then there was no need to be a club member, a railway officer, a member of a well-heeled family or even the sovereign. All you needed to have was the price of the ticket — and this could even be third class.

This concept of specific sets of carriages for particular workings reached its apogee after the grouping and began in Victorian times, so the period under discussion had certain evolutionary qualities,

some of them of quite prime significance. The obvious contender for this type of service was, of course, the already considered Pullman, but the railway companies themselves seemed quite willing, on occasion, to join in the party. During Victorian times, the GWR, MR, WCJS and GER, to mention but a few, had all in their own way produced some splendid 'dedicated' sets of vehicles. The first true corridor train was GWR, the first long-distance corridor was WCJS, the first all-class dining service was GER and the Midland's special sets of the 1890s have been mentioned already, so the idea was not new. But the Edwardian period saw it reach new heights of splendour — and it was not simply in the long-distance field. Even the short-distance railways like the LB & SCR made their mark.

So far, this narrative has not been noteworthy for its praise of the Brighton line, save for its use of Pullmans and a commendatory mention of its late Victorian Royal Train, but there was one rather shining exception to the fairly unmemorable quality of most domestic LB & SCR stock for anyone other than first class passengers. When Billinton introduced his somewhat avant-garde 'Balloon' stock (see page 133), there was included among them a really quite splendid boat train set for the Newhaven services; it was non-corridor but it did have an adequate provision of lavatories for a not too lengthy run, and the opulence went down below the first class level. For the Brighton it was amazing, but sadly was not repeated. The real contribution was to be that of the more long-distance lines, and these were mostly north of the Thames or even north of the Anglo-Scottish border; moreover, the GWR was not exactly to the forefront either!

We have already noted, *en passant* such vehicles as were provided for the Caledonian 'Grampian' corridor trains, the NBR Fife and Lothian coast expresses, the LYR 'Fireproof' stock for its business trains and the GNR and/or East Coast twelve-wheelers, all superb in their own way, but if asked to provide a couple of prime examples, then I would argue that the LNWR/WCJS contribution stood supreme at this time. However, such a categorical statement needs qualification.

Wolverton (LNWR) was by no means the only carriage building establishment of merit. It has already been described how it was that many railways moved rapidly from late Victorian complacency to early-twentieth-century achievement; but it does seem, as already averred in the twelve-wheel field, that Wolverton managed somehow to get the overall

mix more consistent than anywhere else. Its only serious rivals were Swindon (GWR), Doncaster (GNR), York (NER) and, conceivably, Derby (MR), but none of these places managed to deliver with quite such panache as did this venerable Buckinghamshire establishment during 1907-8, when it put into service probably the finest sets of carriages ever built in Britain for the *non-supplementary fare-paying passenger*. The emphasized qualification is important.

I refer, of course, to the celebrated '2 pm' and 'American Boat Train' stock. In a sense, they could well have come into Chapter 10, but somehow they seem more appropriate here. As vehicles, they were probably no better, technologically, than those of maybe half a dozen other lines, but conceptually they were real pioneers, setting standards which were never approached, let alone exceeded, for decades. They were so good, in fact, that the LMS (in succession to the LNWR) did not feel the need to replace them on their original designated service until more than twenty years after they were introduced.

Left and right *These interior views sum up the luxurious character of the 'American Special' and '2 pm' trains. They depict, in order: 'small' first class compartment, American stock; second class compartment, American stock (the American and '2 pm' thirds were all but identical to this); first class compartment, '2 pm' stock; second class dining car, American stock. The dining areas of all three classes on both trains were virtually indistinguishable from the version shown.*

To get this into perspective, one only needs remark that the famous Deltics and their 100 mph trains of the more modern BR era lasted only some 16 years (1962-78) with at least three changes of coach style and at the time of writing the 1978 HSTs are likely to be replaced in 1991 after only 12-13 years of operation on the East Coast Main Line, and even so they have needed an intermediate face-lift (1985-7) on the way!

The sets of coaches provided in 1907-8 by the LNWR for its services — the '2 pm' was, in fact, WCJS but the design was pure LNW — embodied the classic twelve-wheel design philosphy which had gradually evolved over a fifteen-year period (1893-1907). Apart from the full kitchens and full brakes of the Boat Trains which were eight-wheelers, all were mounted on the well-proven LNWR twelve-wheel chassis and it does seem likely that no compromises were ever made in such mundane matters as weight per seat. They were opulent trains; even if one was travelling second or third class, one had no draughty compartment doors, the diners were superb and nowhere else in Britain was there anything quite like them. To be candid, they were ahead of their time, drawing much of their quality from the immediately preceding LNWR royal coaches of 1902-3, not to mention the 1904-6 sleeping and dining cars, themselves a considerable cut above average.

The 'American Boat Trains' — designated for the Liverpool (Riverside) to Euston services — were undoubtedly designed to impress the transatlantic clientele, and probably copied, if only subconsciously, some American ideas. Even so, an 11 ft 9 in by 6 ft first class compartment with but three arm-chairs and a settee was going some, even by USA criteria, especially when the journey time was no more than about four hours maximum! Nevertheless, since these splendid carriages were still somewhat restricted in their patronage being boat trains, it was the '2 pm' which turned out to be the real show-stopper.

In superficial terms, the '2 pm' West Coast stock was not perhaps quite as lavish as that of the American specials, although externally it looked much the same. The diners were, in fact, a few years older and still deployed the clerestory roof, but they were extremely elegant and, moreover, first and third class only. The side corridor stock was orthodox insofar as a five-compartment brake third, some 65 ft 6 in long without compartment doors and weighing some 40 tons could be considered orthodox. Even at maximum capacity (40 passengers) it was one ton per *third* class traveller, and the said traveller did not have to pay a penny extra for the privilege. Suggest that to a harassed second class commuter into London in the 1980s, crammed six-a-side in non-corridor side-door compartment stock of much more recent build!

The pictures appended herewith probably tell it all. The LMS and LNER could not improve on matters until the 1930s, while the Southern and GWR never did so as far as the third class passenger was concerned, so it does not seem unreasonable to conclude our review of pre-group conventional carriages on this mid-Edwardian high point. Nothing better was ever offered to the ordinary traveller, even though objectivity forces me to admit that the same LNWR, only five or six years later, produced some distinctly mean 57-foot eight-wheel coaches for the 10.00 am WCJS train, almost as though it knew it had gone too far. Although it made quite a splash about them at the time, one feels it was a sort of hollow claim — and there we will leave it for the moment.

14. 'They also served'

Before leaving the realm of conventional locomotive-hauled carriages, we must not forget the many thousands of vehicles which found their way into passenger trains but which did not carry passengers as such. Their importance has already been touched on in Chapter 6, but we must now take a closer look at this very important aspect of railway travel. First, however, a brief word about the subject in general.

From almost the very beginning of railways, the speed of transit afforded by the passenger train relative to most other contemporary forms of surface transport, has always been a key factor in terms of patronage, and from the earliest days there have always been certain types of cargo whose nature was such as to make time in transit an important consideration. Probably the earliest manifestation of this type of demand was the carriage of mail, and as early as 1830 the railways began to carry mail on their best trains. This concept was gradually expanded to embrace all manner of traffic until a whole generic group of vehicles had been evolved whose running characteristics in terms of their vehicular quality was fully compatible with passenger carriages but whose body structure was adapted to a whole range of different uses. Collectively, this group of vehicles is usually referred to as 'non-passenger-carrying coaching stock' — a cumbersome phrase but pretty well self-descriptive. These are the vehicles with which this chapter is concerned.

Obviously, there is a degree of blurring at the edges, for we are dealing with vehicles whose cargo could, in some cases, equally well have found itself forming part of the more humble goods or freight train, but from the earliest days there have always been certain types of commodity whose nature was such as to encourage their owners to pay a little more for the speedier transit which a passenger train would guarantee. This in turn stimulated the railways to make rather superior vehicles with better brakes, running gear and so on, the higher capital cost of the construction of which would, all things being equal, pay for itself by virtue of the higher charges which could be commanded for their use. These vehicles tended to fall into quite distinct categories, and this will be the basis of the analysis which follows.

The brake, luggage and parcels van group

The 'passenger full brake', to use its proper title, is the most obvious extension of the passenger carriage into the non-passenger sphere and, in purely vehicular terms, is no more than the logical consequence of expanding the van portion of many a brake-ended carriage to the point where one can do without any passenger-carrying compartments. The logic behind this course of action was no more than the natural outcome of the sheer volume of luggage which, increasingly during late Victorian and Edwardian days, the ever-growing number of passengers wished to take with them on their journeys. This led quite regularly to situations where, especially on the longer-distance trains, the luggage capacity of a normal brake-ended coach was insufficient, and the railways found it expedient to make carriages purely for luggage. It was equally logical to let the guard ride in them and, if the service so demanded, fit them with gangways as well. They were cheaper to build than a passenger-carrying vehicle and offered useful extra capacity for conveying other things than passengers' luggage should space and demand permit.

Of the various 'extras' which could be conveyed in this fashion, there soon turned out to be a profitable trade in such things as parcels and newspapers. In both cases, there was a degree of urgency in terms of transit time and the railways soon discovered that by putting a full brake into the train instead of a brake-ended passenger carriage, there was often sufficient space available to convey this extra trade without disadvantage to the original primary luggage function. Of course, many of them were pure luggage vans but increasingly the sheer versatility of a 'carry-all' vehicle unencumbered by the demands of the passengers themselves led to a situation where special-purpose vehicles purely for parcels or newspapers were built *without* guard's accommodation and also added to the main trains. This was an even cheaper option than the full brake with guard's space, and became extremely popular with those railways which had a fair volume of this traffic. All that really mattered in these cases was that the carriage itself should be capable of operating at passenger train speed. In fact, so lucrative did this trade become in some cases that special workings consisting of nothing but parcels and newspaper vans became quite common, the only condition then being that one of them, at least, should have somewhere for the guard to ride and also be fitted with the mandatory handbrake.

In the earlier days, it was more customary for such vehicles to copy standard passenger carriage styling, since more often than not they would be formed up as part of a passenger train, but it was not absolutely necessary and more than one railway could see no point in spending too much money on the vehicle itself. Thus, provided the couplings and brake gear were compatible with passenger train operation, it

A typical passenger-rated bogie full brake van from the turn of the century — LB & SCR No 438, built in 1900. Note the huge 'chimneys' for the oil pot lamps.

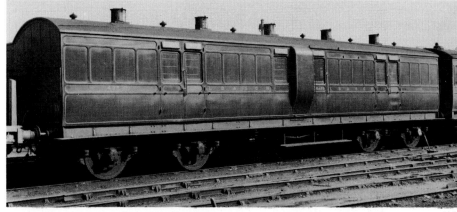

East Coast gangwayed bogie full brake No 6 was typical of many hundreds used on long-distance services by most major companies. The 'Luggage' branding, though wholly appropriate, was by no means universal on such vehicles.

A 70-foot twelve-wheel luggage van was a distinct rarity, but GWR No 876 was one of a pair built in 1910 as high-capacity baggage vans for the Fishguard boat trains. They could carry 20 tons of passenger luggage and after the Great War were re-classified as newspaper vans (T.J. Edgington collection).

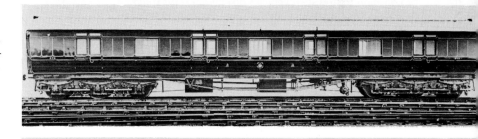

The SE & CR adopted very much a 'goods vehicle' outline for its passenger luggage vans with no concession to 'coach' styling. This design became the basis for the ubiquitous Southern Railway general utility vans in the post-group period. In spite of appearances, their running gear had all the necessary refinement for high-speed operation and the design was long-lived. Many later examples survived well into the 1980s.

*This non-gangwayed newspaper van No 208 of the NER was also
a full brake — note the guard's lookout. There was always a degree
of blurring at the edges in the description of this group of vehicles,
and after 1923 the LNER simply classed them as full brakes.*

was not unusual to find some of these vehicles being
built to quite a utilitarian, almost freight-vehicle
outline. This in turn led to a further sub-classification
of 'general utility van' (GUV) to cover almost any
kind of vehicle which might be expected to find itself
either attached to a passenger train or forming part
of a parcels or newspaper train merely by virtue of
the load it carried. This type of operation continues
to the present day and in the 1980 it is rather more
common to find such vehicles displaying semi-freight
wagon characteristics than purely passenger vehicle
styling.

The dedicated mail vehicle group

The carrying of mail by train has always been an
important part of railway operation, and right from
the very beginning the Post Office has always insisted
on speedy transit. In fact, during the seminal period
of railway development, the mail trains were always
the fastest in the business and in some cases
passengers were prepared to pay extra to be conveyed
on the postal trains. Indeed, famous named trains
such as the 'Irish Mail' can trace their origins right
back to this evolutionary time.

In most cases, mail vehicles ran as part of a mixed
passenger and mail train and only rarely were all-
mail formations operated. However, whether in
mixed formation or exclusively mail, at heart of the
postal operation was that unique vehicle, the
'Travelling Post Office' (TPO). This type of carriage
could trace its origins back to the start of Victoria's
reign, and by the turn of the century had developed
very sophisticated characteristics. Its name was self-
descriptive and many of them actually carried a late

fee posting box into which one could post one's letters
direct.

In structural terms, the TPO almost always
mirrored that which was most up-to-date in
contemporary coachbuilding practice. Typically, it
would contain a multiplicity of sorting racks and
shelves along one side of the carriage at which
employees of the Post Office could sort the mail traffic
as the train proceeded. Until very recently (1971),
these facilities were regularly supplemented by the
unique apparatus devised originally in 1838 whereby
mail bags could be despatched from or collected by
the train without the need to stop or even slow down.
There were few more spectacular sights than to see
a postal train exchanging its mail bags at high speed
during the time when this practice was customary.

Because the mail pick-up apparatus was always at
the near side of the line, TPO vehicles were usually
built one-sided with the pick-up nets on the near side
and the sorting racks on the off side of the carriage.
Furthermore, in order to give an uninterrupted run
of sorting shelves, it was equally customary to offset
the gangways to the near or pick-up side of the
carriages. These structural constraints meant that the
vehicles not only had to be turned before their return
journeys, but also could not be gangwayed to the
normal centre-gangway passenger-carrying vehicles
in the train. This, of course, ensured the security of
the mail vehicles but also meant that all mail vehicles
had to be marshalled together rather than mixed up
with the passenger vehicles, the ultimate form being
a full mail train. The most celebrated of these was
the 'Night Mail' or 'West Coast Postal', whose
departure from Euston (LNWR) at 8.30 pm, was not
only more than normally ritualistic but whose
operation itself was given the sort of special attention
which might normally have been expected only if it
was carrying a full load of the most influential people
in the land.

Of course, not all mail vehicles were dedicated TPOs, and even the main users of these specialized vehicles also needed many carriages purely for the storage of mail bags and parcels *en route*. These coaches were little different from the normal luggage/parcels/brake vans already considered, and some railways owned only these types. In fact, there was more than a little chopping and changing of usage, and once again the categories could become blurred. Indeed, at peak times all manner of non-passenger coaching stock could be pressed into service for the carriage of mail, and it was always common for a few mail bags to be carried in the guard's van of many ordinary passenger trains, especially those operating in the more sparsely populated areas.

Top to bottom *Although not strictly twentieth-century (it was built in 1895), this GWR Dean clerestory No 596 merits inclusion if only for its most unusual configuration. It was a third class and Post Office van, fully equipped with mail pick-up apparatus and gangwayed only at the mail van end. It was not unusual for passenger accommodation to be provided on mail trains, but not normally in the Travelling Post Office itself!*

This is the classic form of TPO from the route which made most use of the type, the West Coast main line. WCJS No 437 was a 57-foot sorting van, built in 1910 with pick-up apparatus, and is shown here posed with its nets extended. Note the offset gangway to allow more space on the far (sorting) side of the carriage

This rather noble-looking clerestory mail van, No 351 of the LB & SCR, was built in 1897 but is seen here with King Edward VII's monogram. It was converted to a full brake in 1921.

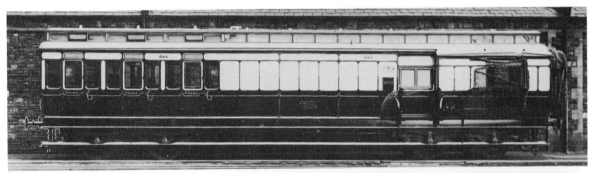

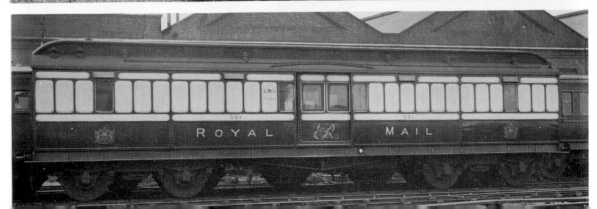

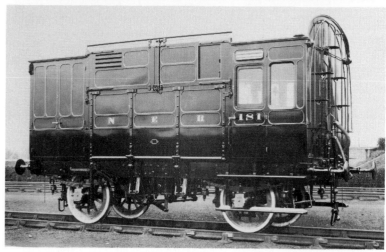

Left and below left *LNWR No 329 and NER No 181 are entirely typical of the better horse box designs of the pre-group period. They look very different but both embody similar features: (from left to right) fodder and 'tack' compartment, livestock area and the groom's compartment in the form of a coupé*

Left *The demands of circus traffic gave rise to the need to carry elephants. The size and weight of these animals precluded the use of normal livestock vehicles so the more robust covered carriage truck was commonly adapted for the purpose, the animals entering the vehicle through the end doors. This is NER No 167 in LNER days.*

The livestock group

The bulk of animals carried by the railways were conveyed in normal freight trains utilizing cattle wagons, vehicles of little sophistication and scarcely better than open wagons with added roofs. They were partially open-sided above the waist as a rule and there was no provision at all for any accompanying stock handler or herdsman. Most of them had but rudimentary brakes and suspension and only a few had any capability for high speed. For the most part, these vehicles sufficed for large-scale stock movements but there was one group of livestock whose movement demanded (and received) better treatment. These were the high-value animals normally conveyed in considerably smaller numbers than the large herds of cattle and flocks of sheep which formed the bulk of livestock traffic.

The dominant species was the horse, and the most characteristic passenger-train-rated livestock vehicle was a horsebox. These were normally four-wheelers with accommodation for no more than two or three animals in well-padded stalls, along with storage space for tack, fodder and bedding straw and almost always with a half compartment for the groom. These distinctly superior vehicles arose from the fact that, as a general rule, horse traffic was very much up-market, being confined in the main to racehorses in transit to meetings and private carriage horses accompanying their usually wealthy owners on holiday or elsewhere. The so-called 'horse and carriage' trade was a very lucrative source of revenue for the railways and even quite modestly sized stations were expected to keep at least one horsebox and carriage truck (see below) in readiness for whatever business might arise. For this reason, even the smallest railways could muster quite a few horseboxes, while the larger organizations could number them by the hundred. Because of the high-value nature of the animals themselves and their rather more important status, the railways charged more for their conveyance and, in consequence, were able to provide vehicles which could safely be attached to passenger trains, or even be operated in special trains should occasion demand. They were usually finished in passenger carriage styling.

There were two main offshoots from this principal category. First was the carriage of prize cattle, almost always pedigree breeding bulls. These animals were less common than horses, but their conveyance, when called for, was just as important and the resultant vehicles were rather similar, if somewhat less elaborate. The second category was the travelling circus animal. In the days before motorized heavy road transport, the railways were sometimes called upon to convey complete circuses and deploy all manner of specialized vehicles, but again speedy transit was of the essence — frequently overnight — so passenger-rated vehicles were called for, not just for the animals but also for the human artistes and their accompanying scenery, tents and other paraphernalia. The livestock could often be accommodated in conventional horseboxes or prize cattle vans, but some species, for example elephants, needed somewhat stronger provisioning. This regularly took the form of specially strengthened carriage trucks or similar vehicles. In this context, there was much in common between the circus train and the requirements of the travelling theatrical companies; their transport problems also embraced personnel, costumes and scenery.

These needs, and many others too numerous to mention, gave rise to the considerable growth in demand for provision of one or more items from the next group of vehicles to be considered.

The carriage truck group

The carriage truck, as its name implies, was developed originally for the conveyance of horse-drawn carriages by rail, usually in company with the horses themselves (see above). The origins of the type go back to the dawn of the steam railway when, as an alternative to the conventional railway carriage, it was not unheard of for the more wealthy folk to travel in their own horse carriages firmly strapped down on to the top of a flat truck. Even when conventional coaches improved and the railways stopped allowing owners to travel in this way, the gentry still liked to take their equippage with them and the carriage truck continued to develop. By the time of this survey, the basic vehicle had developed into two specific variants, the 'Covered Carriage Truck' (CCT) and the 'Open Carriage Truck' (OCT). The names are self descriptive, the open version being, of course, the lineal descendant of the pioneer type. Whether open or covered, they were built to a variety of sizes and lengths, most common being four-wheel and six-wheel examples.

As a general rule, covered carriage trucks were usually fewer in number and confined to what were reckoned to be more valuable loads. In Edwardian terms, this often meant the newfangled motor car, and this new usage is worthy of more than a passing mention. In a curious anticipation of the modern 'Motorail', and before the real threat of the car had become apparent, the railways seemed to go out of their way to encourage the conveyance of motor cars, and produced some very stylish CCTs branded for motor car traffic. Of course, the modern trunk roads did not exist in the form we now know them; many indeed had not been built. With the benefit of

Left *Caledonian Railway CCT No 138 was a typical six-wheeler with visual points in common with both passenger and freight stock. It had spoked wheels, a very goods-truck-like handbrake and the end doors are simply tongue and groove boarding, but the bodyside styling is pure coachbuilding.*

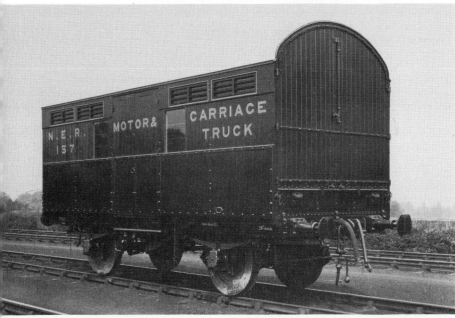

Left and below left *These two views show contrasting examples of CCTs adapted for motor car traffic in the early days. NER No 157 has distinctly 'freight vehicle' characteristics, but LNWR No 603 was clearly designed and painted to draw attention to itself*

Opposite page *The open carriage truck came in a variety of forms and these three examples are typical. LYR No 147 is a very long wheelbase four-wheeler with no side planking; LNWR No 280 probably represents the most numerous single type, a fairly conventional four-wheeler with side members of modest height; and LNWR No 12015 is an example of the somewhat less common bogie type. It started life as a scenery truck but is seen here modified to carry containers of joint LNWR/LYR ownership.*

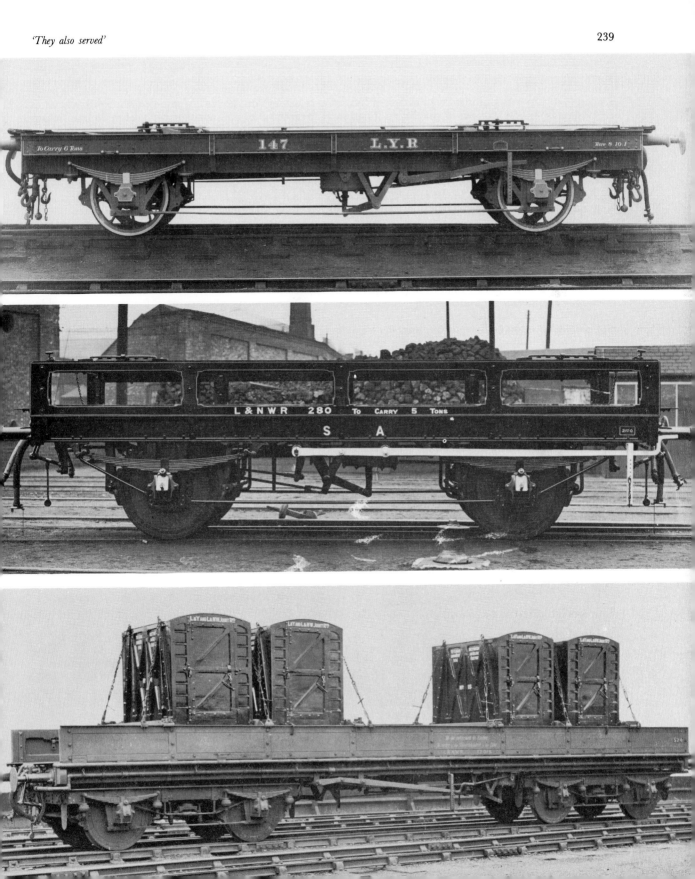

hindsight, it does rather seem that the railways never realized that the car would be a serious long-distance threat to their basic passenger trade, but rather tended to regard it as a substitute for the older 'horse and carriage' traffic. It was, of course, confined in those days mostly to the more wealthy who, presumably, would want to take their cars with them on their travels just as they had hitherto conveyed their horse-drawn rigs. This development saw a more or less continuous growth throughout the first half of the century and it is only in the more modern era that the whole business has had to be re-marketed in a somewhat different way.

The OCT could be used for a whole range of vehicles from horse-drawn furniture vans to farm machinery, but as with the covered version the principal distinguishing factor was the ability to be loaded 'over the end' rather than from the side. This was done by means of 'end loading' docks at the larger stations, where there would be some form of flat plate above the buffers connecting the vehicle floor with the loading bay itself. This had obvious advantages when the cargo needed to be wheeled on to the vehicle, but did not prevent side loading in some cases or even a quite different form of use for theatrical scenery, containers or any other high-speed cargo whose nature made the provision of an easily loaded passenger-rated vehicle with a large floor desirable. There was thus a degree of overlap between the carriage truck and general utility categories, and different railways had different names for them. However, the pure carriage truck was always recognizable by its ability to be loaded from the end. Thus, if an otherwise similar vehicle did not have this end-loading facility, including end doors if of the covered variety, it could not properly be called a carriage truck. The accompanying pictures indicate just some of the variety to be seen in this very large group of vehicles. There were many more and they earned much revenue.

The perishable cargo group

The final group of non-passenger-carrying coaching stock to be considered is that which most closely approximated to conventional goods vehicles. Some of them were, in fact, no more than goods trucks which had been given brakes and running gear to allow them to be worked safely in passenger trains. Their origin is obscure and almost certainly bound up with the total inability of the typical nineteenth century British goods train to be operated at anything like the transit speed required for perishable goods, and although this book is essentially about passenger carriages it is necessary at this point to refer briefly to the other side of railway operation, freight traffic.

It is one of the more severe indictments of the development of railways in Britain that their sheer success in capturing just about all the available land transport market in the nineteenth century bred a degree of monumental complacency in the board rooms of most railway companies when it came to vehicle provisioning for cargo handling. This typical four-wheeled British goods wagon was a poor thing indeed, usually devoid of both automatic brakes or any degree of sophistication, but for almost a century it had a virtual monopoly of the traffic so there was no real incentive to change its nature, particularly in terms of the speed at which it could run. In fact, it was not really until the 1950s and later that any real improvement began to take place on a widespread basis, by which time it was often too late to avoid losing the traffic to the road competitor with results which are now obvious to all.

Nevertheless, there were a few readily definable high-value traffics which demanded a higher transit speed even in the early days, and the railways were never slow in addressing the problem if they thought there was revenue to be gained, so in some areas they genuinely 'tried harder'. One way was to add the odd perishable goods vehicle to a passenger train, thus guaranteeing better speed provided the vehicle could operate in this mode. In effect, this was one of the first tentative moves on the part of the railway towards the much higher-speed freight service which is now commonplace. However, during the steam period it never went much further than an occasional fully braked freight train and, in consequence, there was always a place for those somewhat rare vehicles which could be hitched on to a passenger train.

The types of commodity carried should occasion no surprise: milk, fish, meat, vegetables and so forth. Many areas of the country could usually generate a wagon load or two of such items on almost a daily basis, so what more natural than to load them into a passenger-rated vehicle which would not have to endure the interminable delay of the loose-coupled and unbraked freight train? There can have been few places in rural Britain which did not respond to the undoubted advantages of being able to despatch the odd load of surplus fresh meat or liquid milk to the ever-growing towns with the guaranteed assurance that the railway would get the produce to market still fresh, usually the same day or, at worst, the next morning. In consequence, there grew up a considerable wagon-load traffic of perishables which would regularly find themselves attached to the first passenger train of the day — the 'early morning milk train' in very truth. Of course, the vehicles provided were more sophisticated and the rates for their use more expensive, but on the whole it was a valuable service in the pre-motorized era and the fact that

Right *The LNWR was the biggest single British operator of non-passenger coaching stock, so no apologies are necessary for yet another example from its diverse fleet. This is open fish truck No 439, one of many specifically built for carrying loaded boxes of fresh fish. It may not have looked like a conventional carriage but its mechanical specification allowed it to be treated as such in terms of the speed at which it was allowed to operate*

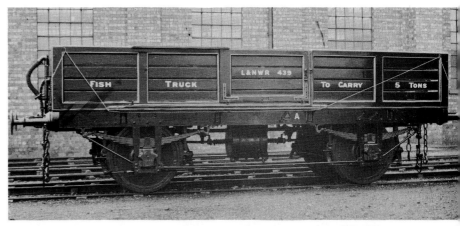

Above right and right *The covered van with slatted sides was a very common solution to the problem of handling several different kinds of perishable traffic. These two very similar vehicles, MR No 95 and LYR No 25 are for fish and milk traffic respectively* (Top R.J. Essery collection).

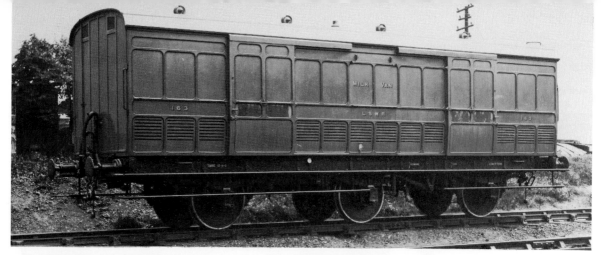

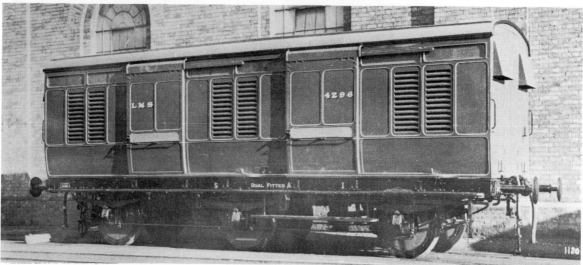

These stylish six-wheelers are very much in the carriage building tradition. LSWR No 163 was for milk traffic, and LMS No 4296 was built at Wolverton in pre-group days for West Coast fish traffic. After the grouping, it was re-designated as a meat van. Such change of usage in the 'perishable cargo' category was by no means uncommon

there may have been no more than one vehicle load from any one location posed no real problem while ever there was a passenger service to which it could be attached.

To some extent, the coming together of these individual loads at more central locations enabled the railways to operate high-speed 'perishable' trains under full passenger-rated regulations, much in the manner of mail and parcels trains, but it was not necessary *per se* and it was just as common to see such vehicles working to London, Birmingham and other big cities as part of the passenger service. Of course, in exceptional cases it paid the railways to operate

all-fish, all-meat and all-milk trains, especially from those locations where one might reasonably expect to be able to load a full train from the outset. The Aberdeen and Grimsby fish trains spring immediately to mind in this context. In some cases, the railways even transported *live* fish in mobile 'fish tank' vehicles so as to ensure even greater freshness on arrival.

In purely vehicular terms, the demands of this sort of traffic could be met by wagons and/or vans which could span the range from vacuum-braked open goods trucks to purpose-built and elaborate vans, scarcely distinguishable in appearance from most other coaching stock. At the margin there was always a degree of uncertainty as to whether a particular vehicle constituted a fully-braked goods vehicle or was genuinely non-passenger coaching stock. Some railways hedged their bets and classified in both ways, so it is difficult to be more specific; it was all part of the passenger business in the broadest sense.

15. Alternatives to convention

As has already been related in the context of many different types of vehicles, the first two decades of the present century were a time of great change in railway travelling habits culminating in the move to ever more grandiose conveyances for the more prestigious trains. All of the vehicles so far considered, however, be they humble suburban coaches or palatial special saloons, have one point in common; they were marshalled into trains and hauled along by locomotives. The same period, however, was also noteworthy for the first significant moves to some form of self-propelled passenger-carrying vehicle. This quite distinctive alternative form of passenger conveyance in the form of the ubiquitous diesel or electric multiple unit is very much the norm on many parts of the current railway scene and is likely to become more so during the next century, but it was the first twenty years or so of the present century which saw the real beginnings after a few late nineteenth century experiments.

The spur to change was the growing road competition, first in the form of the street tramway (see Chapter 8), supplemented increasingly by the motor omnibus and road coach; while the 1920s were probably the first decade during which the private motor car was first seen as a threat. To be honest, the railways did not seem to give this last competitor much serious thought until after the Second World War but it did have an effect, particularly in the country areas before then. However, in the context of this volume the real threat was the rapid rise of alternative forms of mechanized *public* transport and it was this aspect which lay at the heart of the new ideas.

The railway, for all its many virtues (not least its solidarity, reliability and safety), is by nature a somewhat inflexible form of transport with a multiplicity of fixed structures to maintain, not to mention its vehicles, even the meanest of which are normally heavier, stronger and more expensive to built than the road equivalent. To combat road competition, the railways therefore had to seek more economical ways of doing a task which hitherto had enjoyed something of a methodological monopoly even though the railways themselves competed with each other for custom. They were now all under threat.

The self-propelled option offers quite a few theoretical and practical advantages for short-to-medium-distance operations. It avoids the extra expense of a separate locomotive, it offers some greater degree of design freedom, its power output can, be more exactly matched to the load to be carried and it affords at least a possibility of trying to avoid the railway equivalent of using a sledgehammer to crack a walnut by providing vehicles just sufficiently large, but not too large, for the task. This latter point, however, can also be its undoing.

Electrification

Perhaps surprisingly to some people, the oldest alternative *form* of propulsion to steam was electricity, which first emerged on the scene in 1879 and was destined to become the principal motive force for much of the world's railways. In Britain, electrification was a slow process and its development, while beginning to achieve some dominance in certain specific areas during the Edwardian period, was much more spectacular during the periods covered by the second and third volumes of this series. However, its origins were Edwardian and can conveniently be considered here.

Without doubt, the various activities of the Metropolitan and District Railways and the London Underground group, all later to become part of the unified London Passenger Transport Board (LPTB), were the most striking single manifestation of railway electric traction during the first part of the twentieth century, but their story merits more detailed treatment than can be given at this first general encounter with alternatives. In any case, their own version of the grouping did not take place until 1933, well into the period covered by Part II.   Since the formation of the LPTB was so pivotal in the whole development of London's transport needs, along with the Southern Railway electrification of the 1920s and 1930s. I have chosen to consider the fuller story in that context; but one cannot dismiss the entire subject quite so baldly, even at this stage.

The establishment at the turn of the century of both the pioneer deep-level 'tube' lines in London (always electrically powered) and the electrification of the so-called 'surface' routes of the Metropolitan and the Metropolitan District Railways can be seen, in retrospect, to have had an influence well beyond the confines of the routes concerned. On the technical side they began to establish standards of traction and current collection which became widely influential; in operational terms they began to develop a pattern of frequent trains at such short intervals as to make a knowledge of the timetable unnecessary (at least in the principal built-up area) and, perhaps above all, they were amongst the first railways to undertake a major 're-think' in terms of vehicle design. It is with this particular aspect of the story that this part of the

from North American inter-urban and 'streetcar' design, the end product was a distinctly new look.

That many of the new electric trains should draw some inspiration from contemporary road practice is not entirely surprising, given the early history of railway carriages (see Chapter 1). Moreover, several of them arose out of competition with the new electric street tramways which were proving very popular. Thus the end door with the transverse *and* longitudinal seating, so characteristic of the typical British tramcar, was also a commonly seen 'new' arrangement on the electric trains. It had considerable merits in terms of fairly speedy loading and unloading, it gave plenty of room for standees and, supplemented by intermediate central doors, is still a very characteristic form on the London Underground network of the present day.

Of course, the highly characteristic double-deck tramcar body style could not readily be translated into railway form — it was too tall — but the railway lent itself to longer, wider and more massively built vehicles, so it is hardly surprising that many systems looked across the Atlantic to America where the street-car had taken on a much longer bogie form, of more orthodox railway carriage shape. Neither must one discount the influence of developments in mainland Europe where railway electrification was pursued with rather more vigour than in Britain in the early days.

Whatever the precise reasons, many new electric carriages in the London area and elsewhere took this new form and, particularly in the case of systems which had no pre-history of compartment stock such as the deep-level tube lines, it became a standard type. The forefather of them all was probably the celebrated 'padded cell'-type carriage design of the City and South London Railway of which an example is happily preserved at the London Transport Museum, but this quickly gave way to altogether more elegantly styled vehicles on such pioneer cross-London routes as the 'Central London', 'Great Northern, Piccadilly and Brompton' and so forth. The circular geometry of the tube tunnels forced, of course, a characteristic profile for these new carriages which must, at first, have seemed strange, but which is now so familiar as to cause scarcely a second glance.

The so-called 'surface' routes of what was to become London Transport, the Metropolitan and the Metropolitan District (later, more simply, the 'District') lines, had much older origins and began life as steam systems with conventional compartment stock. In consequence, when they were electrified a mixture of purpose built open EMU stock and conventional compartment stock hauled by electric locomotives was to be seen, and this division of style

account will be concerned, for therein lay a strong link with those few of the main-line railways which assayed electrification.

Given that there have been and will always be exceptions to any generalization, it does seem to me that the most dominant design feature of early electrical multiple unit (EMU) stock, as it is called, compared with its locomotive-hauled predecessors is the more widespread use of an open-plan interior layout, relatively uninfluenced by any previous kind of railway vehicle. When this was married to a form of exterior styling which drew much of its inspiration

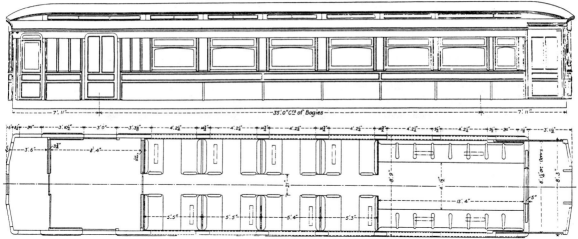

Electrically Operated Carriages, Metropolitan Railway.—Motor Car.

Above left *The now familiar mixture of transverse and longitudinal seating in deep-level tube stock is well illustrated by this view of a Charing Cross, Euston and Hampstead carriage of 1920. This route is now part of the much longer Northern Line of London Transport.*

Left *Two 1905 Metropolitan open motor cars flank four carriages of bogie compartment stock originally built for steam services in a typical mixed formation operation* en route to Baker St, *circa 1910.*

This page Figure 61 *Elevations and plans of the stylish clerestory open stock introduced by the Metropolitan Railway in 1905.*

Electrically Operated Carriages, Metropolitan Railway.—Trailer Car.

Scale 3mm = 1ft

End View & Cross Section of Motur & Trailer Cars, Metropolitan Railway.

was exceedingly long-lived, surviving on the Metropolitan until well after the Second World War. However, when the Metropolitan and the District built EMU carriages, they too chose the new open-plan layout for the most part and even adopted the clerestory roof form which made the carriages look even more transatlantic.

Compared with the purely 'London' railways, and with two notable northern exceptions, the main-line railway companies were somewhat slow to adopt electrification for suburban purposes, and even by the time of the railway grouping by far the bulk of

the short-haul commuter traffic was still firmly in the hands of the old faithful steam train with its individual carriages. Competition forced improvements to the actual vehicles (see Chapter 8) but the capital investment in locomotives was, presumably, such as to oblige most railways to look long and hard at the economics of electrification before making changes. It is a matter of history that many of them never did, but where the change was justified it tended to be more than usually interesting.

Remaining for the moment in the London area, the effect of the new underground electric lines, was

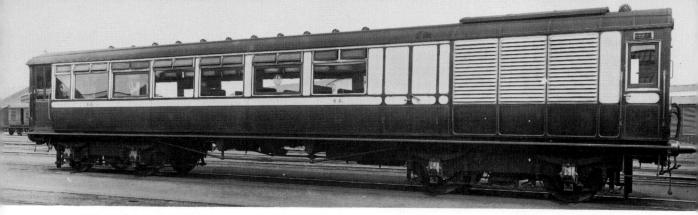

This third class motor driving car from the LNWR shows off the neat lines of the celebrated 'Oerlikon' stock of 1914. This stock was the only major instance of the LNWR panelled livery being applied to a non-beaded exterior.

beginning to have some effect, both in operating and in terms of attitude. Thus, for example, the GWR got into the act via the Hammersmith and City route by collaborating with the Metropolitan, while the London, Tilbury and Southend Railway went into joint ownership with the District Railway in some stock for through working.

North of the Thames, the only other railway seriously to entertain electrification was the LNWR which put conductor rails on to its Watford local lines and built for them some very stylish new carriages, again mostly end door and open plan. Memory recalls them as being of more than normally fine riding quality. Like the GWR and LT & SR, the LNWR also had a link with one of the London-based systems, but this time, rather unusually, it was a deep-level tube system, the forerunner of the present Bakerloo Line. This meant that the normally dimensioned LNWR stock could not penetrate the tube system, so the tube trains went out to Watford instead, wearing LNWR colours and joint insignia for a while and looking distinctly diminutive out in the open alongside the LNWR main-line trains. Even today, Queens Park station on the Bakerloo still bears witness to this historical curiosity.

It was, however, south of the River Thames where the main-line companies seriously considered and eventually embarked upon electrification during the 1910-23 period. In all cases the catalyst of change was the electrified tramway, and the reason for it being more prevalent south of the river was a consequence of the somewhat peculiar geography of the railways in and around London. If one looks at the familiar system map on any London Underground station, one cannot fail to notice that the bulk of the routes lie to the north of the Thames. The Metropolitan and District lines and all the deep-level tubes are predominantly found in this area, and this goes right back to the time when these various lines were in private ownership. Consequently, it was mostly the underground lines which met tramway competition in North London.

In part, this fundamental difference was accentuated by the fact that many of the main lines north of the Thames were not only genuine long-distance concerns (GWR, GER, LNWR, MR, GNR and so on) but also since the earliest days their termini had been forbidden to penetrate central London any further south than the line of the modern Marylebone and Euston Roads. Moreover, the traffic patterns of these longer-distance routes was subtly different from those in south and south-west London, even that of the LSWR. In effect, therefore, what is now London Transport filled the gap between the two sets of London-based railways and established a pattern which, for all its subsequent augmentation and change, persists to this very day.

Thus, the SE & CR, LB & SCR and LSWR could all bring their lines right up to Thames-side, and had done so. This was through the very heart of tramway territory in the 1900-20 period, and the first line to meet the new challenge was the Brighton. Adopting what was, for Britain, a very unusual single phase, high-voltage AC systems with overhead pick-up wires, the LB & SCR installed very successful pioneer electric trains on the South London line from London Bridge to Victoria via Denmark Hill in 1909, the whole service going electric by 1912. Meantime, a second overhead service on the Crystal Palace lines had started in 1911. These 'elevated' electric routes, as they were called (by virtue of the overhead current collection), were the pioneers of what was to become the whole Southern Railway electric network, but they did not survive long after the grouping in their original form — and this seems an appropriate point at which to raise the more technical business of current collection as far as trains are concerned.

In essence, an electric train, be it a multiple unit (ie traction motors mounted on some or all of the passenger carriages) or a locomotive pulling carriages, must both pick up and return the current. Pick-up can be either from a trackside conductor rail or an overhead conductor wire, return being either via the running rails or a fourth conductor rail. This in itself can be complicated enough, but when taken with the fact that the supply voltage can be anything from 5-600 volts DC to 25,000 volts AC, the potential for lack of standardization is enormous — and so it turned out to be as far as the Southern Railway was concerned in 1923. By the way, the London Underground systems and their associated links with the main lines were to a still different system, the now familiar fourth conductor rail method seen all over London Transport.

Although the Brighton pioneered South London suburban electrification, close on its heels was the LSWR which brought in a 600-volt DC conductor rail method in 1915 and by 1923 had well over twice as many actual vehicles in service than on the earlier Brighton system (300 out of an SR total of 434 to be exact) and rather more routes electrified. By now, the SE & CR had also got as far as the planning stage and was proposing a 1500-volt system with two conductor rails. The new Southern Railway, quite logically, should see no sense in all this; *force majeure* prevailed and the LSWR 600-volt DC method was adopted as standard although the Brighton overhead lines were developed for a short period before conversion to 600 volts. Naturally, the former SE & CR routes, after grouping, were electrified on the LSWR system from the outset, and basically, apart from subsequent slight voltage upgrading, the Southern electric, to this day, betrays its pre-group history in terms of current collection. Ironically, the Brighton had chosen an overhead collection AC method which, modified to 25kv, is now regarded as the BR standard!

Although this narrative may seem at times to have strayed somewhat from the specifics of vehicle design, the peculiar and unique nature of the London area electrification cannot really be ignored for fuller understanding of a rather complex subject. Moreover, it will need to be readdressed frequently in the context of both post-grouping and post-nationalization developments. In its own way it turned out to be just as powerful a manifestation of the complex relationship between people and railway vehicles as any of the other issues so far considered.

The Brighton actually built new stock for its 'elevated' electrics but did not copy the new open-plan style of the underground railways. Instead, it adopted a modified compartment style with an internal passageway (not a true corridor) and partition heights less than full height of the roof, save for the divisions between the 1st and 3rd and smoking and non-smoking areas. Stylistically, the South London stock exhibited square-cornered panelling and a somewhat more rounded arc roof, but the Crystal Palace sets reverted to customary LB & SCR

styling and both versions were very much in the traditional mode.

This was even more so with the LSWR services where all the 'new' electric three-car trains were, in fact, rebuilds from the older (1904 vintage) four-vehicle 'bogie block' sets and thus very much in the customary LSW stylistic idiom. However, their new driving cabs, with a pronounced 'V' shape (often nicknamed 'torpedo' ends), along with the new all-green livery, gave them a superficial air of newness. They were, however, just as traditionally non-corridor as in their steam-hauled days.

This non-corridor compartment type of EMU, adopted by both the LB & SCR and the LSWR in their different ways, not unnaturally became the SR norm after 1923, and when the ex-SE & CR lines were added to the electric system in the 1920s, they too made much use of rebuilt ex-SE & CR steam stock. In fact, all three constituents of the SR contributed steam-hauled coaches to the new company

The diminutive appearance of the tube stock on the 'open road' is seen in this view of a five-car set of London Electric Railway/LNWR joint stock on the LNWR 'new' lines near Kenton. Two styles of vehicle are featured on this northward extension of the Bakerloo line.

This page top to bottom *A three-car train of LB & SCR South London stock on the overhead electrified system at Wandsworth Road. The distinctive square-cornered panelling is readily apparent.*

This Southern Railway view shows a very characteristic form of operation — an eight-car train made up entirely of converted steam stock from the LSWR and LB & SCR.

The substantial American-built stock for the original LSWR Waterloo and City services was astonishingly well finished for such a short distance operation. The attention to detail, especially in the woodwork, would not have disgraced a main-line express.

Above right *The LYR electrics were built in several batches over a period of years, starting with clerestories in 1904 and followed by elliptical roof stock from 1910. This view shows a mixed four-car set with two of each type. The driving ends when originally built had a pronounced inwards taper to the front windows, later altered to the full width arrangement shown here. Note the elaborate lining.*

Right *The distinctive lines of the later LYR elliptical roof stock are well shown in this 'works grey' view of third class motor car No 3065.*

which were subsequently converted to EMU form, so even after 'Southern Electric' had become something of a household phrase, the pre-group origins of many of the new electric trains remained obvious for decades.

Before finally leaving the London area, brief mention should also be made of that mildy curious operation, the 'Waterloo and City Line'. Built, as its name implies, to link Waterloo (LSWR) with the City of London, it was the only pure deep-level tube line never to be integrated with London Transport. Its first cars were both American in style and origin, and to this day it is the only pure tube line which is operated by British Railways.

Outside the London area, and disregarding such odd freaks as the Swansea and Mumbles (incidentally, the oldest passenger-carrying line in the world opened in 1807), the Grimsby and Immingham and the Burton and Ashby Light Railway routes (all of them

essentially no more than glorified tramways somewhat in the American 'inter-urban' mode), the only two main-line railway companies which made any sort of progress with electrification in the pre-group era were the LYR and NER. It is interesting that, yet again, these two companies whose carriage building has often tended to be ignored (because they did not go to London?) were both pioneers in the new technology — and neither of them did it by converting elderly hand-me-down steam stock either. Moreover, the LYR was actually the first railway in Britain to electrify what amounted to a main line (1904).

Both companies adopted the new open interior, end door approach and did it in some style with, if anything, the palm going to the LYR for its efforts north and north-east of Liverpool. In truth, there was probably little in it either way, for the Tyneside electrics of the NER were distinctly attractive and well found vehicles; but the LYR efforts were on a

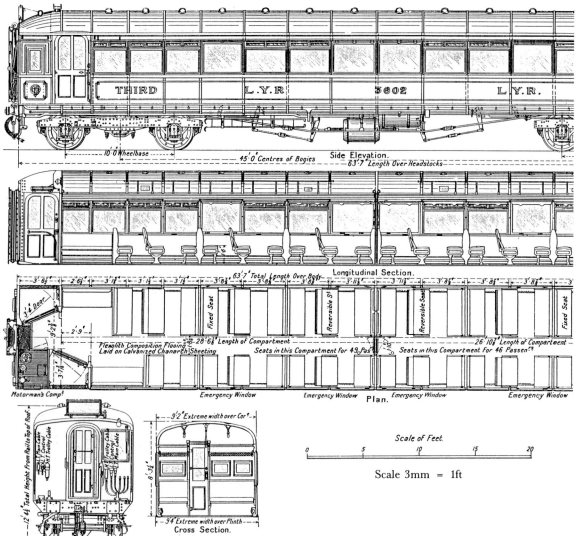

Figure 62 *Elevations and plan of the 1915-built third class LYR trailer cars.*

truly spectacular scale in terms of both vehicle shape, construction and size. They were of all-steel construction, of almost GWR 'Dreadnought' proportions and even wider (10 feet) in the case of those carriages reserved exclusively for the Liverpool-Southport and Liverpool-Ormskirk services which had a generous loading gauge. They were in fact the widest railway vehicles ever built in Britain and decorated most flamboyantly with, for the LYR, a massive amount of lining and florid insignia which must have looked good set against the rather sombre basic colours. Their interiors, too, were different. Drawing from both contemporary American inter-urban and British tramway styling, they managed

to provide what to me seems to be an attractive and acceptable improvement on conventional contemporary suburban coaches, for they were, after all, only commuter trains. Perhaps the somewhat fashionable nature of the residential districts between Liverpool and Southport had something to do with it.

Scarcely less attractive were the somewhat smaller vehicles of the so-called 'lightweight' stock, built for through running on to the Liverpool Overhead system. If anything, these were even more flamboyantly decorated than those on the Southport services. Clearly this was the dawn of a new era, and the LYR could see no reason why it should be, or need be, too coy about its achievements.

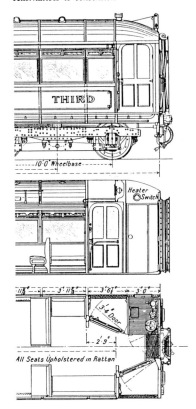

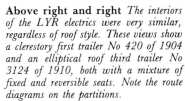

Above right and right *The interiors of the LYR electrics were very similar, regardless of roof style. These views show a clerestory first trailer No 420 of 1904 and an elliptical roof third trailer No 3124 of 1910, both with a mixture of fixed and reversible seats. Note the route diagrams on the partitions.*

Below *Composite No 1005, one of the flamboyantly decorated 'lightweight' LYR cars for working on to the Liverpool Overhead system.*

This page top to bottom *Interior of prototype LYR 'lightweight' car No 1000. The first class areas were much the same as on normal LYR electrics, but these slatted benches with their 'carpeted' seats were much inferior to normal third class LYR practice.*

The markedly American nature of the Mersey Railway electric stock is well exemplified by this mixed set of later elliptical roof motors and original clerestory trailers at Birkenhead Park.

Three typical NER Tyneside electric cars — a motor luggage first is nearest the camera and behind is a pair of full thirds.

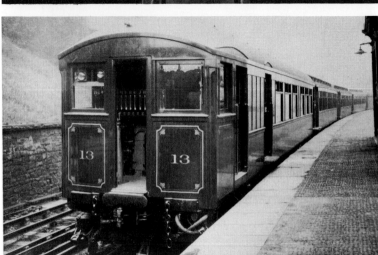

Right *A single-unit Tyneside electric train — NER Motor luggage composite No 3770 with a cab at both ends.*

Below right *The Midland's rather half-hearted attempt at electrification in the Morecambe area took the form of central motor cars flanked by two trailers. The carriages, though not very good in either style or comfort, were, however, different from all other MR stock*

Furthermore, it augmented its electrified system by tackling the Manchester-Bury route some eleven years later with some equally fine vehicles. The carriages built for all these services lasted well into the LMS era and the first replacements did not appear until 1940-41.

Mention of the Liverpool Overhead in the context of the LYR serves as a reminder that London was not unique in having its own 'dedicated' electric railways. Liverpool could sport two such. The 'Overhead' was a quite distinctive operation in the dockland area which, by virtue of its route set on gantries above the streets and docks, was the nearest thing Britain ever came to having an 'elevated' urban railway in the American sense of the word. 'American' too were its carriages, as indeed were those of that other Liverpool system, the Mersey

Railway, which operated what amounted to not much more than a shuttle service from the Wirral peninsula, under the Mersey itself and into the heart of Liverpool. The 'Overhead', sadly, is no more, but the old Mersey lines along with those of the Wirral Railway and the LYR Southport lines still form the nucleus of the modern 'MerseyRail'.

Just as the LYR had adopted electrification in advance of the London-based companies, so too did that other large English regional company, the North Eastern, when in 1904 it began to operate electric trains in the Tyneside area. They were somewhat similar, if slightly smaller in overall dimensions, to the LYR carriages, but whereas the LYR broke entirely new stylistic grounds, the NER vehicles did perhaps carry a slight hint of contemporary company fashion, save for their livery, a striking new red and

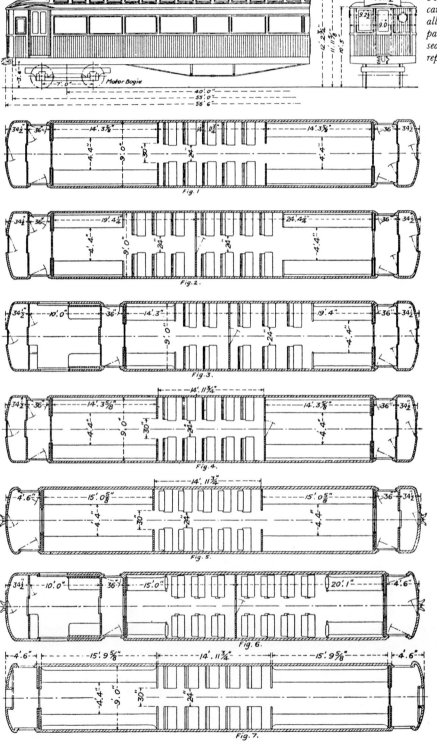

Figure 63 *The original Tyneside electrics came in quite a variety of internal layouts, all displaying the characteristic mixed pattern of transverse and longitudinal seating. No fewer than nine variations are represented by these contemporary plans.*

1. Third Class Carriage (Motor). Third class compts. 64 seats. Two driver's compts. Two vestibules. Weight, 29 tons 1 cwt.

2. Third Class Carriage (Motor). Two third class compts. 60 seats. Two driver's compts. Two vestibules. Weight, 29 tons 1 cwt.

3. Third Class Carriage (Motor). Two third class compts. 42 seats. One luggage compt. Two driver's compts. Two vestibules. Weight 29 tons 1 cwt.

4. Third Class Carriage (Trailer). Third class compts. 64 seats. Two driver's compts. Two vestibules. Weight, 23 tons 1 cwt.

5. Third Class Carriage (Motor). Three third class compts. 64 seats. One driver's compt. Two vestibules. Weight, 28 tons 19 cwts.

6. First Class Carriage (Motor). Two first class compts. 44 seats. One luggage compt. One driver's compt. Weight, 28 tons 17 cwt.

7. Third Class Carriage (Trailer). Three third class compts. 68 seats. Two vestibules. Weight, 21 tons 5 cwt.

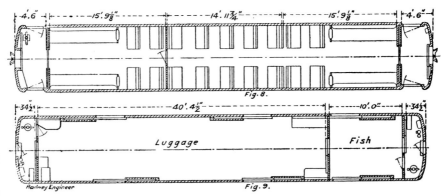

8. Third Class Carriage (Trailer).
Three third class compts.
64 seats. Two vestibules.
Weight, 21 tons 15 cwt.

9. Luggage Van (Motor).
One luggage compt. One fish compt. Two driver's compts. Weight, 34 tons 10 cwt.

Scale 2mm = 1ft

cream colour scheme. Like those of the LYR, they survived well into the BR period, but the story of their eventual replacement is rather more complex and very much a part of the latter-day BR development to be considered in the final volume.

Of the other main-line companies, wherever located in Britain, none can really be said to have achieved anything of great significance in terms of pioneering electrification. Several had thought about it and, as we have seen, the SE & CR had got as far as the planning stage by the time of the grouping, but of the others only the Midland possessed any purpose-built hardware, aside that is from its interest in the District Line via its ownership from 1912 onwards of the London, Tilbury and Southend Railway. The Midland's own home-produced product was a small clutch of not particularly exciting vehicles for an experimental overhead electrification project carried out in the Lancaster, Morecombe and Heysham area, of all places. It survived well into LMS and BR days but was never of more than marginal significance, save in a quasi-experimental category.

The best, therefore, that can be said about the moves towards electrification during the pre-group era is that they showed an increasing awareness of a growing problem. However, while some were distinctly well thought out, there was no real appreciation of the virtue of some sort of standardization in terms of technology. The legacy of this inconsistency is still with us, albeit perhaps less visibly obvious than in those pioneer days if only by virtue of the somewhat greater vehicle body design harmonization of the BR period.

Perhaps the most surprising feature of the whole business is the lack of interest in electrification shown in the other three great industrial conurbations of Birmingham, the West Riding and Glasgow. True, Glasgow did have its own underground, but this was not much more than a glorified electric train set, devoid of any pointwork and operating on a self-

contained city centre circular route in tube-type tunnels. Even the vehicles had to be placed on the track with a crane! It was never considered to be a railway in the fullest sense and was usually referred to as the 'subway'. It was, however, full of character and, re-equipped in the early 1980s, still survives to this day.

Glasgow, as the centre of a large industrial complex, had to wait until BR days for a proper electrified suburban system — and a very good one too — but the West Midlands and the West Riding are at the time of writing still waiting for the sort of electrified suburban network which would be normal in almost any other comparably sized industrial regions of the world. Perhaps this is because, unlike London, Lancashire and the North East, neither the West Midlands nor the West Riding during the company period were served by but one big company which regarded these areas as its home territory. In Birmingham, the GWR, LNWR and MR eyed each other suspiciously while at the same time having bigger fish to fry, while in the West Riding, although almost everybody got into the act (GNR, NER, LYR, LNWR, MR, GCR et al), nobody seemed to be able to capture the leading role. The modern-day legacy of these competitive nonsenses is still there for everyone to see.

If electrification was less than universally successful in the pre-group period, the other alternatives were no better. It was, one supposes, inevitable that the newfangled internal combustion engine would be tried out somewhere, and this led to a minor outbreak of some pretty comically styled petrol-driven railcars, some of them being 'petrol-electric', ie petrol engines generating electrical energy for traction motors. This was an idea pursued with rather more vigour in North America, but the British contribution was, in global terms, of monumental insignificance. The NER was again to the fore, and, to be fair, probably tried harder than anyone, but the only others worthy of even passing mention are perhaps the GNR and

Left and below *'Dignity and Impudence' seems an apt description of these NER petrol-driven vehicles. No 3711 is a diminutive petrol-engined railcar, employing a form of direct drive, whereas No 3170Y, seen in early LNER days, was described as a 'Petrol-electric-autocar'. The petrol-driven generator was located in the body superstructure at the left-hand end, and the whole ensemble was styled rather in the manner of the contemporary 'enclosed'-type steam railmotors.*

Bottom *LB & SCR petrol-electric railcar No 3 was one of two supplied by Dick Kerr and Co in 1905, broadly identical in size and configuration but with somewhat differently styled bodywork, the tramcar inheritance of which was clear. They did not last for more than five of six years in passenger use, being transferred for inspection use on the overhead electrified lines in 1911.*

the LB & SCR, both of whom tried out some near-identical four-wheel petrol cars of Kerr-Stuart origin. They were quite neat in a sort of 'modified tramcar' style but, like the NER contribution, they came to nought.

In the context of Britain's railways, it did seem that tradition died hard. Perhaps the most astonishing manifestation of this was the building of a brand new *horse-drawn* carriage by the NBR for its Port Carlisle branch as late as 1908! However, this was distinctly maverick.

Steam railcars and derivatives

The real bastion of the traditional approach to the problems of competition was that uniquely Edwardian phenomenon, the steam railcar, or steam railmotor as it was sometimes called, and it is with this vehicle and its derivatives that the rest of this chapter is concerned.

It was entirely predictable that when the pre-group companies began to feel the competitive winds blowing from road and tramway competition, they should try to modify the traditional steam train to a more economical form. What they were striving to do was produce a smaller powered, cheaper to

build and cheaper to operate unit which would not be as much of a drain on financial resources as the larger, more conventional locomotive and carriages approach. This was achieved by making use of what was normally a self-propelled single unit vehicle embodying a combination of a small locomotive portion with a passenger-carrying area. Many were built by a considerable number of railways (see Table 10).

In terms of structural form, two alternatives were to be seen: the 'rigid' railcar, wherein the locomotive part was mounted on the same frames as the carriage portion, and the 'articulated' version whereby the powered end, although semi-permanently attached to the carriage, could pivot independently. On the rigid railcar, the purely engine portion was, in effect, a sort of steam-powered traction bogie, whereas with the articulated type the configuration was somewhat more that of a conventional locomotive whose boiler pivoted along with the driving wheels.

Either variety could be found in either of two styles

Table 10 Purpose-built steam railcars 1902-11

Note: The totals refer to the number of passenger-carrying units — several railways (eg GWR/LYR/Taff Vale) had 'spare' engine units. The list refers to Great Britain, excluding Ireland.

Years built	Company name	Rigid pattern			Articulated pattern			Grand total
		'Open' loco	Enclosed loco	Sub total	'Open' loco	Enclosed loco	Sub total	
1904	Alexandra Docks		2	2				2
1903	Barry		2	2				2
1911	Cardiff*		2	2				2
1905	Furness		2	2				2
1904-5	GCR		3	3				3
1905	GNR				6		6	6
1905	GNSR				2		2	2
1904-5	GSWR				3		3	3
1903-8	GWR		97	97		2	2	99
1906	Isle of Wight Central				1		1	1
1905	LB & SCR					2†	2†	2†
1905-10	LNWR		7	7				7
1904-6	LSWR		15	15				15
1902	LSWR/LB & SCR Joint	2		2				2
1905-11	Lancashire & Yorkshire				17		17	17
1904	Midland		2	2				2
1905-6	North Staffordshire					3†	3†	3†
1907	Port Talbot					1§	1§	1§
1907	Rhymney				2		2	2
1904-5	SE & CR				8		8	8
1903-6	Taff Vale				16		16	16
	Totals	2	132	134	55	8	63	197

* The last British company to introduce the type.
† In effect an 'enclosed' locomotive portion but with 'external' chimney in front of the concealed portion.
§ The only British steam railcar with a *six*-coupled locomotive portion.

which, for convenience, may be described as 'open' or 'enclosed' in relation to the locomotive portion. In the former type, the powered end genuinely resembled a steam locomotive, albeit of diminutive size, whereas in the latter case the power unit was sheathed in an outer casing designed to look like part of the carriage itself. As part of the general attempt to keep down size, weight and cost, wheels were normally quite diminutive and the boiler itself could be either conventional (ie fore-and-aft), transverse or even vertical.

The three principal pre-group practitioners of the steam railcar were the Great Western (by far the most dominant single company), the LYR and Taff Vale, the GWR adopting the 'concealed' styling, the LYR and TVR going for the alternative mode. In both cases the influence of these companies turned out to be stronger than the rest, but, as Table 10 reveals, they were by no means the only operators of these characteristic vehicles. From the table it can also be seen that the rigid type outnumbered the articulated variety by roughly two to one and that, although both body styles could be seen in both structural patterns, the two predominant varieties were the 'rigid enclosed' and 'articulated open' variations.

Paradoxically, however, the first genuine railmotor design (discounting a few eccentric nineteenth century experiments) was not to either of the two common configurations, and its introduction was the brainchild of that celebrated Scotsman Dugald Drummond when, in 1902, as LSWR chief engineer he had built two for the joint services of the LSWR/LB & SCR between Southsea and Fratton. The GWR borrowed the first one and reported quite favourably, but in service they turned out to be feeble machines with insufficient steam raising power to keep going when fully loaded. In this respect they not only pioneered the railmotor type but also accurately anticipated its principal subsequent weakness, regardless of who built it, to what design, or for what purpose.

As built, these two vehicles were quite neat and tidy but the need to rebuild the locomotive portion gave rise to an ensemble which for grotesque ugliness would have taken some beating. One writer has described them as 'loutish' — most apt! Appearance notwithstanding, they nonetheless gave nearly twenty years of service in re-boilered form which was better than many. Nevertheless, the typical British railcar was not to be quite like either variant of these pioneer Drummond conveyances, and from this point it will be convenient to divide the discussion into the two principal structural forms, starting with the rigid type.

Although Drummond's prototype railcars had been of the rigid frame configuration, in the event they turned out to be the only such railcars to display an 'exposed' locomotive portion. All the rest were of the enclosed type and by far and away the leading light in this story was the GWR. In fact, its 'enclosed' rigid railcars made up just about half of the total British fleet of both kinds. They varied somewhat in both superficial appearance and detail design and, to be truthful, were not the most elegantly styled products of this celebrated railway, but they were probably the only really serious attempt on the part of a major company to persevere with a cheaper solution to real operating problems.

In terms of designed utilization, two main varieties were built, the so-called 'suburban' and 'branch line' types, and the nomenclature perhaps revealed a sort of uncertainty about the whole concept which was to bedevil all British steam railmotor building and was to be their subsequent undoing. Not to put too fine a point on it, it is hard to see how the same sort of vehicle could simultaneously be thought to be the right answer both for a lightly trafficked branch *and* for the busy suburbs, even given different seating capacity. However, the GWR (and others) went along with a sort of theory that one way to compete with the suburban tramcar was to provide a vehicle of somewhat similar capacity which, because of the very nature of the railway, could traverse the suburbs at frequent intervals much more quickly than a vehicle on the public highway. It could and it did, and it became so popular that it often turned out to be too small to carry the resultant loads. The generally feeble power of the dedicated locomotive portion was usually incapable of pulling an extra trailer to carry the greater load, thus resulting in a sort of conceptual stalemate. We shall come back to it later.

In the context of the GWR, however, the steam railcar obviously fulfilled a more than useful purpose — or else why build nearly 100 of them? This was especially true in the country areas, and the 'branch' type, always numerically stronger, well outlived the suburban variety by on average some ten years into the mid-1930s when it was often replaced, significantly one feels, either by the auto-train (see below) or the diesel railcar (Chapter 24). It is worth noting that the GWR steam railcar fleet remained at full strength for only the seven years between 1908 and 1914, and one cannot help but think that in the post-Great War era, the motor bus and motor car helped kill it off. However, many of them (most, in fact) had a second lease of life as auto-trailers.

After the LSWR/LB & SCR experiment, the GWR became (in 1903) the first company to embrace this new idea and, that company being so influential, it is likely that some at least of the other railways followed suit on the 'imitative' principle. In terms

Right *NBR horse-drawn Port Carlisle 'Dandy' No 2, built in 1908, must surely have been the most surprising new carriage ever built in the twentieth century for a British main-line company. It was broken up circa 1914.*

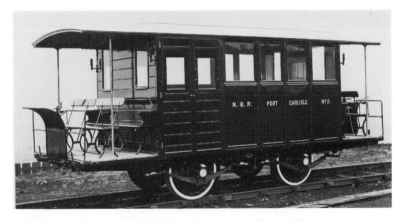

Below *Drummond's pioneering LSW and LB & SCR joint steam railmotors: No 1 with its original too feeble boiler of 1903, and No 2 as rebuilt in a most grotesque fashion a year later.*

Bottom *GWR flat-sided 'enclosed' steam railcar No 17, characteristic of the earlier examples from this company.*

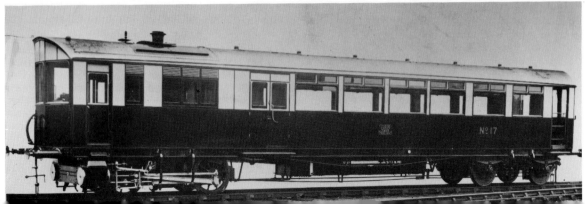

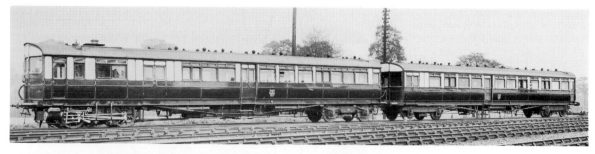

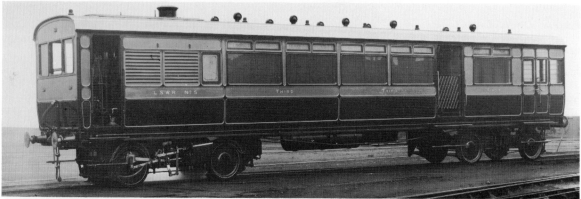

This page top to bottom *Later GWR railcars embodied more traditional vehicle styling with 'proper' panelling. This is No 61 hauling trailer No 34.*

The running gear of LSWR steam railcar No 5 reveals its derivation from Drummond's original efforts, but the enclosed body is far more typical of 'enclosed' steam railmotor practice at the time.

One of the neat Furness railmotors with its equally neat four-wheel trailer at Coniston. The clerestory styling was a distinctively different and attractive stylistic feature

The LNWR steam railmotors were distinctly handsome as can be seen here at Bicester. No 3 was one of six broadly identical 57-foot cars; the engine portion is at the far end.

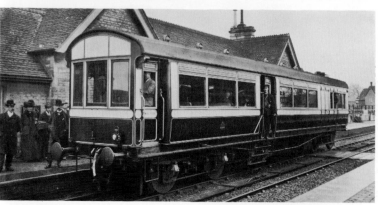

Right *The final LNWR railcar was a solitary 60-foot example with rather more power and designed to run with a trailer. In this view at Lees, near Oldham, in 1910, and now renumbered 507, it had also acquired a horsebox. Unfortunately, this degree of versatility was rare in most rigid steam railmotor designs.*

of those which adopted the enclosed rigid railcar, most seem to have done so on an experimental one-service-only basis if the quantities listed in Table 10 are any guide. Conceptually, all had much in common and some were distinctly stylish, but aside from the GWR the only two railways which tackled the rigid railcar in more than penny numbers were the LSWR and LNWR, and even these two seemed to have their doubts.

The LSWR built a total of fifteen whose running gear was much influenced by the prototype Drummond pair but whose bodywork was somewhat cleaned up in style, with a neatly enclosed portion. The first two of this new style had somewhat brutal, all-encasing platework at the powered end, but the final thirteen were treated in 'coachbuilding' style to vastly better effect. The LSWR seems to have seen them as fulfilling something like the GWR 'branch' role, but in 1906 Drummond moved to his version of the auto-train and the railcars quickly withered on the branch. Three only were left by 1916 and all had gone by 1919.

The LNWR, although much the same size as the GWR, seemed not to espouse the railcar cause with any great enthusiasm, but the few which it did build (six in 1905-7 and an extra one in 1910) were perhaps the most stylish enclosed steam railcars ever seen in Britain. Their nearest rivals in this respect were those of the Furness and GCR, and all three railways seemed to produce a more visually harmonious unit than did the otherwise far more significant GWR. The LNWR examples were particularly well built in body construction terms and were technically interesting in embodying an *inside*-cylindered locomotive unit which made them not only marginally less grotesque when in motion but probably smoother riding than most of their kind, if only because the cylinders were closer to the longitudinal centre-line. For all their small numbers, they lasted better than most and even the

unsentimental LMS found use for most of them until the late 1920s or early 1930s. One lasted until BR days in 1948 and was the final survivor of any of its kind in revenue service in Britain, having outlived its far more numerous GWR contemporaries by some fourteen years.

As for the other rigid railcars, they can be realistically disregarded (except by their devotees) save perhaps for the Midland's experiment, and even then only by accident of history. The MR steam railcars were not the best of the bunch; there were only two of them and internally they displayed a particularly nasty form of pierced plywood seating which they shared with their equally unmemorable electric contemporaries (page 255 above). Their power units were unreliable (one, indeed, if not both had to be changed), but one of them was converted to an officer's saloon which, by one of those strange quirks of history, has survived and is now in the National Collection. It is, ironically, the only such vehicle in Britain which has any remote chance of being restored to its original and once quite characteristic form. It will need a vast sum of money and, at the time of writing, I am unable to state whether it will ever be possible; but it is better than nothing. If only there was a genuine GWR or LNWR example.

Turning now to the articulated form, this approach fared little better than the rigid railcar. It was very much a child of the Lancashire and Yorkshire via the Taff Vale in the person of Mr Hurry Riches who designed the first example for the TVR in 1903. As far as can be seen, Mr Riches, an enthusiastic supporter of the steam railmotor who, *inter alia*, delivered a paper on the subject to the Institution of Mechanical Engineers in 1906, felt that a more powerful unit, articulated to the passenger-carrying portion, might prove to be a better solution to the problem, and he designed a most unusual locomotive portion for TVR examples with a *transverse* boiler with

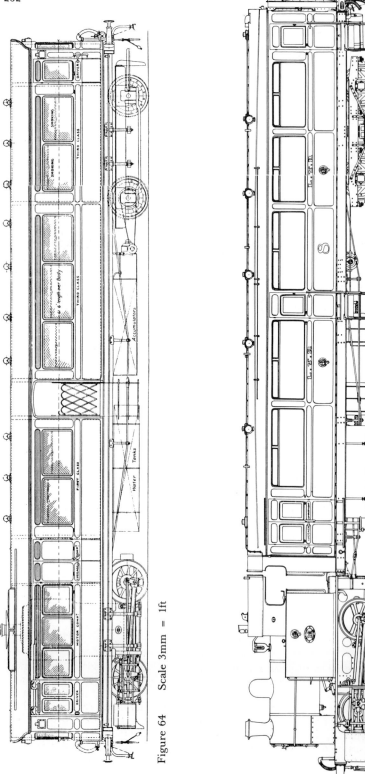

Figure 64   Scale 3mm = 1ft

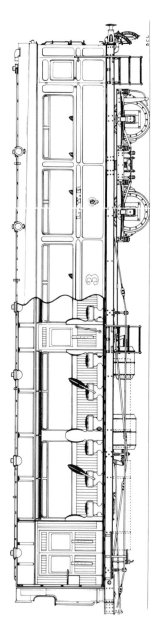

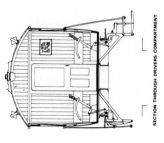

Figure 65   Scale 3mm = 1ft

SECTION THROUGH DRIVERS COMPARTMENT

Figure 64 *This drawing of the GCR composite steam railmotor design reveals that it rivalled that of the LNWR for handsomeness of outline.*

Figure 65 *The upper drawing shows the final form of the LYR railmotors in 1921 livery. The wider chimney on the locomotive and corridor connection to the carriage were pre Great War alterations, but the wide bearing bogie was a later substitution. The lower, sectioned, drawing shows the first of Hughes's carriage sections with the 'truss rod' narrow bearing bogie and fully glazed driving end as built. Numerous other smaller modifications took place through the years to the lighting, gas supply tanks, steps and even the frames (Drawing by B.C. Lane based on LYR originals).*

Above right *Midland steam railmotor No 2234 is seen here receiving attention at Hellifield* circa *1904. The slightly tedious method of taking on water is readily apparent.*

Right *Mr Hurry Riches's pioneering articulated steam railmotor No 1 of the Taff Vale Railway. Its unorthodox boiler worked well on the TVR but did not fully withstand translation to the LYR*

two short 'drums' fed by a single central firebox. By all accounts they had quite formidable steam raising power for their size, and the LYR was persuaded to go for a couple of similar machines in 1905. Avonside and Kerr Stuart were the favoured TVR manufacturers, and the LYR procured two Kerr Stuart examples to the basic TVR design; but, it has to be said, the LYR Chief Engineer, George Hughes, did not seem too enchanted with his new purchase! Accordingly, he decided he could do rather better himself and forthwith designed the LYR variant — a typically neat and efficient Horwich engine unit married to an altogether better-looking passenger-carrying component. This became (marginally) the most numerous, and undeniably the best, articulated steam railmotor ever built in Britain, and by far the

most long-lived. Not for the first time, as this narrative has averred, the oft unsung 'Lanky' turned out to know best.

If the Taff Vale and the LYR vied with each other for *primus inter pares* in this form of alternative steam railcar technology, they were not exactly alone, for the articulated option seemed to attract the attention of more than a few eminent designers. In consequence, although numerically less significant than the rigid option, the articulated railcars seemed to sprout just as many varieties, most of which somehow seemed to be rather better regarded in their day. Perhaps it was because they looked more like 'proper' trains, since most of them had a very visible and obviously 'engine-like' powered end, that they were taken more seriously! Moreover, to be truthful,

Left *Detail view of LYR steam railmotor No 9 in 1920. Another view of this type will be found on page 78.*

Below *SE & CR steam railmotor No 1, built in 1904 and seen here labelled for service on the Isle of Sheppey Light Railway.*

many of the designs were of more than normally pleasant visual aspect, however useful or not they may have been in their primary role.

Of the many which might be mentioned, we can perhaps single out a few of particular interest, partly on numerical terms but also in the context of design originality. The surprising leader of the pack, after the LYR and TVR, was the SE & CR, which built no fewer than eight beautifully stylish examples under the supervision of Harry Wainwright. The carriage portion of the final six differed slightly from that of the first two. As with many other companies, these neat units found work for less than a decade, all being withdrawn by the end of 1914, although the carriage portions were converted for auto-train work.

The only other railway to build more than a token number of articulated railmotors was the GNR with six, built in three pairs and apparently intended by Ivatt for evaluation — there were two contemporary petrol railcars too. All three steam pairs differed slightly in detail, although the basic carriage layout was pretty well the same. Perhaps the most interesting structural feature was the full elliptical roof sported by the first pair (the other four had what amounted to a Howlden roof profile). This was the first use of the soon to be familiar GNR roof shape, and, although Ivatt is credited with the design, the influence of his carriage and wagon chief, Nigel Gresley, was clear. None of the designs was repeated but the GNR railmotors enjoyed twenty years of life before withdrawal — better than most — and, as was quite common, the carriage portions were recovered for further use. Unsurprisingly, Gresley turned pairs of them into articulated 'twins'.

Of the rest of this group, those of the LB & SCR and the NSR had much in common, with a curious

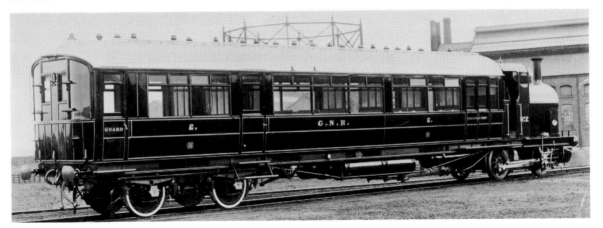

Above *GNR steam railmotors Nos 2 and 8, both built in 1905, show the two carriage styles adopted, the body of No 2 being the first Gresley bow-ended elliptical roof vehicle for the GNR. The power unit of No 8 was built by Avonside, and in both cases the carriage portions were later converted to articulated 'twins'.*

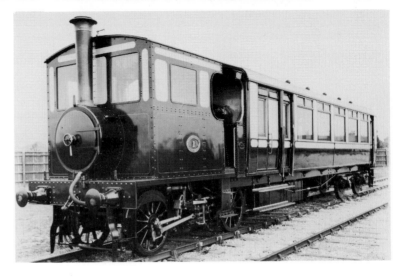

Right *The distinctive 'half and half' styling of the engine unit of LB & SCR steam railmotor No 1 is very clear in this ex-works view. The engine portion of the North Staffordshire examples was identical.*

'cross-bred' engine section, neither fully open nor fully enclosed. The engine portions were identical, but the carriage elements were different with the Brighton probably having the stylistic edge. However, their life was exceedingly short (four years or so) whereas the NSR trio survived until 1922. They were curious, ungainly looking ensembles compared with most of their type but at least they did manage to earn some revenue before going the way of the rest. Mention too should be made of the solitary GWR excursion into this type — a pair of Kerr Stuart units with hideous enclosed cabs and somewhat non-GWR-style bodies. One of them was sold to the Nidd Valley Light Railway in 1920 and outlived all the other GWR steam railcars (of any

kind), not being withdrawn until 1937, by then named *Hill*. It was still in existence in a Leeds scrapyard some 25 years later!

Amongst the rest, perhaps the most interesting, if least successful, design was that of a GNSR pair which used patent boilers with a hemispherical firebox. It gave them a distinctive appearance but they were really rather ineffective and survived only a few years. In this they were in marked contrast to the solitary and quite successful 'enclosed' Port Talbot example, Britain's largest steam railcar of any design. It lasted until 1926, latterly with the Port of London Authority.

All told, however, the articulated railcar fared no better than the rigid type. The GSWR trio lasted until *circa* 1917 and the solitary Isle of Wight example only until 1912 so, apart from the LYR fleet, this interesting experiment was born, matured and died pretty well within the period encompassed by this volume. However, the LYR examples were different. For one thing, they had a powerful enough engine portion to allow a trailer to be attached to the main unit, and this gave them added flexibility in coping with busier traffic. The two Taff Vale units were

Below *This picture reveals the unique hemispherical boiler design adopted by the GNSR for its steam railmotor No 29.*

Bottom *LB & SCR 'Balloon'-type carriage coupled to a 2-4-0T* Boxhill *represents the engine-plus-single-coach form of push-pull train.* Boxhill *was converted to this wheel arrangement from its original 0-6-0 styling for this type of use. It later reverted to an 0-6-0 type and, as such, is preserved at the NRM*

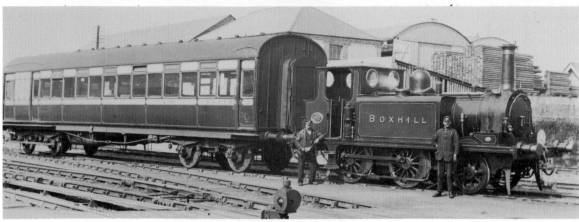

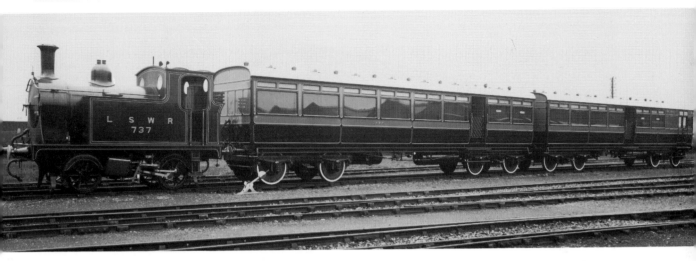

quickly consigned to oblivion (the carriage parts were retained) but the rest survived to the LMS and withdrawal was quite leisurely, not starting until 1927 and only slowly thereafter. The last example, like that of the LNWR (see above), just managed to reach BR.

The steam railmotor, rigid or articulated, was a fascinating if generally abortive attempt by the railways to make a quantum change. It failed because of its inflexibility. Whether in the suburbs or in the country, it was only viable as long as it did not generate too much patronage. The moment that overloading became a problem, the generally feeble engine portions proved unable to cope, and only those with a little extra power could survive. However, the moment one began to think of using a more powerful unit to cope with the extra loads, then most railways concluded that one might as well use a conventionally styled locomotive and separate carriages again. This, in fact, is precisely what happened in the form of the Auto-train, or such other name as the owning railways chose to call them.

This type of operation looked, superficially, rather like the sort of train which the steam railmotor had been designed to replace, but there was a strong technical linkage and this turned out to be the vital factor. More than once, this narrative has remarked on the time-wasting caused by marshalling carriages and by engines having to run round their trains for the return journey. The steam railmotor could be driven either from the locomotive *or* the opposite end of the carriage portion, and the technical modifications to allow this could without too much difficulty be applied to conventional engines and carriages. Thus was born the so-called 'Auto-train', 'push-pull train,' 'motor-train' or whatever.

It consisted of a suitably adapted engine and carriage(s) which remained semi-permanently

These views show the exterior and interior of a rather rare solution to the auto-train problem adopted by the LSWR — using a purpose-built engine rather than adapting an existing type. The neat and stylish exterior was somewhat marred by the frugal interior with its pierced plywood seats.

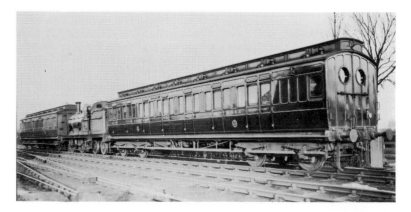

coupled. The driver worked either from the engine itself or a specially modified 'cab' at the opposite end (usually located at the outer end of a brake-ended vehicle), and there was no need to run round. However, at the end of the day, the engine *could* be uncoupled if necessary for other work and the railways rapidly discovered that it was possible to convert *existing* stock for motor-train working if they chose not to build new vehicles for the task. Many companies actually did both, and this push-pull style of operation became a very widespread feature of the British scene almost to the end of steam.

However, its origins were in the hey-day of the steam railmotor and its success undoubtedly hastened the demise of the single-unit railcar. Indeed, as has been more than once remarked, the carriage part of many erstwhile steam railcars was often converted to the new mode. In this role they were often called 'trailers', 'auto-trailers', 'control trailers', 'motor trailers' or some such, and it was perfectly possible to have a push-pull train with several such vehicles, two or three being very common and four not unheard of. During the early days, many distinctly attractive formations were to be seen, some depicted here; in the 1930s the GWR in particular was regularly characterized by a branch line train consisting of a pair of auto-trailers (often ex-railcars) flanking a small engine, or with the engine at one end, either option being possible. The LYR's twelve railmotor trailers were 'ready-made' motor train vehicles and found several decades of use in North Lancashire in 'twin' or even 'quad' sets; as such they lasted until BR days.

Thus the steam railcar lived and died almost within a generation, save for a mild revival in a slightly different form during the 1920s and 1930s (see Section 2), but it did leave its legacy in the form of the motor-fitted train, a much more useful solution to a real problem. Furthermore, the railcar left its

mark on vehicle design too and this seems an appropriate theme with which to round up our pre-group survey.

The steam railcar was almost always of open interior configuration, a style it shared with contemporary electric stock. Seats were usually a mixture of transverse and longitudinal and often quite spartan. There was some attempt to produce composite 1st/3rd accommodation but predominantly and not surprisingly, this was a third class sort of business and thus it remained. In terms of what I have called carriage 'architecture', the railcar — and indeed many of the purpose-built push-pull 'trailers' — often broke new visual ground, sometimes with very pleasing results. There is little doubt in my mind that there is at least some design linkage between this type of operation and the move to electrification in terms of vehicle interior layout; the LNWR, for example, adopted a near identical vehicle body style both for its electrical services and in its push-pull operations.

Thus it is not perhaps too fanciful to state that in the various alternative approaches considered in this chapter, the railways began to sow the seeds of the now customary layout for the shorter-distance train, be it diesel of electric multiple unit or whatever. The traditional compartment, of course, died hard, and many hundreds were still built (or converted) for both EMUs and push-pull trains. However, a new idea was there, just as in the case of the longer-distance carriage (see Chapter 10), where some railways had begun to pioneer the now normal centre passageway open carriage.

PART II — THE YEARS OF CONSOLIDATION: 1923-53

The years between the two world wars, and their immediate aftermath until the early 1950s at the start of public ownership, were a difficult time for British railway operators. Though often described as the high point of the railway age, the final phase of private ownership (ie in the accepted 'all embracing company' sense) was also characterized by a degree of doubt and uncertainty as railways tried to meet the ever-growing competition of the motor vehicle in all its forms. In consequence, there was much worthwhile innovation as railways responded to a new challenge. But some doubts never really went away and this was often seen in a preference for consolidation and conservatism in design terms, which could then result in railways simultaneously building some of their most sublime carriages alongside their most sublimely awful efforts! Even so, during this time, most of the seeds of the present day railway passenger scene were sown.

There can be little doubt that one of the great features of the grouping period was the considerable effort made to improve the lot of the third class passenger on the long-distance trains. Nowhere was this better exemplified than in the Pullman cars of the 1920s. This is an unidentified third class interior, most probably from a 'K' type car

16. The Great Amalgamations and their aftermath

Every now and then, an event occurs in world history which, however important in itself, has a 'spin-off' effect even wider than anyone can have foreseen at the time. Such, in terms of British railway history, was the consequence of the assassination of Archduke Franz Ferdinand at Sarajevo on that fateful day in August 1914 which launched the world into the first of its two holocausts during the first half of the twentieth century. It almost seems tasteless to link the evolution of railway history with these two vast human tragedies, yet such was the case; the effect of these two conflagrations cannot be excluded from our story. This volume takes us through that turbulent time when the world went mad, for the course of British railway history would almost certainly have been different had it not been for those greater realities and what happened in their wake. Of course, it was never that simple, but let me at least try to make the linkage by way of background to this book.

In 1914, so as to serve in the strategic national interest, the many private British railways were brought under centralized Government control and operated by a Railway Executive Committee. Although they continued to operate under their old names, they were, for all practical purposes, nationalized. This continued to be the case during the 1914-18 period and it established a sort of feeling that perhaps things should stay this way after the war. It was, in fact, no new idea; Gladstone had, after all, advocated a form of state ownership as early as his celebrated Railways Act of 1844. However, the country did not seem quite ready for this fundamental re-appraisal and, as is its wont when faced with real decisions, Parliament came up with a compromise solution which we now know as the 'Grouping'.

In this, the railways were retained in private ownership but combined into four 'groups' of existing companies to form new and larger organizations. Most of the old companies — and certainly all those with which this survey is concerned — were known as 'constituents' of the new groups, the latter being determined largely on territorial grounds. There was a degree of competition retained 'at the edges', so to speak, but this was no more than the natural consequence of the decision to keep the former company boundaries inviolate with no attempt to tidy them up where the old borders crossed each other. Thus, for example, the London Midland and Scottish (via its inclusion of the former LNWR and MR) found itself with penetrating arms through GWR territory into South Wales, while the London and North Eastern (having taken charge of the former GCR) now possessed a second main line to London from the north, almost completely surrounded by LMS lines, as well as the old GNR line to King's Cross.

No doubt Parliament was happy to maintain a form of spurious competition but, overall, it fooled no one at the fundamental level and, save for some economies of scale, did not really achieve very much which could not equally well have been expected from the old pre-group companies had they gone back to their old boundaries. In the event, the necessarily 'shot-gun' marriages which were forced on the old companies in consequence of the Grouping, often exacerbated rather than reduced their differences. Prior to the Grouping, each company could take pride in its own achievements and pursue commercial rivalry or co-operation with its contemporaries without any serious fear of loss of identity, or indeed, *esprit de corps*; but when amalgamation with a rival loomed ahead, it was inevitable that something would have to give. Put in a nutshell, there had to be winners and losers in the new amalgamations and this was not, psychologically, the best way to launch these new enterprises. It was one thing to collaborate with a rival in the interests of a better commercial return for both, but it was quite another to be swallowed up — and there was a good deal of the latter in 1923, nowhere more than in the realm of preferred designs to be adopted, be they locomotives, wagons or carriages.

Now it is an interesting fact that whereas in the locomotive field some of the old companies' efforts were far more worthy of continuation than others (not

Above left *Though all railways soon began to build new carriages, there were so many old ones in stock that many had a very long innings -- see also Chapter 10. Here at Tunbridge Wells, a sort of frontier town between the SE & CR and the LB & SCR, the symbolic marriage under Southern colours of a former Brighton 0-4-2T No 2221 and one of the well-found SE & CR 'birdcage' sets makes the sort of pleasing and typical combination that could be witnessed for a generation or more* (Ransome-

Left *Pullman retained its connection with the Brighton line long after the grouping and continued to provide most of the catering services, a typical example being seen here in the form of two quite elderly specimens in the centre of a neat set of low elliptical roof ex-LSWR corridors bound for Eastbourne behind 2-6-0 No 1906*

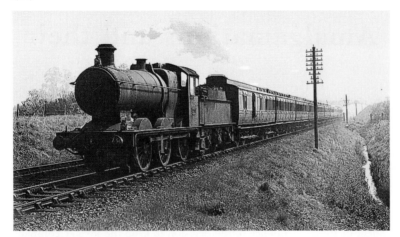

Left *After the grouping, any non-Swindon carriage designs inherited by the GWR mostly stayed confined to their old areas, if not scrapped, and the GWR continued to use its old Dean stock for many years on lesser duties. Here is a fine ten-coach set of non-corridor clerestories near Long Ashton on a down excursion to Weston super Mare at a date well into the 1930s*

Below right *Amongst the finest 'inherited' carriages of the LNER were those of the old North Eastern. Third class dining car No 1031Y was as good as anything built later and is seen here branded 'Restaurant', the LNER's preferred name for catering vehicles*

that this always happened, by the way!), the same was not quite so true in the field of the passenger carriage. Much of the background to this state of affairs has been given in the previous volume but it will do no harm briefly to recapitulate the principal trends which dominated as far as the new grouped companies were concerned, starting with the smallest of them and ending with the most awkward.

The Southern Railway (basically LSWR/LB & SCR/SE & CR) did not face too much of a problem. Each of its constituents held a form of territorial monopoly already, give or take a few exceptions, so the greater company was little different in this respect. It also had an edge-on boundary with the GWR, but this was no whit different than had formerly been the case, since this boundary was almost wholly LSWR/GWR. Furthermore, for reasons given in my first volume, the LSWR was the only SR constituent which had needed seriously to address the long-distance problem, so there could be no real objection to the Southern's long-distance philosophy continuing in the LSWR tradition; it made sense.

There can be no doubt that this was rendered more palatable to the LB & SCR and SE & CR sections by the facts that the new Southern CME, R.E.L. Maunsell, was an ex-SE & CR man and that the Brighton line had never built any true long-distance carriages anyway. In any case, Maunsell continued to develop the already ordered SE & CR corridor stock to some extent and fairly soon moved the new SR standard vehicles to a form which, though mostly LSWR-inspired, was far more obviously 'Southern' than pre-grouping. Moreover, as we shall see, the new Southern carriages were built to various structural 'envelopes' so as to fit the varying loading gauges of the SR constituents. Maunsell was clearly something of a diplomat.

Diplomatic, too, if somewhat 'forced', was the solution to the provisioning of shorter-distance coaching

stock. The SR had, at an early stage, determined on wholesale suburban electrification and the fact that there was something of an unholy row about which system should be adopted (see Chap. 21) did not seriously affect the carriage design side. For one thing, the SR was not a wealthy company and since all three of its constituents had already re-equipped with quite reasonable bogie non-corridor stock, it made eminent sense to convert many of these carriages to electrical multiple unit (EMU) form for the suburban lines. Thus the Brighton electrics continued to look 'LB & SCR', the South Eastern area 'SE & CR' and the trains from Waterloo very much 'LSWR' — honours more or less even all round. Furthermore, when Maunsell built new EMUs for the further extensions of the electrified system, they were distinctly 'Southern' in concept with little harking back to the old days.

Inspired too, if less than visually exciting, was Maunsell's final choice of SR carriage colour scheme. Had he gone for the most attractive of the constituent companies' liveries (arguably the LSWR salmon-pink and brown), this may have been undiplomatic; had he chosen the SE & CR (crimson) or the LB & SCR (umber and cream), the same diplomatic problems might also have occurred, but he would also have adopted liveries very close to those of the LMS and GWR respectively. This may not have seemed the best choice in view of what was probably felt to be a need to establish a new 'corporate identity' in the post-1922 era. He therefore chose the all-over sage green, originally adopted purely for LSWR EMUs but applied to all LSWR stock after March 1921. Some no doubt saw this as a victory for Waterloo, but the chosen scheme had some positive virtues in its own right.

Firstly, it was different from that of the other three 'Big Four' companies — and likely to remain so; secondly it was already identified with 'electric trains', a point which the SR, from an early date, put high on its list of publicity priorities. It also differentiated the Southern Electric trains from those of the often competing London underground lines, even before the latter were amalgamated in 1933. Lastly, it was a very practical and economic livery to apply. That the SR subsequently found itself not quite sure what the precise shade of green either was or should be is a different story!

Thus, the SR achieved a reasonable carriage compromise — and it did the same with Pullman on the catering front too. The latter company maintained its traditional influence on the former LB & SCR and SE & CR operating areas, while the purely Southern catering contribution was mainly concentrated in erstwhile LSWR territory. At all events, it seems to have worked pretty well for over 20 years and when Bulleid, in the 1940s, finally had to address the whole problem of large-scale carriage replacement, it was only to be expected that he would and did come up with totally new designs.

However, if there were no outright 'winners' and 'losers' on the Southern, the same was not the case with the Great Western. Here, everybody 'lost', save for the title company itself. The original GWR was so much bigger than any of the other constituents of the proposed 'Western' group that the old title was kept and the smaller fry were absorbed, almost literally, into the greater GWR. In carriage terms, this made much sense. None of the smaller constituents had developed its carriages to anything like the extent or variety of those produced at Swindon. The Cambrian had, perhaps, come closest, but it was still a very long way behind. In consequence, the evolution of GWR stock continued, without interruption, from the Churchward 'Toplight' phase (see Volume 1).

In a sense this was slightly unfortunate, for whatever the problems of the three other newly grouped companies — and there were many — there is no doubt that the fusion of ideas between their various constituents was ultimately to be of benefit to all, even if occasionally it took some time to befall. On the other hand, the newly enlarged GWR found that there was far less stimulus to change, largely because there was no really meaningful 'alternative' input from its constituents; in consequence, GWR carriage design tended to stagnate in the 1920s and 1930s. By the latter period, the two larger groups, particularly the LMS, had well outstripped the GWR in terms of the quality of their general service long-distance stock.

The LNER inherited many fine carriages from its constituents and many of them were to serve their new owners for quite a few more decades — until well into BR days as it turned out. In the event, however, although the GCR, GER, NER and NBR could all offer some excellent vehicles, it was the GNR influence which prevailed. Volume 1 has explained how this came to be — largely, in fact, in consequence of Nigel Gresley's position and the fact that the East Coast Joint Stock (a sort of pre-group unifying influence) had, for the most part, adopted GN-type styling. By 1923, this had become pure 'Gresley' and, save to the cognoscenti, was virtually indistinguishable from the 'proper' GNR carriages.

Technically, too, there were many good reasons why Gresley's precepts should continue. He was, of course, originally a carriage designer and, by 1923, had given his company by far the best bogie design in Britain; furthermore, his old company (and the ECJS) had long since adopted the more efficient Pullman gangway and buckeye coupling as standard, while Gresley's articulation ideas, of great value in reducing train weight without loss of amenity, had progressed well beyond the experimental stage. None of the other LNER constituents — nor much of Britain either for that matter — could match this. Moreover, the great NER carriage works at York (inevitably bound to play a vital role in the new enlarged LNER) was already experienced in build-

ing Gresley-type carriages for the ECJS, so the transition could perhaps be rendered relatively painless.

On the more cosmetic side, teak was still a favoured and durable material — in spite of the increasing use of sheet steel by other companies — so its continuation by Gresley also made some sense and certainly determined the new LNER carriage livery. The company adopted the ECJS variant of the traditional varnished teak as its new standard scheme. The ECJS differed from that of the GNR and the 'GNR/NER Joint' fleets only in respect of the fine lining down the edges of the gold/yellow stripes on the beading and the colour of the shading to the carriage insignia: GNR — blue; GNR/NER — green; ECJS — vermilion. This meant that, fine lining and insignia shading apart, many thousands of carriages were already correctly finished. Additionally, the GCR also employed a varnished wood finish and many GER carriages were also in this style. The only other conceivable choice for an LNER carriage colour would have been the crimson lake of the NER and NBR (also, to some extent, adopted in its later years by the GER), but since it probably seemed fairly certain that the other three grouped companies would all adopt painted finishes, the LNER would be distinctively different if it continued with varnished natural teak. It proved to be a wise choice since the LMS chose a crimson lake colour scheme.

The biggest 'loser' on the LNER, in strictly carriage terms, was the North Eastern Railway, for reasons outlined in Chapter 7 but it did not vanish without trace. Its main-line stock was distinctly good — some would even argue that it was more advanced and aesthetically more harmonious than the GNR

product — and it lasted well; but so too did much of that of the other LNER constituents. The LNER was always 'stretching' for capital investment and was forced to maintain many older coaches in service. This, as an almost irreverent aside, put it in the rather curious situation of still operating some 50 per cent of the total surviving *British* four-wheel and six-wheel fleet at the same time as it was proudly advertising its celebrated, ultra-modern, streamlined trains!

The LMS, the fourth and largest of the British main-line companies formed in 1923, was the most comprehensive in terms of its inherited carriage fleet. As Volume 1 has revealed, the LNW and Midland railways dominated, but there were significant contributions of both stock and ideas from the LYR and the Caledonian. As it transpired, Midland domination at Board level determined such relatively insignificant matters as carriage livery and external styling (both of which continued in the MR tradition), but conceptually, the needs of the other LMS constituents, particularly but not exclusively the LNWR, had a very considerable influence on the choice and quantity of carriage types built by the new group.

As things turned out, the LMS standard carriage soon began to look very distinctly 'Midland'. It made use of the MR-derived angle-trussed underframe and bogie and deployed Midland-style detail treatment. There were some quite sound technical reasons why this should be so, not simply because the new LMS carriage chief, R.W. Reid, was ex-MR, but mainly for the fact that he, alone of his contemporaries, had begun to address the whole business of more economic carriage building and had, naturally, started the process at Derby. The LMS was soon to benefit

Left *The LNER's inheritance was very mixed, and because the company was never wealthy it kept a far higher proportion of six-wheel carriages in service than anyone else. This delectable assortment of ex-GCR museum pieces probably dated back to nineteenth-century MSLR days, yet it is seen here near Woodhouse in the late 1920s behind 4-6-0 No 5052 with the engine carrying express head lamps. The reporting number on the engine probably indicates excursion use.*

Above right *No amount of tinkering about with new liveries could disguise the Wolverton origins of former West Coat Joint Stock dining car No 10421 dating from 1905; one must also concede that the new livery sat very well on these handsome cars. When this picture was taken in the mid-1920s, the cars had just received a complete refurbishment of the interior — see overleaf*

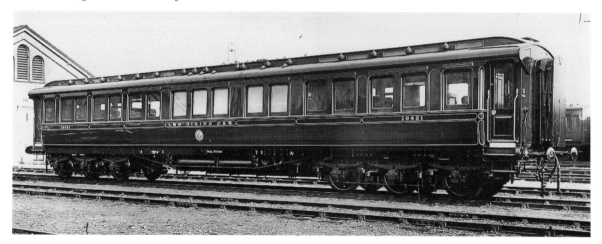

and its carriage building rapidly began to be influenced by Reid's ideas which he fairly smartly soon put into operation at Wolverton (ex-LNWR) and Newton Heath (ex-LYR) as well. By contrast with the contemporary developments in the locomotive department, Reid's changes do not seem to have encountered any real hostility. Like Maunsell on the SR, he seems to have been a bit of a diplomat.

For one thing, although the new LMS carriages looked superficially Midland, Reid really did attempt to come to grips with the realities of the new company. Thus, for example, his first generation LMS twelve-wheel sleeping and dining cars had far more Wolverton (LNWR) thinking in them than Derby (MR). There was, in truth, little to chose in absolute terms between the best of the LNWR and MR coaches at the time, or those of the LYR and CR for that matter, but the LNWR was by far the greatest user of twelve-wheelers at the time; Reid seems to have been aware of the importance of such matters and this particular appreciation of the greater company need was not to be an isolated instance in the LMS carriage building business.

The apparently Midland nature of LMS carriages was, of course, reinforced by the choice of MR livery. But even if the MR influence had not been present at high level, the LMS would probably have had some difficulty in arriving at a universally acceptable standard carriage colour. The MR, GSWR and NSR all used crimson lake (the NSR called its slightly darker shade 'Madder' lake), the LNWR and Caledonian had near-identical carmine lake and off-white liveries, the LYR used a similar carmine lake and 'tan' while the smaller constituents offered blue (Furness) and greens (Highland, and Maryport and Carlisle). One can be fairly certain, however, by virtue of its 'common factor' status amongst most of the constituents, that a dark(ish) red, in some form or

another, was bound to have figured in the LMS carriage scheme, and had the choice been the LNWR/CR style, in all logic the only other real contender apart from a totally new livery, this too would have had its opponents. One could, perhaps, argue that a combination of Midland engine colours with West Coast carriage livery might have been the best of all possible worlds, but this can never be more than a matter of opinion. In purely objective terms, the crimson livery looked good and, like the Southern dark green, was both hard wearing and practical.

All told, therefore, the apparently 'Midland' nature of the first generation LMS coaches was more superficial than real and long before the end of the 1920s the LMS, more than any of the other companies, had begun a significant break-out from the pre-grouping mould. Meantime, like the LNER, it continued to make use of its better pre-grouping stock. The LMS was, however, less constrained in terms of new capital investment than its East Coast rival and, in consequence, was able to do away with a much higher proportion of the older four-wheel and six-wheel carriages. In part, this was made simpler by the high quality of much of the later pre-grouping stock. As new LMS carriages came into service in their hundreds, much of the newer pre-1923 stock was 'cascaded' to replace old bone-shakers in the Highlands and elsewhere. Some of the more fascinating examples of this re-location are offered in Chapter 10.

Having therefore set the background to the dominant influences which were ultimately to prevail after 1922, it only remains necessary at this point to review those carriages which, although appearing after the Grouping, managed to perpetuate pure pre-group (or near enough so) characteristics. This time, however, it seems logical to review them in terms of the speed with which the four new companies settled down after 1922. We thus start with the GWR, since

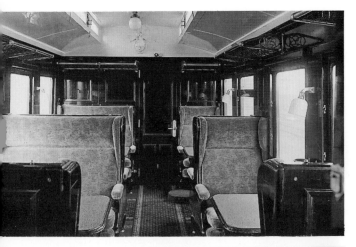

Left *Unlike the GWR (see Chapter 5), the LMS did not rebuild its pre-group dining cars but it did re-work their interiors which allowed them to hold the fort until the massive replacement programme of the 1930s. This is the remodelled interior of No 10421 with cleaned-up surfaces and new 'LMS'-marked luggage racks. The cars were nominally composite and this is the first class end. The third class was identical save for a change in upholstery cloth*

Middle left *The LMS, like the LNER, kept more than a few six-wheelers in gainful employment for many years. Former North Staffordshire Railway brake third No 27770 still looked smart in its fully lined livery at Waterhouses in 1933*

this company needed no settling down period at all; it had already decided what to do in 1922 and the grouping made no difference.

We left the GWR in the previous volume at the end of the 'Toplight' era, a period of carriage design started by Churchward in 1907 in the fully beaded wood-panelled form and concluded in 1922 by the final examples with steel sheet outer panelling with little or no raised mouldings. The 'Toplight' designation arose from the presence in most of them of small, shallow depth, fixed lights in the area between the cantrail and the top of the conventionally positioned main windows. Many other railways — the GNR, LNWR, MR and NER to name but four — had done the same from time to time but the feature was particularly associated with Swindon. These carriages, even when built, were no quantum step ahead of the better competition in terms of size, comfort or amenity, save for the sheer length of the earlier 70-foot examples, but from the outset they were quite recognisably twentieth century in outline and in the

context of their use of smoother outer steel panelling, they accurately predicted one of the most obvious evolutionary characteristics which was eventually to take place in all companies of the 'Big Four' era.

Right at the time of the grouping, 1922 to be precise, the GWR moved away from the 'Toplight' form to a rather dull and uninspiring period of carriage design, generally referred to as the 'Bow-ended' era, which lasted until the mid-1930s and will be considered in later chapters. It is only because the first few examples appeared (literally) as pre-Group vehicles that they are mentioned here at all. The 'Bow-ended' carriages were, in effect, the first post-group GWR standard types.

The next quickest group to resolve its carriage policy was the LNER. Here, the Gresley/ECJS influence dominated and by the end of 1923 the new company had determined that its standard policy would be an uninterrupted continuation of Doncaster (GNR) practice. However, there was a slight difference compared with Swindon in that the LNER (as did the LMS and SR) also inherited existing orders for pre-group stock. In most cases, these were merely fulfilled, after which the old works then moved over to LNER designs. Thus Dukinfield (GCR) and Stratford (GER) merely completed existing orders (basically non-corridor types) before moving to LNER group standard practices. In fact, it was not long before Stratford stopped building new coaches altogether, 1927 seeing its last new vehicles emerge. The transformation in Scotland was even more rapid. Cowlairs (NBR) had nothing new on hand at the grouping and Inverurie (GNSR) merely finished a handful of non-corridors; neither place built another new carriage.

The great exception to this post-1922 pattern was to be found at York, ex-NER. Even before the grouping, there had always been great rivalry between the two great carriage building establishments at York and Doncaster which, at times, had taken on almost tribal characteristics — and when two Yorkshiremen disagree, the consequences can be interesting to say the least! Nowhere was this more the case in the LNER carriage context than at these two places and to understand subsequent LNER policies, one must comprehend this fact.

It all stemmed from the fact that although the NER was bigger than the GNR, the latter's design influence, largely through Gresley, had been dominant in the pre-1923 evolution of the East Coast Joint Stock. But York always felt that it made its carriages rather better than they did at Doncaster regardless of design, and in truth this was almost certainly the case in purely objective terms; principal main-line stock excepted (where there was little difference in quality), the NER operated far superior and better-built carriages than did the GNR. Added to this was the undoubted fact that the absolute building capacity at York was greater than at Doncaster so the LNER had to resolve the problem or face some degree of crisis. That it did so was to the credit of both the two rival works themselves and the LNER CME, Nigel Gresley.

The crucial point was in the field of long-distance carriages where the NER had already proved itself capable of designing very good examples for its own services, being, for example, an early railway to abandon individual outside compartment doors as I have previously noted in Chap. 7. Even though these stylish vehicles were rather few in number compared with

Left *The post-grouping transition on the GWR was so imperceptible that it is difficult to pin-point a time when things were obviously different. This example dates from the mid-1930s, but apart from the obviously more modern bow-ended carriage at No 3, such was the quality of the original Churchward stock that several fully panelled 'Toplights' and at least one 'Dreadnought' still harmonize well with the train, an up South Wales express near Pilning behind 4-6-0 No 5040* Stokesay Castle

Right *After the grouping, Gresley's carriage ideas soon held sway on the non-GNR parts of the system, and remained there for a generation or more. This is a pair of 'Quin-arts' dating from the 1920s at Hackney Downs in 1948 behind 0-6-2T No 9671; and they still had many more years to go*

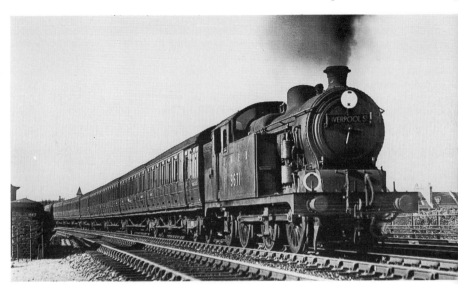

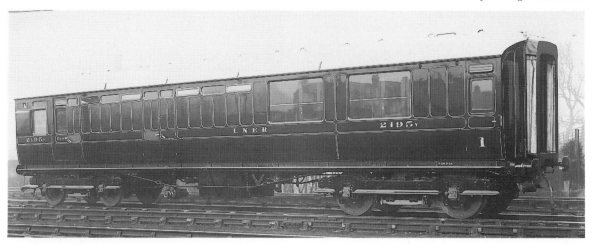

No 2195Y was one of several types of NER-styled coaches built by the LNER for the GE section, though there were only two first brakes of this type. Only the LNER standard gangways, couplings and bogies distinguish it from the pre-1923 version.

the Gresley 'breed', there can be no doubt of their quality or style — better than most. Fortunately, in purely design terms, there was also at York, as well as a fair degree of company pride, a considerable appreciation of Nigel Gresley's talent as a carriage designer and this, in the end, turned out to be the key factor. York had long being building GN-styled vehicles as its share of the ECJS and always felt that it could outdo Doncaster if put to the test, and Gresley probably knew this. It may, therefore, have been a stroke of some genius that led him to order from York some NER-styled carriages for the GER section soon after the grouping!

The GER section, for reasons which even now are not fully understandable — something to do with

platform capacity at Liverpool Street and other problems elsewhere, I believe — was not, after the grouping, immediately able to accept the new LNER standard 61 ft 6 in corridor carriages. In due course the solution turned out to be a 52 ft 6 in version of the LNER standard type, but the interim answer was found in Gresley's decision to give them some pretty well unmodified NER-style 53 ft 6 in corridors, no doubt to the immense satisfaction of the York builders! I have never seen the point put this way before, but this decision may well be a contributory reason for the fact that York never created any real problems during the LNER period and was always the principal LNER carriage building establishment and a considerable exponent of the best of Gresley's LNER practice even though Doncaster continued to build the bulk of the special stock (eg the Stream-

Figure 1 Elevations and plans of the late vintage four-wheelers of Caledonian design built early in 1923.

Scale: 2mm = 1ft

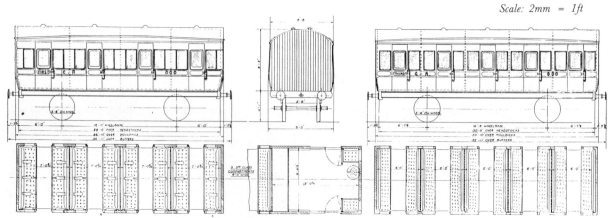

Drawing showing Principal Dimensions of 4-wheeled Coaching Stock built for Suburban Services.

liners — Chapter 25). In more modern BR days, York long outlived Doncaster as a carriage building location and is still active today.

Turning now to the LMS, the ultimate Derby stylistic influence has been mentioned and it is a moot point whether this company or the LNER was the quicker to determine new standards after the grouping. At that time, there was on hand a fair amount of pre-1923 work at all four of the principal LMS works. Wolverton (LNWR) was building some 57-foot non-corridors, Newton Heath (LYR) was turning out both corridor and non-corridor examples of its final standard styles, and up in the north St Rollox was finishing off the final Caledonian designs, including some quite amazingly late examples of the

four-wheel genre for suburban services in fashionable Edinburgh, of all places. This actually took place early in 1923 at that curious time when, for six months, the Caledonian was not legally part of the LMS group to which it was assigned but which it only joined, officially, in mid-year (for the record, the North Staffordshire Railway was similar). It need hardly be said that the unsentimental LMS soon put a stop to all this.

Meantime, Derby Works was not only introducing what turned out to be the first of the true LMS standard carriage types but was, under the direction of R.W. Reid, also being reorganized to produce its carriages in a quite new form of mass production which was to revolutionize the LMS

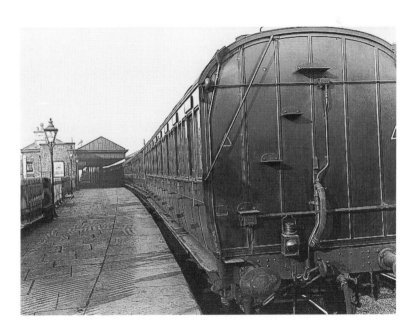

Right *Late period LYR carriages had an almost identical profile to those of the MR, LNWR and CR but were, on the whole, rather smoother sided, a point well illustrated by this steeply angled view of a non-corridor set at Darwen in the early LMS period. Note the inward taper of the sides to the guard's lookout, just visible at the near end of the second vehicle, a typical LYR feature and shared with the LSWR 'Ironclads'. Note too that the nearer coach still carries LYR livery.*

Below *This northbound stopping train at Northchurch tunnel circa 1930 headed by 4-4-0 No 5308 Simoom not only shows the similarity of size and roof profile between the mainly ex-LNWR coaches and the one and only LMS standard type (fifth vehicle) but also illustrates the increasingly common LMS practice of operating 'cascaded' corridor stock on many semi-fast services.*

These methods were, in due course, to be applied at Wolverton, principally, and also, to a lesser extent, at Newton Heath. However, just as on the LNER, there were to be no more new carriages built at many of the old works; and before the 1930s were scarce started, these new manufacturing methods made it possible for Derby and Wolverton to meet virtually all the LMS requirement for new carriages.

The final pre-group carriages built during LMS days to the designs of its principal constituents were much closer together in concept than those of the LNER or Southern constituents and, apart from fine detail, shared many features in common, not least their overall shape and size. Most were within the 54-57 ft long by 9 ft wide 'envelope', embodying full elliptical roofs and not dissimilar forms of construction. Indeed, when the final pre-group designs were actually turned out in full LMS colours, there could often be seen far more closeness in general style between them all than anyone might have supposed. Save for the exterior panelling, the general shape and characteristics of CR, LNWR, LYR and MR carriages, not to mention some from the Furness and GSWR, were all very similar, so when it finally appeared, the new LMS standard carriage was no real surprise.

It was, in fact, the Southern Railway which displayed the most lengthy and interesting transition from pre-Group to post-group practice. By comparison with the other three companies, the Southern had some catching up to do and it is now necessary to devote some space to its consideration, if only to bring the SR to the same point in the broader national story.

New developments were confined entirely to mainline stock, the reasons being bound up very closely with the rather different nature which the Southern had both revealed from the outset and continued to

demonstrate. For instance, the fact that the Southern built no new locomotive-hauled local stock during the whole of its existence is mostly due to its electrification policy. This latter point will be considered in due course but the residual effect on the non-electrified stopping services was to reduce their need for new stock to nothing that could not be and usually was provided by 'cascaded' older vehicles. For one thing, there was a fair chance that within a few years these lines too would be electrified, so why build new coaches? Such need as did arise for something more 'modern' during the later 1930s could still be met, for the most part, by that time-honoured Southern trick, first revealed in quantity during the suburban electrification phase, of rebuilding serviceable older carriage bodies on to new frames. A fair number of robust ex-LSWR non-corridors received a new lease of life in the mid-1930s in consequence.

There was, however, a real need for something better on both the long and medium distance routes; in particular there was a growing demand for gangwayed stock both to bring the Southern up to the standard of the rest of the country and to avoid losing business. With a few noteworthy exceptions, the Southern showed up badly in 1923, compared with the other new companies, largely because its constituents had no real tradition of building long-distance gangwayed stock in any quantity. The Southern was thus able to develop its own style more or less free from too many preconceived prejudices. The fact that it took only some three or four years to evolve a unified style was, in the circumstances, no mean achievement when set against the 20 years or more of corridor coach evolution which had already taken effect on other lines. It was an interesting time in consequence.

I have already opined that the Southern CME,

Maunsell, seems to have been something of a diplomat, a view reinforced by the events of the 1923-26 period. He inherited but two lines of corridor coach development: the relatively recent proposals of his old company, the SE & CR, and the much longer-standing experience, though not in fact translated into too many vehicles, of the LSWR. Like his LMS and LNER counterparts, Maunsell also inherited existing pre-Group orders but, unlike the engineers of the two northern companies, he allowed them to develop, rather than switch abruptly to new styles. He clearly used these pre-Group ideas as a sort of intermediate

stage in the evolution of his own, recognisably 'Southern' carriages of the mid-1920s onwards.

Least changed from their pre-Group forebears, and the first actually to be authorized by the new SR, were further examples of the SE & CR type, side-corridor coaches for the Kent Coast boat trains, the pioneer example of which, a train of eight vehicles, had appeared in 1921. Their flat-sided appearance, with its vertical 'matchboard' panelling below the waist line, was rather attractive in a European sort of way and they were fitted with 'state of the art' Pullman gangways, save at the outer brake ends. Hardly sur-

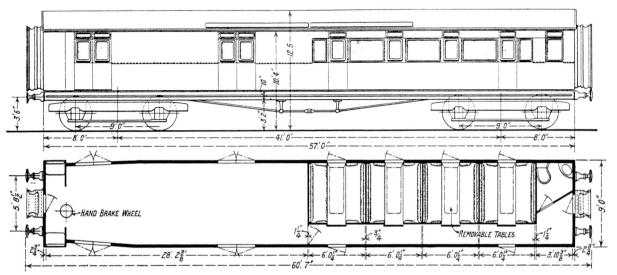

Brake Third-Class Carriage.

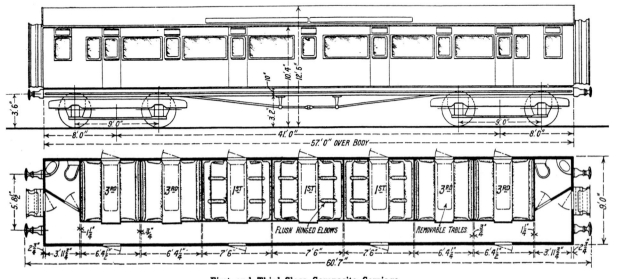

First and Third-Class Composite Carriage.

prisingly, they were often referred to as 'Continental' stock and were usually operated with a Pullman or two somewhere in the middle of the formation. Because of lineside loading gauge restrictions they were kept to a nominal width of 8 ft (actually 8 ft 0¾ in) but they displayed a generous 62-foot length over the body, a dimension not exceeded on the Southern until Bulleid's time.

Some of the extra carriages were actually on order before 1923 and the SR added to this order, the carriages appearing in 1923 and 1924. Those built by the SR itself in 1923 retained the 8-ft nominal width, but those which appeared in 1924 were to a new 8 ft 6 in wide dimension. There was also one final and suprisingly late series of carriages built to this style in 1927 at Eastleigh (LSWR) of all places; previous examples had either come from Ashford (SE & CR) or outside contractors. An interesting minor point about them was that because of their well nigh exclusive boat train usage, they were predominantly first and second class when built, with only one third class type (a third brake) appearing, and that not until the contractor-built batch of 1924. In due course, the seconds were downgraded to third and the Southern adopted its own peculiar solution to the residual second class customers by making use of what it called 'nondescript' carriages — see page 332.

Simultaneously with the continuation of SE & CR designs, Maunsell also went on with the construction of LSWR-type 'Ironclad' corridor coaches. These were of much more traditionally British outline and their nickname derived simply from their steel sheet outer panelling. In this, they were somewhat akin to the more or less contemporary later period GWR 'Toplights' and they shared very similar dimensions (57 ft long, 9 ft wide). Like the SE & CR designs, some had been ordered before the grouping and these came out with the cumbersome and massive looking LSWR outside framed bogies. When Maunsell ordered further 'Ironclads', the later-built examples from this series were fitted with SE & CR type bogies, the type which by then (late 1923) had been adopted as the SR standard.

Further orders followed, including those which provided the first proper corridor stock on the former LB & SCR main line. Its introduction as the 'City Limited' late in 1925, along with some further 'Ironclads' a few months later for services to Bognor and Worthing, marked the end of this particular line of development. By contrast with the SE & CR types, these LSWR-inspired carriages were all fitted with conventional gangways and couplings, the SR not yet having made up its mind which to adopt. It eventually, and sensibly, went for Pullman type gangways plus buckeye couplings for long-distance stock.

The drafting of 'Ironclads' into areas other than ex-LSWR territory gave them a sort of 'standard' status, unlike the SE & CR-styled 'Continental' stock, but they did not, in the event, turn out to be the precursors of the true SR standard types. The more probable contenders for this distinction were some carriages to a new design which Maunsell introduced

The form of the Southern 'Ironclads' is well-revealed in this circa *1936 view of a Brighton-Cardiff train at Patchway behind GWR 2-6-0 No 8323. The first two and last vehicles have the LSWR outside-framed bogies and may even be of LSWR origin, but the third has SR bogies. The smoother appearance of the fourth carriage reveals it to be of post-'Ironclad' vintage*

Close up detail of an early 'Ironclad' at Havant in 1937. Note the inward taper of the guard's lookout and the very heavy outside frame of the bogie

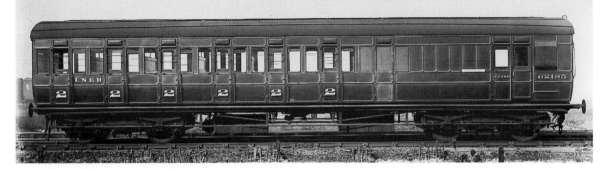

simultaneously with his continuance of the SE & CR and LSWR ideas. Yet again, they arose because of the unsatisfactory nature of existing pre-group provisioning to an important area of the Southern's hinterland, the Kent Coast.

The old SE & CR had provided, for its longer-distance services, some very agreeable bogie non-corridor stock, often with lavatories, during Wainwright's time and later (Chapter 7), but apart from the above-mentioned boat trains, the corridor carriage was almost unknown. By 1923, this was not considered adequate, hence Maunsell's new Kent Coast stock of 1924-25. They looked rather like mini-'Ironclads' and were to the same length and general cross-profile. But, again for structure gauge reasons, their width was kept down to 8 ft 6½ in. They also displayed predominantly SE & CR-type detail fittings, but in their use of British Standard gangways they followed LSWR precedent. They were also given angle-trussed underframes — unlike the 'Ironclads' which had the turnbuckle type — so in every significant way, Maunsell was now beginning to arrive at some form of synthesis for his new railway.

These Kent Coast corridors were built in some quantity and were a familiar enough sight for more than 30 years until the eventual BR electrification. If not the most inspiring of designs, they were no worse in absolute terms than much which was to be seen throughout Britain on many of the longer-established 'corridor' lines, and they certainly provided an adequate basis from which the Southern CME could develop his eventual standard types in 1926 and later.

Thus it was that by the mid-1920s, all four new companies had arrived at their new 'group standards' for carriage construction. To be honest, save for a few noteworthy exceptions — and those mostly attributable to their pre-group constituents — none of them had anything either markedly superior to those of their rivals or, for that matter, anything which would have suprised their forebears either; many Edwardian carriages were just as good as anything which had succeeded them. But it may be helpful briefly to summarize the overall situation in outline before continuing the story.

In the short-distance and medium-distance field, the non-corridor compartment coach reigned

This former Great Eastern brake second No 62185 in LNER colours was, in spite of its quite modern roof shape and general proportions, far too typical of many coaches in the 1920s and 1930s. The very spartan seats — particularly in view of its class designation — can be seen through the windows, but were not unusual. Second class survived for some time in the London area, largely because, at the time, third class season tickets were not available.

supreme, regardless of company. Some had lavatories but far too many did not and there was an altogether too high proportion of four-wheel and six-wheel stock still in regular use. Even the newly electrified Southern lines made use of non-corridor compartment stock. Similarly, in the long-distance field, side corridors were by far the most dominant gangwayed type with very little use being made of the centre aisle open saloon alternative. Virtually all side corridor stock had a full complement of outside compartment doors, in spite of valiant attempts by some companies to wean the public on to something more modern, and there were still far too many so-called expresses making use of non-gangwayed carriages anyway.

Technologically, there was still massive inconsistency between systems in such things as brakes, gangways and couplings. Steam heating was fairly well universal in the locomotive-hauled field, but in the realm of carriage lighting far too many vehicles remained obstinately gas lit in spite of the fact that a satisfactory electrical alternative had existed for a generation. Structurally, the wood-framed body on a steel underframe was all but universal but only the two smaller companies, the GWR and SR, had moved, definitively, away from wood panelled exteriors for new construction.

Neither was there too much evidence of a fundamental change in attitude as the railways embarked on what was to prove their most critical phase so far. They entered the troubled years of the inter-war period in a stolidly traditional way and remained thus for far too long. In the next few chapters, we shall consider in more detail how the situation gradually changed. For all that it seems, in retrospect, to have been frustratingly slow, it was not really seen to be so at the time; it was by no means lacking in interest and, as always, some surprisingly beautiful and enterprising things did eventually emerge.

17. Post-grouping changes in carriage technology

The advent of mass production

The carriage builders of the grouped railways were heirs to almost a century of tradition, and although such matters can be valuable in the right context, one cannot help feel that there was too much slavish adherence to this tradition in the 1920s and 1930s. This was particularly so in the field of carriage design, especially in the long-distance sector where new competition threatened. There were, however, some general moves forward across the board in the specific area of carriage assembly and technology and it is thought helpful to consider these aspects first, leaving the design developments until later chapters. For clarity, this and the next few chapters will concern hauled stock only, leaving the more specialized vehicles, mostly of a self-propelled type, to be covered separately.

Although it is a pity that better assembly and technology were not married to more enterprising basic design, save in a modest number of cases, in pure economic terms it was undoubtedly significant. Like many things, its origins can be discerned in the Great War and, of course, some railways went further down the new route than others. Put at its simplest, the carriage builders began to adopt some of the techniques of mass-production.

Before the 1914-18 war, there were few machine tools available to industry which were capable of mass-production with any great precision, but the demands of the war caused great strides to be made in this field and by the end of the conflict the dream of mass-production in the transport arena had become a reality. This concept was and is, of course, much more familiar in the road vehicle industry, but the very nature of a railway carriage made it extremely unlikely that it could be put on the conveyor belt in the manner of a Model T Ford. However, the commercial advantages of mass-production were such as to make railways look at the idea. In essence, it showed a considerable reduction in labour costs, provided that the capital cost of the machinery could be met and that it was capable of making items to a high standard of dimensional accuracy, thus avoiding much labour-intensive hand finishing.

Left R. W. Reid's mass production methods at the three principal LMS carriage works showing: carriage roof assembly at Derby; carriage side panels under construction at Wolverton; and non-corridor carriage ends being fabricated at Newton Heath

Applied to the traditional and still favourite method of coachbuilding — the timber frame covered with sheets of wood or metal panelling — the techniques lent themselves best to the prefabrication of carriage component parts with the minimum of subsequent 'cleaning up'. To some extent this fought against the traditional idea of roughly machining the joints and components over-size and then allowing the carpenters to finish and fit them by hand. Many felt that this was still the best way — and in the hands of the best coachbuilders it probably was — but its success did rather depend on the individual skills of the carpenters and they were not all uniformly talented.

The leader in the field was undoubtedly the LMS and, in fact, the origins were Midland in the person of R.W.Reid. Before 1923 he had already begun to set up a new method of carriage building at Derby and it was first put to use in building what were to become the first LMS standard carriages. The secret, if such it may be called, was the use of precision jigs in the sawmill. In place of the individual marking out of each component, a single accurate template was used and the machines then cut as many repeats as were required. Each part was, of course, carefully gauged before leaving the sawmill, but once the machined parts had left the mill any one example of a particular component was interchangeable with any other. It did, of course, demand seasoned timber but this was not the problem it is in the 1980s, since railway carriage timber had usually been naturally seasoned for several years before use. There was none of the modern kiln drying and its attendant problems so, as far as can be judged, the amount of defective timber was kept acceptably low.

An obvious disadvantage to mass-production in the modern sense is that, because of the high cost of obtaining and setting up the machines, one has to envisage a good long 'production run' to make the system pay for itself. This can, of course, limit to some extent the variation of or improvement to design, save after a reasonable period of time. Reid was no doubt aware of this but by concentrating his efforts on producing individual components, he could permutate them in a variety of ways to produce the many different carriage types needed. Thus, a typical LMS carriage, of whatever type, would always have identical doors, ventilators, fixed and drop lights, carriage seat ends or any other item which could usefully made in bulk — and most of them could. This

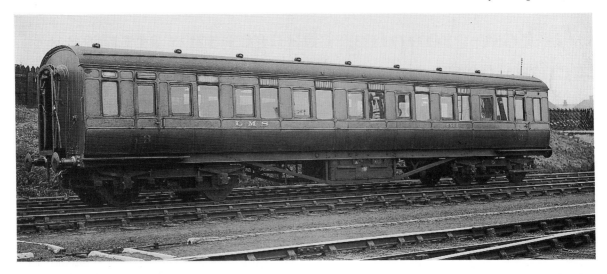

Above *The finished product: LMS standard open third No 8506 photographed in 1939. The view is of additional interest in that it was taken just as the vehicle was about to be converted for wartime ambulance use (see also page 258)* (R.J. Essery Collection).

Figure 3 *Reid's 'Progressive Assembly' layout as adopted at Wolverton (ex-LNWR) for new carriages. Note that where appropriate it was also integrated with wagon-building operations.*

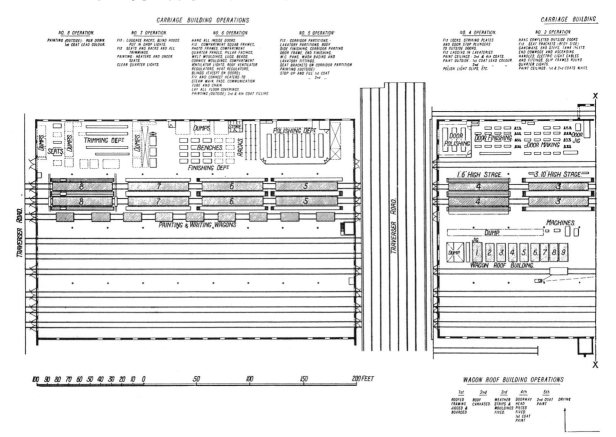

in turn caused a new method of carriage assembly to develop which reduced the building time of a single vehicle from six weeks to six days and the erection time of the basic carcass from floorboard to roof to only one hour!

What it amounted to was the prefabrication from the above-mentioned standard components of all the basic sub-assemblies needed for a particular carriage. These sub-assemblies were known as 'units' and the production of several types of units could be carried out simultaneously, whether it be ends, doors, side panel sections or a complete roof. The latter was, by the way, built on a jig at floor level, again from prefabricated accurately cut components. At the due time, all the necessary 'unit assemblies' would be positioned in the erecting shop, and a complete carriage underframe was then wheeled in on to which was already attached the floor framing and floorboards. Using compressed air power tools, the two completed ends would be pulled down on to the floor tenons, followed by the two side assemblies in rather similar manner and then the completed roof. It was in every sense analogous to using a kit of parts with

the certain knowledge that because of the precision in manufacture, all the pieces would fit together accurately. At this point, the interior fitting out could then commence, again using prefabricated finished components.

To make the best use of this new method of assembly, it was also found desirable to reorganize the layout of the carriage works themselves to a sort of 'flow-line' arrangement and by mid-1925 Reid's methods were also in full operation at Wolverton (ex-LNWR). It was called 'Progressive Construction' and the appended contemporary drawing should be self-explanatory. In effect, the finished components were taken to the appropriate part of the production line in sufficient quantity to be available on demand without delay.

So successful was this progressive approach to carriage building that it was also adopted for carriage repairs at the LMS main shops and it was not long (1927) before Newton Heath (ex-LYR) followed Derby and Wolverton in benefiting from this modernization. While no two works were identical — their structural forms would have precluded exact dupli-

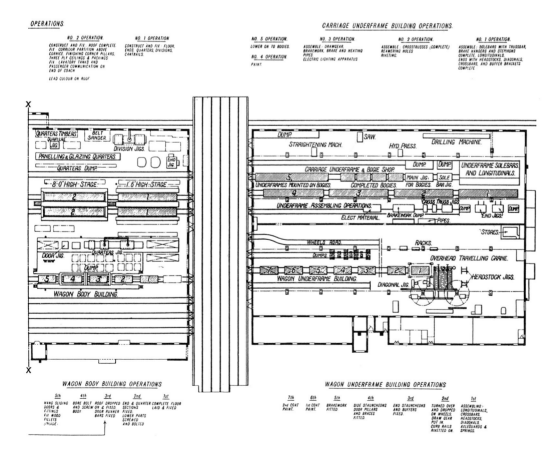

cation — the principles were identical and designed to fulfil several criteria:

a) Elimination of manhandling
b) Allocating a definite type of work to a definite location
c) Allocation of men to specific type of operations
d) Moving work to the men, not men to the work
e) Movements of vehicles between sections of the line at defined times
f) Ensuring all component parts were properly pre-positioned both in terms of type and quantity
g) Making sure (in the case of repairs) that the supply of carriages for attention was kept constant
h) Paying attention to good heating, lighting and working conditions

Students of these matters will detect considerable similarities with the 'belt' system of locomotive repairs introduced by the LMS at Crewe at much the same time and, just as in the case of locomotives, so too with carriages, it enabled the company to make huge works economies by contemporary standards. Railway works rationalization is no modern phenomenon and by 1931 the LMS had dispensed with all but its two biggest carriage works (Derby and Wolver-

ton) as far as new construction was concerned. In fact, Newton Heath was the only other LMS carriage works to build standard design carriages for the new company — and even then, only humble non-corridors — yet even though it had been similarly modernized, there was no call for new carriages from this works after 1931, so efficient had the other two become. And it was not a question of smaller quantities of carriages either. The LMS built massively throughout the pre-war period and it need hardly be stated that its new construction and repair methods stood the test of transition to new materials as the grouping period evolved.

Figure 4 *Southern Railway 'Progressive Repair' layout at Lancing (ex-LB & SCR). On completion of repairs, carriages were moved to the separate paintshop for finishing. The numbered repair roads were used as follows, marked 'stages' on each road being reserved for defined operations within the overall category of that road:*
1-3: Intermediate repairs: bodies, underframes and bogies respectively
4-6: General repairs: bogies, underframes and windows respectively
7-8: General repairs: interior stripping and burning off paintwork
9-12: General repairs: interior refitting, completion of exterior filling and staining
13: General repairs: exterior filling, first stage
14-15: General repairs: bodywork

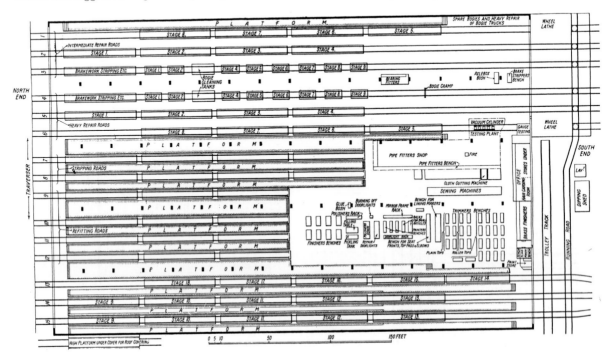

Layout of Carriage Shop for Progressive Repairs, Lancing, Southern Railway.

The LMS experience was not confined to that company, though it was the leader in the field. On the Southern, for example, Maunsell began to rationalize methods along similar if not identical lines. By 1928, he had resolved to reorganize rolling-stock building and repair using his three principal pre-group workshops. Eastleigh (ex-LSWR) and Ashford (ex-SE & CR) became responsible for the building of carriage bodies and the building and repair of wagons, while Lancing (ex-LB & SCR) became a dedicated carriage repair works on a rather similar 'progressive' system to that introduced by the LMS. However, the Southern never adopted the true mass-production techniques of the LMS for new construction and at the height of its electrification in the late 1920s and 1930s it made extensive use of outside contractors for much new EMU stock.

The LNER experience was a little more complex. It had, of course, rather more carriage works than the Southern yet, though smaller than the LMS, it kept more of them actively building new carriages than did its principal rival — at least for a time. But it rarely worked them to capacity as did the LMS and often placed substantial outside orders with 'the trade' even when it might have been supposed that the company works could have tackled more themselves. The LMS did place orders with outside contractors but, with few exceptions — mainly the 'all steel' vehicles (see below) — only when its own works had no spare capacity.

The LNER, like its rivals, reorganized its carriage works in the 1920s along the fashionable 'progressive repair' lines, and this included, as well as York and Doncaster, both Stratford (ex-GER) and Dukinfield (ex-GCR). There was even some modernization at Cowlairs (ex-NBR) but it never took on the wholesale re-shaping that happened on the LMS. As stated in the previous chapter, Stratford built no new carriages after 1927 (it had, in point of fact, plenty of workload in keeping the GE section fleet repaired), but until 1939 York, Doncaster and Dukinfield were all kept busy on new construction. In the LNER case, unlike the LMS, there was also a much greater degree of sub-specialization between works. Thus Doncaster built most of the special stock, including the sleeping and dining cars and the streamliners, the ex-GCR establishment concentrated on non-corridor and much of the non-passenger coaching stock, while York tackled the general service long-distance fleet. After 1939, all new work was concentrated on York and Doncaster.

Even so, the LNER system of carriage building was never as efficient *per se* as that of the LMS. There was little in it for quality, but whereas the LMS had reduced its typical building time per carriage from six weeks to one week by the mid-1920s, the best the

LNER could do was to reduce it from about the same original figure to a value still more than twice that of the LMS. Most of this reduction was achieved by a similar 'unit assembly' method as Reid had initiated at Derby but it did not, at first, go hand in glove with the 'progressive' idea, which approach had been mainly confined to repair work only on the LNER. It was not until well into the 1930s, under A.H. Peppercorn, that a similar type of flowline production, allied with mass-produced components, was introduced for new construction and even then, although several new carriages could be built simultaneously, the LNER never matched the sheer output rate of the LMS works.

The GWR remained stolidly traditional in its constructional methods and, of course, had the indubitable advantage of being able to concentrate activity at Swindon. It actually built a formidable number of new coaches during the grouping period as will be seen but it was distinctly unadventurous both in design and carriage building technology. One wonders just what might have been possible had Swindon been reorganized along similar lines to those of Derby or Wolverton from the outset. It was not, in the event, until after the Second World War that Hawksworth's direct building system began to make Swindon look more like a modern carriage works.

To be fair to GWR carriage building technique, however, it was probably in a better state of health than most of the rest at the time of grouping, and with none of the concomitant problems of the latter event to overcome. Needless to say, much of this was attributable to Churchward who, long before 1923, had re-equipped the carriage works with modern machinery and initiated repair and overhaul procedures which were, for the most part, far superior to the rest of the country. Yet again, there was probably little in it in terms of the absolute quality of carriages built compared with other systems, but the GWR's relatively unchanged status after 1922 once again led to a sort of conceptual complacency both in design and technique. This resulted in little real change in carriage building methods at Swindon for more than 20 years, save for a bit of extra machinery, and by the end of the pre-BR period, GWR carriage building methods were lagging behind more than somewhat. This is not to say, of course, that the GWR made no contribution to the evolution of carriage construction; and it is to this aspect that we must now return.

Timber versus steel construction

At this point, however, it is more important to define a few terms of reference to avoid ambiguity. So far, I have considered only changes in the methods of

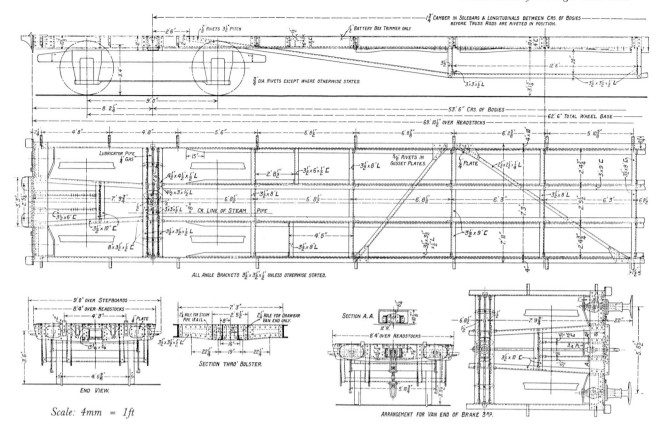

Scale: 4mm = 1ft

Figure 5 *Half elevation and plan of GWR angle-trussed 70-foot underframe for the 1923 bow-ended stock.*

assembling new carriages rather than their fundamental design and construction. In these two latter respects, though the methods of building them may have been changed to some extent, the basic nature of the British locomotive-hauled coach was slow to alter during the grouping period. In the rest of this chapter, hopefully in the interests of greater clarity, attention will be concentrated solely on the forms of construction adopted during this time, and the changing nature of materials used, both within and without the carriage, leaving the matter of general design concept and amenity to be tackled later.

For almost the whole of the 'Big Four' period, the British carriage remained very traditional, at least in terms of its basic construction. Save for a few exceptions, to be considered shortly, it retained the separate body and chassis form described in some detail in the first volume and almost always displayed the familiar timber-framed body, covered with panelling of either timber or steel sheet. Its chassis was by now wholly made from steel and all railways very soon adopted the angle-trussed form, the LNER being the last to abandon the older round bar and turnbuckle style.

As already stated, couplings and gangways retained their Byzantine inconsistency and braking was slow to harmonize, eventually going the wrong way — save on electrified lines — by standardizing on the automatic vacuum rather than the more efficient air brake.

The first railways to break out of this mould — and both did it before 1923 — were the GWR and LSWR when they began to use sheet steel outer panelling. It was, to be sure, but a small step forward, but it eventually became universal. The GWR was the more enterprising since it took the process further and its motivation seems largely to have been so as to overcome the problem of leaking, splitting or rotting panelling and leaky roofs.

Taking panelling first, the GWR used mahogany — an excellent timber in many ways (see   Part I Chapter 3) — but no matter how carefully made, panels were prone to split and the moulded beading could demonstrate a tendency to lift off the panels. These characteristics, in turn, let in water and thus caused rotting. Repairs involved not only replacement panelling but often replacement beading as well and even, occasionally, some repairs to the carriage framework. All of this cost money and the GWR began to experiment with steel and iron panel renewal to see whether savings could be made. For a while this worked, but there then arose the matter of corrosion of the steel, usually from the inside of the panel. On investigation, this turned out to be due to the tannic acid in the oak framing which, in association with the inevitable moisture, began to attack the metal plates. It was eventually overcome by the use of galvanized steel panels. Interestingly, other railways which adopted sheet steel were often slow to

Angle-trussed underframes from the other members of the 'Big Four' showing their remarkable similarity of form both to each other and also to the GWR pattern. They are, in order: LMS 57 ft, SR 59 ft, LNER 60 ft

appreciate the virtues of galvanized panelling (it was, unsurprisingly, more expensive) and it became an unfortunate characteristic of many steel-panelled coaches, well into BR Mk 1 days, to gain an unsavoury reputation as 'rot boxes', usually revealed to the eye by much external patchwork. Even so, it was cheaper than the all-wood option.

The GWR also addressed the roof problem. The traditional tongue and groove roof boards with their impregnated roofing canvas covering were in time subject to the depredations of both perished paintwork and canvas becoming porous. This also caused leaks unless remedied by repainting and/or re-treating the canvas — or even *in extremis* replacing the latter. The GWR therefore began to use galvanized steel for roof sheeting as well. There was also some reduction of fire risk as a result of these moves and the GWR developed matters further by making its carriage floors, not of traditional wooden floorboards, but of

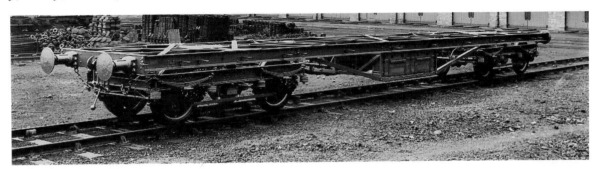

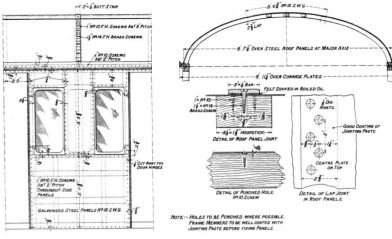

Panelling Methods on Carriage Stock, Great Western Railway.

Figure 6 *Diagram to show the fixing methods adopted by the GWR for steel panels on a timber frame.*

Below left *Close-up of the elaborately executed full lining used on GWR flush-panelled carriages until 1927. The example illustrated is a two-coach 'B' set with a semi-permanent centre coupling (see page 48). Note too the distinctive bowed ends*

Figure 7 *Arrangement of structural framing for the 'all-steel' LMS open stock of 1926-7.*

corrugated steel plates covered with a fireproof material. Steel sheet was also applied to panel replacement on repaired stock on an 'as required' basis. It was no doubt effective but led to a certain degree of external untidiness when a carriage displayed a mixture of original wooden and replacement steel panelling.

For a few years, this was effectively disguised from

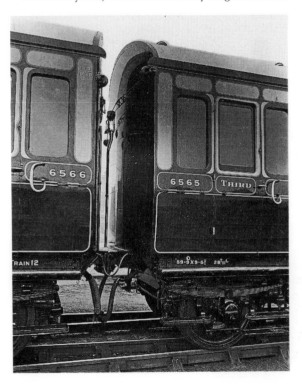

all but the closest examination by the GWR retaining its elaborate and attractive fully lined chocolate and cream livery. This colour scheme was, wisely, reinstated after the grouping in replacement of the erstwhile 'all lake' version, and the painters went to extraordinary lengths to re-create the impression of the fully beaded panelling, with its raised bolection mouldings, even on flush steel stock. It looked very attractive, but one does rather wonder how much of the savings achieved by steel panelling were lost by the retention of expensive painting.

The GWR was not alone in this particular practice — in fact, all four main-line railways did it with their first flush steel coaches — and it was in the end the GWR which was the first to dispense with an elaborate livery when, in 1927, it introduced a new simplified form of carriage decoration. This change was accompanied by a fair degree of self-satisfied justification in publicity terms, based on its apparent 'modernity' compared with the older form of painting. So it was, but it was also a good deal cheaper to put on the carriage and this was the *real* reason for its adoption!

The LSWR 'Ironclads' were the other principal vehicles to display the new steel-panelled technique and the Southern carried on with the idea for all its new carriages. Like the GWR, it too saw the virtues of galvanized sheet as opposed to plain steel and also retained a pseudo-'panelled' livery for many years. In the Southern case, however, the simplification of lining was slow to develop and came about gradually during the 1930s rather than abruptly at one point in time. It was, in fact, left to Oliver Bulleid to take the Southern into a fully simplified painting style in the late 1930s, when he simply suppressed all lining entirely. In one fundamental respect, how-

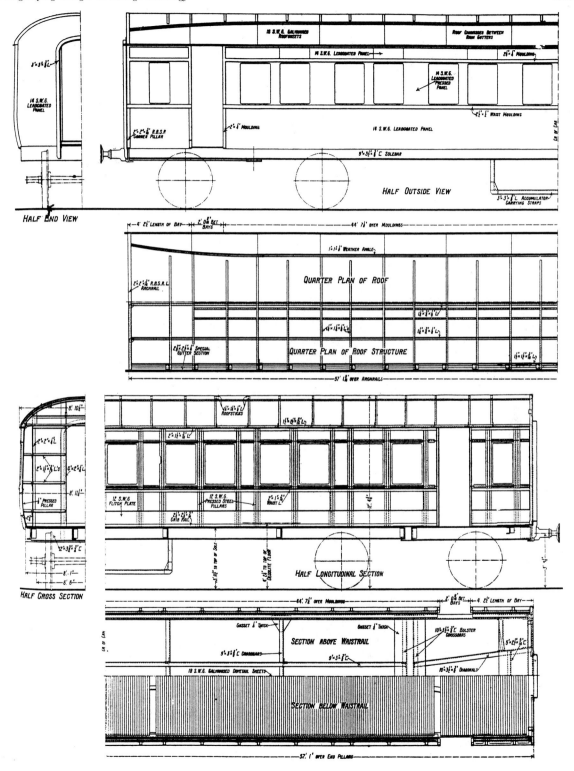

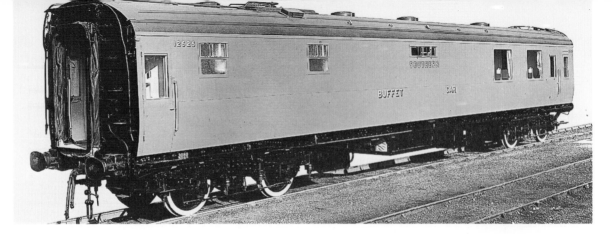

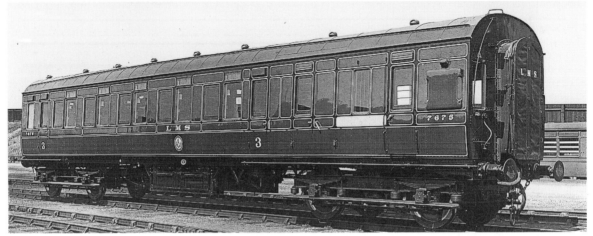

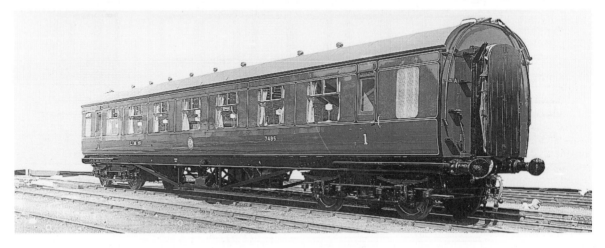

Top *Plain but honest: Bulleid's unlined malachite green was first applied to coaching stock in 1938; this is 'Bognor Buffet' No 12525 from one of the 4BUF sets.*

Middle *Fully panelled livery treatment applied to 'all-steel' LMS open brake third No 7675 in 1927 (BR LMR).*

Bottom *For a year or two after his new carriages appeared, Stanier's flush-sided stock was given a fully lined livery which, though suggestive of traditional panelling, also suited the modern lines of the coaches. This is open first class dining car No 7495 in 1934.*

ever, the Southern did not take matters as far as did, eventually, all the other companies. The company remained faithful to wood and canvas roof construction right into the totally flush-sided period, after the second war.

The next railway to espouse steel panelling in a major way was the LMS and it did so in two ways, the first of which, in 1926, was of more than usual significance. In that year the company introduced the 'all-steel' carriage, rather than the intermediate version adopted by the GWR and Southern. If truth be told, the LMS made rather more of a fuss about it than was perhaps justified, but it was innovatory in constructional terms if for no other reason than that it had no separate underframe.

The superstructure of the vehicle, which was carried on standard LMS bogies, was in the form of a steel box-girder (it was called a tubular girder at the time) whose bottom member was, in effect, the two solebars connected by the corrugated steel floor and whose upper component was formed from the cantrails, roof sticks and roof sheets. Also made of steel were the pressed channel pillars which connected roof and solebar and to which were riveted the body side plates, the whole forming a rigid structure which could withstand considerable compression stress. They were probably the strongest carriage bodies built for general service main-line use in Britain until the early 1950s.

To allow the solebars to take the complete buffing and drawgear stresses without the need for the trussing of a conventional separate underframe, the new LMS carriages had a box girder at each end of the frame which consisted of the customary rolled steel channel headstock and crossbar (which formed the buffing girder) connected at top and bottom by web plates and further reinforced by longitudinal angle members. Further crossbars between the solebars were calculated to carry all the floor loading and at the bogie centres a double channel bolster girder took care of vertical loading and brake stresses. It was claimed for them that the whole formed '. . . a reasonably light and very rigid body to resist all the stress occasioned by travelling at high speeds, and should be very much stronger than a composite wood body and steel underframe under collision conditions'.

The latter claim was tested, under rather dramatic live conditions, in an accident to the 'Royal Highlander' at Dinwoodie in 1928 when the leading 'All Steel' full brake was found to have absorbed much of the collision impact. This led to the LMS trying to adopt a blanket policy that these all-steel brakes should always be run at the head of principal trains. It was, needless to say, very much a forlorn hope — there were simply not enough of them to go round —

but there were many instances where these vehicles could indeed be marshalled at the head of the train.

The principal building of all-steel carriages took place in 1926-7 and all were built by outside contractors, the general consensus being that one reason for their introduction was so as to give tangible assistance to outside industry at a difficult time. Other than the full brakes already mentioned, the only other carriages were of the centre-aisle open type and were exclusively third class. Most were full thirds but some had brake ends and their overall style copied the by now quite typical LMS open carriages (see Chapter 19). The interiors generally followed conventional practice, being finished in wood, but a few were given steel interior seat frames and other details. And there the experiment more or less began and ended! A few years later, a handful of side-corridor brake firsts and brake thirds were built on the same principles, but the LMS clearly seems to have taken a somewhat ambivalent view of these vehicles. Though at the time of their introduction, the Chairman of Cammell Laird (one of the contracting firms), who was also an LMS director, is on record as having stated that the steel coach was here to stay, the LMS clearly thought otherwise and more or less abandoned the idea for more than 20 years.

It is tempting to speculate why this should have been the case, for as far as the types built were concerned, they were in no way inferior to the more conventional vehicles — they weighed no more and their far greater strength was, presumably, a plus factor. However, the railways were not in the habit of wrecking trains with gay abandon, and in any case the conventional separate steel underframe could stand quite a degree of strain. It therefore seems likely that the rarely encountered 'accident factor' would not count too highly when set against the undoubted fact that the LMS carriage workshops were by now geared up to manufacture conventional carriages on mass-production lines and the company always preferred to build its own stock wherever possible.

Thus the LMS eventually decided to follow the GWR and Southern and confine the use of steel to underframes, outer panelling and, of course, the traditional reinforcement of the carriage framing, especially the roof. This it began to do in 1929-30, and within three years the familiar Stanier-pattern flush-sided stock had begun to appear after a short interregnum of more conventionally styled steel-panelled carriages. Needless to say, both the 'All Steel' and the early steel-panelled carriages were all arrayed in the full panoply of the lined crimson livery, only slightly simplified in the earlier 1930s. Interestingly, it was not long after Stanier had assumed responsibility for LMS matters that he introduced a much simpler livery for carriages in 1934. One can perhaps read some of Stanier's old company influence in this move, for the LMS switched immediately to the new style just as had the GWR some seven years earlier and for much the same reasons. We are, however, by mentioning Stanier, moving a little ahead in the chronology for the moment.

Meantime, the LNER continued to produce the handsomely styled Gresley carriages for almost 20 years after the grouping, little changed in superficial outer appearance from those of the GNR. For reasons already stated, they were in fact rather stronger than their wooden bodies might have suggested, partly because teak itself is tough material but also by virtue of their buckeye couplers. The only really surprising fact is the long retention of the turnbuckle underframe, and it was not until 1930-31, largely as a consequence of the introduction of a longer 65-foot chassis, that the angle-trussed underframe became the LNER standard.

Like the LMS, the LNER also toyed with the idea of 'All Steel' carriages but, also like the LMS, their works were geared to the production of wooden-framed vehicles so the idea was not pursued to any significant extent. A few open thirds and full brakes were obtained from 'the trade' in 1927 which, like the LMS equivalent, were devoid of conventional underframes, but whereas the LMS bought hundreds, the LNER settled for but a few dozen all told. It seems that they were more expensive to pro-cure than conventional carriages and, in the LNER case, there was also a slight weight penalty compared with the teak-bodied version. Their livery was a quite extraordinarily complex business for not only did they have full lining (as in the case of the LMS examples), but they were also given an elaborately 'grain-painted' finish to match the normal stock. This was amazingly convincing, but at what cost one wonders.

There can be little doubt that the lack of real enthusiasm for all-steel carriages by the two largest British companies was the prime reason why the idea did not take hold for fully a generation, even though when it did finally re-appear in BR days, slightly modified, the methods adopted for body construction were not dissimilar to those pioneered in the 1920s; but this development must wait its time for the moment. What is, perhaps, more surprising is that Gresley did not, in the 1930s, move in any significant degree to the by now customary British practice of steel panelling on wood frames. By the mid-1930s, economics were causing him to question the cost of teak panelling and some carriages were in fact built with steel panelling (fully 'grain-painted' of course), but teak panelling remained the norm until Thompson swept it into limbo for new building in and after 1944. Before this, however, and perhaps even more unusual, was the use by the LNER of plywood outer panelling on the distinctive green and cream 'Tourist' stock of the 1930s. This

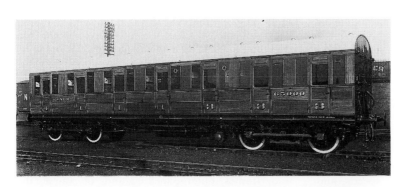

Left *An astonishingly realistic impression of grained teak was always achieved by the LNER painters on the small amount of conventional steel-clad stock which was built between the wars. This example is non-corridor composite No 65000, out-shopped from Dukinfield in 1933. Though this is not an 'all-steel' carriage, the latter were treated in like manner*

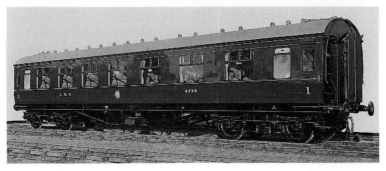

Left *Stanier-pattern corridor composite No 4298, built in 1939, clearly shows the extent to which the LMS had moved styling onwards during the 1930s. Note the suspended-pattern gangway and the welded bogie. The underframe is still, however, riveted*

Figure 8 *This sectional drawing shows the essential differences between the traditional wooden framing and panelling of an early LMS sleeping car (upper elevation) and the later form of part welded steel and part wood framing of the Stanier sleeping cars (centre and below).*

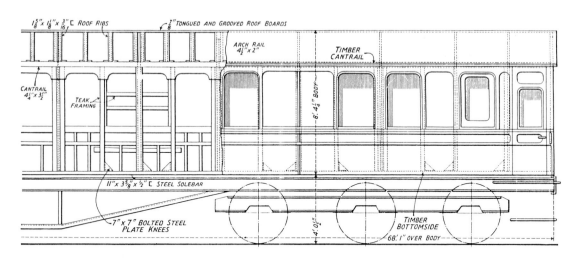

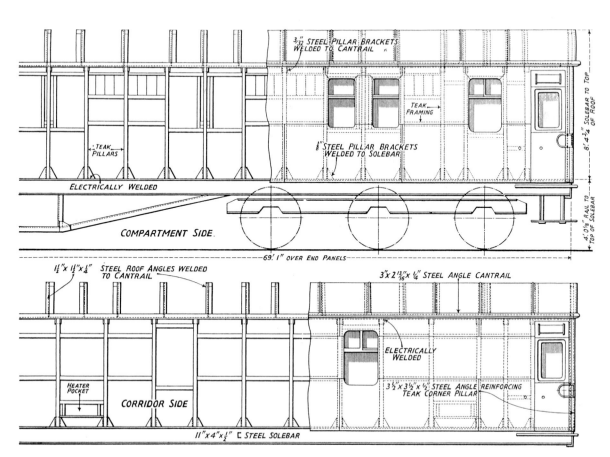

and these changes, when allied to the increasing elimination of capping strips between panel sections and the new simpler liveries, gave carriages far smoother exteriors and, in consequence, a more modern appearance. The modernity was, however, rarely more than skin deep and these slightly newer constructional ideas were rarely made the opportunity for innovative new design concepts for many years, as we shall see.

It was the LMS in the person of William Stanier which first began to marry new constructional methods with changed design ideas and here it is very tempting to draw parallels with his locomotive work on the LMS. He clearly brought the 'flush-clad' method with him from the GWR (which had started the business) and as with locomotives, took it further on his new company than did his old system. The GWR did not really take the design possibilities of flush-clad, steel-panelled carriages to a logical conclusion until late in the 1930s and it was not until after the war, with the new Hawksworth types, that GWR design caught up with that of its famous, but now LMS-employed son! In like manner, the Southern and LNER did not really adopt the flush-clad style in any major way until Bulleid and Thompson took over, well after the Second World War. The more detailed design implications of these changes will be considered later.

As for basic carriage technology itself, little else of consequence really changed in the constructional field and most things which did occur were merely in the form of slight adaptations of existing practice. Thus, for example, the GWR introduced a modified form for the British standard gangway housing in which the familiar lazy tongs (which allowed the moving part to extend from the fixed housing) gave way to a 'suspended' form of attachment at the top of the moving frame. Needless to say, Stanier took this idea to the LMS with him. Likewise, the main change in underframe construction, once all railways had moved to the angle-trussed form, was the gradual introduction of welded rather than riveted fixing from the mid-1930s. It never became exclusive, however, until BR days, even though the underframe was rendered far more rigid if the components were welded together.

An interesting use of welding, particularly on the LMS, was that which allowed the elimination of the bottom horizontal timber frame members for the carriage side. In this revised arrangement, steel 'pockets' were welded to the top of the underframe into which were directly fixed the vertical timber frame pieces, the underframe itself acting as the lower horizontal component. It saved a bit of weight and, possibly, a degree of rotting in the timber frame (the lower member was always the most vulnerable with steel panel-

was an undoubted economy move but was not entirely successful (see Chap. 19).

Perhaps the most visibly obvious changes, consequential upon the gradual supersession of wood by steel panelling over the years, were those of least importance in terms of fundamental carriage construction. Starting with the GWR *circa* 1930 and closely followed by the LMS in 1932-3, the now customary 'flush-clad' carriage made its first widespread appearance. In these vehicles, the only real change was the elimination of the familiar bolection mouldings round the fixed windows. In their place, the glazing was set in a concealed frame immediately behind the outer steel sheets and thus the glass was only the thickness of the outer sheeting behind the panel itself. The fixed lights were often given markedly rounded corners in association with this new form of treatment

Left and right *These three views show different aspects of the later LMS method of carriage body construction. In order: twelve-wheel underframe and floor with steel pockets welded to accept the timber framing uprights; part assembled frame showing composite wood and welded steel framing; and finally, the interior panel fixing. Note particularly the concealed wooden window frame behind the outer steel panelling in the latter view*

Right *LMS six-wheel bogie of totally welded construction save for the components which need to be periodically replaced. Note, however, the retention of Mansell-pattern wood-centred wheels, probably one of the last examples of the use of this type on new stock*

ling if for no other reason than that water gravitated downwards and tended to rest behind the panels above the lower frame itself) but the idea never became universal.

Bogies too remained largely unaltered in basic principle from that described in the previous volume. Welded frames sometimes replaced a riveted assembly, as with underframes, but the 'swing link plus bolster' allied to leaf spring primary suspension was always the norm in the company period. There were, it is true, various categories of bogie available, and the choice of which to use was largely determined by the size and weight of the vehicle carried on them, but this mostly affected such matters as spring strength or wheel journal and axlebox sizes. No one attempted to make any progressive step forward and, in strictly technological terms, the best of the bunch was still the Gresley 'double bolster' bogie adopted as standard by the LNER throughout its lifetime for all its best stock; but even the LNER had a single bolster version for the lesser fry — Gresley's more sophisticated type was somewhat more expensive to build! As an aside, in early BR days the more expensive Gresley bogie was still preferred to the newer BR type for some EMU stock.

In a sense, the latter statement gives a sort of clue as to why basic carriage technology did not change too much in the post-grouping period. For all that I have sometimes remarked on the generally conservative nature of *design* developments during this time,

Traditional upholstery with slightly brighter walls and ceilings in an 'all-steel' LMS open brake third of 1927. The overall effect is still fairly solidly pre-group in flavour

these comments must be set against the fact that viewed *purely as a vehicle*, the British carriage was by no means backward in the pre-grouping era. If post-group technology seemed conservative at times, it was in part because earlier carriage builders had moved matters forward so much, especially when compared with most contemporary practice in other countries, save for the very best examples. In consequence, many of the technical ideas which developed in Britain during the first quarter of the century stood the test of time, not because the railways were unable or unwilling to change but more because there was no need to change. In a very real sense, this statement held true for maybe the first 10-15 years of the BR period too and there, for the moment, we must leave the technicalities of the vehicle itself. There will, of course, be need to come back to the matter from time to time.

Vehicle interiors

Turning now to the vehicle interior, yet again traditional methods remained the norm for by far the bulk of carriages as far as construction was concerned, the biggest changes to be observed being, as indeed they had always been, in response to the changing fashions of the day. Thus — and this had actually started well before the grouping — there was increasing use of simpler and much plainer wood finishes than in earlier days. The florid Victorian excesses had long gone, but even the more restrained and delicate Edwardian styles were in due course to give way to still less elaborate treatments. Much of this will be covered in later chapters, but in general terms the carriages of the 'twenties and 'thirties strove, not always successfully it must be admitted, to give a brighter and more airy appearance than hitherto and painted surfaces often replaced the heavier treatments such as Lincrusta and wood panelling.

This topic is, of course, at the interface between construction and design and it is a moot point whether it should be considered here rather than later. However, since new-style finishes were regularly applied to carriages whose layout was in every other respect thoroughly old-fashioned, it seems better to consider the subject at this point. In fact, though most railways seemed to attempt to move with the times only as far as was possible without seriously incommoding their traditional ways of doing things, their compromises often turned out rather better than might have been expected.

One factor which always militated against a truly avant-garde approach to railway carriage interior design (it still does by the way) is the sheer longevity of the vehicle itself. Forty years was a by no means abnormal life for a carriage and some lasted very much longer, during which time fashions may well

The restrained use of simple, if dark, wood surfaces with only modest detail in combination with plain upholstery material offers a relaxed if not especially avant-garde *environment in this GWR first class compartment of 1935*

panelled style — became quite popular and increasing use was made of plywood which could carry many more varieties of decorative timber (applied in the form of veneer) as its visible layer than were afforded by the traditional solid oak, teak and mahogany of the older carriages. Thus, timber varieties increased rapidly and the LMS in particular made great play of its use of 'Selected Empire Timbers' in its new carriages. Veneered plywood could be worked just as easily, if not more so, than the traditional solid wood, but gave rather more scope for variety and quite a number of new-style surface patterns could be developed by butting together contrasting colours or grain patterns, relying on the texture of the timber surface itself rather than using elaborate mouldings or beading. This became particularly widespread during the 'Art Deco' period of the 1930s and, while not always successful, its better manifestations were of a very high order.

Upholstery, too, underwent changes but here recognition had to be made of the fact that patterned designs and darker colours were less likely to show dirt than plain cloth and lighter shades. The trouble with many of the newer patterns was that while the cloth itself was every bit as good as hitherto, the pattern repeats were often larger than before and since the railways liked to 'centre' the designs on seats and backs. there could be quite a lot of cutting to waste compared with a smaller pattern. Furthermore, a

This rather modish experimental Stanier interior from the mid-1930s shows a not entirely unsuccessful use of Art Deco-style materials. Note the care taken to position the large pattern repeats in exactly the same place on every seat unit.

have changed more than once. It was therefore customary for railways to play safe and adopt somewhat conservatively styled interiors which would not date too quickly nor cause undue offence to their many less fashion conscious customers. As has already been outlined in the previous volume, it was normal railway custom to use the very best materials anyway and these too would have a long life. Interior woodwork might well be expected to last the lifetime of a carriage while upholstery should be good for 15 or more years of even the most vigorous usage. But re-trimming with a newer-fashioned upholstery cloth could not really disguise an older style of basic interior treatment so there was a natural tendency for many otherwise perfectly serviceable and comfortable carriages to look old-fashioned in terms of decor.

It was really only in the realm of new vehicles that any more adventurous ideas began to appear and these mostly tended to be found in wall finishes and, to some extent, light fittings and upholstery cloth. The flush-finished wall — as opposed to the older

large pattern size tends to make a carriage interior seem smaller, so those attempts to use the most popular 'jazz' patterns of the age were not always particularly successful. In general, the better solutions always seemed to be achieved with less strident designs and it became quite common to see small pattern repeats but devoid of the Victorian and Edwardian fussiness of actual design. Thus interiors gradually became simpler and less fussy, often augmented by much simpler picture or mirror frames or even, quite commonly, frameless mirrors.

In the realm of carriage lighting, electricity was, of course, the norm for new construction, and while many railways continued to use bare bulbs in plain holders (particularly in corridors and lavatories), there was increasing and widespread use of more modern lampshade designs, the geometric type being very popular during the 1930s and later. The better examples were often in the open carriages and some railways even went in for concealed cornice lighting in their open saloons giving them a rather 'Odeon'-style character in consequence, but by no means unpleasing in the better examples.

Much more use was made of painted surfaces inside the carriages than hitherto and this gave a much lighter appearance, while a particularly popular innovation from the 1920s onwards was the use of Rexine leathercloth as a finish. The SR actually tried this as an exterior carriage covering on one experimental vehicle, but apart from this and the rather special case of the LNER 'Silver Jubilee' train (see Chapter 11), Rexine was pre-eminently a useful interior material. The advantages were considerable. It cost little to maintain and could be kept clean by washing with soap and water. It was cheaper and quicker to apply to the surface (by glueing in position) and had good scratch-resistant quality. It was available in a considerable variety of patterns and,

not least because it could be applied quickly and by unskilled labour, was also cheaper to replace should a panel become either worn or damaged. Though the GWR and LMS used it to some extent, the Southern and the LNER were probably the major users, standardizing the material for window blinds and, in the case of the Southern, for the lining of door panels. The LNER used it in some of its sleeping cars and it became particularly widespread in buffet cars and other catering vehicles where its 'wipe-down' property was of considerable practical benefit.

Other areas where some slight moves forward were made were in floor coverings and window curtains (where present). Linoleum and carpet were the traditional floor materials and continued to be widespread — indeed, the carpet never lost favour in the better carriages — but rubber composition flooring was increasingly used, laid direct on to wood or steel, often applied in layers up to 1 inch thick and sometimes taken a few inches up the carriage side in the form of a coved skirting to facilitate cleaning. As with upholstery, the patterns used for carpets and curtains were gradually simplified and the better results were achieved with the less 'loud' designs.

In most other respects, little really changed. Carriage ventilation and heating still followed traditional custom and the openable window remained a British favourite throughout the 'Big Four' period. Quite a bit was said in the contemporary technical press about the virtues of full air-conditioning, but it did not happen for the ordinary passenger. The nearest approach was a sort of pressure heating and ventila-

Traditional LNER, and none the worse for that: only the angle-trussed underframe reveals that LNER corridor third brake No 52221 was built in the 1930s (1934 to be exact). Its handsome Gresley-styled body form goes back to the pre-1914 GNR.

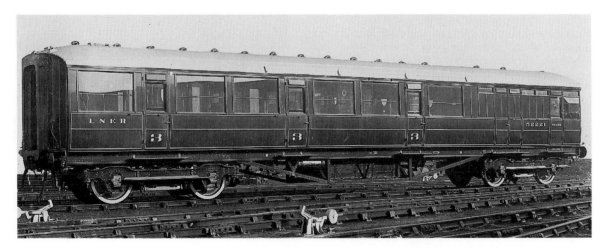

Neat but conservative: a characteristic Maunsell SR exterior of the 1930s, in this case a corridor composite No 5662 from the 1932 series with 'tall' corridor-side windows

tion system adopted in some sleeping cars. Those carriages which did display larger windows — regrettably rather fewer than perhaps should have been the case — eventually mostly settled down to having the top quarter or so fitted with one or two of the familiar sliding elements, but far too many long-distance carriages retained a full array of outside doors to the compartments which prevented more widespread use of larger 'picture' windows; and these doors, of course, always carried the obligatory drop light.

It was mostly these latter features which caused many British carriages to seem obstinately conservative; but conservative or no, the end result was almost always a high-quality product. The 'soft third class' was still very much a British speciality compared with overseas, and as the years progressed the already high standard of accommodation for the average traveller continued to improve. If it had a weakness, it was the lack of much design innovation, most noticeably in the field of interior layout. Some, of course, would argue that this was no bad thing anyway on the basis that if traditional layouts were popular, why change them? The next two chapters take a much closer look at this particular aspect, but by way of concluding this technical overview, a few words on building costs and carriage maintenance will not come amiss.

Building and maintenance costs

Carriages were a major part of railway capital expenditure and, as the next few chapters will reveal, some 27,000 locomotive-hauled coaches were built to company designs over a period of some 30 years. If to these are added the various self-propelled and other vehicles, something like 1,000 new vehicles per year were added to stock between 1923 and 1953, even discounting non-passenger-carrying vehicles. This was probably three times the number of locomotives built during the same time and undoubtedly totalled more actual cash expenditure than did the locomotives which hauled them. Yet it is one of the more surprising features of recorded railway history that little mention is made of the actual costs incurred. Furthermore, not too much detailed contemporary evidence seems to have survived. However, enough does exist to allow a few points to be made.

At this point in time, the ravages of half a century of inflation make the actual number of pounds sterling seem trivial indeed, but, even allowing for this fact, the railway carriage was by no means an expensive item to procure. Some of the detailed figures for the LNER and the SR have survived to reach the NRM records and these show the following actual values:

a) Southern Railway eight-compartment corridor third, 1924-5:

Material:	£1,568 12s 10d (£1,568.64)
Wages etc:	£630 16s 2d (£630.81)
Oncost and Supervision:	£301 19s 2d (£301.96)
Total	£2,501 8s 2d (£2,501.41)

b) LNER five compartment corridor brake third, 1929-30:

Material:	£1,606 13s 8d (£1,606.68)
Wages:	£539 17s 9d (£539.89)
Workshop expenses:	£153 17s 4d (£153.87)
Total	£2,299 18s 9d (£2,299.94)

Though the basis of comparison is not quite the same, there was negligible inflation during the 1920s and 1930s (amazingly, there was actually deflation during some years!) so the figures are broadly the same. However, low though these values are by present-day standards, I still cannot resist making the point that the cost of applying the full varnished teak LNER livery (including all materials and lining out) came to no more than £101 13s 4d (£101.67); which has to be a bargain compared with current NRM restoration costs!

Exact equivalences are not known for the LMS save that when the 1937 'Coronation Scot' sets were built (see Chapter 11), the company reckoned that the average cost for a new corridor vehicle was some £2-2,500. So the LMS may have been reaping benefit from its more modern mass-production methods. Comparable GWR figures do not seem to have survived. However, such figures as have been published for the pre-1914-18 war period suggest that a turn of the century non-corridor came in at about £1,000 and that a 'Dreadnought' sleeping car of 1907 cost over £3,000. The latter type of vehicles were always more expensive on all railways, and there was some quite considerable inflation during the First World War, but since it is known that LNER sleeping and dining cars were only costing about £4,000 in the inter-war years, maybe the GWR vehicles remained a little above the rest.

But in all conscience there can have been little in it between all the companies, and an average figure of some £2,500 per carriage (less for non-corridors, more for special stock) would seem about right. The overall carriage investment in new stock by the 'Big Four' must therefore have been in the order of £75,000,000 over the period — a not inconsiderable sum which probably needs multiplying fortyfold to give a comparable modern figure (BR MkIII stock was quoted at some £100,000 per unit in the early 1980s). To put this into further relevant perspective, brand new LMS Stanier Class '5' 4-6-0s were costing about £6,000 each before the war.

Even allowing for the imprecision of these figures,

their size relative to other aspects of railway expenditure meant that maintenance costs loomed high, and here the SR and LMS seem to have benefited from their 'progressive' system of carriage repairs. Full data is not available, but Table 1 has been compiled from the official Railway Clearing House returns for the last ten years of the company period and the SR performance during the war years can be seen to be quite outstanding, all the more so since it probably bore the brunt of air raid damage. The LMS only got into difficulties towards the end of the period but the poor old GWR had almost a quarter of its stock awaiting repair in 1947[1] and the LNER was little better. Yet all had started from broadly comparable situations in 1938. Though I cannot prove it, this situation may even have had some bearing on the fact that the subsequent BR standard carriages drew more heavily on SR and LMS practice than the rest.

It can therefore be appreciated that however the figures be interpreted, the provisioning and maintenance of carriage stock was a vital and at times costly element in the last years of the private railways of Great Britain as they strove to keep pace with the ever-increasing volume of competition from alternative modes of transport. It is to their credit that the companies did not stint in their efforts, even though at times they may have seemed a little old-fashioned. So, having set the background, we can now take a longer look at what they actually built.

Table 1 Coaches under/awaiting repair 1938-1947 (% of operating stock)

Company	1938	1941	1944	1947
GWR	5.8	7.1	12.8	23.5[1]
LNER	6.4	6.4	9.0	18.5
LMS	6.5	5.0	7.7	9.2
SR	5.3	6.4	5.8	6.4
Great Britain (total)	6.2	5.9	8.5	13.4

Worst Years (%)	Best Years (%)
GWR (23.5%) 1947	GWR (5.8%) 1938
LNER (20.1%) 1946	LNER (5.4%) 1939
LMS (9.2%) 1947	LMS (5.0%) 1941
SR (7.4%) 1946	SR (4.4%) 1940

[1] This figure was probably inflated by the aftermath of a long strike at Swindon Carriage Works in 1946.

18. Design tradition dies hard

In this and the next chapter we turn to the design of the many general service carriages built during the 'Big Four' company period. However, since developments did not take place simultaneously on all four lines, there is some degree of chronological overlap between the two chapters. In general, this chapter tackles the traditional approaches, and the next the more modern ideas. In this context, 'modern' should not be taken to mean the flush-sided form of construction. Many of the latter vehicles were thoroughly old-fashioned in concept and it is with conceptual ideas that we are principally concerned here.

Before analysing the carriages, however, it is useful to know the scale against which the carriage building efforts of the old companies should be measured, and Table 2 attempts to show this. From this it can be seen that the 48,000 or more pre-group carriages inherited by the 'Big Four' were reduced in total by well over 8,000 during the 25 years in question, yet the number of seats actually provided was maintained at broadly the same level until the war years and only slightly reduced thereafter. Some of this may even have been due to war damage or have arisen in consequence of the 'Is your journey really necessary?' campaign. This changeover was entirely the consequence of much new building and although it is not possible to give absolutely precise figures (statistical sources do not always quite correspond), by the time that purely company designs stopped building (*circa* 1953-4), over 27,000 new locomotive-hauled coaches had been built and well over 70 per cent of the inherited pre-group fleet had been replaced. Of the new vehicles, some two thirds were gangwayed, the rest being of the non-corridor variety, and it is with these that we start the review.

Non-gangwayed carriages

Throughout the 'Big Four' period, the non-gang-wayed carriage continued to be built in quantity, though it eventually yielded its numerical superiority over all others. Most of them were of the traditional compartment style with individual side doors and although many new examples were built, their totals were swelled considerably by the many thousands of similar vehicles which had been inherited from the pre-group companies. The latter were often of high quality and a fair proportion served right through to BR days. The new construction is tabulated, as far as available statistics make possible, in Table 3. It came, of course, from only three of the four companies, the Southern, for reasons already given, finding it unnecessary to build new non-gangwayed stock for locomotive-hauled shorter-distance services. To get a fully balanced picture, one should not forget the 'New Build' EMU stock (Chap. 21) which, on the Southern, took the place of the new locomotive-hauled non-corridors of the other lines.

Meantime, the other three carried on much as their constituents had done before and it is a moot point which of them deserves the 'booby prize' for being the least enterprising! In truth, of course, the old-fashioned non-lavatory compartment coach was slowly going out of fashion for most purposes; but it was still one of the best means of moving large numbers of people and getting them on and off the train quickly, so it tended to have no real competition in the suburban and/or short-distance mode. In consequence, the railways tended to go on churning them out much as before but they were increasingly confined to the short-haul mode as years went by. Most of them were like-for-like replacements (in kind if not in size) of earlier four-wheel and six-wheel carriages, usually on the basis of *seats provided* rather than numbers of vehicles. Thus a typical 9-foot wide eight- or nine-compartment third, seating 96 or 108, would probably replace two former five-compartment six-wheelers of narrower width, each seating 50 people.

Table 2 Passenger carriage totals 1923-1947 (including both hauled and multiple-unit stock)

Note These figures are abstracted from official returns to the Board of Trade.

Company	1923			1930			1937			1947		
	Total carriages	Seats (1000s)	Seats per carriage	Total carriages	Seats (1000s)	Seats per carriage	Total carriages	Seats (1000s)	Seats per carriage	Total carriages	Seats (1000s)	Seats per carriage
LMS	19663	1018	51.8	19536	1121	57.4	17409	1057	60.7	16354	1002	61.3
LNER	14314	721	50.3	13620	732	53.7	12430	681	54.8	11567	648	56.0
SR	7469	401	53.7	7089	411	58.0	6682	404	60.5	6318	408	64.6
GWR	6768	350	51.7	6768	371	54.8	6248	362	57.9	5791	340	58.7
Totals	48214	2490	51.6	47013	2635	56.0	42769	2504	58.5	40030	2398	59.9

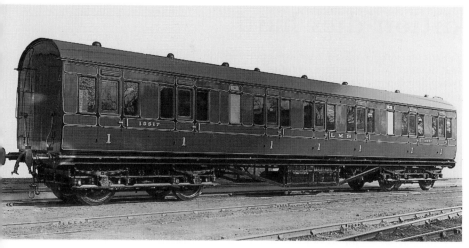

This rather good-looking non-corridor lavatory first, No 15517 of 1927, not only represents the first LMS standard style of wood-panelled and beaded body but was almost certainly the best designed non-corridor carriage type ever built by that company. Even so, three out of seven compartments were denied access to the toilet

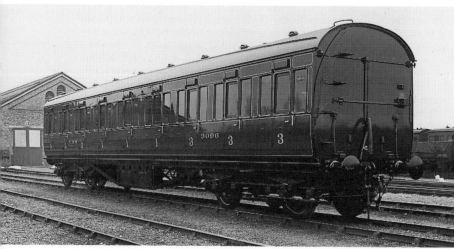

The 57-foot nine-compartment composite No 3096 was the LMS norm in the non-corridor, non-lavatory field from 1923 until the early 1950s. This is a 1931-built example from the initial steel-panelled period, ie with retained window bolection mouldings rather than flush-fitting quarterlights

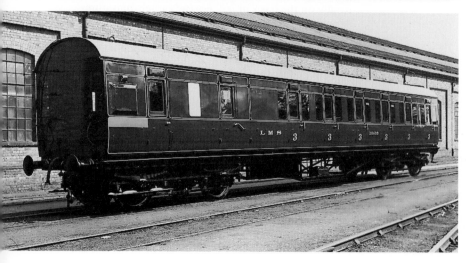

Stanier-pattern LMS 57-foot non-corridor third brake No 20609 was one of the very first flush-panelled examples, dating from 1933, and still carried the fully lined livery abandoned a year or so later

Right *Third class compartment interior of LMS pattern composite No 16751 built by BR in 1949 was in all essentials indistinguishable from its predecessors of a generation earlier*

Table 3 Non-corridor locomotive stock — new build: 1923-54

Note: These values have been extracted from various published works and may contain occasional discrepancies from other sources in the units column. Overall, they represent within 1 per cent of the precise totals and serve adequately for comparative purposes.

Company	Carriage type[1]									
	FL	CL	TL	BTL	F	C	T	BC	BT	Total
LMS	30	200	—	273	132	936	1616	—	1356	4543
LNER	—	310	81	—	132	347	1156	85	898	3009
GWR	—	—	—	—	10	313[2]	542	330[3]	495	1690
Totals	30	510	81	273	274	1596	3314	415	2749	9242

1 Carriage types are identified by standard BR codes of this summary. Each unit of an articulated set counts as one carriage.
Those built as second class are considered 'third' for the purpose
2 Of which 80 were built in 1953 for the LMR and numbered in the ex-LMS series.
3 Of which, all but circa 60 vehicles were built as two-coach 'B-sets'.

In strictly design terms — and in marked contrast to its long-distance achievements — the LMS probably held the palm for sheer stagnation of thought. It established its 57-foot standard non-corridor carriage designs in 1923 and proceeded to produce them in vast quantities for the rest of its life. By far the majority consisted of but three types: nine-compartment thirds and composites (6T + 3F) and six-compartment brake thirds. There were a few eight-compartment full firsts for good measure, plus a few non-standard layouts for the North London line which incorporated second class as well, most of which latter types appeared within the first ten years after grouping. All these carriages were handsome enough from the outside, especially when fully lined, but internally nothing of significance changed for almost 30 years until the last of them appeared in the early 1950s under BR auspices. From 1923 to 1930 they were wooden-bodied with full beading and full lining; 1931-2 saw a change to outer steel panelling (still fully lined out) and from 1933 onwards came the flush-sided 'Stanier' versions, mostly with the simplified 1934 livery. However, throughout the whole period the interior layout or amenities scarce altered; in part, no doubt, this was the inevitable economic consequence of mass-production.

Amongst the vast horde of non-lavatory stock, the LMS also had one last fling at the now largely outmoded non-corridor lavatory style, most of whose sundry ramifications were well covered in the last volume. There were some full firsts, by far and away the best non-corridors ever built by the LMS, but most were brake thirds or composites and these too were quite agreeable withal. They were mostly formed into 'Inter-District lavatory sets' — at least in theory — but if truth be told, none of them were anything like as generous in their lavatory provisioning as the best of the pre-group offerings of the same

type. One still had to be something of a detective to be sure of getting access to a lavatory. None was built after 1930.

Added to this 57-foot proliferation, there was a somewhat smaller number of 54-foot equivalents, differing mainly in their slightly more cramped compartment sizes which, even so, were rather better than those of the LNER. Although some went into general service, the majority were set to work on the Tilbury line in set formations where their marginally shorter length allowed, or so it is said, one extra coach per train to be provided for this busy route. Included amongst them was a quite absurd lavatory composite which, in an otherwise toilet-less eleven-coach formation, allowed but one first and one third class compartment a modicum of creature comfort! When somewhat similar five-coach sets of 'short' stock were built with steel panelling for the Cathcart Circle route

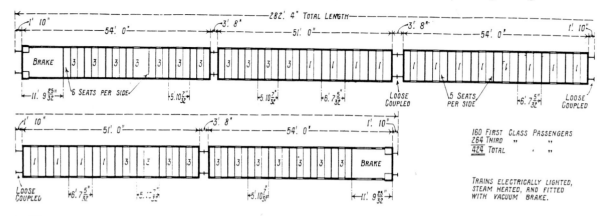

in Glasgow in 1926, the lavatories were left out, the composites in consequence being reduced to a 51-foot length. The LMS claimed great things for these Glasgow area carriages but they had five-per-side firsts without armrests and a contemporary account unconsciously revealed something closer to the real truth:

> 'The interior furnishing of the compartments has been designed with a view to providing the greatest possible comfort for the passengers, and to facilitate cleaning by the eliminating of carved and decorated surfaces, which collect dust. The ceiling is formed of three-ply, finished in glossy white enamel, which surface acts as a reflector for the lights.'

In other words, they were utilitarian...and you can bet that the lights were reduced in number in consequence of the glossy ceilings!

This apart, just about the only other development of interest in the LMS non-corridor field was a half-

Figure 9 *Simplified floor plans of the spartan LMS Cathcart Circle non-corridor stock of 1926.*

hearted attempt at articulation in 1937. Eleven triplet sets were made, none of the operating divisions were wildly enthusiastic about them and they were never repeated; but mention of articulated carriages brings us naturally to their prime exponent, Gresley's LNER.

The LNER was simultaneously better and worse than the LMS in the short-distance field. While many quite reasonable conventional carriages were made (see below), much of the purely suburban effort was concentrated on the celebrated articulated stock designed by Gresley, and in this particular arena the LNER was disgracefully parsimonious with space. The origins and weight-saving advantages of this method of construction were discussed in Chap. 7.

LMS Stanier non-corridor articulated triplet of 60003/4/5 in simplified LMS livery

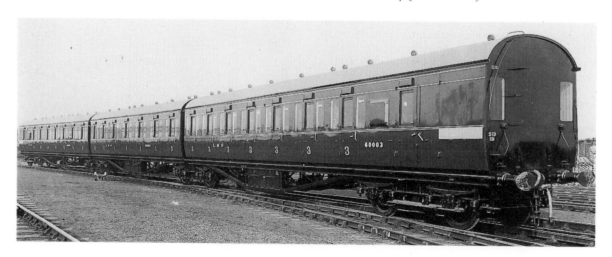

and for quite some time prior to 1923 articulation was also regularly seen as a convenient means of re-using serviceable bodies which had hitherto been carried on four or six wheels. As such it undoubtedly succeeded in giving a better ride quality and no doubt saved money too. New articulated stock, both long-distance and suburban, had also been made before the grouping, but it was only after 1922 that the LNER began to introduce new four-unit and five-unit sets (known as 'Quad-Arts' and 'Quin-Arts') in any real quantity.

From the outside they looked suitably '20th Century' (full elliptical roofs, etc) and the Gresley bogies no doubt improved the ride; they were also given the full works as far as the teak livery was concerned, but the compartment sizes were every bit as mean and cramped as their Howlden predecessors with far less good reason, and the firsts were actually smaller between partitions than most LMS non-corridor *thirds*. In fact, for all their uninspiring nature, LMS non-corridors (including even the parsimonious Cathcart Circle stock) gave a far more comfortable seat to both classes of passenger than ever did their LNER articulated suburban contemporaries. One really would have thought that having saved so much weight on bogies, the LNER could have offered a bit more space between partitions without serious penalty. Maybe platform length had something to do with it, but for nigh on 40 years they trundled commuters to and from King's Cross and Liverpool Street and many other places too. When they finally departed (well into BR days), they were mourned by very few

LNER (GE section) brake tri-composite 'Quad-art' unit No 159, built in 1929, dates from the period when three-class accommodation was still provided by the LNER, mainly for the benefit of season ticket holders at a time when third class season tickets were not issued

save for those who put nostalgia above creature comfort! One 'Quad-Art' set is privately preserved.

By contrast with these spartan-like offerings to the harassed commuters, the LNER's other non-corridors were considerably better and, in one case, of genuine quality. Unlike the LMS, which put its non-corridors on the same length chassis as most of its gangwayed stock, the LNER, for some reason, adopted a much shorter 51-foot length for most of its single unit non-gangwayed stock and also retained conventional side buffers and screw couplings for these vehicles. It also built a fair number of articulated 'twins' with much more generously proportioned compartments than the 'quads' and 'quins', and in this guise the articulated style continued in construction, to a limited extent, well into the steel-panelled era, the last examples appearing during the early 1940s.

In the single unit category, five out of the six theoretically possible types were built, the omitted style being a brake first; in fact, no post-group non-corridor brake firsts appeared from any company. LNER brake composites were also quite rare and confined to Scotland, but brake thirds came in considerable numbers and assorted compartment configurations between three and six. All had quite spacious compartments, generally *circa* 7 ft 3 in first and 6 ft 2 in third, with the composites even more generously dimensioned in both classes; there were also a few second class examples and odd batches of brake thirds and full thirds were built to slightly longer dimensions (54 ft and 56 ft respectively).

In addition to these non-lavatory types, the LNER also introduced some far more agreeable intermediate-distance non-gangwayed lavatory stock than almost anywhere else in Britain. To be more accurate it continued an existing idea, for several LNER constituents had done something similar (the GNR,

NER and NBR to note but three). The carriages mostly took the form of lavatory composites with half-length side corridors leading to a pair of centrally located lavatories, one for each class. All passengers could thus gain access to the toilet rather than 'second guess' the state of affairs as was usually the case on the LMS (if it provided lavatories at all). The basic idea was carried on during Thompson's time in office and after, many being built during the early BR era. There were also a few lavatory thirds, some of which had a sort of open-plan interior.

There seem to have been no hard and fast rules as to which services these better non-corridors should operate, but I have strong personal memories of an odd composite or two scattered amongst the mostly ex-NER non-lavatory stock which was the common carriage choice on many of the West Riding local trains of my youth. Some of them even had folding armrests in the thirds, if I recall aright, and they gave off a characteristic and not entirely disagreeable smell!

Turning now to the GWR, it too offered little of

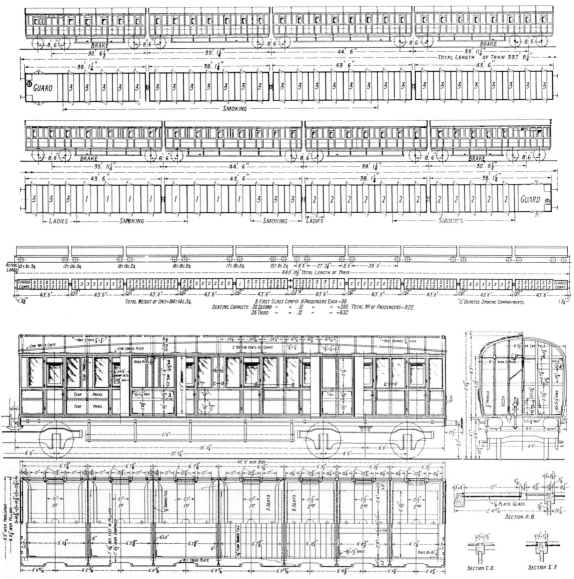

General Arrangement of First and Second Class Composite Coach.

Figure 10 *These drawings and plans of Gresley suburban articulated stock show, from top to bottom:*
a) *Simplified elevations and plans of a typical eight-coach train of 'Quad-arts' with short brake vans.*
b) *Sketch plans of a ten-coach 'Quin-art' train.*
c) *Detailed drawings of the outer (first/second class composite) end of a 'Quin-art' set.*

Scale: ¹/₁₀″ = 1ft

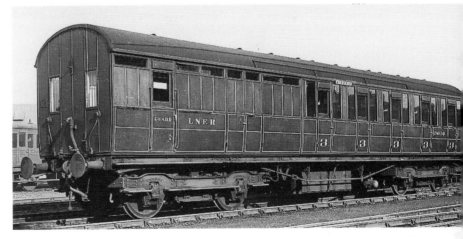

Top *Typical 51-foot five-compartment LNER non-corridor brake third No 3616 of 1925, seen operating in Scotland*

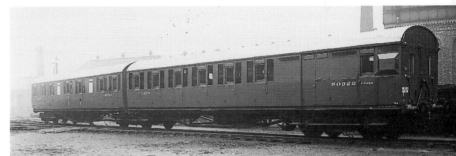

Right *Late period LNER articulated non-corridor twin brake third/lavatory composite No 80322/3 built in 1940 for King's Cross outer suburban use and carrying wartime utility brown livery. This set was steel-panelled, not teak, and anticipated many features of the post-war Thompson stock, but the rectangular-shaped lavatory windows reveal its Gresley origin*

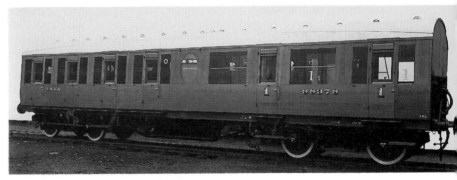

Above right and right *Typical LNER centre-lavatory non-corridor composites: Gresley pattern No 32454 of 1927 and a steel-panelled Thompson version, No 88378 from 1947. They were internally all but identical save for their opposite-handed layout, but the post-war example lasted little more than ten years, swept away by the DMU tide*

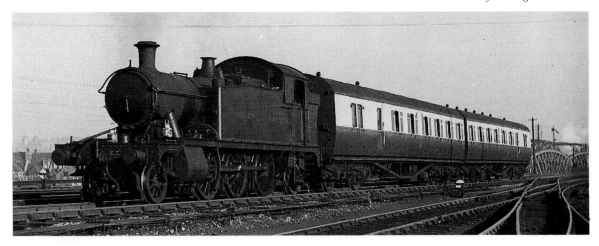

GWR 'B Set' in operation behind 2-6-2T No 5540 circa 1936.
This was one of the later sets with the first class compartment of
each coach next but one to the luggage van. For a close-up of the
centre coupling of a similar set, see page 28

any truly innovatory nature in the non-corridor field, and in terms of conceptual dullness was worse than either of the two companies so far mentioned: it never offered lavatories in non-corridor stock. In part this was because many of its country districts were served by short branch lines where transit time hardly merited lavatories, and in those cases where distances were longer, 'hand-me-down' older corridor stock often sufficed. Furthermore, the GWR's country districts were increasingly to become the home of that characteristic feature, the auto-train (see Chapter 13).

To a considerable extent, the GWR had addressed the more purely suburban problem during the Dean and 'Toplight' eras, culminating in a number of quite substantially sized and up-to-date full elliptical roof vehicles, some of which were illustrated in the first volume. These older carriages had a long innings, many lasting well into BR days, and the bow-ended and subsequent eras saw little if anything better offered to the GWR commuters. In this respect it was no whit different from either the LMS or the LNER. Uninspiring examples came out during the whole of the inter-war period and their external styling merely followed the current contemporary fashion. But there, apart from two quite well-known exceptions, the matter started and finished.

If the GWR can be said to have made any form of distinctively unique non-corridor contribution in the 1923-39 period, it was its espousal of the two-coach 'B Set'. This was a pair of permanently close-coupled brake composites, utilizing a centre coupling, set brake ends outwards, usually with small van portions and each coach containing but *one* first class compartment. There were no lavatories, of course, and there was also some degree of indecision over the years as to where the solitary 'state apartment' should go. As new batches were built, it gradually migrated from the inner ends of the carriages (ie the centre of

the formation) via an intermediate location to a final resting place next but one to the van. They were neat sets, much used on those routes, including many branch lines, where traffic exceeded the capacity of a single auto-coach, and since they did not require a specially adapted locomotive the latter could be gainfully occupied on other duties as well if opportunity allowed — which it regularly did in the more bucolic parts of the GWR empire!

Like the LMS, the GWR also dabbled with articulation in the non-corridor field and, like the LNER, it managed to produce some diabolical compartments in consequence. The carriages concerned were rather mean six-unit formations of which three sets were built in 1925, originally for through working on to the Metropolitan widened lines but which left the London area at the outbreak of the Second World War when through services between the GWR and London Transport were suspended. They were inelegant carriages and, again like the LMS examples of the genre, they led to nothing significant. In fact, only the LNER really made extensive use of this form of construction and even that line found, as years went by, that the articulated principle was only advantageous for universal use on inner suburban work where fixed sets could be virtually guaranteed not to need much alteration. Elsewhere, the need for operational flexibility made single unit stock far more useful as a general rule, albeit often in association with the articulated 'twins' already mentioned.

But if truth be told, when compared with their various efforts in the self-propelled field (see Chapters

23 & 24), none of the three companies which went on building locomotive-hauled non-corridor stock produced any conceptual 'leap forward' beyond those established in the pre-group period. There was, without doubt, no perceived need. The carriages did, however, carry prodigious numbers of customers in the heavily populated areas and should not be despised for their lack of enterprise. Most of them probably earned their keep several times over.

Corridor carriages

I have deliberately used the word 'corridor' rather than 'gangway' for this part of the story in order to concentrate attention on this specific type of carriage, leaving the 'open' and specialized stock for the time being, in the former case largely because it was part of the move to modernity (see Chap 19). In this context, it is rather more helpful to summarize the building of new stock in a different way than for non-corridors, and in Table 4 I have isolated the 1923-43 'build' which forms the basis of the next part of the discussion. To get a truer balance of the long-distance carriage output of each company, the open stock built for general service during the same period

(mostly LMS and LNER) should be added to the totals (see Table 5, p . 324). But regardless of this latter fact, the output of side-corridor stock during the inter-war years was formidable, some twice that achieved in the non-corridor field.

The reason for this rapid expansion seems clear: the side-corridor coach had only become the accepted long-distance norm during the generation or so preceding the grouping. In consequence, many services still remained in the hands of non-gangwayed stock; the companies were anxious to change this state of affairs and they did indeed do so. Perhaps it was because of this need for rapid change in fundamental carriage type and the fact that side-corridors were still (relatively) new, compared with railway carriages in general, that early post-grouping corridor coach developments seemed to move forward but little in pure design terms. In any case, many of the larger railways had entered the amalgamations with a fair number of more than reasonable and quite recently built 'state of the art' offerings, and the concept of the side-corridor carriage was, in the British context, a very sound one for reasons explained in the previous volume; so they may have felt little need to experiment further.

Table 4 Side-corridor stock — new build: 1923-43

Notes: 1. These values have been extracted from various published works and may contain occasional discrepancies from other sources in the units column. Overall, they represent within 1 per cent of the precise totals and serve adequately for comparative purposes.
2. Although built until 1943 in some cases, all carriages listed are to unmodified pre-war design. For postwar continuation, see Table 9, page 536 .

Company Style	Carriage type[1]						
	FK	CK	TK	BFK	BCK	BTK	Totals
LMS/Non-standard (LNW type)[2]	—	—	5	—	—	8	13
LMS/1923-32 standard	23	329	295	47	184[5]	239	1117 } 3182
LMS/1933-40 (Stanier)	41	501	611	12	93	794	2052
LNER/Non-standard (NER type)	—	22	8	2	15	13	60
LNER/Gresley (1923-33)[3]	41	110	291	6	58	235	741 } 2515
LNER/Gresley (1934-43)[3]	37	361	766	16	103	431	1714
GWR/'Toplight'[2]	—	—	25	—	—	22	47
GWR/'Bow-ended' period	6	297	648	6	94	269	1320 } 2402
GWR/1934-40 standard	30	178	493	—	137	197	1035
SR/Non-standard[4]	67	46	76	13	5	67	274 } 1316
SR/1926-36 standard	68	173	405	2	120	274	1042
Totals	313	2017	3623	104	809	2549	9415

1 Carriage types are identified by standard BR codes. Those built as second class are considered 'third' for this summary.
  Each unit of an articulated set counts as one carriage.
2 Ex-First World War Ambulance coaches, not strictly 'new'.
3 Listed separately mainly to give quantitative comparisons with LMS and GWR figures during similar building period.
4 Includes SE&CR, LSWR and 'Kent Coast' designs .
5 Including 100 later (*circa* 1939) rebuilt with 'Stanier' outer panelling.

What is certain is that there was no contemporary feeling that any really fundamental change was necessary. Indeed, the first generation of post-group corridor stock, regardless of company, was often greeted in semi-eulogistic fashion by contemporary writers as though it was something radically new. The reality was somewhat different and, if truth be told, some of the descriptions do rather reveal this when read between the lines with the benefit of hindsight. Take, for example, the new 'Flying Scotsman' sets built for the LNER in 1924. The vehicles were handsome enough from the outside, of course, and the 'triplet' articulated diners (see Chap. 20) were mildly innovatory, but the *Railway Gazette* seems to have had some difficulty in finding evidence of any real improvement in the ordinary coaches (author's comments in [brackets]):

'The ordinary vehicles...correspond substantially with standard East Coast designs [hardly surprising], except that many detail improvements [all unspecified] are included, and advantage has been taken of all good features [again unspecified] ... of the companies now included in the LNER ... It is claimed [by whom?] that these new trains are the most comfortable and luxurious in the world for passengers paying ordinary fares.'

This last statement was palpable nonsense. Both the first class and third class compartments were *smaller* than the equivalent Midland offerings of more than a decade earlier and all compartments still had a full

The LNER was still building much 'all-door' corridor stock in the late 1930s. This is composite No 24359, ex-works from York in 1937. The thirds were now three per side, but note the retained first class half compartment in the centre

Figure 11 *Floor plans and carriage formations of the LNER 'Flying Scotsman' set of 1924 and the Leeds–Glasgow set of 1931.*

set of outside doors on the compartment side. The LNWR (as early as 1907-8) had suppressed these features on its celebrated '2pm' twelve wheelers with larger compartments to boot; the GWR had done it even earlier with its 'Dreadnoughts' and the NER had even produced 'doorless' compartments in the thoroughly modern idiom, ie with large picture windows. The fact was, of course, that individual outside doors were mostly still considered necessary, though whether this desire was felt by the passengers or the railway administrators is hard to determine at this point in time. Either way, it served little useful purpose, but tradition died hard. True, the LNER only claimed six seats per compartment in the third class parts of the 'Scotsman' set, but the carriages lacked the necessary armrests to ensure that this principle held good; one doubts not that eight per compartment (the pre-group norm in a 9-foot wide carriage) were often carried.

A year or so later, the 'Hook Continental' was similarly re-equipped, this time first and second class only (it was a boat train), but the second class seems to have been scarce distinguishable from the thirds of the 'Scotsman' set, at least in terms of seat density or compartment size. And when, as late as 1931, a new Leeds-Glasgow set was proudly announced as embodying the latest LNER practice, all was revealed when the third class was quoted officially as having eight seats per compartment, still with outside doors!

All of which may seem rather unfair to the LNER, but the LMS was no better in the early 1920s. It too put a full set of outside doors on all its corridor coach compartments, though the latter were usually a frac-

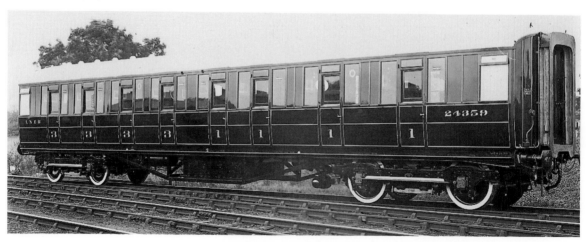

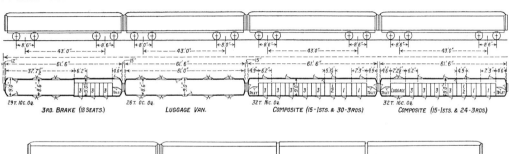

3RD. BRAKE (18 SEATS.) LUGGAGE VAN. COMPOSITE (15-1STS. & 30-3RDS) COMPOSITE (15-1STS. & 24-3RDS)

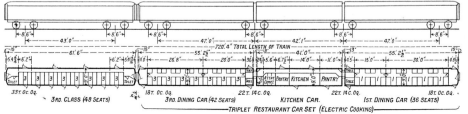

TOTAL LENGTH OF TRAIN

3RD. CLASS (48 SEATS) 3RD. DINING CAR (42 SEATS) KITCHEN CAR. 1ST DINING CAR (36 SEATS)

TRIPLET RESTAURANT CAR SET (ELECTRIC COOKING)

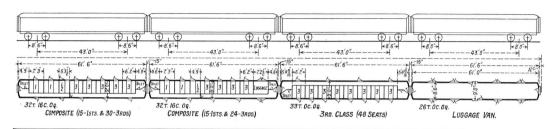

COMPOSITE (15-1STS. & 30-3RDS) COMPOSITE (15-1STS. & 24-3RDS) 3RD. CLASS (48 SEATS) LUGGAGE VAN.

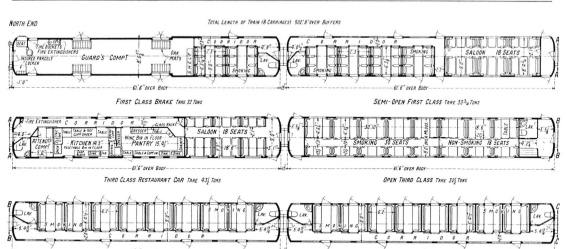

NORTH END

TOTAL LENGTH OF TRAIN (8 CARRIAGES) 502'.9" OVER BUFFERS

FIRST CLASS BRAKE TARE 32 TONS SEMI-OPEN FIRST CLASS TARE 33¾ TONS

THIRD CLASS RESTAURANT CAR TARE 43¼ TONS OPEN THIRD CLASS TARE 32½ TONS

CORRIDOR THIRD CLASS TARE 33½ TONS CORRIDOR THIRD CLASS TARE 33½ TONS

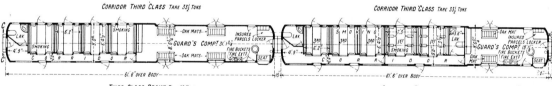

THIRD CLASS BRAKE TARE 32 TONS COMPOSITE BRAKE TARE 33½ TONS SOUTH END

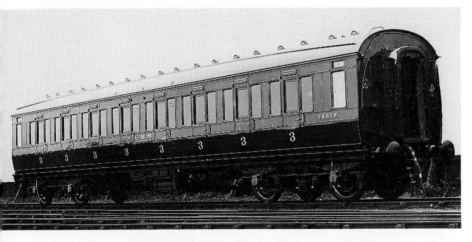

Neat but unimaginative: 'all-door' corridor third No 14318 of 1928 was to be one of the last batch of such vehicles to be turned out by the LMS. A year later, no new corridor coaches from this company had individual outer doors

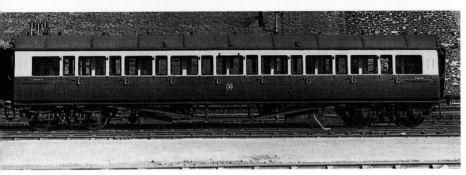

Left and below left *Not much change was seen in GWR main-line stock for many years after the grouping as may be seen by comparing the corridor side of bow-ended corridor third No 4840 of 1926 and brake composite No 6909 of 1934. There is some simplification in the later example but both had a full set of outer doors on the other side*

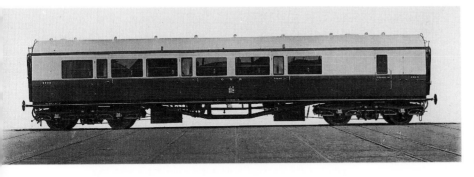

Figure 12 *Detailed drawings and full train plan of the GWR 70-foot bow-ended set of 1923.*

Scale: 3mm = 1 ft (main drawing)

tion larger between partitions than those of the LNER; but its vehicles were shorter and did not have the more up-to-date buckeye couplers and Pullman gangways of the LNER equivalent. Neither, in fact, could claim seriously that they had made any great improvement over their pre-group antecedents in the early days. Perhaps they were taking stock after the great amalgamations, who knows?

No such excuse could, however, be offered for the GWR. Having established a degree of pre-group modernity by introducing steel panelling, it ground

to a conceptual halt for a decade or more. The actual beginning was in 1922 when the 'Toplight' era was succeeded by the so-called 'Bow-ended' period, whose self-descriptive nomenclature needs no real amplification: some of them had curved carriage ends on plan which, with their reversion to the famous GWR 'chocolate and cream' livery after a decade or more of all-over crimson lake, just about says all! A definitive account of this period states: '...the first new post-war coaches to be painted in the reintroduced brown and cream livery...preceded a period of con-

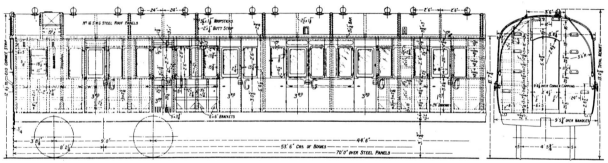

Compartment Side, 70-ft. Composite Carriage.

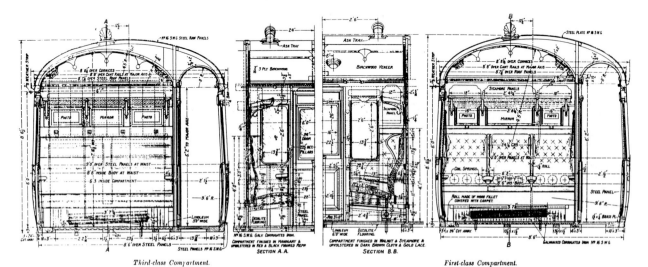

Third-class Compartment.

SECTION A.A.

SECTION B.B.

First-class Compartment.

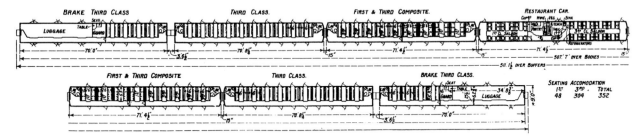

servative design with little inspiration'.*

Now, not unnaturally, contemporary accounts were somewhat less scathing, but let us examine the facts. The first examples marked the last GWR essay at the 70-foot length and some of them even had buckeye couplers. So far so good, but they did not copy the LNER pattern, having hinged 'drop-down' buffers rather than the quasi-standard pull-out type (see

Great Western Coaches, 1890-1954: M.Harris, David and Charles, 1966/72

Chap. 2 page 28); their Pullman pattern gangways were not compatible with the LNER type and not all coaches were so fitted anyway, the outer ends having conventional screw couplings, British Standard gangways and *flat* ends! All told it was a curious mishmash of indecision, and to claim, as did the contemporary *Railway Engineer*, that: '. . .it would, we think, be difficult to plan, within the available loading gauge dimensions, a more roomy and well-appointed set of coaches of the corridor compartment type', was arrant rubbish; others had already done it, years earlier!

Typical GWR four-per-side third class seating and sombre wood finish in brake composite No 6909 (see previous view)

To be fair, the first class was generously dimensioned at 7 ft 6 in between partitions and the carriages looked handsomely distinguished in the reintroduced and fully lined two-tone livery, but the thirds were a bit parsimonious at 6 ft and four-per-side seating, while there was still the matter of outside doors to all compartments. They were put into service on the South Wales and Birmingham/Birkenhead routes, after which time the GWR reverted to a standard 57-foot length from 1923-29. They were simply shortened versions of the 70-foot bow-enders and back came the screw couplings and British Standard gangways, many earlier ones with flat ends to boot. In fact, in all essentials they were indistinguishable in amenity from the earlier 'Toplights', but like most things GW, they were built to last and survived well into BR days.

Much the same continued to be true during the whole of the bow-ended era, and even the much vaunted 'Cornish Riviera' stock of 1929 was no quantum improvement, save for a welcome increase in third class compartment size to some 6 ft 4½ in (6 ft

8 in in the composites); but they still had a full array of outside doors and no armrests. Indeed, I still recall the surprise when, in 1950 (my first venture down the former GWR main line to South Wales), I found myself in a four-per-side third with compartment door and no armrests; the old LMS and LNER lines had long abandoned this sort of thing by then — at least on their longer distance services!

During this at best rather debilitating period, the GWR (inevitably?) had to have a go at articulation (during 1925), making quite a fuss about it in the process. However, the various individual components rarely exceeded a 50 ft 6 in length — the GWR never really showed the flair of Gresley's LNER in this respect — and as far as the passenger was concerned, compartment size and amenity showed no real improvement over the 70-foot and 57-foot standard single unit carriages. The idea never really caught on and they were subsequently rebuilt (being lengthened in the process) to conventional single unit carriages. As such, two of the open third class dining carriages survive in the National Railway Museum collection.

It was all rather sad for such a distinguished company — and the new, so-called 'Modern' livery of 1927 fooled no one at the fundamental level. However, by 1929 the GWR showed that it could do better if wanted when it introduced a slight modification in the form of a modest increase in length to 60 ft, a rather wider carriage profile which gave a bit more space in the thirds (still four-per-side and 'all-door', however) and a more flush-sided form of panelling. Moreover, in the form of its quite magnificent Special and Super Saloons of 1929-31, the GWR also revealed a hitherto unsuspected ability to really 'go to town' if it so desired. We shall have cause to come back to these vehicles later in the book (Chapt. 26) and the real tragedy is that the genuinely advanced ideas which they embodied were not transferred across to the more orthodox side-corridor field. Even the later and generally far better 1935-40 stock (page 344) was uninspiring by comparison.

The Southern Railway, meanwhile, gradually moved itself into a position of more or less full compatability with its more traditionally 'corridor'-orientated contemporaries. Chapter 1 has outlined how Maunsell fairly speedily developed a new 'Southern' approach to the business from very limited beginnings, and by 1926 the first of the true SR 'standard' corridors had appeared. They were actually ordered in 1925 and at 59 ft long by 9 ft wide were, in contemporary terms, usually exceeded in size only by Gresley's LNER offerings. Like the LNER, the SR eventually opted for buckeye couplings and Pullman-type gangways, and, like the GWR, it went for steel panelling from the outset. Some were built

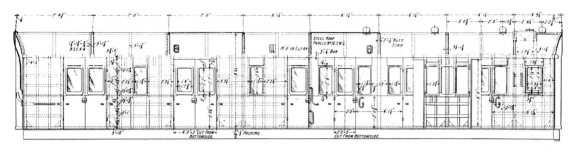

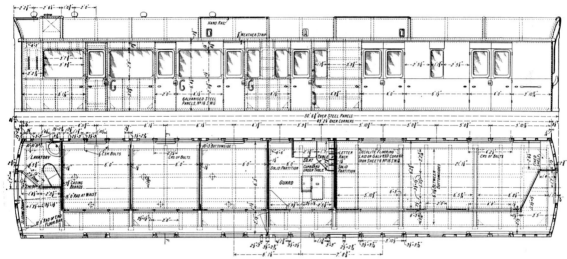

Corridor Brake Third-Class Carriage, G.W.R. Articulated Train.

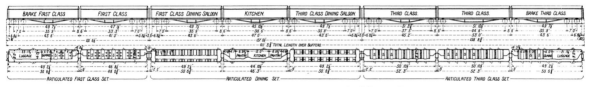

Formation and Leading Dimensions of G.W.R. Articulated Express Train.

Figure 13 *Typical carriage arrangement and full train plan of the 1925 GWR articulated trains.*

Scale: 3mm = 1 ft (main drawing)

The first SR standard corridor style: Maunsell brake third No 3226 of 1925 vintage, built as part of three-coach sets with two brake thirds and a full composite

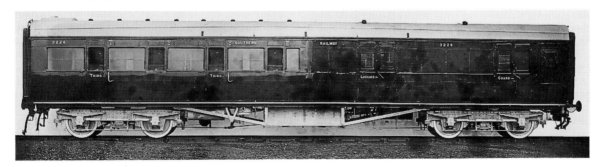

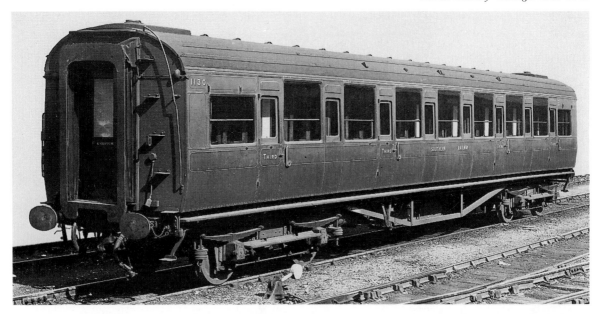

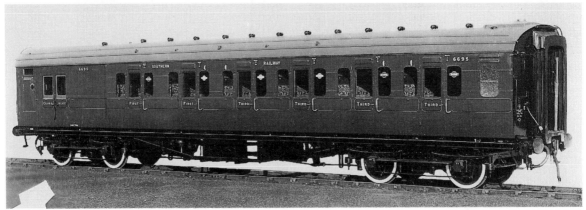

Top *The later Maunsell corridor style with 'tall' corridor windows is exemplified by full third No 1130 of 1930. Note the Pullman gangway and buckeye coupling of this very neatly conceived design*

Above *The Southern's last pre-Bulleid corridors came out in 1935-6. This is brake composite No 6695, almost flush-sided but with a fair amount of visible riveting and still deploying a full set of compartment-side outer doors*

to a narrower and more straight-sided 8 ft 6 in width in 1928 for the Kent Coast.

Loading gauge restrictions always bedevilled the Southern more than any of the other companies and this inevitably fought against true standardization on the LMS pattern; but regardless of width, Maunsell's first stock was every bit as good as most of the opposition, and when he slightly modernized the designs in 1929-30 by introducing full height corridor side windows, a quite distinctly handsome ensemble resulted. By now, there were also 8-foot wide vehi-

cles for the Hastings line to add to the two earlier width dimensions, and in the mid-1930s the Southern moved to a slightly more modern style with almost fully flush-clad carriages. There were not, however, too many in this latter category and the Southern built no more corridor stock after these 1935 orders (built in 1936) until the post-war Bulleid years. During not much more than ten years, however, the Southern had added over 1,000 new corridor coaches to its fleet and had completely revolutionized its longer-distance services in consequence.

The Southern's corridor carriages were mostly very orthodox and all of them had the seemingly inevitable outside doors to all compartments. But in this respect the company was little different from most of the rest. Yet there was an alternative, and by the mid-1930s one of the 'Big Four', the LMS, had already begun to go well down the road in the direction of more modern ideas in the long-distance carriage field.

If one looks in detail at Table 4, it is immediately obvious that some two-thirds of the LMS build of corridor stock in the pre-war period was to the so-called Stanier style, first introduced in 1932. These were the first carriages to be built in quantity which incorporated the sort of design ideas which we would now consider to be 'modern' in the sense that they can be seen as leading to the vehicles of our own time; but it is important to remember that for some years prior to their introduction, the LMS had also been the first company to break out of the interior design mould even while its carriages were otherwise still very much in the traditional exterior form.

The most numerous examples of this were, at first, in the 'open' carriage category, and the large-scale building of this type of vehicle was undoubtedly the reason why the number of new LMS side-corridor coaches were rather smaller than might otherwise have been expected during the pre-Stanier era. However, before analysing the reasons for and the consequences of these changes, it will be useful to conclude this part of the discussion by a further examination of the figures quoted in Table 4, in which I have deliberately isolated the corridor coach construction of the inter-war period, mainly to reveal the extent to which the LMS differed from its rivals.

If one counts only orthodox 'all-door' carriages, then the LMS total in the 1923-32 period is still further reduced, for only some two-thirds of the total listed (752 out of 1,117 to be precise) were in this configuration. The LMS move to new standards began, in fact, during 1927, and after 1930 it built no more side-corridor stock with outside compartment doors, in which respect it was almost alone for many years. As far as the GWR and SR were concerned, their corridor coaches were mostly or wholly of the 'all-door' kind until the late 1940s, and by far the bulk of those built by the LNER also followed the traditional style until the post-war years, though in fairness it must be pointed out that by the late 1930s the LNER and GWR had begun to make something of a move towards change.

None of which, of course, should be taken to imply criticism of the quality of vehicles built by those companies which remained faithful to the older design ideas. The overall quality of the British general service coach, regardless of company, was always high and there was little or nothing to choose between them when it came to quality of workmanship or robustness of construction. But some of them were more old-fashioned than others, and if one discounts the relatively small number of Gresley LNER corridor carriages built without compartment doors, along with the few examples of rather more specialized carriages built by all companies from time to time, then the fact remains that the LMS largely led the way for almost 20 years in terms of interior design as far as the long-distance general traveller was concerned. The next chapter takes a closer look at the causes, nature and implications of this situation.

19. New ideas emerge — but slowly

During the early part of 1925, accompanied by a suitable fanfare from modestly sized trumpets, the LMS announced the introduction of a 'New Type of Set Train' for an accelerated service between London and Bradford via the Midland line. It even went so far as to distribute external views of the train which at first glance seemed no different from many of its predecessors. It was headed by a Midland Compound 4-4-0 (LMS-built, of course!) and the front and rear carriages were seen to be former Midland clerestories, the like of which had not been built for a least half a generation. In fact, the chosen carriages dated from 1909; so what, precisely, was new?

Well, in the literal sense, nothing really, apart from the engine itself and the rest of the carriages. The LYR had built much the same sort of train well before the First World War, but for some reason, this LMS revival of the old LYR venture did catch on. Its so-called newness stemmed solely from the fact that it was wholly composed of open, centre-aisle stock, most of which was of the latest LMS standard pattern... and the Midland brakes? They were simply included because at this time the LMS had not yet introduced its own design of brake-ended open carriage and the Midland happened to have a few, which it regarded as 'Excursion' stock, by the way. In the event it turned out to be the forerunner of almost every InterCity express of our present day so it behoves us to look at it in a little detail.

The train plan is appended herewith (Figure 14) and is self-explanatory. Its stated aim was: '...to meet the needs of the considerable business travel between Bradford and Sheffield and London'. It was later

The so-called 'new' LMS train of 1925, though only the really clever could tell it apart from its Midland forbears, did in fact represent some genuinely fresh thinking

known as the 'Yorkshireman', but its schedule would rather surprise the modern-day business traveller on the same route, even if its interior layout might well seem rather familiar. It left Bradford at 9.10 am, arrived in London at 1.25 pm, '...thus allowing for a full afternoon's business in London...', and departed St Pancras at 4.55 pm. One can only conclude that in the 1920s, business must have been concluded rather more rapidly if 3½ hours represented a 'full' afternoon! Joking apart, however, it was the start of a new concept in long-distance travel and the LMS was the prime instigator; indeed, it was almost the sole protagonist in the main-line sense until late in the 1930s, when the LNER began to copy.

Open stock, as such, was nothing new — see Chapter 10, for a more somewhat detailed analysis of its origins — but apart from a few specifically dedicated cases, like that of the LYR above mentioned and, of course, dining purposes, most railways tended to regard the open saloon carriage as best suited for excursion and similar duties, perhaps on the basis that its internal layout was more friendly and sociable than the conventional corridor carriage. But even that was only partly true, for the railways also continued to make widespread use of compartment stock, both corridor and non-corridor, for much of their widespread excursion and holiday traffic. To find a more long-lasting reason for the LMS attempt to change emphasis, we need to look a little below the surface, and contemporary accounts of the pioneering Bradford train give a few clues.

The *Railway Gazette* of 1925 records, *inter alia*:

'...the new Bradford train includes six passenger coaches, arranged three each side of the kitchen car...All vehicles are of the central gangway type...and every seat in the train has table equipment...Obviously, in the ordinary way,

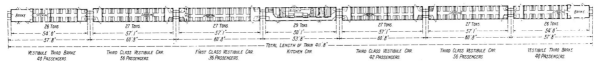

Plan of New Vestibuled Train with Kitchen Car for London-Bradford Services, L.M.S.R.

Seating Capacity: 234 Third-Class; 36 First-Class; Total 270. Total Weight of Train, 189 tons. Steam Heated and Electrically Lighted.

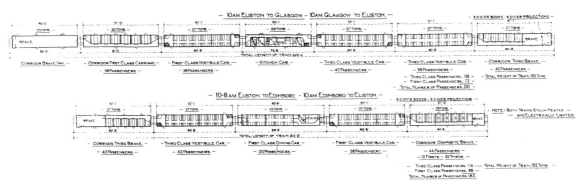

Figure 14 *Sketch plans of the LMS 'Bradford' set (above) and the morning Euston to Scotland train (below) of 1925.*

passengers taking lunch or dinner will be concentrated, as far as possible, in the vehicles immediately adjacent to the kitchen car, but if there is sufficient demand the kitchen car staff will be prepared to serve meals in any part of the train...Even if not required for meal purposes the tables will no doubt be appreciated very greatly by passengers, in that business men will be able to attend to correspondence, &c, while travelling...

'Another point of interest is that some, if not all, of the third class cars have practically the same seating and other dimensions as the first class cars, so that no inconvenience arises when two passengers (particularly if substantially built) are seated on the same side of a table, as it does in some third class dining cars, which may at times be somewhat uncomfortably crowded for this reason...notwithstanding the comfort of the seating accommodation and the high quality of the appointment and fittings of the train, no charge is incurred beyond the payment of ordinary fares.'

No doubt the magazine's correspondent was well looked after by his hosts, but even allowing some reservation for literary licence, there is a clear hint that the LMS was making a conscious attempt to produce an improved travelling environment for the long-distance ordinary traveller. The train was very heavily biased in favour of third class seats and would that the modern BR was prepared to serve meals 'in

any part of the train'! As a second (sorry, *standard*!) class passenger these days, it is almost impossible to find a full dining car service; such is the price of progress.

There were also some very practical issues. Open stock was rather cheaper to build, having less outer doors and inner partitions, and well-suited to Reid's new mass-production techniques. It also weighed slightly less, seat for seat, than corridor stock and thus, no doubt, suited the rapidly developing cost-conscious management approach of the new LMS; it is therefore no surprise that the very first carriages to be constructed on the mass-production principle were these new generation open saloons. They also, by way of bonus, gave marginally more comfortable seats in the 'two plus two' configuration than was offered by a four-per-side third class corridor compartment. Given these facts, it must have seemed sensible to the LMS to try and sell its new conceptual ideas in a positive way and this it proceeded to do.

On the same day as it introduced its Bradford service, the LMS did much the same sort of thing with its well-known 10.00 am train from Euston to Glasgow and Edinburgh. Once again it seems to have been anxious to get its new ideas into the public domain as soon as possible, for perusal of the train plan (Figure 14) reveals that the dining car of the Edinburgh section was of turn of the century LNWR vintage. This time, however, there was a mix of corridor and open stock, all of new LMS standard style, and it is interesting to speculate whether this was because of an absence of open saloon brakes or whether the company was deliberately offering a comparison to its patrons as part of the 'educational' process. At this time, the corridor coaches had doors to all compartments, of course, but it is also interesting to note the pair of 'two plus one' third class opens as opposed to only one 'two plus two' version. This was ostensibly to allow more seat space for dining but the LMS did encourage 'all the way' travel in this kind of vehicle and was by no means parsimonious in its provisioning as the years went by.

There was, however, undoubtedly a psychological barrier to overcome on the issue of compartment versus open stock as far as the passenger was concerned. The British like their privacy, the compartment provided it and events were to show that the LMS eventually built more corridor stock than open coaches. But the fact remains that during the early and mid-1920s, the company produced far more open carriages than side-corridors and one cannot help but feel that their weight-saving quality was paramount — this was the era of the Midland-inspired 'small engine and train' policy on the LMS, be it remembered, and much remained subservient to this basic philosophy for a few years. Be that as it may, within five years of the grouping, by far the bulk of the early standard open stock listed in Table 5 was in service and they were not all for excursion use, though many were employed in that mode.

The carriages themselves were rather traditional and very much in the Midland mode; in fact, the very

Figure 15 _Elevations, plans and sections of the characteristic LMS-pattern open thirds and third brakes of the 1920s. These are in fact the 'all-steel' versions (see page 31) but the wooden-bodied stock was identically laid out. The upper set show the brake thirds from the Leeds Forge Co and the lower drawings are of a full third from the Metropolitan C & W series._

Scale: 4mm = 1ft

first of all the hundreds of open thirds was to a Midland design and the LMS standard version only differed significantly in the matter of outer door handles! Their most distinctive outer feature was the 'twin window per seating bay' which derived mostly from MR practice but was not, if truth be told, unknown on the LNWR lines. There was, needless to say, much use of dark polished walnut and blue cloth in the first class while mahogany with velvet or moquette served for the thirds. They were very well made and I can vouch for the high quality and durability of their interior finish, having been much involved in the restoration of those in the NRM collection. Only a few were first class or composite, the main thrust to a new style of accommodation being directed towards the third class traveller, and in 1926 the LMS-built wooden-bodied third class versions were supplemented by the several hundred 'all-steel'

Table 5 Open gangwayed stock — new build: 1923-39

Notes: 1. These values have been extracted from various published works and may contain occasional discrepancies from other sources in the units column. Overall, they represent within 1 per cent of precise totals and serve adequately for comparative purposes.
2. The tables include all non-kitchen vehicles built for dining purposes.

Company/Style	Carriage type[1]						
	FO	CO	TO	BFO	BCO	BTO	Totals
LMS/1923-32 standard	106[2]	20	1305	5[4]	—	90	1526 } 2515
LMS/1933-39 (Stanier)	86	50	664	—	—	189	989
LNER/Non-standard (NER type)	5	—	5	—	—	—	10
LNER/Gresley (1923-33)[3]	20[2]	—	142	—	—	12	174 } 1029
LNER/Gresley (1934-43)[3]	34[2]	—	675	—	—	136	845
GWR/'Bow-ended'	6	6	32	—	—	—	44 } 131
GWR/1934-40 standard	—	—	75	—	—	12	87
SR Maunsell standard	—	63[5]	159	—	20[5]	—	242
Totals	257	139	3057	5	20	439	3917

1 Carriage types are identified by standard BR codes
  Each unit of an articulated set counts as one carriage.   Those built as second class are considered 'third' for this summary.
2 Includes some semi-FO types.
3 Listed separately mainly to give quantitative comparisons with LMS and GWR figures during similar building period.
4 Lounge brakes.
5 Classed as 'Nondescript' but effectively for either class.

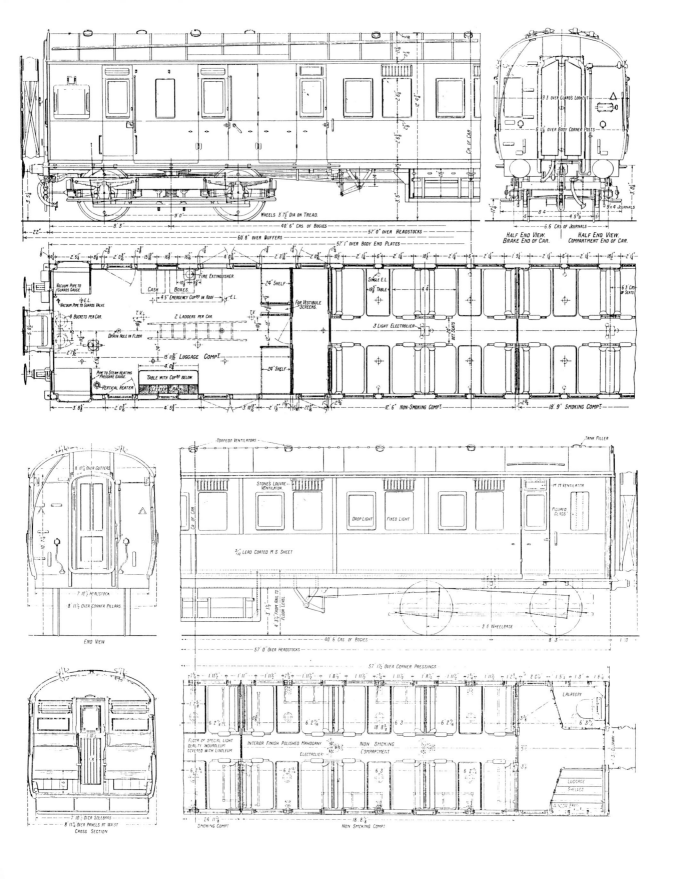

equivalents purchased from trade sources and already mentioned in Chapter 17. Taken as a group, these thousand or more third class carriages marked a significant milestone in British carriage history, if only by virtue of their sheer numbers. It is fortunate that we still have a few to be examined.

Meantime, the other companies seem either to have ignored this major LMS innovation or were not convinced of its relevance. In any case, one of them, the Southern, was probably far too busy with its attempts to catch up in the basic corridor mode to be overly concerned about yet another conceptual idea; but the attitude of the GWR and LNER does merit a few words.

If, indeed, the matter of weight-saving was the key factor in the LMS decision to build so many of these carriages in the 1920s, then the GWR and LNER could reasonably claim that such matters were not applicable to them; in the early days they both had express locomotives which, however pro-LMS one might be, were a quantum leap better than anything running out of Euston or St Pancras. Things were, of course, eventually to change, but Table 5 reveals the extent to which both companies largely set their faces against open stock for at least ten years after the grouping. In the case of the GWR, this attitude applied throughout the whole of the inter-war period as well and it built none at all after the war. The fact is that the GWR always took the view that open stock was not for general service use and in consequence made no long-term or lasting contribution in this arena, which was a pity, for its later excursion stock was more than agreeably founded.

The LNER was not very different in the first decade after 1922 and much of its teak-bodied open stock was for dedicated dining use, including some agreeable semi-open firsts. However, it did issue one design of 'two plus two' open third designated for excursion or 'Tourist' use and thereby hangs one of those delightfully inconsequential little tales which bring such joy to the student of railway carriages. The current and long-accepted descriptive BR coach coding (see page 285) was based on the old LNER system and an open third was classified as TO (Third Open) and assumed to have 2 + 1 seating, since most were originally used for dining. If the seat arrangement was 2 + 2, it was therefore regarded as Tourist stock by the LNER, being described, in consequence, as a Tourist Third Open (TTO). When third became second class in 1956, this then translated to TSO, the now universal description for general service *standard* class open carriages, simply because their seats are arranged 2 + 2. How many, I wonder, realise, when they ride in these parts of the HST 125s or other BR stock of similar ilk, that they are officially classified as Tourists...?

However, the LNER did not multiply this high-density type to any extent and it was only the outside purchase of a few all-steel coaches in 1927 that made even the 1923-32 total of open thirds reach even the modest 142 vehicles which Table 5 reveals. These carriages were the LNER equivalent of the much larger LMS purchase — see page 295 — but did not have anything like the same degree of significance to the parent company at the time. However, unlike the GWR, the LNER did eventually espouse the open carriage to a somewhat greater extent during the 1930s and we shall have cause to come back to them.

Meantime, the LMS continued almost alone with its 'great experiment' in open stock, if thus it may be called, so it must have been slightly surprising in contemporary circles when it, of all companies, chose also to tackle, head on, the almost total conceptual stagnation in the side-corridor field. This must have been most unexpected. It may be a tenable hypothesis that the motive power crisis on the LMS was instrumental in its choosing the 'open' solution to the carriage problem, thus advancing the long-term cause of carriage development in quite a noteworthy way, but weight-saving can hardly have been the prime consideration when, in 1926-7, the LMS decided to make very radical changes in its design of conventional side-corridor carriages by getting rid, once and for all, of the individual side doors to the compartments.

As already indicated, this was no new idea. The GWR, LNWR and NER had all tried it in earlier days to various degrees and without universal acclaim, so it is by no means clear why the LMS, in 1927, chose finally to abandon the use of traditional outside doors on the compartment side of its corridor stock, but the coincidence of date suggests that it had more than a little to do with the growth of commercial rivalry between the LMS and LNER for the Anglo-Scottish trade. This was first revealed in the post-1922 era by the introduction of the 'Royal Scot' locomotives in 1927 and a new train of the same name between London and Scotland — or more correctly, the naming, for quite overt publicity purposes, of the long-established 10.00 am service (see above) as a counterblast to the 'Flying Scotsman' train of the LNER. Hitherto the latter company, with its Gresley 4-6-2 'Pacific' locomotives, had made most of the running, the LMS cause not being in any way helped by the total confusion of purpose in the locomotive department which, for five years, denied it a suitable large locomotive for long-distance work. The 'Royal Scot' 4-6-0s changed all that with their ability to pull heavier trains, and this may have been the key to the new carriage designs.

In strictly carriage terms, if one abandons outside doors in the interest of offering much greater pas-

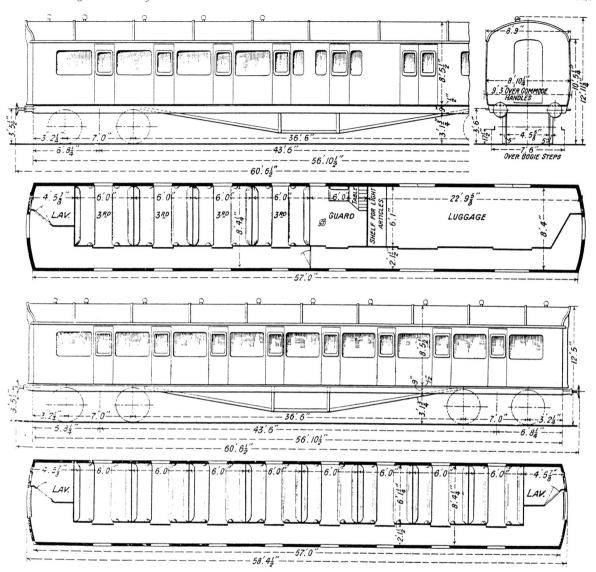

Figure 16 *Even for excursion purposes, the GWR was slow to adopt open stock; these 57-foot bow-ended thirds were its preferred alternative in 1929.*

Scale: $^1/_{10}$" = 1ft

Right *This stylish 48-seat open third No 21308 of 1934 typified most of the earlier traditional teak-bodied LNER open stock in being classed as TO-ie having 2 + 1 seating (see text). It was also a very early LNER example with a welded underframe*

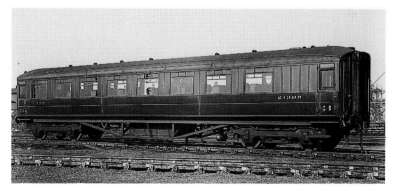

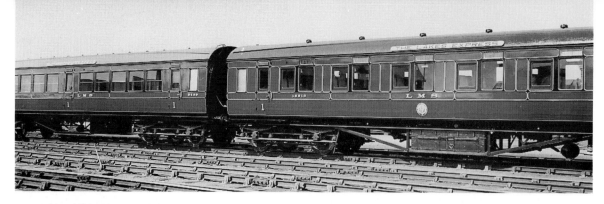

senger amenity, then some form of entrance lobby (or vestibule) has to be provided from which to gain access to the compartments via the corridor. This takes space and, customarily, reduces by one the number of compartments which can be provided in a given carriage length. The carriage weight per seat must therefore increase and this inevitably means a heavier train for the same number of people, whether by virtue of more carriages of a given size or the same number of larger vehicles. Given that the Anglo-Scottish schedules were, by agreement, pegged to something like eight hours, thus preventing the LNER striking back by speeding up its services on a somewhat less adversely graded route, the LMS clearly felt it could gain a worthwhile edge by offering a much better passenger environment than its rival, using its new engines to overcome the inevitable weight penalty.

At first, given the improvements to the third class environment in the form of the open stock already mentioned, the enhancements were confined to the first class passenger in the form of some palatial side-corridors with, rather curiously, 4½ compartments in the brakes but only 5½ in the full firsts; note, by the way, the happy revival of the much loved half-compartment, not that it ever did quite go out of fashion (see Part 1). In exterior styling, the carriages themselves were still rather old-fashioned and

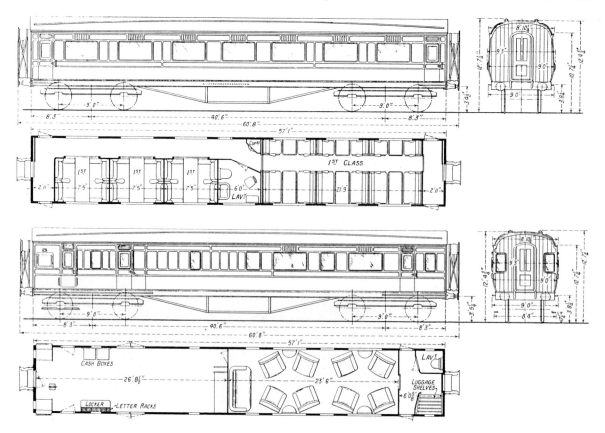

had 'twinned' windows in the compartments, rather in the manner of the now familiar open carriages, but they were soon followed in 1928 by something rather better: a first class semi-open carriage (or 'corridor-vestibule car' as the LMS preferred to style it) with large single picture windows in both the compartments and the dining bays. There were three of the latter, all given the conventional 2 + 1 seating, and they were separated from the three first class compartments by a quite splendid toilet compartment of almost 'powder room' size. But it was the compartments themselves which took the prize, for there were only four seats in each of them; every passenger thus had a corner position and all three compartments were differently trimmed and furnished. When to this is added the fact that the LMS also threw in for good measure a first-class lounge brake with armchairs and settees, picture windows and occasional tables, it will be appreciated that something distinctly new was in the wind.

To this was then added a very agreeable design of 2 + 1 open third class carriage, dedicated to dining purposes and also given large picture windows, and the whole lot rapidly became referred to as the '1928 Royal Scot Stock'. Even though the third class ordi-

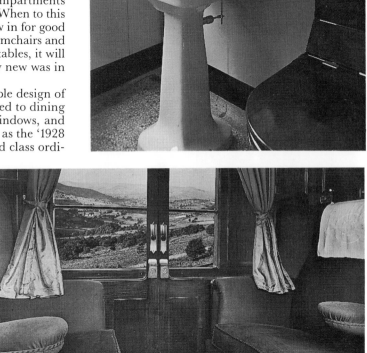

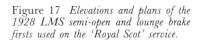

Above left The new LMS carriage ideas were wrapped in very traditional exterior form at first. Here are seen part of corridor first No 3499 (left) and open first No 15913 (right), both of 1927 vintage; but the left-hand carriage had 'twin' windows (rather in the manner of the open first) on its compartment side, and there were only 5½ compartments in its whole length

Figure 17 *Elevations and plans of the 1928 LMS semi-open and lounge brake firsts used on the 'Royal Scot' service.*

Scale: 2mm = 1ft

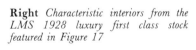

Right *Characteristic interiors from the LMS 1928 luxury first class stock featured in Figure 17*

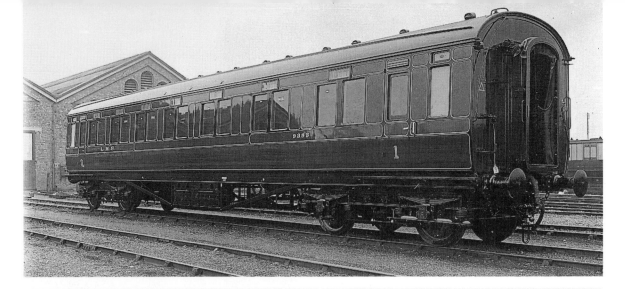

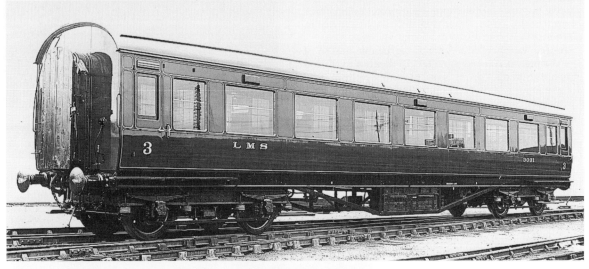

Top *This stylish LMS twin-window corridor composite design No 9383 of 1929 was still rather traditional in body form and construction but much improved in passenger amenity*

Above and left *Further LMS third class improvements in 1930: corridor third No 3031 showing the new low waist and large picture windows (now fitted to both sides of the carriage), and an interior view of a contemporary open third class dining carriage*

Figure 18 'All-steel' corridor brake third to the new 1930 LMS style.

Scale: ¹/₁₀" = 1ft

nary was still partly confined to four per side compartments with outside doors, the signs of change were there, and within two years the LMS went several stages further.

As early as 1929, the third class passenger gained advantage from the new thinking as a result of the introduction of some splendid corridor composite carriages (both brake-ended and orthodox) which combined twin windows in the compartments (and no outside doors) with large picture windows on the corridor side, and these introduced a new 60-foot carriage length to LMS design. In the previous volume, I indicated how the demands of differentially sized first and third class compartments could fight against total standardization of carriage length, and the LMS in 1929-30 seems finally to have accepted that the best solution was to add an extra 3 ft of length to its composites. The net result was to the benefit of everybody.

Only a year later, the LMS made a further stylistic change to its long-distance carriages, this time by lowering the waist level by a few inches and suppressing the separate exterior waist panelling, thus giving the passenger a much improved outlook from the large picture windows and also imparting an altogether more 'svelte' look to its offerings from the outside. The semi-open firsts and the corridor composites and brakes were repeated in this style, as were the open diners — the latter were also enhanced to a 60-foot length; but the lounge brakes gave way to well-appointed brake firsts of conventional compartment style, but still four per compartment, however. These were altogether some of the most stylish carriages ever offered to the non-supplementary passenger at the time and the whole re-appraisal was culminated by giving to the *third* class passenger a 60 ft long side-corridor coach with similar lavish facilities — large

windows, low waist, only seven compartments (each 6 ft 6 in long and designated for six passengers only) and no outside doors. Only two years after it had put the 1928 stock into service, the LMS again re-equipped the 'Royal Scot' train with these new offerings.

To be fair, the LMS did not build too many of these new vehicles at the time, but their speed of conception and introduction puts our own age to shame. When to this is added the fact that, simultaneously, the company was finally moving to a new policy of steel-panelled exteriors — best exemplified by the quite magnificent twelve-wheel sleeping and dining cars of 1930-31 (see Chap. 20) — then it may be appreciated how significant, in retrospect, were these changes. The final flowering of this highly creative period of design evolution was to be witnessed during 1930-2 when the LMS added to its laurels by building some 300 orthodox 2 + 2 open thirds to the new style, this time to the conventional 57-foot length, along with some further outside procurement of all-steel brake firsts and thirds from 'the trade'. In all this rapid development, the credit may justly be given to Reid for first establishing the wherewithal by which it could be achieved, but tribute must also be awarded to his successor, Ernest Lemon, for seeing it through to such a splendid conclusion.

Thus it was that by the time William Stanier arrived on the scene in 1932, and in quite stark contrast to the semi-chaos which existed on the locomotive front, the LMS was exceptionally well placed to take advantage of any 'Wiltshire Wisdom' which the new man might wish to impose in the carriage building field. In the event, all that Stanier seems to have done is to introduce the mostly GWR-inspired 'suspended' gangway and encourage the quick move to

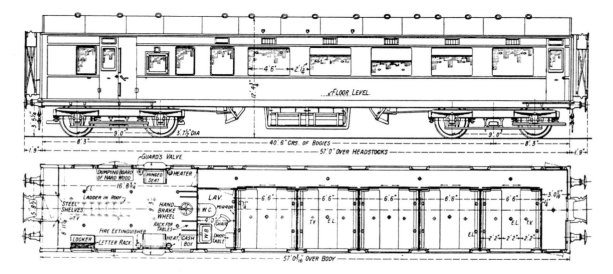

Left *Picture window and superb light-toned woodwork in one of the 1930 LMS brake thirds. Courtesy lights over the seats have also appeared, and the individual armrests soon followed*

Below *This luxury LMS 4½-compartment brake No 2554 was the contemporary 'all-steel' first class equipment of the third class type shown in Figure 18, and appeared in 1931*

totally flush-clad carriage exteriors, including some of their smaller detail points, already well-established at Swindon (see below). The first exemplar of this fusion of ideas was quick to emerge: the quite magnificent Stanier corridor brake composites of 1932, the pioneer carriages built by the LMS in the Stanier era, in which stood revealed all the essential ingredients of the modern long-distance railway carriage. However, before coming on to discuss these carriages, we must first take stock of what was happening elsewhere.

The year 1930 seems to have marked something of a watershed for all the British companies, for if the LMS was the most active, the others were at least beginning to re-assess matters. By now the Southern was well into its stride with its corridor building activities, and its 1930 programme included its own first essay into the open third field which took the form of some rather well thought out carriages with large single windows. Each of the latter was in effect

a frameless droplight and could be lowered in its frame, somewhat in the manner of those fitted to the new generation LMS carriages. The Southern thirds were initially intended to run with first class dining cars — the Southern in pre-Bulleid days never offering a third class kitchen/diner (see Chap. 20) — but they were of 'general service' configuration and over the next few years the SR built rather more of them and their successors than could ever have been needed in the dining mode. Two worthwhile features of their design would do well to have been copied by other railways: the spacious 'L'-shaped entrance vestibules and the very useful luggage 'baskets' which were fixed above all seats. The final pre-war examples, to a new design in 1934, were the first SR coaches to exhibit flush-sided body construction and rounded window corners.

It was the Southern too which made use of that lovely word 'Nondescript' in describing some of its open stock. Two varieties were built, the first, also

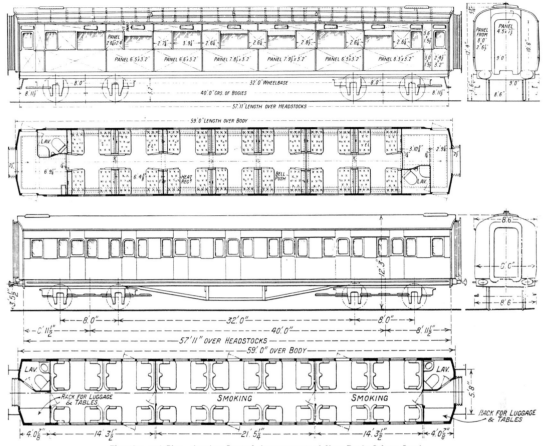

Elevation and Plan, showing General Arrangement of New Bogie Saloon Coach.
NEW BOGIE SALOON COACHES, SOUTHERN RAILWAY.

Figure 19 *Elevations and plans of the first Southern Railway essay in the third class open stock field, the 56-seaters of 1930, and the nondescript saloons of 1931.*

Scale 2mm: 1ft

Right *The well-finished interior of an earlier SR saloon, No 7988 of 1928, seems hardly to justify the description 'nondescript'; it was clearly of first class quality*

termed 'General Saloons', dating from 1928, while a brake-ended version of rather more modern exterior styling appeared in 1933. Both were built to the 8 ft 6 in width for greater availability and embodied a 2 + 1 seating configuration. They were anything but 'nondescript' in quality, being in all vital respects first class in standard, but they had detachable 'class'

boards and were used as second class for the continental boat trains (which retained three class travel) and the brakes were almost exclusively confined to this purpose. The full saloons were even regarded as third class for school use; but then the SR had some very plushy schools in its bailiwick! Both versions had intermediate side doors to some of the seating bays,

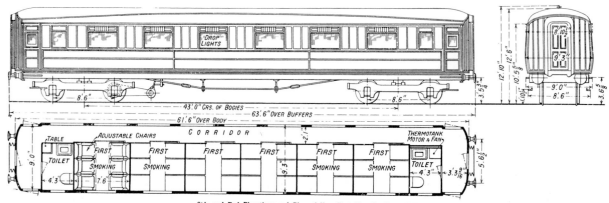

Side and End Elevations and Plan of New First-Class Carriages, L.N.E.R.

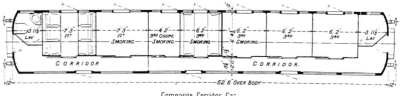

Composite Corridor Car.

Figure 20 *Elevations and plan of the spacious LNER corridor firsts of 1930, together with detailed floor plans of the more traditional 52 ft 6 in long LNER corridor coaches for use on the GE section of the system.*

Scale: 2mm = 1ft

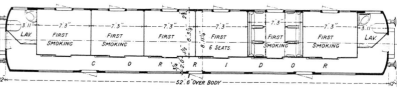

First-Class Corridor Car.

Top right *The one batch of SR brake-ended 'non-descripts' dated from 1933 and were almost wholly used for boat trains. Their large windows where there were no outside doors gave them a more modern look. This crisp official view of No 4448 when new clearly shows the almost flat sides in consequence of their 8 ft 6 in width*

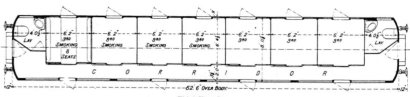

Third-Class Car.

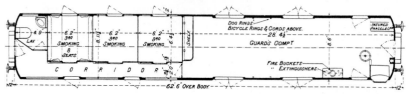

Composite Third-Class Brake Car.

Above right *The much improved look which the suppression of compartment doors gave to LNER stock is well shown in this view of corridor composite No 32386 when new in 1937*

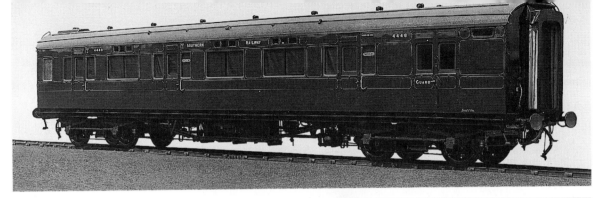

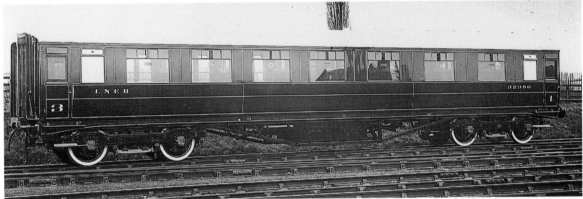

and though only one batch of brakes was ever built, the earlier design was repeated at intervals.

The Southern Railway was not really in serious competition with any other railway save the GWR, and its main-line carriages could now certainly stand favourable comparison with all but the best of those from Swindon, but the same was not true of the LNER in relation to its chief rival, the LMS. Many of its trains connected the same terminal points, and by 1930, though the standard Gresley corridor was still without peer as far as its vehicular quality was concerned, in all other respects it showed the same uninspired standards throughout the 1920s as did all but the latest LMS offerings.

Contemporary sources do not give precise reasons for the subsequent LNER changes which began to emerge from 1930 onwards, but it is hard not to see the competition from the LMS as being partly responsible. What is certain is that in 1930 (first class) and 1932 (third class), the LNER too abandoned side doors on at least some of its new main-line stock in favour of large side windows and entrance lobbies — and some exceedingly handsome vehicles resulted, both inside and out. They were, of course, still fully teak-bodied in the traditional East Coast style, but the new carriages, devoid of the interruptions to the styling consequential upon many outer doors, revealed an exterior elegance which, in the view of this writer, made already good-looking carriages even bet-

ter, and whose visual harmony was rarely bettered.

Nor was it a case, as so often transpired in these matters, of flattering to deceive; the interiors were every bit as good and the first class version, in particular, was just as comfortable as its LMS contemporary. It was also quite definitely more modern in its styling and only suffered in comparison because six people were still seated therein. However, the LMS four-seaters were very thin on the ground and six per compartment was its usual standard, so honours were just about even. This applied to the third class too which, like the latest LMS offerings, also gave a 6 ft 6 in compartment to its patrons with a single large outer window. In due course, brake-ended and composite versions followed in all categories save that of brake composite, and all were built to the new standard 9 ft 3 in width, this having largely superseded the slightly narrower 9 ft dimension which, hitherto, the LNER had built turn and turn about with its slightly wider stock.

There was only one adverse aspect to this welcome change on the LNER; it also chose to retain the 'all-door' alternative and, indeed, it was to be 1936 before any brake thirds to the new style appeared. Furthermore, none of the more modern corridors were ever built to the shorter standard 52 ft 6 in length which the LNER employed very widely in its former GER territory. These remained entirely conventional, being mostly one compartment less in length than their

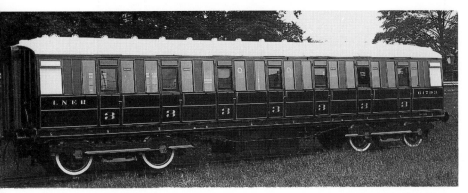

Left *Undoubtedly very smart but equally rather dated: LNER (GE section) 'short' corridor third No 61793 of 1934*

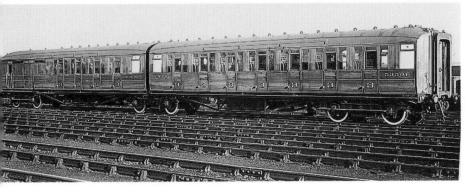

Left and below left *Though dated in concept with their retained outside doors, these two examples of flush-sided steel-panelled LNER stock leave one lost in admiration for the brilliant representation of teak livery achieved by the painters, all the more so since they were finished in August and November 1939 respectively, right on the outbreak of war. They are articulated twin third brake No 53500/1 and composite No 58107, both seen ex-works at York*

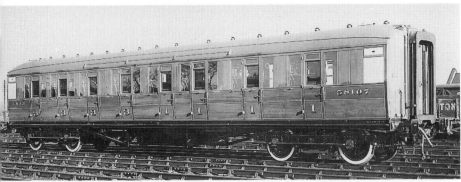

Left *Green and cream LNER 'Tourist' open brake third No 43500, ex-works at Doncaster in 1933*

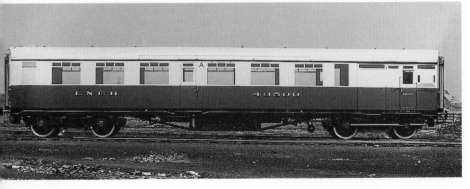

Right *LNER 'Tourist' stock interior, complete with the innovatory but not much loved 'bucket' seats*

61 ft 6 in contemporaries. Thus there never was as much consistency in the accommodation offered in its main long-distance trains as the LMS achieved during the 1930s. Even so, the LNER did build more than a token number of corridor carriages to this new standard, and personal recollection of riding in them brings back happy memories of the relaxed environment they offered, and especially their superb riding quality.

The later 1930s period also marked a somewhat half-hearted LNER attempt to produce steel-panelled main-line stock, teak having increased in cost. All that happened was that steel sheet replaced teak on the outer surfaces of otherwise unaltered designs. This went on intermittently until the war years, but no real attempt was made to re-style the vehicles to suit the new material, and the steel-panelled versions were by no means the most distinguished of the genre, being generally employed on more secondary workings, leaving the main lines almost exclusively in the hands of the orthodox teak carriages. And there such matters rested (save for the celebrated special stock — see Chap. 26) until the end of the teak-bodied era.

At the same time as it began to improve at least some of its side-corridor stock, the LNER also began to adopt the open configuration in the third class to a much greater extent than in its first ten years. As with the LMS, one cannot be certain of the precise thinking which went behind them, but it does seem that their Tourist and excursion potential came high on the list of considerations and, indeed, they came in two forms.

First on to the stage were some dedicated 'Tourist' trains in 1933 which made a serious if not always successful attempt to offer new design thinking in an important new market area, that of competition with the growing road coach excursion business. Their most striking external feature was their bright and cheerful green and cream livery, hitherto associated only with steam railcars (see Chap. 24) and their most innovatory constructional detail was the use of plywood outer panelling. In fact, they were built to something of a budget and lacked the form and comeliness of traditional teak-bodied stock, being devoid of domed roof ends, for example. A full set of them did, however, look rather good, and their external lines gave more than a hint of the soon to emerge special streamlined trains of the later 1930s. The brake ends and buffet cars were single units, but the bulk were built as articulated third class 'twins'. They became popular with the public and further sets, some of the later ones with slight modifications, emerged at intervals until 1939.

Within the vehicles, the interiors were somewhat brightly spartan with much glossy paint and pale-coloured Rexine replacing former wood finishes, and naked lamp bulbs were considered sufficient to illuminate the interiors. There was much use of fashionable chrome-plated fittings, rather in the manner of the best contemporary cinema interior practice, especially in the buffet cars (see Chap. 20) which also had chrome-plated tubular steel chairs of fairly atrocious aspect and comfort! The main seats, however, were distinctly new and clearly reckoned to be of pioneering importance. They were of a semi-bucket type with Alpax legs, and were designed to allow each passenger a seat to himself with, and I quote, '. . .the maximum of room and the greatest comfort'. Would that this had been so. Having got over their novelty value — which did not take long — they were amongst the most diabolically uncomfortable seats which I have ever experienced in a railway carriage, and many were subsequently replaced by more conventional straight-backed versions.

Very similar general service carriages with conventional teak-panelled bodies also emerged during the same time and were given an all but identical interior arrangement, including the dreaded bucket seats which were eventually all replaced. In this case, there were quite a number built to the GE section 52 ft 6 in length. Like the pure 'Tourist' sets, the teak-bodied coaches were mostly used for excursion work and the LNER never used its considerable fleet of

open thirds for pure main-line use to anything like the extent as did the LMS. The teak-bodied examples lasted rather better than the painted carriages, whose plywood panelling gave considerable trouble in later years.

Turning now to the GWR, this company has not received too many plaudits so far in its post-1922 carriage building activities, but it finally began to make forward progress again at almost exactly the same time as the great LMS changes in the side-corridor field already mentioned. Though still regarded as part of the 'Bow-ended' era and not married to any radical re-design of carriage interiors, the new GWR main-line coaches of 1929 and later are noteworthy as being the first British vehicles to embody flush-sided exteriors in recognisably modern form. Even the door handles were recessed, and on its 'Cornish Riviera' stock of 1929-30 the GWR also permitted

itself, for almost the first time since Churchward's huge 'Dreadnoughts' (Chapter 7) to take advantage of its more generous structure gauge and build carriages to a near 9 ft 7 in width. It also extended them to a 60-foot length and this, even allowing for some sterility in terms of interior amenity, gave them a far more spacious look.

The non-kitchen dining cars of this series also embodied large windows with sliding top sections to afford ventilation, and this produced a very pleasing if simple outline. When the GWR then proceeded to put further 9 ft and 9 ft 3 in wide coaches of broadly similar style on to its other services, it did seem for

Figure 21 *Floor plans showing the spacious interior dimensions of the 1929 GWR 'Cornish Riviera' stock.*

Scale: $^1/_{10}$" = 1ft

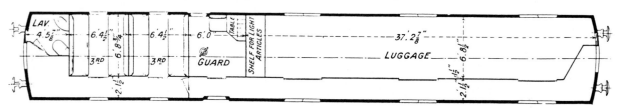

Brake Third Coach.

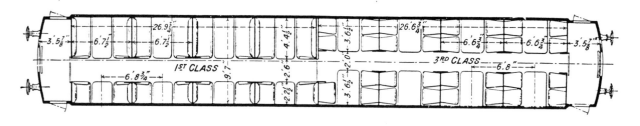

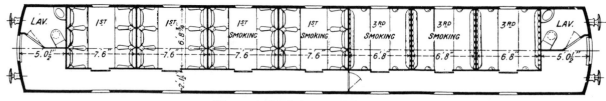

First and Third Composite Coach.

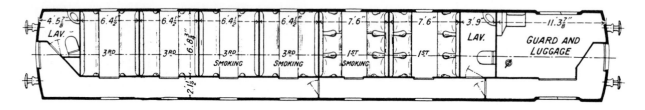

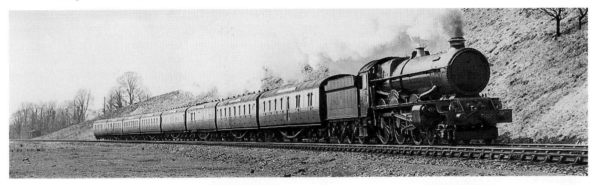

Top *This splendid view of the up 'Cornish Riviera' at Somerton circa 1935, headed by 4-6-0 No 6023* King Edward II *and almost wholly composed of 1929 stock, clearly shows the smooth exterior of this first British flush-sided carriage style and the pronounced widening at the waist which the GWR loading gauge permitted. The particularly clean lines of the dining cars (vehicles three and four) in consequence of their large windows and few doors is especially noticeable. It was, however, rather rare for a GWR train to be visually so neat and tidy at this point in time!*

Above *Stanier's first carriage essay: No 9318, one of the excellent and trend-setting brake composites, ex-works at Wolverton in 1932, in the short-lived but very attractive fully lined livery which was only to survive until 1934 on new stock*

a while as if things had changed. But apart from the dining saloons, a full set of doors on the compartment side was still considered essential, so some of the apparent modernity was lost. Furthermore, from 1933-6 the company then went back to the 57-foot length, reinstated flat ends and stubbornly persisted with 'high-waisted' carriages when other lines, particularly the LMS, were giving the passenger the benefit of a lower window-sill for a better view out. One writer has described them as '. . .probably the most undistinguished of GWR coaches'.*

In several respects, however, the GWR influence was greater than may have been supposed. For one thing, it was simultaneously building some very fine special stock (see Chap. 26) and, perhaps even more important, a considerable infusion of its constructional practices seem to have gone to the LMS in 1932

Great Western Coaches: M.Harris (*ibid*)

in the person of William Stanier. Just as in the case of locomotives, so too in the realm of carriages, it was left to the LMS to develop Swindon's ideas to a far greater extent than on the parent company, and it was not until the late 1930s and 1940s that any degree of re-importation took place. So it is to the LMS that we once again must turn to continue the story.

When William Stanier arrived on the LMS, its newest long-distance stock displayed considerable interior design innovation but was associated with somewhat traditional constructional practices. Stanier seems to have almost instantaneously grafted the best of the new GWR constructional techniques on to the carriages of his new company, and before his first year with the LMS was out, there had emerged the first of what were to become possibly the most familiar outline main-line carriages in the pre-BR MkI era, the pioneering essay being a quite splendid brake composite on a 60-foot chassis.

It set new standards in two quite specific ways. First and most obviously, it established a totally new body construction style of quite definitely modern aspect. The GWR-inspired flush-sided form of bodyside

Figure 22 Elevations and plans, plus typical detail features, of characteristic Stanier corridor stock from 1934 onwards. Note that the contemporary draughtsman put a non-existent rain strip on the carriage roof!

Scale of whole elevations: ¹/₁₆" = 1ft

panelling was married to the already existing LMS espousal of large windows in all its main-line stock to produce a very distinguished-looking ensemble. Even the fact that it was given a fully lined livery suggestive of panelling did not impart a pseudo feeling, and there were many who later wished that Stanier had not moved to the pretty uninspired exterior decoration which became so boringly familiar after 1934! Stanier main-line stock in the more fully lined form always looked good.

Constructionally, apart from the changes consequential upon the use of flush-sided outer panelling, one could also note such 'GWR' touches as 'shell'-pattern roof ventilators, upper window 'sliders', steel sheet roof covering in place of roofboards and canvas, 'suspended'-pattern British Standard gangways and the very practical water-filling pipes which, doubling as end handrails, allowed the water tanks to be filled from platform level by means of a hosepipe, rather than scaling the roof to open the top hatches. The underframe retained all its essential LMS characteristics and Stanier clearly saw no need to change the excellent LMS bogie or the 'Wolverton' lighting system. If there was one fault it was that the LMS chose not to go the 'whole hog' and adopt buckeye couplings and Pullman gangways. Given the sheer weight of numbers of Stanier carriages eventually to be built, it would have been a worthwhile change.

Within the vehicle, the already existing LMS improvements were further refined. The LMS was very much wedded to timber finishes so its compartment interiors remained rather more sombre than some of the newer LNER offerings in this respect,

but this apart, it led the field. First class compartments were variously two or three per side, depending on whether classed as 'luxury' stock, and the thirds were now consistently three per side only and were given the luxury of folding armrests and additional courtesy lights above the seat position; these modifications were also made retrospectively to much of the better older stock. A particularly practical touch was the use of double sliding doors to the corridor which opened wide enough to give more than sufficient space for passengers to manoeuvre their luggage. This idea actually stemmed from the immediate pre-Stanier corridor stock but remained an exclusively LMS feature. Other lines would have done well to copy it and it is a surprising if not very happy thought to recall that the BR standard stock did not copy it either.

With regard to seat and other interior design features, Stanier LMS stock continued the simplification of styles which had first appeared in the 1930-32 era and, at long last, the LMS moved permanently away from the somewhat stodgy upholstery patterns which had hitherto found favour. To be candid, some of the new styles of trimming did not work — especially if they tried to ape too closely the various currently fashionable 'jazz' patterns and the like — but on the whole such a good standard was achieved as to stand the test of time for almost 20 years. The very last Stanier-type corridors did not emerge until the early 1950s — they were hardly changed from those of the early 1930s and they still looked as modern as anything which the other companies had designed later.

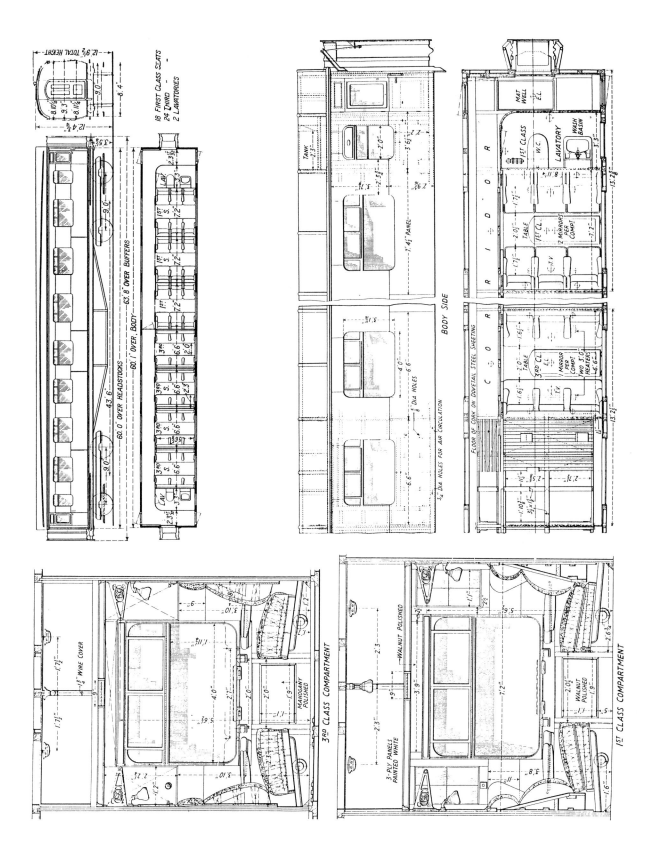

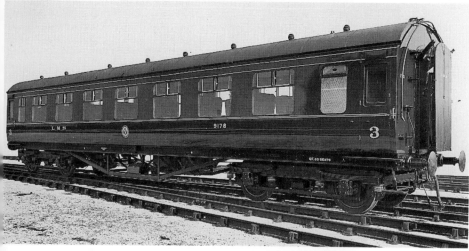

Left *The more typical pattern of sliding window ventilator and the new simplified carriage livery are both seen in this 1936 high-capacity (60-seat) LMS open third No 9178. Note the half bay of seats at the far end of the coach.*

Below left *The favoured 'Empire timber' is well seen in the veneers used in this LMS open third brake interior of 1938. The neat door label (always a feature of LMS coaches of this era) states it to be Indian Laurel in this particular example*

A couple of not much more than cosmetic changes took place quite early in the evolution of the Stanier coach. The first design of single unit sliding upper window section does not seem to have been too effective and quickly gave way to a rather deeper double-opening window slider which afterwards remained standard. Secondly, from late 1934, the LMS adopted, as had the GWR a few years earlier, a much simpler carriage livery in the interests of economy. It did not have the redeeming virtues of the GWR two-colour scheme to make it particularly attractive, but from the passenger standpoint this made no difference to the high quality product that was being offered within its walls.

Stanier carriages were built in all the existing types and, from time to time, half bays (open stock) or coupés (corridor types) were incorporated to make up the vehicle length. The coupés were most usually found in the brake composites, including the first ever examples (see above), but in the pre-war full firsts only 5½ compartments were offered on a 57-foot chassis which, like its pre-1932 predecessor, was wildly extravagant of space. After 1945, a small reduction in compartment size was adopted to give a full six compartment form — a much more logical solution to the problem. This apart and taken overall, the Stanier revolution — and this is not an over-extravagant use of language — was almost completely successful. Having said this, however, it would not be correct to infer that all was sweetness and light after Stanier arrived on the LMS, and one aspect of the Stanier coaching stock era is worthy of further mention; it forms a sort of curious interlude in the generally self-confident evolution of LMS carriage design during the 1932-47 period.

Earlier in the chapter I tried to explain, as best I could, how the LMS made a quite deliberate attempt

Close-up detail of flush-sided Stanier articulated third class open stock of 1937, again with a welded bogie.

to move long-distance travel — especially in the third class — away from the conventional side-corridor style in favour of the open configuration. The Stanier era continued this principle to some extent, but perusal of Table 4 (p. 313) in comparison with Table 5 (p. 324) will reveal that it was only partly successful. During the 1932-9 period, in spite of the huge building of open stock prior to Stanier's arrival, the fact remains that the company still felt it expedient to build more than twice as many side-corridors during his first seven years than were offered in the open style. Yet one senses that the LMS still remained to be totally convinced, for amongst all this it decided to have yet another radical 'go' at open stock and it took the form of a more than experimental flirtation with articulated construction.

In 1936-7, the LMS was still, in spite of its more puissant Stanier locomotives, clearly concerned with weight-saving in terms of carriage building, and even built an experimental brake third with a new type of centrally trussed, lightweight underframe so as to evaluate its new ideas. In the event, the full realization of these thoughts was to achieve fruition in the form of a series of articulated open 'twins' which, collectively, numbered over 100 individual carriage units. Why the open configuration was preferred to the side-corridor form is not at all certain — it probably had something to do with reducing the cost of excursion stock, eg the LNER 'Tourist' experience (see above) — but, by using a 2 + 2 layout the LMS managed to accommodate 112 passengers in a less than 50 ton 'twin pair' of open thirds, compared with the approximately 60 tons which two single unit vehicles with the same capacity would have tared. It is interesting to note, *en passant,* that the design of the BR Mk 1 underframe followed, quite closely, that of these 1937 LMS designs.

Although these new LMS carriages may have originally been mostly intended for excursion use, in due course they found their way into normal workings, an event of far more significance than the somewhat half-hearted effort at non-corridor articulation mentioned in the previous chapter. It also had more than a degree of design spin-off into the radically conceived articulated sets of carriages for the re-vamped 'Coronation Scot' of 1939 (see Chap. 26). It is more than sad that the Second World War intervened at this interesting point in carriage evolution and we can but speculate what the eventual LMS solution might have been. What can be said — and this without any caveat whatsoever — is that the LMS, before the war, does seem to have been addressing the carriage business with a far greater degree of thoroughness than any of its rivals.

Given this virtual revolution in carriage design by the LMS, it remains a source of some surprise that the other companies did not copy it until very much later, but the LNER, as has been noted, made some move in the direction of the LMS approach to matters. This was by no means whole-hearted, but did copy the LMS to the extent of putting armrests and courtesy lights in the third class (whether with outer doors or no) and again, like the LMS, made some modifications of like kind to older stock. The Southern, however, never offered side-corridor stock with picture windows in the compartments, nor did it offer three per side in the thirds (save in restricted dimension stock) and never with armrests. Its final pre-war offerings were in the fashionable flush-clad idiom, superficially quite modern looking, but most certainly not revolutionary in quality. In fact, the Southern's move to flush-sided carriages was hesitant, interrupted by a curious short-lived period wherein all the screw heads fixing the outer steel sheets were

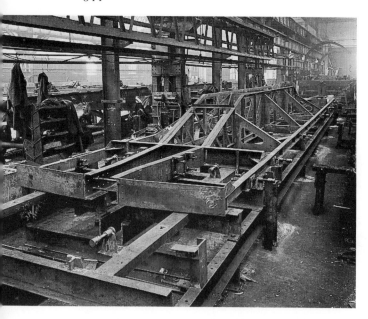

left rather prominently visible. The Southern built no new corridor stock after 1936 until the post-war Bulleid era when it did eventually move to the more modern style, more or less coincidentally with the similar adoption of more modern carriage designs by the LNER and GWR as well.

Meantime, what of the latter company? Its best pre-war contributions were, without doubt, the 'Centenary' and 'Special' stock (see Chap 26), but in the later 1930s it finally recognized some of the new thinking in its so-called 'Sunshine' corridor stock of 1936 which finally suppressed the outside doors in favour of end entrances only and low-waisted configuration. Stylistically, and stripped of GWR livery and bogies, they might well have been cloned from Stanier via Derby or Wolverton, save that they never had three-per-side thirds. A few years later, however,

there was a modest reinstatement of corridor-side doors, and in some of the later examples one compartment reverted to the outer door style, presumably to speed up the boarding and leaving of vehicles at intermediate points. These styles became, in effect, the design basis for the post-war GWR carriages.

Slightly before this modest move forward, the GWR had introduced its first recognizably 'modern' carriages in the form of its final series of open stock, again classified for excursion use, though they were undoubtedly also used for summer relief workings as well. Designed for use with intermediate kitchen cars with an implicit promise of 'meals at all seats' (did it actually happen, one wonders?), the early examples had nice big drop windows while later examples were given double sliding top sections much in the fashion of Stanier's LMS or the GWR's own 'Sunshine' stock, but the ledges of the windows were retained at an old-fashioned higher level, thus impeding the view to some extent. They were roughly contemporary with the LNER Tourist sets but rather better furnished. Lamps had shades, for example, and the interiors, though still light and airy, did not entirely eschew the use of wood finishes. Very much in the Art Deco idiom, a particularly nice touch was the low-backed seating which would undoubtedly permit passengers a better view across the aisle, but there were insufficient of them to make an appreciable impact on general GWR philosophy.

Thus, but for these well-recorded exceptions, the LMS gradually moved itself well ahead of the competition in the long distance carriage field and Table 6 attempts to show how dominant it became. Bearing in mind that of its more than 5,000 side-corridors, only some 750 had outside doors to the compartments and well over 4,000 were to the Stanier pattern, then its leading role is quite clear. Even allowing that it would always hold the primacy in absolute numbers simply by virtue of its larger size, it is still worth noting that its new gangwayed coaches represented some

Table 6 Gangwayed coaches: new build, all types 1923-53

Note: This table summarises the data in Tables 4, 5 and 9 (Chapter 14). The latter gives a full analysis of the post-war continuation.

Company	Corridor stock			Open stock			Grand total
	Pre-war	Post-war	Sub total	Pre-war	Post-war	Sub total	
LMS	3182	2067	5249	2515	370	2885	8134
LNER	2515	830	3345	1029	42	1071	4416
GWR	2402	495	2897	131	—	131	3028
SR	1316	494	1810	242	350	592	2402
Totals	9415	3886	13301	3917	762	4679	17980

45 per cent or more of all new British main-line stock built during the final 30 years or so of pure company designs as opposed to its only some 40 per cent share of the total British carriage fleet in 1923. Table 6 includes for completeness the post-war carriages built by all four companies and again the LMS dominates. However, to maintain some element of chronology to the story, these will not be covered until the final chapter.

But if the LMS was absolutely dominant in the general service 'ordinary' field, there was a rather greater parity of achievement in the realm of the more specialized carriage stock during the 'Big Four' period, and to some of these vehicles we must now turn our attention.

Left *A new type of 'lightweight', centrally-trussed mostly welded underframe under construction at Derby in 1936 for the LMS articulated sets. Note the far lighter solebar sections.*

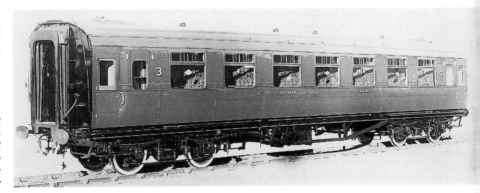

Right and below right *These two views of Southern open thirds Nos 1311 and 1450 of 1935 and 1936 respectively show how a somewhat half-hearted attempt at flush-sided treatment quickly gave way to a rather more conventional form with visible window frames. Honesty compels one to admit that in this case, the older concept was of rather more handsome aspect.*

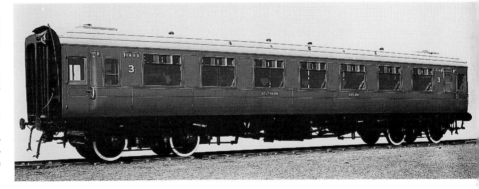

Below *This fine view of the up GWR 'Bristolian' somewhere between Bristol and Filton Junction circa 1936-7, headed by 4-6-0 No 6014* King Henry VII, *is of especial interest in showing how very stylish an almost complete train of the newly introduced 'Sunshine' coaches could look, compared with the previous high-waisted form, here represented solely by the 'quick lunch' buffet car (see page 369), halfway down the formation. The engine still carries some of the absurd streamline fairings fitted in 1935 (see page 482)*

20. Sleeping and dining car development

The fundamental characteristics of railway sleeping and dining cars had been well established during the pre-group period and they changed but little afterwards; there was no real need in most cases since the ideas were soundly based in the first place. The post-grouping period was therefore mostly one of consolidation and improvement rather than outright innovation. Having said that, however, the period in question was also full of great interest, not least in the sheer number of such vehicles built after 1922. This latter point is even more surprising when one considers both the large number of generally quite modern overnight and catering vehicles which the 'Big Four' had inherited and, in many cases, their long revenue life thereafter. It was, for instance, not at all unusual for pre-group examples to outlast the company period itself, albeit by then somewhat relegated in terms of service status.

Table 7 attempts to summarize the situation for the post-1922 'new' build of 'mobile hotel' vehicles, and two basic points should be made. Firstly, the grand total was high in absolute terms and secondly, expressed as a fraction of all new carriages, it represented some 3.5 per cent of the total. This may not

Table 7 Sleeping and dining cars: new build, 1923-52

Notes: 1. These values have been extracted from various published works and may show odd discrepancies from other sources. This should not affect their value for comparative purposes.
2. It should be appreciated that much of the post-war build in these categories took place after the nationalisation of the British railway system in 1948.
3. Individual elements of articulated 'sets' are counted as one unit.

Company/Style	Sleeping cars				Dining/Kitchen cars						Grand Total
	SLF	SLC	SLT	Total	RF	RC	RT	RK	RB	Total	
LMS/1923-32 standard	52	12	85	149	24	18	—	73	1	116	265
LMS/Stanier, 1933-1939	26	13	15	54	20	13	44	35	4	116	170
LMS/Stanier, 1945 on	25	—	25	50	1[1]	—	—	—	—[2]	1[1]	50
Sub totals	103	25	125	253	44	31	44	108	5	232	485
LNER/Gresley (to 1933)	33	11	46	90	27	—	4	10	12[3]	53	143
LNER/Gresley (from 1934)	16	3	—	19	22	16	7	4	37	86	105
LNER/Thompson	5	—	17	22	13	—	—	11	2	26	48
Sub totals	54	14	63	131	62	16	11	25	51	165	296
GWR/1930-34	9	1	15[4]	25	10	15	—	13	9	47	72
GWR/1934-40	—	—	—	—	4	5	—	10	9	28	28
GWR/Hawksworth	4	—	—	4	—	—	—	—	—	—	4
Sub totals	13	1	15	29	14	20	—	23	18	75	104
SR/Non standard	—	—	—	—	—	—	8	—	—	8	8
SR/Maunsell	—	—	—	—	46	—	—	—	—	46	46
SR/Bulleid	1[5]	—	—	1	—	—	11	—	8[6]	19	20
Sub totals	1	—	—	1	46	—	19	—	8	73	74
Grand totals	171	40	203	414	166	67	74	156	82	545	959

[1] Rebuilt former pre-war carriage.
[2] Many old sleeping/kitchen/dining cars in old LMS series were rebuilt to this form in early BR days.
[3] Including 'Tourist' stock.
[4] Two were later converted to corridor third, one to SLC.
[5] Not for general service, classified Inspection Saloon
[6] Tavern Cars, later converted to RKB (ie. Kitchen and Buffet).

Table 8 Comparative analysis of ordinary and special stock

Company	All stock[1]		Specialized stock[2]					
			Sleeping		Dining		All special stock	
	Total	per cent	Total	per cent	Total	per cent	Total	per cent
LMS	16354	40.8	253	61.1	232	42.55	485	50.6
LNER	11567	28.9	131	31.65	165	30.3	296	30.9
GWR	6318	15.8	29	7.0	75	13.75	104	10.8
SR	5791	14.5	1	0.25	73	13.4	74	7.7
Totals	40030	100	414	100	545	100	959	100

[1] 1947 values used for comparison (see Table 2).
[2] Post-1922 builds as a proportion of all stock owned. If pre-group vehicles are added, LMS/LNER dominance is increased.

at first glance seem very high, but when one considers the thousands of non-corridor carriages included in those totals which could never run with sleeping or catering carriages anyway, the matter takes on a somewhat different perspective. When expressed as a proportion of new *gangwayed* stock — perhaps a more reasonable comparator — the figure rises to over 5 per cent and even this is still probably misleading since, like non-corridor carriages, much gangwayed ordinary stock was used for services devoid of 'hotel' facilities.

A more realistic assessment of the figures might therefore be that up to 10 per cent of the principal main-line stock was of the specialized kind, and this would certainly be true if one added to the tabulated totals the hundreds of non-kitchen open coaches used for dining purposes. In fact, it is this latter aspect alone which explains why the sleeping car total is almost as big as the catering fleet; the latter only includes carriages which had cooking facilities as part of their make-up.

It is thus readily apparent that the railways, in spite of the higher unit cost of specialized vehicles, felt obliged to provide them in some abundance, and the rationale for their construction can only be explained in terms of meeting the increased competition from other modes of transport combined with a greater public expectation of what ought to be provided. One doubts not that the four railways of the final company years were just as aware of the deadweight and potential non-revenue earning characteristics of these vehicles as is their BR successor! This, perhaps, merits a little more explanation.

Sleeping and dining vehicles are heavier, passenger for passenger, than ordinary stock and their capacity for revenue generation is therefore not as high per ton weight as a conventional day carriage. A typical twelve-wheel sleeping car of the inter-war period, for example, would weigh 40 tons or more yet only accommodate maybe 12 berths. These would, addi-

tional to the fares paid, only earn the equivalent in supplementary berth charges of a few more passengers in normal seats at standard fare; and the carriages stood idle for over half the day anyway! One orthodox corridor carriage (of whatever class) could earn as much revenue as at least two sleeping cars. Much the same is true of dining vehicles. In this case, the traditional car was 100 per cent deadweight, save for the profit from meal service, since the passengers were most usually accommodated elsewhere in the train. Small wonder that the LMS (probably the most cost-conscious of them all) felt it expedient to offer meals at seats with a kitchen-only car somewhere in the train (see page 323)

All things considered, therefore, it is remarkable how lavish were the provisions made for what can, at best, have been only a marginally profitable operation, and at worst a heavy loss-maker. But the railways were clearly convinced (as indeed to a lesser extent is the BR management of the present time) that travellers will pay due regard to 'on train' facilities in making the fundamental decision whether to travel by rail at all. For this reason, the railways continued to build their mostly magnificent dining and sleeping cars — and glad we should be that they did. In fact, it is not too far off the mark to state that it was in this field that most of the more interesting developments, both in terms of interior amenity and vehicle technology, first began to appear.

Hardly surprisingly, the two bigger long-distance companies led the field both in quantity and quality and, as with gangwayed stock in general, the LMS led the way with over 50 per cent of the total, a rather higher proportion than was true for its coaching stock taken overall (see Table 8). The LNER too had a higher than expected quota of these vehicles; but perhaps the most revealing is the low proportion represented in the GWR and SR fleets. In the latter case, the absence of sleeping cars — save for Mr Bulleid's one-off 'maverick' (see page 532) — and the

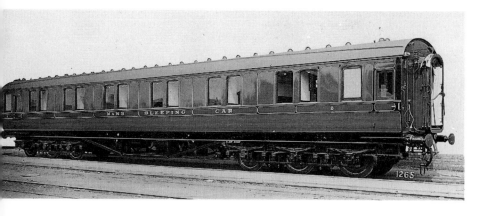

Left *The first generation LMS sleeping cars are well exemplified by this 1927 example, M & NB No 2. Ownership markings apart (see text), it was to the pure LMS pattern and painted in LMS colours*

Figure 23 *Comparative floor plan diagrams of LNER single unit and articulated twin sleeping cars.*

presence of Pullman on the catering side are, no doubt, much of the explanation, but what of the GWR? Overall, though owning more than half as many coaches as the LNER and approaching 40 per cent of the LMS total, it possessed but 35 and 21 per cent respectively of their specialized fleets.

One should not make too much of statistics — they can only reveal facts and not causes — but the variation in the figures quoted does seem to reveal something about the different characteristics of the four post-grouping railways. On the whole, it seems likely that the high LMS/LNER values were in part caused by their mutual competition for much of the traffic to the Midlands, North of England and Scotland, whereas the GWR had more of a monopoly in its hinterland, save 'at the edges', so to speak. There was therefore probably some element of over-provisioning on the LMS and LNER (for competitive reasons?) which was not felt to be needed by the GWR. The latter company also had more holiday traffic (as, indeed, did the SR) which clearly would not warrant very much catering provision in the traditional form.

But whatever the precise reasons, there was less difference in carriage quality between the coaches which were built than might be supposed from the unevenness of the totals quoted. Sleeping and dining cars were always the type of vehicles which gave railways publicity and status, especially on their more celebrated trains and all four companies made significant forward steps during the period in question. Some ideas were more far-reaching than others, and a few bordered on the ridiculous, but they were rarely without interest.

Sleeping cars

In all seriousness, there were really only two significant sleeping car companies during the 'Big Four' period, the LMS and the LNER, and both were rather good at it, though in very different ways at first. Towards the end of their independent existence —

and indeed the design and construction spilled over into early BR days — there was a great deal of coming together of ideas, and this proved to be both influential and fortuitous when it came to designing the first generation BR standard sleeping cars of the 1950s. In effect, the LMS and LNER had done most of the hard work!

The traditional British sleeping car layout (side-corridor giving access to a series of compartments with berths set transversely to the longitudinal axis) never varied during the whole of the grouping period, but the individual LMS and LNER solutions to it were often quite different in fundamental structural terms, especially in the first class arena. This, of course, was the only type existing in 1923 and it was not until 1928 that the overnight third class patron got his shout. Interestingly, it was the need to meet this eventuality which caused the first convergence of ideas between the two main companies...but back to 1923.

In this year, the inherited LMS sleeping car tradition was dominated by the two English giants, the LNWR and Midland, for reasons given in Volume 1. But it was really no contest, for the LNWR had far more experience of the business than had the MR and, unlike most things during early LMS days, the LNWR's ideas were to prevail. This resulted in a quick standardization of the 68-foot twelve-wheel car, based on final Wolverton LNWR practice; in fact, Wolverton Works built every single first class twelve-wheel sleeping car constructed to LMS design. The first ones even looked mostly like LNWR carriages and a few even had LNWR rather than the new LMS standard bogies, though they all made use of the new angle-trussed underframe. They had handsome, conventionally timber-built bodies and their panelling, save for a modest bit of deepening at the waist to more Midland-like proportions, was pure 'Wolverton'. Dozens were made down to 1930 and the later examples saw some important internal changes.

Within the cars, 12 single first class berths was normal, some having interconnecting (lockable) doors to make double berths if needed. The lavatories and attendant's compartment completed the assemblage and the first series had ponderously heavy interior treatment, mostly in the form of seemingly endless acres of traditional mahogany panelling from floor to cornice. They were, needless to say, magnificently appointed, their ride quality was without peer and they were wonderfully well finished, but they were rather old-fashioned.

In the later series, the LMS improved the interiors by painting the walls above the dado in white enamel and, in the final batches, began to fit the now-familiar corner washbasins in place of the older fold-away type. The company also coved the floor angles (see p. 302) to facilitate cleaning. All of them were given more than adequate heating, and individual electric fans supplemented the conventional ventilation. One interesting small point was the fitting of frameless droplights to the compartment and the provision of vertical 'rolling' shutters rather than conventional window blinds to give, as it was said, '...a general appearance of warmth and cosiness...' One rather interesting aspect of this long-lived series of cars (most lasted well into the early 1960s) was that a pair of them were built in 1927 for the M & NB joint stock for service between St Pancras and Edinburgh. This stock was not formally divided between the LMS and LNER until 1928, and the LNER got one of them in its share of spoils. It was fairly swiftly transferred back to LMS stock!

Almost at the end of the building period of this style of car, in 1929, the LMS equipped one of them with a new type of ventilation system known as the 'Thermotank' apparatus. This was a fan-driven air circulation system, driven by a 250 watt electric motor fed from the 24-32 volt carriage lighting circuit. This served each compartment through a 'Punkah' louvre from a roof level air duct installed below the corridor ceiling. It could be arranged either to deliver fresh air or extract stale air from the compartment, and the compartment louvre — which was under passenger control — could also be swivelled to direct the air over a wide area. Its capacity was 40 cubic feet per minute per berth and the passenger could, if desired, close it off completely. It proved a remarkably successful idea and became the basis of the method which was designed into the later LMS and BR standard sleeping cars right until the Mk III era.

No less comfortable than these opulent but somewhat dated sleeping cars — and arguably more technically innovative — were some of the contemporary LNER offerings wherein, of course, the hand of Nigel Gresley was to be seen at work. In 1923, the LNER — no doubt influenced by cost and weight consider-

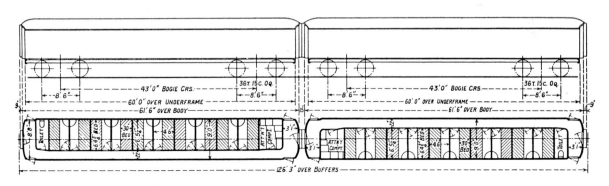

Diagram giving proportions of Two Single Unit Sleeping Carriages.

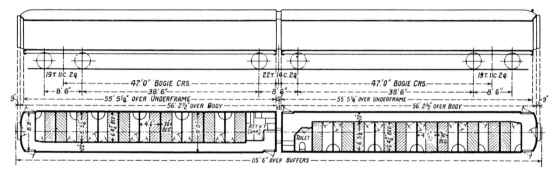

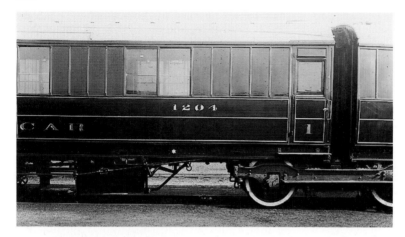

Close-up detail of LNER twin sleeper first No 1204/5 of 1926, taken in 1930 when the set was fitted with the shower compartment (whose door is just visible through the window) in place of one berth, so as to match the later single unit series — see text

Compartment-side elevation of LMS third class sleeping car No 14247. Along with the LNER equivalents (see Figure 24), these were the first of any post-grouping third class side-corridor carriages to dispense with outer compartment-side doors

Figure 24 *Elevation and plan of LNER third class sleeping car of 1928; the LMS version was identically arranged.*

Scale: $^1/_{10}$" = 1 ft

ations — set in motion an interesting comparison between single unit and articulated sleeping car pairs. The individual vehicles were ten-berth carriages on a standard eight-wheel underframe and conceptually no different from the LMS examples, save that their shorter length was reflected in their smaller carrying capacity. The twins, however did make quite a weight saving. Each half still had ten births, but length and weight were saved both by articulation and by only offering one toilet and one attendant's compartment, each now serving 20 berths. The basic arrangement is given in the appended drawings and it gave a nearly 8 per cent length reduction and an almost 16 per cent weight advantage compared with two single cars. The problem was that they could not be operated unless a destination required at least 20 berths to be offered. Many did not, so there was still a need for the single unit type; but the twin sleepers remained a characteristic feature on the East Coast route for many a long year.

Outwardly, the new LNER sleeping cars showed even less change from pre-group days than did those of the LMS, being solidly in the GNR tradition as

would be expected, but in purely interior terms they were marginally better in that they had corner wash-basins and white enamel paint above the dado from the outset. There seems little doubt that in this respect the LMS may have copied the LNER. But this 'anything you can do' attitude was quite characteristic of these two great companies during this period and the traffic in ideas was by no means one way. Thus the LNER, in 1929, copied the idea long used by the LMS when it substituted sliding window shutters for blinds and curtains, but the LNER shutters slid horizontally, were each panelled to match the compartment interiors and had auxiliary louvres opposite those in the windows themselves.

Likewise, the LNER began to experiment with 'forced' ventilation of its sleeping cars in 1929. It called it 'Pressure Ventilation' and according to *The Railway Engineer*, the system was developed by J Stone & Co rather than by Thermotank Ltd as on the LMS. However, another source states the system to have been of 'Thermotank pattern'* and the mode of oper-

---

* *Gresley's Coaches*, M.Harris, David and Charles, 1973

ation was identical; no doubt each company made full publicity value out of its 'different' system!

In one respect, however, the LNER was more adventurous than its LMS rival: water heating. Here, after experiments involving keeping pre-heated water warm by using the train lighting circuits, Gresley managed to install what amounted to a totally self-contained water heating system in sleeping cars by fitting a supplementary belt-driven generator and storage cells, fully independent of the lighting system. This added weight but eliminated the need for the use of oil gas water heating. The LNER was more keen than the LMS in ridding itself of oil gas for heating and conducted considerable experiments in both the sleeping and dining car field in pursuance of this aim (see below). Meantime, large gas tanks for heating were always to be found below the floors of LMS twelve-wheelers.

Honours were, therefore, just about even between the LMS and LNER during the 1920s and remained so during the 1930s, but before resuming the story of first class developments on the two principal railways, we must first turn to the introduction of third class sleeping cars and also catch up with the GWR contribution to the story, such as it was!

On 24 September 1928 — and in a spirit of harmony between the railway companies — the GWR, LMS and LNER simultaneously introduced the final phase in the emancipation of the ordinary traveller (which had begun so long ago with the nineteenth century Midland Railway) when they offered proper sleeping cars to third class passengers. As usual, the two northern companies led the way both in terms of concept and quantity and each offered what amounted to an identical vehicle, an eight-wheeler on a 60-foot underframe, the LNER examples being

61 ft 6 in over body because of their bow ends, of course. Within these new carriages, layouts were identical: seven compartments to which access was gained from end entrance lobbies, each of which also had access to lavatory and toilet.

In both cases compartments were 6 ft 4 in between partitions, neither type had outside compartment doors and both of them featured two quarterlights flanking a central frameless droplight on the compartment side, combined with large picture windows on the corridor side. Within the compartments, a convertible arrangement was offered with four berths at night, the upper ones folding against the partition by day to produce a fairly orthodox side-corridor third with eight seats per compartment. Pillows and rugs were provided for night use at a modest supplement, 6s (30p) or 7s (35p) per passenger depending on the distance travelled.

They were uncommonly handsome vehicles and proved deservedly popular, so much so that repeat orders were soon forthcoming by both companies, the LMS, as usual, building about twice as many as the LNER. It seems likely, in view of their striking similarity, that there must have been some sort of collaboration between the two companies in terms of their design. Happily, a fully restored LMS example from the very first batch is preserved at the NRM.

Meantime, the first GWR offering was rather different and consisted of but three carriages which did not display much imagination compared with the new LMS and LNER carriages. They followed the customary 'bow-ended' stylistic practice, having eight compartments without entrance vestibules; but only three had the convertible berth arrangement with no outside compartment doors, pretty well identical to the LMS and LNER versions. The remaining five

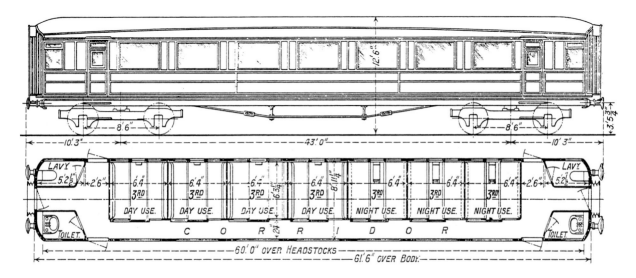

*This view of an up GWR express at Somerton circa 1935 behind
4-6-0 No 4097* Kenilworth Castle *shows a very characteristic
mixture of GWR carriage styling, dominant amongst which is the
bulging profile of the leading first class sleeping car and the similar
profile of the third class version at vehicle No 3. For the record,
other identifiable types are the three 'Sunshine' corridor coaches in
the middle of the train and a 'Dreadnought' diner, third from the
rear. Unfortunately the train itself is not identified*

compartments were arranged very conventionally
with day seats only and outside doors. On the corridor side, long lights alternated with outside doors
save at the sleeping end, where there were simply
droplights in place of doors. In 1935, the GWR
brought this experiment to an end when it converted
two of them to orthodox corridor thirds, the odd man
out becoming a composite sleeping car.

Clearly, the GWR had been over-cautious and only
a few months later, in 1929, its own genuine third
class sleeping cars on the LMS/LNER pattern began
to emerge. There were only nine of them but they
were much better than the original trio. For one thing,
they made full use of the generous GWR structure
gauge and were given bulging sides in order to
lengthen the berths slightly. They also had recessed
end entrance doors, and in these two respects they
also set the pattern for the few first class sleeping cars

which the GWR built during the grouping period.
Three further third class sleepers with rather more
restricted dimensions for cross-country working were
built in 1934.

In 1930 and 1931, coincidental with the bulging-
side third class cars, the GWR introduced the only
first class sleeping cars built by the company proper
between 1923 and 1947. Again nine only in total, their
appearance almost exactly matched that of the third
class carriages, save that they had six-wheel bogies
to carry the extra weight, and they were by no means
ill-looking vehicles in a ponderous sort of way. But
their ten-berth interiors were stodgy in the extreme
and not as good as even the most conservative of the
first post-1923 LMS offerings, leave alone the better
ideas which both it and the LNER were actively pursuing by this time.

In fact, despite William Dean's fine pioneering
work in late Victorian times (Chapter 11), the subsequent GWR contribution to twentieth century British sleeping car development was minimal to

*Until purpose-built composite sleeping cars were introduced, the
two-class form was usually first class sleeping plus third class
ordinary. This LNER example No 10207J, built in 1925, was
typical. The 'J' suffix denoted East Coast main line allocation*

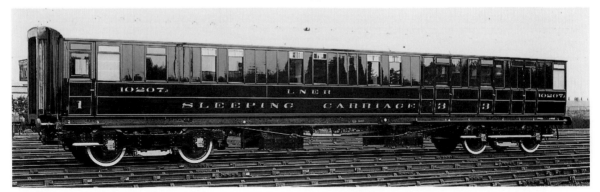

Figure 25 *Elevations and plan of the LMS composite sleeping carriages of 1930 and 1931. In later years, part of the compartment immediately to the left of the first class section was converted into a third lavatory (for the first class section only) by inserting a partition where a pecked line is marked and moving the corridor door into line with it. At the same time, the remaining 14 convertible third class berths were altered to a fixed arrangement.*

Scale: ¹/₁₀″ = 1 ft

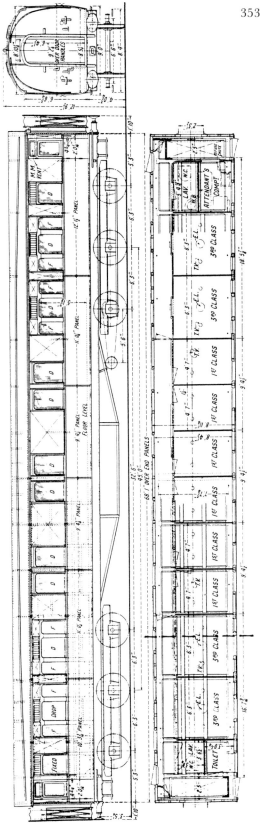

non-existent. Apart from a couple of equally unexciting composites (the above-mentioned conversion and one further example to the bulging-side style), the only other sleeping cars built to GWR design after its final trio of third class carriages in 1934 were four first class examples to the Hawksworth pattern in 1951, after nationalisation. These were ten-berth twelve-wheelers, like their predecessors, but it is a sad measure of the generally uninspired situation at Swindon in this particular field that these were the first and only GWR-design sleeping cars to have air conditioning in any form — and even this was only pressure ventilation of the kind introduced by the LMS and LNER more than 20 years previously! So it is to these two companies that we must turn again to round out the British sleeping car story.

It is not too surprising that after the introduction of proper third class sleeping cars, there should also develop a demand for a composite pattern which would offer both classes of sleeping accommodation to many of the destinations served by the railways which did not warrant more than one through carriage. In this respect, the LMS took the lead in 1930 — probably because it had rather more of such destinations — in the form of some quite splendid twelve-wheelers in which one could also discern the last fling of pure 'Wolverton'(LNWR) as opposed to LMS standard styling. It was by now the start of the LMS steel-panelled era so these new cars were devoid of external beading, but their window style and general configuration harked back to LNWR days and their layout was both logical and well-balanced: six conventional first class berths in the centre (between the bogies), flanked by two convertible third class compartments on each side. Fully lined out, they were a considerable credit to the company. They were later modified to fixed berth arrangement in the third class and lasted until the 1960s.

Meantime, the contemporary LNER composite contribution was rather muted, taking the form of a single vehicle (for the former M & NB service) plus, perhaps inevitably, a pair of articulated twins, each half first and half third class, (one of the compartments from a third class portion is beautifully preserved at the NRM). But if the LNER was slow to follow the LMS lead in terms of numbers (it built very few composites even in later years), it most certainly set the pace in terms of better amenity inside

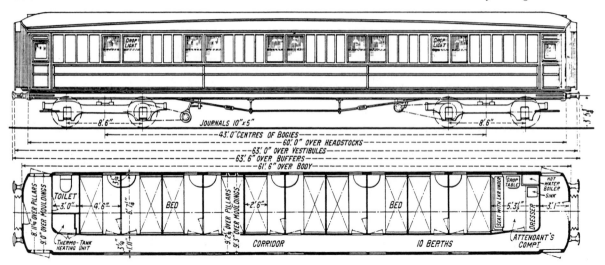

the cars themselves. As early as 1931, a clutch of dedicated thirds (ie non-convertible with fixed berths) was built on a new 65-foot design of underframe. This permitted eight compartments, all of which were given much more lavish facilities including mirrors, individual bedhead lights and coathooks, while a supply of filtered drinking water was a very welcome addition.

Even before this, however, in 1930, the LNER had taken further important steps forward in terms of compartment comfort in the first class. These were to banish forever the somewhat dated and at times gloomy interiors of most British sleeping cars to date. It would seem that Messrs Waring and Gillow were called in to decorate the berths in two of these cars

and decided upon a totally new-style painted finish of light colour (blue was chosen). This had the effect of making the berths seem more spacious and henceforth became the standard LNER treatment. In spite of their internal modernity, these 1930 carriages were still mounted on the standard 60-foot underframe with turnbuckle trussing, and it was not until 1932 that the newly introduced 65-foot chassis was used beneath first class sleeping cars; it was this new length of underframe which caused the LNER to adopt the more modern angle-trussed form for all stock.

Within these new 65-foot first class cars, the LNER did not, as might other railways, add an extra berth to the layout; instead it fitted a shower cubicle, the

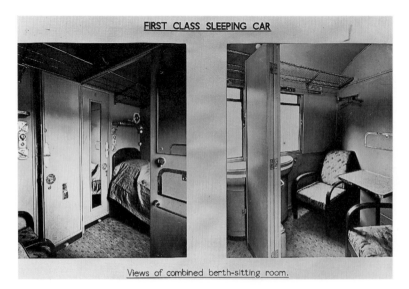

FIRST CLASS SLEEPING CAR

Views of combined berth-sitting room.

Figure 26 *Elevation and plan of a typical LNER first class sleeping car of 1930.*

Scale: $^1/_{10}$*" = 1 ft*

Left *The new and lighter-toned interior decor of LNER sleeping cars based on Rexine finishes is seen to good advantage in this posed publicity view of a combined berth and sitting room in twin sleeping car No 1156/7 of 1932*

Above right *Compartment-side view of LMS fixed berth third class sleeping car No 585 of 1933. This was the prototype which toured in North America with* Royal Scot *(see text)*

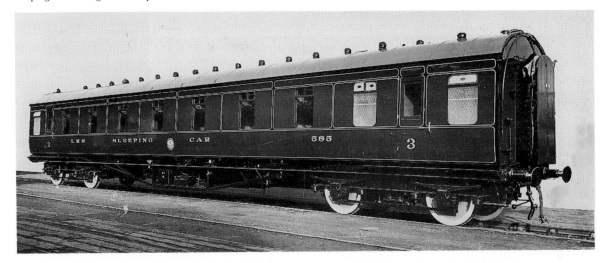

first such example in a British sleeping car. The 1934 examples in the same idiom were even better and a fine model of one of them may be seen at the NRM. However, despite the changes wrought by the LNER in terms of interior design and amenity, the cars themselves somewhat belied their modern nature by still maintaining a traditional panelled teak finish, handsome though it was, and it was left to the LMS (as in the general service arena) to put a properly modern interior into a vehicle whose exterior also indicated an up-to-date approach to the subject. The instigator was, of course, William Stanier.

Interestingly, the first beneficiaries were the third class travellers when in 1933 the LMS introduced what were undeniably some of the most handsomely styled carriages ever to emerge in the modern flush-sided idiom. They, like those of the LNER, also used a new 65-foot underframe and their fixed berths and other internal accoutrements undoubtedly imitated those of the 1931 Gresley vehicles, but there were still only seven compartments since, for the first time ever in a third class-car, an attendant's compartment was provided. Moreover, by means of outside air-scoops on the corridor side of the body, fresh air (passed through oil filters) could enter the carriage and be admitted to compartments by floor-level grills in the compartment doors. The first of these fine carriages was sent with *Royal Scot* on its tour of North America in 1933 where, largely in consequence of the overall quality offered to 'ordinary' passengers, it caused something of a mild sensation by contrast with American 'coach' class travel.

Finally, in 1935, the Stanier approach was applied to first class sleeping cars. The twelve-wheel, twelve-berth style was retained but, for no readily apparent reason, the body length was increased by another foot to 69 ft; the attendant was the sole beneficiary of this

expensive largesse! The cars also displayed a slightly bulging profile (ex-GWR via Stanier again?) and this added some 3 ins to the berth length. By some margin, these were the largest passenger carrying vehicles ever built by the LMS but, for all that, were commendably light in weight at 42 tons, only 5 tons more than the above-mentioned 65-foot third class cars.

This was undoubtedly achieved largely by means of a whole host of new constructional features which Stanier incorporated into their design and which were given considerable publicity in the contemporary press. Most of the change was in the extensive use made of electric arc welding in the bogies, underframe and carriage roof frames. The elimination of most rivets not only saved weight in itself but also enabled lighter steel sections to be used in some parts of the carriage, simply because there were no rivet holes to weaken the structure. This was augmented by the elimination of the heavy bottom bodyside timber members (see p 298), the simplification and lightening of the basic timber body frame and the use of a steel cantrail. Many of these new ideas were also embodied in contemporary corridor stock, yet the rigidity of the structure was, if anything, better than the traditional form. It is, in fact, rather surprising that the LMS did not wholly standardize this form of construction from then on.

Inside the cars, the decor largely copied that which had been LNER practice for some four or five years and represented one of the few occasions in which the LMS made use of Rexine in any great quantity. A slightly new touch was the use of four different interior colours within each car (three compartments each in yellow, green, blue and beige) with sanitary ware to match in an unconscious and early anticipation of 1970s 'Habitat' styling! However, the corridors

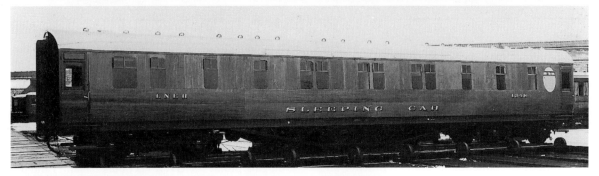

Top *The final LMS twelve-wheel sleeping car form was 69 ft long. This is Derby-built composite No 713 of 1936. Note the recessed handles to allow a little more width at the waist and the late use of Mansell wood-centred wheels, probably for a quieter ride*

Above and left *Exterior and interior views of experimental Thompson LNER third class sleeping car No 1348 of 1947. The compartment shown is one of the twin berth types with high-level beds — see the sections and plans in Figure 27*

Below *Quite apart from its flush-sided form, the post-war LNER pattern first class sleeping cars differed from tradition in having single rather than 'twinned' compartment side windows. No E1257 was the first of five in 1950*

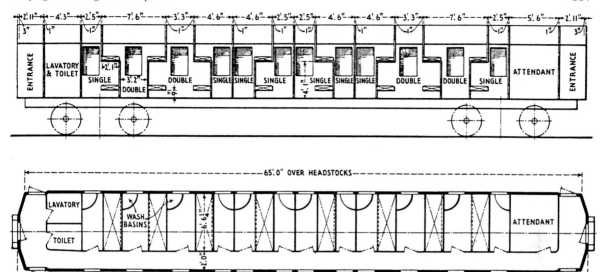

Figure 27 *Longitudinal section and plan of Thompson's experimental third class 'interlocking berth' sleeping car for the LNER.*

faithfully maintained the LMS traditions; walnut and sycamore. All the internal passenger facilities which had evolved after the grouping were installed and one of them, slightly modified, also went to the USA, this time in 1939 accompanying the new 'Coronation Scot' set (see page 493). A model of the standard type is also at the NRM.

Very soon afterwards, the LMS produced some composite sleeping cars to the new Stanier pattern. These too were 69-foot vehicles and the only twelve-wheel LMS pattern sleeping cars to be built at Derby. The latter works had been the source of supply of all the LMS third class sleeping cars and rather more than half the LMS twelve-wheel diners (see below), but the old LNWR tradition seems to have more or less ensured that *first* class sleeping cars were a Wolverton speciality; maybe composites were different! In them, the fixed berth compartments of the 1933 third class type were combined with the single berths of the 1935 first class cars to produce a predictable end product. Unlike the earlier composites, they were arranged with first class at one end, third at the other.

Thus it was that by the outbreak of war, there was little to choose in terms of quality between the best of the LMS and LNER fleet, and the final coming together of design after the war was probably inevitable. By then, the LNER had gone to the flush-sided style and only built one further sleeping car in its own name. This was a mildly experimental Thompson third class car in 1947 which, by means of an interlocking berth layout, enabled both single and double

compartments to be contrived. But in its anticipation of providing fewer than four berths in a third class compartment, it probably had some influence on the final designs which were to post-date the onset of BR. Outwardly, this first Thompson sleeping car was (ersatz teak livery excepted) much more akin to the LMS styling than any of its Gresley forbears.

Apart from this one car, the final LMS and LNER sleeping car designs all post-dated BR in terms of entry to service. This was quite characteristic of many of the final company designs of carriage (see Chapter 29). The LMS ordered up another batch of Stanier-style first class twelve-wheelers (built 1950-51), which were almost identical to the pre-war series, and Thompson on the LNER produced what amounted to a ten-berth equivalent on an eight-wheel chassis. Length apart, and the fact that there were far more of the LMS pattern, there was little significant difference; and Gresley's shower cubicle did not return in the LNER type, more's the pity.

It was finally in the third class (soon to become second class) field that the ultimate fusion of ideas took place. Here, in 1951-2, both Doncaster (ex-LNER) and Derby (ex-LMS), came up with a new concept for overnight third class travel. Unsurprisingly, both places used a 65-foot chassis and the layout was conventionally side-corridor, but all compartments in both series were twin berth only and given first class type pressure heating and ventilation. Their origins may have had something of Thompson's influence in them, but a further factor may have been the not uncommon practice during the war of adding upper berths to some first class compartments. Be that as it may, they, along with their first class con-

temporaries, were so nearly identical as to be the inevitable influence on future development — and there we must leave it.

Catering vehicles

The dedicated catering vehicle — and in this chapter the discussion will be confined solely to carriages with some form of on-board cooking facility — came in but one of the three basic types during the final years of the company period: the Dining Car 'proper' (ie a vehicle with kitchen, pantry and seats at which passengers could take their meals), its 'poor' relation the Buffet Car, and the Kitchen Only Car, usually called simply a Kitchen Car — ie a carriage which is completely full of kitchen and pantry equipment without seats for patrons. To some extent, the type of vehicle favoured reflected the differing approaches of the companies themselves. Thus, for example, the LMS was by far the largest user of kitchen cars just as the LNER was well ahead of the field in its early espousal of the buffet car; but this was by no means a clear-cut distinction. It therefore seems helpful to start this section with a general look at the nature of on-train catering in the 1920s and 1930s.

The desirability of having catering facilities on a train went way back into Victorian times, so by the

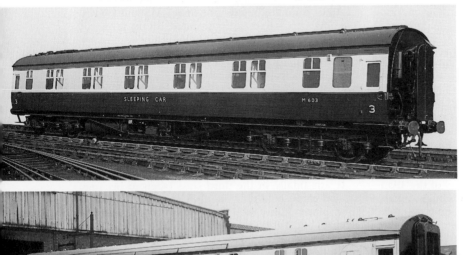

Above left *This wartime conversion to twin berth of an LMS first class sleeping car not only typifies final LMS pattern sleeping car interior styling but undoubtedly set the style for the post-BR twin-berth third class form adopted by the successors to both the LMS and LNER*

Left *The considerable similarity between final LMS and LNER third class design practice is well shown in these ex-works views of LMS type twin-berth car No M603 of 1951 and LNER pattern No E1763E of 1952. Both were built new carrying BR standard red and cream livery, a style which suited the 'LNER' cars far better than painted 'teak'!*

Figure 28 *The twin-berth third class sleeping car arrangement adopted by the London Midland Region. The final 'LNER' version was similar.*

Right *The classic kitchen/dining car: LNER third class No 10215J, built in 1925 for East Coast main line service*

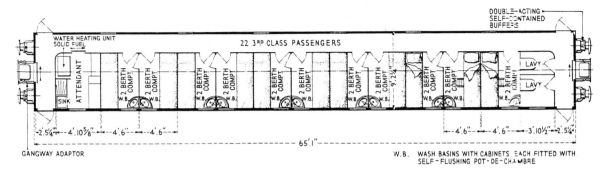

time of the grouping the general idea was well established. At the time it mostly took the form of a full dining car, but there had already been some mild experiments with kitchen and buffet cars and the grouping was to see further changes. Even though the modern proliferation of mini- and micro-buffet cars, griddle cars or what have you was still to come, one can detect its seeds in the activities of the inter-war period.

Starting with the full dining car, its earliest form was designed to serve the first class passenger exclusively and this was to remain the most common form of conventional car right through the grouping period (see Table 7). But the growing demands of the third class passenger did not have to wait long. Even by the grouping, such famous companies as the LNWR had long been building both composite and third class dining cars in the traditional mode — often inserting one of each type into the more important trains — while such as the Midland had long realized that the kitchen of the dining car proper was well able to produce far more meals than the typically 18-24 seat capacity of the car itself could consume, and had therefore settled on an almost semi-standardized arrangement of first class diner plus open third class diner for its main trains. The composite type, characteristically with about 30 seats (12 first plus 18 third) was often sufficient for the smaller trains and this had an interesting alternative: the so-called 'common' or 'unclassed' dining car. This was an all-comers vehicles and the nearest approach the British companies ever came to the typical Wagons-Lits approach which was so popular in mainland Europe. In fact, the preserved ex-MR dining car at the National Railway Museum, though built to a third class design, was mostly used in this mode.

Several alternatives also began to find favour. One of these reversed the normal pattern and operated a third class dining car with an open first. Though this happened before 1923, it became much more common thereafter, often with the first class dining seats occupying only half of the adjacent non-kitchen carriage which could, therefore, be of either semi-open configuration or even composite in its layout, thus giving more flexibility. This became particularly favoured on the LMS. But such was the growing demand for meals that the bigger trains could not always be served in this fashion and a very typical 1920s and 1930s solution was to place a full kitchen car between at least two fully open carriages (one first, one third). In some cases, three or even four open carriages could be thus served. The LMS was a great protagonist of this method but the LNER and GWR also found it advantageous, the former often in the form of an articulated 'triplet' set. The GWR also tried articulation, but fairly swiftly rebuilt its offerings into single unit carriages (see page 318)

The buffet car solution was very much a child of

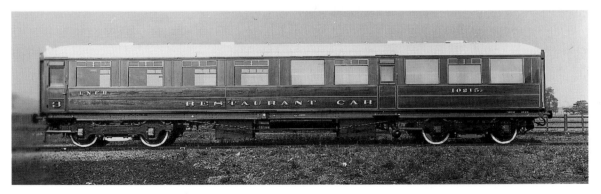

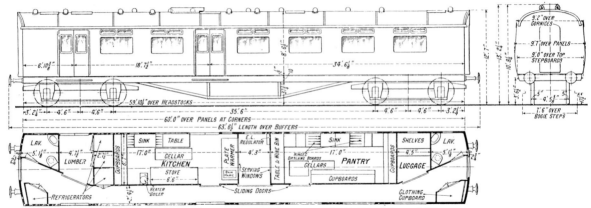

Side and End Elevations and Plan of New Kitchen Car, "Cornish Riviera" Express, G.W.R. 1929

Figure 29 Elevations and floor plan of the GWR 1929 'Cornish Riviera' stock kitchen cars, very typical of the facilities to be found in most examples of the genre.

Scale: 2mm = 1 ft

Left *Equally classic LMS dining car interiors: twin window open first class No 3716 of 1925 (which would normally be served from a full kitchen car), and kitchen/first No 3129 of 1930.*

Above right *LNER Buffet car No 61496 was converted from a former GER coach and was one of several such in the early 1930s which led to the building of many new examples of the type*

the LNER and met with considerable success as the numbers in Table 7 reveal. What is perhaps most surprising is that the other companies did not seem to see it the same way. The GWR had a few but the LMS merely tinkered with the idea and the SR did not bother at all until Bulleid's time, and even this post-dated the formation of BR except for EMU stock. To the modern traveller, even discounting the cost advantage compared with the full dining car, the buffet car is so well established as the normal form of train catering that it is rarely possible to get the full meal service unless travelling first class — full circle indeed. We are told that there is no longer a demand for such things — and this may be true — but one cannot help but think that the intrinsic cost disadvantages of a full catering service, adumbrated on page 83, have at last been allowed to govern the overall policy.

We have perhaps strayed a little forward of the grouping period in this regard, so these issues will mostly have to await the next volume to discuss more fully. Meantime, what it meant in practical terms was that the proper dining car, with a few exceptions, probably reached its apogee during the final company period and nothing built since nationalization displayed any conceptual improvement. In fact, looking back to early BR days, it is noteworthy how often the catering facilities were regularly provided by company-designed vehicles in an otherwise BR standard carriage formation; few of the LMS standard dining cars, for example, were withdrawn before the late 1950s and most served into the early 1960s.

As with sleeping cars, the two major Anglo-Scottish companies were also dominant in the catering field (see Tables 7 and 8) and if buffet cars are excluded, the LMS again occupied an even more leading role (almost 50 per cent) in terms of its more conventional catering stock. To some extent, this degree of imbalance is to be expected, given the nature of the

services operated by both it and the LNER; and undoubtedly the latter company redressed the balance more than somewhat by using buffet cars where the LMS would offer a more conventional alternative. But what it is perhaps most surprising is that unlike sleeping cars, where the northern lines would naturally take precedence, train catering is a daytime activity so one would have expected the GWR in particular to have been rather better represented. It did, of course, have a fine inheritance of catering vehicles in 1923 so perhaps the need was less, but whereas the LMS and LNER went on building newer and better vehicles to supplement their own, usually quite excellent, pre-1923 fleets, the GWR yet again seems to have taken a rather complacent line.

In earlier chapter I stated that the grouping probably did the GWR no favours in terms of carriage design compared with its rivals and this does seem to be reflected in much of its inter-war activities. Supporters of this company may well feel that this is a somewhat harsh judgement, but it is hard not to make it — and catering vehicles were no exception. Even one of its most noted apologists has written that GWR dining cars after the grouping were often 'unremarkable' and 'without any special distinctions' * and this seems to have extended to the numbers built as well.

The Southern's situation was rather different and in many respects its approach to the train catering problem was the most praiseworthy of the four companies. It started from a low point compared with the others (a handful of ex-LSWR dining cars and little else) while two of its three constituents had put all their catering into the hands of the Pullman Company. Although this latter situation was to be maintained (and even increased — see Chapter 27), the SR, never the richest of companies, managed to build

* *Great Western Coaches*: M.Harris *(ibid)*

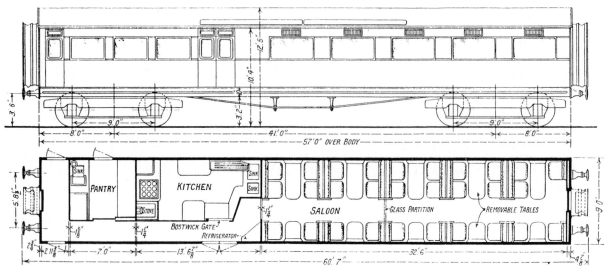

Figure 30 *Elevation and plan of Maunsell's first SR dining car, the 29-seat third class carriages built in 1925 as part of the final 'Ironclad' series (see page 18).*

Scale: $^1/_{10}"$ = 1ft

Figure 31 *Elevation and plan of the initial Maunsell SR standard first class dining cars of 1927, along with schematic floor plans of the normal Southern Railway dining car pairing.*

Scale: $^1/_{10}"$ = 1ft

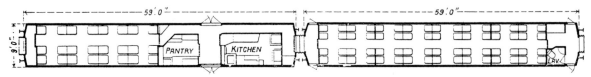

COMBINED 1ST CLASS DINING SALOON & KITCHEN CAR   THIRD CLASS DINING SALOON

The final Maunsell diners appeared in 1934 and No 7998 was one of them. It differed very little from the 1927 type in Figure 31, save for the outer end passenger doors

more first class dining cars than did the LMS and only marginally fewer than did the LNER. The LMS position was, of course, influenced by its large number of third class dining cars and kitchen cars, but offsetting this was the fact that the Southern's fleet was almost exclusively devoted to the former LSWR lines where it probably deployed almost as many dining cars as did the GWR on the whole of its larger system.

The Southern Railway, of course, though perhaps better known for its great electrification programmes, was pre-eminently a passenger railway throughout its whole territory for reasons given in the previous volume, and this fact alone clearly influenced all its activities. Indeed, one writer has stated, *inter alia*: 'The coaches of Richard Maunsell were the last to be designed for the Southern with the absolute right of passenger preference in mind.'* Given the lack of cash resources in absolute terms which it often suffered (hence its major reconstruction of old steam stock for electric services), the Southern made a quite remarkable effort to woo its customers, and the fleet of dining cars can clearly be seen as part of this endeavour.

So much, then, by way of overview; what of the vehicles themselves?

In terms of vehicle design, and in spite of my strictures about the GWR, there was probably little to choose between any of them in terms of fundamental quality and constructional excellence. By now this was an expected attribute of British carriage builders and was almost always present. The major interest, therefore, lies more in the slight variations of concept between the companies combined with those few design innovations and technical improvements which some of them began to make. And having arrived on

* *Maunsell's SR Steam Passenger Stock*: David Gould, Oakwood Press, 1978

the Southern Railway, we might as well remain there for the moment.

In 1923, in association with those determined efforts to improve the long-distance image of the company mentioned in previous chapters, Maunsell seems to have resolved that all the principal West of England services should have proper catering facilities. At the time, such few as were available were provided by centre-kitchen composite dining cars running in the centre of fixed, usually five-coach, corridor sets. At first, Maunsell took these as his role model, and in 1923 and 1925, as part of the last 'Ironclad' series — see Chapter 16 — a further eight diners were built, this time end-kitchen, officially third class and seating 29, though it appears likely that they may often have operated as 'common' cars.

Very soon thereafter, the capacity of these LSWR-inspired carriages was considered inadequate, and by 1927 the first of the Maunsell standard dining cars appeared. They were end-kitchen first class only, seating 24, but were designed from the outset to run with a full open third dining car, and this became the standard Southern arrangement until Bulleid's time. The open thirds were 64-seaters and the SR never adopted the more generous 2 + 1 seating arrangement in its third class open diners. This, in fact, was probably the only slightly parsimonious feature of Southern catering and compared less than favourably with the LMS and LNER which, as already indicated, generally favoured the more spacious arrangement in their third class dining vehicles. From the Southern standpoint, however, it doubtless made economic sense since its GWR rival also favoured 2 + 2 seating in

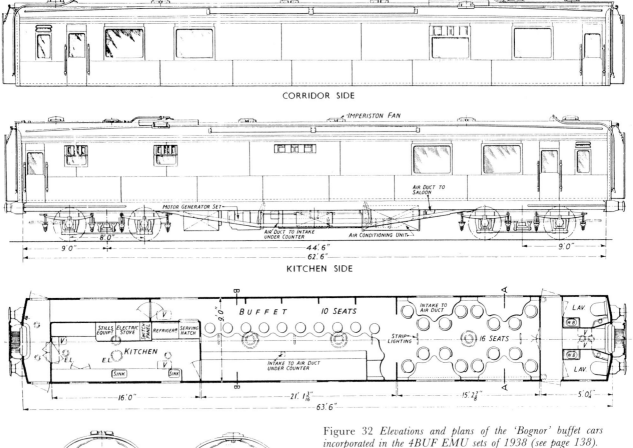

CORRIDOR SIDE

KITCHEN SIDE

Figure 32 *Elevations and plans of the 'Bognor' buffet cars incorporated in the 4BUF EMU sets of 1938 (see page 138).*

Scale: ¹/₁₀″ = 1ft

Below right *The 'Bognor' buffet car interior was certainly different, but the lack of side windows at the counter end was not well liked. The later 'Tavern' cars repeated this mistake*

the third class, and if all 64 seats could be filled with happily eating customers, so much the better!

The dining cars themselves were to the standard 59-foot length, eight wheeled and of characteristically solid Maunsell style. The design scarcely altered until the last of them was built in 1934, save that the earlier examples were built without the outside passenger entrance doors which later versions sported. They were handsomely proportioned vehicles, with more than a hint of Pullman in their decor— including individual table lamps — and a fairly mandatory quota of wood panelling and moquette. The more avant-garde interior decor ideas, much favoured by Gresley on the LNER, never penetrated the Southern until Bulleid's time, and then in much different form.

Their lack of external doors and very soundly conceived window ventilation gave them quite a modern look compared with most Maunsell corridor stock, but the fact that they were identical in size and shape to the general service carriages meant that they did not stand out in the train compared with their pre-group clerestory ancestors; but then the best Southern expresses of the 1920s and 1930s were mostly very neat and tidy.

Maunsell had achieved so much by the mid-1930s that there was no need for Bulleid to do very much at all for more than ten years afterwards in terms of new catering vehicles, and of course, the war intervened to slow things down even further. But needless to say, when this extraordinary man began to address the problem it would have been surprising indeed had there been no changes — and so there were. Bulleid was a fine carriage designer and, as will be seen in Chapter 14, most of his stylistic ideas were probably more in tune with modern ideas than any of his contemporaries. In terms of conventional dining provision, this was also made evident when he reversed the Maunsell policy of adding a first class dining car plus open third to almost any express formation by adopting a fully integrated dining facility in the main set of carriages.

Bulleid employed a third class dining car plus open first arrangement. In fact, it was a semi-open first, still offering 24 dining seats, but this then made it possible to put another open third at the opposite end of the dining car and all 11 of the new-style dining cars were thus employed in fixed formation sets for the Waterloo-Bournemouth services. Clearly, the existing first class accommodation was considered adequate and it was the third class which was given augmented provisioning. The only mean thing about it was the retention of 2 + 2 seating in the third class dining areas, and history does not tell us how capable Bulleid's kitchens were of serving meals to 24 first class and no fewer than 96 third class passengers on a two-hour trip. One wonders if they ever tried — the LMS would undoubtedly have used a full kitchen car and double-strength catering crew for this level of patronage! But at the very least it indicated a willingness to think about the problem.

It was Bulleid too who first addressed the 'buffet car' concept on the SR with any degree of conviction. In this, it is hard not to see his experience of LNER buffet cars at work; he was, after all, Gresley's chief assistant until 1937. At its most successful, the buffet car was first seen on the newly electrified medium-distance services to the south coast from 1937 onwards in the form of the well-known '4BUF' units which are also considered in context in the next chapter. At this juncture, therefore, it is perhaps sufficient to say that in them he first displayed his old master Gresley's characteristic of 'daring to be different' in the context of interior carriage decor. The 'Bognor' buffets, as they were fairly quickly christened, were most certainly that, and by no means to everybody's taste, unlike the often 'French-inspired' interiors adopted by his old LNER chief which almost always got a good press. But they did fill a conceptual gap in SR catering and were regularly well patronized; so maybe it is best left there!

But in his final years, after nationalization, the very final fling in the railway carriage field of this highly idiosyncratic man was to cause even more than the normal controversy which usually surrounded him. I have repeatedly said or inferred, in both this and the previous volume, that railway carriages are as much about people as about technology, and nowhere can this have been more true than in the case of Bulleid's celebrated 'Tavern' cars of 1949. They were, of course, officially 'BR'; and even though they will return in the next volume in the context of BR's own developments in catering vehicles, no one can reasonably doubt that they were also a final manifestation of company individuality and, as such, should equally be considered here.

In essence, the Tavern cars were buffet cars with kitchen and pantry plus the usual passenger seating facilities; but there all resemblance to any other catering vehicle for British service before or since, or even overseas for that matter, ended. It is a moot point whether they were so awful as to break through the taste barrier and come out the other side unscathed or whether they were simply vulgar in the extreme; for what Bulleid had done was to try and put an English (not British, be it noted!) 'pub' into a roughly 64 ft long by 9 ft wide 'envelope' and put it on to railway wheels. Even the new BR red and cream livery helped him, for he could paint the exteriors in imitation half-timbering above the waist and 'English Bond' brickwork on the lower portions — and he even had the temerity to put 'traditional' pub signs on the outside! As if to compound this presumption, it was applied to the 'Tavern' end of the carriage only, the other bit having conventional BR red/cream livery, while within the carriages, dark oak settles and 'ye olde'-type tables, not to mention pseudo half-timbering, were employed in profusion, the latter wall treatment being mostly at the expense of any outside

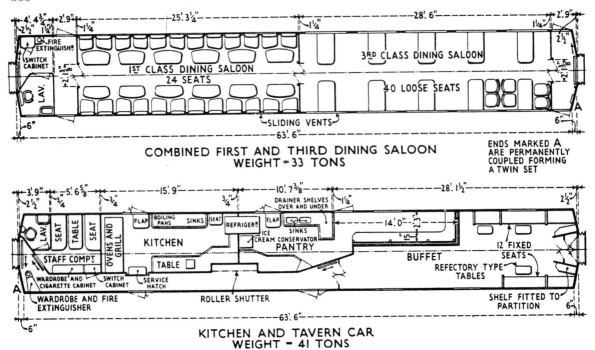

COMBINED FIRST AND THIRD DINING SALOON
WEIGHT = 33 TONS

KITCHEN AND TAVERN CAR
WEIGHT = 41 TONS

Figure 33 *Floor plans of Bulleid's controversial 'Tavern' cars and the equally unorthodox composite open dining saloons which ran with them. Neither the 'back to the wall' seating in the first class or the almost windowless refectory end of the Taverns met with much approval.*

windows through which the passenger could see out! The whole pastiche was completed (or betrayed, according to opinion) by the bar area then being given a superabundance of 'state of the art' stainless steel, chrome plate and plastic. In general, passengers were less than well pleased and were not long in complaining.

It was all most curious, and those who never saw them — they were not to remain long in their original form — may, even now, doubt their very existence; but was it any worse in principle that the currently fashionable vogue for the spurious and inappropriate 'Edwardianization' of many licensed premises, the re-using of grounded ex-Pullman Car bodies as 'Yuppie' annexes to fashionable restaurants, or pretending that by renovating old Pullman and Wagons-Lits carriages and whirling them at £600 per throw to Venice and elsewhere we are somehow re-creating the days of the great trains? Frankly I don't know, but I think I would rather have liked to have experienced one of Mr Bulleid's 'Taverns' for all that. They most certainly brought some life to the scene in those rather grey austerity post-war years and, who

knows, their less outrageous features may even have made some small contribution to later developments in the BR rail catering field — and there we must leave them for the time being.

If the Southern was most remarkable for its speedy meeting of customer demand in the 1920s and 1930s, and for its adventurous innovations in the 1940s, then the GWR must surely have been one of the last bastions of tradition in the railway scene — and none the worse for that, if truth be told. So maybe this is the right moment at which to redress some of the balance concerning this great railway which has, so far, received little praise in these pages in terms of its post-1922 contribution to carriage building developments.

In purely catering terms, the GWR was well established at the grouping and its pre-1923 dining cars could stand comparison with the very best — see, for example,Chapter 11 pages 204-5 — and maybe this was the problem. For, as has been suggested already, there was probably a degree of complacency about the post-1922 GWR which all but its most bigoted supporters must concede. It had good cause, for a variety of reasons, and it is a measure of the absolute quality of its pre-1923 contribution, whether in the realm of locomotives or carriages, that there was no perceived need to make too many changes. After all, even the GWR had to pay dividends and, no matter what one's personal views may be, the hard-nosed

Above *Detail of a Bulleid Tavern car in service on the 'Atlantic Coast Express', showing the painted fake brickwork and half timbering, the 'pub sign' and the very small high-level windows*

Above right *The 'Olde Englishe' interior of a Bulleid Tavern*

railway management of the 1920s and 1930s, even that of the highly image-conscious GWR, would be indisposed to make too many changes unless they were needed. If proof be needed of this fact, one has merely to consider the GWR's highly significant pioneering work in the field of cross-country diesel traction (see Chap 24), where its contribution to future development was probably as important as its conventional carriage building was not!

The fact is that the GWR probably did not need to improve its main-line services with quite the sense of urgency as did its rivals. For one thing, its principal competitor to the West of England — and even then not all parts — was the LSWR, and there was no real threat there until after the grouping when Maunsell had turned the Southern Railway round, so to speak (see above). On its other flank, the GWR mostly had the LMS to contend with, but not to any great extent save for the Birmingham traffic and, to a much lesser extent, some degree of more penetrating competition into Wales and the Welsh Marchlands, plus an element of *frisson* in the Wirral region

north of Chester. It may, therefore, reasonably be assumed that Paddington took the view that a relatively modest and economically acceptable injection of new ideas would suffice for most purposes — and so it was to prove. In effect, the GWR had a fair degree of territorial monopoly and while it would not deliberately 'short change' its patrons, it probably did not see the need to try as hard as did the LMS and LNER in their mutual rivalry nor even the Southern in its commendable attempts to match its larger rivals.

Given this assessment, which does not seem too unreasonable, the GWR carriage building activities of the 1920s and 1930s make rather more sense. At all events, the GWR catering contribution was characteristically one of quite cautious change rather than staggering innovation. Symptomatic of this approach — and by no means the least of the reasons why there were less new dining cars than might otherwise have been expected — was the extensive rebuilding of many of the Churchward era dining cars during the 1930s at a time when the LMS and LNER were scrapping their more or less contemporary vehicles. Such was the high quality of the Edwardian GWR diners that a dozen or so were thus treated when they were between 20 and 30 years old; with new flush-style exteriors replacing their former beaded configuration, they were scarce distinguishable from the new vehicles with which they ran. Some

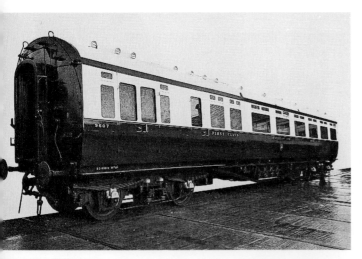

Left *GWR composite restaurant car No 9607 was built in 1930 and typifies the bow-ended, bulging-side style. These cars were the subject of two separate rebuildings — see the next views*

Middle left *This view shows the first class saloon of No 9602 after some changes to the windows — but there has been no real change in style. It is still very traditional*

Bottom left *Post-war Hampton-style conversion of an unidentified GWR composite restaurant car. This is the same first class area of the car as shown in the previous view but now looking in the opposite direction. The transformation was complete; note particularly the new-style roof treatment and the third class saloon with its glass-screened seating bays, just visible through the door*

Right *Exterior and interior views of the GWR 'quick lunch' buffet car No 9631 when new in 1934*

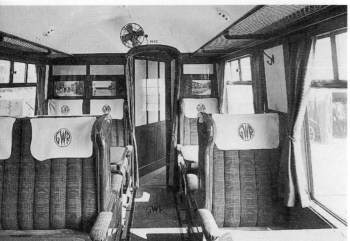

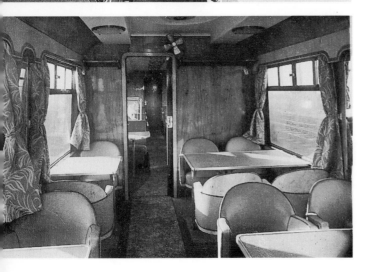

were, additionally, mounted on heavier duty six-wheel bogies and most remained active until the late 1950s and early 1960s. In fact, the rebuilding of older dining cars — or at very least a comprehensive internal refurbishment — was a characteristic GWR policy and was to be repeated after the Second World War in 1947 with the well-known 'Hampton' conversions, some of which were in fact 'second time round' rebuilds of later pre-group stock of 1922 vintage which had already had one major pre-war face-lift.

Turning now to new carriages, the bow-ended era saw the introduction of further dining cars of no great pioneering significance, though they were, of course, very well built. But there were no signs that the company wished to make any striking changes. Thus, even the celebrated articulated triplets of 1923 seem, in retrospect, to have been more of a gesture than anything else. The open first plus kitchen car plus open third made eminently good sense, and was a common GWR arrangement, but one senses that the articulated versions were introduced with no great conviction and their subsequent rebuilding as single unit vehicles was to prove this point.

Approximately equal in emphasis to the use of a kitchen car flanked by open stock was the familiar pairing of first class dining car plus open third but, and proportionally rather more so than on other lines, the single unit composite diner devoid of supplementary open carriages was almost as common a solution on the GWR as the other two ideas added together.

In terms of styling, the new GWR carriages followed contemporary company practice, including the bulging-side profile of the later bow-ended period, but internally there were no great innovations and, like the Southern, the GWR also favoured 2 + 2 seating in the third class. Even the above-mentioned

rebuilds often retained much of their original interior and it was not until the post-war era that anything distinctively different began to appear. As far as can be judged, this was probably inspired by the final series of pre-war buffet and dining cars wherein the GWR made a rather attractive attempt at combining the then fashionable Art Deco styling with the favoured traditional interior layout. The best of them were undoubtedly the 'Centenary' diners of 1935, but these have their own place in a later chapter. Of the others, the 1938 twelve-wheel buffet cars and composite dining cars were probably the most significant.

One of them was singled out for renovation as a post-war prototype and in fairly short order many more were so treated. Most of the inspiration came from the firm of Hamptons and took the form of installing a somewhat 'Odeon'-style interior into older vehicles, along with better and more modern windows. Typically, the first class areas were given individual revolving 'bucket' seats in grey leather while the thirds, retaining the 2 + 2 arrangement, were offered low-backed green leather bench-type seating, often with decorative glass screens above the seat backs bearing Art Deco pictorial motifs. False ceilings with flat centre sections and concealed lighting, along with modern flush-veneered wood panelling, completed the ensemble. It was certainly different, but such was the strength of tradition that not all approved. While many of the older vehicles undoubtedly needed some form of brightening up, it was perhaps unfortunate that this treatment was also given to the aforementioned Centenary diners; they most certainly did not need it and the preserved example would undoubtedly have said more about the best Swindon practice had it retained its original interior.

Although not as lavish as the LNER in its provi-

sioning, the GWR was a very good runner-up in the buffet car arena, being far better than either the LMS or SR in this respect. Like the LNER, its first efforts were conversions from older pre-group stock, but with its new vehicles of the middle and later 1930s it may even be said to have been the leader of the pack in conceptual terms when it pioneered two particularly interesting new ideas. One of them was the by now well-known 'quick lunch' buffet car of 1934, preserved in the National Collection.This vehicle consists simply of a long bar counter running the length of the carriage at which passengers can either stand or sit on fixed stools. A small kitchen is at one end but otherwise the essential facilities are all neatly stowed either under the bar or at the back, all within easy reach of the staff.

Even better than this type (of which only two were

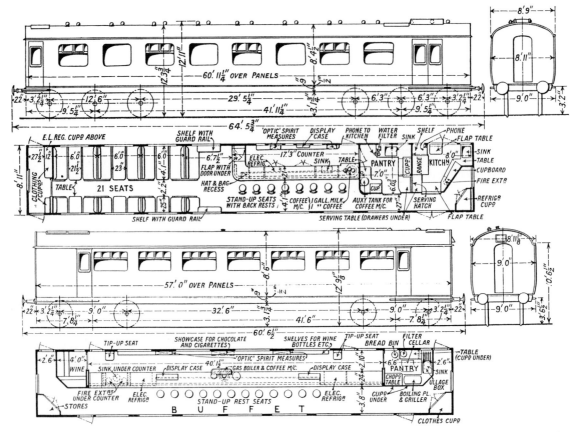

Figure 34 Two good examples of GWR buffet car layout. The upper was the most favoured type, while the lower shows the 'quick lunch' buffet car.

Scale: 2mm = 1ft

built) were the twelve-wheel buffet cars of 1938. These combined a somewhat similar bar arrangement with fixed stools (occupying the middle third of the carriage) with, at one end, 21 fixed low-backed leather seats of a type similar to the post-war Hampton conversions and at the opposite end a very adequate kitchen and pantry. As all-purpose catering vehicles they were hard to better and were amongst the very last GWR examples to be withdrawn in the mid-1960s.

Thus, in its final years, the GWR was by no means without enterprise in the catering field, after a somewhat stodgy middle period, and it too dared to innovate. It even put a small and well-designed buffet bar across the end of some of its diesel railcars (see Chapter 9), which was far more comprehensive in its offerings than many a larger more modern BR train!

Turning now to the two big companies, it is easier,

as with their sleeping car designs, to deal with them together, for in a very real sense their catering vehicles were as much a manifestation of their mutual competition as anything else. Each of them built more new dining cars during the company period proper than the GWR and SR between them, and if the LMS built twice as many kitchen cars as all three of its rivals added together, then the LNER buffet car fleet was equally dominant in this particular genre, also representing some two-thirds of the British total.

Quite apart from the purely cosmetic variations caused by their differing liveries and forms of carriage construction, the LMS and LNER tended to adopt rather different approaches to the whole business of train catering. In part, this may have been deliberate in the interests of promoting their individual images, but it was also a consequence of their pre-group inheritance.

Take, for instance, that very characteristic LMS feature, the twelve-wheel diner. It was not that the LNER did not have any, for it inherited a fair number of superb examples from its constituents, but it never built any more after 1922, preferring instead to concentrate its efforts either on the articulated option or the standard length eight-wheel vehicle. By contrast, the LMS never built a full dining car which did not have twelve wheels, and even though the GWR occasionally assayed the type, the LMS was without doubt the last convinced adherent to the form.

In this it seems reasonable to presume that the inherited experience of the LNWR and the MR, particularly the former, were the decisive factors, and it could be significant that the very first of the post-group LMS twelve-wheel dining cars of 1925 (a 30-seat composite) was, like the contemporary sleeping cars, almost undilutedly LNWR in its styling and was fitted with LNWR bogies. However, apart from these few cars it did seem that the LMS had abandoned the full dining car as it proceeded to put into service a quite colossal tranche of more than 70 dedicated kitchen cars between 1924 and 1928. This sudden move to an idea which, though not unheard of, had never been practised to this extent before and was never matched in such quantity by any other company, was almost certainly tied in with the building of large quantities of open stock explained in Chapter 19.

It is not known whether the LMS seriously contemplated an almost total standardization on the kitchen car plus open carriage format. Demand was, of course, rising, but although the full kitchen car could offer a greater number of meals than a conventional dining car, and soon became a feature of most of the bigger trains, there were still many services which would be over-provisioned if this idea was universally adopted. Here, the fact that the LMS had acquired a very good fleet of conventional dining cars from both the LNWR and MR, many of which were of no great age, became relevant; for these were most certainly not put out to grass. However, when they were reaching about 30 years of age, the LMS chose not to rebuild them as had the GWR in similar circumstances, but to replace them almost like-for-like. Thus, the 1930s saw a great resurgence of the twelve-wheel catering vehicle. In the event, this was to prove the final flowering of the twelve-wheel idea in terms of British catering vehicles, and a fine climax it made.

Meantime, the LNER took rather a different line and tended to follow GNR practice, which was also the dominant influence on the East Coast Joint Stock. Here, Gresley had begun to move away from the bigger, all-purpose dining car and fairly soon two principle alternatives began to be the preferred LNER

Figure 35 *Probably the most favoured LNER catering arrangements: articulated triplet set and the first class dining car plus open third pairing.*

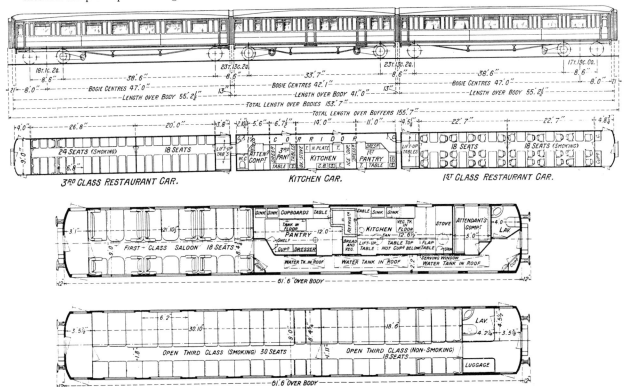

forms. Most celebrated were the articulated triplets in which a central kitchen unit was flanked by open first and third class elements. These were used on the busier services, while simultaneously the alternative preferred form settled down to a conventional non-articulated first class diner plus open third pairing, the thirds being quite often of the type which contained a small pantry (with cupboards and hotplate only) at one end. Like the LMS, the LNER also made full use of its inherited fleet for many years, so the variety to be seen on both lines was rather greater than the above-described standard procedures might suggest. Also, like the LMS, the LNER chose not to rebuild its older cars and let them run on to the end of their useful life — in the event, often quite long.

Technically, there was little remarkable about the vehicles built by either company which was not shared with other general service carriages, and the only serious experiments were connected with a wish to dispense with compressed oil gas as a cooking medium in the kitchens, whether they be in kitchen cars or proper dining cars. This was tied in with a general desire to eliminate gas lighting as well, this time in all carriage stock. The fear, of course, was the greater fire risk, a hazard which had been instrumental in consuming some gas-lit carriages earlier in the century.

Gresley favoured all-electric cooking and had first demonstrated his ideas with the celebrated quintuplet dining car set for the GNR Leeds services in 1921. The method relied on a multiplicity of ground points and battery charging facilities throughout the system, not to mention a far greater battery storage capability on the carriage itself. But the sheer economics of eliminating gas (it was still needed for carriage lighting in many older vehicles) meant that the full economy of completely closing the gas plants could not be achieved. Another disadvantage was the fact that

since they relied on ground facilities, the all-electric dining cars were not self-sufficient and this militated against their use on cross-country services. During 1937, therefore, in conjunction with J.Stone and Co, the LNER conducted experiments with solid fuel cooking which would reduce the call-off on the carriage electrical supply. Anthracite was used to heat the water and main ovens while electricity did the rest. These anthracite-electric cars soon became familiar, and all new construction was to employ this form from 1938 onwards.

The LMS was not quite as concerned about the problems of gas cooking as the LNER, even though its own constituents had been just as prone to having gas fire accidents in their history as had those of the LNER. It thus continued to remain faithful to oil gas until 1933 when, as part of Stanier's reassessment of the situation, an experimental new all-electric kitchen car was built. In this vehicle, the electricity was provided by two on-board diesel generators, one at each end, and these took up some 11 ft 6 in of the vehicle length, thus causing an enlargement of the whole vehicle from the customary 50 ft of the gas-fitted kitchen cars to a 60-foot length. Again, a handsome modern-looking vehicle resulted, and it too went to North America with *Royal Scot* in 1933. A second car of the same type was finished in 1934, but thereafter the experiment ended with little in the way of published evidence to indicate its success or failure. One does rather suppose that the noise of the generators may well have been an irritant to the catering crews if no one else. Suffice to say that all subsequent Stanier kitchen cars, of which there were a fair number, reverted to the traditional 50-foot length with gas cooking to which the LMS thereafter remained faithful, save for one experiment with solid fuel cooking in the kitchen car of the ill-fated 1939 'Coronation Scot' set (see Chapter 26)

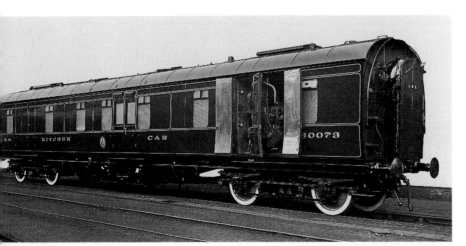

Left *Prototype LMS diesel-electric kitchen car No 30073 showing, at the near end with the doors open, one of the two generator sets. This car went to North America with* Royal Scot.

Above right *Though not perhaps quite as celebrated as the 'French'-style interiors of ten years earlier, the LNER 'Flying Scotsman' first class dining ends of the 1938 articulated triplets had a very light and airy interior in a restrained Art Deco style, and were perhaps more typical of British practice generally.*

An interesting conclusion to the LNER and LMS experiments with electric cooking finally arrived in the early 1960s. The two LMS kitchen cars had long been scrapped and the LNER electric cars (of both types) were still proving either expensive to maintain or, in the case of the all-electric versions, were often incapable of operating all their equipment while on the move. BR therefore decided to dispense with electric cooking and standardized all catering vehicles with gas, this time of the bottled propane variety. It was not until our modern Mk III era that electricity returned in the form of microwaves and the like.

Turning now to the general design of dining cars on the LMS and LNER as it affected the passenger, it seems fair to say that they were both, in their way, rather more forward looking than either the GWR or SR. While they were both capable of producing uninspired carriages, they were equally capable of offering vehicles whose internal decor and ambience was the equal of anything which had gone before. Naturally enough, the first class passenger was at the head of the list of clients to be satisfied, and in sheer panache the LNER probably took the prize. In 1928, as part of some new triplet dining sets for the re-equipped and soon to be non-stop 'Flying Scotsman' train, Gresley adopted a new 'French' style of decor. It was a deliberate attempt to produce a sort of eighteenth-century feel to the coaches and the design was put in the hands of White, Allom and Co. This company had also been involved with the experimental re-decoration of the LNER sleeping cars (see above) where its ideas took second place to those of Waring and Gillow and were not adopted; not so in the dining cars.

All natural timber finishes were suppressed, the first class areas being finished in either soft blue and stone (fawn) or red and stone, and individual armchairs were provided instead of fixed seating. Decorative pelmets surmounted the curtained windows and the whole impression was one of relaxed elegance. And it was carried through into the third class as well. Here, fixed seating was adopted with a green and stone colour scheme, but again a most gracious effect resulted, which was rather unusual for the LNER whose third class interiors were not usually as good as those of its rival.

Of course, not all LNER dining cars were given such special treatment and Harris records that public reaction was not particularly favourable*. I must confess that I find this rather suprising, having enjoyed travelling in some later LNER examples of the 'French' style, but the fact remains that the 1929 build of new carriages for the East Anglian services reverted to a somewhat uninspired and very traditional form. However, in 1935 a first class variant of

*Gresley's Coaches: M.Harris (ibid)

the 'French' style was again offered on the Anglo-Scottish services and this too seems in retrospect to have been rather good. The LNER's prime achievement in this area was, of course, in its special stream-lined stock; but this will have to wait its turn (Chapter 26.

The LMS took no risks with any form of avant-garde interior decor in the pre-Stanier period, but its own development of the traditional forms was very well done. It first appeared in the dining ends of its first class semi-open stock of 1928-30 for the 'Royal Scot' train (see page 65), but was then used in splendidly opulent form in a magnificent series of first class twelve-wheelers built between 1930 and 1932 in the new steel-panelled style. Rarely had a traditional dining car been so agreeably finished, and if it lacked the flair of Gresley's best efforts, it more than compensated in terms of sumptuous comfort.

There were two conceptual aspects which usually differentiated LMS and LNER first class dining cars. In general, the LNER examples were smaller, being mounted on standard 60-foot underframes and having but 18 seats, while the LMS equivalent always offered 24 (hence the need for 12 wheels); secondly, the LNER had rather more of them in spite of it being a smaller company. Whether the 18-seat capacity was always adequate is not known, but presumably it must have sufficed. In any case, both companies retained the option of operating a full open diner in conjunction with a kitchen car for the busier trains, whether articulated or in the form of individual vehicles.

Another difference in principle was that the LMS, even after Stanier's arrival, was still very disposed to

Opulent LMS first class dining car No 1864 ex-works at Wolverton in 1932. The interior of an earlier batch of these cars can be seen on page 96

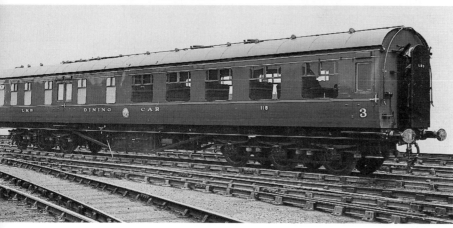

LMS Stanier-pattern third class dining car No 118 of early 1934, just after the change to simplified exterior livery

Figure 36 *Elevation, plan and interior seating detail of Stanier's initial first class LMS dining cars of 1933.*

Scale: $^1/_{12}$" = 1ft (main elevation)

adopt traditional finishes, whereas the LNER continued to experiment, particularly in the first class. But if the LNER was more enterprising in this respect, it was in the third class arena that the LMS seems to have redressed the balance. For the most part this is explained by the fact that the LMS built composite and third class dining cars to a much greater extent than did the LNER, and here it showed its strength.

In 1932, coincidental with the above-mentioned first class cars, the LMS also built a clutch of equally splended 30-seat composites for cross-country working. They were, in fact, generally regarded as 'common' diners and had detachable class designation boards in the windows. Apart from slightly smaller seating bay dimensions, they were every bit as well founded as the first class version, and this was to be the prelude to a period when it became harder and harder to differentiate between the first and third class parts of an LMS dining car set. The instigator, once again, was probably William Stanier.

Within his first year or so, the new modern flush-sided exterior styling was applied to the twelve-wheel dining car and no fewer than 77 new diners emerged from both Derby and Wolverton between 1933 and 1937 in all three types. This was the most concentrated building of dedicated dining cars in Britain since Wolverton's LNWR/WCJS efforts early in the century, and was not unconnected with the fact that these new Stanier cars were designed mostly to take their place. From 1936 onwards, most were given pressure heating and ventilation of the type newly developed for the sleeping car fleet. The firsts had the customary 24 seats, the composites and thirds had 30 and it was the third class version which was numerically dominant. Within the cars, though the traditional timber finishes were retained, much variation in timber type and upholstery material was to be found and the seat design was altered to a suitably modern look. The main difference between the first and third class was the provision of window curtains and generally softer upholstery and more heavily padded armrests in the firsts, but in all conscience there was little to choose between them and all, of course, had 2 + 1 seating, this being customary LMS and LNER practice in dining vehicles.

These twelve-wheelers were to be the last of a famous breed and they, together with a few more kitchen cars and, of course, associated open stock, were to see the LMS through to nationalization and, for the most part, for another 10 to 15 years afterwards.

But if the LMS had the edge in third class dining cars, the LNER was undoubtedly the trend-setter when it came to the buffet car alternative. This idea could trace itself back, as far as the LNER was concerned, to pioneering turn of the century efforts by the GCR, and in 1932 the LNER began to experiment with the conversion of some pre-group GER and NER stock, though contemporary accounts rather tried to give the impression that they were new. It quite soon settled down in 1933 to a more or less

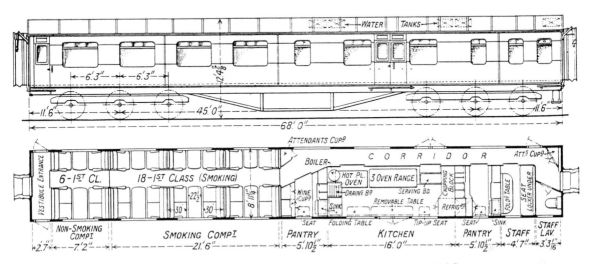

General arrangement of first class dining and kitchen car, L.M.S.R.

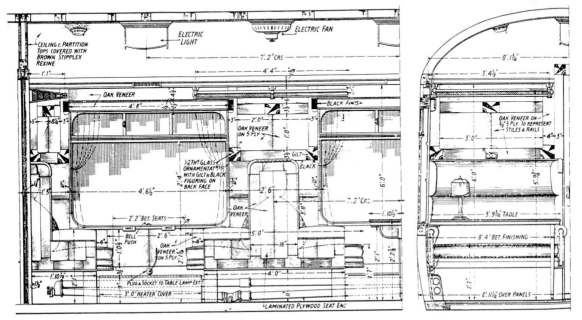

Longitudinal and cross sections of new first class dining car, L.M.S.R.

Left and below left *First and third class ends of LMS composite open dining car No 9755 of 1939; one almost needs the label over the doors to tell them apart. This type of carriage usually operated with the third class diners shown in the previous picture*

Below *LNER buffet car No 648 when new in 1935. These were the most common LNER buffets and were to prove the very last Gresley-type vehicles to remain in passenger service on BR. Several are preserved, including one at the NRM*

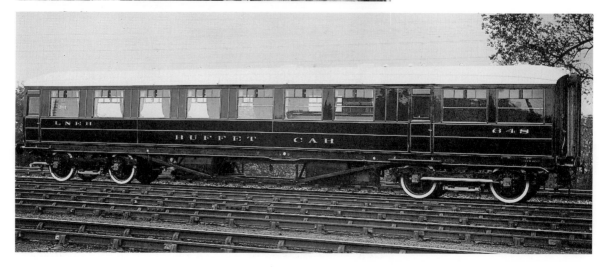

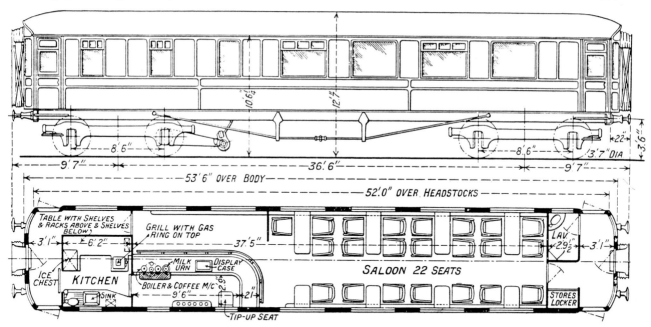

standard arrangement of a kitchen and serving bar at one end with 24 seats at the other, all mounted on the standard 60-foot underframe. It was not, perhaps, quite as well thought out as the later GWR type (see above), nor was the interior decoration anything like as attractive, but in terms of sheer numbers it was undoubtedly more significant, and in them can easily be seen the start of the modern most favoured train catering provision.

The vast majority were trimmed in Rexine with stark chromium-plated seats of dubious aesthetic merit and no comfort whatsoever. They also had painted ceilings and bare light bulbs and were certainly no place to linger, but maybe that was deliberate. Moreover, the value for money in terms of the bill of fare was of a high order. They were destined to become the last Gresley carriages in regular BR service, by now re-equipped and re-trimmed with almost equally awful 1950s-style laminated plastic. Several are preserved, including one at the National Railway Museum.

Paradoxically, though it never really developed the idea, the LMS actually introduced its first buffet car slightly ahead of the LNER. This took the form of a one-off vehicle in 1932, just a few months ahead of the LNER experiment, and it was launched with

Figure 37 Elevation and plan of the prototype LNER buffet car converted from an ex-NER vehicle. This basic layout became the LNER standard.

Scale: 3mm = 1ft

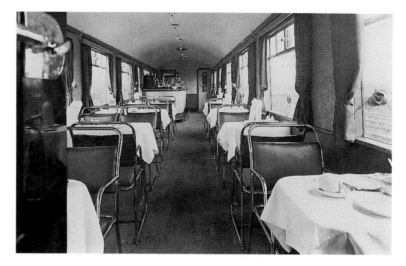

Right *Interior of Gresley LNER buffet car No 24082, showing tables laid up with the favourite 'Keswick'-pattern crockery. The seats were very uncomfortable!*

a great deal of fuss and palaver, most of it probably unjustified. The LMS called it a 'Cafeteria' car, though it said 'Buffet' on the outside, and it certainly embodied an interesting layout. The LMS stated 'If the innovation proves as popular as it is anticipated, an order will be placed for a large number of these cars...' So much for fond hopes! Its interior fittings — chrome-plated, naturally, to suit the fashion of the day — were as awesomely bad as those in the later LNER cars and nothing much else happened until 1936 when four more were built to the Stanier pattern but copying the by now normal LNER internal layout. A fair attempt was made to improve the interior decor, and with some success, but the LMS never seemed to know just what to do with the type; although all five lasted until the early 1960s they were

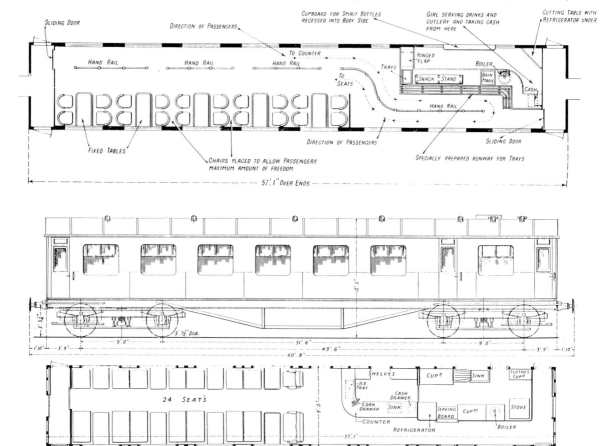

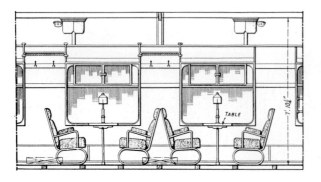

Scale: $^1/_{10}" = 1ft$

Figure 38 *The two LMS buffet car designs. The upper plan shows the 'Cafeteria' layout first adopted in the proto-type car. Its layout was fairly soon altered to something like that of the Stanier-pattern cars shown in the rest of the drawings.*

Right and below right *Contrasting LMS buffet car interiors, separated by only four years in time. The older car shows the rearranged interior of the prototype car whose original floor plan is shown in Figure 38*

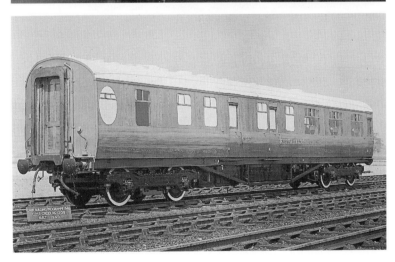

Right *The few post-war LNER-style first class dining cars of 1949, though stylish enough from the outside, were very dreary by comparison with the Gresley breed. This is the first of them, No E1657, outshopped in ersatz teak livery when new*

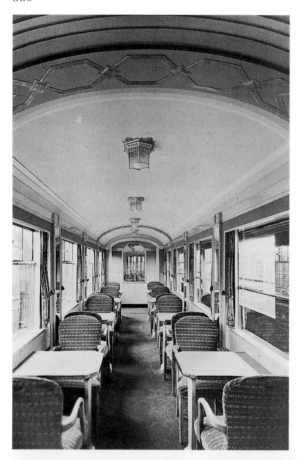

never repeated. A rather clever re-creation of one of them has been built by the Severn Valley Railway in the shell of an orthodox LMS carriage.

Summing up the story, the final verdict between these two great companies is probably 'honours easy', to use the phrase first coined by an earlier writer in reference to their locomotive achievements; and maybe that is as it should be. The great achievements were all made before 1940, and after the war the only new catering vehicles were some not wildly memorable Thompson coaches of very dated and dreary character, most of which actually came out after BR was formed. The LMS contribution was even less, taking the form of two rebuilt carriages in 1947, one open first and one proper diner. They were given loose individual chairs plus a few fixed seats, both of very utilitarian appearance, and although the LMS made its usual publicity meal out of them, it somehow seemed hollow compared with pre-war days. Sadly, and for some unaccountable reason, these really quite awful interiors, particularly the loose chairs, took root in the BR mind and resulted in some of the worst dining car designs ever to be seen emerging as a later BR standard.

Meantime, let no one doubt the real quality of the specialized vehicles which were built by the old private companies. They may not have been perfect, but it is a measure of their quality that, with few exceptions, BR was unable to produce anything better until the days of the Mk III sleeping and dining cars, wherein at last could be seen some real improvements. However, the story of the slow build-up to these events must wait its time for the moment.

Above left *The stylish buffet lounge in the 1938 LNER 'Flying Scotsman' set allowed eating passengers some considerable privacy by means of the by-pass corridor on the right*

Left *The dated and not very elegant interior of refurbished LMS open first class dining car No 7555 in 1947. It started life with an interior such as that shown on page 112.*

21. Southern Electric

Regardless of their individual favourites, few would seriously deny that the most far-reaching change in the conceptual development of British carriages during the company period was that wrought by the Southern Railway in its rapid and widespread adoption of electric traction during the 1920s and 1930s. It was not so much that the vehicles themselves were particularly different (they were in fact mostly rather old-fashioned and ordinary for reasons which will be explained), but in the context of a totally changed approach to the business of operating passenger traffic, the Southern stood supreme. One says this, notwithstanding the role of London Transport (see Chap 22), largely because, unlike the services run by the LPTB, the Southern, within 15 years of the grouping, had transformed a few rather modest suburban ideas in South London into what amounted to a totally integrated electrification policy, embracing almost all categories of passenger transport from inner suburban to main-line operations.

The achievement was all the more remarkable because of the straitened financial circumstances against which it was carried out, and here the major share of the credit must surely go to the Southern's wily General Manager, Sir Herbert Walker KCB. Walker was a dedicated proponent of electrification as the means whereby to counter ever growing road competition. Unfortunately, Southern financial resources were insufficient to meet this threat in the manner which Sir Herbert might well have preferred — brand new rolling-stock to suit a brand new system — but this was not going to stop him. Thus there began that quite astonishing element of carriage rebuilding, often best described as 'make do and mend', which both typified the first 25 years of 'Southern Electric' and also gave it much of its undoubted character. And in this regard, Sir Herbert Walker was more than ably abetted by his CME, Richard Maunsell, whose many other fine achievements have more than once received acclamation in these pages.

The background goes back well before the grouping and was briefly touched upon in the final chapter of the previous volume, but it will be helpful in understanding the fuller development of the whole Southern system if the basic outlines are briefly recapitulated here so that they can be followed through without break into the post-1922 era.

The historical background

The first electrification was that of the Brighton's South London line in 1909 between Victoria and London Bridge via Denmark Hill, closely followed by the Crystal Palace lines well before the First World War. These were electrified on what was, at the time, an advanced 6.7kV AC system: the 'Elevated Electrics', as they were called by virtue of their overhead catenary. Before the grouping, plans were well advanced for further extensions to Coulsdon and Sutton, to the extent that the Brighton overhead system was indeed extended to these two places in 1925 under the auspices of the new Southern Railway. Meantime, from 1915, the LSWR had tackled its own inner suburban services over the Kingston 'roundabout' and from Waterloo to Wimbledon via Putney (plus a few other associated bits and pieces), by means of a radically different 600V DC third rail system. Finally, the SE & CR was planning to go into the electrification business by means of a yet different 1500V DC system, though its ideas had not yet taken tangible form.

There was thus the making of an unholy muddle for the newly amalgamated Southern Railway, and although Walker allowed the Brighton line extensions to go ahead, even by the time they were opened he had realized that the SR must have a unified system of electrification. The final decision was by no means as clear cut as is sometimes supposed, and followed several years of debate, which at times took on quite acrimonious character, between the several protagonists of the various conflicting ideas. The eventual outcome was that the former LSWR three-rail system, later in the field than that of the LB & SCR though arguably less technically advanced, became the new Southern standard. In its favour, however, it did extend over more route mileage than the Brighton overhead in 1923 and was probably more economical to install.*

Added to the economic advantages of the LSWR system was the fact that it made use of rebuilt ex-steam stock, whereas the Brighton overhead had employed new vehicles. The LSWR philosophy in this respect was also adopted, for the most part, by the new Southern Railway and this left a legacy which even today (1988) is by no mean wholly eradicated and which also, curiously enough, represents not the least reason why, in terms of modernity, the Southern Region electrics of the BR period often lingered behind those of other regions until the late 1980s. The

---

* For a far more detailed technical account of the debate surrounding the final adoption of the LSWR 600V system, see *Triumph of the Third Rail* by J.N.Faulkner: 'Railways South East', Vol.1 No.2, Summer 1988.

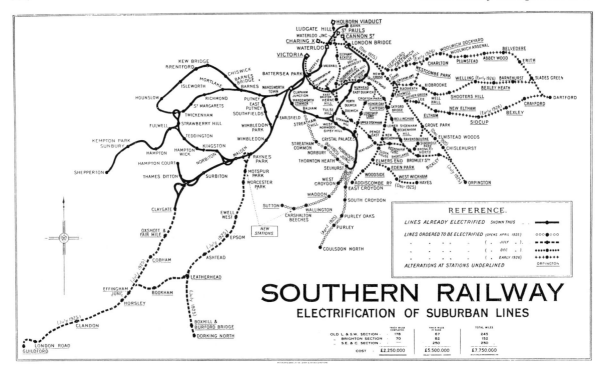

SOUTHERN RAILWAY
ELECTRIFICATION OF SUBURBAN LINES

	TRACK MILES COMPLETE	TRACK MILES IN HAND	TOTAL MILES
OLD L. & S.W. SECTION	178	67	245
„ BRIGHTON SECTION	70	82	152
„ S.E. & C. SECTION	250		250
COST	£2.250.000	£5.500.000	£7.750.000

full story thus embraces both the grouping period and the BR continuation and will figure both here and in the next volume. At this point, therefore, we shall concentrate on the period from the First World War to the end of the Bulleid era, starting with the very disparate inherited offerings.

In 1918, the LB & SCR had two sorts of new stock in operation on its overhead lines, the original South London stock, quite wide bodied and to a new square-panelled exterior style, and the later Crystal Palace units, more traditionally 'Brighton' and much narrower in body profile. These were pretty conventional EMUs, ie with passenger-carrying power cars and non-powered trailers, but the extensions to Coulsdon and Sutton added a third approach, though still very much in the Brighton visual idiom, with round-cornered panelling and arc roofs. For these services the SR adopted a quite new (and never

Figure 39 *Map showing the early stages of the Southern Railway electrification proposals down to 1926.*

Left *Ex-LB & SCR South London two-car unit at South Bermondsey in March 1928, 'wide-bodied' driving motor leading* (H.C. Casserley).

Five-car train of 'Crystal Palace' stock at Victoria early in the SR period. These sets had carriages of much more traditional 'Brighton' outline.

Newly-built third class driving trailer No 9171 for the Coulsdon and Sutton 1925 extensions of the 'elevated electrics'. The lineaments are still very firmly LB & SCR.

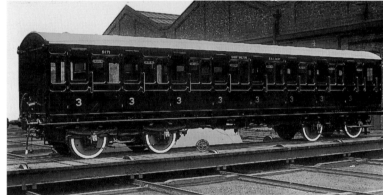

Southern Railway power car No 10101 when new in 1925. Note the guard and luggage space in the centre.

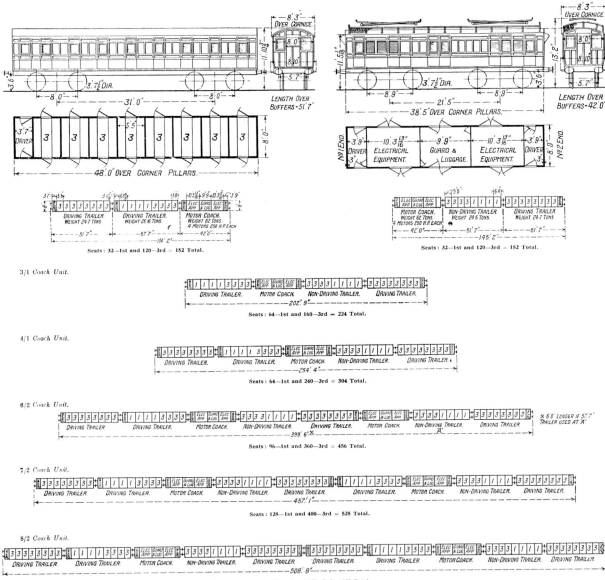

3/1 Coach Unit.

Seats: 32—1st and 120—3rd = 152 Total.

Seats: 32—1st and 120—3rd = 152 Total.

4/1 Coach Unit.

Seats: 64—1st and 160—3rd = 224 Total.

6/2 Coach Unit.

Seats: 64—1st and 240—3rd = 304 Total.

7/2 Coach Unit.

Seats: 96—1st and 360—3rd = 456 Total.

8/2 Coach Unit.

Seats: 128—1st and 400—3rd = 528 Total.

Seats: 128—1st and 480—3rd = 608 Total.

repeated) system of twin-bogie dedicated power cars. They were never called locomotives, presumably because they also incorporated the guard and luggage space, though that is what in effect they were. Commonly nicknamed 'milk vans', they were designed to run with non-powered passenger-carrying trailers in a whole variety of formations, dependent upon traffic demand — see Figure 40 — though the most common was probably one power unit in the centre of a four-car formation. Most of the trailers also had driving cabs to facilitate maximum flexibility of operation.

At the same time, the LSWR had gone for a basic three-car conventional EMU (motor/trailer/motor) with a driving cab at each end and passenger seats in all three carriages. Here, the desired operational flexibility was achieved by means of a single unit for off-peak services, two in multiple being used for busier operations. The vehicles themselves were converted from former suburban steam stock and retained the full LSWR-style panelling and other features. Their new driving cabs, however, displayed distinctively styled 'torpedo'-shaped ends which gave them a very jaunty and highly distinctive appearance.

In only one respect were the Brighton and LSWR carriages remotely similar: their use of conventional compartments. True, some of the LB & SCR first class trailers had a sort of internal 'open' side corridor, but each bay of seats had its own side door and this feature was to remain the norm on SR suburban units, whether the word stood for 'Railway' or 'Region', well into the 1960s. Both of the pre-group companies had offered first and third class accommodation, so the SR continued in this mode. However, the LSWR had used the introduction of its electrics as an excuse to abandon *three*-class provisioning and this too was to prove prophetic when, in logical continuation, first class accommodation was also abandoned on the inner suburban routes throughout the London area in October 1941.

From the outset, the Southern Railway had to reconcile these operational parameters if it was to achieve some sort of uniformity. Fortunately, at this time its immediate thoughts were solely concerned with suburban operations so it is with these that the analysis will start.

Suburban developments, 1925 onwards

'When the present programme is completed, expected before the end of 1926, the Southern Railway will have what is believed to be the most extensive system of Suburban Electrification to be found in this or any other country.'

Thus proclaimed *The Railway Gazette* in March 1925 in the first of what were to prove to be a whole series of highly detailed accounts of Southern electrification for the next 15 years which I am more than happy to acknowledge as a prime source of information for much of the account which follows. In fact, the Southern Electric has attracted to itself a very fine

and detailed literature which makes this writer's task abundantly simpler in terms of trying to distil its essence into a more general overview, and readers who would know more of this fascinating subject are well advised to consult the Bibliography.

The prime reason for Sir Herbert Walker's dedication to electrification seems to have been the substantial success achieved by both the LSWR and the LB & SCR in meeting the challenge of the urban street tramway and reviving their flagging fortunes to a level almost equal to that which pertained before the onset of the electric tramcar. Thus it was not surprising that very soon after the grouping, the various strands of development, independently determined by the three constituents of the SR, were brought together in a comprehensive plan for the wholesale conversion of the South London suburban services to electric operation. Having determined the system to be used (low voltage three-rail DC), the main issue, after meeting the actual cost of the necessary civil and electrical engineering work to effect the change-over, was to determine the most effective and economic way of solving the rolling-stock problem.

In this respect, the LSWR's pre-grouping *modus operandi* seemed, overall, to offer the best way forward. The first intention was, apart from the already agreed 'Brighton' expansion (see above), to extend the existing LSWR system out to Dorking and Guildford and simultaneously inaugurate the former SE & CR proposals from London Bridge as far as Dartford (by all routes) and to Orpington, from Victoria and Holborn Viaduct (via Bromley) and London Bridge (via Chiselhurst), not to mention the considerable 'cat's cradle' of interconnecting lines which, then as now, so characterizes the railways of this part of the country. The SR could only do this within its budget by an extensive rebuilding of steam stock to EMU pat-

Figure 40 *Simplified elevations and plans of the 1925 'elevated' stock together with sketch plans of the many possible train formations which could be made up from this stock.*

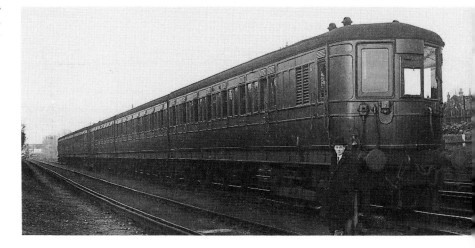

Right *The very first LSWR three-rail EMU, No E1, seen at the head of a six-car train at Strawberry Hill only two months after the grouping. Note the characteristic 'torpedo' front (H.C. Casserley).*

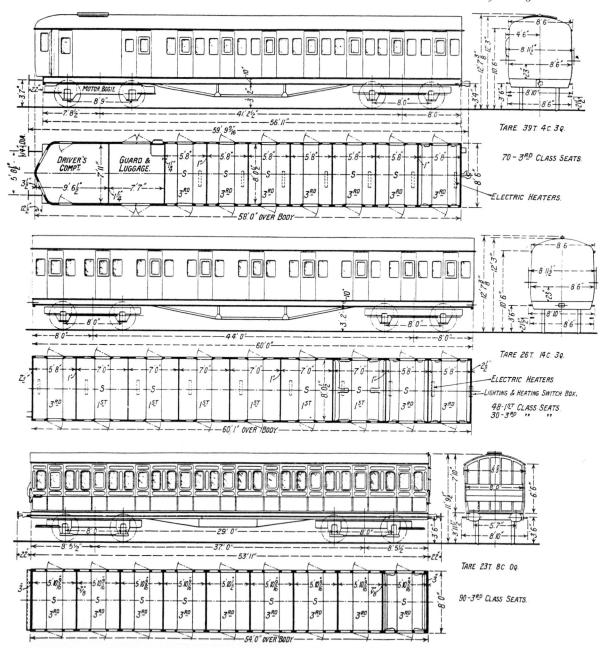

Figure 41 *Elevations and plans of the 'Western' section new-build EMUs of 1925, together with the converted ex-LB & SCR 'augmentation' trailers.*

Scale: 2mm = 1ft

tern, but even this could not wholly solve the problem. Thus began the seemingly unending business of combining newly built with re-worked older stock, the interplay between which constituting much of the fascination of the whole story. Apart from the 'overhead' stock already discussed, the basic LSWR three-car principle was adopted for the rest of the expansion

(motor/trailer/motor), but even so this took three quite distinctive forms.

On the former LSWR lines, now known as the 'Western' section, a tranche of new EMUs was built to supplement the existing converted ex-LSWR steam stock. These consisted of 'torpedo'-fronted 58 ft long third class motor cars and 60-foot composite trailers. Stylistically, they were very much in the newly established, albeit conventional 'Maunsell' SR style with steel outer panelling on timber framing. But their distinctive 'torpedo'-shaped front-end treatment, along with their fully lined 'pseudo-panelled' livery (albeit square-cornered) gave them a strong family resemblance to their LSWR ancestors. In later years they sported round-cornered painted panelling of more orthodox Southern style, and as such one motor car survives in the National Railway Museum at York.

By contrast, the former SE & CR lines, now regarded as the 'Eastern' section, were offered a slight variant of this type, though still retaining the basic 'two motor third plus composite trailer' formation. These too had a mixture of new-build and rebuilt ex-

steam stock, but in this case the former SE & CR carriage length dominated. Thus, the ex-steam stock rebuilds displayed SE & CR lengths and panelling and the corresponding new-built units were to slightly greater (SE & CR) length than their 'Western' section contemporaries. Whether new or rebuilt, motor thirds therefore had eight compartments (rather than seven) and the composites were 7F + 2T rather than the 6F + 3T of the ex-LSWR area. Thus, all Eastern section units were 62 ft long over frames. They also had a very different front-end treatment, much less pointed and conceivably more modern than the shape of the ex-LSWR and new-built 'Western' section units. This revised front-end styling was given to both the ex-SECR steam stock rebuilds and to the new build Eastern section carriages and was, with some slight variations, to become the Southern 'standard' for all EMU stock until the Bulleid era, as indeed was their greater length. Like the new Western section units, the new build Eastern section cars also came into service with square-cornered 'panelling', but before long, round-cornered styling became the Southern norm.

Figure 42 Elevations and plans of the new 'Eastern' section EMUs of 1925 which ran with similar trailers to those shown in Figure 41.

Scale: 2mm = 1ft

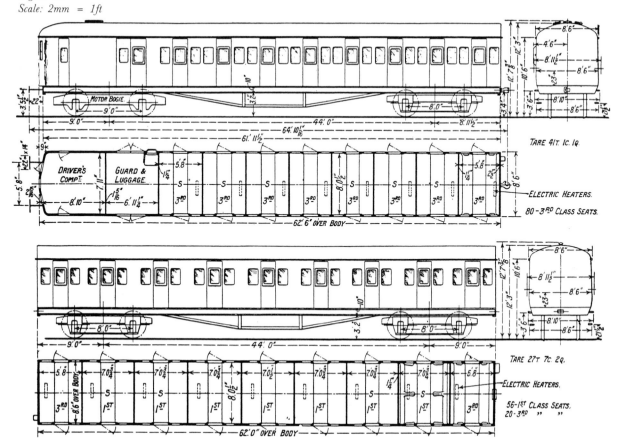

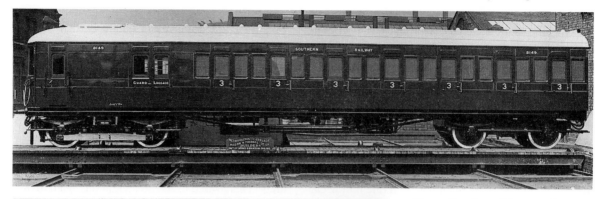

Above *Brand new Western section motor third No 8149 outside Saltley works in the 'square-panelled' version of the Southern livery. The Eastern section units were similarly finished*

Left *Third class (formerly composite) trailer coach No 9575 in Eastern section set No 1495, one of many which were converted from former steam stock, in this case two four-wheelers. Note the characteristic form of SE & CR carriage beading, devoid of continuous waist and eaves panels*

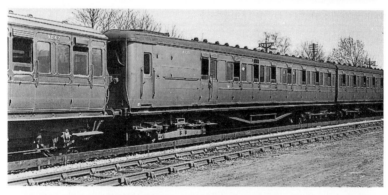

The view shows former LB & SCR augmentation trailer No 9042 coupled to the cab end of motor third No 8833 (set No 1698) which was one of the Southern conversions from LSWR stock embodying the post-grouping standard cab style

4SUB unit No 4105 was one of the first ten new Bulleid suburban sets, most of which emerged right at the end of the war. It is seen here new, ex-works at Eastleigh

Not surprisingly, given the publicity approach of the day, the Southern Railway tried its level best to kid the public that all these EMU sets were genuinely new vehicles, but since by far the majority (regardless of operating section) were rebuilds, no-one can seriously have been fooled for long! What is more, the pre-group origin of most of the Eastern section fleet was even more obvious than the Western section rebuilds, simply by the lack of genuine waist panelling, ex-SE & CR stock mostly having displayed the 'Wolverton' style of body treatment (see Part 1, Chapter 7). Perhaps the most beneficial aspect of the whole business all round was the genuinely high quality of both the ex-LSWR and ex-SE & CR steam stock which even allowed such subterfuges to be contemplated!

But that was not all; there was a further 'Joker' in the Southern pack at this fascinating time. The basic three-car (off-peak) and six-car (rush-hour) formation had already been called into question at really busy periods, even at the time of introducing these new Western and Eastern section developments, so the SR, strapped for cash as always, hastily came up with a swift panacea: the insertion of a two-car non-powered third class trailer unit between two of the conventional three-car EMUs. This idea dated back to the LSWR in 1919, but the dead give-away was that these new SR augmentation trailers were neither LSWR, SE & CR nor even new build, but were in fact rebuilds of surplus *Brighton* line steam stock whose length (54 ft) and arc roof profile matched up with neither that of the LSWR nor SE & CR! It was all most democratic, and students of carriage evolution must have been quite fascinated. The appended drawings of the various alternatives will, hopefully, make matters more clear.

The amazing thing was that it all seemed to work and attract still more traffic, so when it was finally determined that the erstwhile 6.7kV Brighton line overhead system should be converted to the now standard three-rail system, it can have occasioned no surprise whatsoever that the basis of many 'new' DC EMUs for the suburban workings on the 'Central' section of the Southern Railway (as the ex-LB & SCR operating area was now called) should now become a fairly catholic mixture of converted ex-steam and overhead stock. They too were mostly rebuilt into the standard three-car Southern EMU form (motor third/composite/motor third), though the wide-bodied 'South London' motors were rebuilt as twin units (now motor plus driving trailer) and went back to their old haunts because of loading gauge restrictions. With their combination of 'Brighton' arc roof carriage styling and quasi-standard Southern front-end treatment (based on that first applied to the ex-SE & CR rebuilds mentioned above), not to mention the

augmentation two-car trailer units, the Central section units became yet another variant to be added to the vast proliferation of styles to be seen on what is even now regarded as having been a very boring railway at the time!

For the Central section suburban services, in addition to the conversion of former Brighton stock, further ex-SE & CR steam stock was also turned into the now standard EMU form in 1928. This gave breathing space for the conversion to DC of the final overhead carriages, and the last overhead electrics ran in 1929.

These first stages of what was a quite remarkable transformation had, therefore, all taken place before 1930 and at an amazingly low cost, all things considered. Certainly nothing like it was happening on any of the other three main-line systems; yet hardly had the SR sorted out this first phase of its suburban affairs than it also started to address the medium and long-distance possibilities of electrification. These developments, even though they were soon to be happening simultaneously, will be left until after the end of the suburban story in the interests of clarity.

When the Central section conversion to DC was approaching completion in 1928, there began a further period of very large-scale ex-LSWR steam stock conversions. These were mostly from the old 'bogie block' sets, but the 1931 examples came from two six-wheelers mounted on a single new underframe. This 'second helping' of ex-LSWR EMUs differed from the original 1915 stock by having the new 'Southern' front-end instead of the old 'torpedo' shape and by being mounted on the now standard SR 62-foot EMU chassis. This was then followed by a lengthening of the original LSWR electric stock to the new standard SR 62-foot dimension by adding two compartments per coach and putting these too on to new frames; but their retained 'torpedo' cabs always identified them as the pioneer three-rail carriages.

Steam stock conversion to the purely inner suburban style went on until 1937, again involving ex-LSWR stock, by which time by far the bulk of the suburban fleet was of one of three styles, each readily identifying its former company of origin, though now all on new SR 62-foot chassis. However, such was the standardization achieved in running equipment, that the three styles were by no means confined to their original pre-group routes. Moreover, the new EMUs built in 1925 were now in a distinct minority. Regardless of exact origin, virtually all the stock was running in three-car units (now known as 3SUB). It remained thus throughout most of the Southern Railway period.

Throughout this time, the strengthening two-car trailer units continued to be used at peak periods. The twin trailer idea, though it originated on the

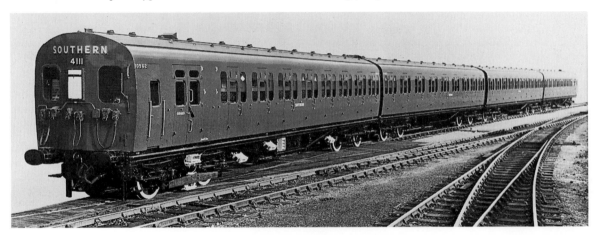

LSWR in 1919, had by the late 1930s been extended to all lines, while the trailers themselves, also converted from pre-group steam-hauled carriages, were by now a thoroughly heterogeneous mixture of stock from all three companies, by no means always marshalled with 3SUBs of the same architectural parentage. Furthermore, because of their lack of driving cabs, the trailers could occasionally cause operational problems when operating in support of a single 3SUB, it being not unknown for the motor set, *in extremis*, to have to run round its trailers for the reverse working. Oliver Bulleid fairly soon put a stop to this nonsense by taking the obvious step (or at least it seems obvious enough in retrospect) of separating the two trailers and inserting one each into a 3SUB unit, thereby creating the 4SUB, the familiar formation in more modern days.

The idea came from Bulleid's first venture into new stock building for the Southern Electric when, in 1941, he introduced the prototype 4SUB unit No 4101 as the first brand new stock for the purely suburban section of the Southern Railway since the 1925 cars. In them he revealed for the first time the new 'Bulleid' body profile, eventually (in the late 1940s/early 1950s) to become very familiar throughout the system. Its continuously curving side contour enabled six per side, while the compartments were of almost Gresley LNER-like meanness in their inter-partition dimensions. There were ten compartments in the motors and 11 in the third class trailer; maybe there was some inherited influence from Bulleid's old company, who knows? Only one set was built in 1941 and its second trailer was a ten-compartment composite, but at much the same time the railways abolished first class on London's suburban lines and the composite was immediately downgraded. The remaining nine sets of this type appeared in 1944 and 1945 and had two trailer thirds from the start.

In spite of their cramped interiors, the prototype 4SUBs were rather handsome looking sets in which were combined the cab style of the 1939 2HAL units (see page 138) with Bulleid's distinctively new body profile. They certainly looked far more modern than most of their predecessors. But the passengers did not like the cramped compartments and said so; accordingly, the next new 4SUBs in 1946 had one less compartment in each of the two types of carriage. More to the point, however, these new units also had quite different non-domed front-end which thereafter increasingly came to symbolize the Southern Electric in almost all its forms as stock was replaced. Even more significantly — unlike the prototype 4SUBs which retained traditional wood/canvas roofs — they were also all-steel in construction, being built by assembling prefabricated cab and compartment 'modules' on to the standard Southern chassis.

During the next five years until well into BR days (1951), the new Bulleid 4SUBs came into service seemingly by the bucketful. There were subtle

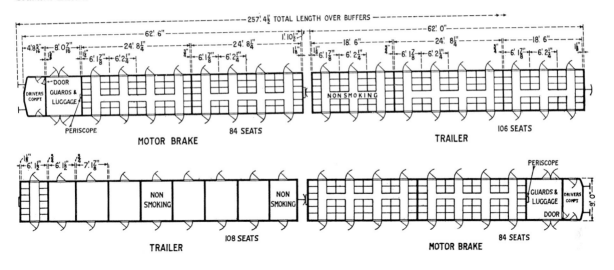

MOTOR BRAKE — 84 SEATS

TRAILER — 106 SEATS

TRAILER — 108 SEATS

MOTOR BRAKE — 84 SEATS

Above left *This close-up view of the new-style cab on motor third No 10950 of 4SUB No 4105 also gives clear detail of Bulleid's new curved-side carriage profile*

Below left *The familiar face of the post-war Southern: prototype vertical front 4SUB No 4111 when new in 1946*

Figure 43 *Floor plans of the later centre-aisle 4SUBs together with elevations, plans and perspectives of the experimental 4DD unit. Note the larger centre compartments of the non-open 4SUB trailer, a legacy of the fact that they were designed before the abolition of first class on London suburban workings.*

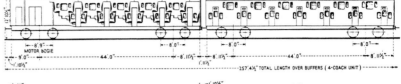

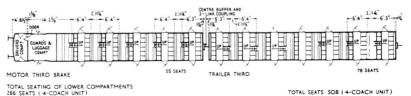

TOTAL SEATING OF UPPER COMPARTMENTS 242 SEATS (4-COACH UNIT)   55 SEATS   66 SEATS

MOTOR THIRD BRAKE   55 SEATS   TRAILER THIRD   78 SEATS

TOTAL SEATING OF LOWER COMPARTMENTS 266 SEATS (4-COACH UNIT)   TOTAL SEATS 508 (4-COACH UNIT)

changes between batches, well covered by the more specialized literature, but the only really important innovation in most of the later series was to substitute an 'open'-style interior layout in many of the cars. They still retained a full set of outside doors, but the absence of compartment partitions, combined with a centre aisle, enabled passengers to distribute themselves more evenly through the carriages. Seats were arranged 2 + 3.

Meanwhile, the older units were gradually phased out, but before this happened almost all of them had been, as stated above, converted to 4SUB form by the insertion of an extra trailer. It so transpired that there were not enough pre-group-style trailers to allow all former 3SUBs to be thus enhanced, so a fair number of new augmentation trailers were also built.

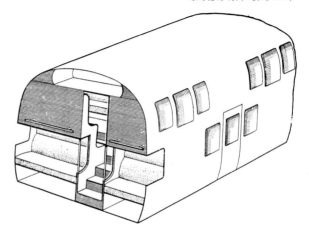

These, naturally, followed the new Bulleid profile so there were ultimately some very odd-looking hybrid units indeed whose constant formation and re-formation no doubt brought great delight to perceptive observers. Almost any theoretical combination of styles could be and probably was seen. However, large-scale withdrawal of the early pre-war-style units was also being carried out simultaneously with the introduction of new Bulleid 4SUBs, and this led to the final phase in the story.

When the old units were withdrawn, their rebuilt pre-group bodies were by now, of course, mostly running on new SR standard chassis. It will therefore occasion no surprise that when the final new-style 4SUBs were built, all but a few of them utilized the salvaged frames. They were mostly also given the still quite new Bulleid-style augmentation trailers (see above) which, naturally, were not withdrawn when the old 3SUB units went to the scrapyards. Thus, the final 4SUBs were not quite as new as they might have seemed — Southern tradition died hard and was still by no means over, as the next volume will reveal. But at least with the massive re-equipment of the 1945-51 period, Southern suburban services were operated by a far more homogeneous fleet than ever before. It was made even more so when the first genuinely 'BR' continuation came into service in the form of the 4EPB units in 1951 — visual 'clones' of Bulleid stock but with very different traction equipment. But they too must wait their time until Volume 3.

The final purely 'Southern' contribution to the suburban story actually dated from 1949 and was yet another example of Bulleid's rather idiosyncratic approach. This time, however, though the intention was sound, the end product was a bit of a disaster; it was, of course, the celebrated eight-car train, made from two units each type-classified 4DD (Double-Deck). It should, more properly, have been described as a split level design, and came about as a valiant attempt to increase train capacity without adding to train length.

Even though the by now standard 4SUB unit with six-per-side seating, and working in multiple to give an eight-car train at busy times, gave more seats than the old '3SUB plus augmentation trailers' approach, there was still much overcrowding. The 4DD units were a brave attempt to cope but were conceptually flawed on several counts. For one thing, they were, of necessity, built to the maximum possible structure gauge and were thus confined to only a few of the overcrowded routes (Charing Cross and Cannon Street to Dartford and Gravesend) and there were only half as many outside doors as compartments, so loading and unloading took longer. Passengers also complained about the lack of room, lack of comfort and poor ventilation. After about a years's trial, it was decided not to repeat the idea but instead to lengthen station platforms to allow ten-car sets of conventional stock to be used. The experimental set did, however, go on serving the Dartford line for 20 years, so maybe it earned its keep. When finally withdrawn in 1971, it probably departed the scene unloved by any save the enthusiast fraternity who could not understand why no one would preserve it! Later, two motors and a trailer were preserved at Ashford and though the trailer was subsequently scrapped, a motor coach still survives.

Main-line electrification, 1932 onwards

During the earlier stages of the Southern's electrification, there was a degree of uncertainty as to the wisdom of extending the new system much beyond the 20 to 30 mile distance which the above-mentioned suburban routes mostly represented, partly because the distances involved were considered to be rather

more 'main line' in their characteristics and not wholly appropriate to being served by multiple unit sets of the then 'state of the art' technology. In retrospect, this seems rather absurd considering the non-corridor nature of most long-distance trains on the constituents of the Southern Railway (save for a few LSWR exceptions), but be that as it may, there was a fairly strong feeling that any medium to long-distance services ought to have locomotive haulage, and there was a sound technical reason why this would be difficult to achieve with the now standard three-rail system.

The large number of complicated junctions on the Southern decreed that there had to be numerous gaps in the conductor rails. This posed no problem with multiple unit stock with current collectors at each end, but third rail locomotives might not be able to

Top left *'Hybrid' 4SUB (believed to be set No 4479) consisting of a new Bulleid post-war trailer inserted into a pre-war 3SUB whose carriages are of SE & CR origin*

Above left *4DD unit No 4001 in service, clearly showing the full extent made of the structure gauge in achieving the extra seats*

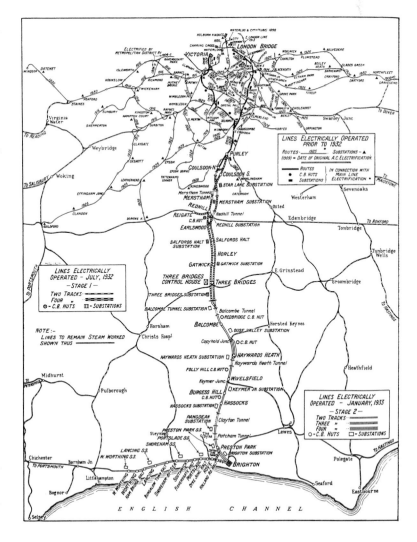

Figure 44 *Map showing the scope of the Brighton line electrifications. Though through services to Brighton did not commence until 1933, the Purley-Three Bridges section was in use by mid-1932.*

bridge such gaps and in consequence there would probably be the need for expensive overhead wiring at junctions, combined with dual standard collecting equipment. In the event, the company resolved on the EMU solution for the most pressing of the longer-distance routes (that of the former LB & SCR to Brighton) and took advantage of a Government remission of passenger duty in 1929 to help finance not only the extension of the third rail, but also the building of a completely new range of EMU stock.

The full service commenced on 1 January 1933, and the design of the new stock was intended to reflect its main-line nature, but the implementation was, in reality, more in the nature of a long-distance suburban operation than that of a genuine main line. In the context of the Brighton route this was not, perhaps, too unreasonable, but in the event it proved so successful that in due time the EMU concept was extended to most Southern lines and eventually took over routes extending to well over 100 miles from London in the BR period.

The original intention was to alternate express and semi-fast services, and to this end two basic types of unit were introduced. The semi-fast sets were of four cars and not much more than glorified suburban units. They were given the classification 4LAV in the then semi-descriptive form of coding used by the Southern, but there was but a single lavatory-equipped composite to mark them out from their purely suburban brethren. This composite had a side corridor (but no gangway to adjacent vehicles) and a lavatory at each end. Stylistically, they were pure Maunsell, with perhaps a hint of LSWR in their general shape, and they featured the new and rather handsome 'Southern' standard driving cabs with domed roof-end first seen on the Eastern section suburban units of 1925.

For the so-called 'express' services, something distinctly superior was both felt to be desirable and was actually achieved. These were the celebrated six-car sets, the first genuinely long-distance EMUs built in Britain and a quantum leap forward from most stock which had ever served the Brighton line, save for the few decent lavatory and/or Pullman sets in LB & SCR days (Chapter 7) or the early post-group steam-hauled corridor coaches (see p. 282). They mostly came in standard formation, but there were two noteworthy groups of 'special' sets and it is worth remarking that Pullman insisted on having its shout in all of them, this being a residue from the pre-group arrangement with the Brighton company.

In all cases, the motor cars were all-steel in construction and came from outside contractors, the order being equally split between Metro-Cammell and the Birmingham RCW Co, following a prototype

from each of these two firms. One of these, that from the Birmingham RCW Co, was a slab-sided unit, whose external lines were rather reminiscent of the SE & CR 'Continental' boat stock (see page 18), but the other prototype followed the more traditional Southern appearance and was to set the style adopted for the production series from both firms. These driving motor thirds were very heavy at 57 tons, they had open-style interiors and were arguably by far the most handsome-looking of the new coaches with their large picture windows and well-schemed front-ends. They were by no means inferior within the walls either.

The standard formation was a 6PUL 'express' unit, gangwayed throughout its length with a mixture of corridor and open accommodation in the third class, side corridor only for the first class ordinary and a Pullman composite kitchen car for the dining provision — hence the 'PUL' in the type designation. The Pullman cars were of a new interior style, there never having been composite kitchen cars (or EMU Pullmans for that matter) before. They made no exterior visual concessions in either style or livery to the new order and added an incongruous look to the sets, in spite of their self-evident appeal. This visual nonconformity between 'inserted' Pullmans and ordinary stock was to last well into BR days on the Southern lines. The side-corridor stock was built by the SR to the now standard Maunsell style (steel body panelling on timber framing with wood/canvas roof) and had the new-style 'tall' corridor windows, but inside a very useful improvement was the double sliding doors to the compartments from the corridors. Regrettably, this very practical idea — also characteristic of most LMS side-corridor stock from this same time onwards — did not long remain a standard Southern offering.

The two special groups were the three 6CIT units for the 'City Limited' service and the celebrated five-car all-Pullman sets for the 'Brighton Belle', type designated 5BEL. The latter will be considered in the Pullman chapter, but it is convenient to mention the 6CIT units here. They were very similar to the 6PULs save that the three side-corridor coaches were all first class and the only third class seats were in the driving motors. The Pullman diner was exactly the same as in the 6PUL sets. The prototype motor thirds (see above) were both used in 6CIT units, but after the war, when first class accommodation was less sought after, some of the cars were downgraded and the units became 6PULs. Plans of the three main types of units (express and semi-fast) are appended, along with more detailed drawings of some of the individual types.

In the event, the designed division between the express services and the slow/semi-fast operations, which justified the different forms of sets, did not

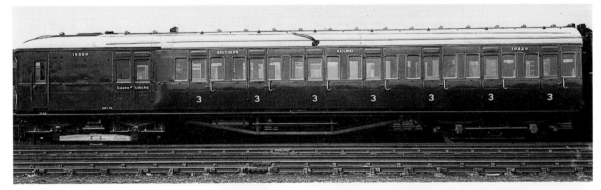

Above *Motor third No 10520 from 4LAV set No 1930, showing its basically suburban nature. By now (see page 123) the Southern EMU livery had settled down to a 'round-panelled' form*

Right *4LAV unit No 1934 in service near Oxshott in 1932, motor third brake No 10527 leading. Note the recessed outer ends, typical of Maunsell's company-built brake-ended 9 ft wide carriages of all types, also the destination boards, typical of much pre-war Southern working, by the guard's door. The high-windowed corridor-side configuration of the lavatory composite can also clearly be seen*

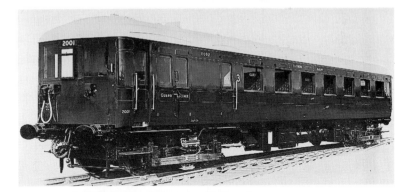

The dignified motor brake third design for the 6PUL/6CIT sets. This is No 11002 from set No 2001.

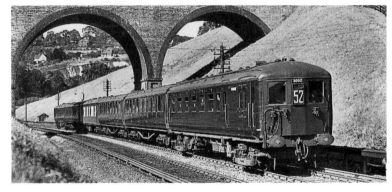

6PUL set No 3002 in service on a down Eastbourne express on the Quarry Line, taken at some time after the set was re-numbered from 2002 in 1937.

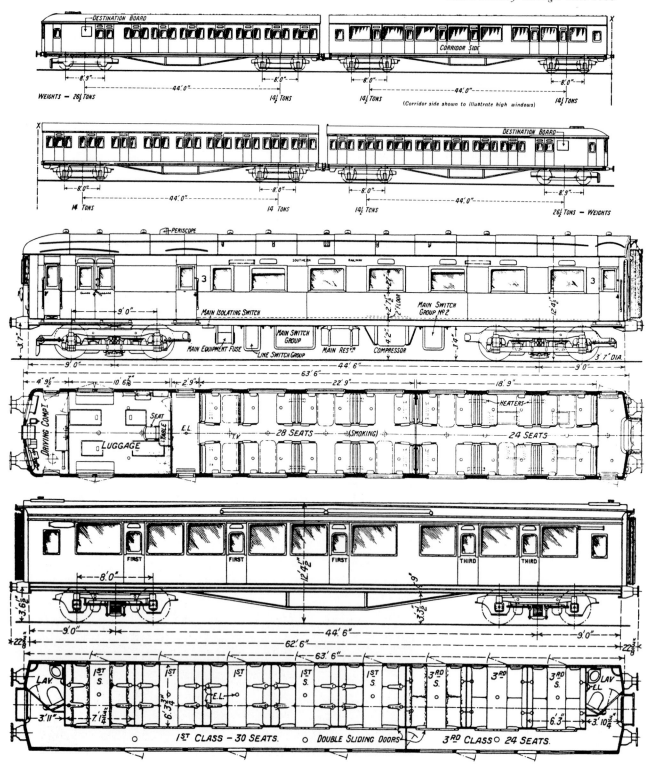

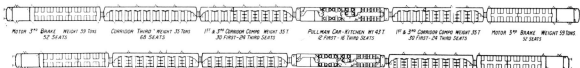

| MOTOR 3RD BRAKE. WEIGHT 41 TONS | 1ST & 3RD LAV. COMPOSITE WEIGHT 29 TONS | 1ST & 3RD COMPOSITE. WEIGHT 28 TONS | MOTOR 3RD BRAKE. WEIGHT 41 TONS |
| 70 SEATS | 30 FIRST - 24 THIRD SEATS | 40 FIRST - 40 THIRD SEATS | 70 SEATS |

| MOTOR 3RD BRAKE WEIGHT 59 TONS | CORRIDOR THIRD WEIGHT 35 TONS | 1ST & 3RD CORRIDOR COMPO WEIGHT 35 T | PULLMAN CAR-KITCHEN WT 43 T | 1ST & 3RD CORRIDOR COMPO WEIGHT 35 T | MOTOR 3RD BRAKE WEIGHT 59 TONS. |
| 52 SEATS | 68 SEATS | 30 FIRST-24 THIRD SEATS | 12 FIRST - 16 THIRD SEATS | 30 FIRST-24 THIRD SEATS | 52 SEATS |

| MOTOR 3RD BRAKE WEIGHT 59 TONS | CORRIDOR 1ST WEIGHT 34 TONS | CORRIDOR 1ST WEIGHT 34 TONS | PULLMAN CAR-KITCHEN.WEIGHT 43 TONS | CORRIDOR 1ST WEIGHT 34 TONS | MOTOR 3RD BRAKE WEIGHT 59 TONS |
| 52 SEATS | 42 SEATS | 42 SEATS | 12 FIRST - 16 THIRD SEATS | 42 SEATS | 52 SEATS |

work out quite as perfectly as might have been expected, and it was by no means rare to see a twelve-car train consisting of three 4LAV units pressed into use on the faster workings — and vice-versa with the express sets, one supposes. BR tried again when it replaced them in the 1960s with two differently conceived units, but met with not much greater success. Some of this nonsense still persists as Volume 3 will reveal.

That apart, the Brighton scheme was a huge success, and before long it was the turn of Eastbourne, Hastings and most points adjacent, to which locations the third rail had penetrated by mid-1935. Once again, new stock was provided, and though the basic Brighton line philosophy was followed, it was not slavishly copied. In this instance the six-car express sets were wholly SR, Pullman only providing the catering crews, not being able to afford further new cars. In consequence, the new trains were altogether neater-looking than the 6PUL sets and were known as 6PANs because their catering was provided from a PANtry in one of the first class vehicles. This car also had its first class side-corridor accommodation arranged without exterior compartment doors, a well nigh revolutionary concept for the Southern but all the more welcome for that. But the single door to the corridor returned, and outside compartment doors were found on all other carriages.

Other than the pantry first, the basic formation employed similarly styled coaches to the Brighton sets, but instead of two composites a full first and full third were offered (see appended plans). The motor thirds were also slightly different in that they featured sliding ventilators above their big picture windows. All told, the 6PANs were a considerable aesthetic improvement on the 6PULs and a fine advertisement for the Southern system. In due course, the 6PANs and 6PULs worked turn and turn about on both the Brighton and the Hastings lines and a sort of standardized 6PUL-6PAN formation became the common twelve-car train for some 30 years.

For the semi-fast and slow services on this latest section of the Southern Electric, including its 'out of town' branches and the shorter purely coastal runs, the 4LAV idea was not repeated; instead, two-car units were provided, one of which was a completely new design — the 2BIL (BI-Lavatory). Though of basic side-corridor form, there was no inter-connecting gangway and each half had its own toilet. One element was a motor third, the other a composite trailer with driving cab, and the idea was that they could be made up into four, six or even eight cars as needed. It was a nice thought — and successful when practical — but there were none too many of

Figure 45 Typical first generation Brighton line EMUs are featured in this set of drawings. They are, from the top: a) Simplified elevations of the 4LAV sets. b) Detailed elevations and plans of the motor third brakes and the corridor composite trailers from the 6PUL sets. NB The Pullman drawings to match these cars will be found on page 506).

Scale: 1/10" = 1ft

c) (above) Sketch plans of the 4LAV, 6PUL and 6CIT units of which 33, 20 and 3 sets respectively were introduced.

Right *The clean lines of the 6PAN units — and the different arrangement of the window ventilators on the motor brakes — are seen in this view of set No 2036 circa 1936*

Left *Compartment side of motor third brake No 10574 from 2BIL unit No 1897, one of the ten new 1935 sets. This time, the brake ends were not recessed.*

Figure 46 *These drawings show the new stock introduced for the Hastings and Eastbourne extensions and show, from the top:*
a) Sketch plans of a 6PAN set together with semi-detailed elevations and plans of the four carriage types involved.
b) Elevations and plans of the new 2BIL units.
c) Elevations and plans of the 2NOL units, but omitting all evidence of their former LSWR panelling!

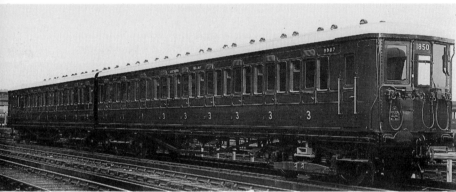

Left *2NOL unit No 1850, one of 78 such sets built from former LSWR steam stock in 1935-6*

them at first (only ten sets) and to complete the re-equipment the SR, possibly financially exhausted by its unaccustomed building of so much new EMU stock for the new express services, resorted to its familiar 'make do and mend' approach by offering the rest of the 'new' two-car fleet in the form of rebuilt pre-group LSWR steam stock.

So, out again from sundry highways and byways came the old warriors, this time to re-emerge as two-car non-corridor units (motor brake third plus driving trailer composite). They were in effect 2SUBs, but for some reason which is by no means clear, the SR this time preferred to indicate their comfort status (or lack of it!) by classifying them 2NOL (NOn-Lavatory).

The next phase of the main-line electrification was soon destined to reveal itself as the most ambitious to be tackled yet: the direct line of the old LSWR to Portsmouth from Waterloo. By now, some of the limitations of the six-car main-line units were beginning to be clear, not least the lack of gangways between sets. Furthermore, the all-steel motor cars were very heavy and not kind to the track. They were also expensive and the Southern was, yet again, watching its pockets. The consequence of all this was that the new Portsmouth main-line express stock was to a possibly less pleasing exterior design and built

more to a budget. For the first time for main-line EMU stock, the motor cars were built with timber frames and wood/canvas roofs (to save weight), and by the SR not outside contractors. Yet they were also probably the most familiar of all the Southern express EMU types.

Other than the constructional form of the motor thirds, the most obvious change from the earlier main-line express sets was the reduction in number of carriages per set from six to four, combined with through gangway connections at the driving ends. This gave the stock a sort of untidy look compared with the earlier six-car sets, and the slightly asymmetrical one-eyed look of the driving ends caused the units instantly to be nicknamed 'Nelsons', no doubt augmented by the Portsmouth connection. But they were vastly more practical, and the through-gangwayed form set the style for all subsequent main-line EMU stock on the Southern lines right down to the Class 442 'Wessex Electrics' of 1988.

Two types of standard four-car set were offered (see Figure 47), a non-dining 4COR (CORridor) and a dining 4RES (REStaurant) unit. Normally they operated as eight or twelve-car formations with one 4RES per train, but over the years formations tended to change and some of the dining cars were converted to buffets after the war. A rather retrograde step was

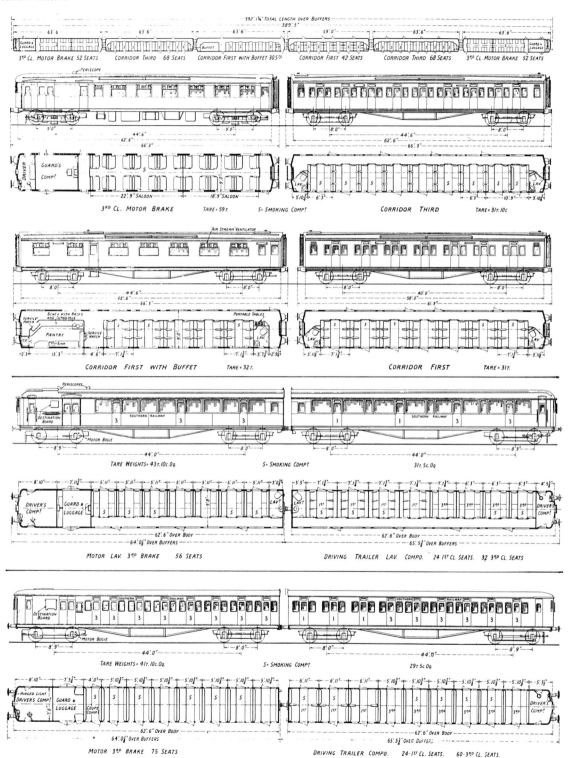

392' 1¼" TOTAL LENGTH OVER BUFFERS

389' 5"

63' 6" | 63' 6" | 63' 6" | 59' 0" | 63' 6" | 63' 6"

3ᴿᴰ CL. MOTOR BRAKE 52 SEATS — CORRIDOR THIRD 68 SEATS — CORRIDOR FIRST WITH BUFFET 30 Sᵀˢ — CORRIDOR FIRST 42 SEATS — CORRIDOR THIRD 68 SEATS — 3ᴿᴰ CL MOTOR BRAKE 52 SEATS

PERISCOPE

9' 0" — 9' 0" — 8' 0" — 8' 0"

44' 6" — 44' 6"

62' 6" — 62' 6"

66' 3" — 66' 3"

GUARD'S COMP.ᵀ — DRIVER

22' 9" SALOON — 18' 9" SALOON

LAV. — 6' 3" — 6' 3" — 10' 9" — 3' 10½"

3ᴿᴰ CL. MOTOR BRAKE — TARE = 59 T. — S = SMOKING COMP.ᵀ — CORRIDOR THIRD — TARE = 31 T. 10 c.

AIR STREAM VENTILATOR

8' 0" — 8' 0" — 8' 0" — 8' 0"

44' 6" — 40' 0"

62' 6" — 58' 0"

66' — 61' 9"

SERVICE HATCH — BENCH WITH RACKS AND CUPBOARDS — PORTABLE TABLES — SERVICE HATCH — PANTRY — SINK — LAV. — LAV.

CORRIDOR FIRST WITH BUFFET — TARE = 32 T. — CORRIDOR FIRST — TARE = 31 T.

PERISCOPES

DESTINATION BOARD — 3 — SOUTHERN RAILWAY — 3 — 3 — 1 — 1 — SOUTHERN RAILWAY — 3 — 3 — DESTINATION BOARD

MOTOR BOGIE

8' 9" — 44' 0" — 8' 0" — 8' 0" — 44' 0" — 8' 9"

TARE WEIGHTS = 43 T. 10 c. 0 q. — S = SMOKING COMP.ᵀ — 31 T. 5 c. 0 q.

DRIVER'S COMP.ᵀ — GUARD & LUGGAGE — LAV. — LAV. — DRIVER'S COMP.ᵀ

62' 6" OVER BODY — 62' 6" OVER BODY

64' 0¼" OVER BUFFERS — 65' 5½" OVER BUFFERS

MOTOR LAV. 3ᴿᴰ BRAKE 56 SEATS — DRIVING TRAILER LAV. COMPO. 24 1ˢᵀ CL. SEATS. 32 3ᴿᴰ CL. SEATS

DESTINATION BOARD — 3 — SOUTHERN RAILWAY — 3 — 3 — 3 — 1 — 1 — 1 — SOUTHERN RAILWAY — 3 — 3 — 3 — 3

MOTOR BOGIE

8' 9" — 44' 0" — 8' 0" — 8' 0" — 44' 0" — 8' 9"

TARE WEIGHTS = 41 T. 10 c. 0 q. — S = SMOKING COMP.ᵀ — 29 T. 5 c. 0 q.

HINGED LIGHT DRIVER'S COMP.ᵀ — GUARD & LUGGAGE — COUPE COMP.ᵀ — DRIVER'S COMP.ᵀ

62' 6" OVER BODY — 62' 6" OVER BODY

64' 0¼" OVER BUFFERS — 65' 5½" OVER BUFFERS

MOTOR 3ᴿᴰ BRAKE 75 SEATS — DRIVING TRAILER COMPO. 24 1ˢᵀ CL. SEATS. 60 3ᴿᴰ CL. SEATS.

the fitting of screw couplings and non-Pullman gangways to the outer ends, all the more odd since the SR had virtually adopted the more modern alternative by then.

Augmenting the main-line express stock was a modest infusion of additional 3SUBs, augmentation trailer pairs and 2NOLs for inner suburban use (ex-steam stock rebuilds, of course) and a very considerable provisioning of 38 brand new 2BIL sets for semi-

fast working. The latter were obviously proving a boon to the Southern and their ability to be operated in a variety of combinations from two cars upwards no doubt made them very acceptable throughout the system.

The Portsmouth line went all-electric in 1937, and when it was completed there remained only the mid-Sussex area from Dorking to Bognor, Littlehampton and Worthing (via Angmering) to be infilled in order

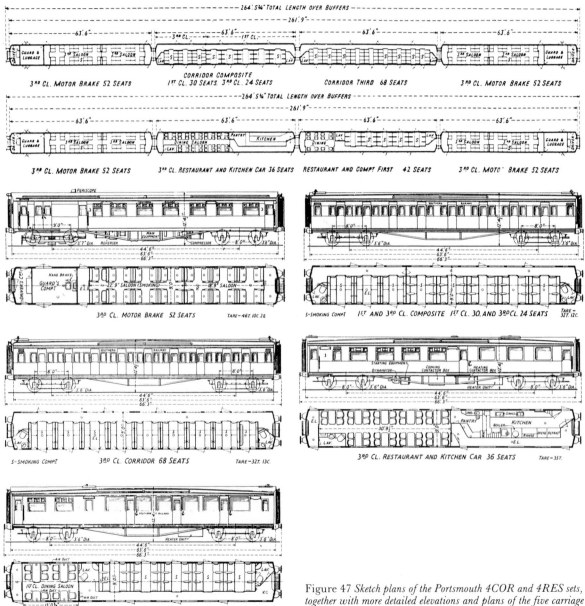

Figure 47 *Sketch plans of the Portsmouth 4COR and 4RES sets, together with more detailed elevations and plans of the five carriage varieties built for the 1937 services.*

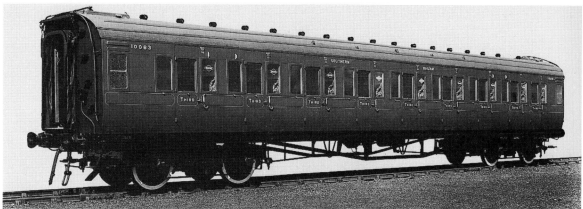

Top *Motor brake third No 11159 from 4RES unit No 3064, showing the first version of the simplified Southern livery which began to emerge at this time — waist 'panelling' only*

Above *Compartment side of corridor third No 10083 from 4COR unit No 3129. Note the half compartment at the far end and the fact that only two compartments were non-smoking!*

Above right *Two 4COR units working in multiple in 1937 headed by set No 3056, which is interesting because No 3056 was actually listed as a 4RES. There are, however, no diners in this train. From this angle, the wood and canvas roof structure of all cars is very clear.*

Right *The first class restaurant car interiors of the Portsmouth 4RES units were a little old-fashioned but by no means undignified.*

The 4BUF sets came out in 1938 in even more simplified livery — two yellow lines only — and the buffets carried the new unlined Malachite green scheme. Both these features are clearly seen here on set No 3074, the second of the series; for further details of the buffet cars, see page 100

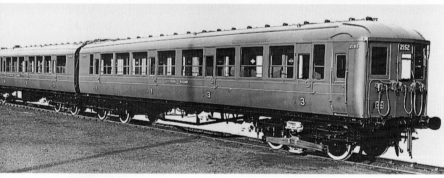

Corridor-side elevation of 2BIL unit No 2152, the last of the 1937-8 batch built in consequence of the Portsmouth and mid-Sussex extensions. Note again the much simplified lining, possibly even malachite green livery too, judging by the light tone

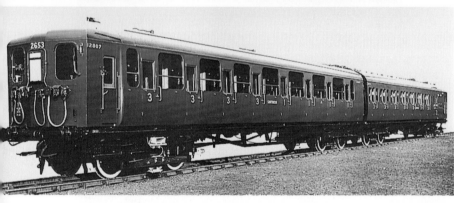

The 2HALs, exemplified here by unit No 2653 built in 1939, were the first SR vehicles to reveal some of Bulleid's new carriage styling ideas: flush sides and round-cornered fixed lights, for example. They also displayed a new-style EMU cab treatment and were finished in unlined malachite green

Right *The comfortless interior of a Bulleid 2HAL*

to virtually complete the electrification of the former LSWR and LB & SCR lines to the south coast. This was in turn completed in 1938 and further 4COR units were built for it along with a new type, the 4BUF (BUFfet), in place of the Portsmouth 4RES units. The new buffet cars in these units were amongst the first SR carriages to display Oliver Bulleid's new Malachite green livery and looked slightly incongruous in the middle of an otherwise olive green train. They also revealed in their interiors some of Mr Bulleid's more *outré* design fancies!

As with the Portsmouth line, the mid-Sussex extensions also received yet another large flotilla of brand new and by now almost ubiquitous 2BIL sets, this time no fewer than 68 twin units being provided. It

is very fitting that the NRM has preserved one of these highly characteristic sets in full working order and left it in the south of England where it makes occasional forays on some of its old stamping ground for the benefit of enthusiasts, often in aid of charity. A Portsmouth motor third is also preserved at York in non-operational order.

After the completion of the mid-Sussex scheme in 1938, the Southern, quite naturally, turned to the Kentish area of its parish, but its long-term plans were to be frustrated by the war and, in the event, the electrification of the main lines to the Kent Coast had to await BR days. There was, of course, slightly less urgency since Maunsell had already equipped these services with new steam-hauled corridor stock in the

1920s (see page 19) but there was opportunity for some modest expansion in the Eastern section in 1939 wherein the hand of Oliver Bulleid was first revealed in the EMU mode (Bognor buffet cars excepted). This took the form of a new two-car unit based on the 2BIL but with only one of the two coaches (the driving trailer composite) given a side corridor with lavatory access. It was, of course, called a 2HAL (HAlf Lavatory).

These units turned out to be the last purely 'Southern' EMUs to be built for main-line as opposed to suburban use, and their rather indeterminate nature (the motor third end was conventionally non-corridor) was a sort of conceptual reflection of the lines on which they were first used — extensions to Gillingham and Maidstone, more outer suburban than main-line in character. The coaches themselves were fairly typically Southern, but Bulleid fitted a new angular cab unit on them made of welded steel sheet. The bodyside fixed lights were flush to the outer panelling with rounded corners, rather in the style of Maunsell's final main-line corridor stock, and the ensemble represented a sort of uneasy halfway house towards Bulleid's familiar post-war style. They were far more spartanly finished than the 2BILs and by all accounts much more uncomfortable. In a much refined form, the cab style of the 2HALs re-appeared on the prototype 4SUB in 1941 (see page 390), but it was not to become a true Southern standard. When the 2HAL style was revived, briefly, after the formation of BR, the final few units embodied the new flat-fronted style, profile and all-steel construction of the Bulleid 4SUB.

Overall, however, in summarizing the first phase of the Southern Electric story, one can only admire the dedication and speed with which this not very wealthy railway, the smallest of the 'Big Four', made its valiant attempt to modernize one of the most complex railway networks in the world, even though some of its more quaint carriage efforts added a sort of 'comic opera' quality to the scene by their infinite variety. It had virtually completed the task (Kent Coast lines and a few other minor branches excepted) within but 16 years of the grouping, and one doubts not that but for the war, Dover and Folkstone would probably have joined Portsmouth and Brighton on the third rail network. It was a rate of progress which BR would have done well to copy after 1947. Yet nearly 40 more years were to pass before some of the former Southern Railway lines were finally converted — and not too far away from Central London either; the Oxted line did not get its third rail until 1987!

Partly as a result of the slow post-1948 progress, the former Southern EMUs of most types were to enjoy, collectively, the longest post-company active life of any of the 'Big Four' carriage designs, some last-ing well into the 1970s and, in BR-derived form, the 1980s too. By then they were well behind the times as also were some of their BR successors; but this is no slur on the original SR concepts of the 1920s and 1930s. It is more properly a compliment to their rugged and robust nature that these vehicles could carry on for so long under such intensive use; but that part of their story must await the next volume to resolve, save for one rather noteworthy exception to round out the story.

The Waterloo and City tube stock

It is, perhaps entirely typical of the Southern Railway that some of its most modern electric stock should have been built — and during the war at that — for its most unusual route, the deep-level tube between Waterloo station and the Bank of England. It is also entirely typical that at the time of writing this stock is still in active use, now almost 50 years old and still looking quite smart and modern in spite of the quite awful Network SouthEast livery which it now carries! However, the story started much earlier, and since it was given but fleeting mention in the first volume, this seems another case where the mainly post-grouping parameters of this present survey must be exceeded.

The Waterloo and City Railway arose from a desire by the LSWR to have a terminus nearer to the City of London than Waterloo, and some early mutterings were to be heard as far back as 1846. However, it was not until the success of the first deep-level tube, opened in 1890, had been appreciated (The City and South London — see Chap. 22) that the LSWR real-

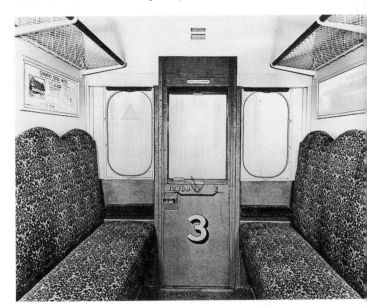

ized that an underground electric connection to the City might give the facilities needed. Powers to construct the line were obtained in 1893 and though it was built to the new tube style, the diameter was set at a rather larger dimension (12 ft 1¾ in normally, but 12 ft 9 in on curves) than that of the C & SL. The line itself was opened in 1898 and has been carrying commuters to the city ever since.

During that time there have only been two fleets of carriages, and the first of them, built in 1898, was responsible for services during most of the Southern Railway period as well as that of the LSWR. While I cannot prove it, it seems to me that to run such an intensive service for over 90 years with only one complete re-equipment probably constitutes some sort of record.

The first cars were built in the USA by Jackson & Sharp of Wilmerding in 1898. The roller-bearing bogies — an unusual idea at the time for such stock — were assembled at Eastleigh and five four-car sets

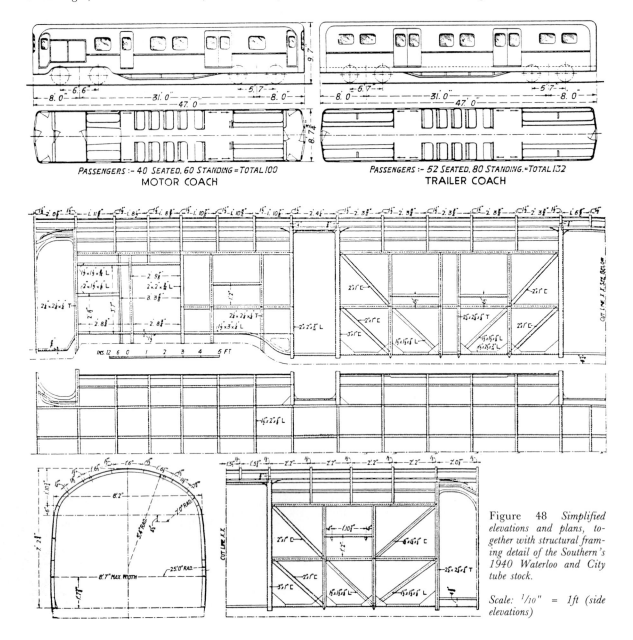

PASSENGERS :- 40 SEATED, 60 STANDING = TOTAL 100
MOTOR COACH

PASSENGERS :- 52 SEATED, 80 STANDING. = TOTAL 132
TRAILER COACH

Figure 48 *Simplified elevations and plans, together with structural framing detail of the Southern's 1940 Waterloo and City tube stock.*

Scale: ¹/₁₀" = 1ft *(side elevations)*

(motor/trailer/trailer/motor) were supplied. A year later, five single unit motor cars were built by Dick, Kerr and Co for non-rush-hour services. All vehicles were of quite definite American style and displayed wooden-bodied construction with vertical matchboarding below a pronounced waist rail. Inward-sloping windows above the waist were adopted so as to fit the tube profile, and the cars were given a natural varnished livery. They were very well finished considering they were for a route less than 1½ miles long, and their general quality was probably superior to most other London underground stock for many years. Internally, they displayed the mixture of transverse and longitudinal seats which eventually became characteristic of all underground trains but the seats, though cloth covered, were not upholstered.

Contemporary pictures reveal that great care was taken with the interior detail and the cars were sufficiently well built to last, virtually unchanged, until the SR determined on a complete modernization which took place in 1940. For this modernization, 12 new motors and 16 trailers were procured from the English Electric Co Ltd, the successors to Dick, Kerr. They were in fact made in the old Dick, Kerr premises. The intention was to operate five five-car trains (two motors and three trailers) with a modest amount of spare stock, the off-peak services being taken care of by detached motor cars running singly. Presumably the extra mileage likely to be run by the motor cars in consequence of this policy was the reason for having two spare motors but only one spare trailer.

The stock itself was distinctly modern-looking but had proportionally less window area than the old cars and within rather more standing space relative to seating areas. When fully loaded, some 60 per cent of the passenger capacity was represented by 'standees'. In general design terms they were rather similar to the pre-1938 London Transport tube stock in terms of the 'upswept' lower bodyside adjacent to the power bogie but thereafter most resemblance to LT stock was muted. Though they had pneumatically operated sliding doors and the usual mixture of transverse and longitudinal seats, their bodyside profile was continuously curved to gain maximum benefit from the tube shape, and one cannot help but wonder whether there was some design linkage between this stock and Bulleid's later adoption of a similar continuous curve on his conventional post-war carriages.

Basic body construction was of welded steel panels on a steel frame, the whole being mounted on an all-welded underframe. Again one wonders whether Mr Bulleid had a good look at the form of construction when designing his own post-war stock. Inside the cars, the finish was light and airy with rather less ceiling space devoted to advertising than on London

Replacement of old with new stock on the Waterloo and City line in 1940 at the point on the north side of Waterloo station where the tube lines connect with the surface system.

Transport — or, at least, it seemed that way. Light-coloured two-tone Rexine with discreet mahogany mouldings was adopted and the transverse seats were more akin to omnibus than railway practice. This time round, seats were upholstered, rust-coloured uncut moquette being the chosen material. All timber was treated with fireproof paint.

The cars were built to a robust standard and, given their short length of 47 ft, were quite heavy (motors 29½ tons, trailers 18¾ tons). There is little doubt that this substantial form of construction — and the fact that they spend most of their life underground, thus minimizing the rust problem — is a major reason why they have given almost 50 years' service so far and show no signs yet (1988) of being withdrawn. When they are eventually replaced, one of them would form a far more worthy candidate for permanent preservation than many other items I could think of.*

The Southern's Waterloo and City stock of 1940 probably represented the most advanced design of commuter vehicle ever built by the company & was also unusual in being operated on the only deep-level underground line not to come under the control of London Transport; and it is to that mammoth operation which we must now turn attention.

(NB This later happened and one preserved car can now (1996) be seen at the NRM)

22. The London Transport story

By almost any objective criteria, the history of the 'dedicated' London area railways forms something of a special case. Moreover, its distinctive nature has always been recognized in and reflected by railway literature, not least in the very extensive coverage with which the Metropolitan area has always been well blessed. Thus, as in the case of the Southern Electric, readers are recommended to consult the Bibliography for more detailed sources. This special pleading holds equally true in respect of the carriages built for those railways which eventually became amalgamated as 'London Transport' in 1933; so, within the space available, this chapter can never hope to be more than a general overview to help point the way to a basic understanding of a very complex subject. There will certainly be no space for consideration of every type of vehicle built.

However — and available literature notwithstanding — even to understand the nature of London Transport rolling-stock at no more than the most general level, we must first devote some space to an examination of the main historical factors. Furthermore, as I stated in my introduction, this chapter will also stray rather more from the strict 1923-53 period in terms of vehicle coverage. Just as with the four main-line companies, so too with London Transport, the post-amalgamation developments were very much a consequence of the inherited situation, and since little was said in earlier chapters, I shall try to make modest restitution here.

The historical background

The peculiar railway needs of London were probably first identified in mid-Victorian days and arose, in part, because of the success of the Metropolis in attracting so many trunk railway systems. For the most part — and for sound historical reasons — they either stopped close to the south bank of the Thames or along the general line of the Marylebone and Euston Roads in the north. This left a void in the centre, broadly that area now identified as the Cities of London and Westminster. In more strictly railway terms, it is the area inside the route of the London Transport Circle Line and, indeed, the familiar map of the London Underground is probably the best single aid to understanding. It is not reproduced here because it is meaningless in black and white, but I have ventured to assume that most readers will be familiar enough with its symbolism to enable me to use it as a 'hidden' visual aid.

On matters of terminology, London's railways have undergone several name changes since 1933 when the London Passenger Transport Board was established. After 1947, following the nationalization of the railways, it became the London Transport Executive and today, following the 1986 de-regulation, its railways are operated as London Underground Limited, itself answerable to London Regional Transport. All told, it seems simpler to forget the semantics and call it London Transport throughout; that is what most peo-

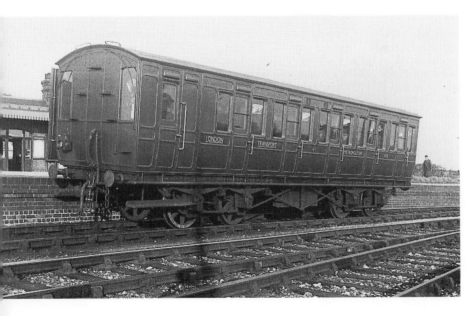

Undoubtedly the oldest coaches to serve the unified London Transport system were the rigid eight-wheelers originally built as long ago as 1866 by the Oldbury Carriage Company. They somehow or other managed to stagger on until 1935, largely because the Metropolitan had retained a handful for use on its steam-hauled Brill branch (formerly the Wotton Tramway). They were survivors of the original Metropolitan stock and known at one time as 'Long Charleys'. This view of No 41, believed to have been taken at Quainton Road circa 1934, could well have gone into Chapter 10, but it seemed best here as a symbol of the incredible variety which was a Metropolitan characteristic at the start of the London Transport era

ple still do! Fortunately, the names of most individual routes still link back to their pre-1933 origins.

By a long way the earliest lines to penetrate the inner London area were those which now form the Metropolitan and District lines (dark purple and green, respectively, on the famous map). These are different from all the others in that they originated well back in Victorian times as steam-hauled systems and were built to the normal structural dimensions of all other British railways. Much of their mileage is in the open air, and when they penetrated Central London they did so in tunnels made by the 'cut and cover' method just below street level. They are often referred to as 'surface' lines in consequence.

The two companies which owned them, the Metropolitan and the Metropolitan District Railways, were jointly responsible for operating the well-known Circle Line (originally the 'Inner' Circle and coloured yellow on the LT map), which was in effect created by linking together their two separate entries to London, the Metropolitan in the north and the District along Thames-side. Though never easy bedfellows, their interests were more compatible than contrary, so they rubbed along. The Metropolitan was the larger and even had some delusions of grandeur in that it always regarded itself as more of a proper railway than the District. It did, indeed, have some pretensions to main-line status because of its extended route from Baker Street to the Chiltern suburbs — 'Metroland' as the Company publicity department called it from 1915 — but it was always essentially a passenger commuter system, however much it might have liked to pretend otherwise.

Because of both their structural parameters and their early status, the two surface systems always operated rather different sorts of carriages from the rest of the London underground and even, in the early days, from each other. In purely dimensional terms, this difference still holds true today.

The remainder of the London system consists of deep-level 'tube' lines whose history goes back to 1890 when the pioneer City and South London Railway was formed. This was an independent locomotive-hauled system, electrified from the outset — as, indeed, were all the tube lines — and because its tubes were less than 11 ft in diameter it was more restricted than later similar systems which adopted a more or less standard 12-foot diameter tube, give or take a few inches. It was not until much later in the 1920s that the C & SLR became fully integrated with the main system by the expedient of enlarging its tubes to the standard size and linking it to the Hampstead Line (see below). It now forms the 'City' branch of the LT Northern Line (coloured black on the famous map) from Euston to Kennington via the Bank.

After the C & SLR came the unique Waterloo and City line of the LSWR, discussed in the last chapter. This never became part of London Transport, but the next oldest tube, the Central London Railway dating from 1900, did. It too was a locomotive-hauled line at first, but by 1903 had begun to adopt the EMU configuration which thereafter became standard for all tube lines. The CLR remained independent for some time and its original portion forms the middle section (between Shepherd's Bush, Bank and Liverpool Street) of the now much more comprehensive

The handsome and substantial nature of the Metropolitan's early clerestory electric stock is well seen in this close-up of a Harrow-bound train taken during the major reconstruction of Baker Street station which started in 1910

Central Line (bright red on the map). It was perhaps most famous in its early days for its name — 'The Tuppeny Tube' — a reference to its original 'flat fare' policy.

The remaining tube lines during the early period all dated from 1906-7 and shared common ownership and styling, though they were each physically separate and their original promotion was by different people. Before opening, they came into the ownership of an American company founded by Charles Yerkes, which also controlled the District Railway (see below), and from 1910 onwards the tube lines were operated under the corporate name of the London Electric Railway. In due course they were to form the central sections of the Bakerloo Line (originally Baker Street and Waterloo, map colour brown), the Piccadilly Line (originally Great Northern, Piccadilly and Brompton, map colour dark blue) and the West End branch of the Northern Line (originally Charing Cross, Euston and Hampstead, map colour black). Interestingly, after this first flush of deep-level tube lines, no more were built until the Victoria Line was opened some 60 years later.

In effect, the first deep-level tubes criss-crossed the area defined by the Circle Line and it was not until much later that they extended outwards into the suburbs. Though the expansion of the network is not part of their carriage history *per se*, it did of course involve extra stock provisioning and, as time went by, the extended underground lines, mostly still keeping north of the Thames, began to perform very similar functions to the electrified commuter lines which the main-line companies were developing south of the river. This pattern of differentiated approaches north and south of the Thames still underlays most of London's rail-borne commuter traffic to this day.

Because of their different origins, each of the various private underground lines developed its own styles of carriage and this was always more than simply a differentiation between surface and tube lines. For many years there was no way that a District train could be mistaken for a Metropolitan one, nor a Central London tube train be confused with its Bakerloo equivalent. To a large extent this is still reflected in the present-day scene (albeit rather more subtly than in older days), and stems from the fact that even after London Transport was formed in 1933, most stock replacement tended to be on a line by line basis, each route being operated by a broadly similar class of vehicle. There has, of course, been much coming together, and it will be the purpose of the rest of this chapter to examine the extent to which this had taken place by *circa* 1953.

Surface stock: 1905-1936

The twentieth-century history of London Transport railway carriages is mostly the history of electric stock, especially in the period covered by this volume, but even though this will form the remaining bulk of this chapter, it must be recalled that both the Metropolitan and the District Railways started as steam-hauled systems and, in the case of the Metropolitan, locomotive haulage remained a feature of its activity well into the post-nationalization era. Even then, some of its services were still steam hauled in the more rural suburbs though, of course, they were handed over to electric locomotives well out of town for the continuation to inner London. Like the Southern Railway, but not to the same extent, the Metropolitan also converted compartment steam stock to EMU form, and even in the early 1930s had new stock built to this traditional layout. Thus, for the whole of the first half of this century — and after — services on the Metropolitan were always a mixture of open saloon EMUs and compartment stock, some of the latter being locomotive hauled.

This thoroughly conventional compartment interior was to be found in Metropolitan Railway first class carriage No 422, built in 1905 as an EMU control trailer but converted in 1910, along with nine others, to form the first two so-called 'Dreadnought' sets for locomotive haulage on the non-electrified lines.

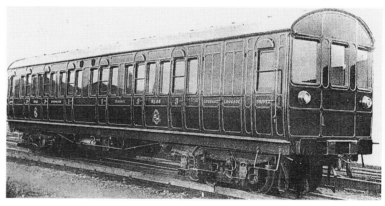

Above *A characteristically neat set of Metropolitan Railway 'Dreadnought' non-corridors out in the country north of Harrow in 1921 behind an unidentified Class 'H' 4-4-4T.*

Right *Metropolitan Railway single-unit 'Shuttle' car No 46 was a conversion in 1910 of a previous accident victim. In converted form, it shared the visual lines of the 'Dreadnought' stock, though not, of course, being intended for locomotive-haulage* (J. Whiting collection)

Each type of stock was confined to a specific service, but where they all converged (on the section between Baker Street and the City) anything was likely to turn up and I well remember my own surprise when, as a student, a pretty scruffy set of dingy brown non-corridors was presented at King's Cross for my trip to Baker Street. Years earlier, and as a child before the war, I had been 'programmed' to expect nice neat red and cream EMUs and had no notion at the time, nor even 15 years later, that these ancient conveyances still existed, much less that they were still in use! However, interesting though these compartment carriages were, they were no whit different, save in minor cosmetic matters, from many a thousand others, and in any case are well recorded in other books; so I have deliberately chosen to give them short weight here.

The real twentieth-century significance of London Transport, whether post-1933 or in its pre-amalgamated state, lies in the gradual evolution of the open saloon multiple unit carriage for purely urban working. And here the District Railway probably merits the pioneering role. As early as 1901, the District, in

an attempt to stem its declining fortunes, had concluded that electrification of its lines might prove the salvation, and this coincided with the arrival in Britain of a group of American businessmen who had made their money from electrified rail systems in the USA. They were headed by Charles Yerkes and took over the District Railway's fortunes. It was the same Mr Yerkes whose company almost simultaneously took control of three of the pioneering deep-level tube lines (see above), though Yerkes himself died before they were open. Thus, from the first Edwardian days, a large slice of what was to become London Transport was under unified control — the so-called Underground Group — and though all the systems were physically separate, the seeds were sown from an early date for the later development of common ideas.

In the event, this early amalgamation was to turn out to be the dominant influence in the subsequent development of London's underground system and was consolidated in 1913 when the City and South London, already in close proximity to the Yerkes lines at Euston and Kennington, also threw in its lot with

This 1934 view of a pair of older District Line clerestories gives a good impression of the difference between the steel-bodied 1923 stock with straight-through clerestories (on the left) and pre-First World War wooden-bodied trailer with domed-end clerestory (on the right). Both had hand-operated doors (London Transport Museum)

the Underground Group, as eventually did the Central London Railway. During all this time, the Metropolitan stayed aloof, and even when the final 1933 amalgamations were imposed it was a very reluctant guest at the wedding! In effect, though by far the largest of the constituent parts of London Transport, the Metropolitan was taken over by the group whose long-established 'UndergrounD' symbol rather set the style for the new organization.

In strictly carriage terms on the surface lines, the District and its rival followed quite different approaches, even discounting the Metropolitan's long espousal of compartments alongside its open EMUs. In a nutshell, the Metropolitan was very British while the District, hardly surprisingly, began to be influenced by American ideas from the onset of its electrification policies. This led both to the espousal of a clerestory roof form which survived for almost 70 years on the District Line itself, and to an interior layout concept which is now dominant throughout London Transport. Furthermore, in the early stock built for the District one can also see many ideas which, as Volume 1 has explained, were not slow to be taken up outside London — on Merseyside and Tyneside for example.

Essentially, the District philosophy was one of a mixture of motor and trailer cars, all from any one batch being of broadly similar appearance, with open interiors and both intermediate and end sliding doors. Within the cars, a mixture of longitudinal and transverse seating was adopted. Styling was always very 'American', especially in the earlier wooden-bodied days, when the vertical matchboarding for the lower panels, a pronounced waist rail and 'Gothic'-type side windows were a commonplace. There were many subtle changes over the years, and District Line trains were run in so many bewildering combinations of

stock that they were often amongst the most untidy to be seen on London Transport. Space precludes a full analysis here, but it is well recorded elsewhere, and even the final steel-bodied clerestory carriages of 1935 displayed a toned-down and suitably modernized version of the styling first adopted more than 30 years earlier.[*]

By then, there had been more than a bit of design 'spin-off' from the District surface stock to the new standard tube stock (see below), while the 1930s interior design treatment of the final clerestories formed the essential basis of the deservedly celebrated 1937 'Metadyne' surface stock and 1938 tube stock, both of which will be considered in due course.

Turning now to the actual carriages built for the District during the main period covered by this volume, the first vehicles which may be said to have had real significance in respect of the final London Transport synthesis were the 'F' stock cars of 1920 — incidentally, the District not only introduced 'car' to the EMU vocabulary (an American term, naturally enough) but also chose to identify successive designs by reference letters in alphabetical order. This again helped to establish a common London Transport feature, but there was no hidden meaning to the letters used, save for ease of identification. These 'F' stock vehicles were built by the Metropolitan Carriage Wagon and Finance Company in Birmingham with the aid of post-war Government financial assistance; they were the only departure from the clerestory form until after 1935 and were by quite some way more modern looking than almost anything else which appeared until the late 1930s on any of the LT lines. They were distinctly more rapid and powerful than anything which had preceded them and dimensionally, at 9 ft 7 in wide, took full advantage of the structure gauge.

Rather unusually, they were not, at first, used for dedicated services, and were reckoned as providing 'additional facilities' to normal services, especially by

[*] For a particularly useful summary of early District stock see *Clerestories on the District* by Piers Connor: 'Railways South East', Vol 1 No 2, Summer 1988.

way of improving the various 'non-stop' operations which, in the interests of arriving at their destination earlier, regularly omitted calls at some stations. At this point it must be understood that 'non-stop' in the UndergrounD context never meant quite the same thing as on the main-line railways; any train which omitted even a few intermediate stations in the interests of speeding commuters to or from work was instantly classified as 'non-stopping'! Thus, the 'F' stock tended to gain a sort of superior status which finally reached its apogee in 1950 when, no less than 30 years old, the cars were renovated and transferred to the Metropolitan Line for use on the semi-fast Harrow and Uxbridge services from 1951 onwards, a task probably more suited to their performance capability than any they had previously assayed.

Because of technical incompatibility with other cars, the 'F' stock always ran in tidy formations of up to eight cars and never formed part of the hybrid compositions characteristic of most District trains until quite recent times. In this respect they were probably the first examples of the universally 'tidy' formations now to be seen throughout London Transport, be it surface or tube. Certainly, until the advent of 1937 (surface) and 1938 (tube) stock (see below) there was never anything quite as visibly homogeneous as an 'F' Stock train, though the Metropolitan open stock ran it close.

The 'F' stock was also interesting in one rather

Figure 49 *Elevation and plan of a District Railway 'F' stock motor car as originally built.*

more cosmetic sense: the cars were first put into service in a darker shade of red than had hitherto been used by the District or was subsequently to become familiar. Referred to at the time as 'Engine Lake', it did not find favour. However, from the passenger viewpoint, these cars also had two features which were to prove of much longer-term significance to the later London Transport scene than their colour: they had rather more doors relative to train length than almost anything which had gone before, and they were possessed of seemingly vast standing space relative to seating, the central area between the doors being wholly equipped with lateral seats. Whether this was considered beneficial at the time is hard to assess, but it did not reappear in quite such profusion until brand new tube cars were built for the Victoria Line in the late 1960s; but maybe I digress!

After the 'F' stock, the District reverted to its long-standing love affair with the clerestory, and from 1923-4 until 1935-6 a whole series of gradually evolving cars came into service, some illustrated here, which took up most of the traditional alphabetical classifications from 'G' to 'N' ('H' were rebuilds of older stock; 'I' and 'J' were never used). There were in fact but two basic visual styles: the earlier 'G' series with 'straight through' clerestories, and the almost identical 'K' to 'N' series with domed-end clerestories and generally rather more modern outline. Though they did not have quite as many doors as the 'F' stock nor as much standing space, in terms of interior styling these final District clerestories were well on the way to establishing the LT standard. They also had the interesting distinction of being the last

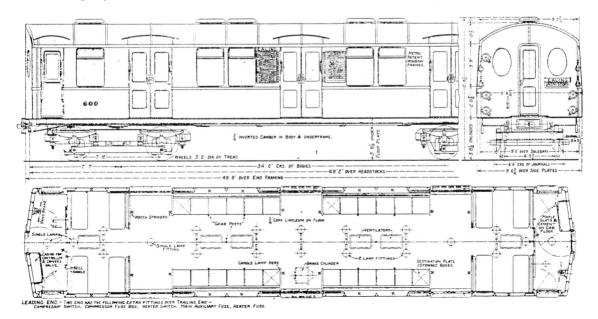

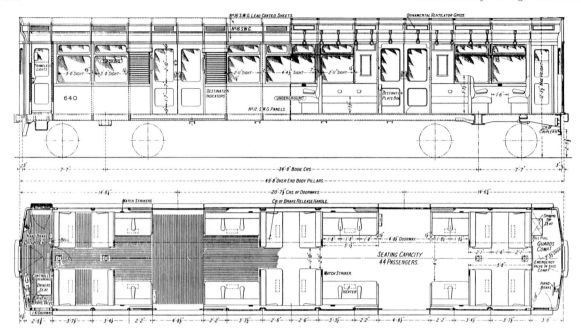

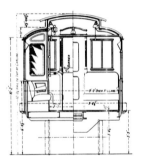

Figure 50 *Detailed elevations and plan of the last 'straight through' clerestory carriages built for the District, the 'G' stock motor cars of 1923-4. Note the hand-operated sliding doors, a feature of the District Line trains for many a long year.*

Figure 51 *Elevation and plan of a 'K' stock domed-end clerestory motor car of the series ordered for the District in 1927. Remaining District Line clerestory carriages of the subsequent 'L', 'M' and 'N' series were styled broadly in this fashion.*

Below *The clerestory-roofed 'M' stock, originally built for the Metropolitan line and seen here at Hammersmith when new, represented the last new stock to have this distinctive roof form. When later transferred to the District Line, these cars eventually became the last clerestories to run on London Transport (London Transport Museum).*

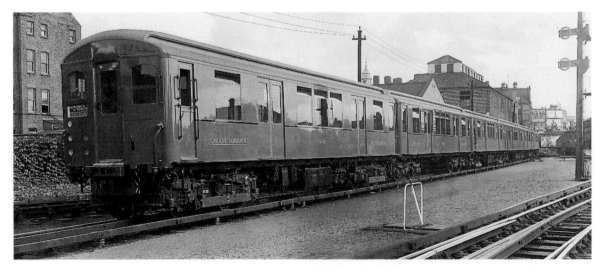

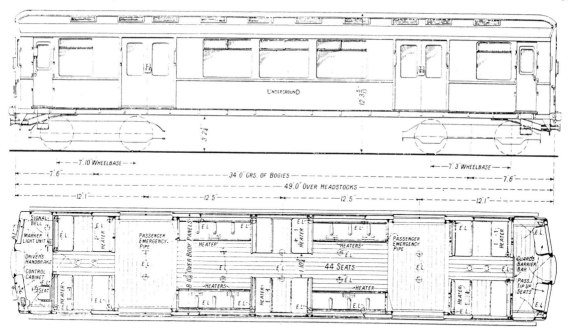

clerestory-roofed railway carriages to be built for service in Britain.

Of these various batches of clerestory carriages we might perhaps single out two more than interesting sub-groups. The first 'domed-end' series were the 'K' Class, and some of them were for a time owned by the LMS in consequence of its financial interest (having inherited the London, Tilbury and Southend line via the Midland Railway) in the District Line's extensions to Upminster. It may perhaps be of appropriate if quite inconsequential interest to note that these 'K' cars were the last District carriages to incorporate dark red (Midland Lake?) in their livery, but only on the doors. Some of the very similar 'L' class of 1931 (all eight of its motors in fact) were similarly LMS owned. In fact, the LMS, technically, owned some 110 District Line cars, but they were always viewed as part of the District fleet. This apart, however, far more relevant was the allocation of some of the final clerestories to the Metropolitan Line after the formation of the LPTB in 1933. These were the 1935 cars of the 'M' series and they were put to use on the Hammersmith services. This marked the start of the Metropolitan's assimilation into the 'mainstream' development of London Transport, and will be addressed later.

Much of the post-1923 clerestory stock survived until the late 1960s and the last of them was not withdrawn until 1971. Speaking from experience, it was by no means outclassed by its later brethren (save, perhaps, for its rather dated appearance) in either ambience or ride quality and, during the late 1960s, it was readily possible at one place in particular (Victoria) to transfer quite regularly on the same day from the progenitor of the modern London Transport approach on the District Line to its very latest manifestation on the still new Victoria Line tube stock.

The final District clerestories — along with the earlier 'F' stock — were indeed significant carriages in the evolution of London Transport, and in their latter days all the post-1923 clerestory cars were reclassified as 'Q' stock; but before getting to that particular complication, it is time to return to that other and geographically much larger surface element of the London Transport system, the Metropolitan.

The Metropolitan Railway had addressed the electrification issue at more or less the same time as the District (to Uxbridge in 1905 to be precise) and although it did, eventually, compromise between compartment and open stock, its very first EMUs could lay sound claim to have been amongst the most handsome of any carriages of the genre to have worked in the London area, or anywhere else for that matter (see also Chap. 15, page 245). Though they had open-style interiors in the 'American' manner, their general styling was much more 'British' in outline with traditional panelling and incurved lower side sheets. In fact, when, a few years later, similarly styled stock appeared on both the Circle and the Hammersmith and City Lines (the latter jointly owned with the GWR), it may have seemed for a while as though this was to become the new 'London' style EMU. In

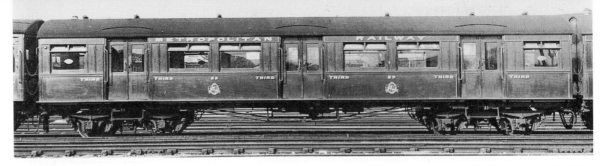

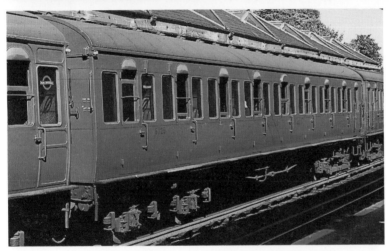

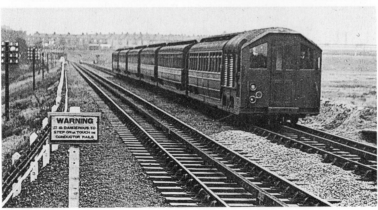

Top *Metropolitan Railway open third class car No 89 with its three pairs of sliding doors typifies the 1921 elliptical roof stock, built to operate with the earlier 1913 vehicles. Compared with the earlier type, these post-war carriages had more doors, flat sides and rather more restrained panelling* (J. Whiting collection).

Above *This, the first five-car Circle Line train of elliptical roof stock, was refurbished as part of the 1934 improvement programme. The motor cars are of 1913 stock and the trailers from the 1921 continuation* (London Transport Museum).

Above left *Flush-sided control trailer No 6725 (note the driving cab at the far end replacing a ninth compartment), photographed at Rickmansworth in the drab London Transport brown livery in August 1951, typifies the final style of compartment-type carriage built for the Metropolitan. By now classed as 'T' stock, the vehicle had entered service in 1929 as one of the new MW fleet, designed from the outset to operate in emu rather than locomotive-hauled form* (John H. Meredith).

Left *The ungainly front-end appearance of the early Central London Railway gate stock EMUs is well caught in this 1924 view of a Liverpool Street to Ealing train entering East Acton station. Note the third rail system used at that time*

purely aesthetic terms this might have been preferable, but events were to prove otherwise.

Unlike the District cars, the first generation of Metropolitan open stock was devoid of central doors and this tended to slow down the boarding of and alighting from trains, especially at busy times. In this respect, compartment stock was better, and this may have been something of a contributory reason for the Metropolitan continuing to operate both open and compartment EMUs as well as deciding to convert much of its redundant hauled stock to the latter form. There was also, of course, the perfectly valid point that out in the country steam haulage was normal for many years between Harrow on the Hill (Rickmansworth after 1925) and Aylesbury, and although these trains were electric hauled to the City, their stock remained conventional. Even after the formation of London Transport, it was to be 1960 before EMUs finally reached Amersham and made LT a fully EMU system, at which time through running to Aylesbury terminated.

Before the formation of the LPTB, the Metropolitan had developed its open EMU style into another visibly attractive form, mainly for the Circle Line. These had centre and end doors, as on the District, but the styling was thoroughly 'British'. It also introduced a full elliptical roof to the London underground; but though conceptually sound, the 1913 stock turned out to be the last open design by the Metropolitan, apart from a few post-war experimental rebuilds which came to little and a further purchase in 1921 of another tranche of 1913-style open stock, this time with three pairs of side doors to each car. Thus, by 1933, the open EMUs which were inherited by the LPTB were dominated by those displaying UndergrounD rather than Metropolitan influence. Even so, one of the first things which took place after 1933 was a thorough renovation of the 1913 and 1921 cars whose handsome outlines thereafter remained on the Circle Line until 1952.

Meantime, the Metropolitan was still uncertain about saloon or compartment stock, and its final pre-1933 EMUs reverted to the latter form. To be honest, this was not for want of trying again in the open mode during 1925. However, the Met's well-heeled long-distance commuters were obdurately conservative and preferred compartments. Thus, new compartment-style EMUs were introduced in 1927, the fleet being gradually enlarged until 1932. This time, though many of the trailers were ex-hauled stock, all the motors and a considerable number of the later trailers were built new. They were handsome of form in a thoroughly conventional way, being in essence styled on the last series of new hauled stock — the so-called 'Dreadnoughts' of the Edwardian era — and in their fully lined Metropolitan livery they must have looked

magnificent. In due course they were designated 'T' stock by the LPTB, following the District-inspired system, and proved to be the last pure Metropolitan EMUs to remain in service, the last to carry fare-paying passengers doing so in October 1962.

A natural consequence of the Metropolitan's 'blow hot, blow cold' policy in regard to carriages was that in 1933 it bequeathed no fewer than 11 types to the new unified system*, many of which were incompatible not only with each other but also with that of the District. There was, to be sure, almost as much visible variation on the District too but conceptually they were all of one form (open EMU with plenty of side doors) and there was more mutual compatibility and system standardization. It was no real surprise therefore when, as a start towards uniformity, the new LPTB initially re-equipped the Hammersmith services with District-style cars (see above). Furthermore, it was only four years after the formation of London Transport that the first recognizably 'unified' designs began to appear on the surface lines — the famous and stylish 'Metadyne' stock — and there was more than a bit of the District experience in their design too. But before going on to consider this particular episode, it will be as well to bring the tube story up to the same point in time.

Tube stock: 1900-1934

When the Central London Railway opened in 1900, there were already two systems of operation in use on the two existing tubes. The City and South London used locomotive haulage and the Waterloo and City adopted the EMU form. The 'Tuppenny Tube' went for locomotive haulage, but within three years had changed its mind because of excessive track damage by the heavy 44-ton locomotives and thereafter the EMU was to dominate.

The CLR had made a heavy investment in trailer cars and these were, of course, retained and the locomotives replaced by motor cars whose general style matched the trailers. This was a handsome 'British' sort of bodywork with a nice domed-end shallow clerestory roof — a sort of tube version of the original Metropolitan EMUs would be no bad description. A mixture of transverse and lateral seats was offered and access was gained via end platforms with gates.

Unfortunately, however, the driving ends of the motor cars in no way came to match the stylish bodywork of the passenger portions of the vehicles. The control gear was housed in a sort of tin tabernacle which bore no stylistic relationship to the rest of the ensemble, looking as though it had been grafted on

---

* *Steam to Silver*: J.G.Bruce, Capital Transport, 1983

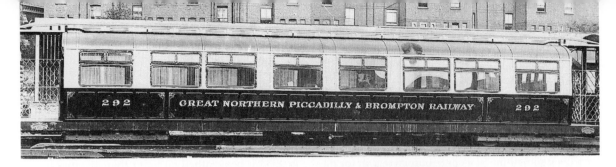

as an afterthought and terminating in a curious and ungainly-looking 'beetle-browed' cab whose quite uniquely ugly lineaments differentiated many of the Central Line trains from those of the rest of the tube system right until the Second World War. When approaching at a steep angle in the open air, one of these sets looked for all the world like an electrically propelled and somewhat morose caterpillar! In one respect, however, these pioneer CLR vehicles set the pattern for every new tube motor car built until 1934: they initiated the characteristic upward sweep of the sideframes above the power bogie.

By contrast with the CLR, the Yerkes tubes went for a far more cheerful-looking and upright-fronted motor car whose cab and control compartment was, more or less, fully integrated into the overall design. Though all three lines went to different builders for their stock, there was a recognizably common approach and their operating systems were mutually compatible. Furthermore, in their front-end treatment they set a design style which was not to change in a basic sense until after the last of the standard tube cars was built in 1934, and which could still be seen in use until the late 1980s on the Isle of Wight, where some of the standard tube stock came to rest during 1967 and later.

Like the Central London cars, the first Yerkes tube stock had a mixture of longitudinal and transverse seats and used end platform entrances with gates, the normal operating procedure on all lines being to use 'gatemen' between each pair of adjacent entrances to take care of passenger safety at stopping places. The gatemen rode the train with the guard(s) and the driving crew. This 'gate' stock as it was called,

though somewhat extravagant in staff per train, remained in use for many years, and the final gate stock train did not run until 1930. Before then, however, the basic nature of most newer tube cars had changed quite considerably.

Like the first generation Metropolitan EMUs, the first gate stock tube cars suffered from having entrances at the ends only, and by 1914-15, when the first Bakerloo and Central London extensions were mooted, intermediate hand-operated side doors had been incorporated in the design, sometimes retaining end gates but often with the end entrances now totally enclosed, also with hand-operated doors. Several varieties were produced over the next few years and included amongst them in 1920 were some more than agreeable jointly-owned cars (LNWR & LER) for the Watford run with rather less standing space, rather more transverse seating and even small luggage racks. Their smaller doors did, however, cause them to take rather longer to load and unload at stations, and the stock was replaced only ten years later. Some of it went to the LMS and was used on the Rickmansworth-Watford branch.

When the Watford stock was introduced, experiments were already being carried out on the Piccadilly Line with sliding air-operated doors of the kind now familiar. This reduced the size of train crew considerably and was applied to both new cars and some conversions of former gate stock and hand-operated door stock. This led directly to the introduction in 1923 of the first of the so-called 'Standard' tube cars for use on all lines coming under the control of the Underground Group. This included the City and South London, which was now expensively

Left *Gate stock clerestory trailer car No 292 in the florid livery of the Great Northern Piccadilly & Brompton Railway, the forerunner of the modern Piccadilly line.*

Below left *Central London motor car No 275 of the 1913 series, with intermediate side door and enclosed entrances, was an altogether more stylish essay than its predecessors.*

Right *The upright-fronted driving motors of the Yerkes tube lines are represented here by this Bakerloo/LNWR jointly-owned version, No 3J, seen at Queens Park circa 1920. The styling is clearly part way to that of the London Transport 'Standard' tube stock.*

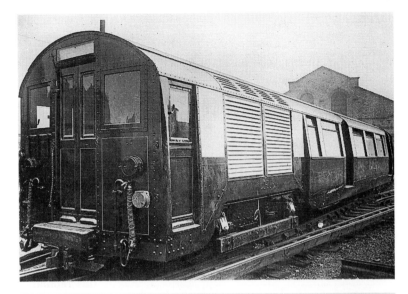

Middle right *Trailer car No 407J, also from the LNWR/LER joint stock, was built in 1920. This view clearly shows the quite small central entrance and, through the windows, the large amount of transverse seating, neither of which features proved particularly helpful either in terms of passenger capacity or ease of loading.*

Below *Now reconstructed with air-operated doors, this six-car Central Line train of former gate stock at Wood Lane clearly shows the retention of the original 1903-pattern cab styling and clerestory roof.*

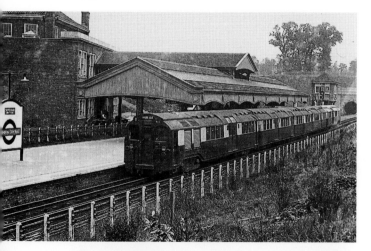

converted to standard tube diameter and linked up properly with the Hampstead tube to form the basis of the modern Northern Line in 1926. It will thus be seen that whereas on the District Railway the basically correct EMU concept had been established from the outset on at least some parts of the surface lines of what was to become London Transport, it took about 20 years for tube stock to arrive at much the same configuration, size apart.

Air-operated doors were obviously the key to the many problems, so before going on to discuss the Standard stock which was its first major consequence, it must also be recorded that much of the former gate stock on the Central London, Piccadilly and Bakerloo lines was planned to be converted to air-door operation. The Central London stock was tackled first, between 1926 and 1928, by enclosing the ends and fitting two sets of twin doors along the sides (one set only on the motors) and although most cars lost their distinctly different side panelling in consequence of this rebuilding, their quaint old-fashioned driving ends remained as clear indication of their origin.

By this time, it had also been discovered, as a consequence of completely re-equipping the Hampstead line, that new Standard cars could be built almost as cheaply as converting gate stock, and these were therefore put on the Piccadilly and Bakerloo Lines instead of the planned conversions. However, the Central Line conversions ran on until mid-1939 before finally being replaced by Standard stock. A principal reason for this was that the original CLR had a tube diameter marginally smaller than that of the Yerkes lines and, though by no means as restricted as the C & SLR, could not accept standard dimension tube stock at all locations. It was only the LPTB new works programme of 1935-40, by allowing some realigning of tunnels and lengthening of platforms, which enabled Standard stock to be used from 1939. At much the same time, the Central Line track was converted from its original three-rail system to the Yerkes standard four-rail method which was now the LT standard throughout.

Turning now to the Standard stock itself: viewed in retrospect, it was the tube equivalent of the Dis-

Top left *A four-car Standard stock train entering Hendon Central station in pre-LPTB days during the early years of the Morden-Edgware Line, now far better known as the Northern Line*

Middle left *Head-on view of a pair of 1924-built Standard stock control trailers in Morden depot, soon after the opening of the Northern Line's South London extension* (J. Whiting collection).

Left *Interior view of one of the 1926-built Standard stock trailer cars by Metropolitan* (London Transport Museum).

trict's 1923-35 stock, even down to the clerestory, and there was much common detail in the design, especially in such things as the interior trimming and colour schemes. But its effect was much more widespread, eventually totalling some 1,466 cars, of which all but 26 were in service well before the LPTB was even formed.

It started in 1922 with an order by the Underground Group for six sample trailer cars, five from outside firms and one 'in-house' example with control equipment, so as to try and arrive at the 'perfect' tube car. Though subtly different, all were recognizably similar in concept and were soon followed by the first production batches which surged into service in great waves for most of the next nine years, 1928 being the only blank year. The Hampstead line got them first in consequence of the almost simultaneous extensions to Morden and Edgware, not to mention the incorporation of the former C & SLR. The Bakerloo and Piccadilly Lines were not long afterwards, again with quantities augmented by vir-

tue of the lengthy extensions into the suburbs, particularly those of the Piccadilly Line both north and west; but total standardization was never quite achieved because by the time the Central Line got these cars in 1939, they were then the 'hand-me-downs' from the Northern and Bakerloo Lines which had by now received replacement 1938 stock (see below).

As for the cars themselves, though there were slight differences between batches, the basic style never seriously changed, nor did the general layout, save for the fact that the 1931 and later batches had single end sliding doors as well as the centrally positioned 'twins', thus slightly reducing the seating but considerably improving passenger access. This apart, however, only three basic types were provided: driving motor cars, non-driving trailers and 'Control'

Figure 52 Elevations and plans of typical 'Standard' tube stock of 1927 from Messrs Cammell Laird and Metropolitan respectively.

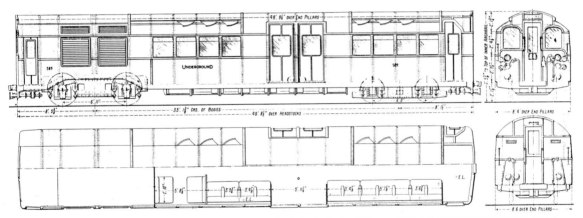

General View, Side Elevation, Plan and End Views of Motor Coach for the London Underground Railways, built by Cammell Laird & Co. Ltd.

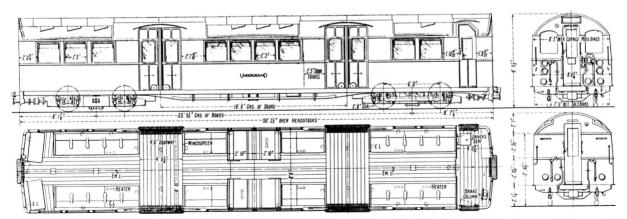

Elevation, Plan and End Views of Control Trailer Coach for the London Underground Railways, built by the Metropolitan Carriage, Wagon & Finance Co. Ltd.

Figure 53 *Elevations and plan of the experimental streamlined tube stock of 1936, the forerunners of the 1938 stock.*

trailers. The most common formation was a seven-car — M-T-T-M + CT-T-M — it being common practice to run the four-car unit on its own at quieter times.

The motor cars were derived from the earlier Yerkes pattern, with upswept frames above the motor bogie, and when all were in service they must surely have represented the most visibly characteristic feature of any stock ever to run on London Transport. As a child they were part of my London scene, along with the Kingsway tram tunnel, and they seemed to give off a particular and by no means unpleasant form of 'electric' odour which, even now, on those rare occasions I sense it in the tube tunnels, has a powerfully nostalgic effect! Their only 'archetype' rivals were probably the 1938 stock cars, and the images of these two styles are still those which come most instantly to my mind whenever I think of the London tubes. The appended drawings of the Cammell Laird and Metropolitan series, first published in 1927, are quite characteristic, the non-control trailers being symmetrically arranged with transverse passenger seats at both ends of the car adjacent to the end doors.

In due course, as stated, much of the Standard stock was cascaded on to the Central Line from 1939 onwards and this, with the Piccadilly Line, was its last regular haunt until well into the period covered by the next volume. On the Central line after the war, eight-car trains were normal and, to avoid two adjacent motor cars right in the centre of the platforms, the formation was modified from two conventional four-car units to M-T + M-T-T-M + T-M.

The great leap forward (1935-1938) and its consequences

In practical terms, the 1923-35 surface stock of the District and the Standard stock of the tube lines was so dominant and had established such a high degree

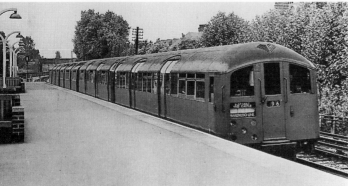

Middle left *This view of a four-car train of 1938 tube stock at Kilburn in 1950 also shows one of the many Standard stock trailers (vehicle No 3) which were modified to run as part of this stock in the Bakerloo line sets — see text (London Transport Museum).*

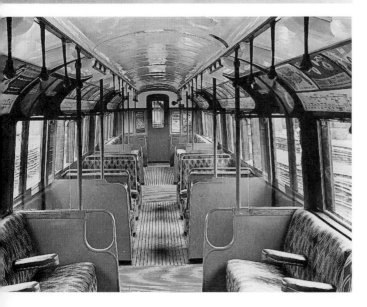

Left *Interior of one of the 1938 stock trailer cars used on the Northern Line (London Transport Museum).*

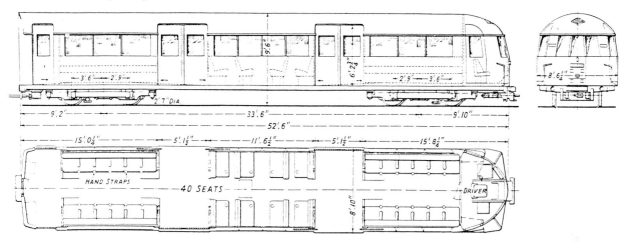

of concept standardization before 1933 that when London Transport was formed only the rebuilt Central London Railway gate stock and most of the Metropolitan fleet stood outwith the general pattern; and even the gate stock had been brought into line with UndergrounD practice as far as possible. It can therefore occasion no great surprise that the subsequent LPTB evolution was an almost direct continuation of that initiated by the former Yerkes empire. As already stated, it actually began mildly enough with the drafting of a new batch of District-type clerestories on to the Metropolitan's Hammersmith Line, but this was merely a start, and in the case of the Metropolitan, short-lived; the new clerestories fairly soon went back to the District as will shortly be explained.

The real catalyst, quite apart from the formation of the LPTB itself, was the burgeoning growth of suburban traffic and the demand for extensions of the LT network. This was made possible by the 1935-40 new works programme which, in terms of new stock provision, resulted in two radically new designs, one each for the tube and surface routes, which, with but one exception, established the design parameters for some 30 or more years. The exception was the new stock for the Metropolitan line to Amersham; that did not arrive until 1960 and must await the next volume to resolve.

It started in 1935 when four new experimental six-car tube trains were ordered from Metro-Cammell, which came into service in 1936. The radical change was to locate all the electrical equipment below the floor, thus dispensing with the switch compartment above the motor bogie, using the vacated space for more passenger seating. In fact, the new motor cars had virtually the same capacity as the trailers and, by way of bonus, since motor cars no longer wasted passenger space, more of them could be provided,

thus enhancing train performance. The experimental trains were therefore all delivered as twin motor pairs. They were operated on the Piccadilly Line in sets of six, this formation having the same capacity as a normal seven-car set of Standard stock.

In design terms they were beautifully conceived save for one quite absurd element, the provision of a streamlined cab on the units of three of the four trains. What possible benefit a streamlined form could confer at not much more than 30 mph down in the depths of the London clay was always obscure, and the idea was soon abandoned. The fourth train was given a much more pleasing semi-flat-fronted but dome-roofed cab design; it was to be the prophetic one.

Streamlining apart, the experimental trains were to form the basis of the largest new build of tube stock since the Standard cars of 1923-31. It was soon known as the '1938 Stock', and although, numerically, the total fleet was some 15 per cent smaller than the Standard stock build, the rate of production was faster, it had far fewer detail variations and was undoubtedly the most consistent tube stock seen so far. In fact, so definitive did it become that the old 'Standard' designation for the earlier stock soon became changed to 'Pre-1938' stock!

The 1938 stock went into service as a total re-equipment of the Northern Line (save for its separated branch from Finsbury Park to the City) and the almost total re-stocking of the Bakerloo Line. On the latter route, some pre-1938 stock was retained and the 1938 stock proper was supplemented by some 58 modified pre-1938 trailers in consequence of the need to augment the fleet when the former Metropolitan Stanmore branch was added to the Bakerloo Line. These vehicles retained their earlier clerestory form, but the only other non-standard cars in the 1938 fleet were the 18 streamliners which, after the war, were

Left *In spite of being well over 40 years old, the 1938 stock never really looked dated even at the end of its working life. This late period view, taken at Kingsbury on the Bakerloo line in 1979, shows a set wearing the final LT red livery with a plain emblem on the carriage sides rather than 'LONDON TRANSPORT' in full* (J. Whiting).

Figure 54 Elevations and plans of a two-car twin-motor 'O' stock unit of the 1937 Metadyne-equipped series.

Right *Exterior view of two-car 'O' Stock for the Hammersmith and City line in July 1937* (London Transport Museum).

converted into trailers. They revealed their origin by having three rather than four windows between centre and end doors; that subtle point apart, which few if any noticed, they were then identical to the 1938 cars proper.

The 1938 stock was generally operated in seven cars trains — M-M-T-M + M-T-M — the intermediate motor in the four-car unit having no driving cab. As with the pre-1938 stock, the intention was to operate single four-car units at off-peak times, and this was indeed the case until well into the 1950s when seven-car trains became the all-day norm. The 1938 stock was also supplemented after the war by a modest complement of 'Shunting Control Motors' which dispensed with a driving cab at the inner end of a three car unit yet which could, in the sidings, be driven from that end when making up a seven-car formation, thus gaining additional passenger space and saving the cost of a full driving cab.

As for the rest of the design, it could hardly be faulted. A smooth and stylish flush-sided exterior was combined with a clean and uncluttered interior. The 'upsweep' of the frames over the motor bogie was,

of course, no more and neither was the clerestory — at least from the outside; but within the cars, it came back as an attractively raised centre section of the roof with some few inches of practical advantage for standees. As for the seat comfort — and here I speak from years of using them — it has never been bettered in any London Transport EMU I have ever experienced, and I have ridden in most of them from the Metropolitan compartment and Circle stock dating from the pre-LPTB era to the latest 1980s offerings. So well-conceived were they, in fact, that 20 years later, the so-called 1959 stock for the Piccadilly and Central Lines was a virtual carbon copy, except that its seats were far more uncomfortable — but that is for others to resolve!

The reader may well, by now, have deduced that I have a sort of 'soft spot' for the 1938 tube stock, and he would not be wrong. I consider it to have been quite exceptional for its time and I write from the experience of being carried in it many a thousand times when I was resident both in Northern and Bakerloo hinterland; but it was not unique. Between the building of the experimental 1936 stock and the

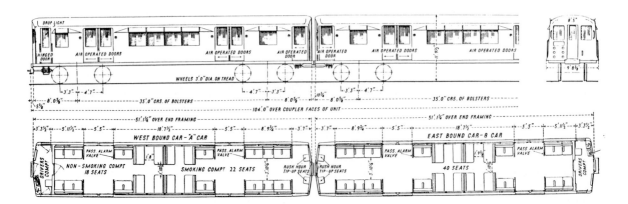

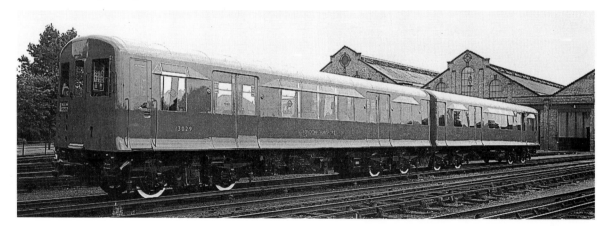

full 1938 fleet, London Transport completed a re-markable double act when it also offered an equally trend-setting new design for the surface routes: the so-called 'Metadyne' stock.

The word 'Metadyne' simply referred to a new form of much improved control equipment which had been evaluated on older cars during 1934, but because it was first put to widespread use in a large batch of brand new surface stock its name became attached to the stock itself. In fact, the new stock, continuing the District line tradition, was more correctly called 'O', 'P', 'Q' and 'R' stock, and though Metadyne equipment was universally used in the 'O' and 'P' stock when new, it was not universal on all cars of the new shape.

Like the 1938 tube stock, the new surface stock also displayed a radical re-think in terms of body styling, and the first examples actually came into service between the experimental 1936 tube stock and the 1938 stock proper. Despite the great difference in size between the tube and surface stock, there was clearly much interlinking of design as far as it affected the passenger areas, and it is a moot point which of the two types of stock influenced which. Later cars of the 'O' to 'Q' fleet were slightly delayed by the war and the whole order was not completed until 1941. Even so, given the simultaneous introduction of the almost twice as large 1938 tube stock fleet, the overall achievement was remarkable. The 'R' stock did not appear until after the war.

The new surface cars shared their flush-sided exterior styling with the 1938 tube stock, but the lower body panels were flared out in an attractive and quite unique way to avoid the need for running boards yet also reduce platform edge gaps. It also prevented any foolish-minded passenger trying to hang on the out-side when the doors closed! They had the usual pair of twin doors along each side and single sliding doors at the inner car ends, all the original 'O' stock com-

ing into service as twin motor pairs with outer end driving cabs, much in the manner of the experimen-tal 1936 tube stock.

Within the cars, furnishing was very like the new tube stock, including the false interior clerestory, and the seats were just as comfortable. A nice styling point was the attractive exterior ventilator treatment above the side windows. The pairs of twin doors were proportionally rather further apart than on the 1938 tube cars, and this gave a fairly lengthy central sec-tion which combined both transverse and lateral seats. The end seating sections had all lateral seat-ing so, except at the car centres, there was a fair amount of standing space, most of which was sensi-bly located in the vicinity of the doors. Once again, the first impression gained by the passenger was wholly favourable.

The 'O' stock was intended for use on the Ham-mersmith and City Line, operating in six-car trains of three twin units alongside the 1935 clerestory stock already provided for this service (see above). This it began to do late in 1937, but in 1938 trailers were inserted into the original twin units, making an M-T-M set, two of which could form a train. This allowed the clerestories to go to the District, along-side their stylistic bedfellows, after only a relatively short spell on the Metropolitan Line. In fact, suffi-cient 'O' stock existed for some of it to go on to the Metropolitan main line as well.

The 'P' stock was almost identical to the 'O' stock save that the guard's controls were brought into the car body, as on the tube stock, rather than in the rear driving cab as previously. Though there were other smaller technical differences, the 'P' cars were styled exactly like their predecessors and also built in con-siderable quantities. They began operation in mid-1939, but their formations were slightly different from those of the 'O' stock.

They were intended for replacement of all the

older-style open EMU stock on the Metropolitan, where eight-car formations were also required. They were thus formed up as M-T-M + M-T-M + M-M, all close-coupled. All motor cars had driving cabs and, as can be seen, the arrangement also permitted a five-car set if required. This was in fact done at about the time the 'F' stock (see page 147) was transferred to the Uxbridge route, after which five-car formations of released 'Metadyne' stock could be moved on to the Circle line. The 'P' stock trailers were also interesting in that they had a hinged door at one end which had fixed transverse seating behind it against the car end, rather in the manner of the earlier pre-1938 tube stock trailers. This was to facilitate later conversion to motor form if so desired, the hinged door then becoming the cab door. Indeed, many were so converted, especially after the war when the 'R' stock came into service. But before dealing with that story, the complicated 'Q' stock must first be outlined.

The 'Q' stock was thus designated as part of the programme which started in 1938 to rid the District of some of its more antiquated clerestories and also to introduce air-operated doors to District Line trains. It is now an almost forgotten fact that the District Line itself, though the pioneer of much which later became an LT standard, suffered the lot of most pioneers in having the earliest equipment. A consequence of this was that hand-operated sliding doors remained universal until 1938, save for the 'M' stock which was, in any case, designated for the Metropolitan line (see above).

There was no economical way by which all the hand-door stock could be converted immediately, and some of the earlier types could not be converted at all, so the rational choice was made to concentrate all the hand-door stock into certain formations and

provide air-doors on the rest. The hand-door stock was later referred to as 'H' stock, and the new air-door style was the 'Q' stock.

So far so good, but the nature of the conversions meant that while all the 1923 and later clerestory *motor* cars could be and were converted, some of their hand-door trailers were needed for the hand-door sets — even including some of the 1935 air-door trailers returned from the Hammersmith line which therefore had to have their doors converted to the older type in 1938! This then left a total shortage of trailers for the air-door stock, and to meet it new ones were built to the new 1937 car profile. These were the original 'Q' cars and the new fleet also included a few motors as well. The converted clerestories were known as 'Q-converted' stock. The net result was that although the District now had a rather more up-do-date fleet, it was still of two technically incompatible types, each of which exhibited an unbelievably cosmopolitan mixture of car styles to enchant the connoisseur of these things!

Thus matters remained, more or less, until after the war, save for purely technical changes to the running and traction equipment which are outwith this survey. The final transformation of the District stock had to await the later 1940s to resolve, the main instrument of which being the 'R' stock. This was the final step in the elimination of all hand-door stock on London Transport, save for the Metropolitan's compartment carriages. Its implementation had a curiously 'ring-a-ring o' roses' characteristic to it!

By now, hand-door open EMU stock was confined to the District and Circle Lines, the latter still in charge of the renovated 1913 stock (see p. 415). The intention was to put the new 'R' stock on to the District to replace all the 'H' stock (see above), eventually in sufficient quantity also to release the 'F' stock for the Uxbridge line, thus allowing the already-mentioned transfer of sufficient 'O' and 'P' stock to work the Circle Line in five-car formation. The whole conversion was in fact done in two stages, the first being to replace the hand-operated District fleet. This was implemented in 1949 by means of the first of the 'R' stock sets.

'R' stock looked just like the 'O', 'P' and 'Q' cars but differed in that all were motor cars, most of which were of non-driving configuration, an idea copied from some of the 1938 tube stock cars. These were all newly built and occupied the central positions in the formations which were either six-car or eight-car. By contrast, all but a few of the *driving* motors were obtained by conversion of the pre-war trailers which had been designed for such a contingency (see above). Many of these were original 'Q' stock which in turn caused some of the more modern hand-door clerestory trailers from the now-withdrawn 'H' stock sets

Left *The well-designed interior of the 'O' Stock and the substantial nature of its upholstery is well seen in this view of an ex-works example in July 1937* (London Transport Museum).

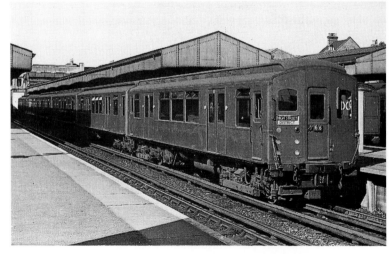

Right *The 'Q'-converted stock was a real mixture, though this example at Wimbledon in 1954 is tidier than many. It is a six-car formation composed of four domed-roof clerestories followed by a 1938-pattern trailer and a square-ended clerestory* (J.H. Aston).

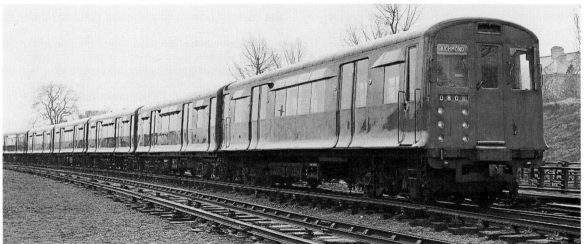

Above *When new, the 'R' stock was almost identical to the pre-war 'O', 'P' and 'Q' series and the various batches of 'flared sided' EMUs were always difficult to tell apart. The destination blinds above the cab window differentiated the 'R' stock from the pre-war 'O' and 'P' stock and this view shows a six-car formation of 'R' stock as used on the Richmond services* (J. Whiting collection).

Right *This 'R' stock driving motor No 22610, taken at Hanger Lane Junction in 1971, shows a* circa *1950 conversion of a 1938 car built as a 'Q' stock trailer. It is now in silver painted livery to match the new aluminium-bodied stock alongside which it ran* (R.J. Greenaway).

to be turned into 'Q-converted' form. Thus, while in one respect (the 'R' stock) District trains were getting tidier, the 'Q' stock became ever more Byzantine!

Within the cars, the 'R' stock was just as agreeable as all the rest of this style of vehicle had been and even brighter of aspect, for all the cars had fluorescent lighting tubes very neatly installed along the lower edges of the ever-present false clerestory. And the whole thing reached its climax with the second batch of 'R' stock which allowed the planned 'F' stock-Uxbridge route-Circle Line waltz to take place!

When the second generation 'R' stock cars were ordered, the trains were again a mixture of new (mostly non-driving) and converted ex-'Q' stock trailers (driving); but it was also resolved that the new cars should make extensive use of aluminium alloy in both underframes and bodies to reduce weight. Furthermore, one car was left unpainted to see whether it might also be possible to dispense with costly paintwork. There were, so it would seem, some worries about the cleanliness factor, but all seemed well and a further full eight-car set soon followed. In consequence, 1953 was to see the first 'silver' train running on London Transport — a prophetic event as it turned out.

Completing the 'R' stock story, though now straying well into the Volume 3 period, a further and final series of these distinctive-looking cars followed in 1959 to enable the release of further 'Q' trailers to augment Circle Line sets from five to six cars. The new cars of this final series were also unpainted, though, as usual, there were further conversions too. However, the older stock was now painted in aluminium colour to match the new unpainted cars, and this was to represent the start of the modern livery for the system. This final build of 'flared-side' EMUs was also to complete the first standardization stage of the unified post-1932 London Transport scheme, and forms a fitting conclusion to our story for the moment, for in them were sown the final seeds of the present-day plant. And it is worth reiterating that although the final examples did not appear until the late 1950s, all their essentials were in position by as early as 1938.

Thus it was that in the building of the 1936 and its derived series of modern EMUs, London Transport finally brought together the various elements of its disparate inheritance. It was a fine achievement, and though at the end of this phase there was still much variety to be seen — and still is, for that matter — there can be little doubt that the fundamental form of trains on the modern London Underground was determined by those significant events which started with that rather odd-looking tube train on the Piccadilly Line way back in the streamline era. From small acorns. . .

23. Other electrifications

Though it is hard to conceive that anyone has not heard of the Southern and London Transport systems already covered, it is by no means as certain that popular awareness is quite so acute when it comes to the other electrified areas of Britain during the company period, and this can only be because they were relatively small and rather scattered. On all other counts, they have sound cause for primacy because many of them actually preceded their more famous cousins in the London area, and on more than one occasion they were technically well in the vanguard of contemporary developments.

There was much individuality, of course — and that may have been part of the trouble; but another factor which may help explain their relatively low profile was that they were mostly both 'provincial' and individualistic, none of them having formed the basis of a complete system as was usually the case in the London area. Nevertheless, they did fall mostly into two readily definable geographical areas, plus one or two oddball London contributions outwith the Southern/LPTB systems. On balance, these regional differentiations seem to form the best basis for this part of the story. Yet again, to afford some degree of continuity, it will be necessary to go back before 1923 in many cases, simply because there was no space in Volume 15 to do more than mention most of them.

Lancashire and the North-West

With the solitary exception of the City and South London tube line, which was hardly typical of anything save itself in the early days, by far the bulk of the pioneering work in suburban electrification was to be found on Merseyside. No doubt my Lancastrian readers will read much significance into this comment but, as in London, the first example was a bit of a maverick with little long-term significance. It was, of course, the Liverpool Overhead Railway which opened in 1893 and, electrically powered from the start, was the world's first 'overhead' line in the generally accepted sense of operating on a continuous viaduct above the city streets. Looking back over the years, it is interesting to note how the pioneer electric railways were all by nature of unique one-offs; even the third of them (the Waterloo and City line — Chapter 21, the only one which still survives more or less as built, can hardly be called typical.

The Liverpool Overhead ran the length of the Docks and was electrified on the third rail system at 500V DC with the conductor rail in the 'six-foot'. Its

Figure 55 *Map showing the scattered nature of the various electrified lines in South Lancashire and the Wirral area during the grouping period.*

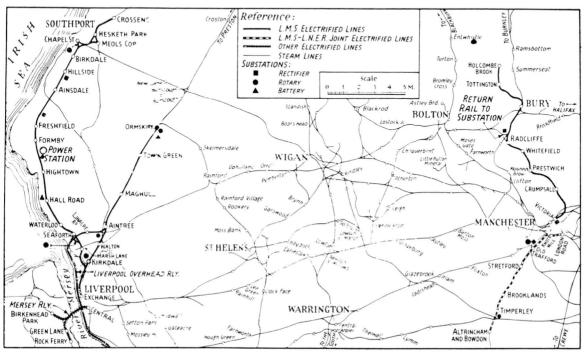

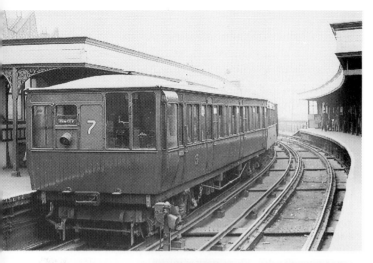

major contribution may well have been to pioneer the modern EMU concept, trains being formed from three-car units (motor/trailer/motor) with interiors of semi-open type. The cars themselves were 'American' in style, serving for the whole life of the system. Eight sets were refurbished, but when life-expired, in 1956, they were never renewed and the line was closed. Thus their design, save perhaps in setting new ideas, was not a significant contribution to twentieth-century carriage development; but they did run throughout much of the period covered by this book and the system itself is surely worthy of mention. Indeed, had it survived, what a boon it would have been to the new and exciting developments in Liverpool's dockland of the 1980s. There were, in fact, many who felt its demise was premature.

Far more significant than the Liverpool Overhead in the long run was the tiny Mersey Railway, by any criterion worthy of mention if only because it was the first underground railway in Britain to be converted from steam to electric traction — in 1903. Furthermore, it was also, by a year or so, the precursor of London's surface lines in terms of carriage concept and power supply system, utilizing open motor and trailer cars running on a 650V DC system with side conductor rail and centre-rail return. In its early days it employed 'American'-pattern clerestory cars with end doors only, and this was one aspect where the Mersey line did not adopt the more familiar 'end plus centre doors' arrangement which became commonplace in the London region.

Right at the time of the grouping, the Mersey Railway had so increased its traffic that it needed to strengthen its fleet and the new cars, while retaining much of the previous clerestory styling, displayed a bow-ended body surmounted by a new type of semi-elliptical roof with domed ends — a handsome combination, repeated in even more cleaned-up form when the fleet was further strengthened in 1936. Two classes were always offered, though in all conscience the five-ply veneered (third class) and rattan upholstered (first class) seating recorded for the 1923 cars

Top left *Original pattern matchboard-panelled Liverpool Overhead Railway stock: motor car No 7 brings up the rear of a train at Seaforth Sands in April 1955* (T.J. Edgington).

Middle left *Refurbished steel-panelled LOR stock: motor car No 29 heads a train into Liverpool Pier Head in October 1956, shortly before closure of the line* (T.J. Edgington).

Left *This nice mixture of domed-roof stock at Birkenhead typified the best of the Mersey Railway in the immediate pre-1938 period — note the fourth rail still in evidence. The first and last three vehicles are the 1923 motors and trailers, while the second and third cars are the 1936 trailers.*

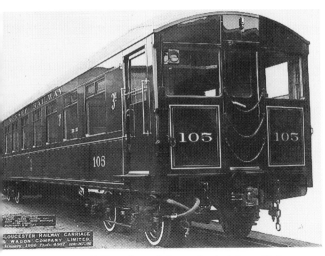

The new 1936 steel-panelled cars for the Mersey Railway were still very 'American' in appearance. This is third class trailer No 105, brand new in January 1936.

The stylish LMS EMUs for the 1938 Mersey-Wirral scheme were formed into three-car units: driving motor third, trailer composite, driving trailer third. This view shows motor third No 28683 at the head of one such formation, soon after its introduction.

can hardly have been the acme of comfort. Even so, it must be stated that in basic quality, the Mersey was probably rather better than the District line at this time, even though it remained faithful to the exclusively end-door arrangement. One of the earlier clerestory cars was badly damaged during the war and was rebuilt at Wolverton into a very modern-looking open first with rather more agreeable seating. The more modern Mersey cars remained in service until 1956.

The system itself was very small, nothing more than a tunnel section from Liverpool Central under the Mersey to the Wirral peninsula, where it divided into two short open-air 'stub' branches to Birkenhead Park and Rock Ferry. The former route was extended to New Brighton when, in 1938, the Mersey Railway shared in one of the more interesting and far-reaching developments of electric traction during the company period. This was achieved in conjunction with the former Wirral Railway section of the LMS when conductor rails were extended beyond the Mersey's routes into ex-Wirral Railway territory and the two systems were then operated as one rather more extended, but still quite small network. The enlarged system adopted conventional three-rail traction and the two companies retained their nominal independence until 1948.

As its share of the expansion, the LMS introduced a large fleet of brand new and, by contemporary standards, fairly revolutionary-styled EMUs as far as the main-line companies were concerned. Up to now, the LMS, when building its own electric stock, had been

as stodgily conservative as the Metropolitan on its long-distance services and had stuck rigidly to the compartment style. For the new Mersey-Wirral scheme, handsome new lightweight three-car units were built, every bit as modern as the latest London Transport flared body stock but whose interior was, if anything, even better. For one thing it still had two classes, and for another the seating was almost wholly transverse. Considering that even at its longest distance, the new network could not match the length of most of the London Transport routes, this was a very superior provisioning for a purely suburban system. Over 20 per cent of the seating was first class with carpeted floors; but then, the Wirral was a relatively well-heeled sort of place, one supposes, and it was to be some time before these trains became one class only. After the war, in 1956, a further batch of near-identical stock was built by BR to replace the original Mersey railway cars.

The Mersey-Wirral scheme eventually formed the city centre nucleus of the modern 'MerseyRail' network, and the LMS-style cars worked well into the 1980s before their eventual replacement. They were the first genuinely modern sliding door EMUs to be built in quantity for the main line as opposed to the London Transport network. One pre-war unit of this significant LMS design is, happily, preserved in operational order.

The next oldest component of the modern 'MerseyRail' owes its origins to the pioneering work of the old Lancashire and Yorkshire Railway which, in 1904, had electrified its Southport line out of Liver-

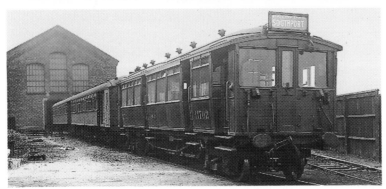

Above *Five-car train of wide-bodied ex-LYR Liverpool–Southport EMU stock in LMS colours during the 1920s, motor third No 14565 leading. The LMS livery for these sets, with its ostentatiously sized running numbers, was rather more reminiscent of former LYR than LMS standard practice; it looked most impressive.*

Left *The leading vehicle of this group of former LYR stock at Horwich in 1932 is one of the lightweight motor composites built for through running on to the Liverpool Overhead. It now carries LMS No 11702, again with a distinctive livery.*

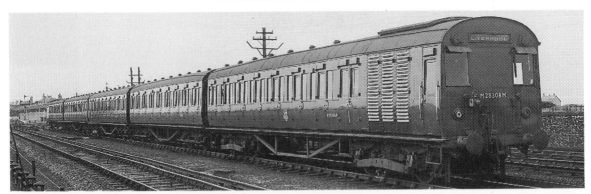

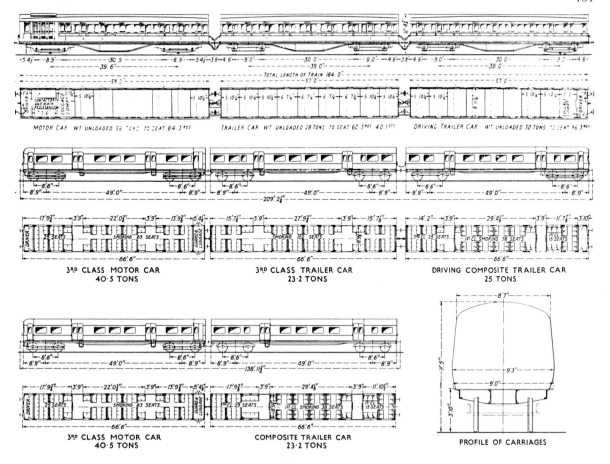

3RD CLASS MOTOR CAR 40·5 TONS   **3RD CLASS TRAILER CAR 23·2 TONS**   **DRIVING COMPOSITE TRAILER CAR 25 TONS**

3RD CLASS MOTOR CAR 40·5 TONS   **COMPOSITE TRAILER CAR 23·2 TONS**   **PROFILE OF CARRIAGES**

pool Exchange. This, by a short head (see page 170) could claim to be the first main-line electrification in Britain and was followed in 1913 by similar electrification to Ormskirk. The 600V DC third rail system was adopted. The LYR trains built for these services were very distinctive (see, for example, Chapter 15 pages 249-51) and by LMS days it was difficult to determine what, exactly, constituted a set formation. They were a mixture of mostly driving motors and orthodox trailers with a few driving trailers and a threesome of parcels vans thrown in for good measure. Some were of lightweight construc-

Above left *A train of the 1927 compartment-style LMS Liverpool–Southport EMU stock seen in early BR days in five-car formation. The first three cars are arranged in conventional formation (see Figure 56) but the rear pair have lost their intermediate composite.*

Left *Three-car unit of LMS 1939 Southport stock in operation with the motor third, No 28315, at the rear of the formation and the driving trailer composite leading.*

Figure 56 *Simplified elevations and plans of the LMS-built EMU stock of 1927 and 1939 for the Liverpool–Southport line.*

tion for working on to the Liverpool Overhead line and all lasted well into the LMS period.

Some stock augmentation was found to be needed very soon and this was provided in the form of some stultifyingly dull compartment stock in 1927 whose only real virtue was that they were some of the first LMS carriages to dispense with outer wood panelling. They were, of course, fully lined out to suggest otherwise, but, that apart, put them behind a 2-4-2T and no one would have noticed that they were one whit different from normal non-corridor stock.

However, just as in the Wirral, so too on the Southport line. When the LMS built new stock to replace the original LYR cars, something positive seems to have happened in the upper hierarchy, for the new Southport trains were even bigger versions of the handsome new Wirral sets and just as well appointed. They could, of course, take advantage of the generous LYR loading gauge which had permitted their predecessors to be, at 10 ft, the widest carriages ever to operate in Britain, but though they were over 66 ft long, the LMS stopped at a full 9 ft 3 in body width. Even this slight increase over normal LMS dimensions allowed 3 + 2 seating in the third class and 2 + 2 in the first without real discomfort. Most seats in both classes were transverse. These excellent cars came into service during 1939-43, their speed of introduction being slowed down by the war. They were designed to operate in three-car and two-car sets whose formations remained fairly stable throughout their lives. Unlike the Wirral sets, they were company-built at Derby rather than by outside contractors.

Constructionally, the bodies were of particular interest in that they were of all-steel welded construction and, in characteristic LMS fashion, the cars were put together from completely prefabricated sides and ends. The bogies and underframes were also of all-welded nature and the whole body structure from underframe to roof formed a completely welded box girder. This form of carriage construction, hardly modified, became a universal standard when the BR Mk I stock was built during the 1950s, though only one batch of conventional carriages of this type was ever built to LMS design. They were also very powerful sets, the rating for a single motor car being 940 hp (one hour) or 736 hp (continuous). This gave the trains, typically formed from either five or six cars, a maximum speed fully loaded of 70 mph and the ability to effect a 10 per cent reduction in the overall journey time, inclusive of all stops.

Of the two broadly similar styles of LMS-pattern

Merseyside EMUs, those on the Southport route were slightly the earlier to be withdrawn; they had probably had a harder life since, unlike the Wirral sets, the fleet was never augmented in BR days. A fully operational pair was claimed for the National Railway Museum, which had already decided that either a Wirral or Southport set merited saving. The Southport stock was assessed as marginally more significant from the technical standpoint and the writer was privileged to take receipt of it at Southport station in 1980 on behalf of the Museum. It is still outstationed there, maintained in full operational order and, now restored to LMS colours, makes occasional forays down its old stamping ground to remind the world, as does its Wirral contemporary (whose retention was an inspired and very welcome gesture by the BR Merseyside folk themselves), that the modern-style British EMU on the main-line system was well and truly a creation of the company period, no matter how long it might have taken finally to penetrate south of the Thames!

Elsewhere in the former LYR heartland, the old company had only electrified one other route, that from Manchester to Bury and Holcombe Brook. It was not, apparently, done to save money but to attract more traffic. The Bury-Holcombe Brook stretch had been the site of an interesting 1913 experiment using 3,500V DC collected from overhead conductor wires, and this indicated the advantages of using a higher voltage. In the event, the final choice settled on 1,200V DC, the maximum which the Board of Trade would sanction for third rail collection. The third rail was of side-contact configuration (the top surface being covered in wood to give extra protection) and a fourth rail between the running rails gave extra conductivity. The line opened in 1915.

To operate these services, including the Holcombe Brook section which was, of course, converted to 1,200V, the LYR produced another attractive design, not quite as wide as the Southport stock, but very similar in styling. They were the first 'all-steel' cars to be built for a British main-line company and were of open type, gangwayed throughout, and featured an offset driver's compartment to allow through movement (see the drawing on pages 250-1 of Volume 1). In this respect, they predicted, by more than 20 years, the arrangement provided in 1937 by the Southern Railway in its Portsmouth stock. The LYR cars, however, could be formed up in any way required, since all of them had driving cabs at both ends; they took up very little space. A typical formation was five cars (three motors plus two trailers) and this produced a very respectable 2,400 hp. Throughout the LMS period, these substantial and well-built carriages continued to operate the service and were not replaced until the late 1950s.

Below left *Third class interior of the 1939 LMS Southport stock*

Above *This typical five-car Manchester–Bury EMU formation of ex-LYR stock is seen in 1925, again carrying the distinctive LYR-inspired form of livery. The leading motor is No 14579*

Right *The MSJA stock was all but identical to all other compartment-style LMS EMUs of the 1920s, but its green livery and overhead pantographs gave it some distinction. This is an unidentified six-car train on special duty when new*

The final electrified line to be considered in the Lancashire conurbation was the LMS/LNER joint operation whose formal title was the pompous sounding Manchester, South Junction and Altrincham Railway — MSJA for short; and it was less than nine miles long! The 1,500V DC overhead contact system was chosen, it being generally believed at that time, 1931, that this would become the British standard for all future electrifications outside the London underground and the Southern systems. The stock itself was all contractor-built and turned out to be of pure LMS non-corridor type, right down to most of the detail fittings. There appears to have been no attempt to come up with a new design, and save for an increase in length from 57 ft to 58 ft and, of course,

the traction equipment, the carriages were much the same as those the LMS had already built for the Southport and Watford lines.

One must concede that if non-corridor stock had to be used, then the LMS design was rather better than that of the LNER for reasons already given in Chap 18 . But it is rather surprising that a more serious attempt was not made to provide something radically new to go with the more modern traction system. Just about the only thing which differentiated it from either LMS or LNER stock was its attractive new mid-green livery, lined black and yellow in LMS style and bearing the MSJA monogram and its florid heraldic emblem. Though they were in concept quite dull, they were indubitably attractive from the out-

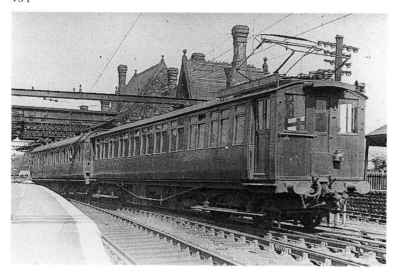

Figure 57 *Elevation and plan of a North Tyneside composite motor car from the 1920-22 fire replacement series.*

Scale: 3mm = 1ft

Figure 58 *Map of the North Tyneside electrified lines, also showing most of the route of the southern line to South Shields, electrified by the LNER in 1936.*

side in an old-fashioned kind of way. Metro-Cammell built them and a form of 'all-steel' construction was employed, best revealed by their riveted roof panelling.

The carriages were no lightweights, the trailers being 30-31 tons and the driving motors no less than 57 tons. In this they rivalled the near-contemporary Brighton line main-line motors (see page 394) but they packed more punch: no less than 330 hp per traction motor of which four were provided in each motor car. This gave no less than 2,640 hp for a typical six-car train, compared with 2,200 hp for the Brighton line sets which had much further to go. MSJA six-car trains were formed from two of the 22 standard three-car units which made up the total fleet (driving motor third/trailer composite/driving trailer third). There was so much power available that a half-hearted attempt was made in 1939 to strengthen peak hour trains to seven cars by inserting an augmentation trailer between two sets — Southern style — but it came to little. The eight vehicles were standard 57-foot LMS non-corridors mostly taken from the Southport stock, but most were soon stored out of use and in 1954 were converted to locomotive haulage.

The original MSJA sets survived, with very little withdrawal, throughout the 1960s, and by quite a long margin gave the railway enthusiast his last regular chance to ride in undiluted LMS-pattern non-corridor stock. Two have been privately preserved, now converted for locomotive haulage.

The last electrically-powered operation in the North West was, like that of the Brighton 'overhead', technically more interesting than most but seemingly rather ahead of its time. However, because the modest little ex-Midland system between Lancaster, Morecambe and Heysham was physically isolated from any

other electrified lines, it retained its 6,600V AC overhead power supply throughout the company period. Only a handful of cars were made for it (three motors and four trailers) and these survived into LMS days. They were, rather surprisingly in view of their owning company, of no great credit to the Midland in terms of either styling or passenger comfort, having ungracious-looking arc-roofed bodies and abominable pierced plywood seats. In later years, though the LMS did not build new stock for the line, a few odd steam-hauled non-corridors (of both ex-MR and LMS standard origin) were converted into driving trailers and added to the character of what was, essentially, a relatively insignificant system. But its time was eventually to come. Paradoxically, its marginal importance, together with its physical isolation, made it an ideal choice for experimental use in connection with the BR move to 25kV AC traction. As such we shall meet it again in the next volume.

The Tyneside electrics

The only group of electric lines outside the London area which could lay even modest claim to form a system in its own right was that of the LNER on the north and south banks of the River Tyne. Its origins were only marginally less venerable than those of the LYR line to Southport, being beaten to the post by a matter of one week only in March 1904 in terms of the first train to run.

Like many of the London area developments at this time, the Tyneside area electrification was stimulated by tramway competition, and as early as 1902 the NER had resolved to electrify its lines running east from Newcastle along the north bank of the Tyne. The selected lines formed a sort of closed 'loop': out from

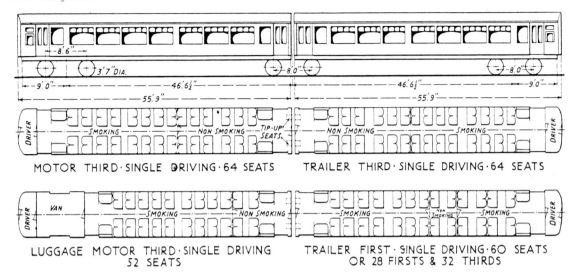

MOTOR THIRD · SINGLE DRIVING · 64 SEATS

TRAILER THIRD · SINGLE DRIVING · 64 SEATS

LUGGAGE MOTOR THIRD · SINGLE DRIVING
52 SEATS

TRAILER FIRST · SINGLE DRIVING · 60 SEATS
OR 28 FIRSTS & 32 THIRDS

Newcastle via two routes to Percy Main and Tynemouth and back inland via Monkseaton, Gosforth and Jesmond, plus a cut-off along the East Coast Main Line from Benton to Newcastle via Heaton. As stated, it was a genuine system rather than a one-off conversion of a single route.

The 600V DC three-rail scheme was inaugurated in 1904 utilizing a series of handsome clerestory cars of new design, many of which were illustrated in Chap. 15 (pages 252-5). During NER days, the original fleet of some 125 vehicles sufficed to provide an excellent service until a disastrous fire in the carriage sheds destroyed 34 cars in 1918. These were fairly speedily replaced during 1920-22 by new stock, still embodying the matchboard panelling and other general styling points of the original stock but now with a domed-end semi-elliptical roof. However,

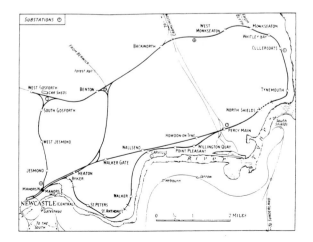

rather than the distinctive red and cream livery adopted for the original cars, the post-war replacements carried traditional NER crimson lake livery; they were still very smart.

Thus matters remained, more or less, for the first 15 years or so of LNER ownership save that the fleet was finished in a drab ersatz teak livery which did not suit its distinctive outlines. But in 1933-4, the LNER began to review the operations of the 'North Tyneside' lines, as they were generally known, and new stock was planned. This was followed by a 1935 anouncement that the South Tyneside line to South Shields was also to be electrified and connected at Newcastle to the older system. Setting aside a few motorized parcels vans, one of which is preserved by the NRM, this LNER modernization was to be the cause of the wholesale withdrawal of the 1904 clerestory cars from the North Tyneside lines and their replacement by brand new stock. Meantime, the South Tyneside route was to be operated by the replacement 1920-22 elliptical roof stock in fully refurbished form.

The new stock for North Tyneside was built by Metro-Cammell, and no one was surprised when it turned out to be articulated pairs in four different varieties as follows:

a) Driving motor third plus trailer first (18 sets)
b) Driving motor third plus trailer third (18 sets)
c) Driving luggage motor third plus driving trailer first (16 sets)
d) Driving motor third plus driving trailer third (12 sets)

These were almost as bewildering as the many clerestory varieties they had replaced; they could be and

Left *Rebuilt set of NER replacement coaches for the South Tyneside lines at Newcastle in the wartime blue and off-white livery; note the LNER emblem on the side. The replacement bucket seats can just be distinguished through the windows.*

Figure 59 *Simplified elevations and plans of typical LNER 1936 articulated North Tyneside stock.*

Scale: 3mm = 1ft

were operated in all manner of permutations. But, *mirabile dictu*, the LNER reinstated the old NER red and cream livery to greatly beneficial effect. No doubt this was inspired by the success of the green and cream tourist livery in terms of public perception, but it did not last long. In 1941 it gave way to a blue and off-white livery — one source stating that this was to reduce visibility from the air in wartime — and this is how most of my generation will recall them. Either way, they gave the Newcastle area a quite dis-

tinctive identity in terms of its suburban electric services which remained unique outside the London Transport area until well into the modern era.

The new cars themselves, if not quite as modern as those of the LMS a few years later, were still very stylish. They were of integral steel construction as far as body and underframe were concerned but they were not all-welded. They had flush-sided exteriors but the sliding doors were hand-operated and fitted only at the ends of the cars. Furthermore, although

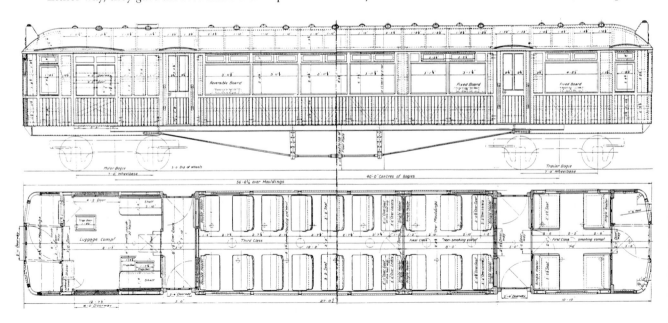

The familiar east end of Newcastle Central is graced on this occasion by an eight-car formation of articulated Metro-Cammell EMUs entering from the Manors direction; on the extreme right, a train of rebuilt ex-NER stock is about to cross the river en route to South Shields. Note the almost 'blanked out' driver's window of the approaching EMU, undoubtedly a wartime safety precaution.

it was decided, not before time, to improve the comfort compared with the old reversible rattan seats of the clerestories, the LNER chose to install its dreaded bucket-seat alternative (see Chap 19). They looked quite good and maybe the shorter distances of the suburban mode made them more tolerable than on long-distance stock. The first class was also arranged 2 + 2 with no quantum improvement over the thirds.

Four single unit parcels and luggage cars were added to the fleet in 1938 which thereafter served its time out on the North Tyneside lines (except for a few early withdrawals due to enemy action or accident damage) until wholesale withdrawal began in 1967, it having been decided to de-electrify the North Tyneside lines for economy reasons. By then, the Metro-Cammell electrics were all in BR green livery, the distinctive Tyneside colours not having been retained after 1947. Like the MSJA stock (see above), so too with the LNER Tyneside cars, the vehicles represented the last company survivors of a specific type to remain in regular service, this time the articulated configuration. Indeed, it was surprising how often it was to be EMU stock which, throughout Britain, kept the old images alive, rather than their locomotive-hauled contemporaries.

The rebuilt stock for South Tyneside was not much changed in appearance from its original form, retaining the matchboard panelling and handsome roof shape. The major internal change was to fit them with bucket seats in place of the old rattan, and the upper windows were given more modern sliding ventilator units similar to those of the new stock. In the reinstated two-tone livery, a surprising degree of visual harmony was achieved both on the cars themselves

and between them and the newer stock. If anything, the older cars had the slight edge in appearance terms, possibly because of their domed roofs and far better styled cab treatment. They lasted until the mid-1950s, being replaced by BR compartment-style EMUs of basically Southern style.

London area developments

Discounting the GWR (Hammersmith and City) and LMS (District and Bakerloo) involvements with the London Transport routes, on which the cars themselves were entirely to the various London Underground patterns, there were only two important company developments in the London area, outside the London Transport or Southern Railway orbit. These were one each from the LMS and LNER, and of them the LNER version did not actually happen until after BR was formed.

The LMS activity was the more long-established, in the form of its line from Euston to Watford and the associated North London route from Broad Street via Willesden Junction to Richmond and Kew. The origins were firmly London and North Western which, at around the time of the First World War, had embarked upon an extensive modernization and widening in the Chalk Farm/Primrose Hill area, combined with the electrification of the above-mentioned routes. The chosen method of electrification was the London Electric Railway UndergrounD fourth rail system to allow compatibility with the Bakerloo tube trains which would join the route at Queen's Park and run through to Watford in association with the

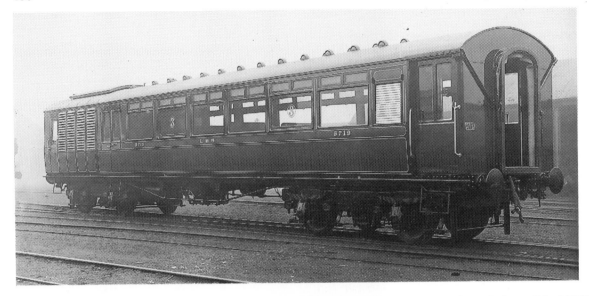

Above *One of the stylish LNWR Oerlikon cars, motor third No 5719, is seen here in LMS livery in the 1920s.*

Left *An Ilford-bound train of LNER-designed Shenfield stock, newly in service in 1949 in BR green livery.*

LNWR's own surface stock from Euston and Broad Street. The programme was ambitious and, because of the war, took some eight years to complete, the first electric trains not using Euston until 1922.

Inititially, the stock provided was predominantly of the famous end-door, open-interior Oerlikon type (there were also a few cars from Siemens), some of the most agreeable outer-suburban EMUs ever built, one of which is deservedly preserved by the NRM. These went on being supplied until early LMS days, the final units coming out from new in LMS colours. But when further new stock was required in the later 1920s, the LMS took one of its periodic yet quite out of character steps backward and augmented the fleet with dated compartment stock. The contemporary

argument (as on the Southern and Metropolitan) was that such stock speeded loading and unloading at busy times, and this was undoubtedly true; but one cannot help but remark that something more akin to Oerlikons with maybe a set of central as well as end doors would have been far better.

Be that as it may, the new trains, all contractor built, were exactly like those already described for the Southport and MSJA routes, and little more needs be said. They ran in standard three-car sets (driving motor third/trailer composite/driving trailer third) with a few spare motors, but were never kept in regular formations. Six cars formed a normal train at busy times, and in 1929 a few augmentation trailers were added to produce seven-car formations. A second batch of similar stock was ordered in 1932, but these were of the main three varieties only. This allowed a more frequent service of six-car trains, thus reducing the need for seven-car sets, so no more augmentation trailers were provided; seven-car trains ceased to operate in 1941 when first class was abolished. Most of the stock, of both builds, was withdrawn *en bloc* in 1963.

The last electrification proposal to be considered here was that of the LNER which, in the later 1930s, had made quite widespread proposals for the electrification of two of its busiest routes. Up in the north of England, the Manchester, Sheffield and Wath line (MSW) via Woodhead Tunnel was, of course, the well-known route and eventually became the first British main line to be electrified for all traffic, using a 1500V DC overhead system. This took place in the early 1950s and it was the same system which the LNER had proposed for its London suburban services out of Liverpool Street and Fenchurch Street to Shenfield. Orders for new EMU stock were made before the war and the same design was chosen both for the London services and the smaller Hadfield and Glossop service from the MSW line.

The war prevented further progress, but afterwards work resumed and in 1946 the part-finished stock was available for inspection. It was not, in the event, to go into traffic until 1949, by then in BR colours. But it was wholly LNER in design as were the similar sets which started work between Manchester and Glossop in 1954.

The carriages were of all-steel construction with air-operated sliding doors and a general configuration very like those of the LMS in the Wirral and Southport areas. Three-coach sets were provided and the driving motor ends had a depressed roof area for the pantographs, but there was little in general to choose between the final LMS and LNER designs. Only the fact of war prevented the LNER stock ever carrying its company colours (though heaven only knows what they would have been!) and the only difference between the Shenfield and MSW sets was the provision of two-class accommodation in the latter.

In the event, of course, the 1500V DC system was not adopted for future standardization, but although up in the north the MSW Glossop-Hadfield section and the MSJA lines remained on this standard until the 1970s and 1980s, the Shenfield line, by virtue of the need for it to be fully integrated into the broader GE section electrification as soon as possible, was eventually converted to the now standard 25kV overhead system, the cars themselves being extensively modified during 1958-9.

24. Steam railcars — and other alternatives

Since the turn of the century, the railways have been striving to find some sort of solution to the increasing problems of road competition, and we have seen how the large-scale electrification of inner suburban routes often helped in the context of urban tramway and, later, bus competition. Likewise, higher speed and improved amenity generally served to maintain the viability of long-distance operations. But the middle ground was often a problem and, interestingly, still is perhaps the major area where, even in the 1980s, the railway is hardest pressed to compete. In more modern days, of course, the solution has often been simply to abandon the unequal struggle and close the service, letting the road competitor take over, if he can — and far too often in recent years, he too has been found wanting. This situation has been made all the more familiar by the Beeching closures of the 1960s and the end result has been to the benefit of nobody in the long run save the makers of tarmac!

Now at this point I must make it clear that I do not believe that the railway has or ever had a divine right to take preference over the roads; the two should, ideally, live in harmony, each playing to and feeding from the relative strengths of the other. But in the curiously unregulated nature of *public* transport which has been the bane of this nation since early Victorian times, things have never been that simple. We have never had an overall public transport policy, and yet the private railways, above all, were instrumental in creating a strong public perception that there ought to be some form of minimal public service *as a matter of right*, and it is to their eternal credit that they often managed to provide such a service from a purely commercial base. However, by the time of the period covered by this book, it was clear that such problems as might have existed before the First World War were as nothing compared with those likely to ensue during the inter-war era and the vehicles to be described in this chapter were a tangible realization of that fact.

Yet again, but in a rather different way from that considered so far, we are at the interface between people and technology. Up to now, the discussion has been mostly confined to an examination of how the railways met the ever-increasing demands and expectations of travellers in terms of vehicular type and on-train amenity, but the grouped railways also had to face the problem of how to provide some sort of service for those who had no choice, when an increasing number of the population were no longer using the railway at all. In the last analysis, the issue is, of course, a political one and I shall have cause to return to it very much in the context of the third volume of this series. But what can be said at this stage is that the four grouped railways did not meekly cave in under this new sort of pressure and simply give up; they made strenuous attempts to find solutions in this marginal area and in some of them could be seen the seeds of much modern railway practice.

The bottom line of the problem was, then as now, one of costs; and to make any significant reduction meant some form of unit which was cheaper to build and operate than the conventional full train. There was nothing radically new in this perception, the steam railmotors of the Edwardian era having been a first attempt to cope; but as Volume 1 has already shown, these mostly came and went like butterflies in summer, and the 1920s dawned with little forward technical progress save for electrification where the high infrastructure cost could be justified — hardly a relevant issue in the area we are now discussing.

The fact is that in the first quarter of the century technology had not really produced any sort of answer for the middle ground, and it was only during the grouping period that railway engineers at last began to come up with ideas which gave some real prospect of success. They did not all work, of course, and some distinctly comical ideas came and went, almost without trace, but overall there were some significant forward moves, and even the relative failures were not without their own bizarre interest. In consequence, it was an interesting time for students of these things and although we may now smile at some of the ideas which were propounded, it is well to recall that they were offered in all seriousness in a quite genuine attempt to solve very real problems.

In essence, the most favoured solution seemed to be a light railcar in one form or another, and the basic purposes for which they were most suited were admirably summarized in an article in *The Railway Engineer* for April 1934:

a) To meet road competition in sparsely populated districts
b) To develop branch-line traffic
c) To pick up and distribute between main-line junctions
d) To provide economical high speed inter-urban services for light loads

There were only two likely sources of motive power

to be tapped: steam and internal combustion. These will form the basis of the rest of this chapter.

The second coming of the steam railcar

It would have been a rare person who, after the mainly disastrous failures of most of the Edwardian steam railmotors, could have predicted that the idea would have a second and rather more successful 'bite at the cherry' during the 1920s and 1930s; yet such it was and here, as in other fields, it was mainly due to the persistence of but one of the four companies, this time the LNER.

The LNER was in many ways the most poverty-stricken of the 'Big Four'. It had some good routes, but its industrial hinterland probably suffered more from the depression, relative to the whole system, than did that of its rivals, and this may have been a part cause. But whatever the reasons, very soon after the grouping the LNER began to take a very serious interest in a new form of steam railcar developed by the Sentinel Waggon Works Ltd in association with Cammell Laird & Co Ltd. This interest went with a renewed assessment of the role of the railcar and it will be helpful briefly to discuss this aspect before going on to the cars themselves.

Traditionally, the older type of steam railmotor had suffered from two principal faults: it was generally seen as merely replacing existing and more expensive conventional trains and, for the most part, its construction kept too closely to design practices associated with conventional stock. The result of this was that it rarely improved the quality of service frequency, and even where it was successful in attracting more traffic, it was either too feeble to cope with it or, if made more powerful, it then did not show the hoped-for cost savings. Many railways therefore resorted to the push-pull option as outlined at the end of Volume 1.

The new approach to railcars started from the rather different presumption that, properly designed, a railcar need not simply replace existing trains — of which only a few per day might have run — but actually provide a better service by operating more frequently. This would reduce the need to add vehicles to the unit which it was self-evidently incapable of pulling (as had often been tried, usually without success, with the steam railmotor) but instead, simply operate more railcars and offer a greater service frequency. Interestingly, as I pen these words, this very policy has fairly recently proved the main cause for much increased patronage of my own local railway. The introduction of four-wheel 'Pacer' railcars now allows BR to offer an hourly service to York and a half-hourly service to Leeds, which policy has both

effectively killed off the bus competition to York and provided better local services to both cities than ever the steam trains, or even the first generation DMUs, managed to do.

However, to do this in the steam context, just as in the modern day, meant using a vehicle which, owing to its lightness and simplicity, needed a smaller and less complicated power unit than was offered by the conventional locomotive style of construction. It was a tricky balancing act, because railway vehicles need to be much stronger than their road equivalent, thus risking imposing a weight penalty, but the Sentinel-Cammell cars were a very fine attempt.

The very first of all was put to work in 1923 on the hitherto unmentioned Jersey Railways & Tramways Ltd in the Channel Islands, thus giving this now long-closed narrow-gauge system an interesting and by no means irrelevant footnote in railway history. But it was its espousal by the LNER which was to be the significant breakthrough. In 1924, trials were conducted in Durham and North Yorkshire of a slightly more powerful version of the Jersey car, and the outcome seems to have been successful, for in 1925 two were purchased and put to use in East Anglia to operate between Norwich and Lowestoft and King's Lynn and Hunstanton. Two years later, two more, slightly modified, were acquired, and 1928 was to see another 20 of this type added to the fleet, giving a total of 24 cars of what later was to be seen as the 'first generation' Sentinel type.

Basically, these first cars made use of the standard boiler and engine unit also used in the well-known Sentinel steam road wagons. This was a proven and economical power unit and was fitted inside a cab unit articulated to the main passenger portion of the railcar. The engine itself was of two-cylinder double-acting configuration and drive to the wheels was by two chains to the rear axle from the sprockets at the end of the crankshaft. The first four (1925-27) cars were finished in ersatz teak, fully panelled, but the final 20 were given the striking red and cream livery of the former NER electrics, almost certainly reflecting the fact that all were put to work in former NER territory. Before long, both these schemes were abandoned in favour of the familiar green and cream livery which most who remember them at all will no doubt recall. This series of cars also introduced the LNER tradition of naming its railcars, old stagecoach names being the chosen theme.

At much the same time as the LNER was conducting its tests on these new-style railcars, the LMS also tried them out. In 1925, trials were conducted on the Ripley branch and a production order of 13 cars was put in service during 1926-7, a year or so ahead of the main LNER order. The LMS cars were driven in the same way as those of the LNER but were rather

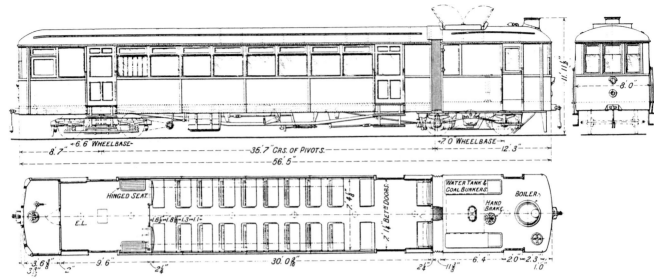

General View, Side Elevation, and Plan of Sentinel-Cammell Steel Rail-Car, L.M.S.R.

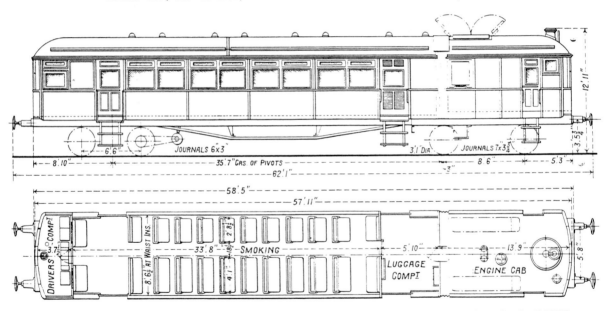

more low-slung in appearance with less of the working parts exposed below the frames. They were finished in standard lined crimson lake and were unnamed. They were also rather shorter and narrower, presumably for even greater route availability, and were thus some 4½ tons lighter (21 t 7 cwt as opposed to 25 t 18 cwt), but this gave them only 75 per cent of the LNER seating capacity (44 rather than 59) since their seats were arranged 2 + 2 rather than the LNER 2 + 3. Both types had reversible 'walk over' seat backs and mahogany interior finish,

LMS seats being green and those in the LNER cars being quoted as having 'standard LNER pattern' material. Comparative drawings of the two types are appended.

Though subsequent events were to demonstrate that the Sentinel-Cammell railcars were to be the definitive steam type, it is necessary, before going on with their later development, to keep the chronology in order by introducing the second LNER approach to the problem. This was a purchase of the rival railcar type offered by Clayton Wagons Ltd of Lincoln,

Left Figure 60 *These elevations and plans of the articulated Sentinel railcars provided for the LMS and LNER respectively clearly indicate the difference in size between the two designs.*

Scale: ¹/₁₀" = 1ft

Right *A trio of LNER articulated railcars in service, the leading example being No 29 'Rockingham' and the second in line No 212 'Eclipse'. The third example is unidentified.*

Below Figure 61 *Elevation and plan of the Clayton-type steam railcar for the LNER.*

Scale: ¹/₁₀" = 1ft

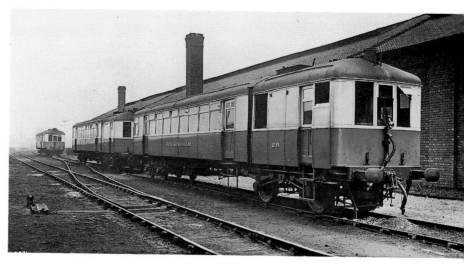

its evaluation being conducted more or less in parallel with that of the first Sentinel cars.

The Clayton cars originated in 1925, originally for use in New Zealand, and in 1927 the LNER acquired one (as also, simultaneously, did the Egyptian State Railways) for test purposes. Again, the company was reasonably satisfied and a production order for ten more was placed in 1928. In these cars, steam road vehicle practice was again adopted, but since the actual power unit was quite differently conceived, it made quite a noticeable difference to the configuration of the powered end.

The Clayton cars used essentially the same stan-

dard engine and boiler unit as fitted to Clayton 'undertype' road wagons. This unit, like the chain-driven Sentinels, also employed a two-cylinder layout but the engine (totally enclosed and mounted above the leading axle of the driving bogie) drove the wheels by a crankshaft pinion in connection with a spur wheel on the axle. The two axles of the driving bogie were then connected by outside coupling rods attached to the wheels in conventional locomotive fashion. The centre of the power bogie carried a conventional bogie bolster and pivot, to which was fixed the leading end of the car body. This placed the boiler within the body but left the coal bunker and water

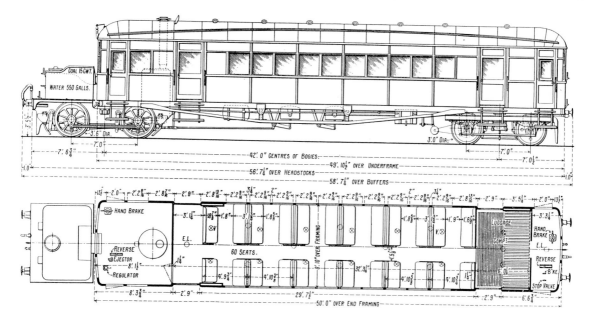

Prototype LNER Clayton railcar No 41 seen here in service at Lintz Green, near Newcastle, when still finished in pseudo 'teak' livery, the only Clayton car so treated. When later repainted in conventional two-colour style, it received the name 'Rapid'.

Opposite side views of LNER rigid chassis railcars No 31 'Flower of Yarrow' and No 38 'Pearl' built in 1928 and 1929 respectively. This type was by far the most common LNER version.

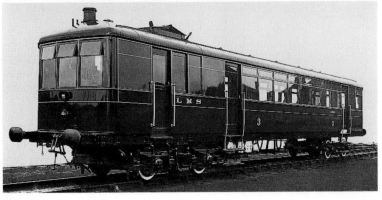

The solitary LMS rigid chassis Sentinel railcar No 4349 of 1930 was undoubtedly both well proportioned and finished, but the LMS seemed to have far less faith in the type than the LNER and never repeated the order. It was scrapped in 1939.

Figure 62 Elevation and plan of the 48-seat LNER Sentinel steam railcars with twin 'engines' introduced in 1932, Nos 220, 246 and 248. They were given bucket seats and classed as luxury cars (sic!), being named 'Defence', 'Royal Sovereign' and 'Tantivy' respectively.

tanks in full view ahead of the bodywork. It was thus, in effect, a rigid railcar with a pivoting power bogie, part of which was exposed to view. The effect was mildly comical.

Like the Sentinels, the first Clayton car was finished in 'teak' livery, the main order mostly being delivered in red and cream. All eventually ended up with green and cream livery and were again named after stage-coaches. The last of the series, a 44-seater with 'more comfortable' bucket seats (sic!) and a few technical refinements, wore green and cream livery from the outset and probably established this style. It carried the wonderfully ambiguous name *Bang Up!*

As things turned out, the LNER seems to have decided to concentrate on the Sentinel alternative very soon after it had put its Claytons into service, and 1928 was also to see the ordering of by far the biggest batch of new steam railcars ever placed by a British railway company. They were all Sentinels and were derived from an experimental 'one-off' car of a new design, tested early in 1928 and named *Integrity*. It seems possible that this car was Sentinel's answer to Clayton, for it embodied gear drive in combination with the existing two-cylinder power unit and was mounted on a rigid chassis, the steam and exhaust pipes having flexible joints to allow for the differential movement of the engine portion (mounted direct to the power bogie) and the boiler unit (fixed to the main chassis). This was to lead directly to a revised version with a six-cylinder single acting engine employing gear and cardan shaft drive.

During 1928 and 1929, no fewer than 50 of these new-type six-cylinder railcars were ordered, 49 for the LNER and one for the Axholme Joint Railway (LMS/LNER), later taken over by the LNER in 1933. They were undoubtedly the most successful Sentinel design and went into service in many areas though, as usual, by far the bulk of them went to the by now traditional ex-NER territory. Stage-coach names were yet again favoured, but this time a few more regionally appropriate titles were also employed. Four similar cars were provided for the CLC in 1929, and the LMS also obtained a similar example in 1930, but, as with its articulated purchase, this was to a generally smaller size and was of much lighter weight (25 t compared with 28 t 15 cwt).

The LNER railcar purchase was completed in 1930 and 1932 with five more rigid Sentinel cars in two separate batches, each embodying a beefed-up 12-cylinder engine configuration for the more hilly routes on the NE Yorkshire coast. In fact, two sets of standard six-cylinder power units were used, each driving one of the two bogies. There were some technical changes between the batches and the passenger accommodation was reduced from the customary 59, first to 54 and then to 48, the latter being in 2 + 2 'luxury' configuration. Finally, mention should also be made of the solitary twin articulated Sentinel, *Phenomena* of 1930. This too had 12-cylinder propulsion, this time with the two 'engines' driving the leading and central bogies. The powered end seated 39 and the 'trailer' portion 83.

Mention of trailers serves as a reminder that to run with its railcars, the LNER also procured some sin-

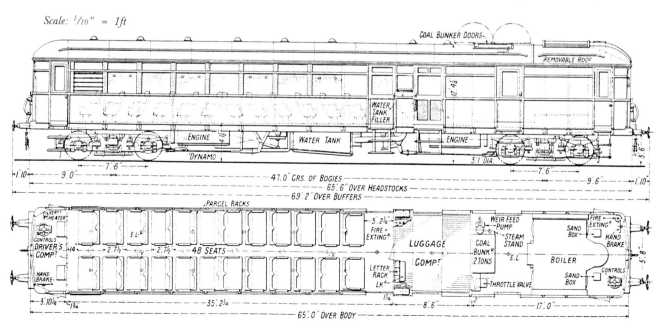

Scale: $^1/_{10}"$ = 1ft

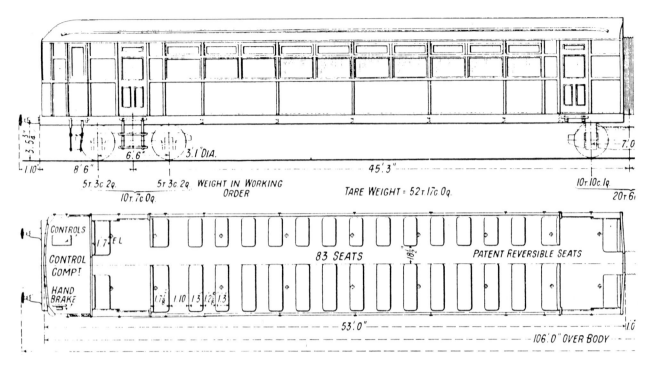

gularly unlovely four-wheel examples of the genre in 1929 from Claytons. Classed as 'Trailer Brake Thirds', eight only were built and never seem to have been very popular. Their final disposal is unknown.

In terms of usefulness in service, the LNER rail-cars clearly had a longer innings than most of the pre-1914 steam railmotors, and its fleet of some 91 units from all sources must have effected quite substantial savings during the 15-20 years when they were operational. The Claytons were the shortest lived, faring no better than the older-type steam railmotors, maybe for much the same reasons, and mostly went out of

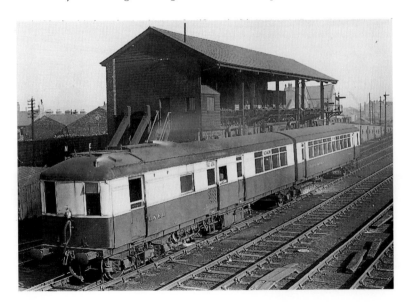

Figure 63 *Elevation and plan of the unique LNER twin Sentinel steam railcar No 2291 'Phenomena'.*

Scale: 3mm = 1ft

Left *Twin Sentinel 'Phenomena' is seen here at South Blyth Shed, during the time when it was used in regular service along the north-east coast between Monkseaton and Blyth*

Figure 64 *Elevations and plan of the rather unmemorable four-wheel Clayton trailers of 1929, designed to run with the railcars.*

Scale: 3mm = 1ft

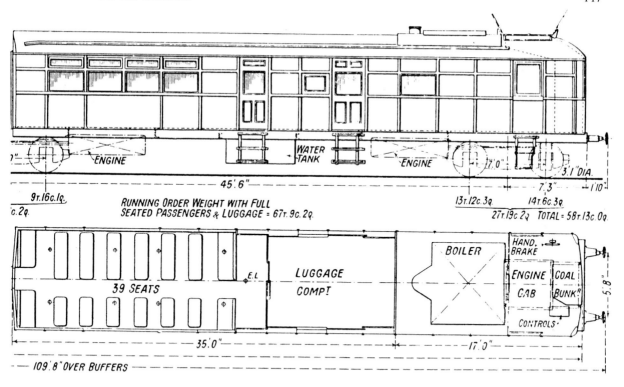

RUNNING ORDER WEIGHT WITH FULL
SEATED PASSENGERS & LUGGAGE = 67T.9C.2Q.

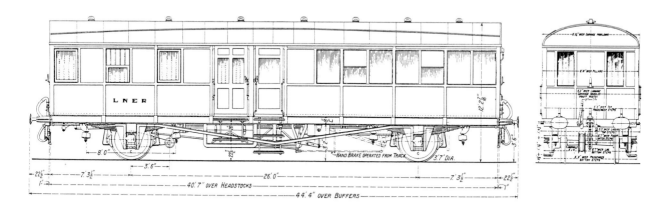

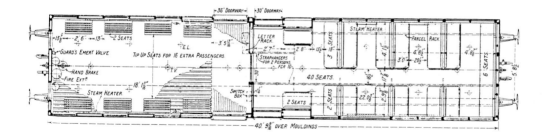

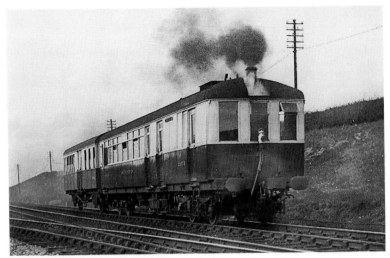

Pictures of Clayton trailers actually in use are somewhat rare, but this view taken near Darlington shows one of them being hauled by rigid Sentinel railcar No 2271 'Industry' (of the 1929-built series) on the Richmond branch service in 1934 (T.J. Edgington Collection).

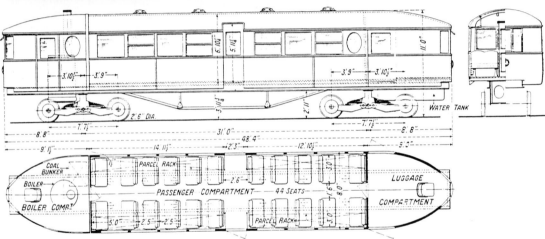

Figure 65 *Elevations and plan of the unique Sentinel steam railbus for the Southern Railway.*

Scale: $^1/_{10}$" = 1ft

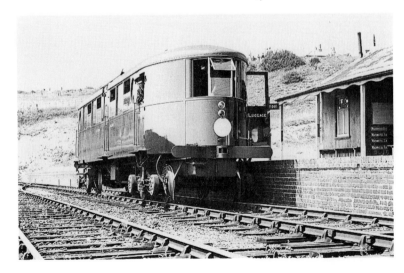

The Southern's Sentinel railbus at The Dyke station circa 1933.

service *circa* 1936. But the Sentinels lasted rather better. The 12-cylinder cars were not too long-lived but the two big batches mostly served until the mid-1940s, many until after the war. One of them, No 2136 *Hope*, just reached BR. Withdrawn early in 1948 it would have been a worthy candidate for preservation, but maybe its name was too symbolic of the whole story of the steam railcar. The fact is that none of them actually gave 20 years of revenue service, and although on average they did rather better than the steam railmotors, the final examples of the latter (those of the LYR and LNWR — see Chap. 15), which also lasted until the late 1940s, had enjoyed a far longer working life. As for the LMS Sentinels, they lasted less than ten years!

The Sentinel steam railcar story was not quite finished in the British context with the building of the last LNER cars in 1932, though it were well had it been so, for its final fling, a sort of Ruritanian creation built for the Southern Railway, was almost in the nature of a tragic farce. In fact, were its existence not confirmed photographically, it could well have been some flight of fancy doodled on the drawing board of an over-imaginative designer working for the tinplate toy manufacturers of the day!

At much the same time as the SR was introducing its new electric services to Brighton, it also put into operation a single unit Sentinel steam railcar on the steeply-graded branch line from Hove to Devil's Dyke, high up in the South Downs to the north-west of Brighton. This in itself would have made some sense, for the branch was both steep and sharply curved; but instead of using one of the well-proved LNER-type cars (or even, for that matter, the lighter-weight LMS alternatives), the whole operation was made the excuse for creating a new sort of one-man-operated bus unit. The engine part appears to have been a two-cylinder compound of unproven quality, slung on the driving axle and fed from a standard Sentinel boiler fitted with a patent automatic stoker embodying a screw feed plus crusher.

It seemed like a lot of technology to crack a very small nut and was then made worse by marrying it to a fashionably streamlined Zeppelin-type body which seemed to be perched on top as an after-thought. Maybe I am too cruel, but when I first saw a picture of this extraordinary creation and realized that on its introduction it had been taken quite seriously, I simply burst out laughing. It appears to have survived until 1942, but actually ceased work in 1937. One cannot envisage even Oliver Bulleid seeing much merit in the thing, and the fact that it was actually authorized by the normally rather conservative Richard Maunsell makes it all the more odd.

However, strange though it may seem, this was indeed the very last self-propelled steam-powered passenger-carrying vehicle to be devised for use in Britain, and as such has its place in our story. But it only served to point out, along with the other Sentinels, Claytons and their railmotor ancestors, that as far as steam propulsion was concerned, the light-weight single unit was still not the full answer, even though the railcars had made a better fist of it than most. If steam could still compete, then push-pull was the far better answer (see Chapter 25); meantime, the lightweight prize was to go to internal combustion.

The rising tide of internal combustion

The internal combustion engine undoubtedly 'grew up' during the First World War, stimulated both on the land and in the air by the demands of the military. In consequence, many ex-servicemen resumed their civilian lives with more than an adequate working knowledge of this relatively new form of prime mover. Aided by a vast supply of government surplus ex-military buses and lorries sold off at knockdown prices, thousands of former soldiers set up their own road transport businesses, both passenger and freight. The latter was, in the longer run, to be the more damaging to railway fortunes, but even in the former case the rise of the motor bus during the 1920s and 1930s was a very real threat to the railway passenger business, nowhere more so than in the sort of services with which this chapter is concerned.

At first, there were many who advocated a straight transfer of this new form of road technology to the rail, believing in all seriousness that all that was needed was to purchase a cheap lorry or bus engine, mount it on something approximating to a rail-borne equivalent of a road vehicle chassis, add some form of appropriate bodywork and off we go. They probably knew that a prime characteristic of rail transport meant that a given unit of power can shift between four and six times as large a load on smooth rails than on the rougher-surfaced roads. It still can, of course, and this realization goes right back to the days when it was discovered that one horse could move the same sort of stage-coach body mounted on railway wheels as it would take four or six to shift along the highway. But in terms of mechanical power it was by no means as simple as that.

Essentially, the road-type power unit and transmission really came into its own when allied with pneumatic tyres which cushioned the vibrations. Even the solid tyres of many old vehicles gave some help in this regard; but the high-frequency vibrations and rigid quality of most railway track were less forgiving and caused problems. Moreover, the lower power to weight ratio needed on the railways led to disappointing performance and a tendency to overload, simply because it was in theory within the engine capacity

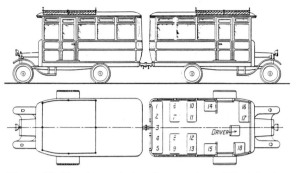

Figure 66 *Elevations and plan of an experimental Ford Duplex petrol engined railcar unit devised for the Derwent Valley Light Railway near York in the early 1920s, a solution not untypical of many which were tried out at this time.*

to cope with such loads.

Thus, the first internal combustion railway vehicles in the post-grouping era mostly seemed like fugitives from the highways. Though they did have some success, they were mostly in the nature of individual experiments and few, if any, were multiplied beyond the first one or two units to be built. Some of them were distinctly comical, viewed in retrospect, and for maybe ten years or so after the grouping, the advocates of steam probably saw no threat; in any case, were not the new steam railcars (see above) proving far more effective? This may well have been so, up to a point, but some of the ideas introduced are still interesting to review in the context of later evolution.

The North Eastern Railway, often underrated for reasons stated more than once in this survey, had long been a pioneer in 'alternative' solutions, and right to the very end of its existence was actively looking at both petrol-electric and direct-drive solutions, some of which were illustrated in Chap. 15; but if truth be told, not much seems to have happened beyond this point until the LMS, in conjunction with Karrier Motors Ltd of Huddersfield, made a very interesting attempt to provide a genuine dual-purpose vehicle with its celebrated but never duplicated 'Ro-Railer'. The idea was so logical and obvious that even now one wonders why it was not pursued with more vigour; it would surely have had many applications even in more modern circumstances.

The episode is well recorded, thus needing but brief mention here, but in essence involved a conventional single-deck motor bus, little modified in basic appearance save for having entrance doors on both sides to suit the 'rail' mode, which was fitted with both road and rail wheels. In 'road' configuration, the railway wheels, being smaller in diameter, simply rotated idly out of harm's way behind the road wheels, but on transfer to rail the steering was locked and, with the road wheels raised by means of eccentrics between wheel hub and rim, the unit became a railcar. The modal transfer took only two or three minutes and one of the unit's more celebrated uses was on the road journey between Stratford-upon-Avon and the nearby LMS Welcombe Hotel, having travelled by rail from Blisworth to Stratford. Maybe it was rather small for more widespread use, who knows, but like so many other ideas it withered on the branch.

The LMS 'Ro-Railer' in service when operating between Blisworth and the Welcombe Hotel, Stratford-on-Avon. It has even been scurrilously suggested that one of the reasons for its failure was that it was too undignified and low-brow for the well-heeled patrons of this very exclusive hotel. This may well be true! (T.J. Edgington Collection).

Figure 67 *This series of drawings represents the several experimental ideas which were evaluated by the LMS during the 1930s — see the text. They are, from top to bottom: Karrier 'Ro-Railer' of 1930-31; 'La Micheline' of 1932; and a standard Michelin pneumatic-tyred railcar of 1935. None of them turned out to have any long-term significance.*   *Scale: 3mm = 1ft*

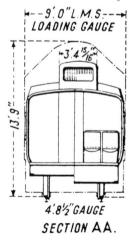

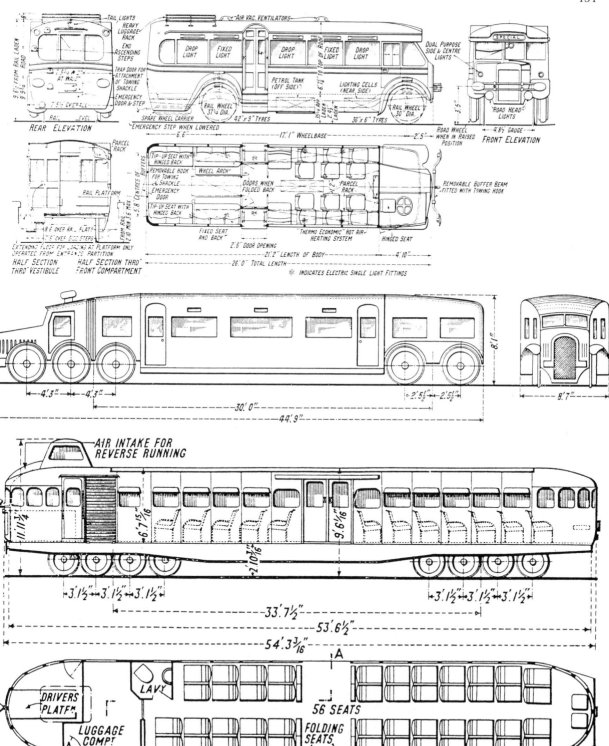

This near head-on view of 'La Micheline' clearly reveals the nature of the wheel treads and flanges of this interesting experiment; above the cab roof were radiators of the water-cooled engine, designed to function adequately in both directions of motion. The car was claimed to save 25 per cent in travelling time on the existing 42-minute Bletchley to Bicester service on which it was evaluated, a distance of nearly 20 miles with six intermediate stops (T.J. Edgington Collection).

The next and final British attempts to marry conventional road technology to the requirements of rail transport were again of LMS inspiration, this time in conjunction with the celebrated Michelin tyre company of France. In these experiments, the shock-absorbing properties of pneumatic tyres, mentioned above, were to be made the justification for evaluating ultra-lightweight construction, for the vehicles were designed in such a way that the rubber tyres actually ran on the rail surface, thus replacing the normal steel tyres and leaving the steel flange to do its normal task. The first example, entirely French-built and known as 'La Micheline', was a ten-wheel vehicle entirely in the road-coach stylistic idiom but far more luxuriously appointed than the near-contemporary 'Ro-Railer'. It seated only 24, as opposed to 26, but was nearly twice as long (almost 45 ft compared with 26 ft) and at 5 tons was more than 2 tons lighter in weight. It had carpeted floors and a mixture of armchairs and conventionally transverse seats and was tested between Bletchley and Oxford in 1932.

That said, little more seems to have been recorded of this experiment than that of the 'Ro-Railer'; maybe both were too limited in their scope or too low in seating capacity. But the next pneumatic-tyred experiment was an altogether more ambitious affair. In 1935, sponsored by Armstrong-Siddeley Motors Ltd who provided the engine unit, the LMS introduced a 56-seat Michelin railcar on its Oxford-Cambridge service. The car itself was the standard Michelin 16-wheel type (two eight-wheel bogies with a raised 'turret' driving cab) and represented a concept already quite well known in France. Its trial performance was most impressive, nearly 70 mph achieved in almost total silence. It weighed in at little more than 8 tons and its seating capacity was fully comparable with any other contemporary railcars but, yet again, no one seems to have been impressed enough to cause the LMS — or anyone else for that matter — to repeat the idea. The odd thing is that ever since that time, the French have always found some application for pneumatic-tyred railway vehicles, best known these days in the context of some lines on the Paris Metro; but then there are those who would argue that in the present century, French railway engineers have often been well ahead of their British counterparts,

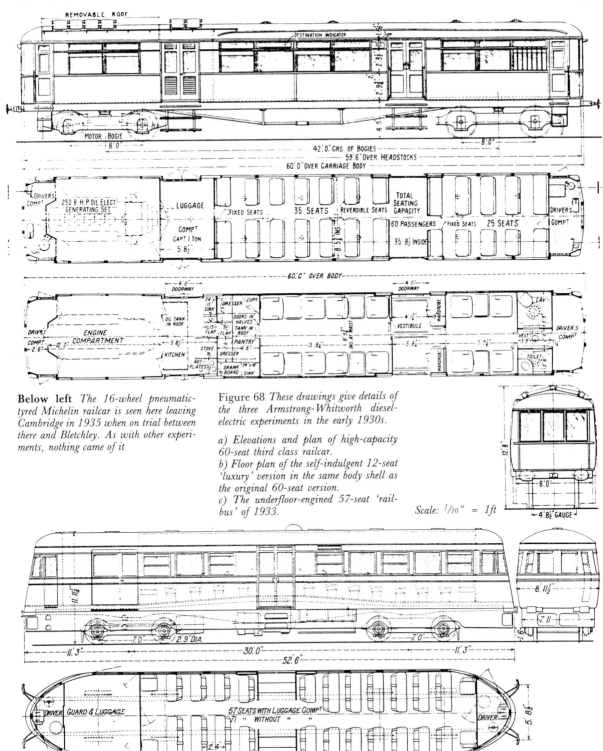

Below left *The 16-wheel pneumatic-tyred Michelin railcar is seen here leaving Cambridge in 1935 when on trial between there and Bletchley. As with other experiments, nothing came of it*

Figure 68 *These drawings give details of the three Armstrong-Whitworth diesel-electric experiments in the early 1930s.*

a) *Elevations and plan of high-capacity 60-seat third class railcar.*
b) *Floor plan of the self-indulgent 12-seat 'luxury' version in the same body shell as the original 60-seat version.*
c) *The underfloor-engined 57-seat 'railbus' of 1933.*

Scale: $^1/_{10}$" = 1ft

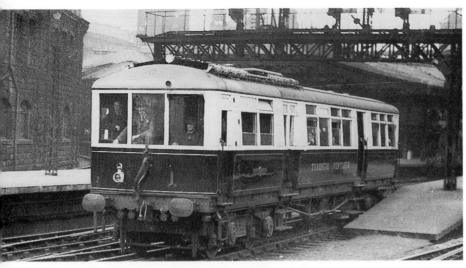

Opposite side views of the first high-capacity Armstrong-Whitworth units 'Tyneside Venturer and 'Northumbrian' in service on the LNER at Newcastle and York in 1932 and 1935 respectively. A third similar unit was named 'Lady Hamilton' (both T.J. Edgington Collection).

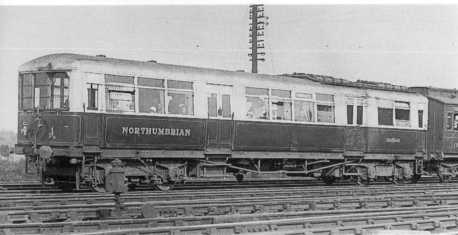

The luxury 'Armstrong-Shell Express' unit at Wolverton in 1933.

at least at the technological level — maybe Euro-Tunnel will sort it out!

Concurrently with the generally unsuccessful British efforts to adapt road practice to railway use, the early 1930s were also characterized by another clutch of experiments whereby internal combustion engines were fitted to more 'railway-like' vehicles. This led to a further modest rash of experiments, of which we may, perhaps, single out for further mention those of Messrs Armstrong Whitworth in the diesel-electric field during 1931-3. These brought two new factors into the equation: the diesel engine and electric transmission of power to the wheels. Though probably unappreciated at the time, both were to prove rather important in the longer term, and although this book is not a technical treatise of railway traction methods, we do need to consider both of them.

So far, all the internal combustion experiments reviewed had used petrol engines, and this may well have been a partial cause of their usually less than successful outcome. As more modern experience has well and truly demonstrated, the compression-ignition engine, invented by Dr Rudolph Diesel, is, by its very nature, far more suited to the rigours of commercial operation and is also able to be enlarged to give a greater power output at greater economy than its petrol-fuelled, spark-ignition equivalent. This was already becoming obvious in the road transport field, as witness the fairly rapid change-over from petrol to diesel in the commercial bus and lorry business; and since railways need, if anything, even bigger engines for their normally heavier vehicles, it should cause no real surprise that the successful application of internal combustion in the railway arena had to await the development of newer and more powerful diesel engines. However, the transmission of power from engine to wheels was different.

In this regard, we have already noted that the vibration characteristics of the railway vehicle were different from those of the road equivalent and that the various solutions to the problem of getting power to railway wheels were, at the time, less than perfect. Under the circumstances, therefore, it is hardly surprising that attention turned to the possibility of using 'state of the art' electric traction motor technology, by now well understood by railway engineers, and combine it with the ability of an internal combustion engine to produce electric power by the simple expedient of letting it drive a generator rather than the wheels themselves. This is indeed the basic principle behind the vast majority of modern high-powered diesel-electric locomotives. But, as might well be imagined, there was a snag, particularly in the realm of the self-contained passenger-carrying vehicle where weight-saving is paramount in order to achieve operational economy. Here, the fundamental dilemma was that a generator big enough to produce adequate electric power was no lightweight component.

This factor was and is usually acceptable in the purely locomotive field, but as far as the lightweight diesel-powered railcar was concerned, the future had to be with some better form of weight-saving mechanical transmission if at all possible, but this was easier said than done in the early 1930s, hence the Armstrong-Whitworth experiments.

It began in 1931-2 with an undeniably well-conceived railcar design which bore more than a passing resemblance to the now familiar Sentinel offerings and with much the same seating capacity — 60 third class passengers in a 2 + 3 arrangement with 'reversible' seat backs. They were given 250hp Sulzer engines manufactured under licence and were designed either to work in multiple or to handle an additional 30-ton trailing load at their designed maximum speed of 65 mph. In fact, the cars were designed to a composite loading gauge enabling them to run anywhere in Britain; but they were rather heavy at 42½ tons. A very successful trial of two in multiple was carried out on the LNER in February 1932 from Newcastle to Hexham and back.

A year later, the LMS also evaluated one of these cars in a very different mode: a fast service from London to the British Industries Fair site at Castle Bromwich. This was claimed to be the first diesel-powered express service in Britain, and so indeed it was, but compared with the LNER experiment this new version, known as the 'Armstrong-Shell Express', seems to have been little more than an extravagant publicity stunt. The car was, in fact, specially refurbished for this service, and within the same body shell the original 60 seats had given way to but 12 Pullman-like armchairs and tables, a small kitchen and pantry and separate toilet and lavatory compartments. No doubt it was all great fun, but 42 tons of railcar for but a dozen passengers was no way to run a railway, then or now!

The last Armstrong-Whitworth experiment is far less well known than the previous two, but from the details given at the time ought to have been a real challenger for honours. It appeared in June 1933 and was an extremely well thought out 57-seater with compact underfloor diesel-electric equipment. Two engine options were stated to be available, either 95bhp or 140bhp, the whole lot coming out at something over 17½ tons with the smaller engine, or slightly under 19 tons with the larger, both being less than half the weight of the 1932 cars. It was regarded as a railbus, had attractive bodywork styled by Park Royal, the well-known London bus builders, and, like so many more of these things at the time, was tried out in Northumberland and Durham by the LNER.

In a sense, 1933 was the critical year for the inter-

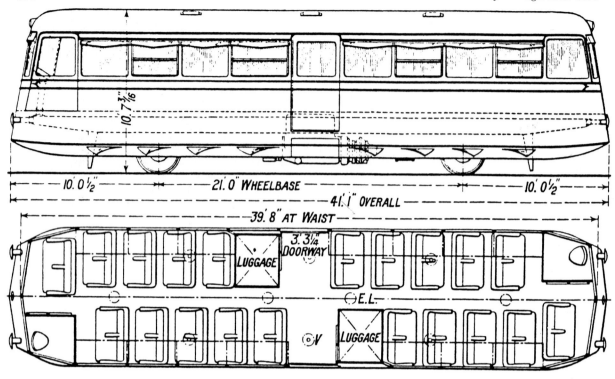

nal combustion engine as far as the British railways were concerned, for it marked both the end of the experimental phase — save for one dramatic later LMS venture in 1938 — and also the start of the only real development which had any significantly long-lasting consequences. The last 1933 experiment was a trio of Leyland four-wheel railbuses for the LMS. They seated 40, weighed only 10 tons and were exactly symmetrical end-to-end about their centre-line, whereon were positioned the outer doors. They had transverse seats facing outwards from the centre of the cars whose enclosed bodywork was of characteristic bus style. They were, in effect, the last throw of the pure road vehicle approach and appear to have been rather more successful than most, surviving until 1951, but right at the time of their introduction, as indeed was also true of the final diesel-electric design from Armstrong-Whitworth, the way ahead was pointed by the first truly trend-setting design to emerge during the grouping era; and it came from an unlikely source.

I refer, of course, to the pioneering diesel railcars of the Great Western Railway, by quite a long way the most properly integrated internal combustion railway passenger vehicles so far seen in this country. In them could be seen not only a proper appreciation of the different needs of a railway as opposed to a road vehicle, but also a properly designed form of mechanical transmission which took care of the technical problems mentioned above. They were also more than normally well styled, being entirely appropriate to their era, yet having a timeless quality which does not always go with being in the height of fashion. Fortunately, like the Southern Electrics and the London Underground carriages already considered, they too have attracted their own dedicated literature — see Bibliography — so it is not necessary to pick their bones here. What is maybe most surprising is that in spite of their longer-term influence, there were less than 40 of them all told.

The story started in quite a modest way in 1933 when a quite new design of diesel railcar was designed by Hardy Motors Ltd of Southall in association with Messrs AEC Ltd, who provided the 130hp power plant, and the GWR which agreed to operate the car on its services between Slough, Reading, Didcot and Oxford. The fully streamlined car body was evolved in wind tunnel tests and was put together by Park Royal Coachworks Ltd. There was thus a very considerable injection of contemporary road vehicle technology; but where it differed from previous attempts to marry road to rail was in the use of a diesel engine, the design of a more robust chassis (lightweight but suitable to railway use) and the development of a

Figure 69 *Elevation and plan of the 1933 Leyland diesel railbus for the LMS.*

Scale: *4mm = 1ft*

Right *Pioneer GWR streamlined railcar No 1 near Maidenhead circa 1934. Note the driver's separate access door, a feature never repeated in any of the subsequent GWR railcars*

Figure 70 *Side elevations and plans of streamlined GWR railcars Nos 2-4 (above) and 5-7 (below).*

Scale: *¹/₁₀" = 1ft*

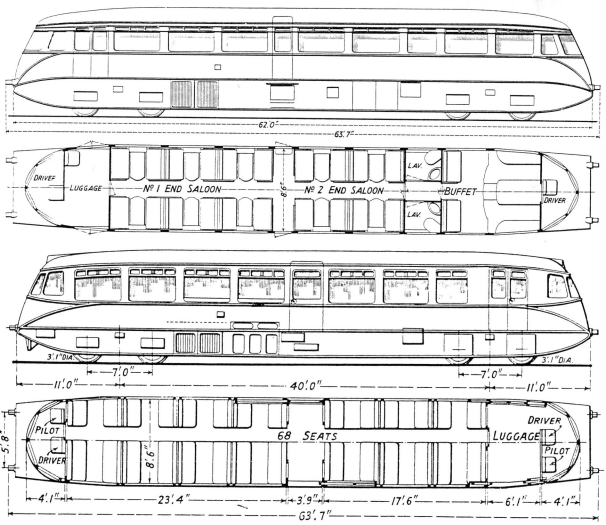

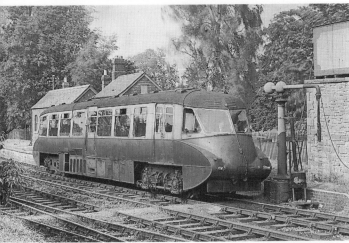

direct-drive transmission system which would be both reliable and capable of operating with equal facility in either direction of travel, the car being double-ended. When it finally emerged, it was a stylistic *tour de force* whose appearance met with immediate approval and brought the GWR much kudos. Though the company itself had little or nothing to do with its design, it was perfectly entitled to take credit for having introduced the car on to its routes.

After considerable evaluation, the GWR then resolved to order a further series of cars which embodied improvements on the prototype, not least being the provision of twin engines for much needed greater power, and by 1936 no fewer than 17 were in service. Though all shared the basic streamlined shape of the prototype, they were not all alike, either in appearance or seating capacity.

The first 'production' series (Nos 2-4) were low-capacity, 44-seat cars for longer-distance work, each having lavatories and a small but extremely well-equipped buffet section at one end; they were used for express service between Birmingham and Cardiff and represented the first regular diesel workings in Britain of this kind, the earlier Armstrong example (see above) having been essentially a one-off operation. Seats were arranged 2 + 2 in bays of eight with tables between them, exactly in the manner of conventional open stock, and a pair of centre doors was provided, one on each side. The driver gained access to his cab from the passenger saloon, unlike Car No 1 where there was an outer door to the cab, and there was a small guard's luggage compartment at the end opposite the buffet counter.

The next three cars (Nos 5-7) reverted to the high density 3 + 2 seating of No 1, and this time the bodywork was made by the Gloucester RC & W Co Ltd, but was slightly differently styled in that the side windows were much deeper, thus improving the outlook, and the centre doors were of the sliding type. The waistline was slightly upswept at the driving ends which, allied to the two-tone colour scheme, gave them a slightly boat-like appearance. The roof line also curved down slightly more over the cab ends, and the effect of both these small-style changes was to result in a most charming variant from the original rather high-waisted appearance of the first four. This low-waisted style was to be the standard for the rest of the streamlined series, whose bodies were also built by the Gloucester company.

The last ten streamlined cars (Nos 8-17) were ordered before the previous batch were all in service, such was the faith of the GWR in this new idea, and all were similar in lines to the No 5-7 series, save that the waistline was now horizontal rather than upswept at the ends. Of these ten, six were exactly as Nos 5-7, ie 70-seaters with no lavatories; three (Nos

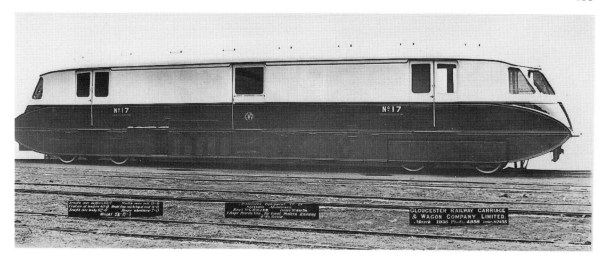

10-12) had lavatories for longer-distance work (but no buffet) and seated 63 in consequence, still in 3 + 2 configuration; while the last, No 17, was a dedicated express parcels car whose purpose was to speed up local passenger services in the London area. This it did by taking over all the 'pick-up' parcels traffic which hitherto had caused extended stops to be made by many local trains. This experiment clearly proved successful, though whether it needed to be streamlined to do the job is rather conjectural.

By mid-1936, therefore, the GWR had put a fleet of 16 passenger-carrying cars into service, and such was their success that the company could claim later the same year that it was operating them on something like 20 per cent of its network and they were putting up over 1,000,000 miles per year. This represented about 2-3 per cent of the GWR passenger mileage, most of which was extra business since, at that time, the railcars were supplementing existing services. In some cases they drummed up so much new business that conventional trains had to be substituted. This seems undoubtedly to have been the reason why, in 1937, the GWR put a new and experimental car into service, No 18. This, while still semi-streamlined, had lost some of the graceful lines of the earlier cars and was also given railway-pattern buffing and drawgear, the purpose being to evaluate whether a railcar could haul a trailing load and still give the same or similar performance to the single unit cars. No 18 was given a much stronger underframe in consequence and was geared differently; it more than exceeded expectations and from it were derived the final GWR railcar types.

One of the obvious differences between No 18 and

Left *These views allow comparison to be made of the subtle visual changes between the three main series of GWR streamlined railcars. They show, in order: 'high-waisted' Buffet Car No 3 undergoing trials on the Brentford branch in 1934; 'low-waisted' No 7 with 'upswept' driving-end waist panelling, still in GWR livery at Coleford in 1950; and No W10W (representing the lavatory version of the most common type) in BR red/cream livery at Campden in 1954 on a Worcester service*

Above *The one-off streamlined parcels railcar, No 17*

Figure 71 *Map showing the extent of GWR railcar operations in 1936.*

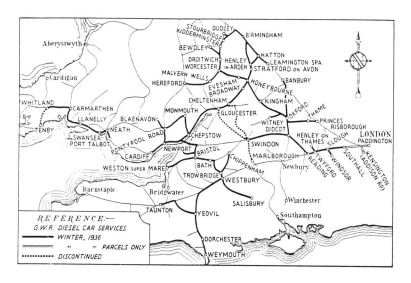

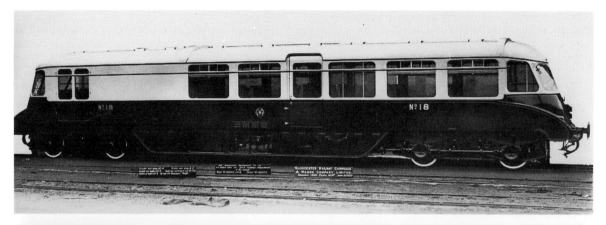

Top *Experimental semi-streamlined rail-car No 18 of 1937, the first to be fitted with conventional buffing and drawgear.*

Above *Swindon-built railcar No W26W at Birmingham Snow Hill on 19 June 1954, having just arrived with the 11.15 from Dudley (T.J. Edgington).*

Left *Twin railcars Nos 35-6 on trial with an intermediate trailer on the Brentford branch circa 1941.*

Right *Interior of the buffet portion of GWR twin railcars Nos 35-6 when new in 1941.*

its predecessors was the much larger luggage van portion, which also contained a steam heating boiler for use when a trailer was in tow. Seating, in consequence, was reduced to 49, still 3 + 2 and arranged in five bays, one seat being 'lost' at the central door to the van portion. However, the loss in seating capacity was deemed to be acceptable in view of the ability to pull a trailer, since the larger van space would obviously serve for both components. This, accordingly, was made the basis for the next main batch, Nos 19-33. This time, however, the bodies were built at Swindon and they emerged during the early war years in 1940 and 1941.

To those who had seen the earlier railcars, the new Swindon cars were a bit brutish in appearance, having angular bodies and little real resemblance to their stylish forbears. They seemed to be all angles and corners in consequence; but this undoubtedly saved cost and time at a difficult period, and in all other respects they were more versatile because of their trailer-hauling capability. Inside, seating now reverted to 2 + 2 throughout and they had six bays, though still with a pretty large van and steam generator compartment. A final car to this same general outline was built in 1941, and was another dedicated parcels railcar, in the manner of No 17.

It was not very long before the obvious next step was taken of making a twin railcar unit to cope with bigger loads, and the final phase saw two of these pairs produced, one each in 1941 and 1942: Nos 35/36 and 37/38. They were well-appointed cars with driving cabs at the outer ends only, and seated 104 in combination. They also had a very well-equipped buffet counter and the first pair replaced the original Nos 2-4 on the Cardiff-Birmingham run. Like the 19-33 series, these twins were also designed to take an auxiliary trailer, this time marshalled between the two components; an ordinary corridor third was used, but at no time does the GWR ever seem to have contemplated designing a purpose-built trailer in matching style for this task, though one was sketched out (but never built) for Car No 18 in 1936.

It was perhaps surprising that this final series of 'angular' cars, whether singles or twins, was actually allowed to go ahead early in the war, and because of their timing into service their early utilization is mostly obscured, largely in consequence of the clampdown on information. However, what can be said is that in them, the GWR had fairly accurately predicted quite a number of aspects which would be copied in the BR DMUs of the mid-1950s and later, in particular the twin formation. In some areas the GWR versions were actually better (the buffets for example). Furthermore, the cars themselves, unlike almost all other non-electric self-propelled stock from the company period, mostly enjoyed a near-normal

length of service life, the last of them not being withdrawn until late 1962. On all counts, though but few in number, they can perhaps be regarded as the most significant company contribution in this particular field.

The only other contender for longer-standing influence in the diesel arena is the final project to be considered in this chapter, a fairly spectacular one-off experimental train introduced by the LMS in 1938. However, its long-term development and possible evolution, like so many other things, were both cut short by the war. The project took the form of a triple articulated railcar set driven by no fewer than six 125hp diesel engines, the drive being of the hydraulic pattern. Each engine drove a single axle and only the extreme outer axles of the unit were unpowered. The train was designed for multiple unit control, thus making it the first genuine British DMU, even though it never had a partner with which to work in multiple, though one was planned. All power and transmission equipment was underfloor, and the articulated bogies were of what was called the 'LMS type'; a clever double pivot arrangement (one above each end of the bogies concerned) allowed rather longer car units to be envisaged within the load gauge 'throwover' limits than was possible with the more conventional Gresley-pattern centre pivot articulation. This allowed the outer ends to be some 64 ft long. The same system was adopted for the equally ill-fated 1939 'Coronation Scot' sets (see Chapt. 26).

From the outside, the train was neatly streamlined with a very stylish end treatment, though maybe not quite so striking as that of the first GWR railcars. The cars themselves were built to conventional LMS

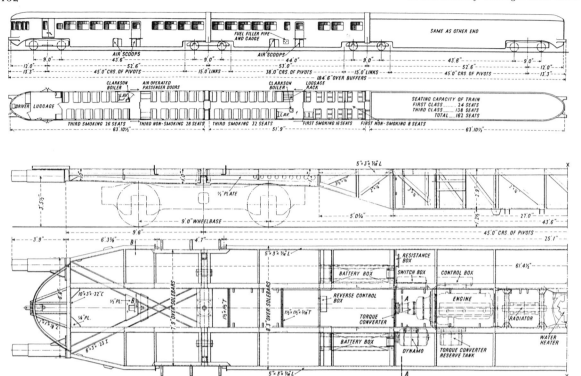

Figure 72 *Simplified elevations and plans, together with underframe construction detail, of the experimental LMS articulated DMU of 1938.*

Scale: 4mm = 1ft (underframe)

pattern practice (flush steel panels on timber frames) and underframes were centrally trussed in the manner of the 1937 articulated stock. Given its overall length (184 ft 6 in) it was a commendably lightweight unit at 73 tons, more than one ton lighter than the above-described GWR twins. The interiors were, if truth be told, more than a bit nondescript, and apart from lavatories there were no buffet or other refined facilities. It seated 162, of whom 24 were first class. An interesting innovation was the provision of air-operated sliding doors, and the seats, except where mounted against sides or bulkheads, were of the reversible 'throw-over' type. It carried a quite spectacular new livery of Post Office red and ivory, topped

LMS articulated diesel units Nos 80001-3 at Derby in 1939, fitted with stone guards over the driving windows.

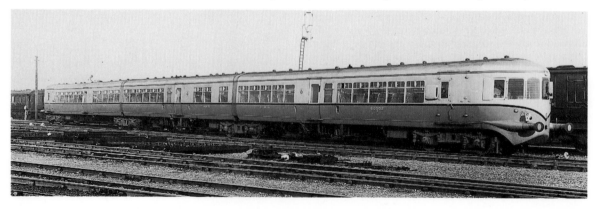

by a 'silver' painted roof, the three tones being separated by black bands.

It is not quite clear what utilization the LMS had in mind for this type of vehicle. The two-class accommodation put it one up on the one-class GWR cars, but the lack of catering provision seemed to point the other way — ie outer suburban rather than true long-distance. It was, therefore, rather surprising that after testing it was put to use on the Midland main line from St Pancras as far out as Leicester and Nottingham. It worked a complex six-service roster of 350 miles daily but little seems to have been recorded of its success or failure and it remained out of use during the war. Afterwards it was converted to a two-car maintenance unit for the MSJA electric line, losing four of its six engines in the process.

Whether or not the LMS form of transmission would have proved itself will never now be known, but post-war events were to establish that for the most part the hydraulic form was not usually the best way forward in British terms in any of its several modes of application, and that the mechanical alternative was the best option for railcar use. Even though the mechanical transmission adopted by BR was different in form from that of the GWR, maybe the influence of that company was the significant factor. Likewise, articulation was not to find any place in the BR solution, whereas the GWR 'twin' idea did. On the other hand, in terms of internal layout, though the LMS idea seems to have suffered from some confusion as to exact purpose, its two-class layout plus lavatories was very much the way that many early BR DMUs were set up.

Perhaps it is reading too much into these final designs to try and trace any profound longer-term influence on subsequent BR practice, for there were, in all conscience, very few of them anyway and the BR examples followed neither of them very closely. But however much or little they may have contributed to the post-war scene, they did at least demonstrate, especially those of the GWR, that at last the long hoped for self-propelled passenger unit was a realistic possibility and they both offered not a few significant ideas on the way.

25. An interlude with the 'old-timers'

There can be no doubt that one of the most fascinating aspects of the post-1922 scene was the fate which befell the older carriages inherited by the 'Big Four'. I have already touched on some relevant aspects in Chapter 1, but the trouble is that their subsequent use, apart from a modest few cases where some form of quite positive statement can be made, usually defies any form of logical analysis; yet somehow or other it seemed quite wrong to exclude them. After all, as Table 2 (p 305) has shown, there were over 48,000 of them in 1923, and even in 1947 more than 25 per cent of this total still remained in service. What I have therefore elected to do is to break the normal pattern of the book in this chapter so as to enable me to illustrate a little more of the variety which was to be seen than would otherwise be possible.

I have chosen to call it an 'interlude', since there will be more than a bit of nostalgia to it, but I hope that this change of approach will not detract from the accuracy of the information. I have grouped the pictures mostly by company simply to avoid total chaos, but they are for the most part 'stand-alones', so I have therefore used extended captions rather than continuous text to tell most of the story. First, however, we need to devote a few paragraphs to establish such general principles as do seem to have been followed.

In general, the old coaches, hardly surprisingly, were usually scrapped on the basis of age, so the first to go were mostly the four-and six-wheelers; but of the bogie stock, much was quite new and even those which had some 20 years of life under their belt already were by no means life-expired. Many of them

were in fact to give a further generation or more of faithful service to their new owners. Indeed, the ex-LNWR sleeping and dining cars and the pre-group GWR diners have already been noted in this category. It was rather more rare for complete trains to survive undiluted after 1922, but there were exceptions. Perhaps the best known example of this was the celebrated WCJS '2 pm' set of twelve-wheelers (see Chap. 13, page 230) which, in spite of the many late-1920s LMS improvements, was not to become ousted from its traditional role until 1930. To this might well be added the Caledonian 'Grampian' and the North British 'Fife and Lothian' sets, the stylish NER formations on the Newcastle-Liverpool run and the celebrated GNR 'quintuplet' dining set on the King's Cross-Leeds workings. There were others too, no doubt, and even when the old sets had been broken up, their vehicles were rarely scrapped; it was far more likely that they would turn up on some lesser services, maybe even as individual vehicles which could at least add interest to and quite often improve

For several years after the grouping, the LMS retained the famous West Coast 1908 '2 pm' twelve-wheelers on their original working. This view at Crewe in 1928 behind 4-6-0 No 6112 Sherwood Forester shows them still in use as the first four carriages (the Glasgow portion) of the down train, now named the 'Mid-Day Scot'. The Edinburgh section (to the rear) has been given some new stock but still retains the old dining car. It is perhaps significant that these 1908 carriages had no outer doors to the compartments and were not replaced until the LMS could offer something similar from its own new designs — see Chapter 19

the general tone of an otherwise fairly humdrum service.

This process was and is known as 'cascading' and could take many forms. First was the straight transfer, without change of passenger classification, to a lower-order working, thus giving better accommodation and/or facilities to this type of service. Secondly could be a downgrading of class from first to third, again with beneficial effect, and I well recall my own first conscious experience of this sort of thing, early in BR days. I was going by rail from Leeds to the Lake District with the young lady who eventually became my wife and I can still see the look of stark astonishment on her face when I directed her towards what was undoubtedly the scruffiest-looking carriage on the train; I had spotted that it was a downgraded 'twin window' open first of early LMS parentage! It gave us a wonderfully comfortable trip at a third class 'day return' price!

Other possibilities were extensive rebuilding of old stock without change of use — the GWR, as stated, was very good at doing this sort of thing with its dining cars — or a more comprehensive rebuilding for alternative use, such as the already discussed Southern Electrics and the often intriguing conversions to push-pull mode, some of which will be looked at in due course. One could also find the use of older corridor stock in place of lavatory non-corridors on some of the longer cross-country or even express services, or maybe the substitution of lavatory non-corridor for older non-lavatory stock. There was often, in fact, a sort of multiple cascading right down the pecking order as a consequence of new main-line stock being put into service on the main trains.

At the other extreme, those pre-group carriages which were, save for age, in no way inferior to their post-group equivalents, would continue to ply their trade unchanged. And this could apply from the most exalted to the most humble. There could even be transfer of broadly equivalent stock from one operating area to another, especially where it was felt that one constituent of the newly grouped system had produced a rather better solution than another. The LMS was particularly fond of this sort of thing in Scotland, where a whole panoply of former English pre-group stock regularly found a whole new lease of life on many a former Highland Railway service. It even, *in extremis*, led to such unthinkable pre-1923 concepts as ex-MR dining cars being drafted on to former LNWR lines; now *that* was indeed unusual, but it happened!

Another widespread function of older pre-group stock was to enable the railways to meet the huge seasonal demands of the holiday and excursion trade. In our present day it is almost impossible to conceive just how much additional demand this represented,

but it was by no means unusual for the companies to keep hundreds of older coaches on not much more than a 'care and maintenance' basis for wheeling out only on high days and holidays during the summer. This profligate maintenance of such large fleets would certainly not meet with the approval of the accountancy-orientated modern railway. The supreme irony is that though these were still the days of private companies which were working for a commercial return, they nevertheless still managed to provide a service which in many cases was far more comprehensive than is offered by our current publicly-owned organization which might be *presumed* to do such things as of right. We are, it needs hardly be stated, on political ground here, and even though I do not believe that it is the fault of the modern railway *per se* that these things are no longer done, it is a relevant aspect of the overall subject.

Closely allied to this use of old stock was the equally common use of such vehicles for 'strengthening' purposes, as it was called. This was the very common practice at weekends and other times of heavier traffic, whereby extra carriages were regularly added to the normal formations of trains to meet extra demand, it being tacitly assumed that the locomotives could haul the extra loads, even if at slightly reduced speed, and that there would be stock available. Yet again, the modern railway generally finds it too much trouble to do this sort of thing, usually being most often excused by the feeble statement that there is no spare stock — but whose fault is that? My guess is that there are very many current travellers who would not mind finding a few older carriages in their train on a Friday evening, as in older days, if that was the price of having a seat rather than standing in the aisles for two or three hours. But again I digress.

The fact is that the older carriages were an integral, if often randomly disposed, element of the total passenger package in company days and extended well into the 1950s and early 1960s before the old order changed out of all recognition. It therefore seems proper to give some space to the later days of these old warriors, whose very existence, though perhaps of little relevance in evolutionary terms, was very much a part of the total carriage scene in and amongst the newer offerings; and it certainly gave great joy to those who liked to look beyond the locomotive draw-hook. For the most part I have simply arranged the 'orthodox' examples under company headings alphabetically, though I have not even tried to apportion a total balance between the systems, preferring instead to choose those which seemed most interesting. I have, however, added a couple of thematic subject headings, but Pullmans have been excluded; they have their place in Chapter 27.

Great Western Railway

As the previous chapter has revealed, the steam railmotor quickly fell out of favour after the 1914-18 war, which left the railways with quite a few vehicles which, while their prime movers may have been too feeble to pull much save themselves, were often associated with passenger-carrying portions which could be persuaded to yield a few more years of useful life. Most railways had a few and the vast majority served out their time in the push-pull mode (see page 269) but every now and then something different happened. Such was the case with Taff Vale Railway Steam Railmotor No 15. In 1922, it was rebuilt into a corridor third rather than the usual push-pull trailer and, amazingly, it ran for more than another 30 years in this form. It is seen here at Caerphilly Works in 1954 as W4024W, still looking quite spruce. (T.J. Edgington).

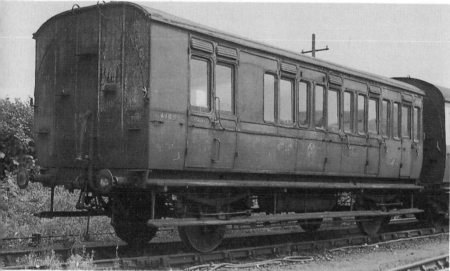

Although the GWR may have been less adventurous than most, the company did not operate anything like as many super-annuated relics as did the LNER or even the LMS. All the more surprising therefore that as late as 1950, this Dean four-wheeler No 4189 was found still in use at Neath Bridge Street. However, judging from the presence of the 1930s 'shirt button' company emblem, the carriage had not been painted for at least a dozen years. But most of its panelling remained intact (T.J. Edgington).

Below left and top right *Dean's GWR clerestory carriages must have been some of the toughest and most resilient vehicles ever built, and they gave valuable service throughout the grouping period. An excursion set was featured on p 272, and here are two more interesting reminders of the time. In the first view at Stapleton Road in 1934, very unusual use is being made of a heavy freight 2-8-0T No 5224 to haul a featherweight two-coach train of lavatory non-corridors which, on examination, can be seen to feature two types of bogie. The leading brake composite has the long wheelbase version while the brake third has the short type.*

The second view shows 4-4-0 No 3363 Alfred Baldwin on a nine-coach train from Cardiff to Bristol near Ashley Hill a year or two later with no fewer than seven Dean non-corridors in the formation. The two extreme end vehicles are probably

added strengtheners, for the rest of the train looks suspiciously like a pair of more up-to-date (but not too modern!) corridor brake composites sandwiching an otherwise third class non-corridor set. This is a good example of the 'cascading' of older corridor stock.

Because Churchward was so much ahead of his time, even his earlier stock tended to look more or less at home amongst the later offerings. Here is seen one of his celebrated 'Dreadnought' composites — an idea well in advance of the field (see Chapter 7) — at the front of a down Brighton to Cardiff train at Patchway, headed by 2-6-0 No 7321. A later fully panelled 'Toplight' is seen as the third carriage. This working was undoubtedly similar to that shown at the same location on page 18, this time it being the GWR's turn to provide the stock. During pre-BR days, it was normal for both companies to provide stock on such joint services.

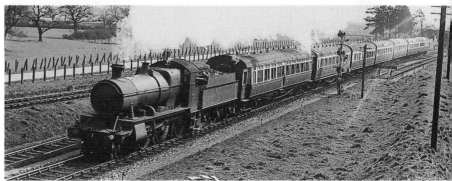

In this circa 1935 view, an Ilfracombe-Paddington train enters Bristol under the Bath Road bridge behind 4-6-0 King Stephen, the most interesting feature being the fact that of the first four carriages, only the dining car is not of Edwardian vintage. A 'Dreadnought' brake third leads and behind the diner can be seen two of the distinctive, if rather absurdly conceived, 'Concertina' corridors which preceded the 'Toplights'

This last view on GWR territory, shows a fascinating scene and makes a nice link to the next section. The train, headed by 4-6-0 No 4038 Queen Berengaria, is at Stoke Gifford on what the photographer described as a Bristol– Swindon local train. But this can hardly be so, for the stock is wholly ex-Great Central in origin, including two six-wheelers, one at least of which may well even be of pre-GCR Manchester, Sheffield and Lincolnshire origin. Moreover, both these vehicles are saloons, probably now designated as Picnic Saloons. The middle carriage is a full brake followed by a later GCR corridor composite; while what appears to be another saloon brings up the rear. My guess is that it was a returning excursion or private charter which turned north at Didcot to re-enter former GCR country at Banbury Junction

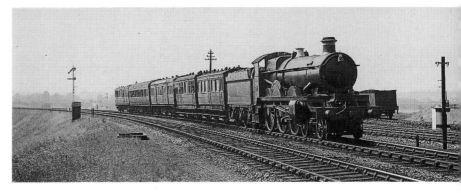

London and North Eastern Railway

The LNER had a higher proportion of older carriages in use than any of its rivals, including no less than 50 per cent of all surviving four- and six-wheelers in Britain. Many of the old stagers were of GER origin (which says much about the quality of their original construction) and remained in GER territory, such as the three prime specimens seen here, all photographed at Stratford in March 1938: six-wheel lavatory third, No 61119; six-wheel corridor(!) brake second, believed to be No 62351; and clerestory corridor first No 6407 tucked between a later GER corridor (left) and a matchboard ex-NER non-corridor. Note too that all three classes were represented (all H.C. Casserley).

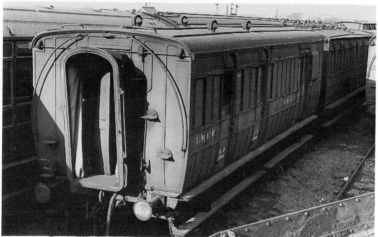

Right and middle right *The LNER was rather more fond of taking posed official views of its older coaches than the other companies, especially where there was something slightly out of the ordinary about their use. The first view shows six-wheel full brake No 3251 in LNER days, still displaying every last inch of its original NBR wooden panelling with its distinctive double layer (see Chapter 7 Page 103); but in 1931, the elaborate branding, including a very passable representation of the 'banner head' of the* Scotsman *newspaper, reveals that it was used exclusively for special newspaper service.*

The second view of LNER Club Saloon No 22113 in 1925 shows a former GCR coach, now well off its original home patch, having been reallocated to the Harrogate–Bradford service of the former NER.

Bottom and overleaf top *Matters remained very 'North British' on the LNER in Scotland during the inter-war years. In the first view of 4-4-0 No 9291* Glen Quoich *on a Thornton train at Inverkeithing in 1927, the train is wholly composed of six-wheelers, at least as far as can be seen. The third vehicle seems to be a first class semi-saloon, or some such, probably with at least some lavatory provision, but the rest is traditionally non-corridor.*

The second view at Inverkeithing, shows bogie stock and 4-4-2T No 9039 in charge. The train is almost equally solidly NBR in composition — again without lavatories — but this time augmented by one of David Bain's handsome turn-of-the-century clerestories from the old NER, now very far from home

Overleaf middle *In the later 1930s, the LNER took over the whole responsibility for the hitherto jointly owned Midland and Great Northern Railway, many of whose better carriages were of pre-group LMS constituent origin, including this particularly interesting ex-Midland clerestory type. They were semi-open thirds, half side-corridor and half in the open 'Picnic' configuration (the far end as seen from this viewpoint). The whole batch of 12 was transferred to the M & GN in 1936. No 99 is seen here at South Lynn in May 1937, still wearing its simplified LMS livery, but in due course it would be repainted in LNER 'teak'* (H.C. Casserley).

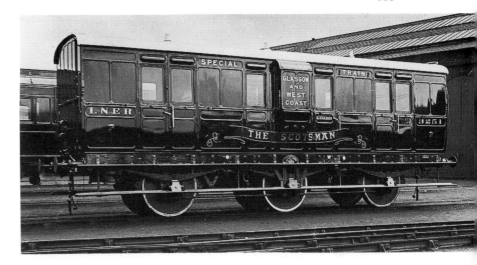

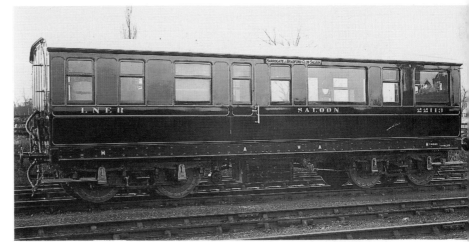

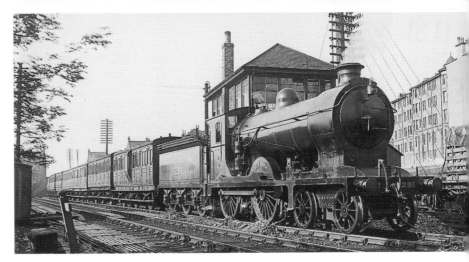

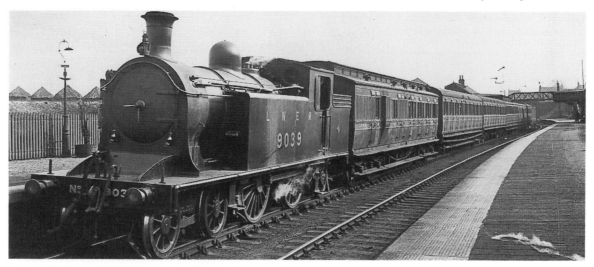

London, Midland and Scottish Railway

Top two right *The former Highland Railway branches of the LMS could be very happy hunting grounds for carriage enthusiasts well into BR days. The process of coach 'cascading' started back in pre-group days and these two early LMS views show how the new company carried on the well-established Highland tradition on just one of its routes, that from Dingwall to Strathpeffer Spa. In the first view in 1925, 4-4-0T No 101, still carrying HR livery, is at Dingwall, and although the first two six-wheel carriages are of typical HR matchboard style, LMS influence is present in the form of two former Midland clerestories, a six-wheel brake*

and a bogie corridor composite, no less.

The second view, a year later with Stroudley 0-6-0T No 16118 in charge, still reveals a Highland six-wheeler at the head of the train, but there is now a nineteenth-century MR six-wheeler in place of the older HR third, while a former LNWR lavatory composite (still in pre-group colours and probably even of radial underframe origin) brings up the rear. In both cases, the former HR stock was already in LMS livery, the Highland area being particularly quick to make use of the new-style colours after 1922.

Right *The Highland main line of the LMS north of Perth was the gathering ground for the most astonishingly motley*

assemblages of carriages both before and after the grouping. All lines converged on this mostly single track lifeline to Inverness, and things were slow to change. In this magnificent study from the mid-1920s, 4-6-0 No 14691 Brodie Castle sets off for Inverness with a wondrous assortment of stock in its nine-coach formation. What is particularly interesting is that it carries stopping headlamps, so it is a fair bet that quite a few of these many and various carriages were not working through from elsewhere but had been drafted on to the Highland by the LMS. As far as can be ascertained, their origins were, in order from the engine: MR, HR, LNWR, LMS standard, LNWR(2), LMS standard, LNWR and, possibly, Caledonian!

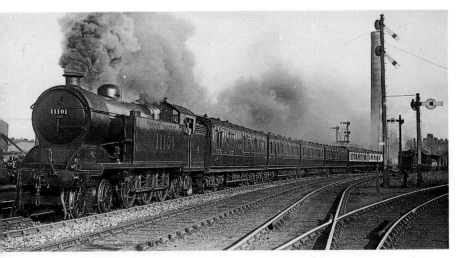

On the old Furness Railway, it was quite customary for many of the through trains to be of 'foreign' stock, so a full set of LNWR carriages would cause little comment. By early LMS days, these were often of high standard and this circa 1925 view shows a Carnforth–Lakeside train headed by 4-6-4T No 11101 and composed wholly of LNWR corridor rather than non-corridor stock. Already four out of the six carriages are in their new colours, but the back pair are one each from the two styles of design which preceded and succeeded the neat four-coach set which forms the main part of the train.

By contrast with the last view, here is a good example of non-corridor pre-group stock on a fairly substantial working in 1937. The train is headed by 4-6-0 No 25797 on the former LNWR direct route between Leeds and Manchester at Marsden. Two ex-LNWR non-corridor lavatory thirds sit between the leading LNWR corridor brake composite and the Stanier open third. Behind this comes an 'all-steel' open third. The relative dearth of first class accommodation and the generally mixed nature of the stock gives every reason to believe that this was a typical excursion or weekend holiday working, maybe to one of the Lancashire coast resorts

In spite of its standardization policy, many LMS trains, even on the main lines, were no tidier than anyone else's in the grouping period. This 1935 view behind 4-6-0 No 5639 taken at an unidentified fell country location, is typical. It too is likely to have been an 'extra' of some kind, probably formed up from whatever happened to be lying around in the carriage sidings at the time. The first four carriages are LNWR, WCJS, WCJS, LNWR and include but one composite, a double brake-ended former 'slip' carriage with only two first class compartments; they are followed by a heterogeneous mixture of LMS types, again with very little first class seating. There is no dining car visible, though there may have been one out of sight, but at least there is a continuous corridor.

Southern Railway

The Southern Railway, as has been seen, re-used much of its old stock in EMU form, but it was just as capable as the rest of upgrading its locomotive-hauled local services (of which it retained not a few) with a modest amount of 'cascading' from time to time, and this crisp late 1930s view shows one such example, an up local near Littlehampton behind 2-6-0 No 1808. The second and third carriages are ex-LSWR lavatory non-corridor thirds, but the leading LSWR brake composite is gangwayed and the fourth vehicle looks suspiciously like one of the 'Continental' SE & CR-pattern corridors.

On the main line also, the SR followed similar ideas to those of the other companies, often retaining much of its older stock in full main-line use. Of course, it did not have too much, but the former LSWR low-roof corridors were of high quality and here a trio of them (still formed up into a set, albeit now three coaches instead of the original five) forms the front of this up West of England express passing through Woking in July 1938 behind 4-6-0 No 747 Elaine. One can be almost certain that the rest of the train was Maunsell standard stock, and, judging from the odd brake composite at vehicle No 4, may well have started from several destinations, whose through carriages were added to the front of the train as it proceeded towards London

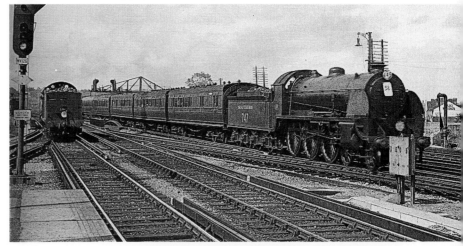

Outwith its electrified territory, the Southern was blessed with numerous bucolic rural branches, none more celebrated than the Brighton's line to Hayling Island. In pre-motor car days many would make the trip by rail, and this nostalgic view reminds us of those long gone high-days of summer when lots of excited children, not to mention their parents, would cause the normal formation to be stretched to such as seen here: four non-corridors (two ex-LSWR and two from the 'home team') in charge of a diminutive 'Terrier' tank, in this case No 2678.

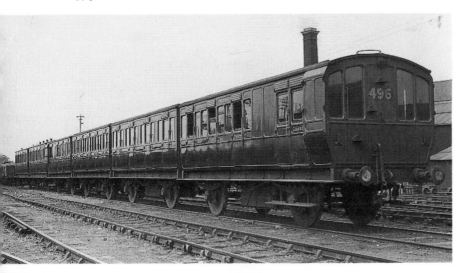

A second remarkable area of the Southern's parish was to be found on the Isle of Wight, and ever since the grouping its trains have almost always been composed of 'hand-me-downs' from elsewhere, a process which continues to this day. In early Southern days things were getting a bit desperate, and in this view, former LB & SCR close-coupled four-wheel set No 496 along with a pair of similar fugitives from the old London Chatham and Dover Railway, all of pre-1900 vintage, make a brave show and still look remarkably smart at Newport, probably soon after they were moved there in the mid-1920s.

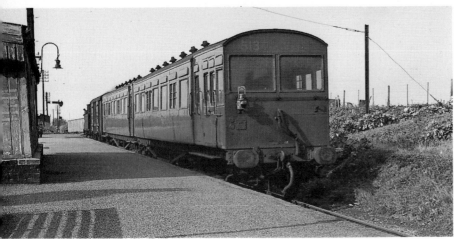

A particularly interesting example of Southern branch line ingenuity was represented by articulated 'twin' unit Nos 513/4 which worked the Sheppey Light Railway from Leysdown to Queenborough from 1924 until 1950. It was built from two former SE & CR steam railcar bodies, and after the Sheppey line closed it enjoyed a further few years of active life in central London. Here the unit is seen at Queenborough, almost at the end of its sojourn in north Kent, during September 1950 (R.F. Roberts).

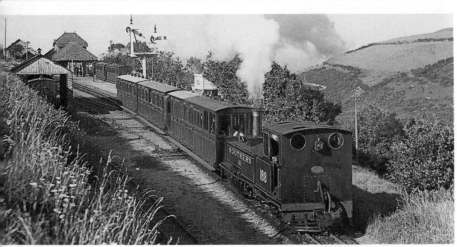

Few would deny that the charming narrow-gauge Lynton and Barnstaple Railway was one of the most regrettable 'lost causes' of the grouping era. It was almost doomed to failure from the outset, but the Southern put on a brave show right to the end as is seen in this delightful view of 2-6-2T No 188 Lew leaving Lyton with a three-coach train of typical 'narrow gauge'-type stock, set so close to the ground that the running gear is out of sight. If truth be told, the British railways had very little influence on the development of this type of carriage, but it is pleasing to record that the leading (and unique) brake composite saloon survives intact at the National Railway Museum, having spent 40 or more years in use as a summerhouse in Devon! Sadly, and largely through lack of funding or resources on the part of the Museum, it has not yet been restored; yet some would argue that it is a much more worthy candidate for public funding than most.

Push-pull trains

The origins of the push-pull train were covered in Chapter 15 and the few totally new examples which the grouped railways built are considered in Chapter 28. However, most such coaches during the grouping period had their origins with older pre-group stock and the Southern was probably the leader of the field. Indeed, this part of the story continued well into BR days. Meantime, this reminder of a typical Isle of Wight operation has an interesting link with a previous view, for the carriages, former saloons of LCDR origin seen here at Ventnor West with 0-6-0T No. W11, came from the Sheppey Light Railway when the articulated twin was sent there. When the SR put them to work on the Isle of Wight in 1924, they were converted to push-pull operation at the same time.

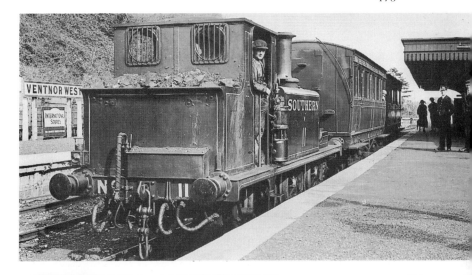

The GWR was another great advocate of the push-pull mode, though its chosen name was 'auto-train'. Most of the carriages came from converted steam railmotors of which it had by far the largest stock of any British company (see Chapter 15). They enjoyed a greatly extended lease of life after conversion, none more so than the pioneer railmotor itself, the not particularly stylish No 1. It is seen here at Caerphilly works in May 1954 as W1W, no less than 51 years after it had gone into service as a self-propelled vehicle. It was still in remarkably good order. Note, too, another glimpse of the ex-Taff Vale Railway's former steam railmotor No W4024W (see page 466) (T.J. Edgington).

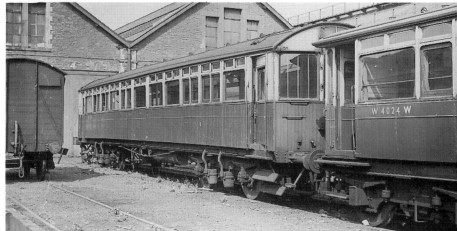

GWR conventional carriages in push-pull mode were little different from those of the others and its vehicles were often just as venerable. This is a pair of low-roof Dean bogie non-corridors near Southcote Junction, Reading. It illustrates the advantage of push-pull over the steam railmotor: note the added horsebox at the rear, such extra loads being possible because of the greater power of a 'proper' engine

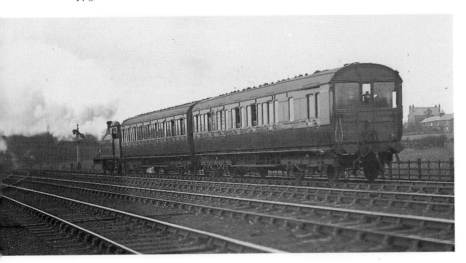

On the LMS, push-pull trains were usually known as 'motor trains' and more often than not utilized conventional-type carriages, a practice going back to pre-group days. Though not quite of LMS vintage, the idea is well shown here in this 1922 view of what the LYR liked to call a 'reversible steam train'. Apart from the brake end driver's windows, it looks just like a normal two-coach non-corridor set. Though the LNWR and LYR did have a few, more or less purpose-built push-pulls and the LMS converted a few more from old corridor stock, this view shows the typical LMS form

Camping coaches

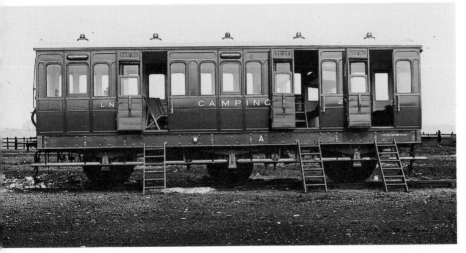

This view is believed to be the first official picture ever taken of a type of vehicle first introduced by the LNER in 1933 which not only became popular during the grouping period, but also became the last resting ground for hundreds of very venerable old coaches. The 'Camping Coach' was the railway equivalent of the modern residential seaside holiday cara-van, and was usually found in similar locations. Indeed, the LMS called them 'Caravans'. In this picture, formerly Lan-cashire, Derbyshire and East Coast six-wheeler No 25 shows the early form with some compartments opened out into a kitchen-cum-day area, the others being left as separate two- or four-berth sleeping compartments. These coaches cost £2 10s (£2.50) per week to hire, but later examples with internal connecting doors cost £3!

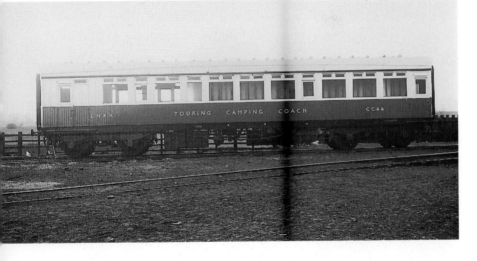

The LNER introduced a novelty variation in 1935 in the form of a 'Touring Camp-ing Coach' which left York every Saturday and visited a different place every day. Six or seven people could enjoy the fun for between £16 and £20 per week for the whole party, including the cost of travel to the various Yorkshire beauty spots! The prototype vehicle was No CC.66 which, though painted in appropriate green and cream tourist livery, could not disguise its original NER matchboard styling of 1905

Above *By 1939, the LNER was converting some pretty plushy-looking coaches to camping form, though they were still quite elderly. Here is a former GCR (ex-MSLR) clerestory brake third of 1895, fully refurbished more than 40 years later in 1939, its fleet number CC.118 being indicative of the success of the whole idea. The impressive quality of these venerable vehicles was noteworthy and may well have been one of the main criteria determining which of them were chosen for conversion*

As might be expected, the LMS weighed in very soon after the LNER and eventually built more of them than did its rival concern. They were also slightly larger and cost more to hire in consequence — all of £3 10s (£3.50)! The hirer also had to book at least four monthly return tickets to get the use of one. This view shows a former LNWR corridor third of circa 1900 running as No 46000 in 1934, the LMS simply using numbers in its standard series rather than giving them a special allocation. Note the fine finish — fully lined company livery, no less. There appear to be a surprisingly large number of the original carriage fittings left intact after conversion

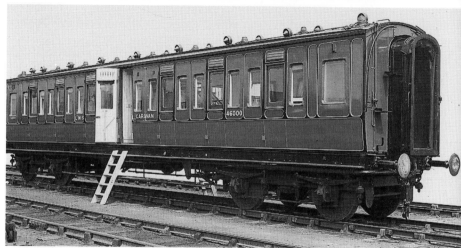

Equipping a camping coach was no mean task, and this view at Derby in 1937 of a string of LMS 'Caravans' being fitted out gives a vivid impression of just what was involved. This time, at least one set of lucky campers is going to get the benefit of a spacious former Midland Railway clerestory composite brake, while next in line a former LYR corridor composite gets the treatment.

Above *The Southern was a bit later in the field and built relatively fewer camping coaches than did the LMS or LNER, but it claimed to be the first to offer wireless aerials and internal water tanks — plus an alarm clock! Thus, even though its first essay, formed from an ex-LCDR six-wheeler early in 1935, was almost exactly like the LNER £3-per-week offering, the Southern charged the same rate as did the LMS and imposed the same travel ticket requirement. No 1 is shown here, once again in remarkably good order*

Below *We take temporary leave of the old timers in some of their many and various guises with this fine view of an altogether more*

impressive SR camping coach. No 18 was converted from one of the ex-LSWR lavatory non-corridors which, in original form, had no fewer than six lavatories to serve six compartments. The window arrangement of the conversion still betrays this fact, but like all camping coaches, though washing-up and drinking water was provided, none of the pre-war examples acutally retained their internal 'comfort stations' — patrons were expected to use the nearby station facilities. One can only presume that the mandatory instruction prohibiting use '. . . while standing in the station' applied to a camping coach just as much if not more so than the mobile variety; but the lavatories were omitted just in case!

26. 'Supertrains' of the 1930s

The decade which preceded the Second World War represented probably the apogee of public perception of transport in all its modes. The Schneider Trophy and the developments of the first great international flying boats and airliners stood for the air, the great ocean liners like *Queen Mary* and *Normandie* vied with each other for supremacy across the Atlantic, Malcolm Campbell and others of his ilk were regularly breaking the land speed record for cars, and the railways had recovered from the first great conflict to the point where they could offer trains and services the like of which had never before been seen. It was, of course, an international phenomenon and the British railway contribution was merely a part. But in those days, we were perhaps more innocent — or at least less cynical — as a result of which almost every new improvement could be guaranteed if not headline treatment in the newspapers, then at the very least some degree of prominence. Even the engine drivers' names were as much part of the common currency as are the Grand Prix racing drivers of today.

Within the British railway field, the starting point seems to have been the improved vehicles offered by the LMS and LNER for the principal day services between London and Scotland in 1928. The LMS 'Royal Scot' stock of that year has already been discussed (p 329) in the context of the general improvement of carriages across the board for that company, and in the event was to set the overall tone of future LMS practice. There was never a complete train of such vehicles, despite occasional claims to the contrary, and after that time the LMS rarely bothered to offer dedicated special sets, save for the one exception of the 'Coronation Scot' train of 1937 (see below). It preferred instead to concentrate on the mass improvement of all its services typified by its huge new building programme of all varieties of modern coaching stock. It was thus rare for any of its better trains not to be in receipt of the latest 'state of the art' vehicles at very regular intervals, often of only two or three years.

The LNER was rather different, and in its 'Flying Scotsman' sets of 1928 can be seen the first seeds from which grew its celebrated streamliners and other dedicated trains of the 1930s, eventually expanding to the point where Gresley's company was without doubt the leader of the field in this sort of thing. The splendid dining cars of this train have already been considered (page 373), but we must now put the whole formation into perspective.

The stimulus was the forthcoming non-stop feature of the service which was an overt publicity stunt to capture traffic. There were rather slow and man-datory timings still in existence, and the only way either the LMS or the LNER could compete was to offer better passenger facilities. Non-stop running was thought to give a degree of exclusivity — which of course it did — but it was hardly necessary given the timings concerned, nor did it allow for any intermediate points to be served. But it did the trick and was continued in the form of the 'Capitals Limited' and the 'Elizabethan' express well into the last years of steam haulage down the East Coast route. The gradual up-grading of the train itself was all part of the same process.

At first, only the dining cars were radically different but, as already stated, their reception was mixed and the new-style 'French' decor was not put into the ordinary stock. However, over the next few years the LNER added more new features to the train such as cocktail bars, a 'unisex' hairdressing saloon, a ladies retiring room and so forth (the LMS only countered this with a first class lounge and pretty soon abandoned the idea), but the real step forward could never come until the old eight-hour schedule (an outdated legacy from the late Victorian 'racing' trains to Scotland) was abandoned in 1932. Following this long overdue step, the LNER concentrated effort on taking full advantage of its Gresley 'Pacifics' along with their East Coast racing track, which was a far more straight and level route than the LMS could offer. Three years later, in 1935, the first of the streamliners emerged, and thereafter speed was king.

But before going on with the speed rivalry between the LMS and LNER, we must first turn to Swindon where, at long last, the GWR was beginning to awake from its post-1922 slumber. It started modestly enough in 1930 when a pair of beautifully appointed and self-contained first class saloons to the same basic styling as the 1929 'Cornish Riviera' stock were put into service. They were intended for private hire, attached to any appropriate service, and there was accommodation for about 14-15 passengers in great comfort. At one end an open saloon with two settees and two armchairs (plus a writing table and chair) gave seats for eight or nine, and this was supplemented by a conventional six-seat compartment. At the opposite end, a 14-seat dining saloon in basically Pullman style (ie individual armchairs and table lamps) was served from a central kitchen and pantry which separated the two seating areas. They were solidly traditional in decor: polished walnut panelling and beige moquette upholstery with brown and black figuring. Modernized in 1947 with newer-style windows and the compartment removed to make space for a much enlarged saloon portion, they were

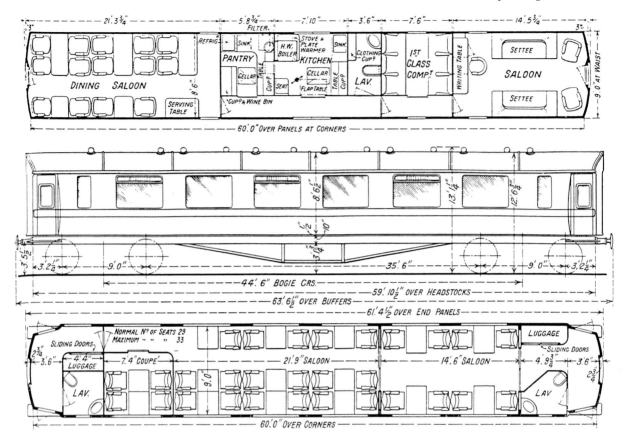

transferred to VIP and Royal service and as such remained in service well into the 1960s. Both survive in preservation.

If these two new carriages were not exactly 'general service', they did give promise of better things to come and the GWR was not long in obliging, this time with a quite superbly conceived series of luxury first-class-only saloons for the Plymouth boat train traffic. 'Super Saloons' the GWR called them, and it was no vain boast for they were probably the grandest vehicles built for general service by any of the 'Big Four' and revealed that the GWR was well able to match the LMS and LNER when it so wished. They were unashamedly up-market and aimed at the high class clientèle of the transatlantic liners. They took full advantage of the GWR structure gauge, being 9 ft 7in wide at the waist and a full 9 ft wide inside, and were mounted on standard 59 ft 10½ in chassis.

In design terms, their styling was quite new, for although they displayed the familiar bow-ends and roof treatment of this particular GWR period, they were given deeply recessed end doors set at an angle and seemingly huge windows compared with all

previous GWR stock. Within, they were clearly the GWR answer to Pullman, with whom there had been a somewhat unsuccessful experiment in 1929-30. Indeed, a quite common nickname for the Super Saloons was 'Pullmans' or 'Cunarders', both terms reflecting their usage.

The interior treatment was, however, the equal of, if not superior to, Pullman — and that is rare praise indeed. They had light French walnut veneers, highly polished, with coved ceilings, concealed lighting and, of course, table lamps. These and the individual armchairs, not to mention a small coupé compartment at one end only, all contributed to the Pullman feel, but the overall effect was far more spacious. Seats were usually trimmed in brown patterned moquette while gold silk damask curtains, framed pictures, dark brown wall-to-wall Wilton carpet and a multiplicity of smaller detail touches served to complete the ensemble.

Two had been finished by November 1931 and six more soon followed, all eight being named after members of the Royal Family. A 10s (50p) supplement was charged for their use which was double that which

Figure 73 *Floor plan of the 1930 GWR special saloons together with elevation and floor plans of the 1931 'Super Saloons'.*

Scale: $^{1}/_{10}$" = 1ft

Interior view of 'Super Saloon' No 9112, looking from the smaller to the larger saloon, the coupé being at the far end

'Super Saloon' No 9112 'Queen Mary' when new

the LNER charged for its first Streamliner (see below). A common boat train formation was four or five saloons plus a kitchen car and brake vans, but there were many occasions when only a small number needed to be accommodated and in this instance a full kitchen was extravagant. Accordingly (in 1935) the last two ('Princess Mary' and 'Princess Elizabeth') were turned into the GWR equivalent of a Pullman Kitchen/Parlour car, the coupé area and part of the larger saloon being used for the new kitchen and pantry.

Some post-war refurbishment and redecoration took place, including new round-cornered windows with top sliders, and after the boat trains ceased to run in 1962 these splendid vehicles were then mostly used for race specials to Newbury and the like. They were also regularly used throughout their lives for numerous special occasions. No fewer than five have been privately preserved, a fine tribute to a fine set of vehicles.

Completing the GWR 'hat trick', so to speak, was the famous 'Centenary' stock for the 'Cornish Riviera Limited' in 1935, wherein at last the needs

of the ordinary fare-paying passengers were met in very fine style. Two complete sets were built, following the general outline of the Super Saloons but this time with accommodation for both classes and a full range of vehicle types. Not since the celebrated West Coast '2 pm' twelve-wheel sets appeared from Wolverton in 1908 (Chapter 13) had anything quite so good been offered to the ordinary traveller without supplementary fare. Indeed, the Centenary stock was almost identical in concept to the old WCJS train and displayed a similar series of sub-formations (for different destinations) within its make-up.

Everything was superlatively well done: light oak and walnut with blue, green or brown upholstery in the firsts; gaboon mahogany and walnut with brown upholstery in the thirds — and large curtained windows for everybody. Mirrors replaced the dreary pictures and the whole impression was of light and space. Under the circumstances it seems churlish to point out that four per side was still offered in the thirds! The dining facilities were in the form of full open thirds with tip-up seats plus kitchen firsts with luxurious fixed seating and stainless steel wall sheeting

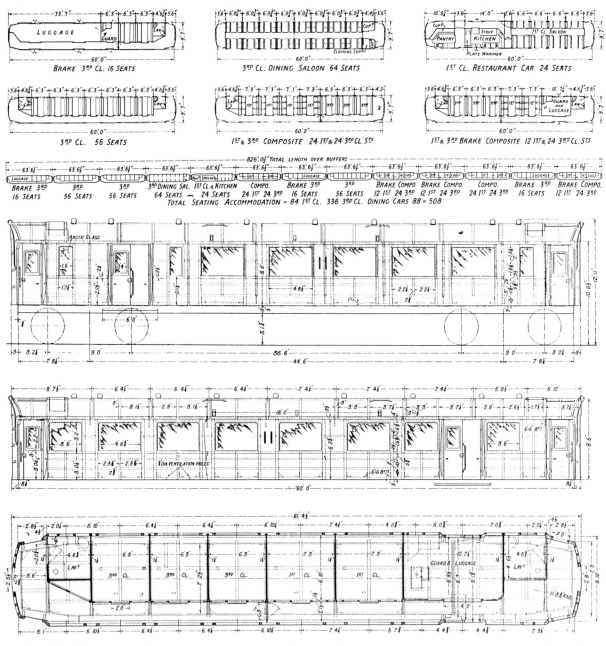

Figure 74 *Individual carriage plans along with the train formation and detailed drawings of the brake composite from the 1935 GWR 'Centenary' stock.*

Scale of main drawing: $^1/_{10}'' = 1ft$

in the kitchens.

The only disfigurement to the complete ensemble when it first went into service was the ridiculous partial streamlining applied to its locomotive in what seems to have been a rather foolish and last-minute attempt to leap on to the contemporary bandwagon. The Centenary stock, though thoroughly modern in its approach, was not in the streamlined idiom, nor

did it need to be thus promoted. Fortunately, most of this nonsense was later removed, but poor old No 6014 *King Henry VII* kept some signs of it to the very

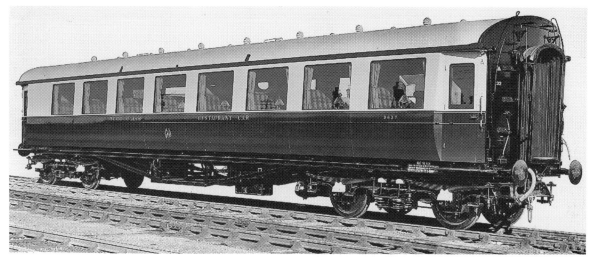

end in the form of its 'V'-fronted cab.

Little change was made to the stock, save for replacing the original large drop windows with fixed lights surmounted by top sliders, but the first class diners were, rather unfortunately, given the new swivelling seats of the earlier-mentioned Hampton conversions (see Chap. 20). It did nothing for their overall ambience and it is ironic that the only carriage to survive from this splendid train is one of these modified dining cars, now in private preservation. Even so, and in spite of its unfortunate upholstery, it still gives off much of the feel of those more leisured times.

With these three quite different sets of vehicles, the GWR went a long way to redeem itself in terms of carriage design, and it is significant that only a year later the very much more up-to-date 'Sunshine' stock (see p. 344) began to appear. so in a very real sense the GWR's contribution in the 'Supertrain' era can be said to have had more significance than mere numbers might suggest. And this was certainly true of the next phase in the story, the exciting though short-lived streamline era of the late 1930s.

It is probably true to say that of all the trains ever introduced on to the British scene, those which the LNER and LMS put into service during just four short years between mid-1935 and mid-1939 caught the public imagination in a way which nothing had done before or has done since. It was a curious mixture of imperial jingoism, national pride, 'hyped' publicity, technical innovation and a renewed outburst of fierce competition between two companies, and even now it is only partly understood. What can be said is that it seems to have captured the spirit of the times, and in purely performance terms it represented the undoubted high point of the British steam railway. That it was tragically foreshortened

Above *Open third class restaurant car No 9637 from the 'Centenary' stock. Note the provision, even in the third class, of table laps in the Pullman manner.*

Below *Solidly 'Art Deco' but light, airy and undoubtedly stylish, the well-finished interior of a first class GWR 'Centenary' stock dining car, complete with posed staff and passengers.*

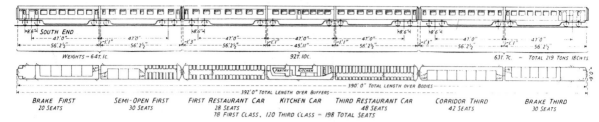

BRAKE FIRST	SEMI-OPEN FIRST	FIRST RESTAURANT CAR	KITCHEN CAR	THIRD RESTAURANT CAR	CORRIDOR THIRD	BRAKE THIRD
20 SEATS	30 SEATS	28 SEATS		48 SEATS	42 SEATS	30 SEATS

78 FIRST CLASS, 120 THIRD CLASS = 198 TOTAL SEATS

by the Second World War is only another example of the point made in the first paragraph of Chapter 1 of this volume; and we can only indulge in daydreams as to what its ultimate conclusion might have been.

The pace-setter throughout was the LNER, and the origins of the first LNER streamliner are well recorded: a conviction on the part of Gresley (aided and supported by his chief general manager, Sir Ralph Wedgwood) that a steam-hauled train could perform just as well as the newly developing diesel 'flyers' in Germany with a far greater passenger load and much better amenity. The happy coincidence of King George V's Silver Jubilee in 1935 was the chosen hook on which the whole business was to be hung; the rest, as they say, is history.

The order was placed as late as February 1935, the whole effort reaching a triumphant conclusion on 27 September 1935 when an amazing silver and grey streamlined train on its first public demonstration outing streaked along for no fewer than 43 miles at a speed greater than 100 mph, reaching a new absolute maximum of 112½ mph in the process. It went into full public service on 30 September and was an instant commercial success. It was, of course, the 'Silver Jubilee' and launched the British railways into a new speed era, a process which, with a few hiccups on the way, is still evolving in our modern 125-150 mph era.

Our concern here is with the carriages, so we must resist the temptation to dwell too long on the prime movers which helped make things possible. They were, of course, an integral part of the whole concept, but are well covered elsewhere. Suffice to say that as with most of the more significant events in railway history, it was in fact a successful combination of all the different strands of the business which helped make it possible, and here the carriage-builders played their own important part.

Articulation was chosen for weight-saving reasons — two pairs and a triplet dining set — and this enabled 198 seats (78 first, 120 third) to be offered with full dining facility in a train weight of fractionally below 220 tons. This showed an approximate 10 per cent weight saving compared with normal stock — well worth having. A contemporary plan is appended

(Figure 75), but later internal changes were made and in 1938 a central element was added to the third class corridor pair, making it a triplet and adding 35 more third class seats to the total (one of the six compartments in the new section had but five seats to allow corridor space to the adjacent vehicle). The seating was split between open and side-corridor style, but it is not known whether there was ever any seat exchanging between areas to allow more meals to be served. Generally, if one wanted to eat, one reserved in the dining portion of the train.

Although the interior arrangements were of the highest quality, there were, for example, only four seats per first class compartment, the whole train layout was thoroughly conventional and it was the exterior which stole the show. Covered in silver-grey Rexine with stainless steel trimmings and with raised stainless steel cut-out carriage insignia, nothing like it had ever been seen before. Combined with the grey-painted underframe fairings and bogie side frames, not to mention the in-fill rubber gussets between carriages, the whole train from the front of the locomotive to the back of the rear carriage gave the most unified appearance ever seen in these islands. A supplementary charge was levied (as with Pullman trains), but there is no evidence that this proved any deterrent to patronage.

It was, in fact, a bit of a 'con': it looked completely different, *de facto* it *was* completely different. But the appointments were thoroughly traditional and the coaches were built in the customary way; there was, to be fair, better sound insulation and the carriages were pressure ventilated, but one might well argue that the contemporary GWR Centenary sets were probably better finished. But speed counted, and since this was always the railway's best marketing feature (it still is, by the way) this was the emphasized aspect, and in this regard the 'Silver Jubilee' set had its problems.

For one thing, continuous high speed imposed far greater wear and tear on brake and running gear, thus adding to the cost, while in spite of beefing up the side springing to avoid sudden lurches, the articulated bogies were not wholly successful in their proclaimed property of improving stability. I never rode in the 'Silver Jubilee' set (though I did ex-

'Supertrains' of the 1930s

Figure 75 *Simplified elevations and plans of the LNER 'Silver Jubilee' train as first operated. Later, the third class side-corridor brake twin was converted into a triple unit.*

High-level view of the 'Silver Jubilee' leaving King's Cross, twin brake third leading

First class compartment interior of the 'Silver Jubilee'; note the cushions and footstools.

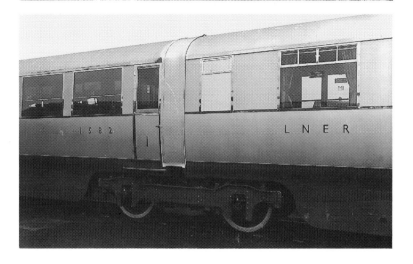

Close-up detail of the twin semi-open brake first Nos 1581/2 of the 'Silver Jubilee', showing the lower body fairings and the in-fill between the carriage units

perience the later LNER streamliners) but those of my friends who have hell me that it was always a bit 'lively'! Maybe this was why it never came back to full East Coast use after the war. There was only ever one set of vehicles and they were stored during the war. Afterwards, the five side-corridor vehicles were used on the rather more leisurely 'Fife Coast Express', while the dining triplet went into routine East Coast service. All carriages were withdrawn in the early 1960s.

The 'Silver Jubilee' was, for all its handicaps, the most long-lived of the streamliners and by no means a failure. It hardly ever 'failed' in service and it had no back-up set, but it was clear that changes would be needed if the idea was to be extended to other services. This was no doubt the rationale behind the rather different streamlined trains which the LNER introduced in 1937, but before coming to them, what of the LMS?

There is little doubt that the LMS was not too convinced of streamlining, or indeed any form of dedicated special train sets during the mid-1930s. It preferred instead to follow a much more general upgrading both in terms of carriage quality and overall average speeds. Thus, though it never operated the real flyers of the LNER or even the GWR, it could offer far more services at 60 mph average than the whole of the rest of the British system put together. In fact, its main contribution to the 1935 celebrations was no more than a single Stanier 4-6-0, tarted up in black and chromium plate livery!

However, there can be no doubt that the success of the 'Silver Jubilee' had caused second thoughts at Euston, and it was a fairly open secret that Gresley would probably try something equally spectacular in Coronation year (1937) and probably tackle the Anglo-Scottish traffic in the process. Now high-speed flyers to Newcastle were no worry to the LMS, but the Scottish business was different. Accordingly, therefore, in 1936 Stanier 4-6-2 *Princess Elizabeth* was duly sent stomping off at great speed from London to Glasgow, coming back the next day and comprehensively breaking the six-hour barrier in both directions with a fair-sized though by no means heavy train on each occasion. No one really believed that this had anything to do with locomotive trials *per se*, any more than they did two years later when Gresley's *Mallard* went bucketing down Stoke bank at 126 mph. Brake tests? It was all part of the contemporary game! What the 1936 LMS jaunt presaged was its entry into the streamline stakes in Coronation year.

Like Gresley, Stanier too designed a new locomotive and it was duly given the mandatory streamlining which, as far as can be judged, was designed to be as different as possible from that of the LNER. Quite naturally, it was given a suitable train to match

and they called it the 'Coronation Scot'. On closer examination, however, and fine train though it was, the LMS had cheated a bit by using mostly refurbished existing coaches, probably so as to get their train out ahead of its LNER competitor which was known to be under construction. In this they were successful and undoubtedly stole a publicity march on the LNER when, in the then obligatory press run in June 1937, *Coronation* and her new train set a fresh speed record of 114 mph — and none of the experts really believed *that* either! But the public loved this LMS re-run of the 1935 LNER 'Silver Jubilee' junketing — in a different colour too — and that was all that mattered. There was a film made and even a special piece of music (later to become far better known as the theme tune for the BBC's 'Paul Temple' radio serial).

Like the 'Silver Jubilee' set, the 'Coronation Scot' was a conventionally arranged train — see the appended plan — and the LMS built three full sets, two working and one standing in reserve. Moreover, to be fair to the LMS, its new standard Stanier stock, being totally flush-sided, was far more capable of being given the streamline 'image' than the traditional teak-bodied LNER carriages. It was done by giving all carriages a luxury finish (two per side in the firsts for example, as with the 'Silver Jubilee') and installing pressure heating and ventilation, revealed by the presence of long ventilation ducts along the roof tops of the otherwise mostly unaltered carriages. Stanier also fitted auxiliary lateral bogie bolster control gear on the end vehicles of the train to counteract the rolling side movements which these vehicles would be likely to experience. But, just as with the 'Silver Jubilee', the striking new blue and silver livery served to distract attention from technical changes and indeed from the relatively orthodox nature of the accommodation offered. And it also worked, the 'Coronation Scot' going into trouble-free service until the outbreak of the Second World War.

The sets themselves were beautifully finished in the traditional LMS fashion and advantage was taken to have each of the three trains trimmed with different upholstery, blue, green and brown being the principal themes. Each coach within the set had different timber finishes, this being the time when the LMS made great play of its use of 'selected Empire timbers', and in the first class dining areas a different finishing timber was used for each train. The variety was, therefore, considerable, and the overall effect was spacious and dignified. Two full kitchen cars undoubtedly made meal service simpler than on the 'Silver Jubilee', but the train was covering a much longer journey. All seats were reservable at a standard 2/6 (12½p) supplement, first or third class, and all told it was a more than commendable effort, though its

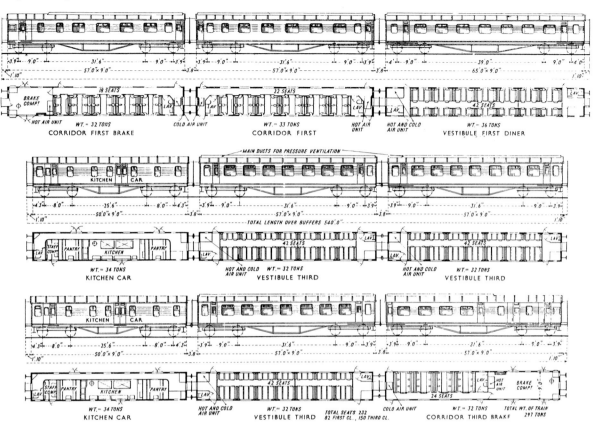

Figure 76 Semi-detailed elevations and plans of the 1937 LMS 'Coronation Scot'. The first class was at the London end of the train. Scale: 1" = 30ft

The northbound 'Coronation Scot' in full cry near Preston in 1937, headed by 4-6-2 No 6224 Princess Alexandra (Eric Treacy).

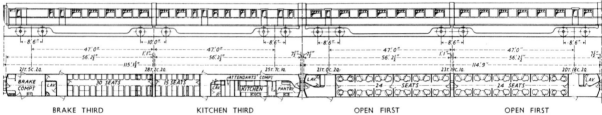

BRAKE THIRD   KITCHEN THIRD   OPEN FIRST   OPEN FIRST

OPEN THIRD   KITCHEN THIRD   OPEN THIRD   BRAKE THIRD

Top *No 30084 was one of six kitchen cars used in the 1937 'Coronation Scot' sets. They not only embodied the normal LMS compressed oil gas form of cooking but, astonishingly, were also given gas lighting as can be seen from the roof detail .*

Figure 77 Schematic elevations and plans of the LNER 'Coronation' and 'West Riding Limited' (both trains were identical), together with the observation car, summer only, of the 'Coronation'. Scale: 1" = 20ft

Below and below right *Posed front and rear views of the 'Coronation' train on the up slow line at Retford in July 1937.*

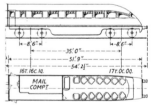

OBSERVATION SALOON

mostly 'second-hand' origins did rather prove that the LMS had been late to be convinced of the need. The company made ample amends, however, two years later (see below).

Back on the LNER, Gresley was developing his 'Silver Jubilee' ideas, and in July 1937 launched the 'Coronation' as the counterblast to the 'Coronation Scot'. He had to wait another year to get the speed record back, but it was pretty well game set and match to the LNER when it came to the train itself. Not only was it half an hour faster to Edinburgh than was the LMS train to Glasgow, but it really was brand new both in concept and decor.

Starting from the sound basis of the 'Silver Jubilee' set, Gresley produced a basic eight-car formation of articulated pairs but completely abandoned the side-corridor arrangement in favour of a fully open interior and, interestingly, gave most of the seating to the third class passengers, there being 168 of them and only 48 firsts (the 'Coronation Scot' had 82 first, 150 third). He then topped it off with a new innovation, an observation car whose shape reflected that of the 'A4' locomotive which would, of course, be at the front of the train. If truth be told, it was a pretty useless observation car since its roof came down so low at the back as to preclude much observation save that of receding sleepers, but no matter, it was different; that was the important point.

Different too was its livery: a striking two-tone blue, light 'Marlborough' blue above the waist and darker 'Garter' blue below, the latter matching the shade of the new series of locomotives built for the service. The usual 'Silver Jubilee'-type stainless steel trimmings were applied along with the bodyside fairings and so forth. Externally it was clearly from the same stable, and when running in winter without the observation car, only the exterior colours differentiated the two trains from all save the *cognoscenti*.

It is interesting, though probably quite coincidental, that both companies chose blue as their 1937 thematic image. Personally, I have some reservations about blue as an overall train colour, though it seems

to work when confined to the locomotive, and I cannot say I particularly liked the shade of either. I saw them both and they seemed rather 'cold' and unwelcoming from the exterior, an impression confirmed when BR began to use much the same carriage colours in 1965. But within the sets it was a different story, and if they shared some external similarities of colour, the pre-war LMS and LNER streamliners gave quite different impressions once through the door. Once inside the LMS train, one had a feeling of *déjà vu*; the luxury and quality was there, but one rather expected this from the best LMS trains, so there was not quite the same feeling of something 'special' which the LNER trains offered on first acquaintance.

Though I saw them from the outside in their blue form, I never actually got to ride in the LNER carriages until after the war when they had been repainted BR red and cream and were, *inter alia*, marshalled into the old 'West Riding' from Leeds to London. At 7.30 in the morning, having been up since 6.00 am to walk two miles so as to catch the connecting train to Leeds, one did not exactly take in the stock if it was painted the same colours as the rest so I did not notice anything unusual about the carriage I boarded. I can still recall my complete and utter astonishment when I walked into one of the open thirds. The first impression was that I was in the first class bit of the train, so I walked through to find the 'steerage' part. When I finally did arrive at the genuinely first class portion, I realized to my delight that I really was not dreaming and that what I had taken to be first class was indeed third; for the firsts were quite unbelievable.

I mention this personal experience because it is the nearest I can come to understanding the feeling which the 1937 streamliners probably created in their first patrons. Starting with the thirds, they were as nearly like orthodox first class dining cars as anything else. Subtle shades of fawn and green combined with excellent attention to detail and, as far as I recall, marvellous riding quality gave the next best thing to

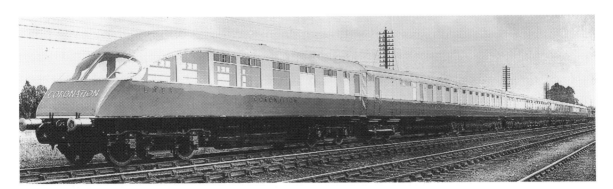

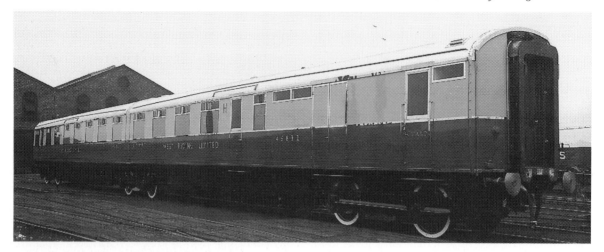

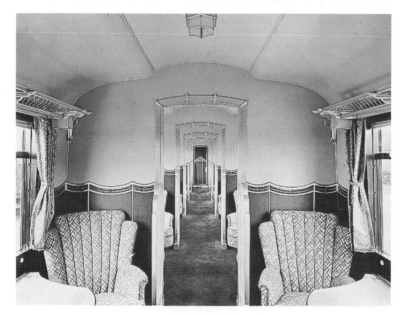

Top *Twin brake open third from the 'West Riding Limited' when new; it is probably the very same vehicle in which the author rode during the early 1950s (see text)*

Above *This posed view of the 'East Anglian' set behind streamlined 4-6-0 No 2859 East Anglian itself is taken from the third class end of the train — see Figure 78*

Left *First class interior of the 'Coronation'*

Right *Contrasting interiors: open firsts and thirds of the 'East Anglian' train. Only the curtains and antimacassars really reveal the first class version, though the uncased light bulbs in the thirds were a bit cheese-paring!*

Pullman travel that I can remember. What was particularly thoughtful was the way in which, when not laid up for meals, the table tops would fold along their long axis to make it much easier to reach the window seats; even the LMS did not do that and neither, it has to be said, does BR in its modern Mk III *first* class stock.

As for the LNER first class, here the 'French' influence crept back a bit, but rather toned down. Single swivelling armchairs were arranged down both sides, and each four-seat bay was divided from its next door neighbour by a full height partition which was not simply a dividing screen but also had lateral 'wings' forming a sort of alcove into which each armchair was snugly ensconced. Privacy was thus assured with all the operating convenience of the open plan layout. Even the table shape, with its scalloped edges, was designed to make eating simpler, and one could even arrange the chair at an angle so as to part face the window while enjoying the meal. They were gorgeous and deservedly popular — 'Supertrains' indeed — and there were four such sets, for as well as the 'Coronation', a further streamliner, 'The West Riding Limited', offered identical privileges, save for the observation car, to the lucky Yorkshire businessman. Two sets were branded 'Coronation', one 'West Riding Limited' and the fourth stood 'spare' for either working.

Like the 'Coronation Scot', the two new LNER trains had but two years of active life before hostilities commenced, when they all went into store. After the war the streamliners were never reinstated, their coaches being scattered about amongst the better LMS and LNER services in the early post-war era. But it was not quite the end of the streamline story, nor of the 'Supertrains'.

Flush with success at the favourable impression created by his streamlined trains, it is hardly surprising that Gresley went on to use some of these ideas elsewhere, and this time East Anglia was to be the beneficiary. Later in 1937, a very nice six-coach set of orthodox teak-panelled stock was constructed for a new fast service from London to Ipswich and Norwich, but inside it was entirely open stock in the manner of the 'Coronation' and trimmed in very similar style. The only difference was that while the third class kept all the nice features of the streamliners, the first class reverted to 2 + 1 fixed seating, but very opulent with it. No supplement was charged and although the train was anything but streamlined in outer appearance, the LNER 'dressed up' two Class 'B17' 4-6-0s in streamline casing to work the 'East Anglian', as it was called. This was almost as ersatz as the earlier GWR experiment, though at least the engine streamlining was properly carried out, although the engines lost their casings after the war.

It was another nice train, for all that.

Finally, in 1938, possibly the most surprising recipient of the new inside styling was a new 11-coach 'Hook Continental' boat train set. In it, third class became mysteriously transmogrified to second, it being a boat train one must understand, that being how they did these things on the other side of the Channel. It was in many ways the best of the bunch, for although encased within conventional teak-bodied exteriors, it combined the best features of both the 'Silver Jubilee' and 'Coronation' sets in offering a mixture of side-corridor and open seating in both classes, the side-corridors having two per side first class seating and the open carriages being of the 'Coronation' type with individual swivelling armchairs in the first class. The second class was identical to the third class of the East Coast sets and there was a mandatory pair of first class Pullmans tucked in between the first class section and the luggage van.

The surprising thing was that all this luxury was provided for a journey which only lasted 1½ hours, and while there was every reason to attract boat train passengers, one doubts not that the patrons of the 'Flying Scotsman', still performing its non-stop daily

pilgrimage with more orthodox day coaches, would have found the new 'Hook' set far more to their liking. One also wonders how much trade the two Pullmans did, given the superb quality of Gresley's open firsts. We were not given much time to find out, for war intervened less than a year after this very fine train was introduced. Boat trains were stopped and the 'Hook' seconds became firsts for the duration; but at least — and unlike the streamliners — it did go back to its proper use after the war was over, the former seconds reverting to their original status, and most of its carriages lasted until circa 1963-4.

While all this jockeying for position was going on between the LMS and LNER, the GWR made no moves to introduce further dedicated sets after its Centenary stock and the Southern seemed not to want to take part at all. Yet the latter railway did make one small gesture which is worth recording in the con-

Figure 78 Plans of the 'East Anglian' of 1937 (above) and the 'Hook Continental' of 1938 (below), Gresley's last two 'Supertrains'.

Scale: 1" = 30ft (upper) and approx 1" = 50ft (lower)

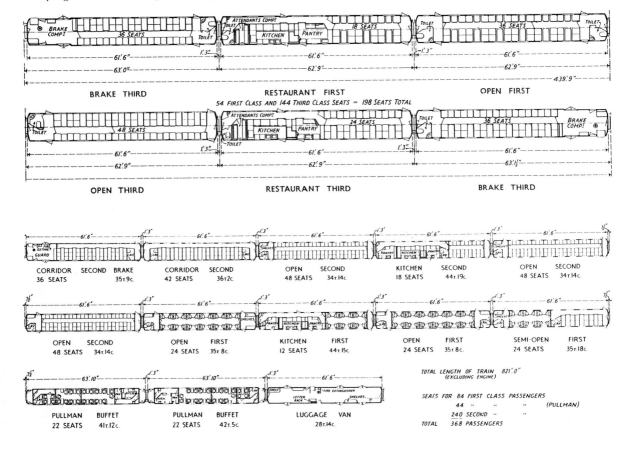

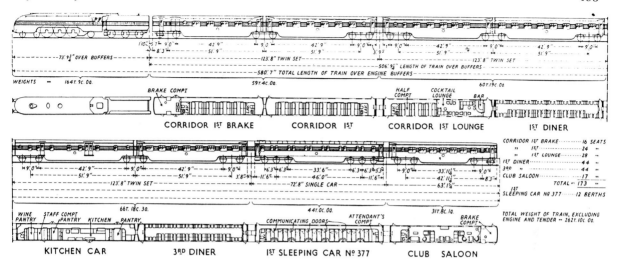

The following labels appear on the elevations and plans:

CORRIDOR 1ST BRAKE   CORRIDOR 1ST   CORRIDOR 1ST LOUNGE   1ST DINER

BRAKE COMPT   HALF COMPT   COCKTAIL LOUNGE   BAR

WEIGHTS — 164T.9C.00.   59T.4C.00.   60T.19C.00.

73'9¼" OVER BUFFERS — 123'8" TWIN SET — 506'5½" LENGTH OF TRAIN OVER BUFFERS — 123'8" TWIN SET — 580'7" TOTAL LENGTH OF TRAIN OVER ENGINE BUFFERS

KITCHEN CAR   3RD DINER   1ST SLEEPING CAR Nº 377   CLUB SALOON

WINE PANTRY   STAFF COMPT   PANTRY   KITCHEN   PANTRY   COMMUNICATING DOORS   ATTENDANT'S COMPT   BRAKE COMPT

66T.18C.30.   44T.10C.00.   31T.8C.10.   123'8" TWIN SET   72'8" SINGLE CAR

CORRIDOR 1ST BRAKE ...... 16 SEATS
„   1ST .... 24 „
„   1ST LOUNGE ...... 28 „
1ST DINER .... 44 „
3RD „ .... 44 „
CLUB SALOON .... 17 „
TOTAL — 173 „
1ST SLEEPING CAR Nº 377 — 12 BERTHS

TOTAL WEIGHT OF TRAIN, EXCLUDING ENGINE AND TENDER — 262T.10C.00.

Figure 79 Simplified elevations and plans of the LMS 1939 'Coronation Scot' set which toured North America. The operational sets in Britain would have seen a further pair of twin thirds in the position occupied by the sleeping and club cars of the American train.

Scale: 1" = 50ft

text of Bulleid's remarkable post-war efforts to up-grade SR main-line services (see Chapter 14). In July 1938, a year after he had taken over from Maunsell, Oliver Bulleid performed a major face lift on a set of Maunsell corridors for the Bournemouth, Weymouth and Swanage service. It was hardly a high-speed flyer, but the renovation was of a major nature. Away went all the dowdy finishes and both new decor and new trimming materials were used, along with numerous technical improvements. The dominant note was simplicity and the tones were subdued, but the light Rexine walls and generally bright interiors gave a pleasing effect. More controversial was the shrieking Malachite green livery which the newly refurbished train sported, devised, according to the Southern, '. . .to give the stock a brighter appearance without being garish'.

Had it not been for the war, the events on the Southern and in East Anglia in 1938 would merely have been a pause in the greater Anglo-Scottish scenario, for the LMS, perhaps smarting under the fact that its 'Coronation Scot' train had been eventually upstaged by Gresley's trains, not to mention *Mallard*'s speed record, was determined to build a real show-stopper for the 'Coronation Scot' service and introduce it in 1940. The catalyst was the decision, taken late in 1937, to accept an invitation to exhibit a complete 'Coronation Scot' train at the New York World's Fair in 1939, coupled with the realization that it would be risky, for operational reasons, to send the 'spare' 1937 set. It was therefore decided to build a new design of train and exhibit this in New York.

Early in 1938 it was then realized that to have simply one new train of a different type and capacity would make things very confusing for the seating reservation clerks when it went into normal service

alongside the old-type sets, so two more new-style sets were also ordered, the intention being that when all three were in traffic, the 1937 sets would take over the working of the 'Royal Scot' service. The background debate regarding the formation and construction of the new train was very complex and occupied much of 1938, and since it has been fully described elsewhere,* need not be repeated here. Suffice to say that the 1939 'Coronation Scot', or at least such of it as was built before hostilities commenced, was the last of the real British streamliners; it would, arguably, have been the best of them all, yet it never 'turned a wheel in anger'.

The concept embodied Stanier's form of articulation, using a double pivot (see p. 461), and the whole formation was envisaged as being five articulated pairs plus an extra 'loose' third at busy times. In the event this was to be slightly modified in the second and third sets (which actually *were* built) when it was decided that the one kitchen car would be an independent vehicle rather than articulated to its third class open diner. The actual train which went to America was three 'normal' pairs from the first set, essentially the first class portion plus the kitchen/third twin, together with a first class staff sleeping car (modified

* *LMS Coaches, an Illustrated History*: D. Jenkinson and R.J. Essery, OPC 1977.

to match the train purely for appearance sake 'on tour') and a special 'Club Car' brake to bring up the rear — again largely for the purposes of the tour. The remaining cars for the first set and the two other sets would be built in time for the full 1940 service.

The train which did go to North America, though incomplete in relation to its planned full formation, was more than sufficient, nevertheless, to give a clear indication of what the new LMS streamliner would look like — and it was breathtaking. This time there was no half-hearted reworking of old stock; just about everything in it was new and, like all the best stream-liners whether in Britain or abroad, it started from the outside. The basic 1937 striped livery was retained, but was now rendered in LMS crimson lake with gold stripes and black/vermilion edging, and the whole effect was vastly more opulent-looking in consequence. The brake ends were 'blind' (ie without gangways), thus giving the stylists a chance to ter-minate the livery properly on the back of the train, and though no observation car was, apparently, ever contemplated, the solution which was adopted came off quite well. Lower bodyside fairings between the bogies and rubber in-fills between all carriages (across which was carried the striping) completed the exterior.

Constructionally, the sets were also very up to date, embodying all-steel body framing and centrally trussed underframes of a similar type to those which had been used on the 1937 excursion sets (see page 343. Though clearly still of Stanier pattern, the car-riages also had a slightly different body profile of somewhat 'sharper' aspect, and opaque circular toi-let windows were provided, matched by similarly shaped clear windows on the corridor sides. Within the train, the LMS had resolved to retain a mixture of open and corridor styling, as with the 1937 sets,

Left *The American tour train from the first class end, showing the 'blind' brake end arrangement*

Below left and right *First class compartment and dining car interiors of the American set: not, perhaps, quite as adventurous as the LNER, but solidly LMS in tradition and of superlative quality. The post-war open stock built to complete the order reverted to traditional carriage cloth rather than leather.*

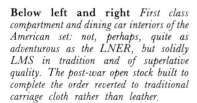

but gave the customers even more space — single seats on either side of the aisle in even the third class at the gangway ends of the dining cars — while the compartment carriages were lavish in the extreme. Each carriage was 59 ft 5 in long, yet there were never more than six compartments to a unit, even in the third class, and the firsts were so spacious that only one lavatory per carriage was provided.

All told, it was one of the most extravagant concepts that had ever come out of a British carriage works — Derby in this case — but it was all to no avail. Though it created a sensation at the New York Fair, the American set languished in the USA until after the war (the engine came home in 1942) and it was well into BR days before the last of the part-finished stock (abandoned as it stood in 1939) was finally completed. Even then, nobody wanted them. They were far too extravagant of space for the crowded post-war austerity years and they drifted off

into general service, just like their 1937 predecessors. Even the trimming of the post-war examples reverted to routine standard finishes, though nothing could change their basic character.

So it was that we were not only denied the chance to see the last of the British streamliners of the pre-war era in all its glory, but we also never saw any of them again in the splendid form they had once displayed. But to those of us who knew a bit about carriages, it was always rather nice to find one of the fugitives in one's train; and just as I had been delighted to find the Gresley stock on my early morning train from Leeds to Kings Cross in 1951, it was with just the same thrill, after I had boarded a train at Carstairs as late as 1966, that I realized I was riding in one of those wonderfully extravagant corridor thirds (now seconds) from the ill-fated 1939 'Coronation Scot' train. One only had to close one's eyes, just a little...

27. *Status quo ante* — Pullman and the Royal Trains

There were perhaps two principal areas during the company period where things never seemed to change in any sort of meaningful way from their established pre-1923 patterns. They scarcely need be specified, for the chapter head says all, but, as usual, their interest far transcends their absolute numbers. And there is some further logic in grouping Pullman and Royal vehicles together in the same chapter, for not only was Pullman travel regally styled in itself, it was also the monarchy's first alternative choice to the Royal Train proper if circumstances decreed that the latter was either unavailable or incapable of traversing a particular route.

In the context of the grouped railways, it is difficult to know where to resume the Pullman story, for the 'markers' in its own line of development did not coincide with those of the greater amalgamations. In fact, the real turning point for Pullman was a few years ahead of the grouping and this seems a more logical start point. The key year was 1915 when Davison Dalziel, the owner of the private Pullman Company, converted it into a public operation and linked it, almost unknown at the time, with the Wagons-Lits company to form the covert association hinted at on page 212 of Chap. 12 From this time onwards, in the British context, Pullman was, of course, as also explained in Chap. 12 , a wholly daytime operation, having long-abandoned its earlier overnight origins.

In 1915, though Pullman had recovered from its early twentieth century low point, it was only really firmly established on a few British lines on which it ran a modest number of cars. These were mostly operated individually in normal trains of the LB & SCR, SE & CR and, very recently in 1914, the Caledonian Railway, whereon Pullman took over most non-West Coast Joint Stock catering operations with a fine fleet of new cars. There were also two Pullman Buffet cars on the Metropolitan, but a far older agreement with the LSWR had gradually declined as the latter company put its own restaurant cars into service. Dalziel's new 1915 company, therefore, owned but 74 cars scattered through the country. Yet before long it was to re-establish itself in no uncertain way.

The catalyst appears to have been the speedy post-1918 re-establishment of a desire to travel in luxury and style, a fact accurately foreseen by Dalziel but which appears to have taken many railways by surprise. Never one to miss a trick, Pullman was ready and waiting, and this was to presage some ten years

of rapid expansion between 1922 and 1932. It was naturally allied to some very shrewd marketing and, by no means the least of the factors, some considerable changes in carriage building technique as far as Pullman was concerned.

Dealing first with some of the new services, the GER had been persuaded to operate a number of first and third class cars between 1920 and 1923, but this did not have any lasting quality save for some long-term survivors which were to be found on the Harwich boat trains for many a long year. Instead, the GER cars were mostly transferred to what was now the GNR section of the new LNER where they met with a much more widespread acceptance, the 'Harrogate Pullman Limited' (later to develop into the 'Queen of Scots') and the 'West Riding Pullman' (later the 'Yorkshire Pullman') being probably the best known. At the same time, Pullman's association with the former LB & SCR and SE & CR was continued and strengthened via the new Southern Railway both in the traditional boat train mode and in a more general sense on many other express services. This was to culminate in the re-establishment of Pullman services on the former LSWR in the shape of Ocean Liner specials to Southampton and, of course, the famous 'Bournemouth Belle'. The Pullman association with the Southern probably reached its pre-war apogee in 1933 with the introduction of all-Pullman EMUs for the 'Brighton Belle' service and, of course, the general incorporation of individual Pullmans in the 6PUL EMU sets already mentioned in the context of the Southern's main-line electrification schemes.

Meantime, up in Scotland, though the LMS was never wildly excited about Pullmans, there was some ten years or more of the Caledonian contract to run, and the LMS seems to have taken the view that it might just as well exploit the situation until the contract could be decently terminated. Accordingly, some Pullman services began to operate in ex-GSWR and ex-HR territory. Thus, even before the Brighton electrics, Pullman had broken out from its SE redoubt and though non-existent in all GWR and most LMS territory, its influence could now claim to extend from the south coast to Inverness and Aberdeen, and it even had a toe-hold in Ireland.

It seems, in retrospect, that two main factors were responsible for this, apart from Dalziel's sheer persistence. One was the 'traditional' nature of the service offered, clearly very popular; second was the extension of Pullman cars to the third class passenger, albeit with a supplementary charge. This too dated back to 1915 when, apart from boat trains and a few suburban survivors, second class was all but dead and third class took its place on most railways. There may well have been a bit of self righteous tut-tutting from some patrons about this democratization of what had hitherto been a very exclusive first class domain, but the proof of the pudding came quickly enough when the new LNER Pullman service of 1923 was seen to have no fewer than four third class cars in its six-car formation — and this was to fashionable Harrogate, of all places! These cars were even given 2 + 1 seating in the third class and may well have been a part cause of the LNER and LMS retention of this form for their own third class diners. South of the Thames, many third class Pullmans remained a little cramped with 2 + 2 seating, including the 'Brighton Belle'; but then, so too did their company equivalents.

Turning now to the developments in Pullman carriage building, the first significant change was revealed in 1922 when, in announcing some new cars for both the Caledonian and LB & SCR, Pullman was able to claim, at least so far as contemporary accounts record: 'A noticeable feature of these new

'Maid of Kent' seen (left) at Preston Park in 1955 was the second car of that name, the first having also been from the identical batch of 1921 cars built on recovered 57-foot LNWR underframes. The first 'Maid' was downgraded to third class in 1948 and sister car 'Formosa' then took over the name. On the right is the twelve-wheel 'Orpheus' dating from 1914. Both cars were withdrawn in 1960 and both are now preserved (B.C. Lane collection).

cars is their low tare as compared with the car of standard Pullman construction, and the reduction in weight has been effected by using all-steel underframes and bogies, which permits of the body framing being made considerably lighter.' So much for the claim, but as was always its wont, Pullman was often economical with the truth when it came to announcing 'new' cars! The bodies were indeed new, and the vehicles were mostly made by outside contractors, but the underframes and bogies were usually from recovered First World War ambulance carriages which had been sold off at low price; a quick glance at the axlebox faces below the floor of these new cars was often quite revealing, as indeed was their length, the 57 ft of the GWR and LNWR being particularly well represented.

Several dozen of these recovered underframes were thus re-used during 1921-2, but no matter, the end product was stylish enough and the underframes were often of the more modern angle-trussed type which, within a year or two, all railways save the LNER had adopted and which Pullman too was eventually to standardize (see below). Bodies, of course, remained wood-framed and traditional, right down to the vertical matchboarding below the waist rail, and many of the new cars came out with British Standard gangways and screw couplings rather than the better Pullman type. This mostly reflected the services to which they would be put. Interiors too remained traditional and, as usual, almost every single car had its own distinctive decor.

Hardly had this early post-war augmentation been completed when in 1923 Pullman came up with its

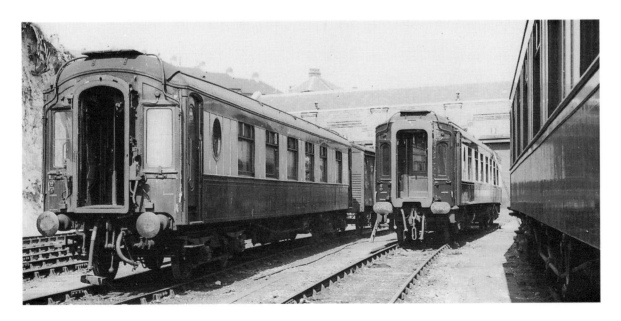

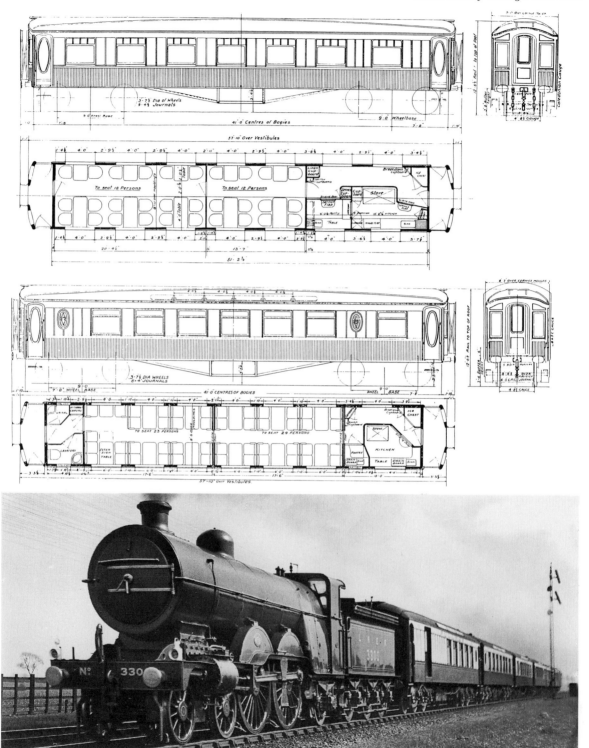

own design of underframe and bogie, in the form of a small clutch of four catering cars for the former Caledonian lines. These saw an extension of length to 63 ft 10 in overall (the frames were slightly shorter at 62 ft 4 in because of the bowed-end body form), and a brand new 10-foot wheelbase bogie with very substantial steel plate sideframes and a massive 13 in wide bolster carried by no fewer than five, differentially tensioned helical springs at each end. While it is always very dangerous to generalize about Pullmans, this bogie and underframe became a sort of standard type for all subsequent new eight-wheel cars for many years. As usual, most of them were con-

tractor-built but they were always designed by Pullman and are generally referred to as 'K' type cars.

Not that Pullman had quite finished with the traditional form of body construction described in the previous volume, or 'American'-style bogies for that matter. When the new 'Harrogate Pullman' was introduced, also in 1923, Messrs Clayton obtained the contract for the eight new third class carriages and built only two to the new style, the remaining six being of the old integral wood body style with compensating beam six-wheel bogies; they were to be not only the last twelve-wheel Pullmans to be built in Britain but also the last to display the traditional

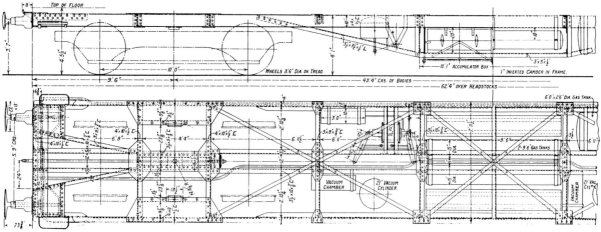

Above left Figure 80 *Elevations and plans of typical Pullmans of the early 1920s utilizing recovered underframes, in this case 57-foot examples of GWR origin. The upper arrangement shows one of two identical dining cars 'Lady Nairn' and 'Bonnie Jean' for the Caledonian in 1922, and the lower example is a third class parlour/ buffet car of which three (Nos 18, 20 and 21) were built for the Brighton line, also in 1922.*

Scale: 2mm = 1ft

Left *The down 'Harrogate Pullman' in the mid-1920s, headed by former GNR 4-4-2 No 3300. Two twelve-wheelers lead the formation of which the leading brake is not one of the types built in 1923. The third car seems to be a 'K' type.*

Right Figure 81 *Pullman standard angle-trussed underframe and 10 ft wheelbase bogie, adopted for 'K' series cars from 1923 onwards.*

Scales: 4mm and 7mm = 1ft

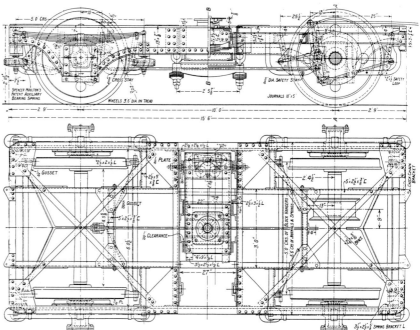

American form of body construction. Of course, such was the longevity of Pullmans that it was to be decades before the older-style cars, be they eight- or twelve-wheel, were to finally disappear. The first class cars for the Harrogate service were to the new 'K'

Below Figure 82 *Floor plans of new cars built* inter alia *for the 'Harrogate Pullman' service of 1923, of which only the first class examples were given the new-type underframes.*

Scale: 2mm = 1ft

Right Figure 83 *This series of elevations and plans shows typical 'K' type Pullman cars from 1923-4. From top to bottom they are as follows:*

a) One of the three first class dining cars for LMS (ex-Caledonian area) service ('Meg Dods', 'Lass o' Ballochmyle' and 'Mauchline Belle').
b) Third class parlour/buffet, No 80, also for the LMS.
c) First class kitchen/parlour cars for the 'White Pullman' service of the SR, later the 'Golden Arrow', typically 'Marjorie', 'Geraldine' or 'Viking'.

Scales: 2mm = 1ft

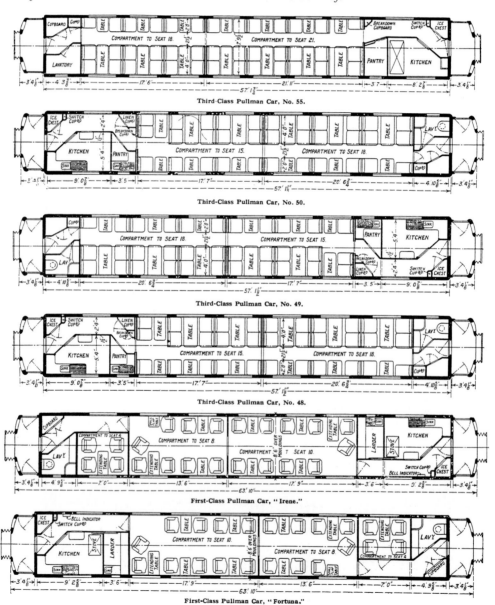

Third-Class Pullman Car, No. 55.

Third-Class Pullman Car, No. 50.

Third-Class Pullman Car, No. 49.

Third-Class Pullman Car, No. 48.

First-Class Pullman Car, "Irene."

First-Class Pullman Car, "Fortuna."

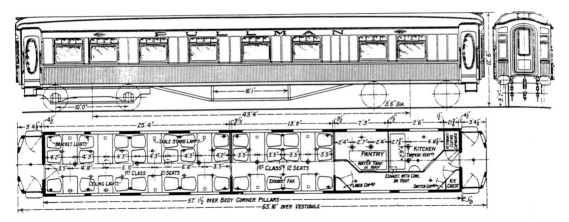

General Arrangement of First-Class Pullman Dining Car.

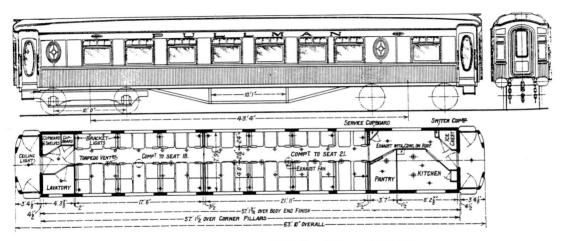

General Arrangement of Third-Class Pullman Buffet Car.

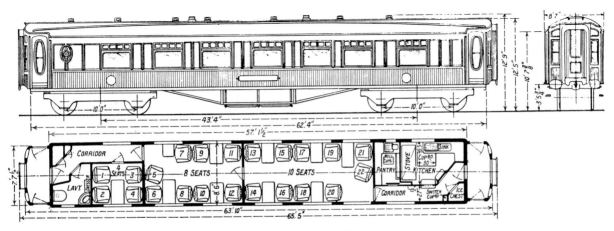

General View and Drawing of New Pullman Car " Marjorie."

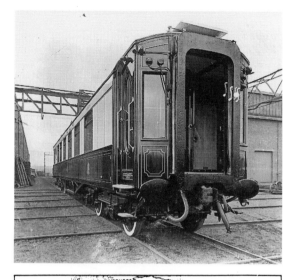

type with separate steel-framed chassis and new-type bogies.

The next recipient, in 1924, of the new-style Pullman cars with separate underframes was to be the traditional boat train operation from Victoria to Dover, and it came in the form of a brand new all-Pullman set which introduced the umber and cream Pullman livery on to former SE & CR metals for the first time, previous SE & CR-operated cars having been finished in the equally dignified all-lake livery to match the SE & CR trains. For a while, it was to be known as the 'White Pullman' in consequence of this change, though its later and much better known official name was, of course, 'Golden Arrow' (from 1929); thereafter all British Pullmans were to carry these colours until well into BR days. This, in fact, represented a slight change of emphasis and this might be the appropriate point at which to address the matter of Pullman's famous British colour scheme.

Until 1924, the Pullmans operating on the LB & SCR and SE & CR had been finished in livery colours which matched that of the company operating the service, as in fact had those on the Metropolitan. Elsewhere, of course, Pullmans generally operated as a fixed set where their own livery made them stand out or, in the case of the Caledonian, on a railway whose livery was not very different from that of Pullman. On this basis, one might have expected, save perhaps for all-Pullman trains, that after the grouping, individually operated cars would have been painted in, say, Southern green or LMS crimson, but it was not so. Thus it was that the old Brighton line colour scheme came to stand for Pullman and the new unified colours did permit Pullman to switch its cars about at will between services without too many folk being aware of the fact. In the early days, the colours were dark brown and just off-white, but when this gave way in 1929 to the version with brown on the headboard as well as below the waist, the brown was lightened and the off-white became a genuine cream. Perhaps 'plain chocolate and spilt milk' giving way to 'milk chocolate and

Above left *This detailed end view of first class 'K' type parlour car 'Rainbow' when new in 1925 shows one of the two cars sold to the Wagons-Lits company which did* not *come back in 1928 — see text.*

Figure 84 *Map showing the extent of Pullman influence by 1928.*

cream' would be a reasonable way to envisage the difference!

The next few years were to see a considerable enlargement of the Pullman fleet. Getting on for another 50 or so were built down to 1928, all being to the new standard constructional form, many of which went to their traditional SR haunts, others going into LNER and LMS use and a handful for Ireland. Ten of them actually spent their first few years of life in Wagons-Lits service on the Nice to Milan run. Eight came back to Britain in 1928, technically having been sold to and bought back from the CIWL, by which date the British Pullman fleet was probably three times its 1915 size, such had been the rapid rate of expansion after 1918.

The key year turned out to be 1928, for a variety of reasons. Firstly, even though the vast bulk of the post-1918 fleet had come from outside builders, it was now clear that the old SE & CR premises at Long-hedge could no longer cope with the extra volume of repair, maintenance and re-building of cars which this much larger fleet entailed. In consequence, Pullman opened its new works at Preston Park, Brighton, and the older premises became a supply depot for the various 'on car' requisites such as linen, silver, etc. Secondly, the year also marked the espousal of all-steel construction for new Pullman cars with a batch of no fewer than 29 being ordered from the

These views show typical 'K' type cars in pre- and post-1929 livery respectively. First class kitchen/parlour car 'Geraldine' was built in 1924 as part of the 'White Pullman' batch. The opposite side is shown in Figure 83. Third class kitchen/parlour No 107 dated from 1927 and was built as first class 'Kathleen'. It was downgraded to third class for the 'Yorkshire Pullman' service in 1946, but its window spacing reveals its true orgins and it was reinstated in this role as 'Thetis' in 1962 — such were the ways of Pullman!

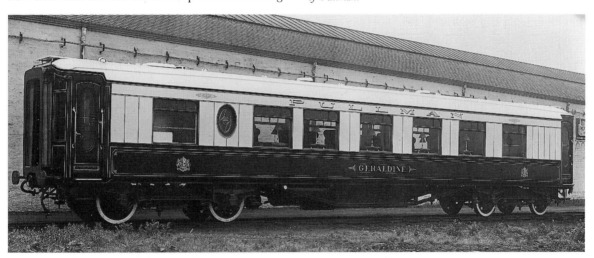

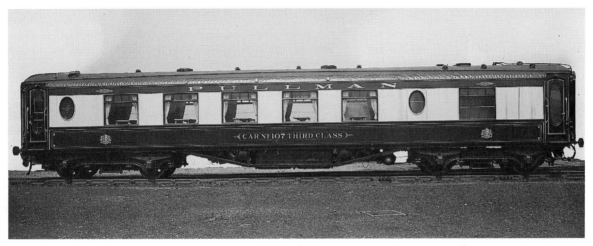

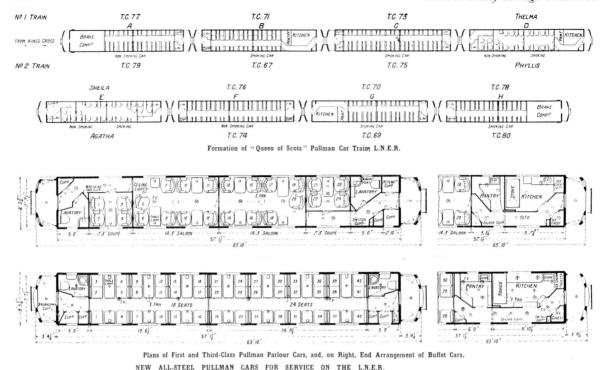

Formation of "Queen of Scots" Pullman Car Train L.N.E.R.

Plans of First and Third-Class Pullman Parlour Cars, and, on Right, End Arrangement of Buffet Cars.

NEW ALL-STEEL PULLMAN CARS FOR SERVICE ON THE L.N.E.R.

Metropolitan C W & F Co Ltd.

In a very real sense, this was a reversion to the original Pullman form of coach construction, save that it was now in steel not wood, for the cars had no separate underframes, being of the integral box-girder structural form rather like those of the LMS and LNER introduced a year or two earlier (see Chapter 17). In consequence, they displayed no separate trussing but, like the LMS/LNER coaches, they did retain their own 'company' bogies, the new 'Pullman' 10 foot wheelbase type. Moreover, their bodies were fashioned in the entirely traditional shape and only their smooth-sided panelling below the waist really gave the game away.

They were extremely handsome cars and became very familiar to those, like myself, whose Pullman

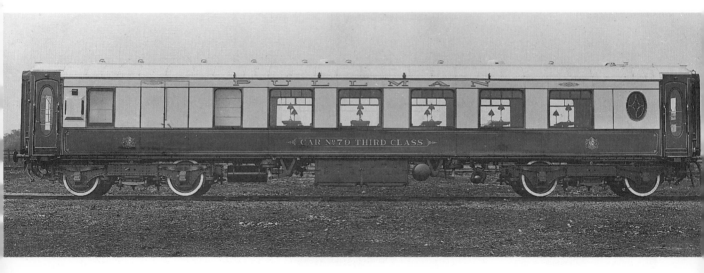

experience was mostly confined to the services operated by the LNER, later BR(ER). In fact, they were in large part built for this very purpose, no fewer than 16 of the original 29 being for the re-equipment of the old 'Harrogate Pullman' which now worked right through to Scotland under that most resonant sounding of all train names, 'Queen of Scots'. Never has a train been better titled or, on its demise, more sadly mourned by its patrons.

As a tangential aside (somehow or other, discussion of Pullman cars always serves to remind one of these things!) what in the event turned out to be my last ride in a 'slab-sided' Pullman car in normal service was in one of these coaches. I had returned from overseas duty one April morning in 1962 and hoped to catch the first train to Harrogate. The best bet was the 'Queen', but I had no reservation. On presenting myself at the booking office it was suggested that as the train was in the platform, I might try my luck with the conductor. His response to my enquiry went something like this: 'I am afraid we only have a few second class seats left, sir, and they are all in the brake-ended car.' He, of course, knew that by then most of the train had been re-equipped with the new 1960 Metro-Cammell cars of BR Mk I profile (and dimension) but that the brake ends were of the old type. So too did I, and I told him that I did not mind at all — in fact I preferred it that way for the proffered car was a 'proper' Pullman. I shall never forget the broad smile on his face which greeted that remark, nor the fact that he 'found' me one of the few remaining 'singles' in the car. Apart from the fare itself, everything else about that trip was first class too! I never encountered another such car in regular service.

While on the subject of tangential asides, for it was

to prove little more than a minor episode, it is perhaps worth mentioning that the majority of the other 1928 all-steel Pullmans were first used on the one and only attempt by Pullman to infiltrate GWR territory. In 1929, Pullman had persuaded a reluctant GWR to allow its cars on to the prestigious Plymouth Ocean Liner Expresses to meet the expectations of the wealthy visitors; but such trains, though popular, only ran on demand and could not keep a set of cars fully employed. Thus there also began in 1929 the 'Torquay Pullman' to give some more work to at least one set of cars. The GWR hardly helped matters, for it had only accepted Pullmans in the first place because of passenger pressure and did not really want them on its lines at all. Pullman gave up the unequal struggle in 1930 and the GWR was obliged, instead, to build its own luxury carriages to meet the demands of its transatlantic clientele, the Super Saloons of 1931, described in the previous chapter. As has been seen, these carriages, though of peerless quality, were a pretty well unashamed crib of Pullman's ideas.

A consequence of this unprofitable move was that Pullman transferred its new cars to the rival Southampton boat train services of the Southern Railway and, in 1931, supplemented these with the new 'Bournemouth Belle', again to increase car utilization rather in the manner of the abortive Torquay service. This time, however, it nicely complemented the Pullman boat specials by giving a regularly scheduled all-year service to Southampton, its only other stop. Both the new 'Belle' and the boat trains became deservedly popular, but when only a few more all-steel Pullmans followed in 1930-31 to augment them, it may have seemed as though Pullman's post-1918 expansion was almost complete. In the pure locomotive-hauled sense this was indeed the case; but there

Figure 85 *Typical floor plans of the 'all-steel' Pullmans of 1928, including the train plan for the 'Queen of Scots'.*

Left *'All-steel' third class brake parlour car No 79 was one of four built in 1928 for the 'Queen of Scots', all of which were retained on the East Coast after 1960 to work with the new Metro-Cammell cars. It was in one of these cars that the author made his last journey in a 'proper' Pullman — see text. No 79 is now preserved by the North York Moors Railway*

Right *The short-lived GWR experiment: The inaugural trip of the 'Torquay Pullman Limited' at Paddington in July 929, probably one of the last times most f these cars ran in the older livery.*

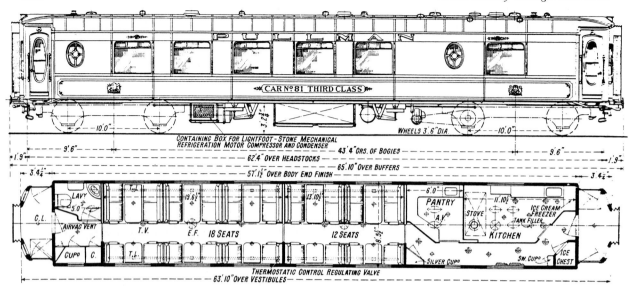

Elevation and Plan showing General Arrangement of All-Steel Pullman Car for Southern Railway Services.

Scale: ¹/₁₀" = 1ft

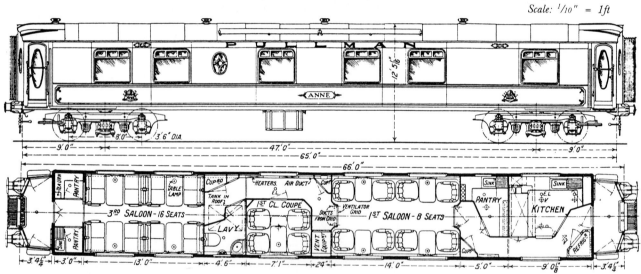

Composite first- and third-class Pullman car, express units

was to be one final flourish, part of which was eventually to become world famous.

I refer, of course, to the celebrated 'Brighton Belle' EMU sets, built in 1932 and first put to use in 1933; but they were only one element of Pullman's involvement with Southern Electric, the other being the insertion of single Pullman cars into the 6PUL units. Both these developments have been considered in their main context in Chap 21 , but the cars themselves were left out of the discussion largely because they actually represented the culmination of ten years

of Pullman evolution and are best considered here. In fact, they formed a logical continuation of the all-steel cars of 1928-31, being structurally very similar. However, their EMU form caused two new types to be introduced.

The first of these was, of course, the driving motor unit of the 5BEL sets whose cab end made it unique. This apart, however, it was a conventional enough parlour third behind the cab end. The other three cars of the 5BEL sets were a single parlour third and two kitchen/parlour firsts, the kitchens of the latter being so arranged as to separate the first and third class portions, thus being able to service both types of accommodation. Two five-car sets would normally work the service in multiple, the third being kept spare, but it was by no means unusual for a single five-car set to operate solo. At first, the train retained the 'Southern Belle' name of its steam-hauled predecessor, but it was renamed the 'Brighton Belle' in 1934 and thus it remained for the rest of its long life.

The second new type of Pullman was the composite kitchen/parlour car for use in the 6PUL sets, of which no fewer than 23 were built in 1932, probably

Figure 86 *Detailed elevations and plans of 'all-steel' Pullmans:*
a) Third class dining car No 81 for general catering service on Southern Railway boat trains and the like.
b) Composite dining car 'Anne', one of 23 built in 1932 for the 6PUL EMU sets (see page 397).

Right *Five-car 'Brighton Belle' Pullman set No 2053 near Hayward's Heath sometime before 1937 when the set was renumbered 3053. From the front, the cars are: third class No 93; third class No 85; first class 'Mona'; first class 'Gwen'; third class No 92. Note the very slight inward batter of the sides between waist and cantrail, a distinctive feature of the 5BEL sets*

Figure 87 *Train and individual car plans of the 5BEL sets.*

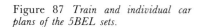

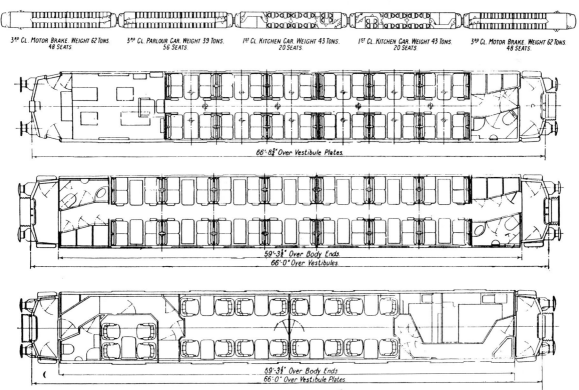

3ᴿᴰ CL. MOTOR BRAKE. WEIGHT 62 TONS. 48 SEATS.   3ᴿᴰ CL. PARLOUR CAR. WEIGHT 39 TONS. 56 SEATS.   1ˢᵀ CL. KITCHEN CAR. WEIGHT 43 TONS. 20 SEATS.   1ˢᵀ CL. KITCHEN CAR. WEIGHT 43 TONS. 20 SEATS.   3ᴿᴰ CL. MOTOR BRAKE. WEIGHT 62 TONS. 48 SEATS.

66'-8¾" Over Vestibule Plates.

59'-3¼" Over Body Ends.
66'-0" Over Vestibules.

59'-3¼" Over Body Ends.
66'-0" Over Vestibule Plates.

establishing some sort of Pullman record for an individual type design. They were ingeniously contrived 28-seaters (12 first plus 16 third) with a kitchen at one end and the usual Pullman-style lavatory separating the two classes. As such, a 28-seat composite was no great leap forward in seating capacity, but the ingenuity arose from the fact that the first class portion still managed to retain the space-consuming single armchair layout on either side of the aisles combined with a typical Pullman-style coupé as well. This was undoubtedly made easier by arranging the third class 2 + 2, a feature also found in the 5BEL sets. It was a little cramped in space when all places were laid for a meal, but the relatively short 1-1½ hour trips probably made it acceptable in a way that would not have been so in the longer-distance locomotive-hauled Pullmans.

These 1932 EMU Pullmans marked not only the end of a ten year period of evolution and expansion, but they were also the last new British Pullmans for almost two decades. Meantime, the others went on for several more years until the outbreak of war, the only main change being the LMS buy-out of the Scottish contract, and from 1934 the erstwhile Pullmans were added to the already large LMS fleet of dining cars. They were soon to become as familiar in Scotland in their new crimson lake livery as they had been in Pullman's own colours. As a result, Pullman there-

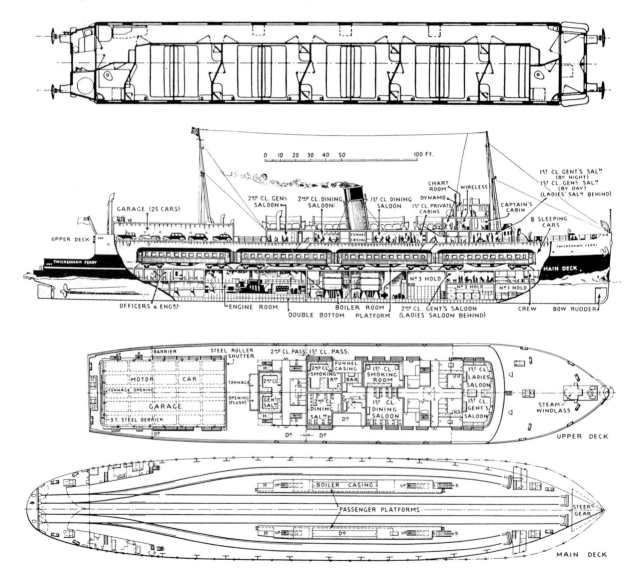

Figure 88 *'Night Ferry' sleeping car plan, and the arrangement of the specially built* Twickenham Ferry *used for the inaugural service in 1936.*

Wagons-Lits Type 'F' 'Night Ferry' sleeping car No 3805 at Victoria, circa 1955. Note especially the combination of traditionally styled compensated beam bogies with roller bearing axleboxes (T.J. Edgington).

after became an operation associated with only two of the 'Big Four' companies, the LNER and SR. During the war years, both these companies paid Pullman an annual compensation to keep the cars intact in storage ready for immediate use thereafter, and this was an undoubted reason why there was such a quick reinstatement of Pullmans in those difficult post-1945 years.

There was, however, one further development of Pullman-style travel before the war intervened, and this was undoubtedly the consequence of the 'hidden' arrangement between Pullman and Wagon-Lits. It had always been the dream of both organizations to forge closer links between Britain and Europe, and in 1936 these achieved reality when there were put into service some overnight Wagons-Lits sleeping cars between London and Paris. They utilized the rail ferry boat terminals at Dover and Dunkerque and were put on board specially built ships designed to carry rail vehicles. The service was known as the 'Night Ferry' and, with the daytime 'Golden Arrow', gave Pullman and Wagons-Lits a near monopoly of the upper end of the cross-Channel trade in pre-airline days.

The sleeping cars themselves were built in France and followed traditional Wagons-Lits style, complete with the famous blue livery and its proliferation of headboard lettering and bold CIWL 'monogram' on the centre of the lower panels. Bilingual inscriptions appeared on the exterior and multi-lingual instructions inside the cars. The only things which distinguished them from their continental cousins were their overall size (small enough to pass the restricted British loading gauge) and their all-metal construction inside and out, this being to minimize fire risk, especially at sea. They were probably the only railway carriages at the time to have life-jackets provided

as a mandatory part of their equipment. As might well be imagined, the latter was very comprehensive.

The service proved very popular, and even though interrupted by the war it soon became a recognized feature of the early morning rush hour to Victoria that in and amongst the many EMUs there would be this rather unusual blue train making its way to London from Dover. It was, in fact, the only regular sleeping car service operated by the Southern Railway or the Southern Region. In spite of airline competition, it was not until 1980 that it was terminated, and then only when the original special-sized cars were life-expired. There was talk of replacement BR-type carriages, but nothing much came of it and we shall have to await the Channel Tunnel for a renewal of through train services to Europe.

Without doubt, travelling on the 'Night Ferry' was a most fascinating and unique experience and I was able to enjoy its distinctive character more than once in connection with the NRM's decision to preserve one of these trend-setting cars. The chosen example was restored at Ostende, but the CIWL offices were in Paris; however, since the 'Night Ferry' by then served Brussels as well as Paris, the two sections being put together at Lille, it seemed only right to use the very service whose vehicle we were trying to preserve. One always tried to remain awake to witness the special loading and unloading on to the ferry boats but somehow, in spite of many who reckoned real sleep was impossible on this train, I always managed to miss it and my two abiding memories are firstly of falling asleep at Lille and waking up amongst the Kentish hop fields or, perhaps more in the spirit of the European 'Great Trains', the sight of a very elegant elderly lady, bedecked in her pink silk robe and fur-lined slippers, sorting out some problem in a most dignified manner with the conductor in the very best

The up Paris–London 'Night Ferry' at Shorncliffe on 25 June 1949 in charge of 4-6-2 No 34074 46 Squadron. The leading luggage vans are French and are followed by the Wagons-Lits, four on this occasion, though it could be anything up to eight or more. The back of the train consists of standard Southern stock, probably including a dining car at this time

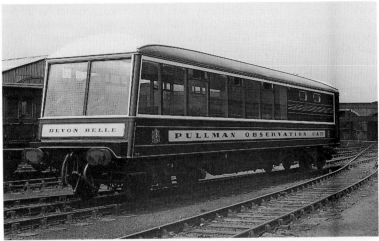

The 'Devon Belle' observation car had one advantage over the Gresley version on the 'Coronation' streamliner: one could actually see out of it more easily! But the styling did not really go well with the more traditional cars in the rest of the train

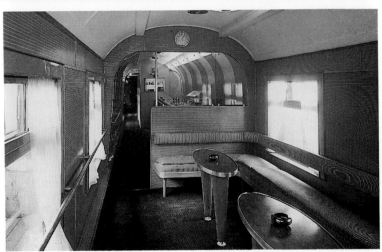

The fashionably trendy first 'Trianon Bar', modelled inside a wooden-bodied twelve-wheeler!

Agatha Christie tradition: right in the middle of the main departure platform at Paris Nord!

During the war itself, like the 'Night Ferry' service, most of the Pullmans were also withdrawn, though the EMU types soon came back, being useful to the general war effort, Catering provision was, of course, limited. A few other cars were used, principally by the LNER, as additional first class carriages and were repainted plain brown. This treatment was also given to some individual Pullmans to render them less conspicuous. A few more were operated in conditions of great secrecy for VVIP use, and even the NAAFI managed to get half a dozen for use as buffet cars in troop trains. But most were far too luxurious in those difficult times and were stored out of use. Some were destroyed in air raids and many were damaged, but a mercifully high proportion did survive to enable a quick reinstatement of many of the pre-war trains, and at least one new one.

The latter was introduced on the Southern's West of England main line in 1947 as the 'Devon Belle' and was designed to attract holidaymakers. For this reason it was given observation cars of really quite nasty design in the then modern idiom, soon to become more familiar to us all in the shape of the 1951 Festival of Britain and all its subsequent imitators. It became dated almost as rapidly as yesterday's newspaper, but in one respect the Pullman tradition was faithfully maintained. Though passed off as 'new', these observation cars made use of ex-LNWR ambulance underframes which had already carried conventional Pullman bodies for nearly 20 years! The rest of the train remained a bastion of tradition in the brave new world of changing ideas and for some years it was very popular, often loading to 14 cars. But the private motor car finally killed it off as it did so much else of the traditional railway scene.

The 'Devon Belle' was, however, not the only instance where Pullman tried to jump on the fashionable post-war stylistic bandwagon. The other well-known example was the multifarious reincarnations of a catering vehicle introduced as part of the 1946 reinstatement of the famous 'Golden Arrow' service. It was known as the 'Trianon Bar' — named as a complement to our French neighbours. The first example displayed the most obnoxiously awful plastic-styled carriage interior which one could possibly conceive and was rebuilt from a much older car. On test, it was involved in an early running incident which caused its temporary withdrawal (some wished that said incident had been more permanent!) and another car substituted of less controversial style. Thereafter, the two cars tended to play ducks and drakes for a month or two, and even Pullman's normally cavalier approach to naming became more than somewhat confused!

Eventually, however, Pullman got it right at the third attempt in 1951, this time in conjunction with a totally new set of cars for the 'Golden Arrow' service. They were to be the last traditional British Pullman cars to be built for the independent Pullman Company and they were a fine finale. Seven came out in 1951 (contractor-built), three more in 1952 from Pullman's own workshops, of which one, inevitably, was a new body on an old set of frames. It was called, not inappropriately, 'Phoenix', though this name could, with justice, have been applied to any one of a dozen or more of its predecessors. The third 'Trianon Bar' was incorporated in 'Pegasus', the very last of the 1951 series to be built.

The new 'Trianon Bar' in this 1951 set went just about as far as seemed proper for a Pullman in terms of its decor and was quite a good example of restrained 1950s styling, but as for the rest of this set

The first substitute 'Trianon' was a 'K' type bar car, formerly 'Diamond' but in 1946, when this view was taken, it had been re-named; the same car also ran as 'One Hundred Bar' and 'New Century Bar', all four names being used in that same year! It reverted eventually to 'Diamond' and was finally named 'Daffodil Bar' for the 'South Wales Pullman' in 1955

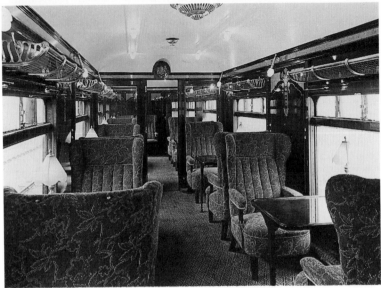

Above *Guard first class parlour car 'Minerva' was built as a 'K' type in 1927 but is seen here completely remodelled with the final type of square toilet windows to run with the new 1951 'Golden Arrow' cars. It is now preserved.*

Left *The remodelled interior of 'Minerva', little changed in essence from all that had gone before.*

Below right *This view of the Southern Railway Royal Train passing St Catherines near Guildford en route to Portsmouth behind 4-4-0 No 716 was taken circa 1938, probably in connection with Coronation year ceremonial. The principal saloon is the second vehicle and the rest of the train is of SE & CR low-roofed style.*

of cars, there was to be no more tinkering about with newfangled ideas, even though it was 'Festival' year. Just about the only obvious changes were the new-shaped toilet windows (rectangular rather than oval) and the LNER-pattern underframe and bogies which gave them a very superior ride quality. They had in fact been conceived as early as 1938 for LNER service and this probably explained the different running gear.

This pre-war origin may also account for the somewhat dated nature of some of the interiors, for much of the decorative panelling had been made before the war and stored during the hostilities. Thus, though admirably well finished as always, the cars saw no really striking innovation, even if there was some slight simplification in detail. They may, of course, deliberately have been designed to reassure, and without doubt they were some of the finest cars ever to see service, but some have averred that maybe Pullman could have been a bit more enterprising. My

own view, for what it is worth, is that there was very little of substance to commend the ultra-modern 1940s and 1950s fashions as far as their application to carriage interiors was concerned and it was not until a decade later that things began to get better. We shall, of course, have cause to come back to this subject in the next volume.

With the building of these 1951-2 cars, we reach an appropriate point at which to terminate this part of the story for the time being, but before leaving the Pullman field, one final point needs to be made, and that concerns the quite astonishing survival rate of many of the old flat-sided Pullmans. Many have been saved privately, including all 15 'Brighton Belle' cars somewhere or other.

The 'Brighton Belle' cars were in fact the very last of the traditional cars to run in BR service, not being finally withdrawn until 1972 — and then not without some protest — but very many of the locomotive-hauled cars lasted well into the 1960s before they were withdrawn, a better survival rate than that of many a company design of newer date. Even then they often refused to lay down and die! Many are preserved privately and some of them indeed are still in main-line use in yet another operational reincarnation entirely characteristic of the company which spawned them. As such, they look set to see the century out; so we have by no means heard the last of them yet, and their story will continue in the next volume.

*   *   *

Just as long-lived as Pullman cars were those other very special vehicles provided for the reigning monarch, and as Volume 1 has already indicated, HM King George V had quite an assemblage from which to choose when the grouping era dawned. However, the circumstances of the grouping caused some adjustments to be made, and although the carriages remained quite splendid, there were some gradual reductions in quantity. However, such was the quality of the mainly Edwardian contribution to the Royal fleet that none of the companies saw any real need to re-equip in full, and only two of them, the LMS and GWR, assayed any new Royal Saloons at all.

Another point to be made is that the grouping saw the increasing use of the more comprehensively equipped Royal Trains on territory other than the lines of the company for which they were built, and this gave the LMS (ex-LNWR) and LNER (ex-ECJS) sets, especially the former, a head start over all the others. This was largely a consequence of the King needing more facilities on his many longer tours than could usually be offered by the mostly daytime-orientated trains of most of the pre-1923 companies. This more extended role of the Royal Train dated, in fact, from well before the grouping when it began to be a very vital element in the King's ability to make his morale-boosting tours during the 1914-18 war. For this purpose, the LNWR train was usually the first choice, but in due time, especially after the grouping, this led to a reduction in role for most of the Royal vehicles save for the LMS train which gradually assumed, if not a total monopoly, then a highly dominant position. It was, all told, a quite complicated evolutionary story, best considered company by company.

The Southern Railway inherited two Royal trains plus a few bits and pieces of a third, a pair of ex-LSWR bogie saloons of 1885 vintage. It was not to be expected that at nearly 40 years old they would last much longer — they had not often been used for Royal purposes in their later years anyway — and they were taken out of Royal use at the grouping, though they survived until the 1930s. A much similar fate was to befall the former Brighton Royal train of 1897 which was, in effect, largely built for King Edward VII when he was Prince of Wales. This was a handsome clerestory train, undoubtedly one of the finest pieces of carriage building ever offered by the LB & SCR, but it too was downgraded in 1923, its vehicles either going into normal service or private charter. Like the ex-LSWR vehicles, they lasted until the 1930s.

The only pre-group Royal vehicles which remained as such on the Southern were those of the SE & CR which had formed up a Royal Train in 1903 but to which I gave but scant mention in Chap. 13. The centrepiece was the fine clerestory saloon by Harry Wain-

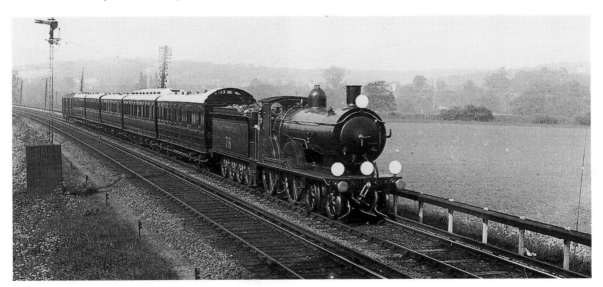

wright, and very soon thereafter the available fleet had been extended to some seven vehicles by means of some characteristically neat and tidy low elliptical roof first class stock, including the mandatory 'bird-cage' brake ends. As I stated in Chap. 7, SE & CR stock was often underrated overall but, like quite a lot of its carriages, its Royal Train was of first class quality and the Southern kept it in being until 1939. Though Maunsell might be accused of some sort of favouritism, being of course ex-SE & CR himself, by any objective standards the Southern only needed one Royal Train and the SE & CR had the best example. It also had the indubitable advantage of having greater route availability than those of the other SR constituents.

Towards the end of the 1930s, however, even this train was showing its age a little, and by then the LMS train had assumed greater dominance anyway. It was already the first choice on the GWR (see below) and regularly made forays into LNER country, so the Southern also tended to use it if possible. This was often not the case but it became increasingly customary for the Southern to hire a few modern Pullmans for Royal use, rather than use the SE & CR train. After 1939, when the latter set made its last Royal trip, Pullmans became the normal Royal conveyances on the SR whenever either the LMS or LNER saloons could not clear the often limited Southern loading gauge.

The GWR's splendid 1897 Royal Train had been rather 'diluted' in the technical sense by Queen Victoria's insistence that her old 1874 carriage be retained, now rebuilt on a new underframe and bogies. Unlike the LNWR, however, which had faced exactly the same problem during the 1890s and come up with a near-identical solution, the GWR did not replace the older carriage when King Edward VII came to the throne. It soldiered on until 1912, having served as a hearse for both the Queen and King Edward VII, and was then scrapped. After this time, the remainder of the fine Dean clerestory set of 1897 remained in Royal use until 1935, when all were withdrawn, life expired. The GWR from then on usually used the LMS (ex-LNWR) train for Royal purposes.

For such a proud railway as the GWR, it is perhaps surprising that no real effort was made to provide a new principal Royal saloon for King George V, and even after the 1897 clerestories had been scrapped, it was to be a few years before the GWR acted. Eventually, however, there was some sort of move forward, and this resulted in four rather splendid vehicles being built during the 1940s. Even so, they were built against the rather tacit assumption that the LMS and LNER trains would be the preferred choice on many occasions — most odd!

The new saloons were built in pairs, first on the scene being two twelve-wheel day saloons (Nos 9001/2), ordered in 1938 and put into service in 1940. They were very fine vehicles but never classified as 'full' Royals at first, being regarded as more general VIP saloons. They were used as such during the war for high-ranking politicians and military men such as Churchill and Eisenhower, but after 1945 they increasingly tended to be regarded as part of the nucleus of a new GWR Royal Train and were indeed often used by Royalty. Both have been privately preserved, one at the Birmingham Railway Museum, the other at the Didcot Railway Centre.

Below far left *GWR Royal Saloon No 9006 in Royal Claret livery. Though it served until 1979, the carriage saw hardly any alterations from its original GWR form. The kitchen is at the near end, the dining room in the centre and the small lounge at the far end*

Below left *The Queen Mother's principal day lounge in GWR Royal Saloon No 9007.*

Right *The East Coast Royal Train photographed between Biggleswade and Sandy in May 1953 on one of its last outings in the varnished teak livery; it was repainted in 1954-5. The engine, 4-6-0 No 61671, was called Royal Sovereign and was always preferred by BR(ER) for Royal Train duty, one of the last examples of railway management going to the trouble of having a dedicated 'Royal' engine. The train itself consists of both principal saloons (in the centre), a dining car, two semi-Royals and two full brakes*

The next major contribution towards the new GWR train was another pair of VIP saloons ordered, rather surprisingly, in 1943. They came into use in 1945 as Nos 9006/7 and had both day and night facilities. In fact, No 9006 was totally self-contained, having a kitchen and dining room as well, but it was not until some years later that they became properly 'Royal'. In 1948 they received a first refurbishment (with air-conditioning) to run with two new Hawksworth brake composites (and Nos 9001/2 if required) as the nucleus of what was hoped to be a new GWR Royal Train. But it was rather too late now for such grandiose plans, given the onset of BR, so the GWR project went no further. The first pair remained as VIP saloons and it was only the consequence of King George VI's premature death in 1952 — and that of Queen Mary in 1953 — which caused Nos 9006/7 to become truly part of the BR Royal fleet.

The principal LMS and LNER saloons were now at the disposal of the present Queen and HRH The Duke of Edinburgh. Accordingly, Nos 9006/7 were extensively refitted in 1955 as the personal saloons for HM Queen Elizabeth the Queen Mother. They usually ran as a pair, No 9007 being Her Majesty's personal saloon (very similarly finished to LMS 799 — see below), No 9006 being for her own personal staff. It was also used to provide the essential catering facilities. No 9007 was the more extensively modified in 1955 so as to enlarge both the Queen's lounge and her principal bedroom, but No 9006 remained virtually pure GWR. At this point they also lost their chocolate and cream colours and were repainted in Royal Train livery. They went on to serve the Queen Mother for nearly a quarter of a century until they made their very last Royal journey to Glasgow in March 1979. Both are now preserved by the National Railway Museum, No 9006 being rendered additionally interesting by having the Queen Mother's own personal china tea and dinner service 'en suite', it having been retained on board the saloon at her special request when the vehicles were saved.

These two saloons were a fitting climax to the GWR carriage story. They are both finished in a restrained but beautifully executed Art Deco style and are just as fine a tribute to the quality of the carriage builders' craft as any of their more elaborate predecessors. It is believed that the Queen Mother was rather sad when their obsolete braking system and running gear in the 100 mph era caused them to be withdrawn; having been privileged to ride inside them on their final journey from Wolverton to York, I can well understand her regret.

During the whole of the grouping period, the LNER Royal Train remained almost exactly as it had been in ECJS days. The normal composition consisted of one or both principal saloons, anything up to four semi-Royal saloons and the two full brakes which served as both staff accommodation and as luggage vans. There was no dedicated dining car as such, the LNER simply using one of its large fleet of first

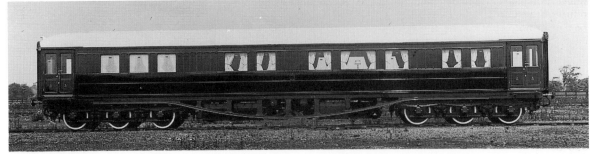

class cars should the need arise. Neither were there any sleeping cars in the formation, which was one reason why it was never as widely used as the LMS train. The only significant change was a form of 'role reversal' for the two principal saloons in 1926.

These splendid twelve-wheelers had been built in 1908-9, one each for King Edward VII (No 395) and Queen Alexandra (No 396). In 1926, No 395 was altered quite extensively for the sole use of HM Queen Mary and was rearranged for day journeys only. In this form it could either form part of the Royal Train or be attached to a service train when the Queen was travelling alone. As far as the internal fittings were concerned, though there was some re-positioning of partitions and doors, the superb quality of the woodwork in both the principal lounge (sycamore and mahogany) and the equerry's compartment (dark and light oak plus boxwood) was not affected. The whole vehicle was refurnished to Queen Mary's personal direction and she used it for the rest of her life. After she died, it was transferred to the use of Queen Elizabeth the Queen Mother, and a further replacement of furniture took place in the mid-1950s, though Queen Mary's personal monograms remained etched into some of the window glazing.

At the same time, No 396 became the principal LNER saloon and exchanged its original outside 'door furniture' with the more elaborate handrails etc which had hitherto been on the King's saloon No 395! In revised form, No 396 became a day saloon for the King and Queen travelling together and in addition to its main lounge had two separate dressing rooms. It also lost quite an amount of its original Edwardian 'Adam'-style plasterwork in the process.

These changes were almost certainly a result of the concentration on the use of the LMS train for all overnight Royal journeys, for until then the LNER saloons could function in this role. After the conversions, this was far less practicable and never, as far as is known, practised. This inevitably meant that the LNER saloons were less often used than the LMS (ex-LNWR) pair, and mainly for this reason they lasted far longer in service. The full LNER set was retained intact until 1961 when it made its last Royal journey in full formation — to York in connection with the wedding of HRH The Duke of Kent. By then, like the LMS set, it had been repainted in Royal Train livery, though not without some sadness at Doncaster when the famous varnished teak scheme

Above *Saloon No 395 after alteration in 1926. HM Queen Mary's monogram was etched into the three obscured glass windows at the left-hand end and is still a feature of the saloon.*

Left *Principal day lounge inside Royal Saloon No 395 showing the furniture provided circa 1955 and subsequently used by HM Queen Elizabeth the Queen Mother.*

Figure 89 *Elevation and plan of East Coast Royal Saloon No 395 as altered by the LNER in 1926 for use by HM Queen Mary.*

Scale: $^1/_{12}'' = 1ft$

was terminated. It is said that some of the old painters refused to be party to such sacrilege, and whether this be true or not, what can be said is that when the luggage van was reinstated to teak livery in the late 1970s (see below), Doncaster did the job with great joy!

The train was disbanded after 1961, but the two principal saloons and one of the luggage vans were retained for another ten years or more, the saloons continuing in use in a variant of their revised 1926 roles, No 396 now being reserved for HM The Queen and the Duke of Edinburgh travelling together, No 396 being an alternative to the GWR pair for the Queen Mother when travelling solely by day. As such they ran well into the 1970s, by which time they had been transferred to Wolverton to be kept alongside the LMS carriages. They were regular visitors to Sandringham, of course, and being marginally less restricted than the LMS saloons were not infrequently used on the Southern system. In the later 1970s, all three were withdrawn for preservation by the National Railway Museum, having had nearly 70 years of active life in Royal service — no mean record. At the time of writing, only the luggage van has been restored to varnished teak (its dark red paintwork was in poor condition when withdrawn) but it is the hope that in due course all three will display the famous East Coast livery and be marshalled together as a single exhibit.

We come now, and finally, to the LMS (ex-LNWR) contribution, without doubt the most celebrated of the pre-BR Royal Trains during the last company phase. This train originated in 1902 with the building of two superb Royal Saloons, followed by six matching semi-Royals a year or so later. It was later augmented by two dining cars and two sleeping cars (eventually there were three of the latter), all of the

standard LNWR pattern, and two staff vehicles, both at first being full brakes. This was the assemblage inherited by the LMS in 1923 and the first change was almost immediate. The two full brakes were replaced by two ex-LNWR corridor brake firsts whose passenger accommodation was modified to offer convertible sleeping berths and whose roofs were given clerestories to match those of the rest of the train. Until the third sleeping car (an elliptical roof example) was added to the fleet, this all-clerestory set was one of the most beautiful trains ever to be seen, especially when running in full formation.

Its beauty was enhanced by the retention of its former LNWR livery at King George V's personal request. Even the Midland-minded LMS had to listen to that, and it remained thus until 1940 when, in the interests of security from air raids and so forth, King George VI agreed to it being painted in standard LMS lake as a sort of camouflage. This apart, the only visible difference for most of the pre-war LMS period was the new company insignia and badges on the carriages replacing those of the old LNWR.

The LMS train was the most fully-integrated formation of any of the Royal Trains and the only one which could provide suitable accommodation for a multi-day operation. For this reason, it was the almost inevitable selection whenever the King needed to be away for several days at a time, and this requirement was increasingly common as years went by. It thus became familiar throughout the land and since the LMS always used it on their own lines anyway for all Royal journeys, its vehicles ran many more miles than those of the other companies.

This was undoubtedly the reason why, in the later 1930s, the LMS began to think about a complete replacement. However, just before this time, the death

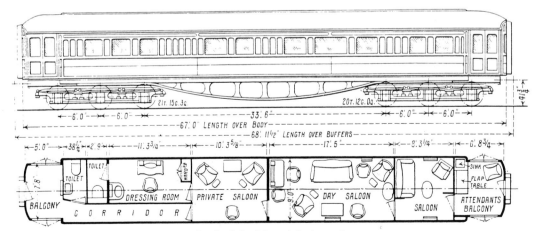

Details of the Saloon as Re-Arranged.

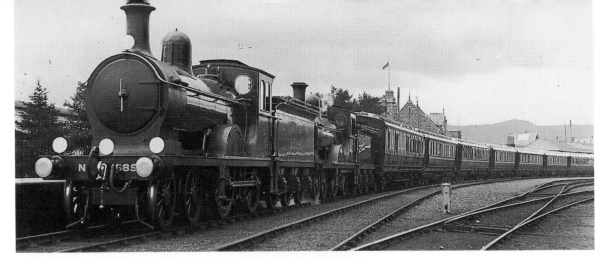

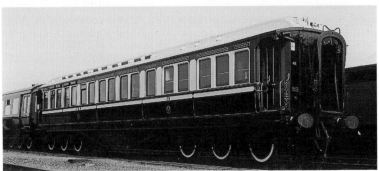

Above *The full LMS Royal Train in its retained LNWR colours at Ballater in August 1928 headed by LNER 4-4-0s Nos 6850* Hatton Castle *and 6846* Benachie. *Only the King appears to have been travelling for the only principal saloon is his, second from the engines. However, there must have been quite a sizeable entourage for there are two semi-Royals, two dining cars and a sleeping car present in the visible portion of the train. A 10–12-coach formation was customary on trips of this nature*

Above left *Royal Dining Car No 76 on its replacement LMS-pattern underframes and now restored to pre-1940 colours*

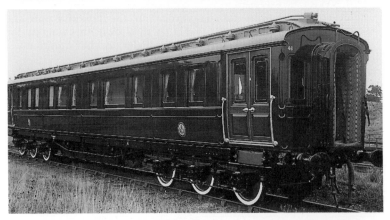

Left *The King's Saloon from the LNWR train in its wartime LMS colours. Note the replacement LMS-pattern axleboxes and side buffers, part of the late 1930s improvements. The carriage, along with its 'twin', has now been restored to its original LNWR livery*

Below left *LMS King's Saloon No 798 in wartime armour plating*

Figure 90 *Diagrams issued after the war giving details of the three new LMS Royal Train vehicles. They show, top to bottom: King's Saloon, Queen's Saloon, Brake and Power Car.*

Scale: $^1/_{12}$*" = 1ft*

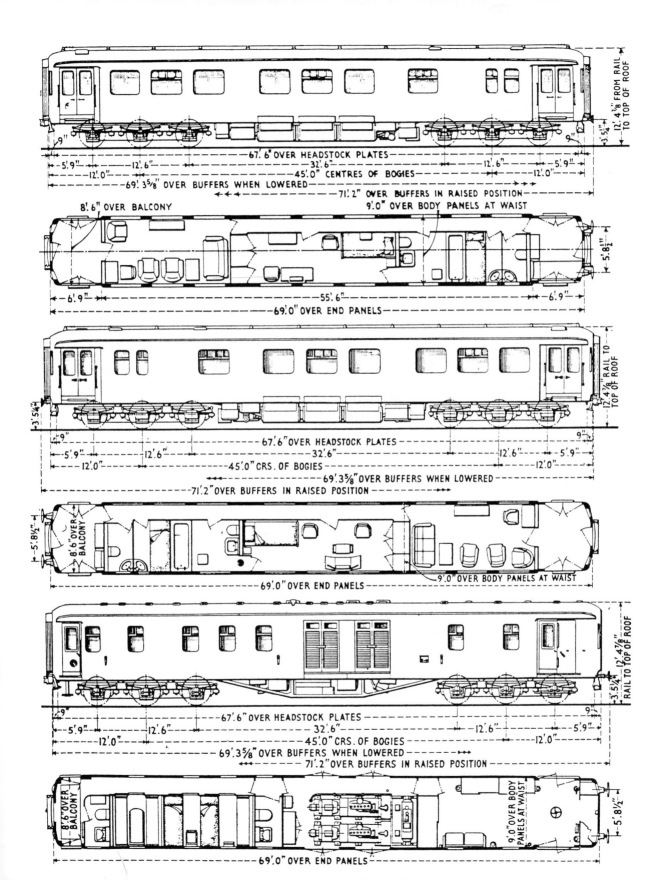

12'.4⅞" FROM RAIL TO TOP OF ROOF

3'.5¼"

9"

67.6' OVER HEADSTOCK PLATES

5'.9" 12'.6" 32.6" 12'.6" 5'.9"

12'.0" 45'.0" CENTRES OF BOGIES 12'.0"

69'.3⅝" OVER BUFFERS WHEN LOWERED

71'.2" OVER BUFFERS IN RAISED POSITION

9.0" OVER BODY PANELS AT WAIST

8'.6" OVER BALCONY

5'.8½"

6'.9" 55'.6" 6'.9"

69'.0" OVER END PANELS

3'.5¼"

12'.4½" RAIL TO TOP OF ROOF

9"

67.6" OVER HEADSTOCK PLATES

5'.9" 12'.6" 32.6" 12'.6" 5'.9"

12'.0" 45'.0" CRS. OF BOGIES 12'.0"

69'.3⅝" OVER BUFFERS WHEN LOWERED

71'.2" OVER BUFFERS IN RAISED POSITION

5'.8½" OVER BALCONY

8'.6" OVER BALCONY

69'.0" OVER END PANELS

9.0" OVER BODY PANELS AT WAIST

12'.4⅞" RAIL TO TOP OF ROOF

3'.5¼"

9"

67.6" OVER HEADSTOCK PLATES

5'.9" 12'.6" 32.6" 12'.6" 5'.9"

12'.0" 45'.0" CRS. OF BOGIES 12'.0"

69'.3⅝" OVER BUFFERS WHEN LOWERED

71'.2" OVER BUFFERS IN RAISED POSITION

8'.6" OVER BALCONY

9.0" OVER BODY PANELS AT WAIST

5'.8½"

69'.0" OVER END PANELS

End detail of Saloon No 798 as preserved, showing the totally smooth finish and the reinstated LMS livery. This vehicle is now on public display at the Museum of Transport, Glasgow, having been lent by the NRM in connection with the opening of the enlarged transport display at Kelvinhall in 1988.

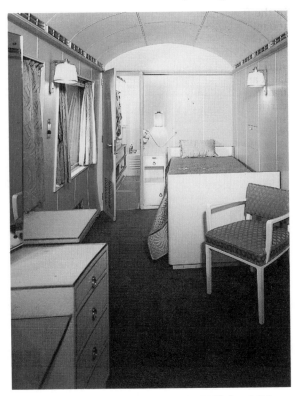

Much attention was given to detail in the LMS Royal Saloons. This is the principal bedroom in Saloon No 799. Note the neatly located air conditioning grilles between sides and roof.

of King George V had made it seem for a while as though there may be no further need for any Royal Trains. King Edward VIII generally preferred motor cars and aeroplanes and, if travelling by train, usually chose to use the LMS President's saloon rather than the full train. But the abdication crisis of 1936 brought another family man to the throne, and the LMS dusted down its plans.

Part of the problem was the age of the train combined with its heavy usage and the fact that railway speeds were increasing. A new train was the ideal answer, but as an interim solution during 1937-8 the LMS fitted heavy-duty axleboxes and drawgear to the whole Royal fleet, put new angle-trussed underframes beneath the Royal dining car and the two staff brakes and replaced the wood-centred Mansell wheels which were fitted to most of the carriages with modern all-steel disc wheels. This, in essence, was how most of the carriages in the train were to see out their lives.

In 1938, the LMS at last issued the order for two new Royal Saloons of ultra-modern type as the first stage of what is thought to have been a total replacement programme, but the war clouds came and the project was shelved. The old train remained in use and, as stated, was repainted to make it somewhat less conspicuous. But its carriages were still wood-bodied, there was an ever-present fear of air raids, and the King and Queen were not noted at the time for keeping clear of danger, regularly visiting many areas of the country which were under air attack. In consequence, the LMS was authorized to build its two new saloons (No 798 for the King, No 799 for the Queen) and fit them with armour plating. This was done in great secrecy during 1941 and they were accompanied by a third vehicle, an escort and power car, which contained a diesel generator to provide electrical power during the many periods when the train was standing overnight during its very regular wartime travels. It was not until after the war that full details of the new vehicles were released, almost simultaneously with the removal of the wartime armour plating from the saloons.

These new carriages have many times been described in detail, some of the sources being listed in the Bibliography, so there is no reason to repeat too much here. Basically they were constructed to an entirely new shape and style but embodying traditional Stanier-period LMS methods. The bodies were steel-panelled on timber frames, heavily sound-insulated and mounted on the latest type of welded underframe. They were also the first and only LMS carriages to feature buckeye couplings and Pullman-style gangways, a fact which caused many of the older Royal carriages to have gangway adapters fitted. The outsides were very smoothly finished with all corners rounded and no obvious cantrail, a sort of early prediction of the BR Mk II shape, if you like. Interiors were thoroughly modern in decor employing traditional LMS timber finishes throughout and soft colour shades. All was done with the utmost simplicity combined with quality and they must have been relaxing vehicles in which to travel. Full air-conditioning was installed in both saloons, using ice-boxes below the floor as the main cooling medium. They were also very heavy, even without their armour plate.

From late 1941, the two new saloons replaced the old LNWR saloons for most journeys, but the two 1902 carriages still remained in reserve, so to speak, and were given modernized bathrooms in the general style of the 1941 carriages. As such, they too remained in regular if less frequent use until 1947, spending much of the wartime period as a sort of permanent stand-by in Scotland. They were finally retired in the autumn of 1947 and went into store at Wolverton. In due course they were put on show in their final LMS livery at the Museum of British Transport at Clapham and came to the NRM in 1975. Since that time, both saloons have been fully repainted inside and out, opportunity being taken at the writer's suggestion to reinstate the famous old LNWR livery at the same time. In the flesh, so to speak, this colour scheme looks even more breathtaking than the most vivid imagination could conjure up.

The need for a power car with the two new LMS saloons caused one of the former LNWR brakes to be further modified as a stand-by in this role and it too was given a generator. From this time onwards, the principal British Royal Train has always carried its own generating capability and all vehicles were modified with through conduits to accept this external power supply both when the train was stationary and even sometimes on the move. Finally, the oldest

vehicle in the Royal Train, the 1900 vintage dining car, had one of its two passenger areas opened out in 1942 to form a more conventional dining room with central table and chairs. No doubt it also formed a very suitable, if small, conference room when required; in fact, this may well be why it was so converted.

Post-war austerity meant that no further new additions could be made to the train and it is rather unlikely that the King, always acutely aware of the hardships faced by his subjects, would have been happy even had this idea been suggested to him. So the planned LMS train never got beyond its first three carriages, and it was not until the mid-1950s that further changes took place.

Thus, most of the old LNWR Royal Train vehicles were to serve many more years of life before they too were able to be replaced. In fact, the next to go was not until well into BR days in 1956, when the Royal Dining Car was replaced along with some of the semi-Royals. The sleeping cars lasted until the late 1960s and the two service vehicles were not to be replaced in principal service until Jubilee year, 1977, and even then were kept in reserve for another year or so until finally released to the NRM in 1979. Very appropriately, one of them, the reserve power car No 5154, made its last Royal trip in March 1979 with the last working of the Queen Mother's GWR saloons (see above).

During the whole of the time between the building of the 1941 saloons and the late 1980s, there was always some former LNWR element incorporated in the Royal Train, which tended in consequence to get ever more untidy looking as gradual changes were made. So strong indeed was the element of continuity throughout its whole history that it is difficult to find a convenient stopping point for this part of the story. Perhaps it will suffice to say for the moment that no fewer than seven of the LNWR carriages have survived (five at the NRM and two in private hands) along with the 1941 LMS pair; and by the time this book appears, an eighth LNWR vehicle in the form of the old LMS President's saloon should have joined the NRM collection. This last pre-group survivor was latterly used for railway officers accompanying the Royal Train, a function it discharged until 1989.

28. Other coaching stock developments

Before concluding the main part of our story, we must first give brief attention to those vehicles which do not fall tidily into any of the categories so far covered, so as to give them at least some passing mention in the interests of overall completeness. Dominant by far will be the non-passenger-carrying stock, but there will be mention of some few types which did carry people, such as push-pull coaches and special saloons.

A few overall points should, however, be made clear from the start: in none of the categories covered in this chapter was there much to be seen in the way of design innovation during the grouping period. For one thing, as Chapter 14 in   Part I   has indicated, the function of most non-passenger-carrying coaching stock had been well and truly identified long before 1923 and often provided for quite lavishly, thus reducing the need for adding too excessively to the existing pre-group fleets. Secondly, some categories of traffic went into a gradual decline as a result of road competition, thus making less demand on the railways anyway. Thirdly, and particularly in the realm of passenger-carrying vehicles, most of the requirements could actually be met by pre-group stock either as it stood or, as Chapter 25 has already half-hinted, by conversion, so there was little need for very much in the way of new construction.

Non-passenger-carrying coaching stock

The categories of vehicle outlined in Chapter 14 remained broadly unchanged during the grouping period, so there is no need for repetition, but it has to be said that even though the traffic they handled represented a fair proportion of railway revenue, there was little to arouse excitement in most of the vehicles built new for the purpose during the final company phase. This was, if you like, a sort of back-handed compliment to the pre-group era in having got it right so often; thus, with few exceptions, the 'Big Four' did not take matters very much further. But then, why should they? I once heard it said: 'If it is not necessary for something to be changed then it is necessary that it should not be changed.' And this certainly seems to have been a principle applied to many vehicles in the non-passenger category.

Take, for example, that most obvious non-passenger type, the full brake, including its closely allied luggage and parcels van relations. Many a hundred more were built but almost all were mostly related to their passenger-carrying contemporaries, especially in visual terms, and that just about says all. They remained basically boxes on wheels for the carriage of all manner of traffic which needed safe high-speed transit in a covered vehicle, and most railways built them on an 'as required' basis, following their usual stylistic pattern. There was a gradual increase in the bogie type but four-wheel and six-wheel variants continued to be offered and one supposes that cost considerations were as like as not the reason for the choices.

Cost considerations too were undoubtedly behind the conversion to full brake form in both the early 1920s and late 1940s of many former ambulance vehicles after the two world wars. These carriages, almost a special study in their own right, were very numerous and usually took the form of purpose-built conversions of former passenger-carrying stock into mobile hospital form. They contained ward, operating and treatment cars, which, together with the essential staff accommodation vehicles, formed one of the very few positive contributions to humanity which may be said to have emerged from these global tragedies.

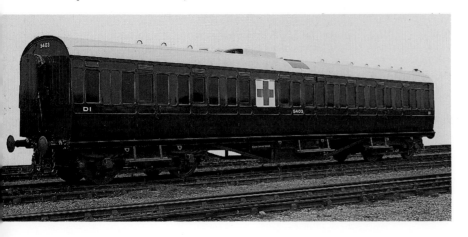

LMS ambulance carriage No 5403 was converted in 1939 from a former eight-compartment corridor third, built during the mid-1920s. It was altered into what was called a 'Kitchen and Sick Officers Car,' but its origins were still visibly obvious from the outside. Inside, however, the conversions often involved completely stripping the interior and this fact, after the war, made them eminently suitable for further use as brake and luggage vans, a much cheaper option than building new ones or even converting them back to their original function. Many hundreds were thus treated, but the ultimate fate of the coach shown here is not known.

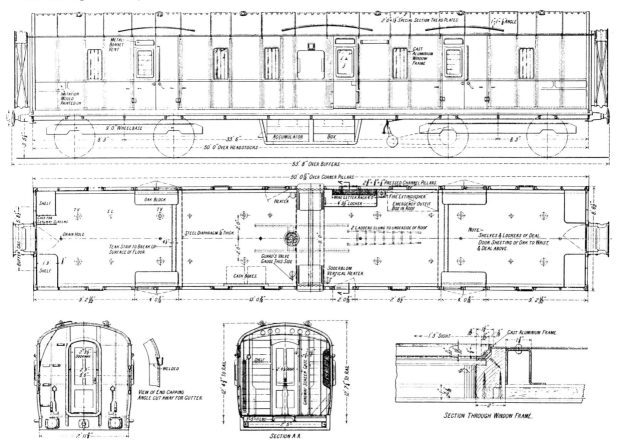

Figure 91 *Detailed drawings of the 'all-steel' LMS full brakes of 1926.*

Scale: 3mm = 1ft

Both conflicts were to see examples of the genre and their company origins were usually readily apparent since the externals remained little changed. Many went overseas for service close to the front lines and were never to return, but many more came back. Some of these were reinstated to their former roles and as we have seen, some of them went to Pullman to enjoy a somewhat more exotic future, at least as far as their running gear was concerned; but far more were simply regarded as a cheap and cheerful way of providing a fresh supply of brake and luggage vans when things got back to normal. The LMS was particularly adept at this sort of thing on both occasions.

The LMS too was responsible for just about the only significant structural change in full brakes built new as such — and even then not overly dramatic — when it experimented with all-steel full brakes from 'the trade' at the same time as its purchase of

similar passenger-carrying stock in the later 1920s. As with the carriages, so with the full brakes: only the knowledgeable could really tell the difference between them and conventionally built examples. One of them was given a vitreous enamelled finish to try and make savings in painting costs, but nothing much came of this experiment and it was not repeated.

Of the 'Big Four' at this time, the Southern seems to have been the least user of passenger full brakes, preferring instead the more versatile 'general utility' van, probably working on the basis that since most of its services were passenger-carrying anyway, there would almost always be a guard's compartment somewhere in the train, thus enabling some manufacturing economies to be made in the non-passenger arena; perusal of many hundreds of pictures of typical locomotive-hauled Southern passenger trains at the time — and well into BR days for that matter — certainly leads to this conclusion.

This led to much building of those most characteristically 'Southern' non-passenger vehicles, the

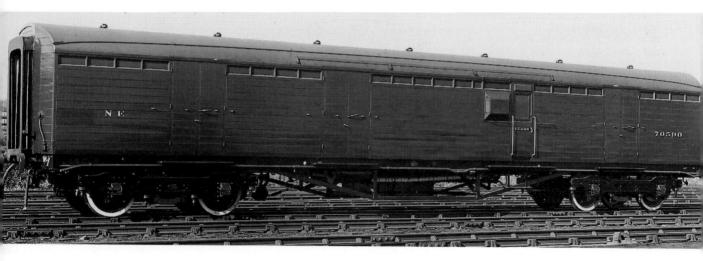

outside framed GUVs, in both four-wheel and eight-wheel form. The latter, it need hardly be said, were often given second-hand underframes. They were to be seen everywhere, not just on the Southern, and were amongst the longest-lived of pre-BR coaching stock. Their inspiration was an original SE & CR four-wheel design which the Southern repeated for many years with little real change, and also developed it into bogie form. Its predominantly 'goods vehicle' structural style undoubtedly saved money, and this particular Southern approach to the business was probably the most distinctively different of any of the 'Big Four' offerings in this field.

After the grouping, the carriage truck business outlined in Chap. 14 was to undergo some quite fundamental changes, usually consequent upon the gradual reduction in horse-drawn traffic compared with its motorized successor. This usually meant that the better open carriage trucks of the pre-group period were normally sufficient to cope with the reducing demand for non-covered movement of vehicular traffic. In fact, they became increasingly used for such things as agricultural machinery and even (suitably modified) for container traffic. The covered version, however, did fare rather better, but not always in the carriage-carrying field. Some indeed were used this way, especially for the growing traffic in the rail-haulage of motor cars where covered vehicles were often preferred, but it was to be well into BR days before this type of vehicle was to be seen in any great quantity. Meantime, the CCTs became ever more versatile in their variety of usage and were increasingly regarded as end-door GUVs (see above).

Thus, when the LNER built a new batch in 1928, although they were styled as CCTs, it is no surprise to note that a contemporary description stated: 'The vehicles are of general utility type — that is to say they are arranged to afford the fullest utility possible in the conveyance of different classes of traffic, so that in addition to the usual folding and falling doors at each end for the admission of wheeled vehicles, theatrical scenery, aeroplanes and other bulky loads, special provision has been made for the reception of parcels, fruit, pigeons, or small livestock which can be carried upon hinged shelves arranged in tiers along each side.' The accompanying drawing should make things clearer, and these vans were entirely typical of the products of all the railways, even down to their re-use of older underframes. In fact, over the years there was to be a gradual blurring of the edges between the use made of CCTs and GUVs and it got to the point where only the end-loading doors of the CCT marked any significant difference between the two.

In the 'valuable livestock' field, increasing road competition also tended to bite into the railways' earlier monopoly, and once again the better pre-group offerings often tended to suffice for much of the trade. But there was enough call to justify some new construction of horse-boxes and prize cattle vans, which process continued at diminishing level right through into BR days. Almost all of them were long-wheelbase four-wheelers whose nature differed little from that of their pre-1923 ancestors; but it only needed a race meeting or something similar for the railways to find reason for turning out whole trains of these vehicles in the pre-motorway age. It is all gone now, but during the company period it remained common enough.

Another category which held up well throughout the grouping period was that of perishable cargo, particularly but not exclusively the carriage of fish and milk. The former trade was increasingly to be han-

Left *In the austerity post-war years, any savings were worth having and Thompson on the LNER experimented with tongue and groove boarding in place of conventional panelling on many passenger brakes. This is No 70590 when new in 1945, one of more than 50 such, covered with deal planking and painted plain brown*

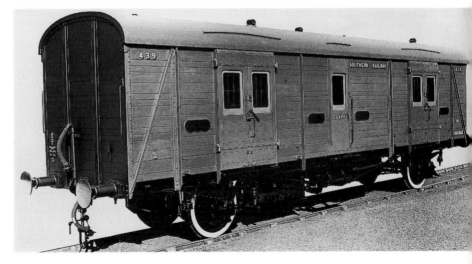

Right and below right *The 'freight vehicle' nature of many Southern Railway luggage vans is emphasized here. Four-wheeler No 439 was one of many variations from the original SE & CR design which went on being built until the end of SR days, while gangwayed bogie van No 2319 dated from 1932, though its running gear was clearly older! Note that the guard was also expected to ride in the four-wheeler*

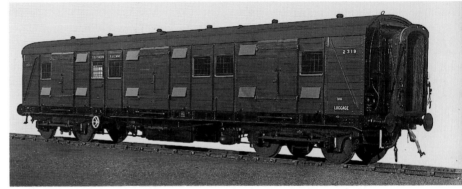

Figure 92 Elevations and plan of the 1928 LNER Covered Carriage Trucks referred to in the text as being of 'general utility' type.

Scale: $^1/_{10}"$ = 1ft

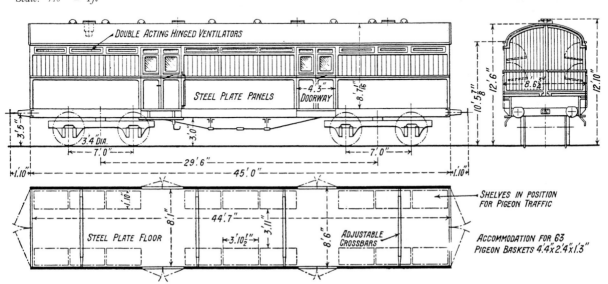

Elevation and Plan of New Covered Carriage Trucks, L.N.E.R.

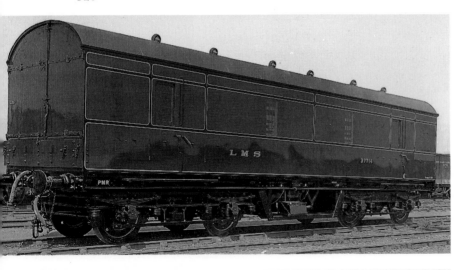

This page *The end-door CCT/GUV became a very common company type, three quite typical examples being shown here. Oddly enough, the oldest by far was the most modern looking: LMS No 37714, built in 1933 with flush steel panelling and fully lined passenger livery. It was classified 'Luggage and Parcels' but was, in fact, a CCT, and probably the major stylistic influence in the BR continuation. The Southern and LNER examples both displayed freight characteristics and were built in 1938 and 1939 respectively. SR No 4596 was classified for the carriage of theatrical scenery, and LNER No 1296 for motor cars, but as with the LMS example one doubts whether these functions remained the exclusive purpose of these versatile vehicles.*

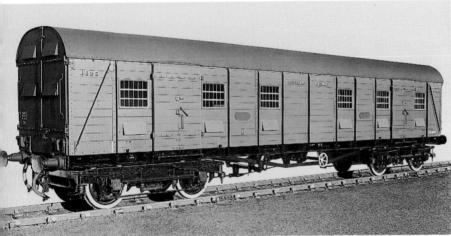

Above right *Though it built quite a few for itself, the LMS also inherited many fine pre-group horse-boxes. This rather handsome if old-fashioned example is ex-Highland Railway No 43792, still in very good condition in the late 1930s*

Middle right *The LNER served much horse-racing territory and 'Return to Leyburn', painted on No 2259, was undoubtedly tied up with the racing stables at close-by Middleham. This was a new horse-box in 1936, one of 50, and by no means the last LNER essay in this field. In fact, the final LNER horse-box design was actually adopted by the London Midland Region after the formation of BR!*

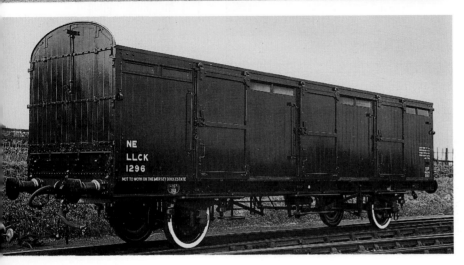

Right *The GWR may well have been the biggest single conveyor of milk in bulk during the company period. This fine view, taken at Patchway in the later 1930s, shows a down working of a characteristically mixed bag of empties from London headed by 4-6-0 No 2902 Lady of the Lake. The leading bogie 'Siphon' was a common GWR type and would handle the churn traffic, as would the third vehicle too, but perhaps most noteworthy is the no fewer than ten six-wheel milk tanks visible in the train. Collectively, these, when loaded, could probably fill well over 200,000 milk bottles!*

dled by covered fish vans which looked very little different from goods wagons, save for the speed at which they ran, and again new building went on throughout the company period, though, as before, there was little change in the nature of the new vehicles provided. In fact, many of them were to unaltered pre-group designs, and even where new versions were offered in later years there was little innovation. Some LMS six-wheel fish vans built at Wolverton in 1947, for example, could just as well have emerged 30 years earlier as far as their general sophistication was concerned! Perhaps there was no perceived need, who can say, but it was to be well into BR days before any even mildly radical new ideas began to emerge, by which time it was too late.

Much the same was true of milk traffic in the first ten years or so after 1923, where, if any new ones were needed at all, pre-group-styled milk vans continued to be built and ply their traditional trade from all corners of the kingdom. The 'early morning milk train' was no flight of literary fancy in those days; but the gradual move from churn milk to bulk milk haulage did cause one of the few genuine design changes to take place. It is a moot point whether the vehicles which emerged should appear in a carriage book at all, for they were in fact tank wagons by any other name, but since the railways always regarded them as 'passenger rated' stock, they do at least warrant brief mention.*

The cause was the gradual concentration of milk distribution at purpose-built depots out in the country to which milk could be brought from the farms in churns but from which it was far simpler to

* For a much more detailed survey of the evolution of rail-borne milk traffic, see *'Milko!'*, by T.W.Bourne: 'Railways South East', Vol 2 No 4, Summer 1989.

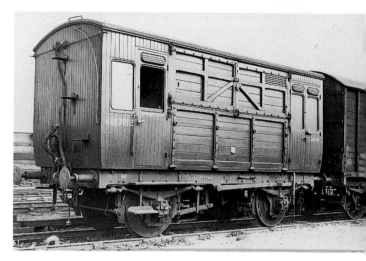

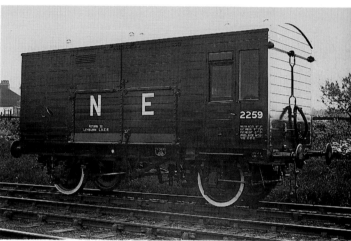

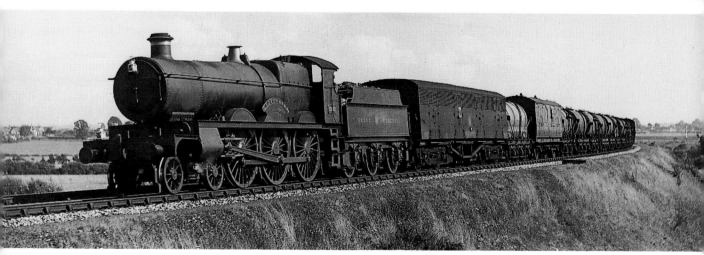

LNER six-wheel 'flat' wagon No 217298 for road/rail milk tanks, built in 1936 and rated for use in passenger trains. The road tanks could be either company or privately owned.

despatch the product in bulk tanks to the large towns and cities. The railways responded in one of two ways. By far the most common was the dedicated milk tank, which was simply a glass-lined tank mounted on a railway chassis capable of passenger speed. At first four-wheelers were used, but the railways soon established that six wheels were needed for this sort of high-speed transit, and from 1937 all milk tanks were thus equipped. An interesting point about them was that the tank belonged to the dairy itself and only the chassis was owned by the railway! But it led to a short-lived and colourful explosion of private owner colour schemes until the Second World War came along.

The second solution was a road/rail milk tank whereby the tank itself was mounted on road wheels (in effect it was the 'trailer' portion of a road unit), the whole being then transhipped at the appropriate railhead to a specially adapted six-wheel rail chassis for its long-distance move. They were not very common compared with the dedicated milk tanks, but did represent a worthy idea which deserved a better long-term outcome.

Milk handling in bulk became ever more widespread, though the traditional churn traffic held up quite well alongside it and milk specials consisting of both forms of vehicle were common well into BR days until they too fell foul of road competition. Fortunately, the NRM has managed to preserve typical examples of both modes of bulk milk haulage.

The last major category of non-passenger coaching stock to be considered is also one of the oldest forms, happily still with us in modern day: the Travelling Post Office (TPO). From a very early stage, the characteristic and specialized vehicles provided for this purpose have always been jointly financed by the railways and the Post Office, though maintained by the former. Their very specialized function and inter-

nal layout is well known and was established long before the grouping period. Furthermore, there were never very many of them in absolute terms, and since their usage was less intensive than most passenger-carrying stock, they tended to enjoy longer service lives. Thus, yet again, the pre-group examples enjoyed many more years of active life after 1923.

When the time came to make some new provision, the vehicular types had settled down, more or less, to but two basic types of carriage, the Post Office Sorting Van (POS) and the Post Office Tender (POT), the latter being mainly a travelling storage vehicle with no *en route* sorting facility. These were, of course, supplemented to a very great extent by the railway-owned luggage and parcels vans of many a hundred orthodox passenger trains which brought the mails to the central distribution points from which the dedicated TPOs would then take over. This basic *modus operandi* may still be observed today, though, I fear, much reduced from its earlier universality.

The biggest provider of dedicated TPOs was, without doubt, the LMS, mainly in consequence of its operation of the key 'Irish Mail' and 'West Coast Postal' services which have always been at the heart of the British mail distribution network; yet even the LMS contribution numbered something less than 70 vehicles built to company designs, the last of which did not appear until 1954. Moreover, such was the resilience of older TPOs that neither the LMS nor the LNER saw fit to provide any new examples at all until 1929. By then, the basic design of POS had settled down to a largely standard layout, well exemplified by the two drawings appended. The GWR equivalent was no whit different in operational status, and the Southern too joined in the act with a few neatly designed contributions. All were, of course, bogie vehicles by now and the companies followed whichever version of their own external styling and livery was currently in vogue, the SR being the only one of the four which did not offer lineside pick-up apparatus. This was perhaps the most publicly understood 'face' of the TPO: an operation immortalized for ever in that wonderful LMS documentary film of the 1930s, 'Night Mail', with its marvellously evocative W.H.Auden commentary poem.

That said, however, little more of significance remains to be mentioned in the general overview context of non-passenger operations. It was an unsung and generally non-glamorous part of the total railway package which, though a very considerable revenue earner throughout the period under review, was also under constant attrition from the fast growing road competition. Whether the grouped railways ever really came to grips with the seriousness of this problem is rather doubtful; this was an issue which

BR had to face in far more dramatic form and which the next volume will try to address. But in so far as the grouped railways were concerned, its outward manifestation seems mostly to have been in the gradual reduction of vehicle types, the coming together of CCT/GUV (see above) being perhaps the most obvious, combined with maybe just a little complacency in vehicle provisioning which led to the design stagnation already hinted at. The fact is, however, that except for a rather reduced level of mail services and some residual CCT/GUV-type traffic, the modern railway has seen the removal of almost all other forms of traditional non-passenger coaching stock revenue from its books. Some of the warning signs were there during the company period, but whether anything more could have been done is perhaps outwith the scope of this survey. And there we will leave it for the moment.

Right *TPOs were another area of non-passenger stock where older vehicles lasted well, and the former Highland Railway was surprisingly well represented (see also page 263). This view shows one of only three sorting vans which it owned, No M30321, still in service in early BR days on the 'Highland TPO' (Gavin Wilson).*

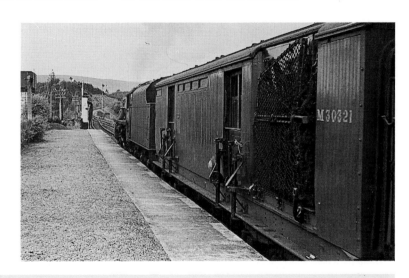

Below *The Post Office Tender, or stowage van, is exemplified by LNER No 30281, built in 1946. Like many GPO-sponsored carriages, it turned out to be a one-off.*

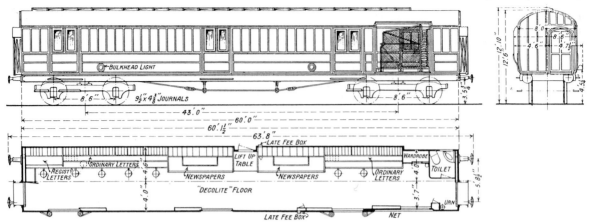

General View, Side and End Elevations and Plan of New Postal Van, L.N.E.R.

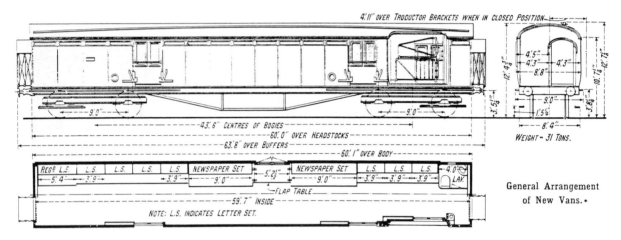

General Arrangement
of New Vans.

Figure 93 *Comparative elevations and plans of the 1928 LNER TPOs for the King's Cross–Newcastle service and the 1932 LMS design for the West Coast Postal and other services.*

Scale: 2mm = 1ft

Other passenger-carrying vehicles

It is almost axiomatic in railway terms that, wherever possible, items of rolling-stock are allowed to perform a useful function for just as long as their basic structure will allow. Historically, this goes back to the very dawn of the railway era, and we have already seen some of the post-grouping consequences in Chapter 25. It was, in large part, a combination of the quality of the original construction with the natural desire of the railways not to spend more than was necessary in order to maintain their traffic. In our present day it still goes on, of course, but is influenced by changing fashion to an extent far

exceeding that which was relevant in the company period. Railway vehicles are, in general, not of the 'throw away after ten years' kind, so prevalent in the modern motor vehicle, and in this lies both their strength and their weakness.

In the passenger-carrying mode, this longevity has proved to be more of a problem in the modern age than during earlier days when fashions changed rather less often. In consequence, the railways were often able to meet many of the new challenges by selective adaptation and rebuilding, and nowhere was this more so than in the realm of special saloons and branch line (or similar) services. In these areas, so much of the post-grouping activity was conducted by means of older vehicles that the need for new items was very small indeed; but those which were built are not without interest.

Starting with the special saloons, it has already been demonstrated that even in the exalted Royal sphere, the pre-group contribution mostly sufficed during the 'Big Four' era, so it would be surprising indeed if the railways had found it needful to augment their lesser saloon fleets, and so it was to prove. In fact, hardly anything at all was added to the 1923 lists. For the most part, this was due to the changing demands of the public in the rapidly motorizing brave new world of the 1920s and 1930s; such firmly established Victorian and Edwardian favourites as family and invalid saloons had no real place in the sort of changing environment where their most likely users were almost certainly amongst the first to adopt the motor car alternative. In consequence, the few residual demands for this sort of thing could be and almost always were met from earlier stock; and even that proved to offer an excessive over-capacity to the point where many were either converted to third class picnic form or given a fresh lease of life in a purely internal railway 'departmental' role. Hardly ever was anything new actually built for this purpose, and even the picnic conversions were mostly a forlorn 'last hope'.

Against this background, therefore, it is rather surprising that such as the 1930 GWR private saloons mentioned in Chapter 11 were built at all, and by any criteria almost amazing that the fairly hard-nosed LMS should witness the building of not only the rather useless but attractive Club Saloon of the 1939

Coronation Scot (see page 230) but had also countenanced a brand new Stanier pattern Manchester-Blackpool Club Car some three years earlier. Even if the 1939 car may well have been justified purely for publicity purposes, the 1935 car seems to have been a quite genuine offering, doubtless very much appreciated by its patrons; but one cannot help but feel that an equally amenable alternative could have been offered by rebuilding at far lower cost, if such was needed at all. It hardly need be stated that the idea was never repeated.

In fact, setting aside these odd few mavericks, the only new saloons which were built during the final company period were mostly of the self-indulgent 'inspection' or 'officers' type whose function was explained in the previous volume. In all cases they had to await the final company years to emerge, if only because there were plenty of pre-group types still available. But when they finally did come out there was no stinting, even though most of them actually appeared during the post-1939 austerity years, some indeed after the formation of BR. Surprisingly, by far the most profligate provider was the LMS which, in the dark days of 1940, introduced the first of an eventual total of 14 new 50-foot bogie inspection saloons to replace its miscellaneous pre-group fleet. They were probably only marginally necessary, but they did at least enjoy a long life, lasting well into the 1980s, and one supposes, saving BR the need to spend much more money on similar provisioning! Some are privately preserved.

But if these carriages were marginal in justification, they were topped out by two wildly extravagant President's Saloons which the LMS built in 1942. In this context it should be appreciated that 'President' was not the title of some foreign dignitary, on which basis they may have had some validity, but was the

One of the most handsome of the few post-grouping additions to the specialist field was the surprising conversion in 1938-9 of former SE & CR carriage No 7919 into an invalid saloon. It was one of a few similar vehicles to be used in the former SE & CR Royal Train and may well have been included in the formation shown on page 513. In fact, its conversion may not have been unconnected with the contemporary disbandment of the Southern Royal Train; such accounts as survive are rather 'thin' on these interesting facts!

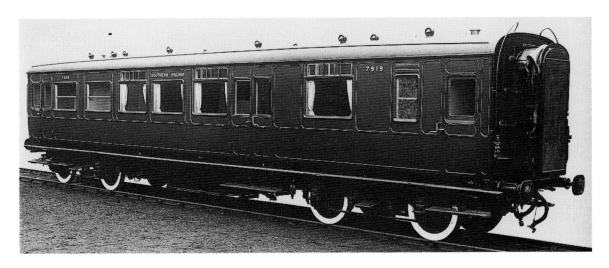

LMS Engineers' Inspection Saloon No 45026 emerged in the dark days of 1944, though heaven only knows why such extravagance was permitted at this time. It is seen in use a year or two later, still bearing the utility unlined LMS livery

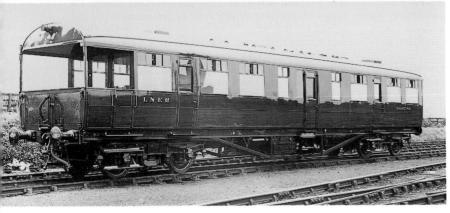

LNER Inspection Saloon No 900580 also emerged during the war in 1943, but was converted to open balcony form in 1945 with a gangway at the opposite end. This April 1945 view shows the end product, perhaps the most odd feature being the extravagant application of a full painted 'teak' livery.

nomenclature of the LMS Chief Executive, in consequence of the LMS running its affairs along American-inspired corporate management methods, unique in British railway administration at that time. This was, in fact, quite a good way of running such a big railway, and the two carriages in question were put to very good use if not quite as originally envisaged. During the war, they were most often put to VVIP use by high-ranking political and military figures, and in 1948 were permanently added to the LMS Royal fleet, at first for the exclusive use of HRH The Princess Elizabeth and Prince Philip after their marriage, but later (1952 onwards) for other members of the Royal Family and/or the Royal Household. As such, they were given Royal Train livery in 1954-5 and could have been included in the previous chapter, but since they were actually built as Officers Saloons they seem more appropriate here. Both of them still survive.

There were also a few modern GWR-designed official saloons, one of which is preserved at the NRM, and a pair of rather nice Thompson-period LNER-pattern offerings, latterly used during the 1980s as

public observation saloons on BR's 'tourist' trains in Scotland after their withdrawal from inspection service; but undoubtedly the most unorthodox of the 'new wave' official coaches was, as might cause no real surprise, the brainchild of that *enfant terrible* of the company era, one Oliver S. Bulleid. It was designated as an inspection saloon, but in fact was the one and only post-1923 Southern Railway attempt at producing a proper form of sleeping car.

Built in 1946, it was, by any criteria, pretty awful. For one thing, it was faced in plywood, a material which, from his LNER experience with the tourist stock, Bulleid ought to have known was doomed to long-term failure, being wholly unsuited to the hurly burly of railway use; but secondly, its internal layout seems to have been designed to be as different as possible from the time-proven LMS, LNER and GWR arrangement as for any other reason. The compartments were arrayed on either side of a central gangway and the berths were longitudinal. There was only one entrance, central on each side of the carriage, while the outside windows were high up on the carriage side in the manner of the worst excesses of the not well-loved 'Tavern Cars' (see page 102). All told, the effect must have been appallingly claustrophobic for those railway officials who had to ride in it, and it is maybe just as well that its style was never adopted for main-line service and that its very existence is mostly unknown! It went, largely unmourned, to the breakers in 1953.

Turning finally to the more publicly accessible vehicles relevant to this section of our survey, we come to that much-loved railway operation, the push-pull train. Chap.15. has explained its origins and Chapter 25 has given a few typical exemplars of the older conversions, but here we shall concentrate on the new examples built during the grouping era. In truth, there were none too many.

We may instantly dismiss the Southern Railway, for although, proportional to its size, it probably made more use of the push-pull mode than any of the 'Big Four', it was achieved entirely by the very clever rebuilding of pre-1923 company stock, and in this context the Southern probably merits almost as much commendation as for its EMU conversions of older stock; they were well thought out and undoubtedly gave much valuable service for a generation or more in such areas as did not justify the third rail. For much the same reason, the LNER also needs but little mention in this regard for it most often tended to espouse the railcar alternative for many of these workings, and made no mean fist of things as Chap 24 has attempted to show. Even though it produced some conventional non-corridor-style push-pull stock as well, these can be realistically ignored in the broader general picture. Which leaves us with the LMS and GWR to consider.

In both cases, the two companies concerned adopted a mixture of pre-group stock and new build. They both had considerable use for such operations, but the end product was rather different and, in the case of the GWR, not uninfluenced by its growing experience with diesel railcars from the mid-1930s onwards. Why they should have been so different is hard to say with certainty, and no doubt prejudiced supporters of the two concerns will advance cogent if not altogether logical reasons for the different approaches, but thus it was.

The LMS was undoubtedly the more conventional. Apart from the LNWR, which had at least tried to devise some new forms of carriage styling for the more bucolic areas of its system, there was no vast inherited tradition of conceptual change as far as the LMS was concerned. Most of its acquired push-pull services were in the hands of converted non-corridor compartment stock, and thus it was to remain both for those and for the new services converted to this mode. True, there were later conversions of a few side-corridor carriages and, of course, the retention of any purpose-built stock which would suffice, but the general feeling seems to have been that orthodox carriage types would suffice for the bulk of these lesser services. In consequence, and added to the conversions of older pre-group stock which it also undertook with great vigour, the best the LMS ever contemplated in terms of new vehicles was merely to adapt its orthodox non-corridor designs for 'motor train' use, as it preferred to call the business. Some were, in fact, conversions of almost new conventional carriages, but others were built new for the job and this went on until *circa* 1950; in fact, just about the only thing which identified an LMS-built push-pull coach from its conventional equivalent were the extra vacuum brake pipes and the windows in the driving versions of the brake ended carriages.

The GWR was very different. For one thing, it had made much greater use of steam railmotors in the pre-1923 period, and although these vehicles had shown quite considerable limitations (Chapter 15)

LMS push-pull driving brake third No 24413 was built new as such in 1933 at the start of the Stanier era, but showed no real innovation in design compared with its conventional non-corridor equivalent; in fact, many more of this type were simply converted from the normal locomotive-hauled fleet than were built new as such

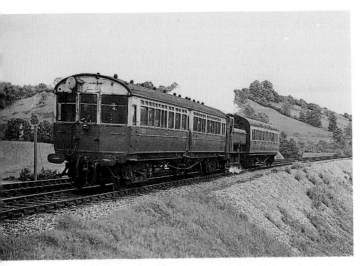

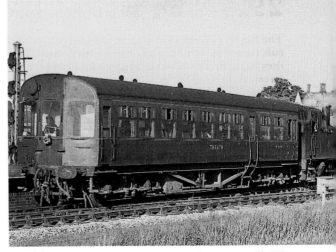

The archetypal GWR local scene of the 1930s: a Castle Cary–Taunton local train consisting of an unidentified Class '54xx' 0-6-0 pannier tank sandwiched between leading auto-trailer No 213, itself converted from steam railmotor No 96, and an unidentified bow-ended corridor third.

BR-built GWR-type auto-trailer No W221W 'Thrush' at Aylesbury in 1962 in the charge of 0-4-2T No 1455 (T.J. Edgington Collection).

they had also helped establish quite a few new ideas in carriage design *per se*, principally their 'open plan' interiors. Moreover, the GWR had quite a considerable number of them, by no means life-expired when it became obvious that the conventional locomotive in push-pull mode was a better answer for the less busy services. In consequence, the GWR had a fine reservoir of potentially convertible stock; this it proceeded to exploit to the tune of almost 90 vehicles down to the late 1920s, and in the process created that most characteristic form, the 'auto-trailer'. So successful was this converted form that it became the norm for most subsequent services of the kind and even led to the building of new auto-trailers as the operations expanded into all parts of the system.

However, in spite of the success of the conversion of railmotors to auto-trailer mode and its consequential enhancement of patronage, such was the size of the original steam railmotor fleet that the GWR did not find it necessary to build any totally new examples of the auto-trailer type until 1929, and even in total, when the programme was completed in 1933, they still represented little more than 33 per cent of the converted railmotor fleet. Furthermore, it has to be stated that they were not particularly distinguished inside. But they did perform an invaluable service, and remained in service well into the final steam days.

So useful, in fact, were the GWR auto-trailers that

well into BR days a final series was felt to be justifiable. These coaches came out during 1951-4, displaying the almost slab-sided profile of the Hawksworth period, and the first pair were even given names 'Wren' and 'Thrush' as the first of what were meant to be a class of 'named' auto-trailers. Though this idea came to nought and the names were soon lost, these carriages in their 1953 refurbished form became a sort of quasi-prototype for the later and ubiquitous DMUs of the 1950s and later. Moreover, the last ten, GWR No Series 235-44, built new in 1954 with the more up-to-date interiors, had the interesting distinction of being the last passenger-carrying carriages to a non-BR standard design. They were not strictly GWR either, but only the pedants complained!

Thus it was that the GWR, whether in the shape of its diesel railcars or in the final series of steam-powered auto-trailers, may be said to have had no small influence on the subsequent evolution of the BR continuation in this specific area. Furthermore, having been more than censorial about the lack of inspiration in most GWR stock of the grouping period, I am more than happy to redress the overall balance by giving Swindon its due share of credit in what was to prove a critical field — and this seems to me an appropriate point at which to take leave of this particular subject.

29. The last of the 'company' carriages

The Second World War was, to put it mildly, a difficult time for all the British railway companies, and they acquitted themselves nobly in the national interest. But they also, undoubtedly, entered the post-war era in the shadow of putative railway nationalization, consequential upon the 1945 General Election results which returned, for the first time ever, a Labour Government with an absolute majority. This carried within it a remit to implement the fundamental tenets of Socialist philosophy which, *inter alia*, implied public control of the overall British transport system. By 1947 the die was cast, and on 1 January 1948 the railways were taken into public ownership. To be candid, some higher echelons of the 'old guard' railway management, and here we may, perhaps, especially single out that of the GWR, could not bring themselves to believe that it would ever happen; but it did and the consequences were widespread. Whether or not they were effective is a very different story to which we shall have cause to return in the next volume; meantime our concern here is to complete the company story as far as carriages were concerned.

In the specific field of vehicle design, it took some years for the newly nationalized organization to settle down, and it was not until *circa* 1951-2 that the first wholly new ideas emerged. In the interim, the old company approaches held sway and this led to a short-lived, but very interesting period of rolling-stock development wherein the final ideas of the 'Big Four' took tangible form against an organizational background which must have been very far from the thoughts of the old board rooms when the ideas were first mooted.

The four main lines had had little chance to develop new ideas during the war years, so in consequence there was probably a degree of pent-up frustration in terms of rolling-stock design, probably made more acute by the ever growing realization of the threat of road competition. In consequence, the main emphasis as far as most aspects of carriage development was concerned was directed to main-line express services, and with the noteworthy exception of the Southern Railway, none of the other railways seem to have been too bothered about their shorter-distance services. There was in any case a sort of monopolistic state of affairs in these areas, given petrol rationing and the like, and there was, in any case, plenty of fairly new short-haul stock available. The Southern was, however, rather different in this respect, so before looking at main-line developments, it seems only proper briefly to address this particular point.

Chapter 21 has indicated how the Southern Railway coped with the carriage consequences of its large-scale pre-war suburban electrification by applying a judicious mixture of rebuilding much of its pre-group locomotive-hauled stock to EMU form with a selective provisioning of new stock where such rebuilding was neither sensible nor practicable, eg the longer-distance routes to such places as Portsmouth, Brighton et al. But by 1945-6, it was quite clear that this process had reached its limit. Furthermore, the converted EMUs formed from pre-group hauled stock were themselves beginning to show signs of their age, many of their bodies being already 40 or more years old. Accordingly, Oliver Bulleid made strenuous attempts to re-equip the short-distance services of the Southern Railway with a new tranche of stock. Now Bulleid has often been much criticized for his rather avant garde and maybe impractical approach to steam locomotive development in the final company years, but it cannot really be gainsaid that in the realm of carriages he showed a far better appreciation of the problem than any of his contemporaries. As a result, the Southern, by the time of nationalization, was not only well down the road to a full reappraisal of its main-line operations, but was also well advanced in the re-equipment of its short-distance operations as well.

To a large extent, this re-equipment took the form of a standardized four-car suburban EMU of a distinctively new external style. Familiarly known as the '4SUB', it merely repeated the ideas of an early generation and, conceptually, was nothing very remarkable, merely taking the form of a tight assemblage of conventional side-door compartments on a basic standard chassis, along with the essential driving and guard's accommodation. The compartments were by no means generously dimensioned, save by comparison with the quite execrable LNER steam hauled quad-arts and quin-arts, but in external terms they established a 'new look' to Southern electric services which remained a familiar sight for nigh on 40 years. Repeated almost to the point of boredom, one cannot say that one looked forward to riding in one of them with any degree of pleasurable anticipation — they were hardly renowned for their spacious quality, nor did they give the passenger the option of first class travel, and their riding could be quite adventurous to say the least — but they surely shifted vast numbers of people in their time, and their outward styling was not without influence in the BR continuation, be it suburban or main-line mode. Later examples, both SR and BR, saw a mixture of compartment and open style and even at the time of

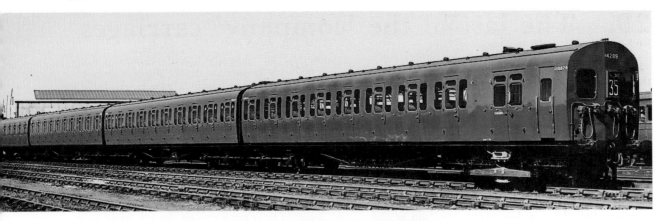

Above *This view of SR type 4SUB unit No S4289 of the 1948-9 build serves as a timely reminder of the fact that Bulleid's final carriage designs dominated the Southern scene for the best part of 20 or more years after the formation of BR. This unit was one of many built with mostly open-plan interiors — see Figure 43, page 391.*

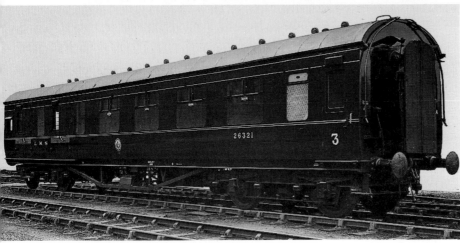

Left *Corridor brake third No 26321 was one of the first LMS carriages to be built after the 1939-45 war as part of that company's determined drive to reinstate its carriage building programme. It embodied welded bogie and underframe construction, but even in this respect it differed little from the pre-war equivalent.*

Table 9 Post-war gangwayed stock to company designs: new build, all types

Notes: 1. These values have been extracted from various published works and may contain occasional discrepancies from other sources in the units column. Overall, they are within 1 per cent of precise totals and serve adequately for comparative purposes.
2. The tables include all non-kitchen vehicles built for dining purposes.

Company	Corridor types[1]							Open types[1]					Grand Total
	FK	CK	TK	BFK	BCK	BTK	Sub Total	FO	CO	TO	BTO	Sub Total	
LMS (Stanier)	42	525	701	15	—	784	2067	20	—	350	—	370	2437
LNER (Thompson)	94	109	488	—	40	99	830	9	—	33	—	42	872
GWR (Hawksworth)	31	36	207	—	44	177	495	—	—	—	—	—	495
SR (Bulleid)	41	246	110	—	53	44	494	11[2]	8	56	275[3]	350	844
Totals	208	916	1506	15	137	1104	3886	40	8	439	275	762	4648

1 Carriage types are identified by standard BR codes when built.
2 All semi-FO.
3 All semi-BTO.

Third Class became Second Class in 1956.

writing   one can still witness some of their lineal descendants at Waterloo, Victoria and Charing Cross, though their days are surely numbered.

In these vehicles, Bulleid adopted a carriage profile which was soon to become familiar throughout the Southern and, later, on the BR system too. In fact, the first BR continuation for the Southern Region was almost a carbon copy of Bulleid's ideas. We cannot be certain why it was chosen, but its essential characteristic was that of a continuous and gentle curve between cantrail and solebar, rather than the usual 'flat' side from roof to waist combined with an in-curve from waist to the solebar. Bulleid put it on his post-war Southern corridors too, and in due course something very similar was adopted as the BR standard for all stock. When applied to main-line stock it had a considerable degree of aesthetic merit and remained the 'current' style until the 1960s. It also served to give BR standard stock a distinctively different look to that of all its company forbears, save for those of Southern origin. However, in mentioning the BR continuation we are moving a little ahead of the story at this point, so we must go back to the finale of the company era.

Apart from Bulleid's valiant efforts on the Southern's suburban lines, the bulk of carriage development during the final company years was connected with the matter of improving main-line stock and here, as Chap. 19 has indicated, only the LMS had much to boast about in the pre-1940 era. Furthermore, it was probably the first of the four companies to get into its stride after the war too. As early as 1945, Derby and Wolverton had resumed their pre-war scale of carriage building activity and, as Table 9 reveals, by the end of the company era LMS designs already represented well over 50 per cent of the total new main-line stock to emerge after the war. However, on this occasion it did, at least, have some competition.

At this point, and by way of mild recapitulation, it may be helpful briefly to compare the main-line stock of the 'Big Four' as it existed at the end of the war, using as a comparison their latest pre-war designs of the common corridor composite type. I have tabulated their comparative details below, and the first thing to note is that in spite of many differences there were also many points in common, not least their very close harmonization in size at about

the 60-foot length and their universal use of an all-steel angle-trussed underframe. It seems, therefore, that in spite of the many stylistic and detail differences, there was also much common ground.

The GWR and LMS used screw couplings and British Standard gangways, the other two preferring the buckeye/Pullman alternative. The GWR and SR never offered three-per-side thirds (save in the SR 'narrow' stock) while the latter company was the only one to retain a full complement of compartment-side doors. The GWR still fitted one or two doors on this side but the LMS and LNER had both suppressed this feature. All lines used the automatic vacuum brake.

For the most part, the LMS simply continued to develop the ideas which Stanier had instigated in the early 1930s. The great man himself left the LMS at the end of 1942, but in the carriage field, as in the locomotive arena, his legacy was such as to necessitate no great quantum change. Just about the only real variation on the pre-war theme was the insertion of one or two extra doors on the corridor side of the main-line carriages, and this is reckoned to have been more to meet the revised safety aspects of the time than representing any basic change of philosophy by the company. None of the older carriages were altered to the new arrangement, so it cannot have been totally mandatory. There was also, in the BR-built examples of Stanier stock, a totally cosmetic change in toilet window shape during 1949-50 to a new circular style (vehicles thus equipped being known colloquially as 'porthole' stock) which derived its shape from the 1939 'Coronation Scot' carriages; but those who have examined the preserved 1937 and 1950 brake thirds in the NRM collection will appreciate how little the fundamentals really changed. In that lies their significance.

Over the years, the LMS had also made increasing use of welding in its bogie and underframe construction — though not exclusively — and there was one particular aspect of welded carriage construction which the LMS was beginning to develop at the very end of its independent existence which turned out to be of more than passing significance. This was the reintroduction of the 'all-steel' form of body construction with a revised design of underframe. It began with the Southport EMUs (p. 431), but afterwards was confined to a series of corridor composites which

Company	Body dimensions	Body construction	Compartments	Seats
LMS	60'1″ × 8'11½″	Flush steel/timber frame	3F + 4T	18F + 24T
LNER	61'6″ × 9'0″	Timber/timber frame	3F + 4T	18F + 24T
GWR	59'10″ × 8'11″	Flush steel/timber frame	4F + 3T	24F + 24T
SR	59'0″ × 9'0″	Steel/timber frame	4F + 3T	24F + 24T

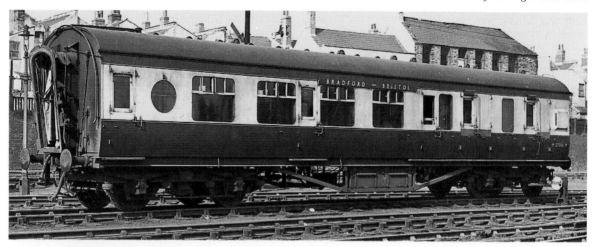

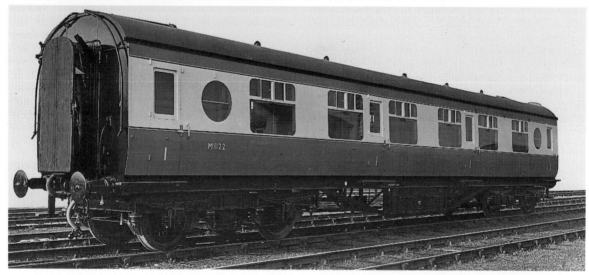

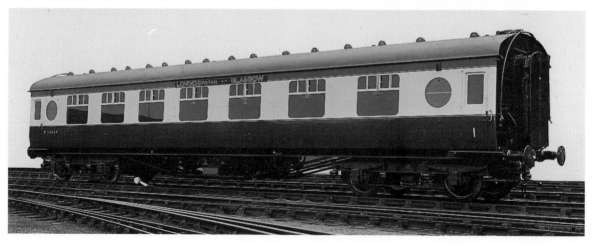

began to emerge in 1949. However, when allied with the generally Bulleid-inspired body form of the BR standard coach, it made the major contribution to the new BR designs of the 1950s and as such we shall return to it in the next volume.

Meantime, the other three companies had more than a little catching up to do in 1945, and it is a matter of history that they all managed to achieve much in a few short years, albeit that many of the results actually came into service after BR was created.

In 1941, the great Sir Nigel Gresley had died before his time and his place on the LNER was taken by Edward Thompson, arguably one of the most controversial figures ever to assume the top position on a British railway. In a sense he was on 'a hiding to nothing', for Gresley's was probably an impossible act to follow, not made any simpler by the straitened circumstances of war. In fact, it is one of the more interesting exercises to speculate how Gresley would have coped during those days, for there was no doubt that some of his preferred methods would need to be changed under wartime conditions. Thompson knew this, but, though oft-times in latter days misunderstood, did not help his cause by the way in which he went about making the necessary changes. If truth be told, he held more than a little admiration for the fairly ruthless standardization which the LMS had been pursuing under Stanier, and though Stanier and Gresley were good friends this was not quite the Gresley way of doing things, however great the economic justification. What is known is that in the locomotive field, Thompson sought advice from some of Stanier's lieutenants who, diplomatically, confined their remarks to such bland statements as 'We would

not have done it quite like that', without actually saying what they *would* have done!

In consequence, Thompson's early efforts on the locomotive front tended to be seen as undoing almost everything that Gresley had done. Given the perhaps rather tactless and insensitive rebuilding of Gresley's first 4-6-2 *Great Northern*, not to mention the equally unmemorable rebuilding of Gresley's fine 'Cock o' the North' 2-8-2s into not very successful 'Pacifics', one could well understand why his activities met with little approval, and when he finally gave way to A.H.Peppercorn in 1946 there were many sighs of relief. Yet the really strange irony is that all post-war LNER carriages are regarded as Thompson not Peppercorn stock, in spite of the fact that relatively few of them were built during Thompson's period of office! And the attribution is fair.

As part of his reassessment of the LNER position, towards the end of the war Thompson realized that the days of the traditional teak-bodied carriage were numbered, not simply on the grounds of dated appearance, but largely because of economic considerations. Some earlier experiments with steel sheeting had been carried out (see p 337), but Thompson's re-think was of a more radical nature and resulted in completely new designs being introduced. Non-corridor stock was little changed in concept but there was a major reappraisal of the main-line fleet, not the least of which was a questionnaire to passengers in 1946.

As a result of these deliberations, the new LNER main-line stock, still maintaining its Gresley-inspired underframe and bogie, though some composites were built on a shorter 58-foot frame to suit the revised interior arrangement, displayed a quite different external style, smooth sided and, in my view, having seen and ridden in many of them, of very pleasing aesthetic character. It further differed from all other contemporary flush-sided stock in having square-cornered windows and very attractive oval-shaped lavatory windows. Within the corridor coaches, a further and very sensible innovation was to divide the compartment areas into sections of two or three with intermediate cross-vestibules, for ease of loading at stations, while the compartment sizes were made a generous 7 ft 6 in and 6 ft 6 in for first and third class respectively. They had bowed ends in plan but no doming to the roof. In them, Thompson gave the new LNER stock quite recognizably modern and different lines which could in no conceivable way be mistaken for its LMS or GWR equivalent; so far so good, but there were snags.

For one thing, the first examples were garbed in ersatz teak livery which, while it might have made some sort of sense while the LNER was building mostly teak-bodied carriages — *vide* the odd steel-

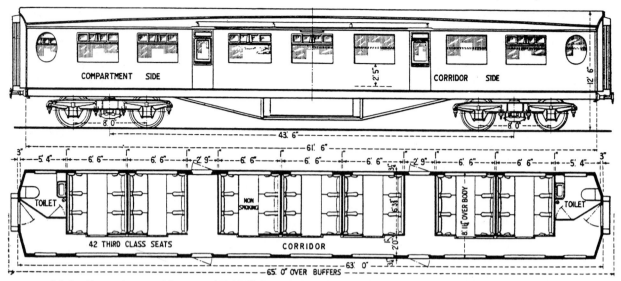

Main dimensions and layout of L.N.E.R. coach with compartments to accommodate six passengers

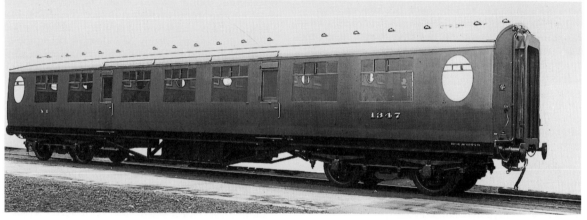

Figure 94 *Elevation and plan of the spacious seven-compartment Thompson LNER corridor third, its cross-vestibules and generously sized compartments being typical of most post-war LNER-type corridor stock.*

Scale: $^1/_{10}"$ = *1ft*

The prototype Thompson LNER carriage, corridor third No 1347 of 1945 finished in pseudo 'teak'. It also embodied Thompson's new design of bogie, but this was not a success and most future examples reverted to the well-proven Gresley type.

panelled experiments in the 1920s and 1930s — it made no sense at all in terms of accentuating the modernity which, presumably, they were meant to represent. Frankly, they looked rather ridiculous and one wonders why the LNER did not adopt a new livery simultaneously with their introduction; the pre-war 'Tourist' scheme would have looked rather nice and, given the LNER's swift post-war reintroduction of apple green engines, would certainly have brightened up the drab post-war years. In this respect, the new BR red and cream livery, applied to many of

them when new and all of them in due course, looked distinctly more appropriate. I have clear memories of these carriages in red and cream hauled by 'A1s' and 'A4s' in the short-lived BR blue locomotive livery, and it really was a most attractive ensemble.

But this is merely a cosmetic consideration, and subjective at that; far more serious were the deficiencies of the carriages themselves. The square-cornered windows turned out to be rust traps and early corrosion was rife; from 1949 onwards, round-cornered windows were adopted to beneficial effect and no detriment to appearance. However, the really major disappointment was within the carriages, where no attempt at all was made to maintain the standards of the pre-war era. Drab upholstery, dreary institutional cream paint, dark woodwork, thoroughly unpleasant plastic trimmings and rather primitive lavatories all combined to make something of a nonsense of the 'modern' image — and the finish was not that good either, as I recall.

Even so, many hundreds were built and though they in no way matched the post-war LMS build in terms of sheer numbers, they represented about 20 per cent of the grand total of LNER-designed main-

line stock when the BR standard types began to take over. They were in every way symptomatic of the post-war 'utility' years and although they rode well, as might be expected of most ex-LNER stock, they generally flattered to deceive. It was a pity, because much of the thinking behind them was sound and with just a bit more care, effort and imagination they could have been very much better. Few are preserved.

By contrast with the LNER, the GWR had adopted flush-sided exterior steel panelling well before the war but, as has been indicated, did not always take full advantage of the stylistic opportunities offered. However, its final pre-war corridor coaches showed that the company was at last emerging from its mid-life crisis, and these were to form the basis of the final and rather stylish vehicles built to the design of Hawksworth. There were not too many of them and most did not emerge, largely for economic reasons, until after the company had given way to BR. But the basic concept and design was wholly Great Western.

These views compare the square- and round-cornered window variants of otherwise identical post-war LNER stock, both being brake composites. The older version, LNER No 1141, came out late in 1947, while No E10159, viewed from the opposite (compartment) side, emerged in 1950. Undeniably handsome of form in both variants, there can be little doubt that the round-cornered version and the more appropriate BR livery had the aesthetic edge

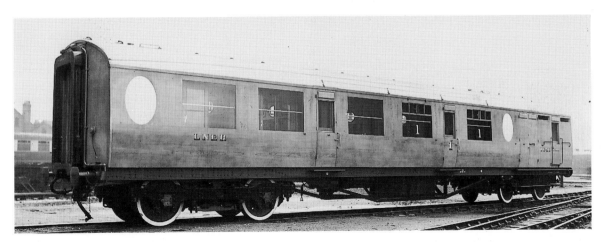

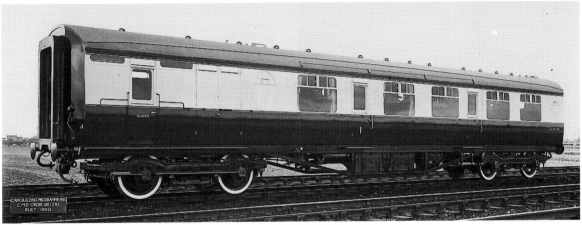

Their origin went back to the final war years when the first orders were issued in 1944, and first indications were that these new GWR carriages were going to be more than normally innovative, given the generally conservative nature of the company. For one thing, they were to have fluorescent lighting, at that time a relatively unknown quantity in terms of carriage building. In the event, very few were turned out in this way, and none after 1947, the general consensus being that the lights were too harsh. Secondly, early examples made use of Formica-type laminated plastic panelling to brighten the interiors and reduce the amount of expensive timber veneers. Unfortunately, and whether it was inspired by the GWR I cannot say, the use of these laminates became rather too widespread after that time in many British carriages, doing little for their aesthetics, however much cost it might have saved.

Another innovation was a new 64-foot length combined with a new body shape, the latter characterized by its almost 'slab' sides but married to an

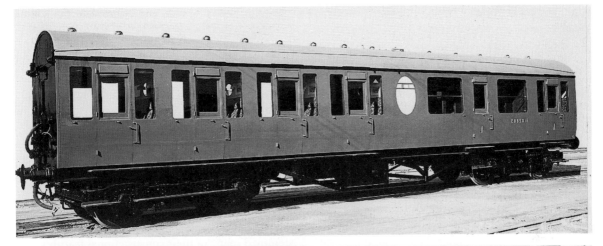

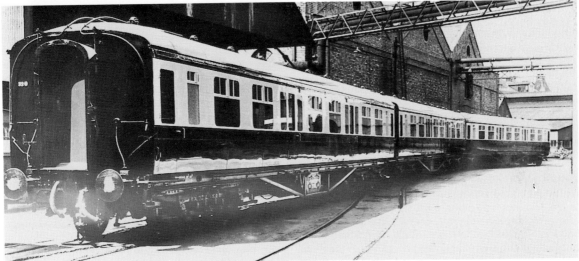

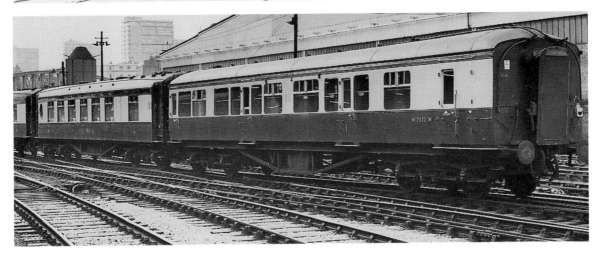

attractive domed end roof very reminiscent of Gresley's LNER carriages. Finally, and at long last, the GWR caught up the rest of the country by adopting a 'direct build' form of carriage assembly. It was not quite mass production on the LMS pattern but was very much based on later LMS (Stanier) practice. The floor now became part of the underframe, as on the LMS, instead of part of the body and, again like the LMS, bottom side members were dispensed with by having brackets fixed directly to the underframe which could receive the body pillars of the preassembled side components. Finally, later LMS practice was also copied in the substitution of steel for wooden cantrails.

All told, a pretty decisive and overdue change was achieved and, taking all into consideration, the only really backward features were the continued use of four-per-side seating in the thirds and the retention of some compartment-side doors. Later production batches also reverted to more solidly traditional wood finishes in the first class, though using enamelled hardboard in the thirds, the latter being far brighter in consequence. In fact, quite a number of interior ideas were tried out in the Hawksworth carriages, some of which, not least the rather more civilized lavatories, seem to have influenced the BR standard types.

But in a sense it was too little and too late. Qualitatively they were far superior to the Thompson LNER stock, but conceptually they still did not match up to the best LMS practice and bequeathed little more than their length (which was shared with Bulleid's SR stock anyway) to the BR period. They did, however, last well into the 1960s, by which time they were almost the only GWR-designed carriages left in service. In this regard, they vanished at much the same time as their other company-designed contemporaries, though perhaps the final irony in the history of the last carriages built to the design of this famous company was the fact that in their final years

they were overhauled at Wolverton, from whence stemmed many of their constructional features, and not Swindon!

Little need be said about the final generation of company-designed non-corridor stock, save that it was all pretty routine and uninspired. However, as an amusing aside, it is probably worth recording that some of the last GWR-pattern non-corridors to be built were issued to a London Midland order because neither Derby nor Wolverton could cope at the time. Since the LMR could not, apparently, accept the new and longer (63 ft) Hawksworth vehicles, the LMR order was delivered to a resurrected pre-war GWR design!

Of all the four companies at the end of the war, the Southern was probably the most old-fashioned in terms of its main-line stock, and this is not really surprising. Most of its carriages were built in the first ten years after 1923, and so successful had Maunsell been in solving the problem that by the time the other companies were starting to modernize their designs in the 1930s, the SR had no immediate need for new vehicles anyway. But this was not the case after the war and, as might well be expected, Oliver Bulleid took full advantage and, it is fair to say, probably made the most significant new contribution to main-line carriage development in the short post-war company period.

His ideas were simultaneously both predictable and unexpected. Ever since 1937 he had been brightening up the interiors of some of Maunsell's carriages, so some of his interior designs probably came as no great surprise; but the new styling given to all new carriages, combined with the introduction of some new types and the concept of a totally integrated set or even train formation, was certainly different. So too was the new malachite green livery which, though introduced to a limited extent before the war, was never really widespread until afterwards. Like it or not, one could not ignore it, and in one respect it was probably the most honest paint scheme of all in that it abandoned all lining with no pretence to be anything but what it was.

Structurally, Bulleid's carriages represented something new both to the Southern and to Britain generally. While not abandoning separate underframes, he did desert traditional timber body framing in favour of a much greater use of steel framing and welding, though there was still some timber used. As many as possible of the fittings were highly standardized, typical being the pressed steel doors with frameless droplights and their characteristic round-ended toplights. As far as possible, Bulleid also moved construction in the general direction followed by the LMS, and complete bodysides were built on a jig. One interesting point, however, was the retention of wood and canvas roofs, largely because the expense of setting up jigs for making a wholly steel-covered coach was thought to be too great in relation to the numbers likely to be built. In this respect, the main-line stock contrasted with the new suburban electrics which were 'all-steel' in basic structure and jig-built; there were, of course, far more of these, thus allowing economies of scale.

Bulleid's first main-line essays — three-coach sets of two brake thirds and a composite — were actually ordered early in the war but did not emerge until 1945-6. They retained the Maunsell length/underframe and, rather surprisingly, still perpetuated most of the old layout features, including a full set of outside doors on the compartment side; but they were otherwise totally new in styling, and this new form became much more familiar when the final length

was determined and the coaches began to emerge in some quantity, all with 64 ft 6 in bow-ended bodies on a 63 ft 5 in underframe. Apart from the flush panelling, the most noticeable feature was the continuous bodyside curve from solebar to cantrail, something quite new to British main-line carriage design, though it had been anticipated with the earlier 4SUB units. It looked very good, and the absence of a gutter strip at the cantrail made the whole body and roof 'flow' together in a most attractive way. The trouble was that the lack of gutters caused passengers to suffer dripping water down the door openings on wet days, and this lack of proper roof drainage was, eventually, to be the cause of much rotting and rusting.

After his first corridor batches, Bulleid finally abandoned the outside compartment doors in all save, for some reason, the third class brakes. In their place came round-cornered large picture windows of a type rather akin to those already common on the LMS. They had upper sliding ventilators of shallow type which eventually gave way (in those examples built during the BR period) to a deeper form. Additionally, there was usually installed a central cross-vestibule somewhat in the Thompson LNER manner; one even wonders if there was some LNER influence at work, since Bulleid was an ex-LNER man. Furthermore, just as did the LNER (see above), the SR also conducted a post-war passenger survey before commencing series production of the new carriages. All conventional corridor and open types were represented (see Table 9) save for a brake first (always a fairly rare breed in Britain until later BR days) but

Above left *This August 1951 view at Whiteball of the down 'Cornish Riviera' headed by 4-6-0 No 6025* King Henry III *reveals that in early BR days even the most important ex-GWR carriage formations were by no means tidy. The leading Hawksworth brake third is stylish enough, save for the intrusive outside door to the first compartment; but just look at the misalignment of roof, waist and solebar levels of the first five coaches!*

Right *A curious mixture of ancient and modern: Bulleid's first corridor stock is represented here by composite No 5726 from the early post war three-coach sets of 1945-6. The new profile is very modern, as is the totally honest plain green livery, but obvious too is the dated retention of a full set of outer doors. Even so, the 'flowing' stylistic nature of the overall body construction was quite new and, in the event, most significant*

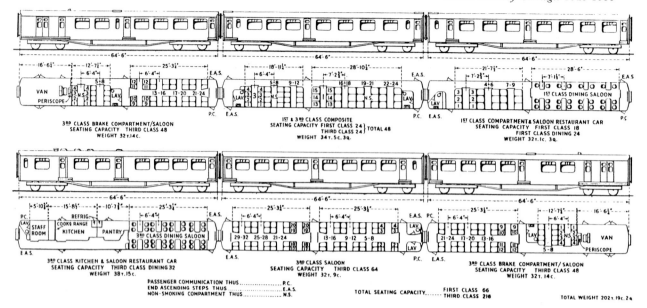

3RD CLASS BRAKE COMPARTMENT/SALOON
SEATING CAPACITY THIRD CLASS 48
WEIGHT 32T.14c.

1ST & 3RD CLASS COMPOSITE
SEATING CAPACITY FIRST CLASS 24 } TOTAL 48
THIRD CLASS 24
WEIGHT 34T.5c.3q.

1ST CLASS COMPARTMENT & SALOON RESTAURANT CAR
SEATING CAPACITY FIRST CLASS 18
FIRST CLASS DINING 24
WEIGHT 32T.1c.3q.

3RD CLASS KITCHEN & SALOON RESTAURANT CAR
SEATING CAPACITY THIRD CLASS DINING 32
WEIGHT 38T.15c.

3RD CLASS SALOON
SEATING CAPACITY THIRD CLASS 64
WEIGHT 32T.9c.

3RD CLASS BRAKE COMPARTMENT/SALOON
SEATING CAPACITY THIRD CLASS 48
WEIGHT 32T.14c.

PASSENGER COMMUNICATION THUS.................P.C.
END ASCENDING STEPS THUS.........................E.A.S.
NON-SMOKING COMPARTMENT THUS...............N.S.

TOTAL SEATING CAPACITY....... FIRST CLASS 66
THIRD CLASS 216

TOTAL WEIGHT 202T.19c.2q.

there was one new variety of carriage which was very much Bulleid's own idea and became the most common single type to be built.

It was a semi-open brake third combining two compartments (a few had one plus a coupé) with four open bays. Several subtle variations existed, as with most of Bulleid's carriages, but the concept was a nice effort to meet the conflicting wishes for both open and compartment type seating in the third class revealed in the post-war survey, though the proportion of open seating was rather higher than passenger preference had indicated. Although Bulleid built quite a few full thirds as well (both open and side corridor), this new-style semi-open was clearly the preferred choice. For one thing, it lent itself to incorporation in fixed sets, especially if of short formation, and must have been a successful compromise; something very like it was often incorporated into several later generations of BR EMU stock for the Southern Region.

In the traditional Southern manner, much of Bulleid's stock was delivered in dedicated formations, including no fewer than 11 handsome six-coach sets for the Waterloo-Bournemouth services which displayed a further nice design touch — the bodyside panelling taken down to conceal the solebars, save at the side-step areas. Great care was taken both with the internal arrangements of the coaches and their order of marshalling: semi-BTO/TO/RT/semi-RFO/CK/semi-BTO. These, of course, were the sets which also contained Bulleid's new approach to dining provision (see p 365), and nothing quite as deliberately well thought out ever emerged from the other companies at the time.

If one can sum up these carriages, the word which springs to my mind is 'harmonious' and this generally extended to their interiors as well. Much thought went into their arrangements, within the economic constraints of the day, and the more revolutionary aspects of Bulleid's first interior design innovations were abandoned in favour of a return to the more popular and traditional wood finishes, usually walnut (first class) and mahogany (third class). Once the proliferation of old-fashioned outside doors had largely gone, there was little to choose between them and the best which the other lines could offer save for the vexed question of compartments versus open and the number of seats per side in the third class areas. Here, the Bulleid stock was to prove slightly prophetic in terms of the BR succession, for not only did the BR standard carriage imitate the Bulleid length and profile, it also copied many of his layouts without too much significant modification. Though much must, perforce, await the next volume to resolve, it is perhaps helpful to address the matter of seating capacity at this stage.

The Southern and Great Western remained wedded to four-per-side thirds to the very end, generally assumed to have been a reflection of their need to offer maximum seat capacity at holiday times, but this seems a poor argument. Given the fold-away nature of the individual armrests provided by the LMS and LNER, it was perfectly possible to get four per side at times of need, yet give the third class passengers a bit more breathing space for most of the year. My guess is that it was probably a mixture of conceptual inertia, a modest saving in cost of seat manufacture and, maybe most important, the problem of seat reservations. A compartment which variously could carry six or eight could not have its seats numbered to suit both forms, and since many of the SR and GWR holiday extra trains were fully reserved it was probably deemed best that the compartments should be labelled in the high density configuration.

The logical solution was, of course, the open style of carriage which the LMS had pioneered in such quantity, and one senses that, at least as far as the SR was concerned, Bulleid was endeavouring to move his line in this direction. But there was considerable contemporary passenger resistance to this approach which none of the companies fully resolved. The LMS probably came nearest, but even it was obliged to build mostly side-corridors after the war (see Table 9).

It is a well-worn cliché that comparisons are odious, but in summing up the carriage designs of the final 25-30 years of the company period, it is almost unavoidable and arguably necessary; so, accepting the limitations which must always qualify a personal assessment, I do not propose to duck the issue. Excluding London Transport and Pullman, of course, and discounting suburban compartment stock, where there seems to me to have been little of fundamental importance to differentiate all four companies, the argument homes in mostly on the main-line contribution along with technical innovation generally.

In terms of overall contribution to the main-line scene, it seems fair to state that the LMS had the best and most 'modern' fleet of carriages as far as the average passenger was concerned; the statistics quoted in this volume lead to this conclusion. It identified the problem earlier than its competitors and if it never quite reached the heights of the LNER's very best efforts, neither did it quite plumb the depths which all three of the others could and did reach from time to time. The LNER, by contrast, was rather more patchy. At its best it was superb, it did have the finest bogie design right to the very end and showed the most dedicated commitment to using more 'modern' gangways and couplings. But the variation in quality between its best sleeping, dining and main-line corridor stock and its worst suburban efforts was really too great to be wholly acceptable. Furthermore, its belated attempt to enter the 'modern' stakes with its post-war carriage designs, though stylish enough from the outside, was rather flawed in terms of quality and design detail.

The Southern had a poor starting base, which was hardly its own fault, and this account has emphasized the steps made by both Maunsell and Bulleid to come to grips with the problem. But not until Bulleid's time could the Southern be said to be really competing (and winning) in terms of the developing mid-twentieth-century passenger needs and expectations; and it never, proportionally, had quite as much up-to-date stock as did, for example, the LMS. As for the GWR, one can only reiterate the view that in main-line terms the first half of the grouping period seems to have been bedevilled by the inevitable complacency which its dominance in its own group after 1923 was almost bound to precipitate. That said, however, there were signs at the end that the GWR had looked over its shoulder and was beginning to make amends; but, as another writer has already put it, its post-war hopes were frustrated by the onset of BR. Even so, in one respect the GWR carriage was still without peer in the late 1940s. Alone of the 'Big Four', its modern flush-sided stock, rather old-fashioned though it may have been in terms of some of its interior design features, was undoubtedly far less prone to rust and corrosion than any of those built elsewhere. The sheer number which have been preserved (relative to the other three) seems to give evidence of that, and cannot wholly be explained by the greater dedication which GWR devotees are usually prone to give to their favourite company!

Outwith the main-line area, the principal electrification prize must go to the Southern whose inter-war

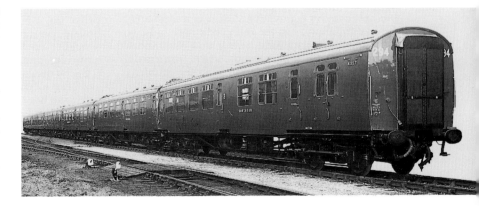

Figure 95 *Simplified elevations and plans of the six-coach Southern Railway corridor sets of 1947 for the Waterloo–Bournemouth services.*

Scale: 1" = 30ft

Right *The beautifully integrated and harmonious visual lines of the final SR corridor stock were nowhere better exemplified than in the six-coach sets for the Waterloo-Bournemouth services in 1947. This view of set No 294 was taken from the left-hand end of the formation as given in Figure 95.*

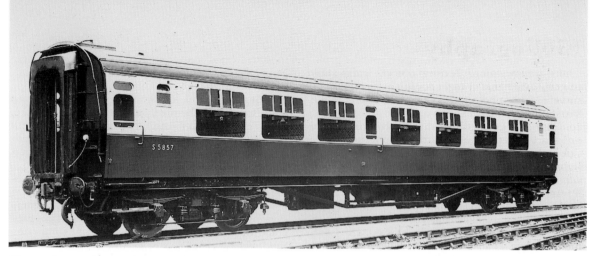

There can be no more appropriate way to end this part of the survey than by offering a view of perhaps the most handsome of the final post-war company-inspired offerings. Bulleid-type corridor composite No S5857 was built in 1950, incorporating the deep window ventilators of the BR period; furthermore, its overall external style predicted the BR continuation more accurately than any other, even though its basic form of construction did not.

efforts, in spite of its financial constraints, were little short of miraculous, suffering only from a degree of design staleness in terms of vehicle type. This was understandable in the circumstances and by no means as worthy of criticism as the surprising lack of interest shown in electrification by the two big companies, both of which had several areas which could have been so treated but which mostly had to await the BR period to be tackled. Offsetting this, however, it also seems fair to say that the final generation of new EMU designs which can be attributed to the LMS and LNER (those with sliding doors for the Wirral, Southport, Shenfield and Tyneside for example) were probably more influential in the long term than their far more numerous Southern contemporaries.

In the other self-propelled areas, the LNER deserves a modest pat on the back for its gallant attempt to revive the steam railcar, albeit ultimately doomed to failure; but the real credit here must go to the GWR for its long-lasting and determined efforts with diesel railcars while others, principally the LMS, were merely tinkering with the problem. The GWR success was clearly of great long-term influence in this field.

Finally, and most subjectively, aesthetics. In the late twentieth century, we are well-accustomed to the exhortations in favour of good design, if only because in a competitive world first impressions count for much. The old companies were not unaware of this,

though they did not have the benefits (?) of the modern-day proliferation of design consultants! Though the private railways did make quite ghastly mistakes at times, on the whole their products mostly stood the 'eyeball' test in a way that some of their BR successors have not. If pressed to an opinion, I would probably award Gresley's coaches the prize in the traditional field, for they almost always showed superb visual balance, especially when the number of outside doors was reduced. They were closely followed by the mid-period LMS offerings, both with and without external beading.

Of the new-wave self-propelled vehicles, few can have been better looking or more right for the time than the earlier GWR railcars, while in the modern flush-sided idiom all four companies had become so similar in their styling as to make the final judgement very difficult. The earlier Stanier breed were quite outstanding in the 1930s context, but eventually became, I suppose, rather too common to attract much attention. Both Thompson's and Hawksworth's offerings looked very good, but it was really only Bulleid who moved things forward, and his fully integrated corridor stock was deservedly the main stylistic influence on later BR design. Somehow it seemed to take external styling further forward from the original pioneering work of the LMS than did either the LNER or GWR alternatives. A set of Bulleid corridor stock was always a pleasure to behold, even though I personally preferred the interior amenities offered by the LMS!

So, by the end of the company period, though there had been much coming together of ideas, there were still quite noticeable differences to be seen and each company could be said to have something worthwhile to offer. This was the problem which the designers of the BR standard stock had to face in the 1950s and later.

Bibliography

There are few comprehensive general works on this subject, other than the well known Hamilton Ellis survey mentioned in the introduction, and most carriage literature is of the semi-dedicated kind, ie confined to specific companies. Although there are noteworthy gaps, the breadth of coverage is considerable and a representative selection is offered. I should also point out the wealth of material which was published in the contemporary issues of the *Railway Engineer* and *Railway Gazette*, particularly the latter (into which was absorbed the *Railway Engineer* from 1935). Little escaped its notice during the period of this review and a little time spent searching through these sources by the dedicated researcher will be well repaid.

Bogie Carriages of the LB&SCR: D.Gould, Oakwood Press, 1995

Bogie Carriages of the SE&CR: D.Gould, Oakwood Press, 1993

British Railcars 1900-1950: D.Jenkinson/B.C.Lane, Atlantic Transport Publishers, 1996

Bulleid's SR Passenger Stock: D.Gould, Oakwood Press, 1994

Carriage Stock of Minor Standard Gauge Railways: R.W.Kidner, Oakwood Press, 1978

Carriage Stock of the LB&SCR: P.J.Newbury, Oakwood Press, 1976

Carriage Stock of the SE&CR: D.Gould, Oakwood Press 1976

Early Electric Trains: R.L.Vickers, Shire Publications, 1991

East Coast Joint Stock: K.Hoole, Oxford Pub.Co.,1993

Great Northern Railway and ECJS Carriages from 1905: M.Harris, Oakwood Press, 1995

Great Western Auto Trailers, Vols I/II: J.Lewis, Wild Swan Publications, 1991, 1995

Great Western Coaches 1890-1954: M.Harris, Atlantic Transport Publishers, 1995

Great Western Coaches (a Pictorial Record of), Vols.1 & 2: J.H.Russell, Oxford Pub.Co., 1972 and 1973

Great Western Diesel Railcars: J.H.Russell, Wild Swan, 1985

Great Western London Suburban Services: T.B.Peacock, Oakwood Press, 1978

GWR Absorbed Coaching Stock: E.R.Mountford, Oakwood Press, 1978

LMS Standard Coaching Stock, Vols I/II: D.Jenkinson/R.J.Essery, Oxford Pub.Co., 1991, 1994

LNER Carriages: M.Harris, Atlantic Transport Publishers, 1995

LNWR Carriages - a concise history: D.Jenkinson, Pendragon Partnership, 1995

LPTB Rolling Stock 1933-1948: B.Hardy, Bradford Barton, undated

LSWR Carriages Vol.I: G.R.Weddell, Wild Swan Publications, 1992

Maunsell's, SR Steam Carriage Stock: D.Gould, Oakwood Press, 1990

Midland Carriages (An Illustrated Review): D.Jenkinson/R.J.Essery, Oxford Pub.Co., 1984

Midland Railway Carriages, Vols. 1 & 2: R.E.Lacy/G.Dow, Wild Swan, 1984 and 1986

North Eastern Electrics: K.Hoole, Oakwood Press, 1987

Palaces on Wheels (Royal Carriages at the NRM): D.Jenkinson/G.Townend, HMSO 1981

Preserved Railway Carriages: J.Lloyd/M.Brown, Silver Link Publishing Ltd., 1992

Pullman: J.Morel, David & Charles, 1983

Pullman Cars on the 'Southern', 1875-1972: R.W.Kidner, Oakwood Press, 1987

Pullman in Europe: G.Behrend, Ian Allan, 1962

Pullman, Travelling in Style: B.Haresnape, Malaga Books (Ian Allan), 1987

Railway Carriage Album: G.M.Kichenside, Ian Allan, 1966

Railway Carriages, 150 years of: G.M.Kichenside, David & Charles, 1981

Railway Carriages in the British Isles, 1830-1914: C.Hamilton Ellis, Allen & Unwin, 1965

Royal Trains: P.Kingston, David & Charles, 1985

Service Stock of the Southern Railway: R.W.Kidner, Oakwood Press, 1980

Southern Electric 1909-79: G.T.Moody, Ian Allan, 1979

Southern Electrics: B.Rayner, Bradford Barton, 1975

Southern Electric Album: A.Williams, Ian Allan, 1977

Southern Railway Branch Line Trains: R.W.Kidner, Oakwood Press, 1984

Southern Railway Passenger Vans: D.Gould, Oakwood Press, 1992

Southern Suburban Steam: R.W.Kidner, Oakwood Press, 1984

"Standard" Tube Stock: B.Hardy, London Underground Railway Society, 1986

Steam to Silver(London Transport Surface Stock): J.G.Bruce, Capital Transport, 1983

Tube Trains Under London: J.G.Bruce, London Transport, 1977

West Coast Joint Stock: R.M.Casserley/P.A.Millard, Historical MRS, 1980

Index